745/-

The Dragon and
The Elephant

The Dragon and The Elephant

Agricultural and Rural Reforms in China and India

EDITED BY ASHOK GULATI AND SHENGGEN FAN

OXFORD

UNIVERSITY PRESS

OXFORD

UNIVERSITY PRESS

YMCA Library Building, Jai Singh Road, New Delhi 110001

Oxford University Press is a department of the University of Oxford.
It furthers the University's objective of excellence in research,
scholarship, and education by publishing worldwide in

Oxford New York

Auckland   Cape Town   Dar es Salaam   Hong Kong   Karachi Kuala Lumpur
Madrid   Melbourne   Mexico City   Nairobi New Delhi   Shanghai   Taipei   Toronto

With offices in
Argentina   Austria   Brazil   Chile   Czech Republic   France   Greece Guatemala
Hungary   Italy   Japan   Poland   Portugal   Singapore South Korea   Switzerland
Thailand   Turkey   Ukraine   Vietnam

Oxford is a registered trade mark of Oxford University Press
in the UK and in certain other countries

Published in India
by Oxford University Press, New Delhi

First Published in the United States by
The International Food Policy Research Institute 2007
First Published in India by Oxford University Press 2008

ISBN-13: 978-0-19-569350 8
ISBN-10: 0-19-569350 7

This edition is reprinted by arrangement with original publisher for sale in India,
Bangladesh, Pakistan, Nepal, Bhutan, Sri Lanka and Myanmar only

Printed in India by De Unique, New Delhi 110 018
Published by Oxford University Press
YMCA Library Building, Jai Singh Road, New Delhi 110 001

Contents

Figures

Tables

Foreword

China and India are the fastest-growing large economies in the world today. Between 2002 and 2006, their gross domestic products (GDP) grew at 10 percent and 7.5 percent per year, respectively. Although both countries embody economic success, their specific experiences diverge. In recent years, China's agricultural GDP growth rate has been almost double that of India's. Less than 10 percent of China's population remains below the poverty line when the international poverty line of one dollar per day is used, compared with more than one-third of India's population.

This comparative study of Chinese and Indian economic reforms, with a focus on agricultural and rural development, is important in at least two respects. First, each country's experience holds lessons for the other. Second, considered together, their experiences can be useful for other developing countries that are formulating economic strategies and aiming to reduce hunger and poverty.

The book highlights the relevance of different institutional arrangements and initial conditions for economic development, and the importance of strategic sequencing of reform steps in order to make overall reform processes pro-poor. Based on comprehensive research on reform in the agricultural and rural sectors, the book shows how agriculture-based reform can pay rich dividends in terms of economic growth that leads to rapid poverty reduction. The book also demonstrates how investment in the rural sector—for example, in rural education and infrastructure—and in agricultural research and development can play a critical role in maximizing the pro-poor effects of reform. Priorities and steps leading to economic transformation are carefully delineated.

This book results from a fascinating, long-term and still ongoing process of consultation and research cooperation that IFPRI is facilitating, mainly among scholars from China and India. The process is focusing on improved understanding of economic change in both the "Dragon" and the "Elephant." The book offers an exhaustive analysis of the agricultural and rural development that has taken place in the two countries since they launched economic reforms. It should form an essential part of policy debates about the dynamics of change in China and India and what those dynamics mean for the rest of the world.

Joachim von Braun
Director General, IFPRI

Preface

Looking back from these heady days of economic success in China and India, it is interesting to note that in 1978 China's per capita income, in terms of purchasing power parity (PPP), was below that of India, and India's per capita income was below that of Sub-Saharan Africa. After a quarter of a century of reforms in China, its per capita income (in PPP) is now double that of India. China began its economic transformation by changing institutional structures in agriculture in particular, by moving toward the household responsibility system in land usage and a free market for agricultural products. It also liberated agricultural prices for its major crops to a significant degree. As a result, Chinese agricultural growth surpassed 7 percent per year during the period 1978–84 and agricultural income increased even more rapidly. Poverty in rural China (using the national poverty line) decreased from 33 percent to 11 percent within a span of just six years (1978–84).

The Indian reform process began with structural adjustment in industrial and trade policies, particularly the removal of bureaucratic red tape. The sector that showed the greatest growth was the service sector, especially information technology. Agriculture also grew rapidly, from 3 percent a year during the 1980s to 4.7 percent during the period 1992–96. But thereafter agricultural growth in India almost collapsed in the wake of falling world prices emanating from the East Asian crisis. There has been marginal recovery since 2004. India's rural poverty (using the national poverty line) decreased from 36 percent in 1993 to 28 percent in 2004–5, a much slower rate of reduction than in China.

What can the two nations learn from each other in terms of their reform experiences and their impact on agricultural growth and poverty? What can countries in transition learn from these two experiments? Providing answers to these questions is the fundamental objective of this book.

In order to understand the dynamics of change in agriculture and rural development in China and India, we brought together experts from both countries. Two conferences were held on this comparative work, one in New Delhi and another in Beijing. The experts attending each conference prepared papers on different aspects of agricultural and rural development, with the objective of understanding how reform has affected agricultural growth and poverty alleviation in rural areas.

Comparative analyses were carried out across ten themes of particular relevance to rural development in the two countries: (1) land reforms, (2) human and social development, (3) public investment, (4) agricultural research and development, (5) irrigation and the water sector, (6) domestic agricultural marketing, (7) World Trade Organization and agricultural trade liberalization, (8) agricultural and rural diversification, (9) the rural nonfarm sector, and (10) antipoverty programs and safety nets. A platform for future dialogue and networking among policymakers, advisers, and researchers from the two countries has also been formed, and it is expected that many such activities will be initiated by both countries in the future.

The results of this comparative exercise have been extremely rewarding. The present study clearly shows that the initial conditions in rural infrastructure (especially roads), agricultural research and development, and rural education are critical in determining the level of growth in agriculture and rural incomes. Appropriate investments in these areas are necessary to boost growth. The volume also shows that institutional reforms related to land use and price policies that favor market orientation can yield high returns in agricultural growth and poverty reduction. China has been much more successful in raising its agricultural growth and thus reducing its poverty. India still has a long way to go, because Indian agriculture and rural areas have not yet been the object of any serious and comprehensive package of reforms.

Both these countries have yet to tackle two key challenges. Inequality has increased significantly in both, albeit faster in China than in India. And the pressure on land is enormous, so that environmental degradation has become a major issue. How the two countries will tackle these problems has yet to be seen.

We hope that this book will be useful to the policymakers of the two countries as well as to those of several transition economies, and to researchers and students investigating the topics covered here. Ultimately we hope that we will have helped in the formulation of policies that can rapidly reduce poverty.

Ashok Gulati   Shenggen Fan

Acknowledgments

This book compares the rural development and agricultural reform experiences of China (the dragon) and India (the elephant) over the past several decades and is the outcome of two international conferences, one held in New Delhi and the other held in Beijing. These events brought together many prominent Chinese and Indian scholars and policymakers and were organized by the International Food Policy Research Institute (IFPRI) in collaboration with Jawaharlal Nehru University, New Delhi, and the Institute of Agricultural Economics of the Chinese Academy of Agricultural Sciences, Beijing.

We sincerely thank the contributors who prepared the research papers, presented them at the conferences, and revised them afterward. Our special thanks also go to the keynote speakers at the conferences, who not only inspired us with their wisdom and commitment but also provided critical insights into the discussion. In particular, we express our gratitude to (in alphabetical order) G. K. Chadha, Peter Hazell, Justin Y. Lin, C. H. Hanumantha Rao, Manmohan Singh, Joachim von Braun, and Huqu Zhai. We are also grateful to two anonymous reviewers who gave very constructive comments on the manuscript, and to Deki Pema, Sara Dalafi, Anuja Saurkar, and Kavery Ganguly for their excellent support during the period of editing and revision. Shirley Raymundo, Joy Fabela, Rowena Natividad did a great job in formatting this manuscript, and John Whitehead and Uday Mohan coordinated the entire process with the publisher. We highly appreciate their contribution and sincerely thank them.

Partial funding provided to Shenggen Fan by the Natural Science Foundation of China (approval number 70525003) is acknowledged.

We are most grateful to Indian Prime Minister Manmohan Singh, the architect of economic reforms in India, who inaugurated the first conference in New Delhi and is still keen to know what each country can learn from the other.

Abbreviations

AMS	aggregate measure of support
APMC	Agricultural Produce Marketing Committee
APP	antipoverty program
BCM	billion cubic meters
BOP	balance of payment
BPL	below the poverty line
CPR	common property resource
CSO	Central Statistical Organization, India
EU	European Union
FCI	Food Corporation of India
FDI	foreign direct investment
GATT	General Agreement on Tariffs and Trade
ha	hectare
HRS	Household Responsibility System
HYV	high-yielding (seed) variety
GMO	genetically modified organism
GOI	Government of India
IMF	International Monetary Fund
IPR	intellectual property rights
MDG	Millennium Development Goal
MFN	most favored nation
m ha	million hectares
MOA	Ministry of Agriculture
MSP	minimum support price
mt	million tons
NBS	National Bureau of Statistics, China
NGO	nongovernmental organization
NPR	nominal protection rate
NSS	National Sample Survey
NTB	nontariff barrier
O&M	operation and maintenance

PDS	Public Distribution System
PIM	participatory irrigation management
PPP	purchasing power parity
QR	quantitative restriction
R&D	research and development
RNF	rural nonfarm sector
RPS	retention price scheme
SC	scheduled caste
SEB	State Electricity Board
SOE	state-owned enterprise
ST	scheduled tribe
TE	triennium ending
TFP	total factor productivity
TOT	terms of trade
TVE	town and village enterprise
URAA	Uruguay Round Agreement on Agriculture
WDI	world development indicator
WTO	World Trade Organization
WUA	Water Users' Association

PART I

Introduction and Overview

This part of the book consists of two chapters. The first sets the scene for the book. It also provides the rationale for the China-India comparison and describes the organization of the book.

Looking at the economic performance of the two countries, some key questions are raised: What reforms made these outcomes possible? What role did the initial conditions of land distribution, rural health, education, and infrastructure play? What are the present challenges confronting these two countries? In moving from low levels of growth to a higher growth trajectory, the experiences of the two countries not only help draw lessons for each other but also provide useful insights for other developing countries. It is of particular interest to researchers and policymakers across the globe to understand the process of economic growth and its implications. They also wish to understand how China and India responded to several critical issues related to rural development, food security, poverty alleviation, and the like. A comparison of their rural and agricultural reforms will result in better understanding and cooperation between the two nations. This in turn will contribute to greater regional development through increased trade and investment opportunities.

The second chapter provides an overview of the reforms and development experience of China and India for the past several decades. Despite differences in timing and approach, a strong political will to implement market-oriented reforms, resulting in greater efficiency in resource allocation, led to higher economic growth in both countries. This outward-looking approach was instrumental in helping the two nations leave behind autarkic regimes and create larger roles for the market and the private sector. In improving their economic performance, the factors that fueled the process resulted in China adopting a bottom-up approach (with reforms starting within the agriculture sector) while India's drive was top-down. Although both countries have made considerable progress in opening up their economies, China pursued more aggressive "open-door" policies in investments and trade. India, on the other hand, has continued to work toward its objective of self-sufficiency and has implemented policies that have helped ensure food-grain security over the decades.

1

Although focused on agriculture and rural development, the overview also covers macroeconomic polices and development outside the agricultural sector, positioning agricultural and rural reforms within a much broader context. China, with its current rapid pace of economic growth, will have to find a way to contain rising income inequalities and ensure the sustainability of its growth momentum. India, in order to ensure efficiency and competitiveness in a growing economy, must overcome the hurdles of stagnation in public investments, infrastructure bottlenecks, lack of institutional reforms, and an incentive environment of input supply and agricultural subsidies

This overview provides a background for later chapters, which will go into greater depth in reviewing and comparing the thematic issues related to land, irrigation, agricultural research, rural public investment, marketing and trade reforms, rural diversification, and antipoverty programs.

1 Introduction

SHENGGEN FAN, ASHOK GULATI,
AND SARA DALAFI

By any yardstick, China and, more recently, India have been striking economic success stories. A few decades ago, both countries were clearly among the world's poorest. Now they top the list of the world's fastest-growing economies and are even being talked about as the economic superpowers of the future.

Over the past 25 years, China and India have experienced a dramatic turn-around in their economic conditions and achieved unprecedented levels of prosperity. In 1978, India's per capita gross domestic product (GDP) of U.S.$1,255 in purchasing power parity (PPP) terms (at constant 2000 price) was lower than the average for Sub-Saharan Africa, which stood at U.S.$1,757. Since then it has climbed steadily upward and more than doubled, to U.S.$2,732 in 2003. Even more spectacularly, the Chinese per capita GDP, which stood at U.S.$1,071 in 1978, a level lower than even India's, increased over four times, to U.S.$4,726 in 2003. China's per capita GDP growth rate, as presented in Figure 1.1, is now almost double that of India.[1]

What is the key to such remarkable success? China, for the past 25 years, and India, for the past 15, have implemented a series of broad economic and rural reforms that have resulted in extraordinary rates of economic growth.[2] From 1978 to 2002, China grew at 8–10 percent per annum, twice the rate of 4–5 percent recorded in the prereform period (NBS 2003).[3] For much of the postindependence era, India had grown at a stubbornly slow rate of 3.5 percent per annum, the so-called Hindu rate of growth, but from 1991 to 2002 it cata-pulted to a growth rate of 6 percent per year (India, CSO, 2004).

During the reform period China not only achieved dramatic economic growth but also successfully reduced its rural poverty (Figure 1.2). The num-

---

1. According to the World Bank income-based classification, lower-middle-income coun-tries are those with a per capita gross national income (GNI) of U.S.$736–2,935 in current U.S. dollars in 2002–3 (Atlas method). With a per capita GNI of U.S.$960 in 2002, China was in this group, while India, with a per capita GNI of U.S.$470, was in the low-income group. See <www .worldbank.org/data/countryclass/OGHIST.xls>.

2. Growth rates are calculated by fitting a linear regression trend line to the logarithmic annual values, except where otherwise indicated.

3. For China, all data used here refer to Mainland China.

FIGURE 1.1 Growth in per capita GDP in China and India

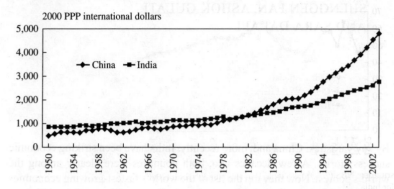

SOURCES: The data for 2000–2003 are taken from WDI (2005), while the data for 1950–99 are extrapolated using the trend of growth in GDP per capita from Maddison (2002).

NOTES: There have been conflicting reports on the per capita GDP of China and India. Maddison (2002) reported that the per capita GDP of China and India, measured in 1990 PPP, were $439 and $619 respectively in 1950 and $3,259 and $1,818 in 1999. Therefore, the ratio of China's per capita GDP to India's increased from 0.7 to 1.8. But the World Bank (WDI 2005) reported a very different trend: as late as in 1978, China's per capita GDP was only $674 measured in 2000 PPP international dollars, which was 56 percent of India's $1,224. But in 2003, per capita GDP in China increased to $4,726 and in India to $2,732. The ratio of China's and India's per capita GDP thus jumped from 0.56 in 1978 to 1.7 in 2003. While we believe the World Bank has done a reasonably good job of estimating GDP in PPP international dollars in more recent years, but it is not clear to us how the World Bank did it for earlier years. On the other hand, Maddison (2002) has documented his estimates for all the years from 1950 to 1999. However, his series ran only to 1999. Therefore, for our purposes in this chapter, we used the World Bank's latest estimates from 2000 to 2003, then used Maddison's trend to estimate the numbers before 2000.

ber of poor declined from 33 percent in 1978 to 3 percent in 2001, according to official sources (NBS 2002), or around 11 percent according to World Bank estimates of 1998 based on U.S.$1 a day measured in terms of PPP (World Bank 2000b). Despite the difference in the two benchmarks and the ongoing controversies regarding poverty measures, there is no denying the steep decline in poverty that has taken place—a reduction of this magnitude over such a short time is extraordinary by any standard. India also logged a sharp decline in poverty before and after reforms, although the outcomes were not as dazzling as in China. According to official estimates, rural poverty in India dropped from 38.9 percent in 1987/88, at the outset of reforms, to 27 percent in 1999/2000, the year for which the latest National Sample Survey (NSS) data are available (NSSO 1999, 2000 estimates).[4]

---

4. The official poverty estimates, based on the 55th round NSS consumption expenditure survey of 1999–2000, generated much debate, because these are not strictly comparable to estimates

FIGURE 1.2 Rural poverty decline in India and China

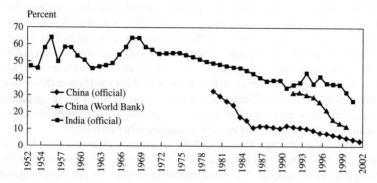

SOURCES: NBS (2002) for China; Datanet India Pvt. Ltd. (2006) and Fan, Thorat, and Rao (2004) for India.

NOTES: The official poverty line in India is defined as Rs. 49 per month at 1973–74 prices (Datanet India Pvt. Ltd. 2006), equivalent to U.S.$0.96 per day (1993 PPP), slightly below the U.S.$1 per day (1985 PPP) used by the World Bank for international comparisons. China's official poverty line used here to plot the poverty trend is U.S.$0.66 per day (1985 PPP).

Together, China and India accounted for a substantial fall in global poverty levels, from 29.6 percent (or 1.3 billion) of the world's population in 1990 to 23.2 percent (or 1.16 billion) in 1999 (World Bank 2003a).[5]

How these successes were accomplished is a mystery that needs to be unraveled to better understand the processes of growth so that the knowledge can not only contribute to the continuing reform process in the two countries

---

based on a similar survey of 1993–94 for the 50th round. The 55th round saw a methodological change, shifting from a 30-day reference period to a 7-day and a 30-day reference period for all food items and intoxicants and a 365-day reference period only for clothing, footwear, education, institutional medical expenditures, and durable goods.

Alternate poverty results have been provided by a number of studies for the period in question. Notable among them are the studies by Sundaram and Tendulkar (2003), who offer comparable results based on the 50th round, in which both 365-day questions and 30-day questions where asked about clothing and so on, which implies an 8.2 percent reduction in the all-India head-count ratio. Deaton (2003) makes use of the fact that a 30-day reference was used for the same group of nonfood items in both the 50th and the 55th rounds, assuming that the probability of being poor has a stable relationship with spending. His head-count ratio for 55th round is 7 pecent lower than the 50th round estimates. The Deaton and Sundarum studies reached a consensus that the absolute number of poor did decline by at least 30 million. A study by Sen and Himanshu (2004) that reviews all the previously mentioned studies estimates poverty based on a mixed reference period (30 or 365 days) and says that the reduction in poverty was not more than 3 percent and that the absolute number of poor did not fall. All these issues were discussed intensely at a seminar organized by the National Sample Survey Organizations (NSSO) in May 2001 and were the subject of a joint Planning Commission–World Bank workshop in January 2002.

5. Excluding poverty decline in China, world poverty actually increased in absolute terms, from 917 million to 945 million people.

but also help us draw lessons from it and highlight implications for other countries from the developing world. What reforms made these outcomes possible? Were they the result of only macroeconomic reforms, were they the cumulative effect of a series of microreforms in the agriculture and nonagriculture sectors, or both? What role did the initial conditions of land distribution, rural health, education, and infrastructure play? Do they explain the disparity in growth rates and poverty outcomes in the postreform period? What could other developing countries learn from the Chinese and Indian experiences? What can China and India learn from each other? What are the challenges confronting these two countries? Are there areas of possible cooperation between them?

This study attempts to answer these questions and also to draw lessons from the experiences of China and India in designing and implementing the economic reform process. The broad objective is to draw lessons that China and India can learn from each other and those that may be applied to the continuation and deepening of their reforms, which could possibly also help other developing and transitional countries in their pursuit of economic growth and poverty reduction.

This first chapter aims to provide the background for the study. To that end, the first section discusses the rationale for comparing the experiences of China and India. The second section outlines how the study is organized to first explain the similarities between the countries and the divergence in the processes and outcomes of reforms in each and to then draw lessons and indicate future progress.

Rationale for Comparison

The most dramatic decline in poverty in China, from 33 percent to 15 percent between 1978 and 1984, took place in the early reform period (Figure 1.2), after the agricultural growth rate jumped to 7.1 percent from 2.5 percent in the prereform period, between 1966 and 1977 (NBS 2003). By contrast, in India agricultural growth of 2.7 percent during the reform period of 1991–2003 was hardly unchanged from—and even marginally lower than—the 1980–90 rate of 2.9 percent (India, CSO, 2004). Clearly, then, compared to the situation in India, in China the primary sector played a more critical role in poverty reduction and overall economic growth, a fact that justifies our focus on agriculture and the attempt to assess the factors that led to this spectacular performance and the resultant drop in poverty.

Many studies have been undertaken in the past to analyze agricultural and rural reforms in China and India, but few have compared the sequence of these reforms and their consequences. There are several reasons why such a comparative effort is necessary.

First, these two countries are major players in the global economy, together accounting for 37 percent (2.3 billion) of the world's population (WDI 2004), producing 17.6 percent of global GDP (in PPP U.S. dollars), and commanding nearly 5 percent of the total trade volumes (World Bank 2003a). Based on World Bank projections, China and India will continue to show strong economic growth, and by 2030 their combined GDP will account for nearly 41 percent of the global economy in PPP terms.[6] By 2040, some expect China to overtake the individual G3 countries (the United States, Japan, and Germany) to become the largest economy, with India following the United States (Wilson and Purushothaman 2003). In fact, in PPP terms, China was already the second largest economy after the United States in 2001, while India's GDP was the fourth largest after those of the United States, China, and Japan (WDI 2003). China is forecast to overtake the economy of Germany in 2008, that of Japan in 2015, and that of the United States in 2039, while India is expected to overtake Germany in 2023 and Japan in 2032 (WDI 2003). In agriculture, China and India are jointly the largest producers of rice, wheat, and cotton, with their production of these commodities accounting for 51, 28, and 36 percent of the global share, respectively (FAOSTAT 2003). Thus, as these two countries integrate into the world economy, with the weight of their large territories and human resources and, more important, with their greater than average economic growth rates, they will increasingly impact global affairs including politics, trade, the environment, and energy conditions.

Second, despite their remarkable achievements, both China and India continue to be characterized by some of the features typical of developing countries: low per capita income and a majority of the population living in rural areas and dependent on agriculture for their livelihood. In 2001 the rural population in India was 72.2 percent of the total, with an agricultural workforce as large as 58 percent of the total. In China, the rural population was 63.3 percent of the total, with an agricultural workforce 50 percent of the total.[7] The Indian experience is particularly useful for African countries. The green revolution initiated in the late 1960s successfully spread to smallholders and transformed India from a food-deficient, poverty-rampant agrarian society to a food-surplus country with a relatively well-developed and diversified dynamic rural sector despite a still high incidence of poverty. But in Africa, the green revolution has yet to arrive. China's successful transition from a rigid centrally planned economy to a dynamic and largely market-driven economy provides important lessons for other formerly centrally planned economies in the former Soviet Union and Central Asia, where the transition has been less successful.

Third, China and India also account for the bulk of the world's poverty. Taking the poverty line of U.S.$1 per day (1985 PPP dollars) used by the World

---

6. The calculations assume an annual growth of 5 percent for both China and India and 2 percent for the world economy.

7. China, Ministry of Agriculture, *China agricultural development report*, 2003; NBS 2003; WDI 2003.

Bank, China still had nearly 106 million rural poor in 1998 (World Bank 2000a), and, according to official data, India had about 196 million rural poor in 1999–2000. Taken together, the poor in the two countries account for more than a quarter of the 1.2 billion poor worldwide.[8] Thus, the achievement of the Millennium Development Goal (MDG) of halving the number of poor by 2015 is critically dependent on the success of these two countries in combating rural poverty. Given China's relatively more remarkable achievements in poverty alleviation, the comparative study of the reforms and rural development can offer valuable lessons for India as well as other developing countries in their continuing effort to eliminate poverty.

Finally, comparing the experiences of China and India is essential for promoting mutual understanding, which has been constrained in the past by political, ideological, and diplomatic factors. If these two countries come together for better understanding and cooperation, it will not only contribute to their development by inducing more trade and investment, scientific and technological exchanges, and cooperation, but will also offer opportunities for neighboring countries in the region to benefit from these two powerhouses of growth. This would increase regional prosperity and stability in Asia and strengthen global peace as well.

Outline of the Study

The study is organized into twenty-two chapters that are thematically clustered into seven sections. Agriculture and microinterventions in rural areas are at the center of the analysis given the phenomenal impact on poverty and growth at different times in China and India, especially with the introduction of reforms in the primary sector. This introductory chapter and Chapter 2 form Part I of the book, which provides an overview of agricultural and rural reforms in both countries and the framework for the subsequent analysis.

Part II focuses on access to land, health and education. These sectors have been highlighted because they form the initial conditions capable of fundamentally influencing the course, implementation, and outcome of rural reforms. Evolution of policies related to education, health, and land and the landmark events and reforms that characterized their progress are highlighted.

Part III examines investments in rural areas, technology, and irrigation, factors that are key determinants of agricultural growth. A microperspective approach has been adopted for the study of agricultural and rural reforms.

The critical topics related to market and trade reforms in agriculture are reviewed in Part IV. With progressive liberalization of the Chinese and Indian economies, the cropping patterns were changed to optimize the comparative

---

8. World Bank 2001 and 2003b; India, Ministry of Agriculture, 2003.

advantage in production, leading to agricultural diversification away from basic staples like wheat and rice. This process was reinforced by increased demand for higher-value products such as those derived from horticulture, livestock, and fisheries, which triggered an increase in per capita income.

Besides the changes in crop mix, growth also led to the diversification in the overall rural economy and the emergence of the rural nonfarm (RNF) sector. Thus, Part V is devoted to rural diversification and vertical integration.

Economic growth was critical in wiping out large pockets of poverty, particularly among poor people close to the poverty line. However, for the most disadvantaged groups, who are located in remote areas or are socially discriminated against because they belong to minority or special castes, as in India, poverty is more intractable and requires well-targeted and sensitively designed antipoverty programs. Thus, antipoverty programs and safety nets are the subjects of detailed analysis in the chapters of Part VI.

Finally, the single chapter of Part VII synthesizes the main findings, distills policy lessons emerging from the Chinese and Indian reform experiences as documented in the previous chapters, and identifies future challenges for the reform agenda for the rural sector in these two Asian giants.

This volume concentrates primarily on understanding the process of growth, especially in agriculture and rural areas, and its impact on rural poverty. However, there are some other important implications of faster growth in these two countries, particularly related to widening inequalities of income and increasing stress on the environment. We well recognize the importance of these two topics, which we reiterate in the concluding chapter of this volume. But they were taken up in detail in another conference organized by IFPRI in Shanghai in 2006, and they form the core of another volume being prepared on the reform experiences of and the social and environmental implications for China and India, the dragon and the elephant.

2 Overview of Reforms and Development in China and India

SHENGGEN FAN, ASHOK GULATI, AND SARA DALAFI

They were giants in the golden past, one closed to the rest of the world, another vulnerable to conquerors. They may become giants again as the world stops to stare. We outline here the major policy and institutional changes that transformed agriculture and rural areas in China and India. Our main goal is to give an overview of major reform events and their sequence to provide the perspective necessary for understanding the subsequent chapters. Despite differences in timing and sequence, change in both countries was prompted by the political will to implement market-oriented reforms in order to improve economic performance and efficiency in resource allocation as well as to gradually integrate with other countries in the world economy. In India's case, short-term contingencies including severe fiscal and current account deficits were major factors pushing the reform movement, which began with liberalization and growth of trade and services, a kind of top-down drive. In the case of China, solid socioeconomic foundations and the communist goal of a better living for the population drove bottom-up change beginning with agriculture, especially through implementation of the Household Responsibility System (HRS). Despite this fundamental difference, in both countries reforms implied a progressive transition from an autarkic to a more deregulated and open policy environment with larger roles for the market and the private sector.

The Transformation of Agriculture and Rural Areas in China

The Chinese reforms can be divided into four phases. The first phase (1978–84) saw major institutional and pricing reforms aimed at improving production incentives. These included the end of collective farming and the decentralization of rural production through a new land tenure system, the HRS, and successive increases in the procurement prices of agricultural output. The second phase (1985–93) was characterized by substantial domestic agricultural marketing reforms, with special reference to the grain market. The pace of policy changes in the third phase (1994–2001) was dictated by China's efforts to enter the World Trade Organization (WTO) and was marked by broad-based trade liberalization.

WTO entry in 2001 marked the start of the fourth stage with a series of policy adjustments, currently under way, for the economy in general and the agrarian and rural sectors in particular, that consists of speedier domestic institutional, marketing, and trade reforms.

The Prereform Era, 1949–1977

Land Reform and Collectivization, 1949–1956

Until the 1949 revolution, land ownership in China was feudal, with 70 to 80 percent of agricultural land held by 10 percent of the landlords (China, Ministry of Agriculture, 1989). Most farmers were landless peasants who rented land from the landowners, usually at exorbitant rates. Between 1949 and 1952, land was confiscated by the government without compensation and redistributed equally among the farmers.

In the very first five-year plan (1952–57), the government needed to deal with the pressing issue of how to increase agricultural production to meet the needs of industry and urban areas. After the distribution of land to farmers, grain purchases and supply to cities at low cost by the government became progressively harder. Thus, beginning in 1952, the government adopted the collective mode of production along the lines of the Soviet model and encouraged farmers to "voluntarily" pool their land and other resources into larger production units called cooperatives. By 1956, most agricultural production was undertaken in cooperatives, each made up of around 200 families (Lin 1990; Putterman 1990).

The government exercised complete control over production by enforcing centrally set targets related to area, yield, output, and so on for each crop. Agricultural produce was subject to the fulfillment of compulsory quotas at fixed procurement prices. Farmers could sell any surplus at the higher above-quota prices (for grains, these were about 30 percent higher than the in-quota price). Trade was monopolized by state agencies, and private trade was limited to the county level and to a few commodities such as tea, tobacco, sugar, eggs, hogs, and so on (Sicular 1988b).

In terms of public investment, top priority was assigned to irrigation, which grew at an impressive rate in the prereform period (Fan, Zhang, and Zhang 2002). Irrigated area as a percentage of arable land grew from 23.25 percent in 1953 to 26.17 percent in 1957, an increase of 5 million hectares (ha) during the period of the first five-year plan alone. All these policies led to rapid growth in both agricultural production and productivity, with annual growth rates of 5.3 percent and 2.7 percent, respectively, from 1953 to 1956 (Figure 2.1).[1]

---

1. The growth rates of agricultural production and productivity used here were calculated using new measures constructed by Fan and Zhang (2002).

FIGURE 2.1 Growth in agricultural output and productivity in China and India

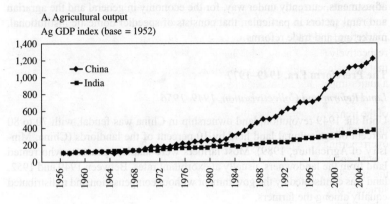

A. Agricultural output
Ag GDP index (base = 1952)

B. Total factor productivity (TFP)
TFP index (base = 1970)

SOURCES: A—Authors' calculations based on NBS, *China Statistical Yearbook,* 2006, and Datanet India Pvt. Ltd. (2006), data from 2003. B—China: Fan, Zhang, and Zhang (2002); India: Fan, Hazell, and Thorat (1999).

The Great Leap Forward and Communization, 1957–1960

The Chinese leaders believed mobilizing the masses could overcome any obstacle and enable China to turn overnight into a First World standard economy. The second five-year plan (1957–62) set the goal for China of overtaking the level of steel production of the United Kingdom. This required a further dramatic increase in agricultural production, and the government embarked on an even more ambitious plan. Advanced cooperatives were merged into "communes" where peasants worked and dined together in collective halls. At the height of the commune movement in 1958–59, the average collective had grown to 5,000 households covering 10,000 acres. The communes owned virtually all means of production, and agricultural labor was rewarded as much on the basis of need as on accumulated work points.[2]

This period also recorded sustained investments in agricultural research, power, and irrigation, which grew at 58.9, 50.0, and 47.2 percent per annum, respectively (Fan, Zhang, and Zhang 2002). The investments, as well as the fact that the state was able to easily mobilize people to work on public projects, gave a major impetus to infrastructure development.

However, farm activities were largely neglected during this phase. As part of the frenzy to catch up with the developed West, farmers were not only engaged in major public works but also involved in the production of steel.[3] There was overreporting of farm output—a common practice in a system without adequate checks and balances—as a result of which the procurement of the surplus for the cities left less food available to rural areas. Even the nature of the incentive structure of collective farming was not conducive to increasing production and productivity. Under the work point system, the role of the farmer was limited to mere supply of labor, and neither was farmers' income related to work effort nor did they have any say in the production decisions made by commune leaders.

As a result, farm output and productivity began to decline sharply: by 6 percent and 5 percent per annum, respectively (Fan, Zhang, and Zhang 2002). Droughts and floods in most of China in 1959 worsened the situation, leading to a famine of staggering proportions, the Great Famine of 1959–61. An estimated 30 million people died of starvation in an insulated economy without access to foreign assistance or a free press to draw attention to what was really happening in the countryside (Lin 1990; Becker 1996; Lin and Yang 2000). This was one of the largest human tragedies in history resulting from a combination of policy and natural failures. The problem of asymmetrical information flow between the top and the bottom of the power chain due to misreporting of output by lower levels of authority was a critical cause of this systemic failure. This catastrophic episode revealed the risks involved in a centralized command system. While on one hand it could effectively catalyze resources to foster rapid growth, on the other it could also lead to immense waste of resources in the absence of checks and balances (Desai 2003).

Economic Adjustments and Cultural Revolution, 1961–1977

The disastrous results of collective agriculture under the Great Leap Forward led to a phase of policy adjustments after 1961. Erstwhile extreme views on

---

2. Work points were an accounting mechanism used by collective leaders to allocate grains and income to farmers and their families. Work points were assigned based on various criteria, such as hours worked as well as political attitude and gender.

3. Encouraged to contribute to steel production, farmers built furnaces in their backyards, and to meet their steel quotas they ended up melting down their personal utensils, such as pots, doorknobs, and even farm tools, which was ultimately detrimental to farm work.

gigantic-scale agriculture were put aside, and production was reorganized into smaller subunits of the commune, called production teams and consisting of only 20 to 30 neighboring families. These were much smaller than even the cooperatives of the early 1950s. By 1962, production teams were the basic unit of operation and accounting in most rural areas. Between 1961 and 1965, controls on household production were relaxed, and farmers were allowed to cultivate private plots for self-consumption and, to a limited extent, sell their produce from private plots at the local markets (Chow 2002). As a result of these measures, production and productivity recovered rapidly, growing at 9.0 and 4.7 percent per annum, respectively, between 1961 and 1965 (Fan, Zhang, and Zhang 2002).

However, agricultural production and productivity growth were again depressed by policy failures during the decade of the Cultural Revolution (1966–76). The government reinstated many controls that had been relaxed during the three-year adjustment period from 1962 to 1965. Although production was organized into small production teams, it was nonetheless tightly controlled by the government. No market transactions of major agricultural products were allowed outside the procurement system, and market exchanges of land between different production units in the commune system were made illegal. Although an increasing amount of resources was poured into irrigation expansion and infrastructure development in the rural areas (Fan, Zhang, and Zhang 2002),[4] the weak incentive structure in agricultural production overrode the positive effects of these investments. Agricultural production in this period slowed to 2.6 percent, and there was virtually no gain in total factor productivity. This called for prompt intervention in the late 1970s (Fan, Zhang, and Zhang 2002).

However, even though the commune system entailed immense costs in terms of efficiency, it benefited the rural population in many significant ways. Provision of free access to education and health services contributed to improving literacy and life expectancy. The collectives were very effective in mobilizing masses for public works and helped build a critical base of irrigation facilities and other public goods in rural areas. Thus, despite tight restrictions, the commune era ended up creating favorable "initial conditions" of human development and basic infrastructure on which postreform China could capitalize.

---

4. Investment in irrigation, agricultural research, and power grew at 8.2, 9.5, and 14.0 percent per annum, respectively, between 1966 and 1977. Agricultural research investment grew from 0.3 to 0.5 of GDP during the 1970s. Between 1962 and 1975, irrigated area as a share of arable land grew from 32.9 percent to 47.6 percent, or from 31 million ha to 43 million ha. New advances in rural electrification drastically increased power consumption from 1.6 billion kW in 1962 to 18.3 billion kW in 1975.

The Reform Period, 1978 to the Present

Two decades (1956–76) of policy failures due to the excesses of the Great Leap Forward and the Cultural Revolution left China in a state of economic and social disarray. The time was ripe for a radical change in economic affairs because the government needed to restore its credibility in the eyes of the masses and deliver on its promise of economic prosperity (Chow 2002). Reforms started in agriculture, and the compulsion to reform came from the perception at the top that stagnation of agricultural productivity was a bottleneck in further development of the economy. Moreover, in many areas peasant unrest was building up and about to explode. The other driver was the need to improve China's status in the international arena. The successful performance of other East Asian countries, thriving under an export-oriented market model, helped to undermine the Chinese policymakers' unshakeable faith in the central planning system (White 1991; Chow 2002). The leaders were eager and determined to see China occupy a strong position in the world, and the only way to achieve this goal was through much higher rates of agricultural and overall economic growth. Improvement in incentives for farmers and the use of market mechanisms for the allocation of resources began to be regarded as the only way to boost efficiency and attain higher levels of growth.

The Decentralization of Agricultural Production and Procurement Price Increases, 1978–1984

One of the first initiatives was to increase incentives to raise the level of agricultural output by launching a new production management system called the Household Responsibility System, which marked the end of collective farming and the beginning of decentralization of agricultural production to the household level. The HRS was a "two-tier" land tenure arrangement in which land was still owned by the communes but user rights and production decisions were decentralized from the production teams to individual households. Farmers were free to decide what to cultivate and could even sell the surplus in the market after they had first met the state quotas, set at around 15–20 percent of output (White 1991; Chow 2002). The revolutionary impact of the new reform lay in the fact that it separated user rights from collective ownership and shifted them directly to producers by linking performance to work efforts. Thus, it improved incentives and eliminated the free rider problems inherent in the old collective system.

The introduction of the HRS was an instance of China's largely "gradual approach" to policy changes, that of "crossing the river while feeling the rocks." The HRS was not introduced from the top by government decree but, starting in the mid-1970s, was pushed through from the bottom as more and more counties abandoned collective farming due to its growing inefficiencies (Lin 1989).

The government sanctioned the new production system in 1979 only when, after extensive experimentation, it seemed to work well in the various localities that had implemented it (Chow 2002; Chapter 3 of this volume). By 1984, the HRS had been adopted nationwide.

Another major step taken during this phase was the government's decision to increase grain procurement prices. After a decade of constant prices, the government raised both in- and above-quota prices for major agricultural commodities. It can be argued that this administrative price hike was not a market-friendly intervention, but the measure nonetheless proved an effective incentive to boost production. By 1979, quota prices for rice and wheat were increased by 18–22 percent (Sicular 1988a, 1995). Above-quota prices for grains, which were 30 percent of the quota price until 1978, were raised to 50 percent of the quota rate. For cotton, quota prices were increased by 20 percent, and an above-quota price of 30 percent was first introduced in 1979 (Sicular 1988a, 1995). In addition, quota prices for oil crops were raised by 26 percent, for sugar crops by 22 percent, and for animal products by 23 percent. In contrast, the average rate of inflation was 2.75 percent between 1978 and 1984, with the overall retail price index rising from 100.0 in 1978 to 117.7 in 1984 (calculations based on NBS 2001). Because all these price increases were covered by the central government budget, the budget deficit as a percentage of gross domestic product (GDP) increased from 0.28 percent in 1978 to 4.23 percent in 1979. The food subsidy as a percentage of GDP also increased gradually, from 0.31 percent in 1978 to 4 percent in 1981. But due to rapid overall economic growth, the budget deficit remained under control after 1981 and was often less than 1 percent of GDP. Some major fiscal and financial indicators are presented in Table 2.1.

The period 1978–84 also saw the implementation of a series of far-reaching reforms aimed at reducing the scope of government planning and procurement while gradually expanding the role of free markets in resource allocation. After 1978, plan targets for yield, output, sown area, and so on were applied to fewer and fewer crops, and they became more a guide than a mandate (Sicular 1988b). This reform indirectly encouraged crop diversification based on local comparative advantages, because farmers were no longer constrained by plan targets. Further, quota levels for grains were lowered by as much as 20 percent between 1978 and 1982 (Sicular 1988b), and the number of commodities subject to public procurement was gradually reduced, leaving more agricultural produce to be sold in the free market (China, Ministry of Agriculture, 1989).[5] By the mid-1980s, marketing activities were completely liberalized for non-staple products such as fruits and vegetables, although the government still

---

5. The number of commodities under procurement dropped from more than 100 in 1978 to fewer than 40 by 1984.

retained tight control over strategic commodities, namely cereals, cotton, and edible oils, which accounted for the bulk of the sown area.

In trade, the state monopoly was broken as private individuals and businesses were allowed to engage in trade alongside state agencies. Rural markets and periodic fairs were encouraged. The government also allowed more products to be exchanged and allowed them to be traded in a larger area.

The impact of these reforms, particularly the HRS, was impressive in terms of agricultural performance and poverty reduction. Many regard the change in farming institutions from collectives to households as the major driver of growth during this phase, with the change in procurement prices and other marketing interventions playing a secondary role.[6] Agricultural production increased by 6.6 percent per annum and productivity by 6.1 percent from 1979–84. China experienced grain surpluses of 300–350 million tons (mt) a year in the early 1980s (FAOSTAT 2003).[7] There was a sharp increase in output and yields of the main agricultural commodities. The output of grain, cotton, and oilseeds increased at rates of 4.8, 7.7, and 13.8 percent, respectively, as opposed to rates of 2.4, 1.0, and 0.8 percent from 1952 to 1978 (Chen, Wang, and Davis 1999). It is clear from Table 2.2 and Figure 2.2 that agricultural GDP grew at a much higher rate in the reform period—7 percent between 1978 and 1984—compared to only 2.3 percent in the prereform period, 1952–77.

As a result, the per capita rural real income growth rate zoomed to 15.5 percent per year (from 220 yuan in 1978 to 522 yuan in 1984 at 1990 prices), contrasting sharply with the pace of 2.3 percent per annum in the prereform period (Fan, Zhang, and Zhang 2002). The striking feature of this phase of reforms is that it showed the biggest fall in poverty of all China's reform stages. According to official estimates, between 1978 and 1984 rural poverty declined from 33 percent to 15 percent of the population (NBS 2002). The number of people living in poverty declined from 260 million to 128 million in a mere six years. This is an unprecedented achievement in the history of development of any country. Unfortunately, this was also accompanied by a considerable increase in income inequality due to decollectivization and the dismantling of the egalitarian redistribution mechanisms of the commune system. Inequality as measured by the Gini coefficient grew from 0.21 in 1978 to 0.26 in 1984 (Fan, Zhang, and Zhang 2002).

---

6. For Lin (1992), the HRS accounted for 60 percent of agricultural output growth and 80 percent of productivity growth over 1978–84. The remainder was attributed to output price changes. McMillan, Whalley, and Zhu (1989) claimed that 80 percent of productivity growth came from the HRS and 20 percent from procurement price increases.

7. The figures refer to cereals and reflect the standard definition of the Food and Agriculture Organization of the United Nations.

TABLE 2.1 Major fiscal and financial indicators in China and India, 1970–2004

Years	Inflation rate[1]		Exchange rate[1]		Foreign reserves (U.S.$ billion)		Food subsidy (% of GDP)		Budget deficit (% of GDP)		Aid (% of GDP)[1]			
	China	India	China	India	China[2]	India[3]	China[4a]	India[5]	China[4]	India[5]	China	India	SSA	LIC
1970	-2.64	1.59	2.46	7.50	—	0.58	—	—	—	—	—	1.37	1.90	—
1971	0.66	5.32	2.46	7.49	—	0.66	—	—	—	—	—	1.53	2.17	—
1972	-0.02	10.89	2.25	7.59	—	0.63	—	—	—	—	—	0.87	2.04	—
1973	0.14	17.90	1.99	7.74	—	0.74	—	—	—	—	—	0.93	2.00	3.58
1974	0.23	16.70	1.96	8.10	—	0.78	—	—	—	—	—	1.26	2.17	4.42
1975	-1.16	-1.55	1.86	8.38	—	1.66	—	0.14	—	—	—	1.65	2.62	4.65
1976	-0.19	5.96	1.94	8.96	—	3.24	—	0.13	—	—	—	1.41	2.29	4.80
1977	1.09	5.58	1.86	8.74	2.35	5.31	—	0.14	—	—	—	0.84	2.44	5.19
1978	1.33	2.52	1.68	8.19	1.56	6.42	0.31	0.16	0.28	—	—	0.85	2.95	5.79
1979	3.56	15.79	1.55	8.13	2.15	6.32	1.36	0.16	4.23	—	0.01	0.92	3.2	6.59
1980	3.78	11.51	1.50	7.86	2.26	5.85	2.28	0.16	1.53	—	0.03	1.21	2.97	7.37
1981	2.31	10.26	1.70	8.66	4.78	3.58	4.09	0.16	0.52	—	0.25	1.05	2.96	6.96
1982	-0.19	7.72	1.89	9.46	11.14	4.28	2.95	0.16	0.55	—	0.26	0.84	3.31	7.31
1983	1.07	8.88	1.98	10.10	14.48	5.10	3.07	0.18	0.73	—	0.29	0.87	3.4	7.37
1984	4.89	7.42	2.32	11.36	16.71	5.48	2.81	0.18	0.62	—	0.31	0.81	4.11	7.40
1985	10.14	7.19	2.94	12.37	11.91	5.97	2.59	0.22	0.24	—	0.31	0.70	4.91	7.81
1986	4.60	6.77	3.45	12.61	10.51	5.92	2.07	0.32	0.69	—	0.37	0.82	5.39	8.64
1987	5.07	9.21	3.72	12.96	15.24	5.62	1.99	0.37	0.67	—	0.52	0.62	5.33	9.08
1988	12.12	8.29	3.72	13.92	17.55	4.23	1.64	0.36	0.53	—	0.63	0.67	5.78	9.46

Year														
1989	8.81	8.35	3.77	16.23	17.02	3.37	1.80	0.38	0.94		0.61	0.61	6.12	9.49
1990	5.68	10.55	4.78	17.50	28.59	2.24	1.67	0.35	0.79	6.60	0.57	0.44	6.38	10.62
1991	6.73	13.82	5.32	22.74	42.66	5.63	1.43	0.41	1.10	4.70	0.51	1.03	6.17	10.38
1992	7.90	8.85	5.51	25.92	19.44	6.43	0.99	0.38	0.97	4.80	0.72	1.00	6.60	11.81
1993	14.55	9.48	5.76	30.49	21.20	15.07	0.74	0.71	0.85	6.40	0.74	0.53	6.31	10.7
1994	19.90	9.68	8.62	31.37	51.62	20.81	0.49	0.61	1.17	4.70	0.58	0.72	7.2	12.77
1995	13.18	8.97	8.35	32.43	73.58	17.04	0.43	0.60	0.99	4.20	0.50	0.49	6.16	11.50
1996	5.92	7.24	8.31	35.43	105.03	22.37	0.50	0.63	0.78	4.10	0.32	0.49	5.13	8.33
1997	0.82	6.51	8.29	36.31	139.89	25.98	0.59	0.78	0.78	4.80	0.23	0.40	4.5	7.39
1998	-2.40	7.89	8.28	41.26	144.96	29.52	0.75	0.84	1.18	5.10	0.26	0.39	4.71	7.01
1999	-2.19	3.85	8.28	43.06	154.68	35.06	0.62	0.82	2.12	5.40	0.24	0.33	4.26	6.84
2000	0.94	3.79	8.28	44.94	165.57	39.55	0.87	1.01	2.78	5.70	0.16	0.32	4.33	6.77
2001	1.18	3.87	8.28	47.19	212.17	51.05	0.63	1.38	2.59	6.20	0.13	0.36	4.62	7.23
2002	-0.29	3.46	8.28	48.61	286.41	71.89	0.51	1.83	2.99	5.90	0.12	0.29	6.32	8.69
2003	—	—	—	—	403.25	107.45	0.47	1.80[b]	2.50	4.60[b]	—	—	—	—
2004	—	—	—	—	609.93		—	—	—	4.60[b]	—	—	—	—

SOURCES: [1]World Development Indicators, 2004; [2]IMF, various years; [3]India, RBI (2006); [4]NBS, *China Statistical Yearbook*, various years; [5]India, Ministry of Finance, *Economic Survey*, 2004–5.

NOTES: — For India 1970 to 2004 refers to the fiscal years, i.e 1970–71, ..., 2004–05.

NOTES: —, data unavailable; SSA, Sub-Saharan Africa; LIC, low-income countries (according to 2003 GNI per capita, calculated using the World Bank Atlas method of U.S.$765 or less).

[a]Food subsidies for China include edible oil, sugar, cotton, and meat.

[b]Provisional data.

TABLE 2.2 GDP and growth in China, by sector

	GDP (billion yuan, 2002 prices)			
	Total	Agriculture	Industry	Services
1952–55	301	339	38	106
1956–60	467	355	99	164
1961–65	436	334	91	153
1966–70	635	444	155	196
1971–75	921	513	276	258
1976–80	1,213	556	409	342
1981–85	1,872	748	636	600
1986–90	3,077	956	1,118	1,124
1991–95	4,899	1,177	2,109	1,711
1996–2000	7,814	1,442	3,807	2,600
2001	9,703	1,566	4,876	3,268
2002	10,479	1,612	5,354	3,513
Annual growth rate (%)[a]				
Prereform period				
1952–56	9.31	4.17	20.47	9.02
1957–60	9.50	–11.47	26.56	12.76
1961–65	10.45	10.06	13.82	6.84
1966–77	6.59	2.49	10.33	5.10
1952–77	*5.43*	*2.29*	*9.42*	*4.18*
Reform period				
1978–84	8.81	7.11	8.23	11.62
1985–93	8.82	4.08	11.33	9.15
1994–2002	8.24	3.38	9.82	8.17
1978–2002	*9.76*	*4.65*	*12.02*	*10.37*

SOURCE: Calculations based on data from NBS, *China Statistical Yearbook,* 2003.

NOTE: Values are simple averages for the time periods indicated.

[a]Growth rates are calculated by fitting a linear regression trend line to the logarithmic annual values.

Domestic Marketing Reform and the Rise of the Rural Nonfarm Sector, 1985–1993

The success of the early reforms encouraged the Chinese government to continue improving incentives in agricultural production through administrative as well as market-oriented interventions. However, these were punctuated by policy reversals to ensure that the new measures did not undermine procurement and self-sufficiency in strategic commodities such as foodgrains.

As cereal production went up steadily, from 280 mt in 1980 to an all-time high of 366 mt in 1984, ensuring the country's food security (FAOSTAT 2004),

FIGURE 2.2 GDP growth in China and India

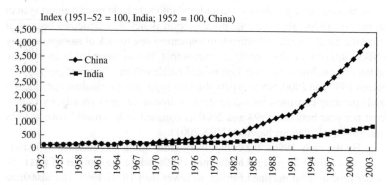

Index (1951–52 = 100, India; 1952 = 100, China)

SOURCES: Calculations for China are based on data from NBS, *China Statistical Yearbook,* 2003; calculations for India are based on India, CSO (2004), and India, RBI (2003).

the procurement system was changed from a mandatory quota system to a contract system in 1985. Quantities for state purchase were to be negotiated between state agencies and farmers and were priced using a unified "proportionate price" that replaced the in- and above-quota prices, which was a weighted average of the two (Sicular 1988b). This eased the pressure on the government's budget, because the government was no longer compelled to buy growing volumes of output above the contracted amounts. However, the indirect effect of the reform was to decrease grain production by 7 percent in 1985. It did not recover to the 1984 level until 1989, primarily because the proportionate contract prices were lower than the old above-quota and market prices, making farmers unwilling to conclude contracts with state agencies (Sicular 1988b).

To boost production of grains and cotton, the reform was reversed and the contract system made mandatory, which in practice amounted to a return to the old quota system. A new wave of quota price increases was also implemented between 1986 and 1988 (Sicular 1988a). The resultant renewed growth in grain output in the late 1980s led to further liberalization of the grain market. Following two years of regional experiments, the rationing system for urban consumers was dismantled in 1993, mainly to ease the pressures on the budget due to increasing price subsidies. The growing gap between the fixed ration (retail) price for consumers and the rising plan prices drained government coffers (Sicular 1988a). By 1985, the total price subsidy had grown to 3 percent of GDP and 13 percent of total revenues (NBS 2001). Some 76 percent of this subsidy went to price increases in grains, cotton, and edible oils.

A grain buffer stock policy was established for the first time in 1990 with a "special grain stock" and a related "grain risk fund" financed at both the central and provincial levels. In response to the fall in grain prices due to domestic oversupply, the government reinstated unlimited purchase of output by state grain bureaus, and the quota system turned into a de facto price support system in the late 1990s. However, the price support policy was criticized because it proved a fiscal burden and difficult to implement due to lack of storage capacity (NBS 2001)). With the growth in grain output, this measure led to an increase in the price subsidy for grain, cotton, and edible oils of 12 percent per year between 1990 and 2000, while expenditure for supporting agricultural production and operating expenses, including stock maintenance, grew rapidly, by 14 percent per year between 1994 and 2000 as opposed to 8 percent between 1978 and 1989 (calculations based on NBS 2001).

By the early 1990s, the compulsory grain quota had declined to 13 percent, down from 20 percent in the mid-1980s, while the number of products under procurement declined further, to fewer than 10 by 1991. Because state procurement was abandoned steadily, the share of all farm produce sold at market prices soared, and by 1993 nearly 80 percent of farm produce was sold on free markets compared with only 5.6 percent in 1978 (Sicular 1995). As a result, private trade expanded remarkably in terms of both numbers of business units and volumes traded (Sicular 1995). Between 1980 and 1993, the number of rural periodic markets increased from 38,000 to 67,000, and that of retail businesses soared from 1.7 million to 10 million, with trade conducted in rural markets rising by 12 percent per year and retail sales by 8 percent per year (Sicular 1995). Thus, as soon as the long-standing restrictions were lifted, the entrepreneurial spirit of Chinese farmers flowered.

Meanwhile, while reforms were apace in output markets, they lagged behind in agricultural inputs during the 1980s. The government controlled the price as well as the distribution of China's major agricultural input, chemical fertilizers, until the early 1990s, when the fertilizer market was liberalized as part of the concessions made to facilitate China's WTO entry. The government's grip on the input market was continued for fear that giving up control of such a strategic sector without putting in place adequate market mechanisms might cause disruption in agricultural production.

The effects of the new wave of marketing reforms on agricultural performance were more moderate than those of the institutional and price reforms of the previous reform phase. The HRS was widely adopted and had exhausted its revolutionary impact. After a while, its deficiencies (in terms of imperfect land use rights) began to take a toll on the performance of the sector. Agricultural production and productivity grew by 3–4 percent and 2 percent per annum, respectively, from 1985 to 1993, which was significant but not as sustained as in the previous phase (Fan, Zhang, and Zhang 2002).

Thus, the decline in rural poverty in this phase was more modest—from 15 percent of the population to 8 percent. This was despite the fact that a formal poverty alleviation policy was adopted for the first time in the mid-1980s with the introduction of major antipoverty programs such as the National Plan for Poverty Reduction, 1986, and the 8–7 Poverty Reduction Plan, 1994.[8] This development lends credence to the argument that such poverty-alleviating spending may be inefficient.

A consequence of the first two waves of reforms was the emergence of a vibrant rural nonfarm sector (RNF), which contributed to the growth and diversification of the rural economy and farmers' income. The RNF was almost absent in China in 1978, but accounted for nearly 25 percent of the country's GDP in the mid-1990s (Fan, Zhang, and Zhang 2002). The rise of the RNF in China was specially stimulated by the growth in agricultural labor productivity and rural incomes, which increased demand for nonagricultural goods and services and released surplus workforce and capital for investment in town and village enterprises (TVEs). More interesting, the growth of rural businesses also put pressure on the urban economy to reform, because TVEs had over time become more competitive than state-owned enterprises (SOEs). The need to reform the urban sector in turn triggered the macroeconomic changes of the mid-1980s.

Pre–WTO Trade Liberalization, 1994–2001

China submitted its formal bid to join the General Agreement on Tariffs and Trade as early as 1986, but it was only after prolonged negotiations that it was officially admitted into the WTO in December 2001. During the intervening 15 years, the foreign trade regime was gradually changed to introduce an export-oriented and more open trade system. Major reforms included the development of regional open-door policies and fiscal and exchange rate measures, liberalization of foreign direct investment (FDI), and improvement of market access (tariff and nontariff) (Huang et al. 1999). Entry into the WTO had the positive effect of giving China "most favored nation" status on a permanent basis, which eliminated the uncertainty over the yearly renewal of this status by the United States and China's other major foreign commercial partners (Agrawal and Sahoo 2003).

To increase its exports and foreign exchange earnings, China had initiated small changes in the fixed exchange rate regime since the first phase of reform.[9] In 1993–94 the exchange rate system was changed from a two-tier system (with an administered official exchange rate and a swap exchange rate)[10] into a unified managed exchange rate pegged to the U.S. dollar (Agrawal and Sahoo 2003).

---

8. This plan focused on 592 designated poor counties with the objective of lifting the remaining 80 million rural poor above the official poverty line during the seven-year plan (1994–2000), and thus was called the 8–7 plan.

9. In 1979 the government introduced the "foreign retention system," which allowed firms to keep foreign exchange subject to improvement in export performance.

10. The swap rate was determined by a swap center where foreign exchange could be traded by businesses based on demand and supply needs. The swap rate was higher than the government-planned rate.

Table 2.1 gives the exchange rates over the past three decades for both China and India. In the prereform period the overvaluation of China's domestic currency negatively affected its overall export environment, but after the launch of economic reforms in 1978 the exchange rate was steadily depreciated, correcting the bias against exports (Agrawal and Sahoo 2003).[11] However, since 1995 the nominal exchange rate has been fixed at 8.3 yuan per U.S. dollar (Agrawal and Sahoo 2003), and at the end of 1996 the yuan was made convertible in the current account of the balance of payment (BOP). With the currency becoming convertible, it is logical to ask if the exchange rate can be fixed even as the BOP current account accumulates surpluses. In other words, is the de facto undervaluation of the currency actually providing hidden export subsidies? This controversy surrounding the Chinese exchange rate is now fueling debates in major international forums in the face of China's growing manufacturing exports.

With regard to market access, across-the-border reductions in product-specific rates were carried out, after which the weighted average import tariff declined from 47.2 percent in 1991 to 16 percent in 2000 (Huang and Rozelle 2002a). In agriculture, the simple average tariff dropped from 42 percent in 1992 to about 21 percent by 2001. The evolution of nominal protection rates for major farm products reveals the extent of improvement in market access over the past two decades. In the late 1970s domestic prices for wheat, rice, and maize were 89, 10, and 92 percent above international prices, respectively, whereas these percentages fell to 26, –2, and 23 percent in 2000 (Huang and Rozelle 2003).

Barring strategic crops such as grains and edible oils, trading of most agricultural commodities was gradually taken out of the monopoly of state agencies. The official agency was the China Oils and Foodstuffs Corporation, which in the late 1990s was restructured to operate on commercial lines and its monopoly ended, allowing nonstate enterprises to enter the market for rice, wheat, and maize.

As a result of 20 years of reforms, China's foreign trade escalated at a rate of 18 percent a year between 1978 and 2002 (FAOSTAT 2004; WDI 2004). Trade has become a major contributor to the country's economic growth, increasing its share from 15 percent of GDP at the start of reform in 1978 to nearly 60 percent in recent years (WDI 2004).

The WTO–induced lowering of tariff and nontariff barriers helped shift trade patterns favoring products in which the country had comparative advantage, including labor-intensive products such as horticultural produce and livestock, at the expense of land-intensive commodities such as traditional cereals. Thus, the share of fruits, vegetables, and animal products in total exports grew from 57 percent in 1985 to 75 percent in 1997, while the share of grains and

---

11. The real exchange rate depreciated by nearly 400 percent from 1979 to the mid-1990s.

edible oils dropped from 33 percent to 21 percent in the same period (Huang et al. 1999).

So, while trade liberalization benefited the producers of labor-intensive products, favoring diversification of agricultural output away from grains, less-developed areas in particular were penalized as they concentrated on grain production. Affected farm households and groups included those lacking the opportunity to shift to nonfarm employment because of poor education and also those dependent on government welfare. Decrease in protection and consequent greater exposure to foreign competition put increasing pressure on the government to restructure SOEs, which traditionally performed several welfare functions ranging from retirement to health and unemployment insurance.

Post–WTO Adjustments, 2002 to the Present

After China entered the WTO, reforms in the marketing of grains were stepped up and remnants of the procurement system were dismantled. The costly food-grain support price system adopted a few years earlier was partially abandoned, maintained only in major producing regions of the northeast. This was necessary not only for fiscal reasons but also due to the need to prevent excessive accumulation of stocks with state grain enterprises even as cheap food imports were rising. Starting in 2002, China took steps to fully liberate the foodgrain marketing system by phasing out state procurement over three years.

Two major breakthrough measures were taken in 2004: the gradual reduction of the agricultural tax by 1 percent a year, to zero in five years, and the introduction of a direct income transfer to farmers, averaging 300 yuan per ha in 13 major grain-producing regions (China Daily 2004). Both these measures, aimed at increasing farmers' income, are significant because they seek to correct the historical industrial bias in China's economic policy. The new emphasis on farmers' interests marked the start of a new strategy in agriculture, swinging from the traditional taxation to subsidization.

In the post–WTO phase, another land reform was implemented to improve tenure security and boost development of land lease markets. In 2003 a new land law, the Agricultural Lease Law, was passed to address some of the drawbacks of the HRS, which had started to impact its performance. The effect of this system on agriculture was telling: growth had decelerated considerably, from 7.1 percent during adoption of the HRS in the period 1978–84 to around 4 percent subsequently (NBS 2003). The shortcomings were in part related to the practice of land redistribution that aimed to give rural households equal access to village land in the event of births or deaths (Chen, Wang, and Davis 1999). Land reallocations led over time to fragmentation of holdings and reduced farmers' incentives to invest in land. The new law aimed at curbing land reallocations by the village authority to improve tenure security and boost agricultural investments and in turn productivity. For some, however, greater tenure security resulting from the new law might not have as much impact as expected due to different informal mechanisms developed in the field over time to counter the impacts of land reallocations.

The law was also a new step toward increased individualization of land rights because it sanctions the right to inherit and sell leaseholds of arable land for 30 years, paving the way to the development of land lease markets (Chen, Wang, and Davis 1999).

In the area of trade liberalization, the trend of declining trade protection is likely to continue. In fact, China committed itself to reducing the average agricultural tariff from 21 to 17 percent by 2004, which would further increase the degree of openness of the primary sector and deepen its integration with world markets. As was the case with the introduction of domestic marketing reforms over the past 20 years, the WTO commitments to further liberalize the economy are regarded as the prime policy measures from which the government expects additional opportunities to deepen the reform process and achieve greater growth.

Finally, population control policies adopted throughout the reform period, mainly the one-child norm, were successful in bringing population growth under control and helped raise overall per capita income (Figure 2.3).

Transformation and Policy Reforms in Indian Agriculture

The green revolution dominated the prereform period in India from 1951 to 1990. Here we briefly review the factors leading to it and the subsequent phases of its growth and impact to set the context for the economic reforms of the 1990s.

The reforms unfolded in three different phases: the first (1991–94) involved changing a broad set of policies outside agriculture, creating pressure for extending the reforms to agriculture. The second phase (1994–98) brought the primary sector under the purview of reforms that aimed at gradually decontrolling agricultural trade flows. As a result of the series of unilateral government initiatives and, to a more limited extent, in response to the signing of the Uruguay Round Agreement on Agriculture under the WTO in 1994, the sector underwent limited changes. The third stage (1998 to the present) extended the reforms to domestic agricultural marketing but left the traditional support system of input subsidies, food procurement at subsidized prices through the Public Distribution System (PDS), and the minimum support prices (MSPs) largely unaltered.

The Prereform Era, 1951–90

Before the Green Revolution, 1951–1965

Right after India achieved independence in 1947, the focus of rural policy was on land reforms and building up rural infrastructure, especially irrigation, both

FIGURE 2.3 Population growth in China and India

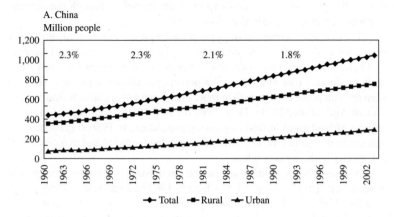

A. China
Million people

2.3%   2.3%   2.1%   1.8%

◆ Total   ■ Rural   ▲ Urban

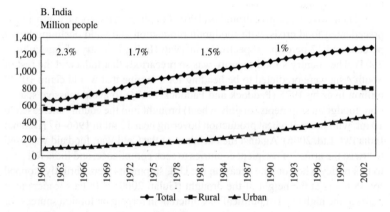

B. India
Million people

2.3%   1.7%   1.5%   1%

◆ Total   ■ Rural   ▲ Urban

SOURCE: WDI, *World Bank Statistics,* 2004.

of which were crucial for agricultural modernization. Overall, implementation of land reforms was only partially successful due to conflicts of interest crippling landlord-controlled state legislatures. The truly successful intervention in this phase was investment in irrigation. The first five-year plan (1951–56) allocated 31 percent of the budget to agricultural development (Chandra, Mukherjee, and Mukherjee 2000), partly the development of potentially 2.5 million ha of irrigated area (Datanet India Pvt. Ltd. 2006). However, rural outlays decreased to 20–25 percent as India formally adopted the socialist strategy of heavy industrialization during the second five-year plan (1956–61). Under this model, agricultural policy was conceived with a built-in pro-urban bias. To provide inexpensive food and basic inputs for industrial development, the farm prices were kept artificially low and agricultural exports were curtailed through quantitative restrictions and an overvalued exchange rate.

The new development strategy put pressure on agriculture because the new investments in capital goods and industrial plants implied a long gestation period before they could translate into higher incomes. Between 1951 and 1966, grain production rose at a rate of 2.8 percent per annum, a rate that failed to keep up with population growth at more than 2 percent per annum (India, Ministry of Agriculture, 2004). Thus, from the mid-1950s India began to rely on imports of foodgrains to feed its growing population. In 1956, India signed the agreement of Public Law 480 (P.L. 480) with the United States to receive food aid, mostly in the form of wheat.

A series of tragic political and natural circumstances increased foreign food dependency. After two wars (with China in 1962 and Pakistan in 1965), India found itself in a deadlock because large amounts of resources had to be channeled to meet defense needs, and, as a result, rural investments were sacrificed (Fan, Thorat, and Rao 2004).

Then two consecutive droughts (1965–66) plunged the country into an unprecedented food crisis, with foodgrain production and yield declining by 19 percent and 17 percent, respectively, in 1966 (India, Ministry of Agriculture, 2004). The country's food security was so precarious that India and the rest of South Asia were predicted to be heading for a famine that would claim 10–20 million lives by 1975 (Paddock and Paddock 1967). To avoid massive starvation, foodgrain shipments (mainly wheat) brought into the country increased to 10 mt, with internal wheat production hovering near 12 mt in 1966–67 (Datanet India Pvt. Ltd. 2006). Against the backdrop of the Cold War, food aid was used to "twist the arms" of recipient countries to seek compliance, and India fell prey to this policy when on one occasion the U.S. shipments were abruptly stopped for 48 hours at the height of the drought (Gulati 2000).[12] India's leaders then realized the high level of political risk inherent in relying on foreign sources for food security and resolved to achieve self-sufficiency in grain production, no matter what it cost. The history of the goal of food self-sufficiency that would shape Indian agricultural policy for the next 40-odd years can be traced back to this period, especially the government's harsh experience with food aid then.

The First Burst of the Green Revolution, 1966–1972

To end its dependence on P.L. 480, India, prompted by the minister of agriculture at the time, C. Subramaniam, adopted a brand-new agricultural strategy to spur grain production. The minister started off by introducing a remunerative

---

12. The order to stop food shipments was a result of U.S. displeasure at India's stance on the Vietnam war and the closer ties with the Soviet Union following Indira Gandhi's visit to Moscow in 1966.

support price for farmers. In January 1965, the Agricultural Prices Commission was set up to recommend a MSP, followed by the Food Corporation of India (FCI) to take charge of the logistics of procuring major agricultural commodities (Gulati 2003). In the same year, India took a bold step by allowing the introduction of new high-yielding seed varieties (HYV) of wheat from Mexico created by CIMMYT (Centro Internacional de Mejoramiento de Maíz y Trigo), an international institute for research on maize and wheat.

The new seeds could yield more than double the existing levels and thus had the potential to dramatically increase wheat production and foodgrain supply. At first there was extensive opposition to the import of large quantities of the HYV seeds, owing partly to the potential inequalities they could create in agriculture and partly also to their lower gluten content and less than optimal baking qualities. However, with the support of Prime Ministers Lal Bahadur Shastri at first and Indira Gandhi later, Subramaniam overcame public resistance. In 1966 India ordered the import of 18,000 tons of HYV wheat seeds that were distributed in the highly irrigated areas of Punjub, Haryana, and western Uttar Pradesh where the past investments in irrigation had paid rich dividends. Under the new agricultural policy, the spread of HYVs was supported by public investments in fertilizers, power, irrigation, and credit (Fan, Thorat, and Rao 2004). The outcome of the experiment was miraculous, leading to a veritable green revolution.

In 1967–68, wheat production in Punjab increased by nearly 30 percent, from 2.5 mt to 3.3 mt, while the all-India average was 16.5 mt, nearly 5 mt more than its best performance in 1964–65 (Datanet India Pvt. Ltd. 2006).[13] The total amount of foodgrains harvested soared from 74 mt in 1966–67 to 105 mt in 1971–72, and that year India became self-sufficient, with grain imports declining to nearly zero (India, Ministry of Agriculture, 2003).

These outcomes would not have been possible without the favorable pricing policy that provided farmers with adequate incentives, the dynamism of the national research system that proceeded to indigenize the new seeds to tackle their shortcomings (Gulati 2003), and the availability of inputs including canal water, fertilizers, power, and credit. In view of the strategic importance of these critical inputs, it was the responsibility of the government to ensure that farmers had affordable access to them. Subsidies thus became an instrument of agricultural policy in the late 1960s and acquired greater importance in the 1970s (Gulati and Narayanan 2002a). The role of credit began to be important after 1969 following the nationalization of banks.

Improved agricultural production resulting from modern input and technologies "trickled down" to the poor and led to a rise in farmer income, while

---

13. It is even reported that there was no place to store this sudden burst of grain, and schools in rural Punjab actually had to be closed to make space for the new harvest to be stored in classrooms.

output growth and increased grain supplies caused a decline in real foodgrain prices, benefiting the poor. Thus, rural poverty declined significantly in this phase, from 64 percent in 1967 to 56 percent in 1973 (Datanet India Pvt. Ltd. 2006). Several government antipoverty programs were also introduced during the fourth five-year plan in the early 1970s.

Debacle and the Second Phase of the Green Revolution, 1973–1980

After the nationalization of the banks, Prime Minister Indira Gandhi took other steps to extend the role of the state in key areas of economic management. In agriculture, private wholesale traders came under attack because, due to their speculative motives, they were regarded as responsible for fluctuations in food-grain prices and supplies. Thus, in 1973–74 the government took over the whole-sale trade in wheat, but the maneuver proved a disaster (Chopra 1981). Wheat procurement was hindered by limited supply resulting from droughts in several states in 1972–73, and the fledgling FCI could not prove itself up to the task.

Procurement dropped to 4.5 mt from more than 5 mt in preceding years, and the cereal price index (base 1961–62 = 100) jumped from 236 to 278 in the course of 1973 (Chopra 1981). The inflationary pressures worsened when the 1973 international oil crisis fueled fertilizer prices. Following two consecutive droughts in 1972–73, foodgrain production decreased by 7.7 percent (India, Ministry of Agriculture, 2003), and India slid back into the trap of foodgrain imports of an average of about 4 mt a year from the United States between 1973 and 1976 (FAOSTAT 2004).

After the oil shock, the government increased fertilizer subsidies to prevent a drop in consumption following the rise in fertilizer prices (Schumacher and Sathaye 1999). In 1977 the retention price scheme was introduced for urea, the predominant fertilizer in Indian agriculture. During the 1970s, other input subsidies grew in importance within the state budget (Fan, Thorat, and Rao 2004), and the subsidy bill excluding fertilizers grew from Rs. 10 billion at constant prices to Rs. 33.2 billion, or from 0.5 percent to 4.0 percent of agricultural GDP, between 1973 and 1980 (Gulati and Narayanan 2002a). The irrigation subsidy was related to a major rebound of investments in projects during the 1974–79 fifth five-year plan. Also during this period, groundwater irrigation increased in importance, with its share rising from 0.55 percent to 19.5 percent between 1960 and 1975 (Datanet India Pvt. Ltd. 2006) on account of private investment in tube wells by farmers who reinvested the income from the earlier burst in foodgrain production. As a result, power subsidies for water pumping grew dramatically, reaching 44 percent of the total input subsidy at the start of the 1980s (Gulati and Narayanan 2002a).

The extension of HYV technology from wheat to rice, favored by the growth of tubewells, spread the green revolution to new areas, marking a new phase in the expansion of domestic production. From 1972–73 to 1979–80, production as well as yields of foodgrains showed remarkable growth, at 3.1 percent and

2.5 percent, respectively, and rural poverty declined from roughly 56 percent to 50 percent (India, Ministry of Agriculture, 2004).

The Third Phase of the Green Revolution, 1981–1990

In the 1980s India consolidated its status as a food self-sufficient country. Rice production soared to 63.8 mt in 1986, up from 37.0 mt in 1964. Wheat output grew, too, from 12 mt to 47 mt in 1986, a year in which India had her first 25.4 mt of grain buffer stocks (India, Ministry of Agriculture, 2004). When in 1987 the "worst drought of the century" struck the country, food needs could be easily met without any loss of lives (Gulati 2003).

During this phase the HYV technology spread eastward to states like West Bengal and Bihar, which experienced surpluses in rice, with output over the 1980s growing at 5.0 and 3.7 percent, respectively (Datanet India Pvt. Ltd. 2006). However, in the rest of the country the green revolution ran out of steam by 1985 once the new seed varieties had been widely adopted in the main producing regions. Yields for rice and wheat that had grown, respectively, by 3.5 percent and 4.5 percent per annum between 1967–68 and 1984–85 slowed down to 2.3 and 2.4 percent per year between 1985–86 and 1999–2000 (IFPRI 2004). With the HYV technology exhausting its impact in the mid-1980s, input subsidies were steadily increased to continue sustaining foodgrain production growth. By 1991, input subsidies had grown to 7.2 percent of agricultural GDP as compared to 4.4 percent in 1980 and to 2.0 percent of total GDP from 1.5 percent in 1980 (Gulati and Narayanan 2002a).

Throughout the green revolution, Indian agriculture labored under a strictly regulated policy regime characterized by wide restrictions on production through licensing requirements and barriers to entry, as well as controls on pricing, movement, and private trading of agricultural produce. On the external front, too, the sector was burdened with various tariff and nontariff barriers to agricultural trade flows.

The high level of protection accorded to industry produced high industrial prices and adverse terms of trade (TOT) for agriculture, reducing the relative profitability of the primary sector.[14] Agriculture was overall net taxed (disprotected) on account of the overvalued rupee,[15] which produced an antiexport environment for agriculture. The objectives of this framework were broadly dictated by the dominant strategy of the prereform era, that is, food self-sufficiency resulting from domestic supplies, aiming to (1) ensure inexpensive food for

---

14. Agricultural TOT, or the quotient of agricultural prices to manufacturing prices, were nearly 0.95 in 1990–91 (India, Ministry of Finance, cited in Gulati, Pursell, and Mullen 2003).

15. In the 1990s the excess of the free trade exchange rate over the official rate increased from about 30 percent in the early 1990s to 40–50 percent by the late 1990s. The overvalued rupee imposed roughly a 20 percent tax on domestic agricultural production (Landes and Gulati 2003).

consumers, (2) protect farmers' incomes from price fluctuations, and (3) keep the balance of payments in check.

In the 1990s, however, the policy framework that had kept Indian agriculture isolated and rigorously regulated for three decades would change in a limited but significant way.

The Reform Period, 1991 to the Present

Macroeconomic and Nonagriculture Sector Reforms, 1991–1994

Starting in 1991, India adopted a series of sweeping macroeconomic and structural reforms in industry, the exchange rate, and foreign trade and investments (World Bank 2003b). The compulsion to reform came as a conditionality of the International Monetary Fund (IMF) and the World Bank, which gave India a loan to tackle one of the most severe macroeconomic crises in decades affecting the country's fiscal and balance of payment situations. By 1990–91, the external position had grown weak and the current account deficit, amounting to 3.1 percent of GDP in 1990, had pushed foreign reserves to historic lows of U.S.$1.5 billion, enough to finance only a few weeks of imports (Desai 2003). Internally, government expenditures, particularly nonplan expenditures financed through borrowing, had soared unchecked in the 1980s and had become unsustainable by 1990–91. The central fiscal deficit and that of the states together added up to 9 percent of GDP, and the short-term debt had grown to an alarming 146.5 percent of foreign reserves (Srinivasan and Tendulkar 2003). Inflation was in the double digits, and the fear of an imminent devaluation led to a flight of capital from the economy.

Against this backdrop, the government of Narasimha Rao came to power in July 1991 and, with Finance Minister Manmohan Singh at the helm, managed to rapidly stabilize the fundamental macroeconomic factors. With a view to redressing the fiscal and current account deficits and under IMF conditionality, the government agreed to cut expenditures and imports and depreciate the nominal exchange rate. As a result, the combined fiscal deficit declined to 7 percent of GDP by 1992–93 and the BOP current account deficit dove from 3.2 percent of GDP in 1990 to 0.3 percent in 1991 (Srinivasan and Tendulkar 2003). Two consecutive devaluations of the rupee, by 22.8 percent and 17.3 percent in 1991 and 1992, respectively, contributed to a further improvement of the BOP situation by increasing exports (Srinivasan and Tendulkar 2003).

It was generally agreed that macroeconomic stabilization was not sustainable in the long term without structural adjustments to revive economic growth and industrial competitiveness. This was so especially because the pervasive regulations and distortions created by the public policies, along with infrastructure shortcomings, had hindered growth of efficiency in the economy. Thus, besides macroeconomic stabilization plans India also adopted an extensive program of longer-term sectoral reforms to liberalize industrial policy and investment as well as trade and the exchange rate regime.

In the area of investment, the government relaxed restrictions on domestic investments and raised the limit on equity participation by foreign capital in the case of foreign direct investment (Gulati and Mullen 2003). For industry, regulations on licensing, barriers to entry, and restrictions on scale expansion were relaxed. The number of industries to which entry required government approval for security and environmental reasons was drastically reduced, and the list of industries reserved for the public sector was trimmed to three: defense, nuclear energy, and railways (Ahluwalia 2002). More recently, the policy of reserving some products for small-scale industries, which aimed at protecting employment by fostering labor-intensive industries, was partially reformed because it had ended up limiting investment and technological innovation. In 2001–2, several products including auto components, garments, and shoes were excluded from this pool of reserved items (Ahluwalia 2002).

Fundamental reforms were also carried out in the exchange rate regime. After the devaluations, the rupee was made partially convertible on the current account in 1993 and the administered system that pegged the rupee to a basket of currency was replaced with a managed floating system, giving the market a greater role in influencing the exchange rate (Srinivasan and Tendulkar 2003). Finally, in the area of trade there was a gradual and substantial reduction in the level of import protection, which had been one of the highest among developing countries. Quantitative restrictions (QRs) on imports were reduced from 93 to 66 percent of tradable GDP by 1995 (Srinivasan and Tendulkar 2003). The weighted average tariff dropped from 72.5 percent in 1991–92 to 24.6 percent in 1996–97 (Ahluwalia 2002). Tariffs on industrial goods declined from as high as 300 percent for some commodities to a simple average of 30 percent between 1991 and 2002.

These policy changes led to a higher rate of economic growth, with GDP recording an impressive 6.5 percent per year growth between 1991–92 and 1996–97 compared to 5.2 percent in the 1980s (Table 2.3).

Overall, the reforms helped accomplish the shift from a closed to a more liberalized and open system. This is reflected in the change of indicators such as FDI inflows and the ratio of trade to GDP. From 1990 to 1995, FDI inflows grew from 0.07 percent to 0.6 percent of GDP, while imports and exports as a share of GDP increased from 17.2 percent to 25.7 percent, as shown in Figure 2.4 (WDI 2004). The foreign exchange situation improved remarkably, reaching U.S.$22.4 billion at the end of 1996 (India, Ministry of Finance, *Economic Survey 1997–98*) after rising from U.S.$1.5 billion at the height of the fiscal crisis in 1990 (Table 2.1).

Although the reforms were implemented in off-farm activities, they affected agriculture in at least two important ways (Landes and Gulati 2003). First, the higher rate of economic growth and the consequent rise in per capita

TABLE 2.3 GDP and growth in India, by sector

	GDP (billion rupees, 1993–94 constant prices, factor cost)			
	Total	Agriculture[a]	Industry	Services
1950–55	1,505	867	166	471
1956–60	1,802	982	223	595
1961–65	2,218	1,110	321	786
1966–70	2,560	1,162	405	993
1971–75	3,042	1,345	498	1,199
1976–80	3,671	1,514	640	1,509
1981–85	4,456	1,723	831	1,903
1986–90	5,757	1,961	1,182	2,614
1991–95	7,504	2,342	1,603	3,559
1996–2000	10,235	2,741	2,294	5,200
2001–4	13,023	2,991	2,839	7,193
Annual growth rate (%)[b]				
Prereform period				
1950–51 to 1959–60	3.62	2.68	5.81	4.43
1960–61 to 1969–70	3.23	1.50	5.03	4.81
1970–71 to 1979–80	3.39	1.72	4.95	4.33
1980–81 to 1989–90	5.24	2.91	7.26	6.26
1950–51 to 1990–91	*3.76*	*2.32*	*5.42*	*4.78*
Reform period				
1991–92 to 1996–97	6.52	4.10	8.65	7.05
1997–98 to 2003–4	5.37	2.01	4.90	7.10
1991–92 to 2003–4	*5.91*	*2.67*	*6.09*	*7.52*

SOURCES: India, CSO (2004); India, RBI (2003).

NOTE: Values are simple averages for the time periods indicated.

[a]Agricultural GDP includes farming and allied sectors (fishery and forestry).

[b]Growth rates are calculated by fitting a linear regression trend line to the logarithmic annual values.

incomes resulting from the 1991–93 reforms had a significant impact on food demand. Higher per capita incomes, growing at 4.5 percent per annum in this phase as opposed to 3.6 percent in the 1980s (WDI 2004), led to the diversification of food demand into nonfoodgrain crops such as fruits and vegetables, as well as meat—mainly poultry—and dairy products. Second, the lowering of industrial protection significantly improved the incentive framework for the sector through improvement in the domestic TOT between agricultural and industrial prices, which rose from 0.9 to 1.2 between 1991 and 2000, as shown in Figure 2.5.

Improved TOT for agriculture in turn resulted in an increase in the profitability of the primary sector relative to industry and led to an increase in private

FIGURE 2.4 Share of trade and agricultural trade in GDP in China and India

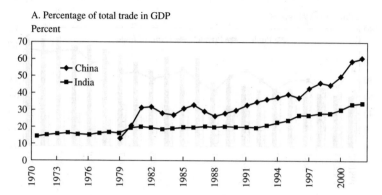

A. Percentage of total trade in GDP
Percent

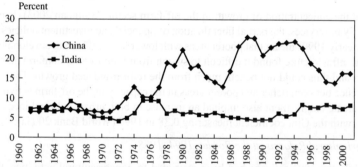

B. Percentage of agricultural trade in agricultural GDP
Percent

SOURCES: WDI, *World Bank Statistics,* 2003; FAOSTAT (2003).

investments, which are now double the public investment in agriculture. These were increasingly directed to the production of horticultural produce, poultry, fish, milk, and eggs in response to booming consumer demand for these high-value agricultural products, leading to a remarkable growth in output of these commodities during the 1990s relative to the previous decade (WDI 2004).

As a result of these developments, agricultural GDP went up from 3 percent in the 1980s to 4.1 percent in the aftermath of reforms between 1991 and 1996 (Datanet India Pvt. Ltd. 2006). However, the higher growth rates did not initially translate into a significant decline in rural poverty, which actually increased during 1991–92, reaching a peak of nearly 43.5 percent in 1992 (Datanet India Pvt. Ltd. 2006). It declined thereafter, fluctuating at the prereform level of 35–39 percent by the mid-1990s. Factors contributing to the lack of poverty reduction included the fiscal contraction imposed by macroeconomic stabilization

FIGURE 2.5 Terms of trade and gross agricultural capital formation in India

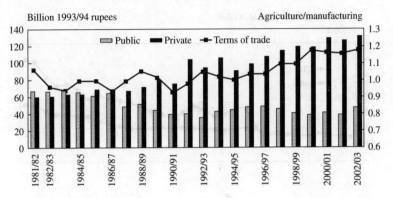

SOURCE: Gulati and Bathla (2002).

and the concentration of growth in the off-farm sector (Waldman 2003). Especially in services, the partial liberalization of financial and investment policies in the early 1990s meant that poorer areas with lower levels of human development and infrastructure found it difficult to switch from farm to rural nonfarm activities and thus could not benefit much from the reform-induced growth. The difference between richer and poorer areas in the capacity of the off-farm activities to create employment also implied an increase in both urban and rural inequality, with the Gini coefficient measuring 0.38 in 1997 (World Bank 2003a).[16]

Agricultural Reforms at the Border, 1994–1998

While the 1991 reforms had been restricted to nonagricultural activities, the signing of the Uruguay Round Agreement on Agriculture (URAA) under the WTO in 1994 officially extended the reform wave to agriculture, albeit limited to the area of trade. The changes were at first contained because there were not many disciplinary prescriptions for India under the URAA. In effect, of the three areas addressed by the URAA, domestic support, export subsidies, and market access, WTO commitments affected India only in the last category (Gulati and Kelley 1999). India was exempted from reducing domestic support because its aggregate measure of support, accounting for the impact of trade policy distortions in favor of domestic prices, was below 10 percent of the value of production, which was the prescribed minimum threshold for developing countries. Input and food subsidies were notified as support to resource-poor

---

16. The Gini coefficient declined to 0.31 in the early 1990s, but increased in the second half of the decade, reaching 0.38 in 1997 (the last year for which data from the World Bank are available).

farmers and as domestic food aid and were not subject to reduction. India was exempted on the export subsidy front, too, because it had none.

With regard to market access, India had been allowed by the WTO to maintain QRs on imports to manage the problems in the country's BOP. However, after the launch of the 1991 trade reforms and the improvement in the BOP by the mid-1990s, the QRs were no longer justifiable. Still, their abolition was very slow for fear of a surge in imports and was completed only in April 2001 (Gulati and Mullen 2003).[17] Even then, a special Standing Group of ministries was set up to monitor trade imports of 300 "sensitive" items, two-thirds of which were farm products (Gulati and Mullen 2003). There was also an emphasis on nontariff barriers, because the 2001 budget put an emphasis on enforcing the sanitary, quality, and labeling requirements of existing legislation in these areas.

Anticipating the phasing out of import restrictions, India bound tariffs at high levels (100 percent for commodities, 150 percent for processed products, and 300 percent for edible oils), including products like some cereals and dairy products they had previously set at zero due to the existence of QRs (Gulati and Mullen 2003). The structure that emerged from the URAA was characterized by a wide gap between bound and applied tariffs, which were 115 percent (simple average) and 35 percent, respectively, as of April 2002 (Gulati and Mullen 2003).[18] There was a general reduction of applied average agricultural tariffs, and some key commodities were opened up for imports. In 1994, imports of oilseeds were allowed, a sector that had until then been highly protected, with domestic prices up to 60 percent higher than world prices (Gulati and Kelley 1999). Wheat imports were also opened up at zero import duty in 1996.[19] Other interventions included the gradual breakup of the agricultural import monopoly by state trading agencies, which by 2002 was limited to a few commodities such as copra, coconut, and cereals.

On the export side, reforms included elimination of minimum export prices, increase in credit lines for exports, setting up of special agricultural export zones, elimination of export quotas except for a few commodities (including onions, paddy, rice bran, and some seeds), and reduction in the number of products canalized by the state agencies (Gulati and Kelley 1999). In 1994–95 the government opened up the export of major foodgrains, first rice and then wheat a year later, which led to a dramatic growth in exports of these two staples.

---

17. The abolition of QRs in 2001 was forced on India by the ruling of the WTO dispute settlement body following complaints by trading partners, particularly the United States, about India's slow pace of improving market access.

18. This gap between actual and bound rates was motivated by the fact that the reduction commitments under the URAA applied only to the latter.

19. Gulati and Mullen 2003. This policy change was meant to benefit roller flour mills in southern India, which had been complaining about the constraints they faced in procuring wheat from northern states.

Rice exports soared, from less than 1 mt to 5 mt in 1995–96, making India the second largest rice exporter that year. Wheat exports grew from 87,000 tons in 1994 to 1.1 mt in 1996. However, although these measures ensured a more liberal agricultural trade environment than in the past, the policy was still under government control and kept changing from year to year. The Ministry of Commerce, for instance, claimed the authority to impose or withdraw export restrictions to ensure an "adequate" domestic supply of key products at "reasonable" prices (Gulati and Mullen 2003).

Thus, the path to agricultural trade liberalization was not smooth, which came to be reflected in the changes in trade flows of India's primary commodities. The reform process was held back by circumstances related to the international market as well as the effect of reversals in domestic agricultural policies in response to the changing world market (Gulati and Mullen 2003). The limited adjustments that the URAA entailed and the prevalence of high world prices in 1995–97 meant that despite the initial trade reforms, agricultural imports were not large enough to generate concern. However, following the Asian financial crisis in June 1997, which hit import demand from Asia, there was a crash in the international prices of major agricultural commodities (IMF 2004).[20] This triggered an abrupt increase in imports, especially of edible oils and wheat, and the government was compelled to implement considerable reversals in the new trade policies. Pressured by domestic producers, the government reinstated barriers that were as high as 50 percent in the case of wheat in 1999 and up to 75 percent for edible oils by 2002 (Gulati and Mullen 2003).

Even the export side was affected by the negative consequences of the falling world prices, as is particularly clear from the changes in rice trade flows after 1998 (Gulati and Narayanan 2002a). The announced world rice price index dropped from 155 in 1997 to 135 in 1998 and further to 82 in 1999 (USDA 2001). Thus, after a peak of 5 mt recorded in 1998, rice exports fell to 1.5–2.5 mt in subsequent years (Gulati and Mullen 2003). The downward trend in the world rice price was believed to have been strengthened by domestic support policies in developed countries, which made their farmers artificially competitive and diverted the burden of adjustment to low international prices for Asian rice exporters, including India (Gulati and Narayanan 2002a).

The domestic support price and buffer stock policies also helped blunt the competitive edge of India's rice and wheat exports. The rising MSPs paid to compensate farmers for the decreasing international prices in the second half of the 1990s resulted in a huge buildup of public stocks, reaching an all-time high of 60 mt in 2001 against a norm of 24 mt (Hoda and Gulati 2003). Rising domestic MSPs against the backdrop of falling world prices in the late 1990s

---

20. As an indication of drastic drop in international prices, the IMF index of market prices of food (1995 = 100) fell to 77.6 by 1999 and then recovered slightly, reaching 81.4 by 2002.

made grain exports less competitive, so to boost exports and get rid of stocks that were getting too unwieldy and expensive to maintain, the government introduced subsidies on freight and stock holding consisting of the sale of foodgrains to traders at concessional rates in 2000–2001. This protective measure raised exports of rice and wheat from 2.1 mt in 2000–2001 to 6.7 mt by October 2002.[21] The domestic situation of growing stocks also justified the protective measures, because it was paradoxical to have huge grain imports coming in while there was an oversupply from domestic sources.

Stagnation in public investment in the sector during the 1990s and the unfavorable international circumstances are regarded as factors contributing to the weakening of India's agricultural and overall economic performance after 1997. In fact, the country's agricultural GDP and total GDP declined to 2 percent and 5.4 percent per annum, respectively, between 1997 and 2003 as opposed to 4.1 percent and 6.5 percent during the early postreform phase (1991–96). It appears, therefore, that there were two distinct stages in postreform Indian agricultural and the country's overall economic performance: the first, between 1991 and 1996, which saw higher growth rates of total and agricultural GDP, and the second, between 1997 and 2003, which saw a deceleration in the pace of growth. Despite this decrease, official estimates found urban and rural poverty declining significantly, from 35 percent in 1993–94 to 26 percent in 1999–2000, although this figure is debated.[22]

Agricultural Reforms behind the Border, 1998 to the Present: A Lagged Response

Compared to reforms on the external front, agricultural reforms in the domestic arena lagged behind. The old support framework with its three main policy interventions—the MSP to ensure remunerative prices to farmers, input subsidies, and the PDS—remained largely unaffected by the changes in the 1990s, except for the PDS, which underwent some targeting modifications in 1997.

Obstacles in the political economy held up efforts by the government to move forward with reforms at home, with pressures from constituencies that were major beneficiaries of the old support system hindering attempts to contain the increasing MSPs and subsidies (Landes and Gulati 2003). By the late

---

21. The new subsidy policy did not incur censorship under the URAA because the government availed itself of Article 9.4 of the agreement, which exempts developing countries from reduction commitments with regard to export marketing and freight costs.

22. Some argue that poverty dropped more rapidly in the 1990s than in previous periods (Bhalla 2003), while others argue that poverty reduction was more sluggish in the 1990s (Sen 1996; Jha 2000; Ravallion 2003). The controversy over actual poverty trends is partly related to modifications in the methodology used for the 55th NSS round (India, Ministry of Statistics and Program Implementation, 2000). The 55th round used differentiated recalls of food consumption (weekly, monthly, and yearly recalls for different items) as opposed to the exclusively monthly recalls of the past surveys.

1990s, these accounted for 2 percent of GDP, 10 percent of agricultural GDP, and a third of the federal fiscal deficit (Gulati and Narayanan 2003). Lavish MSPs paid to producers encouraged excessive grain procurement and stocks, resulting in higher storage and transport costs for the government. Increasing the handling cost of the stockpiles in turn forced a rise in PDS prices, which hit the poorer consumers. Rising subsidies on fertilizers, power, and water limited the scope for productive rural investments, while low user charges encouraged wasteful use of resources and led to environmental externalities (e.g., soil degradation, water salinization, and groundwater depletion).

To address these concerns and extend the reforms to the domestic arena, more than 10 high-level government committees were set up starting in 1998 (Gulati and Mullen 2003). Their reports emphasized the need for implementing reforms, particularly in the three "I" areas—institutions, investments, and incentives—basically calling for the rationalization of markets, agricultural prices, and input subsidies.

Regarding incentives, the government enacted some limited changes in the area of agricultural marketing to reduce the scope of obsolete legislation and thereby improve the environment for private investment. Starting in 2002, the government lifted several restrictions contemplated under the Essential Commodities Act of 1955, which was originally meant to prevent fluctuations in prices and supplies that could result from movement of agricultural produce from surplus to food shortage areas (Gulati and Mullen 2003). The act imposed controls on the storage, trading, and movement of farm products, leading to market fragmentation and limiting private investment in these activities. Reforms involved the temporary removal of these restrictions for major agricultural commodities such as wheat, rice, coarse grains, and edible oils (Landes and Gulati 2003). This intervention is expected to allow the development of a single large market for agricultural produce and give new impetus to private trade and investment, which were highly constrained by the parastatal monopoly in agricultural marketing operations (Vyas and Ke 2004).

Licensing requirements and much-criticized plant scale restrictions were abolished for the main food processing activities, paving the way for the growth of agribusiness (Ahluwalia 2002; Landes and Gulati 2003). Against the backdrop of booming milk production, the Milk and Milk Products Order was reformed to allow large-scale investments in the expansion of processing capacity. Further, restrictions were removed on risk management financial instruments such as futures trading on several commodities, including wheat, rice, pulses, and oil seeds.

At present there are proposals for the reform of regulations by the Agricultural Produce Marketing Committee, including reform of the requirement that agricultural sales occur only in regulated markets, which hinders private investment, and development of a modern vertically integrated marketing chain between producers, traders, and consumers (Landes and Gulati 2003). Other reforms under consideration are legal changes in land laws to facilitate land leasing, in contract farming to encourage market integration, and in food safety laws to align them to international standards and spur exports (Landes and Gulati 2003).

With regard to input subsidies, some reforms were attempted in the late 1990s in the area of fertilizers. But these were limited in scope because of the resistance to any price increase by both farmers and the domestic fertilizer industry, which together make up a broad constituency opposing reforms (Gulati and Narayanan 2003). In 1989–90, immediately before the launch of reforms, the subsidy bill for fertilizers reached a peak of 1.11 percent of GDP, having risen from 0.26 percent in 1981–82. By 1999–2000 it had gone up to nearly Rs. 132 billion, a tenfold increase over the past 20 years (in constant 1981–82 prices). Only very recently were steps taken to reform urea pricing, but imports remain restricted and canalized through state trading agencies. Based on the recommendations of the 2000 Expenditure Reforms Commission, there are plans to gradually increase urea prices by phasing out the retention price scheme over six years (Gulati and Narayanan 2003).

In the area of investment, the committees wanted public spending stepped up in rural areas for their long-term impacts on growth. Despite the increase in private investment in the 1990s, total investment in agriculture was low, at 1.6 percent of GDP at the end of the decade, primarily because of the stagnation in the public investment component (Gulati and Bathla 2002). Increased spending on input subsidies and other domestic support policies (the MSP and PDS) had the effect of crowding out rural public investment,[23] and some have linked this to the stagnation of public gross capital formation and total factor productivity during the 1990s relative to the 1980s. Given the role of public investments and public goods in improving the investment climate through their potential to induce private investment, some of the committees recommended higher government spending on irrigation, rural electrification, and rural roads to foster incentives for the private sector to invest more in agricultural diversification, marketing infrastructure (storage and processing), input supply, extension, and power.

Finally, institutional reforms were recommended in three areas: (1) providing safety nets, (2) enforcing regulations and food standards, and (3) ensuring the transparency and efficiency of government operations with reference to parastatals (e.g., the FCI) and nontradable inputs such as power and irrigation (Gulati, Pursell, and Mullen 2003). The power sector is in a critical situation, plagued by operational inefficiencies and deficient revenue collection. The quality of the services provided by power suppliers such as the state electricity

---

23. During 1980–90, the share of factor subsidies in total revenue expenditure expanded from 44 to 83 percent, with a parallel decrease over time in the share of capital expenditures for long-term capital investments (Smith and Urey 2002; Fan, Thorat, and Rao 2004).

boards deteriorated over time due to widespread power losses and undercharging for consumption, which does not even cover the operating costs. However, some institutional reform measures were taken in the Indian water sector to improve water use efficiency during the 1990s through a community-based approach leading to the introduction of watershed development programs, water user associations, and participatory irrigation management programs.

To summarize, there is a large unfinished agenda in India's domestic arena. As a result of the post-1991 policy changes, the two major constraints of the prereform period, foodgrain shortages and low levels of foreign exchange, have been removed and the country is in a comfortable position on both these counts. But the lack of reforms in the areas of infrastructure, domestic marketing, and investments has been seen as one of the main reasons for the slowdown in both agricultural GDP and total GDP after 1997. Until now, the impact of reforms outside agriculture has been more prominent, but in the future, changes in domestic agricultural policy in the three interrelated areas of incentives, investment, and institutions will be increasingly important (Srinivasan 2003b). Further steps to stimulate strong agricultural growth must include improvements in education and greater emphasis on growing high-value agricultural goods like fruits and vegetables instead of only cereals.

A Comparative Summary

When India and China emerged as new states in the middle of the past century, they shared many features. Both their economies were in bad shape, with low per capita income and widespread poverty, although China was worse off than India in 1950. From the 1950s until the late 1970s, both countries implemented somewhat similar economic development policies inspired by the socialist model. They adopted economic planning, although under different models, namely a mixed economy in India and a command economy in China. Both adopted strategies of heavy industrialization and self-sufficiency in food production and thus subjected agriculture to a panoply of controls to ensure the availability of inexpensive food and inputs for urban development. Both countries chose the industrialization path of import substitution, which led to an autarkic and anti-export policy environment and, overall, gave them an "antiforeign" economic outlook. And both revised and even reversed many of their strategies after a while.

China's reforms began in the late 1970s, while India's started in the 1990s. In the past thirty years, both countries have made remarkable progress, but China, to everybody's surprise, has covered considerable ground and more than caught up with India despite the fact that the latter had better "capitalist infrastructure and commercial culture" (Desai 2003) at the outset of reforms. The truth is that in China, a series of prereform policies and institutions covered a great deal of ground, leading it to catch up as well as laying the foundation for sustained growth once reforms were launched.

A number of factors help explain the difference in the countries' growth outcomes during the prereform era. The collectives in China proved a powerful mechanism for resource mobilization, supported by a high level of national savings, 30–40 percent of GDP, which throughout the prereform period and after was consistently higher than the 20 percent in India (WDI 2003). The commune system, with its focus on universal health and education, ensured better health and literacy for the rural population. Further, the establishment of TVEs laid the foundation for the rapid growth of the RNF. While the green revolution in India did dramatically increase its efficiency in grain production, China has traditionally (since the 1960s) enjoyed much higher grain yields. It is important to also note that between 1952 and 1977, the Chinese population growth rate was around 2 percent per annum and its GDP growth rate 5.4 percent per year, which left more resources for growth in income per capita at 3.4 percent per year. On the other hand, in India, until the 1980s the GDP growth rate was 3.0–3.5 percent, while its population growth rate was roughly 2 percent, which resulted in a lower rate of growth of per capita income of 1.0–1.5 percent per annum (Datanet India Pvt. Ltd. 2006). However, a pertinent issue in China is the growing ratio of aged dependents, which has both economic and social implications for the future.

With the launch of reforms, both countries made substantial progress in increasing the role of markets in the allocation of resources and the degree of openness of the economy, as reflected in the change in FDI inflows and major trade indicators. However, China pursued more aggressive "open door" policies in investments and trade. In 2001 the share of agricultural trade in agricultural GDP was 17 percent in China and 9 percent in India (FAOSTAT 2004). This implies that agricultural liberalization was deeper in China and that the goal of self-sufficiency as a prerequisite for food security was abandoned. By contrast, India is reluctant to let go of the self-sufficiency motif and reform policies that have helped ensure its food security in the past three decades, including MSPs, input subsidies, and the PDS. Finally, continued emphasis on education, high levels of savings, and the development of rural off-farm activities were other major points of difference between the two countries.

As a result of the structural adjustment in marketing and trade over the past few decades, the primary sector's contribution to the economy has progressively shrunk in both countries (Figure 2.6).

In India, the initial fiscal discipline and sectoral reforms in industry, trade, and exports had the effect of improving exports and investments in both agricultural and nonagricultural areas and thus spurring growth. Yet, starting in 1996–97, the effect of these policies began to fade as a mix of factors helped blunt the impact and continuation of reforms. At the same time, trade reforms opened up the economic environment, revealing the lack of efficiency and competitiveness caused by stagnation in public investments, infrastructure bottlenecks, and the lack of reform of the institutional and incentive environment of input supply and agricultural subsidies.

FIGURE 2.6 Sectoral shares in GDP in China and India

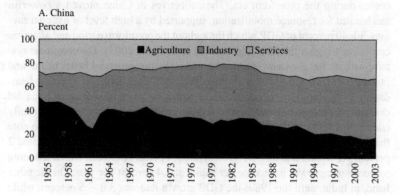

A. China
Percent

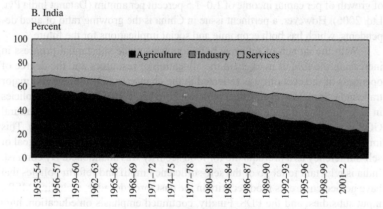

B. India
Percent

SOURCES: Calculations based on India, RBI (2003), and NBS, *China Statistical Yearbook,* 2003.

On the other hand, China, whose success was propelled by the decollectivization of agriculture, pro-market reforms, and dismantling of state planning
and monopolies, as well as implementation of policies favorable to human capital formation and rural off-farm activities, will now have to come to terms with
the issues of rising income inequality and the sustainability of the current pace
of economic growth. These issues are analyzed more extensively in the subsequent chapters.

PART II

Access to Land, Health, and Education: Initial Conditions and Reforms

An overview of the economic and social progress achieved by China and India in the past half century was provided in the previous section. It painted a broad picture of the reform paths followed, particularly in the rural sector, and the different development outcomes in the two countries.

In this part of the book, which comprises Chapters 3–5, we delve deeper into the two fundamental factors: access to land and human capital. It is generally believed that if more equitable land distribution and an advanced state of human capital are provided as initial conditions, reforms are likely to promote faster growth and poverty reduction.

Chapters 3 and 4 provide (1) an overview of the changes in land policy, tenure, and institutions in China and India; (2) insight into the impacts and consequences of these changes with regard to equity, efficiency, agricultural productivity, and poverty; and (3) suggestions for future strategies and policies.

The analysis of the experience in the two countries supports the hypothesis that agriculture-led reforms can accelerate growth and make a profound dent on poverty. While in both cases reforms aimed to give "land to the tiller," the reform trajectories differed in significant ways. The Chinese process showed more volatility due to repeated changes in direction, from family farming to collectivization, then back again to family farming with restricted land rights. However, the centralized system of policymaking and implementation in China ensured uniform implementation and therefore successful pursuit of the reform's equity aspect. India, on the other hand, moved only in one direction— toward the abolishment of landlordism—but the process was slow and showed great regional variation because land reforms were the responsibility of individual states and landlord-dominated state legislatures. Land reforms, therefore, led to different outcomes in states with the landholding structure dominated by marginal (up to 1 ha) and small-sized (up to 2 ha) farms resulting from high population/land ratios, as in China

It is debated in both the countries whether the small size of land units is a disincentive to investments and an obstacle to increasing agricultural productivity and competitiveness. Belief in an inverse relationship between farm size

45

and productivity seemed to hold sway in both China and India, but it has weakened over time with technological changes and growing capital intensity in production. Thus, the question is whether the notion of "small is beautiful" still applies in the present-day context of the increasingly liberalized policy environment promoted under the WTO framework. Liberalization of land markets remains a major area of debate and future reform in both China and India.

Tenure security has been greater in India due to regulation of rent and recording of tenancy. In China, the frequent reallocations of village land to equalize landholdings between villagers has undermined tenancy rights, although the 2003 Chinese Agricultural Lease Law marked an improvement in this regard. What has been the impact of tenure security on investments by farmers? The experiences in the two countries lead to a somewhat surprising answer: there is no unequivocal relationship between investments and securer tenure, because other factors such as access to credit, absenteeism, or level of returns from rental income equally determine investment decisions.

In China, land was distributed evenly among rural households and there were virtually no landless people, although the recent move toward individualization of land rights may increase the polarization of land distribution. In India, land concentration has been higher, with 10 percent of rural households still landless in 1999–2000. In 1991–92, marginal landholdings (less than 1 ha) accounted for 63 percent of holdings but only 16 percent of operated area. Efforts to eradicate landlessness were less effective in India because various interest groups impeded the implementation of reforms. However, improved tenure security had some antipoverty effect given the tenants' improved claims to returns from land and investments (Besley and Burgess 2000).

It is clear that the "redistributive ethos" and vision of an egalitarian society that shaped Chinese land institutions guided health and education policies in the prereform period, although there was a considerable gap in opportunities between rural and urban areas. This egalitarian philosophy, supported by strong political will and the effective operational arm of the collective system, was vital in determining success in the social sector. Social sector spending was sustained over time, which addressed the problem of long gestation lags before investments could translate into improved human indicators.

In India, a similar commitment to improve rural literacy and health was not accompanied by comparable political will and implementation. As a result, although attainments in human development have steadily increased since the 1960s, they are relatively less impressive than the results achieved in China.

It is argued that better achievements in literacy and health resulting from the prereform policies gave China an edge over India at the start of reforms. However, the critical question is whether these outcomes are sustainable in the future given that the market- and profit-oriented approach of reforms implied relinquishing the egalitarian approach and resulted in a decline of public financing and increased privatization of social sector services. Further, is China's success in the social areas to be emulated when viewed in the light of a more comprehensive notion of human development that values not only the final outcomes of policies but also the way in which these are achieved? The comprehensive view sees the merits of a policy framework that provides freedom of choice, accountability, and transparency in the pursuit of better results. These factors can explain, for instance, why India never suffered famines of the gravity experienced by China during the reform period.

Chapter 5 gives a deeper view of the transformations in the Chinese rural healthcare system with regard to coverage, delivery, and financing. It highlights the subtleties in societal and household structures (and therefore of social sector interventions) and challenges the current trend of believing that the market can provide greater efficiency in the rural health sector, discussing in greater detail the replacement of the Chinese egalitarian guiding principle by a pro-market and profit orientation. Suggestions for future direction and strategy are based on household-level study and analysis.

3 The Chinese Land Tenure System: Practice and Perspectives

YANG YAO

With barely a tenth of a hectare of arable land available per capita, China is one of the most land-scarce countries in the world. As a result, the struggle for land has never stopped. Indeed, turbulent change in the land tenure system has been one of the most recurrent themes in the history of China in the past half century.

Thorough land reform in the early 1950s made China's small landholding system even more egalitarian. This reform, although violent and in many cases bloody, substantially increased agricultural productivity. Although the subsequent collectivization during the Great Leap Forward of 1958 led to an unprecedented famine that killed around 30 million people in three years, the commune system, with some changes, remained in place for about 20 years thereafter. Although the growth of Chinese agriculture in this period did not fall short of the international average, the commune system failed to improve the living standard of China's rural population and seriously deprived them of many basic economic and political liberties.

It is not surprising, then, that economic reform started in the rural areas in 1978 after the Cultural Revolution. While the village collective was still the legal owner of the land, reform restored family farming and established farm households as the sole residual claimants of land. The reform was a great success initially, and by 1984 China began to harvest considerable grain surpluses. However, by the end of the 1980s the growth of Chinese agriculture had slowed down considerably and the drawbacks of the mixed land tenure system began to appear. The wheel almost turned full circle with the Agricultural Lease Law that came into force on March 1, 2003, marking a significant step toward de facto private land ownership in China.

In this chapter we provide a review of the 50-year history of the Chinese land tenure system, focusing on the past 20 years. We discuss at length some of the major factors affecting agricultural productivity, including tenure security, land market, and farm size. Next we discuss the role of land tenure in farmers' welfare. Finally, we analyze the relationship between land tenure and rural politics and how this led to the Agricultural Lease Law and also provide an assessment of the new law's implications for rural China. The study does not attempt to provide a complete review of Chinese land tenure history, but rather highlights the issues and policy alternatives aimed at resolving them.

The Chinese Land Tenure System in the Planning Era

A thorough land reform process began in 1949 as soon as the Chinese Communist Party (CCP) assumed power in Mainland China and was completed by 1953. Land was confiscated from landlords and rich farmers and given freely to poor farmers.[1] As a result, landholdings moved toward completely egalitarian distribution. For example, a large survey found that the average farm size after the land reform was between 0.74 and 1.6 hectares (ha) (Bo 1992). The marginal effect of the land reform was substantial in terms of economic efficiency, because grain output increased dramatically in the first years of land reform.[2]

However, polarization began to emerge as soon as the land reform was complete. Even the government found it increasingly difficult to purchase grains and feared that the lack of an inexpensive grain supply might halt industrialization, which the Chinese leaders saw as the most important force for modernizing China (Bo 1992). As a result, agricultural cooperatives were increasingly encouraged. By 1956, almost all farm households had joined the advanced cooperatives in which a group of households pooled their land, production tools, and draft animals and were remunerated only by their labor inputs. While in theory they had the option to leave the cooperative, it was rarely allowed in practice (Kung 1993).

The collectivization movement reached its peak in 1958, when all the cooperatives were consolidated and turned into large communes. History records 1958 as a year of extreme collective hysteria and irrationality in China. The Great Leap Forward set the goal for China of overtaking the United Kingdom in steel production in one year (Bo 1992), and the entire country was mobilized for producing steel. The CCP encouraged the people to think that the dream of

---

1. Land reform actually started earlier than 1949 in communist-occupied areas. In May 1946, the CCP Central Committee issued what is now called the May Fourth Directive to call for land reforms. The initial policy was to compensate landlords with land bonds that would be financed over a long period annually by farmers who received land. However, the subsequent civil war interrupted this policy, and confiscation became a major tool to help boost poor farmers' support of the communists (Luo 2005).

2. Many landlords were killed because of their resistance to the reform. The massive killing was avoided in Taiwan and Japan by compensating landlords. The Taiwanese experience was more successful than the Japanese due to the use of different compensation mechanisms. In Japan landlords were bought out in yen, which promptly declined in value through inflation, leaving many of them stranded, too old to go back to work, and unable to live on the pittance inflation left them. In Taiwan the landlords were compensated in New Taiwan (NT) dollars, but the compensation contracts were tied to a commodity base. The annual payment was computed in terms of the number of NT dollars required to buy a certain quantity of rice or sweetpotatoes. This made the payment reasonably inflation proof. See Cheng (1961).

communism, which for most people meant "two-story houses, electric light bulbs, and telephones," would come true overnight. People began to erect brick and mud-built furnaces to produce steel. In the meantime, rural households began to dine in the communal dining halls, and household cooking became unnecessary and prohibited. In the countryside, people were mobilized to build reservoirs and other irrigation facilities as well.

Contrary to facts, 1958 was portrayed as a year of bumper harvests. Exaggeration of agricultural outputs was effectively the rule of the game, and reports of harvests of a dozen tons per mu of land (one-fifteenth of a hectare) frequently appeared in newspapers. The communal dining system destroyed the saving habit ingrained in the Chinese, and wasteful consumption prevailed (Chang and Wen 1998).

The result of the Great Leap Forward and communization was an unprecedented disaster: around 30 million people died of starvation in the subsequent three years. Following Lin's seminal paper (1990), stream of studies offered diverse explanations of the reasons for the Great Famine.[3] While a summary of these studies is beyond the scope of this chapter, explanations related to the nature of the commune system are worth mentioning.

In his 1990 paper, Lin ascribes the cause of the famine to the lack of the commune's right to exit. He provides a verbal model to show that the lack of the right to exit leads to a serious free-riding problem in the commune system, resulting in a sharp decline of agricultural output. This argument is criticized by Dong and Dow (1993), who argue that the absence of this right could have led to more cooperation inside the commune, just as people in a lifeboat without the option to escape individually decide that it is better to cooperate with others. The general opinion is that it is unlikely that the lack of the right to exit could alone have led to a staggering famine that took millions of lives in a very short time (Kung 1993; Liu 1993) and that multiple factors had more likely been the trigger.

However, the decline in the long-term efficiency of the communes is indisputable. Some authors attribute the failure of the communes to their ill-defined remuneration system. Putterman (1993) believes that the work-point system did not reflect the true contribution of each individual. Others are more critical of the general nature of the commune system, especially its strong tendency to induce opportunistic behavior that is detrimental to group efficiency. This was best demonstrated in Xiaogang, a village that has become a symbol of the decollectivization movement after the Cultural Revolution. Before 1978, a large percentage of Xiaogang's residents went all over the country to beg for food. One winter night in 1977, a dozen farmers gathered in the house of the

---

3. *The Journal of Comparative Economics* and *China Economic Review* each published a special volume (in 1993 and 1998, respectively) on the causes of the Great Famine.

village team leader and decided to give up collective farming even though it was a serious offense and the leader could be sent to jail if detected. In 1978, the first year of the return to family farming, Xiaogang produced enough grain to feed the whole village. The only explanation is that the people of Xiaogang preferred to beg than to work together; in other words, working together had such serious problems that the gains from it were less than those from begging.

However, it would also be a mistake to deny the achievements of the commune system, which granted the state the power to mobilize large amounts of resources and people to engage in irrigation and social projects. In most parts of China today, farmers still rely on the irrigation facilities built in the collective era. In addition, we saw a dramatic decrease in China's rural illiteracy rate and an increase in life expectancy during the period of communes. A basic cooperative healthcare system was established and covered almost the entire rural population. Although its cost-effectiveness can be debated, the system undeniably contributed to the improved health conditions in rural China. In comparing China and India, Sen (1998) argues that China's population was better educated and healthier at the outset of the reform, which gave China a lead over India in terms of preparation for economic growth.

A balanced view could be achieved by weighing the commune's achievements against its costs. While the gains were substantial, the costs were also immense, with significant loss of economic efficiency and immense deprivation for farmers. Under the commune system, farmers were bound to the land by the household registration system; they could not move to the city, even temporarily, nor could they move to another village. They were forced to work together, but could not choose what to plant on their land and had to sell all their surplus grains to the state. A large amount of their surplus was transferred to the city through the "price scissors." When Sen emphasizes the achievements of the collective period, he is defending the values that are embedded in those achievements rather than the commune system itself. It is important to understand and appreciate this when we evaluate China's current land tenure system.

The "Two-Tier" Land Tenure System in the Reform Period

The establishment of the two-tier system known as the Household Responsibility System (HRS) was not realized overnight.[4] At that time, the Chinese economy was on the verge of collapse. Spontaneous breakup of collective farm-

---

4. The term *Household Responsibility System* was used to avoid using nonsocialist terms such as *family farming*. The term emphasizes that the responsibility for taking care of the land had shifted from the village or the state to individual households. The terms *two-tier system* and *HRS* are used here synonymously. The term *two-tier system* was first introduced by Dong (1996).

ing started in 1976, toward the later years of the Cultural Revolution. In the countryside, chronic famine was evident. Farmers were fed up with collective farming, and many of them chose to leave their home villages. Beggars became a serious social problem. Following Xiaogang, many villages in Anhui province (where Xiaogang is located) began to adopt individual or group farming. The party secretary of the province at that time, Wang Li, encouraged this movement and endured strong pressures from the central government.

Following the changes in Anhui province, Zhao Ziyang, party secretary of Sichuan province, also introduced individual and group farming into his province. Sichuan was the most populous province in China (with a population near 100 million at that time), so its action had a significant impact on the rest of the country. The central government, however, was very cautious about the movement because of the fear that socialism was at risk. Thus, only group farming was encouraged at the beginning. However, the initial success of individual farming in Anhui and Sichuan led more provinces to follow suit. By 1984, except for the state farms in the northwest and northeast regions, virtually every village had adopted individual farming. That year, the commune system was formally dismantled. It took six years (1978–84) for the dismantling process to be completed, showing the typical Chinese style of gradual reform.

If there has been one Pareto factor improving institutional change in recent Chinese history, it has been the restoration of family farming. Farmers benefited because they became the residual claimants of the land, able to decide what to plant on the land and whether to keep the surplus. Urban dwellers also benefited from the reform because they were no longer constrained by the strict rationing that had affected almost every aspect of their lives. Finally, the state apparatus realized that the reform eased the pressure to stabilize the countryside and to feed the urban areas, so it was in its interest to sanction the reform.

The energy discharged by the reform was astonishing. In the period between 1979 and 1984, the gross value of agricultural output maintained a real annual growth rate of 7.6 percent, with grain output growing at 4.9 percent. While some people believe that increase in agricultural prices played a significant role in bringing about rapid agricultural growth, Lin (1992) finds that 60 percent of the growth in the early 1980s can be attributed to the adoption of individual farming.

However, the growth of agricultural output decelerated considerably in the second half of the 1980s, although rural industry began to flourish in this period. People linked the deceleration to the inadequacy of the HRS, under which the legal owner of the agricultural land is still the village collective but the land rights are shared between the village collective and the individual household. The point of sharing can be anywhere between complete collective ownership and complete individual ownership, and, as a result, considerable geographic variations came into existence.

Characteristics of the New Land Tenure System

Under the HRS, the village became the most significant player in determining the specific form of land tenure arrangements inside a village. Field research consistently finds that there is a wide variety of land tenure arrangements in the Chinese villages regarding the delineation of rights, the security of rights, and the procedure to be followed to make changes (Liu, Carter, and Yao 1998; Rozelle et al. 2002). Variations in land tenure arrangements are likely to arise around land distribution, far-away households' lease rights, transferability of land, and farmers' rights to their land.

The first arrangement relates to land distribution. Collective land ownership allows each villager to have the same level of claim on the village land. In a village with a limited amount of land, the claim has significant implications for land distribution. The village needs to allocate land to the newly born and the married in order to meet their claims, which means that other people have to give part of their land. In this circumstance, inheritance of land is not guaranteed and a person who permanently leaves the village may need to surrender his or her land to the village. The possibility of redistribution gives rise to tenure insecurity that leads to inefficiency, as described earlier.

The second arrangement concerns farm households' use rights. An individual household can generally decide what to plant on its land and is the sole residual claimant. The state used to enforce grain purchasing quotas on household outputs, and in most cases the quota prices were lower than the market prices. For an average farm household, the quota was between 10 and 20 percent of its total grain output (Liu, Carter, and Yao 1998). In 1993, the quota system together with the urban food rationing was abolished.[5] The government nevertheless maintained official purchase of grains. In recent years, the official purchasing prices were even higher than the market prices because the government wanted to raise farmers' income.[6] However, farmers' use rights are not totally free of infringement by the local government. In some localities, farmers are forced to plant certain cash crops so that the local government can collect an agricultural special product tax. The mixed ownership of the HRS may have provided the local government a sense of the legitimacy of its ordering the farmers to plant certain types of crop.

The third arrangement has to do with the transferability of land, which is restricted by the two-tier land tenure system. Selling land is prohibited. Only partial inheritance is granted: a farmer can pass on his land to his offspring if no reallocation is called for in the village. Land leasing was restricted at the

---

5. However, following inflation at the end of that year, food rationing resumed in several cities. It was again abolished as soon as inflation abated.

6. This practice was put in place during 1998–2000. It stimulated growth of grain output, but it is estimated that the potential loss due to excessive grain storage was worth 300–400 billion yuan.

beginning, but is allowed now. With 5–10 percent of the land and households involved, land leasing has reached the international average.

The last arrangement concerns farmers' rights in conflicts between them and the state. By law, a household has to give up its land when a government-sponsored land development project needs to use the household's land. In a typical land development project in a suburban area, the farm household can receive at most 20 percent of the market value of the land. Conflicts arising from public land development projects have been a major concern of the government.

In sum, under the HRS a farm household's land rights are likely to be incomplete. While conventional wisdom has it that such a system hurts economic efficiency, some authors argue that it is a second-best choice under multiple market failures. We tackle both views in the subsequent sections of this chapter and also discuss the economic and political forces that drive a village toward a specific tenure arrangement. We also describe the geographic variations that result from these different combinations.

Patterns of Land Tenure

From the two-tier land tenure system has emerged a whole spectrum of arrangements that stretch from collective farming to individualized land ownership. Table 3.1 presents data on the number of reallocations during the 1980s and the 1990s in selected provinces for a wider geographic coverage. It is evident that

TABLE 3.1 Land reallocations in selected provinces of China, 1980s and 1990s

	Average number of reallocations per village	Size of most recent reallocation (percentage of land)	Size of most recent reallocation (percentage of households)
Zhejiang*	0.8	n.a.	n.a.
Zhejiang	1.2	60.8	91.8
Jiangxi*	2.1	n.a.	n.a.
Sichuan	0.3	28.6	58.6
Hubei	2.8	55.0	71.1
Shannxi	2.8	34.8	62.8
Shangdong	1.9	74.5	71.2
Henan*	1.7	n.a.	n.a.
Yunnan	0.4	31.3	61.4
Hebei	1.5	75.0	82.5
Liaoning	3.4	91.1	93.1
Jilin*	0.6	n.a.	n.a.
Rozelle et al. average	*1.7*	*57.6*	*74.4*

SOURCES: Rozelle et al. (2002), Yao (2002b).

NOTES: Entries with an * are from Yao (2002b); the rest are from Rozelle et al. (2002). Data from Yao (2002b) are for 1981–93; those from Rozelle et al. (2002) refer to 1984–95. n.a., not available.

large disparities exist across these provinces. It has been a fascinating academic exercise to probe what forces drive a village toward a specific arrangement. Postulated in the institutional change literature is this central question: what are the factors that lead to a specific institution? To answer this question, several theories have been proposed.

The first theory is borrowed directly from the "induced institutional change" hypothesis first introduced by North and Thomas (1973) and later popularized by Ruttan and Hayami (1984). This hypothesis states that the factor whose relative price increases would take a more individualized form of ownership. Applying it to the Chinese case, one would then expect that a village with a tighter land endowment (and thus a higher relative price of land) would adopt a more individualized land tenure arrangement. However, as Hayami (1997) rightly points out, the induced institutional change hypothesis fails to take into account the political process that carries out the institutional change, so it may be too naïve an assessment.

The second theory has its basis in the combination of a rational village and incomplete markets. It implicitly assumes that there is a rational social planner, while the induced institutional change hypothesis takes complete markets for granted. With incomplete markets, the induced institutional change hypothesis may not hold. Turner, Brandt, and Rozelle (2000) build a rational village model on the premise that the land rental market is imperfect in rural China. They model the village as maximizing the sum of agricultural surplus in the village. They predict that administrative reallocation of land can be a substitute for the land rental market's gaining static efficiency by bringing the marginal product of land of individual households closer to the implicit land rental price in the village.

The third theory is a rent-seeking theory that regards land reallocation as a means for the village cadre to explore personal gains (Johnson 1995). To a large extent, this theory matches the reality in rural China. As we will see later in the chapter, it was the conflict between the villagers and the cadre that led to the introduction of a new law whose major aim was to tie the hands of the cadre. However, the political flux in the Chinese village may be quite different from a pure rent-seeking model. The role of ordinary villagers can hardly be ignored. Many village leaders regarded land reallocation as a costly endeavor because it affected the interests of many villagers. At the institutional level, the grass-roots democracy recently introduced into the Chinese villages has empowered ordinary villagers to vote out corrupt village leaders. Therefore, the cadre's rent-seeking capacity can be seriously limited by the political participation of the ordinary villagers. So the rent-seeking model may be best revised as a political model that accommodates a wide variety of political processes.

Empirically, all three theories find supporting evidence. Table 3.1 show clearly that the land-poor provinces (i.e., Zhejiang, Sichuan, and Yunnan) conducted fewer land reallocations than the land-richer provinces (i.e., Liaoning,

Shannxi, and Hubei).[7] This lends strong support to the induced institutional change hypothesis. Yao (2002b) develops a method to test whether the village adopts the rational model or the political model in its decisionmaking about land reallocation. In the rational model, the village maximizes the sum of agricultural surplus of individual households, and thus its prediction is one of the induced institutional change hypotheses. In the political model, the decision is made through a decentralized political process such as majority voting. Under this model, democratic participation blocks land reallocation because it hurts the average household by introducing insecurity to its landholding. Yao (2002b) finds that neither model is strongly rejected, although the political model gains more support from the data. For the imperfect market theory, Carter and Yao (1999b) conclude that land reallocation does respond to the distribution of households' per-unit labor inputs in the village; that is, a village with a more dispersed distribution is more likely to reallocate land. Turner, Brandt, and Rozelle (2000) find evidence to support the assessment that the rational village uses administrative reallocation to explore the static gains from trade.

To summarize, land tenure arrangements in Chinese villages are likely to follow the following patterns: (1) villages with a tighter land endowment tend to adopt more secure and individualized land tenure, (2) greater security in land tenure is more likely to be observed in villages with a better-developed land rental market, and (3) villages with more democratic participation and diversified populations tend to have secure land tenure.

Land Tenure and Agricultural Productivity

Various international organizations have tried to formalize land rights in the developing world by initiating different forms of land titling programs. The goal is to increase agricultural productivity by ensuring secure land rights. In addition, land markets are strongly encouraged as a substitution for mandatory land reforms and customary land allocations. In this section we discuss the three major issues surrounding China's two-tier land tenure system: tenure security, land markets, and farm size, with emphasis on their productivity implications.

Tenure Security, Land Investment, and Agricultural Output

Insecure land tenure is like a random tax levied on a farmer's land investment. Because there is a risk that a farmer will lose his land in the future, he will reduce his investment (Feder 1985; Besley 1995), which in turn adversely affects agricultural productivity. In theory, therefore, there is no doubt that the HRS discourages investment in the land. The point is to determine the significance of the negative effect. Some studies show positive effects of securer

---

7. The exception is Jilin, which is a land-rich province.

land tenure.[8] Yao (1998) finds that in two rice-growing provinces, Zhejiang and Jiangxi, securer land tenure, defined by a synthesized indicator that reflects the frequency of land reallocations and the prospect of a land reallocation in case of a demographic change, increases farmers' incentive to plant more green manures in the winter. However, the impact of securer tenure on land productivity is low. A reduction of one reallocation in a 10-year period would imply a 5 percent increase of output. Li, Rozelle, and Brandt (1998) and Jacoby, Li, and Rozelle (2003) find similar results. A potential problem of these results, however, is that land reallocations are endogenously determined. In particular, farmers may use investment to establish de facto land rights and force the village to reduce its land reallocations, so the estimate of the tenure security effect is biased upward.

The insignificant contribution of securer tenure on land investment may arise as the result of specific arrangements made by the village in the process of land reallocation. First, villages may choose the type of land to be reallocated. For example, it has been found that villages in Hunan and Yunnan reallocate only low-value dry land but do not reallocate high-value rice paddies (Bauhoff and Yao 2002). In addition, villages may also avoid reallocating land with significant land investments such as wells. Second, it has been found that in some areas farmers are compensated for land investments when land is reallocated. Third, many villages set aside land to prepare for population increase so they do not need to take land from farm households when new members of the population need land. All these arrangements mitigate or even eliminate the negative effect of the two-tier land tenure system.

Even if securer tenure encourages land investment, its effect on agricultural output is likely to be limited. This is because land investment plays a minor role in agricultural production compared with other agricultural inputs such as land, labor, and fertilizers. Nevertheless, the lack of long-term investment may hurt the sustainability of Chinese agriculture. While there is no direct evidence showing this long-term negative effect, an international and historical comparison of soil quality by Lindal (1973) shows that China's soil quality has been improving in the past half century. The explanation is that high population pressure forces the country to improve its land. In other words, the effect of factor endowments eventually dominates people's decisions regarding their investment in land. From this point of view, the negative effect of insecure land tenure should not be a concern in the long run.

---

8. Studies conducted in other developing countries have revealed no systematic trend. Feder et al. (1988) found that while land titling in Thailand did not have a direct effect on land investment, it enabled the farmers to get more formal credit, which in turn helped investment. Studies on Africa's land titling program are rather inconclusive (Bruce, Migot-Adholla, and Atherton 1995). Besley's (1995) study of Ghana finds no significant effect of land titling.

TABLE 3.2 Land leases in selected provinces of China, 1988 and 1995

	Land leases allowed by 1995 (percentage of villages)	Land rented in 1988 (percent)	Land rented in 1995 (percent)
Zhejiang	93.8	1.6	6.9
Sichuan	93.8	0.2	2.1
Hubei	59.4	0.3	3.6
Shannxi	65.6	0.8	2.2
Shangdong	46.5	n.a.	1.1
Yunnan	66.7	1.3	0.9
Hebei	80.0	0.3	2.1
Liaoning	62.3	0.1	3.6
Total	*71.6*	*0.6*	*2.9*

SOURCE: Rozelle et al. (2002).
NOTE: n.a., not available.

Land Markets and Efficiency

While private land sales are prohibited, the government encourages land leases. Surveys show that by the mid-1990s the majority of villages allowed land leases, but the incidence of actual land leases was low. Table 3.2 presents summary data from the studies carried out by Rozelle et al. (2002). Overall, 71.6 percent of the sample villages allowed land leases by the mid-1990s, but the percentage of land rented in them was only 2.9 percent. Carter and Yao (1999a) find that about 5 percent of farm households and 2.5 percent of the land are involved in the land lease market, although in some localities, such as Zhejiang province, the percentage of farm households involved in the rental market is as high as 15 percent. These figures are comparable with the data presented in Table 3.2. Kung (2002) finds similar results. The low rate of participation in the land lease market is not surprising and is close to the average of the developing countries.

In terms of China's small landholdings and scant nonfarm activities in most areas, the participation rate is reasonable. The development of the land lease market in a village critically depends on the diversification of the village households in economic activities. Yao (2000b) finds evidence to support this assessment.

As in other developing countries, the agricultural terms of trade have been declining in China. In addition, tax burdens and irregular fees imposed by local governments further lower the income from farming. As a result, land rent is very low. In the coastal and central regions, a landlord has to compensate a tenant for cultivating the land and pay the taxes and fees. Land abandonment has become a serious problem in many localities, and a new form of tenancy has emerged to avoid this. Under this tenancy, individual households whose members do not work their land first rent their land to the village, which in turn rents it to a small group of farmers from poorer counties nearby. This tenancy arrangement greatly reduces the cost involved in contract negotiation and facilitates the adoption of some agricultural technologies, such as irrigation systems. Under this new tenancy arrangement, the amount of land being rented can be as great as 30 percent of the total amount of land in the village (Tian and Chen 2003).

International studies show that the land lease market works better than the land sales market in developing countries (Binswanger and Deininger 1995). In many cases land sales are induced by correlative or idiosyncratic distresses, famine, natural disasters, illness, and other emergencies. In the case of correlative distresses such as famine and natural disasters, the land price is low at the time of the sale, but when the distress is over and the seller wants to buy back his land, the land price rises. As a result, distress land sales hurt the seller in both cases. Because they are not directed to equalize the marginal product of land, land transactions do not necessarily improve economic efficiency. In contrast, land leases are not related to life distresses; they are transacted purely to obtain gains from trade.

In the literature, two kinds of gains from trade are identified for land leases. One is the usual price equalization effect; that is, the marginal product of land is equalized across the farms. The other is proposed by Besley (1995), who shows that better tradability of land increases the chances of trade for land investment purposes. Carter and Yao (1999a) propose a similar hypothesis based on the assessment that improved tradability mitigates a household's concern that land investment could be redundant if there were positive off-farm employment shocks in the future. They call this effect the regret effect of encumbered land transfer rights and verify it in a data set collected in two rice-growing provinces. In their simulation, the authors find that removing the impediments to land transfers will result in a 5 percent increase in total output.

Farm Size and the Competitiveness of Chinese Agriculture

Research carried out in developing countries has established the inverse relationship between farm size and per-unit land output. This finding can be traced back at least to Chayanov's self-exploitation theory (Chayanov 1966 [1925]): small farmers have less expensive family labor, so they tend to exploit themselves and their families by applying more labor to their land; therefore, other things being equal, small farmers tend to have higher per-unit land output. In this scenario, missing or incomplete markets play a pivotal role. Feder (1985) identifies the combinations of missing or incomplete markets that can lead to the inverse relationship as well as combinations that can lead to a positive relationship. For example, if the credit market is featured by rationing and large farmers can access credit more easily than smaller farmers, the positive relationship is possible even when the labor market is imperfect because large farmers can avail themselves of credit to buy more equipment and invest more in their land, so their deficiency in labor input is more than compensated. It is an empirical question, therefore, whether there is an inverse or a positive relationship.

In the Chinese context, however, land consolidation and large farms have long been emphasized, even if there is no evidence showing that large farms have higher profit margins than small farms. Several reasons are usually given for supporting large farms.

First, many people, especially noneconomists, believe that there is a scale economy effect in agriculture. This reason can be readily rejected because agriculture is the sector with the smallest scale effect (if any at all) essentially because of the divisible nature of its inputs. Many have compared Chinese farms with those in the United States in terms of labor productivity, which of course is not suitable for assessing scale economy.

Second, it is believed that it is easier to introduce modern inputs, especially large machines, in large farms than in small farms. This assessment itself is correct, but the question is whether mechanization should be the goal of Chinese agriculture. Yet mechanization was proposed in the 1970s as the central component of modernizing Chinese agriculture. Although agricultural modernization is no longer a policy goal, agricultural mechanization is still regarded by people as a symbol of a modern China. However, in terms of her abundant agricultural labor resources, mechanization can hardly be an appropriate goal for China for at least the next 50 years.

Third, farm consolidation is proposed as a means to increase farm income. However, this proposal misses the point: while the income of the larger farms will increase, consolidation will inevitably leave other farmers landless. Unless the nonfarm sector is large enough to quickly absorb the redundant agricultural labor, land consolidation can increase the income of some farmers only at the expense of others. It is highly unlikely that China's industrial development will quickly absorb the redundant agricultural labor force. Therefore, the proposal of raising farm income through farm consolidation is not a sensible one.

Fourth, since China's accession to the WTO it has been said that China, with its small farms, cannot compete with foreign agricultural imports, so farm consolidation is a prerequisite for Chinese agriculture to survive. Indeed, if China insisted on competing with land-rich countries in land-intensive products such as wheat and corn, China would certainly lose out. However, this is not because Chinese farms are small but because China's land and labor endowments keep the country from having a comparative advantage in these crops. From this point of view, China should not compete with foreign imports in land-intensive products; instead, it should shift to producing more labor-intensive products. For such products, small farms actually have an advantage over large farms because family labor is less expensive.

In practice, farm consolidation is implemented in some localities. For example, villages with relatively large nonfarm sectors in southern Jiangsu province have taken back land from households and given the cultivation of the land to specialized farm teams whose members are paid cash wages. However, the sustainability of such semicommercial farming is in question, because the special farm teams tend to use more machinery and other modern inputs and therefore incur very high costs. In many cases, they have to be subsidized by the village.

Realizing that administrative farm consolidation hurts farmers' interests and freedom, some authors turn to the market for a solution. It is argued that the land sales market helps farm consolidation and improves efficiency because land will tend to concentrate in the hands of those who have an advantage in farming (Liang 1998). However, it is an empirical question whether the land market can achieve farm consolidation, because success depends on the distribution of individual values of land.

Farm consolidation is possible only when the distribution is highly polarized. One circumstance that leads to this kind of distribution occurs when there is a natural disaster whose consequences differ among households depending on their different capabilities to cope with the calamity. Another circumstance occurs when a large portion of the population obtains employment outside agriculture. However, the Taiwanese experience shows that people tend to keep their land even if they move into the cities, because speculation that the land value will increase prevents people from selling off their land. This could be true in the fast-growing suburban areas in Mainland China, where nonfarm employment is growing along with speculation about rising land prices. As a result, it is highly unlikely that farm consolidation will happen quickly.

Egalitarianism and Welfare

For some, the right to private property is the guarantor of individual liberty, which in itself merits being held as the ultimate goal (Buchanan 1993). To the extent that liberty entails only avoidance of the infringement of others, this assessment is largely correct. However, to most economists and ordinary people, liberty not only entails passive avoidance but implies capabilities, that is, the freedom to do something. This notion of freedom and its related implications for development is no more convincingly argued than by Amartya Sen (1998). Sen's approach leads us to view farmers' welfare under China's two-tier land tenure system as a multidimensional issue. While it entails efficiency losses in agricultural production, the system provides a mechanism that takes care of the poorer segment of the population. In this section, we broaden our scope to consider the social welfare effect of the HRS.

At the very basic level, the egalitarian nature of Chinese land tenure alleviates the malnutrition problem of the poor households. Burgess (2003) compares China and India on several welfare indicators (Table 3.3) and attributes China's better performance to her more egalitarian land distribution. His argument relies on land's own price effect.

TABLE 3.3 Welfare indicators in China and India, 1990

	China	India
Per capita GNP (U.S. dollars)	410	370
Daily calorie supply	2,630	2,238
Children 0–5 below –2 s.d. weight for age	17.4	63.9
Children 0–5 below –2 s.d. height for age	31.4	62.1
Infant mortality (per 1,000)	31	97

SOURCE: Burgess (2003).

NOTE: s.d., standard deviation.

When the food market is perfect, land has an effect on a household's consumption only by increasing its income. When the food market is imperfect, land serves as a less expensive device for households to use to generate food consumption. Burgess calls this latter effect the "own price effect" of land. Land is a less expensive device because farm households' labor is inexpensive, and more of it is applied to the land when the outside food market is not perfect. Burgess's econometric analysis of data from Sichuan and Jiangsu provinces verifies the existence of land's own price effect.

To the extent that a farm household with an average landholding can enjoy a reasonable nutrition level, egalitarian land distribution helps alleviate malnutrition in poor households. In this case, the two-tier land tenure system has a built-in mechanism to alleviate extreme poverty. In inland China, most farm households are living at the subsistence level, with most of their income coming from land. Unequal land distribution thus deprives the households with little land of the basic means to make a living, which can hardly be tolerated by the traditional Chinese collective culture (Kung 1994).

At another level, egalitarian land distribution weakens the dependency of human capital investment on family wealth. Dependency of education on family wealth has two adverse effects. One is that families are more likely to embark on diverging wealth trajectories set by their initial wealth stocks, which is not good for social integration. The other is that there could be a misallocation of talents in the sense that children with above-average intelligence in land-poor families do not get enough education, while below-average children in land-rich families do. In this case, economic efficiency is sacrificed.

Land plays two roles in affecting a household's decision regarding children's education (Li, Lin, and Yao 2003). One is that it alleviates the credit constraint faced by the household by providing more self-generated income, and the other is that it increases the household's ability to take risks. The first role is straightforward, but the second role needs more elaboration. Children's education is a risky investment in China. If a child cannot enter college, the marginal benefit of finishing high school is very limited. China's college entrance examination is the most competitive in the world, and the risk of failing the exam is very high. As a result, children's high school education is a very risky investment for a poor household. To the extent that risk aversion is decreased, a larger landholding induces a household to take more risks in its children's education. Li, Lin, and Yao (2003) find significant results from the first role of land for any stage of education, and from the second role for senior high school education.

The egalitarian distribution of land also acts as an insurance mechanism for temporary rural migrants who work in the city. Because employment in the city is subject to external shocks, rural migrants face the risk of losing their jobs in the city. In this case, they can go back home and work on their own land. In the Asian financial crisis of 1997–98, many rural workers lost their jobs and had to return to their home villages. In the privatization process, many rural workers are laid off by the privatized firms and have to go back to work on their own land. Had those workers not had their own land, unemployment in the city would have been much worse.

However, some authors argue that the HRS sets an obstacle to labor migration because migrants cannot finance their migration by selling their land (Yang 1997). Although this argument stands up theoretically, the question is how significant it is in reality. The price for agricultural land is very low. With an average landholding of one-tenth of a hectare in most regions, selling one's land can hardly help one afford to buy a room in the city. On the contrary, Li and Yao (2002) find that more egalitarian land distribution encourages temporary labor migration, because land's role as wealth increases a household's capability to take risks. Egalitarian land distribution increases the propensity for migration of the poorer segment of the population, and because of decreasing risk aversion this positive effect more than offsets the negative impact on the richer section; thus, the net effect is more migration in a more egalitarian village.

In summary, the egalitarianism of the two-tier land tenure system does provide significant benefits to China as a whole. When a value judgment is made, one has to weigh the possible losses in agricultural productivity against the gains in other areas. At the present, social protection in rural China is very weak; the majority of the rural population does not have retirement and healthcare benefits. In this case, land is an inexpensive substitute for cash-based social programs. A land-based social protection program is less expensive because, combined with inexpensive family labor, land can sustain a family's basic living.

Land Tenure, Rural Politics, and the New Agricultural Lease Law

While the efficiency and welfare implications of the two-tier land tenure system are still being debated, it is clear that this mixed system has complicated rural politics. Because the village retains the legal ownership of the land, the village cadre may take advantage of its position to pursue its own interests. As outlined earlier, one explanation for periodic land reallocation points to the cadre's intention to use it as a rent-seeking device. In addition, often the village cadre signs a land contract with an outside contractor without the consent of or proper compensation to the villagers. In such cases, the village cadre is frequently found to have received private benefits. The conflict between cadre and ordinary villagers has led to mass protests and collective petitions to the government. The central government, keen to maintain social stability, is thus very keen to reduce the conflict.

Grassroots democracy brought about by the newly introduced village election does not seem to have eliminated the cadre's rent-seeking behavior, although there have been encouraging signs (Liu, Wang, and Yao 2002; Brandt 2003). China began to experiment with village elections in 1988 when the Village Council Law was publicized. After 10 years of experimenting, the law finally took formal effect in 1998. By now, almost all villages have held at least one round of elections. However, the election of the village council does not automatically lead to better governance, because the classical problem of collective action keeps many villages from benefiting from the new democracy (He 2003). In addition, elections are frequently manipulated by the government, and the elected village council is not under the supervision of the villagers.

The conflicts of interest arising from the HRS have led to serious political pressure on the central government to further individualize land rights (Yao 2002a). In fact, some localities began to move in this direction a long time ago for the purpose of both solving the conflicts and increasing agricultural efficiency. Guizhou province is most radical in this respect. With the help of a group of researchers from the former Development Research Institute and the Experimental Office of Agricultural Reform, Guizhou started an experiment of "two no's"—"no increase of land for the new born, and no decrease of land for the dead"—in Meitan county in 1987 (Zhou and Liu 1998). The two no's policy was quickly adopted by the whole province. After 10 years, the provincial legislature passed a local law in 1998 that formally admitted the policy. In effect, there has been no land reallocation in Guizhou for nearly 20 years.

After long debates, the central government finally passed the Agricultural Lease Law in August 2002, and it took effect on March 1, 2003. The new law defines the relationship between the farm household and the village collective as a lease relationship, that is, the farm household leases land from the village collective. The lease term is set at 30 years for arable land, 30 to 50 years for grassland, and 30 to 70 years for forests.

While most of its contents are no more than a rectification of existing practices that have emerged in the past 20 years, the new law includes the following breakthroughs, which have turned the farm household's lease rights to de facto property rights. First, it stipulates that the village "shall not make adjustments to the lease land in the lease period" (Article 26). Second, the law acknowledges the household's right to inheritance: "The due benefits of the lessee shall be inherited according to the Inheritance Law" (Article 31). Third, the law implicitly gives permission for the sale as well as the lease of land use rights: "Land use rights obtained through family contracting from the village can be transferred to others by way of entrusting, leasing, exchanging, transacting, and other forms of transferring" (Article 32). These articles provide the farm household's lease rights with the three key elements of property rights: clear boundaries and security, transferability, and inheritability.

Although there is a limit to the lease period, the central government has said that the leases will be extended even after the 30-year limit. Therefore, the articles quoted have effectively introduced permanent leasehold of land. In this sense, the new law puts China on the track to de facto private land ownership. However, the law still leaves open the possibility of land reallocation under several special cases, such as natural disasters and state-sponsored land development projects, in which cases the land of some households could be destroyed or taken over by the state. In this sense, the new law has inherited some of the characteristics of the two-tier land tenure system.

While it is premature to provide a complete appraisal of the effects of the new law, several assessments can be made based on the existing research results. These are discussed under three headings: economic consequences, political consequences, and farmer welfare.

Economic Consequences

The impacts of the new law on economic efficiency are likely to be limited. Enhanced tenure security will not have a buoyant effect on agricultural productivity, mainly because, as studies cited in the previous sections have shown, the positive effect of securer land tenure on land investment is quite limited.

The law is also not likely to have a significant impact on land consolidation. In suburban areas, speculation will hinder land consolidation as in Taiwan, where the population is not sufficiently differentiated to induce land consolidation in agricultural areas. In the cases where this does happen, it will probably be associated with distress sales, a consequence that the government wants to avoid. If farm consolidation ever takes place, it would be best if it happened through the land lease market, which allows farmers to keep the option of cashing in the land in the future while obtaining a flow of current income.

Most villages had already allowed for land leases even before the law was introduced; therefore, the law would not induce significant gains by encouraging more land leases. On the other hand, it is also possible that the newly introduced law may encourage more land leases, because securer tenure increases land investment, which in turn raises the value that the tenant places on the land. However, it is an open question how large the effect would be in reality.

On the negative side, individualization of land rights may slow down farm consolidation and other processes that require collective action. In China today, commercial agriculture often takes the form of "company plus farmers," an arrangement in which a leading company provides technology and takes care of the marketing while the farmers undertake production. This form of commercial agriculture realizes farm consolidation through market contracts rather than through ownership concentration. An advantage is that it uses the comparative advantages of both the company and the farmers. In addition, it gives both the company and the farmers flexibility to terminate the contract in a relatively short period of time. In many cases, the company does not sign separate contracts with individual farmers, but signs one contract with one village, and the village takes care of the arrangements within itself. Under the authority of the village, considerable transaction costs are saved in the negotiation and implementation of the contract. Since the new law took effect, the village no longer has the legal right to sign a contract for the village land, and the company has to sign separate contracts with all the participating farmers. Without the village as a buffer, the negotiation and enforcement of the contracts will become much more difficult and costly.

Another situation in which the new Agricultural Lease Law may have a negative effect is when nonfarm development needs a large tract of land. For example, many villages in the Pearl River delta have been turned into industrial parks in the past 10 to 15 years due to the influx of capital from Hong Kong, Taiwan, and some developed countries. In many cases, the village builds standard factory buildings in a predesignated industrial park. After the land rights are individualized, the building of such large industrial parks will become difficult because some households may hold their land hostage for bargaining. At the minimum, the individualization of the land rights will increase the negotiation costs in the processes that involve collective action.

The areas in which the new law is likely to have a significant effect are forests and grasslands. With the lease term formally acknowledged to be 50–70 years, more people will be willing to lease or buy forests and grasslands and to invest in them. In particular, this will open a way for companies to buy mountains and grasslands and engage in commercial agriculture.

Political Consequences

The Agricultural Lease Law is likely to do a better job in the political arena than in the economic sphere. The law stipulates legal liabilities that are to be incurred by the village cadre in case of violation. As a result, individual farmers can take the case to court and ask for legal redress. It is noteworthy that the National People's Congress (NPC) enacted the new law despite existing laws and regulations that were supposedly providing sufficient protection for the farmers.

The NPC seems not to have confidence in the village democracy, the very process that it strongly promotes. Elections empower the villagers as a whole, so there is a free-riding problem when collective action is needed to correct the wrongdoings of the cadre. The Village Council Law allows for an early election, before a council's term ends, if 10 percent of the households sign a written petition. In reality, this is a very stringent requirement under the current power structure.[9] The Agricultural Lease Law gives individual farmers the faculty to sue the cadre in court if they feel that their interests are being infringed. The advantage is therefore the avoidance of the free-riding problem of village democracy.

It also seems that the NPC does not have confidence in the ability of the administration and the party apparatus to curb the village and township cadre's wrongdoings. China is a vast country, and the administrative and party apparatus often loses control at the very end of the system. A centralized inspection and punishment system is not enough to eliminate local corruption. By including the punitive clauses, the Agricultural Lease Law decentralizes checks and balances from the government to individual farmers, so corruption can be easily monitored. Nevertheless, the effectiveness of this decentralized mechanism depends on the effectiveness of the court system as well as the awareness of individual farmers. Given the current weak legal system, it is reasonable to have doubts.

It is worth noting that the Agricultural Lease Law is also likely to create more conflicts between farmers and the government, especially in the case of government-sponsored land development projects. Under Chinese law, the state can procure land from farmers at a predetermined price that is usually lower than the market price. Farmers are in a very weak position in the case of state procurement, especially when the land is to be used for commercial purposes. Farmers are usually compensated at less than 20 percent of the land's value, and private developers as well as various levels of the government corner the rest. Although the new law does not grant individual farmers private ownership of land, it will inevitably increase individual farmers' consciousness of ownership and they will use the law to protect their interests in the case of state procurement of land.

Farmer Welfare

For many people, especially some Chinese scholars, privatization of land is a synonym for polarization and the destitution of some farm households. History seems to support this concern. However, the danger of polarization through land sales may be exaggerated, at least when we are talking about only the short-run effects. In the short run, land concentration may not occur for the reasons discussed previously in this chapter. What should be of greater concern is the fact that the new law takes away the risk-sharing mechanism inherent in the egalitarianism of the HRS. Even without land sales, land distribution will become

---

9. Liu, Wang, and Yao (2002) record a story in which an early election was called by a group of people in a village in Zhejiang province. The leaders of the group never showed up, solicitation of signatures on the petition letter proceeded underground, and the letter was eventually handed to the township congress through lawyers from the county.

quite uneven as household demographics change. In Guizhou, for example, the per capita landholding of the most land-rich family could be 20 times that of the most land-scarce family (Bauhoff and Yao 2002). Because the average landholding is small and can barely sustain a family, a significant portion of the rural Chinese families could suffer from malnutrition.

The new law will also make collective actions more difficult and threaten the current village welfare programs and public investments. There is no government-sponsored social protection program in rural China. Most of the welfare programs, such as those offering old age or retirement benefits, medical insurance, and dividends, are provided by the village based on the income from the village land (Liu, Wang, and Yao 2002). While farmers may receive some of the benefits through individual profits arising from individualized land rights, the cost-sharing nature of some of the programs, such as those for medical insurance, will be lost. The individualization of land rights will considerably weaken the position of villages to obtain revenues, and financing village public projects will become difficult if there is no serious attempt to coordinate individual contributions. It is thus an urgent task to introduce alternative mechanisms to provide social protection to the rural poor.

Conclusion

The Chinese land tenure system has had a volatile history in the past 50 years. The 1950s were dramatic. The small family farming system established by land reform was quickly replaced by collective production under the commune system, destroying many farmers' dreams of accumulating wealth. The historic famine ended the national hysteria of communist fever, and the Chinese agriculture entered nearly 20 years of stagnation. Agricultural reform at the end of the 1970s introduced family farming again, but kept the legal ownership of land in the hands of the village collective. The resultant two-tier land tenure system has been a mixed blessing. On the positive side, it helped alleviate extreme poverty and compensate for the lack of social protection in the rural areas. On the negative side, it entailed dynamic losses to agricultural productivity and magnified the already tilted village power structure by adding another means for the village cadre to seek its own benefits. This last factor was the major consideration behind the introduction of the Agricultural Lease Law.

This law will be a milestone in China's land tenure history. It basically stops land pooling among households, formalizes land lease between the village and the household and sublease between households, and, most important, creates a quasi-market for land sales. It will be very interesting to observe the effects of this law on agricultural productivity, the land market, labor movement, farmers' investment and accumulation portfolios, village inequality and poverty, and village politics. While immediate observations are not possible, some conjectures regarding the working of the new law can be made.

First, it is not realistic to expect an increase of agricultural output at a scale and magnitude achieved by the land reform of the 1950s and the second agricultural reform at the end of the 1970s. The new law's effect on land investment and agricultural output may be quite modest.

Second, farm consolidation will be slow, but the activity of the land lease market is likely to increase, particularly that involving long-term leases. Farm consolidation, if it ever occurs, will probably proceed on the basis of long-term leases.

Third, in the inland areas farmers will be differentiated more on the line of landholdings. In particular, those with small landholdings and little human capital will quickly fall to the bottom of the economic heap. The more active land lease market may help by allowing these families to rent land, but the effect has yet to be verified.

Fourth, farmers' land rights will be more respected, but the collective actions inside the village will become more difficult, and conflicts between individual farmers and the government are likely to become more pronounced, especially in government-sponsored land development projects.

The new law does not end all debate, nor does it exempt the state of its responsibilities in rural China. Rather, it is the starting point for the state to take further actions to complement the implementation of the law. Among these actions, establishing a social safety net and respecting farmers' rights in governmental procurement of land are of foremost importance. The need to develop safety nets for the rural poor is an urgent one, one that is discussed in detail in Chapters 5 and 22.

Compared to the task of establishing a social safety net, respecting farmers' rights in governmental procurement of land is relatively easy, because it basically has to do with redistribution of benefits. The current law gives the state monopolistic power over land conversion and the initial sales of land. This is inconsistent with the village's legal status as the owner of its land. While restrictions on land conversion are necessary, the legal ownership of the village should be fully respected if land conversion is to follow a socially desirable path. The current political balance is tilted toward the state and the developers, and farmers' rights are neglected. This tilted political structure must be righted in order to guarantee a smooth and fruitful implementation of the Agricultural Lease Law.

4 Land Institutions, Policy, and Reforms in India

RAVI SRIVASTAVA, N. C. SAXENA,
AND SUKHADEO K. THORAT

Land is a key productive resource, owned and accessed by the rural poor in India. Nearly three-quarters of the rural population depend on it for their very livelihood, as well as for food, wage and nonwage income, fuel, fodder, and many other requirements.

Of India's landmass of 284 million hectares (m ha) in 1951, 41.6 percent was cultivated, while 14.5 percent was covered by forests and 16.6 percent was either not available for cultivation or was uncultivable wasteland. By 1997, the amount of agricultural land had grown to 46.6 percent and that of forest land to 22.6 percent, while the share of uncultivable land had dropped to 13.9 percent.

The ownership and management of land has very significant implications for equity, growth, and removal of poverty and has been the focus of considerable policy attention in India. Here we analyze the impact of policy changes with respect to different institutional arrangements with reference to their impact on the poor in India. The first section of this chapter reviews major events in land reforms in India since the 1950s, while the next section is devoted to changes in tenancy. The third section reviews the evolution of the landholding structure and trends in the concentration of both owned and operated land. The fourth section considers the effects of input and technology on productivity and efficiency, while the fifth section analyzes the impacts of the land policy changes on poverty reduction. The next section identifies future directions in land reforms, including land markets, women's land rights, and common property resources and is followed by some concluding remarks.

Land Reform Policy

Although the percentage of people dependent on agriculture for a living declined from 70 percent of the population in 1961 to about 60 percent in 2001, about 71 percent of the total population still live in the rural areas, and more than three-fourth of these derive their livelihood from land, wholly or partially. The share of people dependent on land is unlikely to fall drastically in the future. Therefore, relations between various categories of rural households, including

71

large farmers, small and marginal farmers, sharecroppers, and agricultural laborers, and the nature of their respective control over land are of paramount importance. Any strategy for increasing agricultural production in India cannot overlook these structural questions, just as rural poverty and agricultural backwardness cannot be understood without reference to the agrarian structure.

During the colonial period, the British introduced three main types of tenure systems in India, the *zamindari,* the *ryotwari,* and the *mahalwari* systems. Under the *zamindari* tenure system, which prevailed over most of eastern India, land revenue was fixed in perpetuity and land was permanently "settled" with *zamindars.* In the other two forms of tenure, the "settlement" with a class of proprietors was temporary and revenue was periodically revised. In the parts of India that were under indirect sovereignty of the British and were part of various kingdoms, different forms of feudal tenure systems prevailed. In almost all parts of India, those who possessed superior rights over land mostly leased it out. Direct proprietary cultivation, with or without the help of laborers, was rare. However, subinfeudation (with several layers of tenants and subtenants) was the most common in the *zamindari* areas, thus imposing the highest burden on the direct producers.[1] Indebtedness of tenants due to the rental burden and highly inequitable access to land led to waves of peasant revolts in many parts of the country in the late nineteenth and early twentieth centuries.

Abolition of landlordism and other land reforms in the interest of agrarian equity and growth became key policies of the nationalist parties and the government of the newly independent India. Starting in the 1950s, three main sets of land reforms were implemented: (1) abolition of intermediaries (the *zamindari, ryotwari,* and *mahalwari* forms of tenure) and tenancy reforms, (2) introduction of ceilings on landholdings and distribution of surplus land, and (3) distribution of government wastelands and land consolidation programs.

Tenancy Reforms

The goal of the first set of reforms was to enlarge the base of land ownership (i.e., give "land to the tiller"), thus restricting tenancy as well as increasing tenure security. Tenancy legislation was enacted in extensive areas of the country providing for conferment of ownership rights on tenants or allowing cultivating tenants to acquire ownership rights on payment of reasonable compensation to the landlords, subject to limited rights of resumption for self-cultivation to the landowners (Malviya 1954). Some of the states acquired ownership from the landowners and transferred it to the tenants, who paid a certain premium to the state.

Many states enacted the tenancy laws, which severely restricted the conditions under which landowners could lease out land, amounting to a virtual ban

---

1. See, for instance, Chowdhury (1964), Dutt (1970), Whitcombe (1971), Bagchi (1976), Amin (1982), Bharadwaj (1982), Stokes (1983), and Srivastava (1994).

on leasing. These restricted conditions included the imposition of a ceiling on rents (between one-fifth and one-fourth of gross produce) and the guarantee of security of tenure to tenants.

However, the considerable demand for leased land that existed among the peasantry led to the continuation of fairly extensive unrecorded tenancy at rents that were much higher than those stipulated in the laws. Moreover, tenants remained insecure because landlords remained apprehensive that permanent rights could accrue to tenants under the law in case of long-term possession. Further, due to the provision for "voluntary" surrender in tenancy laws, tenants were evicted from lands that they were cultivating. Details of various tenancy conditions in different states are presented in Table 4.1.

The Indian Constitution had put agriculture and land reforms within the purview of the provinces, a state subject. The landed gentry, if powerful in the central government, were even more powerful in the state legislatures and state governments, and exercised considerable influence over the organs of state. The land reform legislation passed in the states in the 1950s (in some cases as late as the early 1970s) provided scope for the substantial landowners to dilute, if not defeat, the intent of the legislation. In particular, they were able to evict large numbers of unrecorded tenants from lands registered as being under their "personal" cultivation (Thorner 1976; Walinsky 1979; Bandopadhyay 1986; Appu 1996).

Nonetheless, the legislation abolishing landlordism achieved a significant transformation of the countryside by enlarging the base of landownership and creating essentially three categories of landholders: those with inheritable and transferable rights over land, those with permanent occupancy rights (which were to gradually transform into the first category), and those with an obligation to pay rent to those in one of the first two categories. As a result of the implementation of these laws, the ownership of nearly 40 percent of cultivable land was transferred to the direct producers, and nearly 12.4 million tenants obtained secure rights or ownership rights over an area of 6.15 m ha, which is around 4.4 percent of India's cultivable area (India, Ministry of Rural Development, 2003).

The Ceiling on Landholdings and Land Distribution

The second prong of land reforms was introduced in the late 1950s and early 1960s and consisted of the imposition of a ceiling on landholdings. The ceiling size was related to the size of an "economic" holding that a family could cultivate with its own resources, including traditional animal-power-based plowing technology. The ceiling size also varied between irrigated and nonirrigated land, with exemptions included for other categories of cultivated land, such as orchards. As in the first phase of land reforms, landowners tried to sidestep reforms by de jure partition and distribution of land among real or fictitious relatives (Bandopadhyay 1986). The failure of the legislation to percolate down to

TABLE 4.1 Conditions of tenancy permitted in different states of India

State or region	Who is permitted to lease out	Consequent landlord and tenant rights
Telangana (Andhra Pradesh)	Smallholders with fewer than three "family holdings" in restricted categories; renewable period of five years	Right of resumption
Andhra area (Andhra Pradesh)	No restrictions	Right of resumption of up to two-thirds of the ceiling area, but the tenant should be left with half the leased area
Assam	No restrictions	The landlord has the right of resumption if the land is required for bona fide self-cultivation
Bihar	Restricted categories. Under the Bihar Tenancy Act, persons with fewer than five acres of irrigated land	Right of resumption
Saurashtra (Gujarat)	Restricted categories	Unauthorized leasing subject to fines
Haryana	Restricted categories	No consequent rights to tenants
Himachal	Permitted	Right of resumption
Jammu and Kashmir	Not permitted	

Karnataka	Restricted categories	
Kerala	Not permitted	
Maharashtra	Permitted	The tenant acquires the right to purchase land after a year unless owner is in a restricted category
Orissa	Restricted categories and "privileged *ryots*"	
Punjab	Permitted	No consequent rights to tenants
Rajasthan	Permitted but restrictions on period, except for restricted categories	
Tamil Nadu	Permitted; agreements have to be recorded	
Uttar Pradesh	Restricted categories	
West Bengal	Permitted	Hereditable *bargadari* rights accrue to tenants; landlords can resume land under specified conditions and subject to a maximum area of holding for themselves and a minimum area to be left with tenants

SOURCE: India, Ministry of Agriculture, various years.

NOTE: "Restricted categories" ordinarily refers to specified categories such as widows, members of the armed forces, persons with disabilities, and so on.

the large segment of the land-poor peasantry whose hunger for land remained acute led to militant movements from 1967 onward that centered on the land issue. The central government recognized the urgency of the agrarian issue and stepped in with a second round of land ceiling legislation in 1972 in which ceilings were lowered and some of the loopholes of the first round were removed.

However, in all but a few states, land ceiling legislation met with very limited success. Besides the reluctance of states to enforce land ceilings vigorously, the other main reasons for this were (1) the exemptions made for plantations as well as land held by religious and charitable institutions, (2) fake transfers, (3) misclassification of lands, and (4) nonapplication of appropriate ceilings on lands newly irrigated by public investment.

By March 2002, about 3 m ha of land (less than 2 percent of the cultivated area) was declared surplus, of which the government took possession of about 2.63 m ha (i.e., 88.2 percent) and distributed an area of 2.18 m ha to 5.65 million rural poor (India, Planning Commission, 2003). However, due mainly to collusive litigation, a large chunk of land (0.46 m ha) out of the declared surplus is under litigation at various levels and has not been available for distribution.

Land Consolidation and Wastelands

The third and final aspect of Indian land reform has been the distribution of government wastelands and the move to consolidate fragmented holdings. Consolidation of holdings in a village could be done after two-third of the landowners had consented. Land of variable quality was then pooled and redistributed among the landowners in consolidated plots, thereby reducing fragmentation and increasing the possibility of adoption of land-augmenting technologies. By 2002, consolidation had taken place on 66.1 m ha out of the 142 m ha of cultivable area, but many states had stopped the process earlier (India, Planning Commission, 2003). Maximum land has been consolidated in the northwestern states of Punjab, Haryana, and Uttar Pradesh and in the western state of Maharashtra. The distribution of government wasteland was most vigorously implemented in the states of Andhra Pradesh (1.7 m ha, or 28.5 percent of the total land distributed in the country), which has a very high percentage of landless laborers, and Uttar Pradesh, involving 1 m ha or 16.9 percent of the total land distributed in the country (India, Ministry of Rural Development, 2003).

Implementation of land reforms varied considerably across regions. Because land reform is within the purview of the individual states, success in its implementation has been varied and has depended most of all on the constellation of political forces at the grassroots and the commitment of the government of the day. Kerala and West Bengal, which were the more successful land-reforming states in India, implemented the reforms with vigor under a Leftist government. They witnessed mass mobilization of the rural poor and had governments with clear and strong commitments to the agenda of land reform. West

Bengal also vigorously implemented a program of registration of sharecropping tenants, thereby providing them security and low rents. More than 1.4 million sharecroppers (*bargadars*) were recorded under "Operation Barga." This was done in collaboration with groups of beneficiaries and with the active assistance of rural farmers' organizations (*krishak sabhas)* and *panchayati raj* institutions (rural local bodies) dominated by poor and middle-class peasants.

The Rationale for Land Reform

Equity, growth, and poverty reduction are the three major goals of any land reform program, and criticism of such reform stems mainly from its supposed negative impact on growth, efficiency, and farmer enterprise.

The equity argument cuts across a spectrum of issues—economic, social, and political—all integrally linked to the development process. A program of transfer of ownership and control over land from the large to the small is expected to increase overall employment and consumption. Access to land not only determines income and wealth but is also the basis of stratification of the village community and the bedrock of rural power relations. Better distribution of land and control over land in favor of sharecroppers and tenants is expected not only to increase employment per unit of land but also to improve the consumption standards of the rural poor, thus enlarging the size of the market for consumer products. Giving the poorest a stake in the land and improving their consumption standards also enables them to invest in their futures. Further, it minimizes the chances of social tensions and conflicts that show signs of increase in states where the landless constitute a substantial proportion of rural society.

The growth, efficiency, and accelerated poverty reduction arguments are partially related to the conditions just discussed. First, land reform is expected to lead to a reduction in unemployment and underemployment and to bring about an increase in incomes of the poorest in the rural areas. It is also believed to help increase production and lead to efficiency, although there is debate regarding the exact nature of this relationship as agriculture undergoes technological change.

From the beginning, the Indian five-year plans have placed considerable emphasis on land reform. As set forth in the national plans, the objectives of the land policy have been, first, to remove the impediments to agricultural production that have arisen from the agrarian structure inherited from the past, and second, to eliminate all elements of exploitation and social injustice within the agrarian system to ensure equality of status and opportunity to all segments of the population. The discrepancy between the ownership and operation of land was regarded as one of the basic maladies of the agrarian structure that acted as a "built-in-depressor." It not only led to inefficient use of scarce resources but also stood in the way of augmenting them. At the same time, contemporary research on the relationship between size and productivity in India during the

1960s (discussed later) principally supported the view that smallholder agriculture is related to higher rates of employment and efficiency and provided an economic rationale for the policy of imposing ceilings on landholdings.

Changes in Tenancy and Their Implications

The forms of tenancy that exist on the ground are not in accordance with the legal framework. Hence tenancy is largely unrecorded and underreported in the various landholding surveys carried out by the National Sample Survey (NSS).[2] Further, careful fieldwork over a long period of time and longitudinal surveys normally show a much higher magnitude of tenancy and a different picture of changes in it than are brought out by short-period surveys (Srivastava 1989; Jha 1997; Swain 1999; Sharma and Dreze 2000; Institute of Human Development 2002).

The percentage of area under tenancy estimated by the Land Holding Surveys has been slowly declining, but the trend reversed in the 1990s. The percentage of area recorded under tenancy in 1954–55 was 20.3.[3] The shares of operated area leased in by rural households declined from 10.7 percent in 1960–61 to 10.6 percent in 1970–71 and 7.2 percent in 1981–82, but rose to 8.3 percent in 1991–92. In absolute numbers, tenant holdings remained stable at 5.5 million from 1960–61 to 1981–82, but their numbers increased sharply, to about 12 million in 1991–92. As a percentage of all holdings, however, the proportion of tenant holdings declined from 23.5 in 1960–61 and 25.7 in 1970–71 to 15.2 in 1981–82 and 11.0 in 1991–92.

Traditional tenancy relations involve large landowners' leasing out land to peasant producers. However, with the rising capital intensity of production and the emergence of economies of scale in agriculture, large capitalist cultivators could lease in land from others, thus also sidestepping ceiling legislation. The latter phenomenon (often termed "reverse tenancy") has been observed in India since the Land Holding Survey of 1954–55 and has been considered quite widespread in some of the northwestern and western states (Vyas 1970; Laxminarayan and Tyagi 1977). This phenomenon is considered to have accelerated during 1981–82 and 1991–92, with both the percentage of operated area leased in and proportion of tenant holdings increasing significantly in the "large holding" category of 10 ha and above. The percentage of operated area leased in for the "marginal holding" category (i.e., below 1 ha) fell from 1971–72 to 1991–92 and remained constant in the "small holding" category (i.e., 1.00–1.99 ha) between 1981–82 and 1991–92. But the percentage of area leased in increased in both the "semimedium holding" (i.e., 2.00–3.99 ha) and "medium holding"

---

2. See NSSO (1954, 1961, 1962, 1972, 1987, 1992b,c, and 1995).
3. However, these figures are not strictly comparable to those of later survey rounds because the land survey of 1954–55 also recorded long-term leases as tenancy.

(i.e., 4.00 to 9.99 ha) categories between 1981–82 and 1991–92, and it rose significantly, from 5.3 percent to 11.4 percent of operated area in the "large holding" category during this period. The proportion of tenant holdings to total holdings also fell in all major categories of landholdings between 1971–72 and 1991–92 except in the case of large holdings, where it increased from 11.5 percent to 16.7 percent in the past decade. Another indication of the increasing concentration of tenancy in large holdings comes from the fact that in a number of states, the percentage of area under tenancy increased quite sharply between 1981–82 and 1991–92 even with a fall in the percentage of tenant holdings (Srivastava 2000).

In numerical terms, households owning less than half a hectare of land account for more than half the households leasing land in 9 out of the 15 major states.[4] Small lessees, owning less than 1 ha, also account for the bulk of land leased in at the state level. An indicator of overall dependence on leasing is the proportion of leased-in area to owned area in the various size groups of land ownership in 1991–92. The proportion of leased to owned area is very high (59.9 percent) in the smallest size category of land ownership (0.00 to 0.49 ha) at the all-India level. It then declines to 10.7 percent in the next category (0.50 to 0.99 ha) and then steadily falls to 4.1 percent in the medium size category (4.00 to 9.99 ha) and 0.8 percent in the large size category (10.00 and above ha).

With regard to terms of lease, studies show that tenancy contracts in India are mostly oral and informal and have been associated with increasing insecurity and a shortening in the period of lease, culminating in the emergence of seasonal leases in several regions in recent decades. Information on the seasonal operation of holdings and seasonal leases collected by the NSS found that during 1991–92, 16 percent of holdings had leased in land, but 7 percent and 1 percent had leased in land *exclusively* during *Kharif* and *Rabi* seasons, respectively. While "*Kharif* only" and "*Rabi* only" tenant holdings were only 0.26 ha and 0.42 ha, respectively, perennial tenant holdings were 1.09 ha on average.

Micro studies throw considerable light on seasonal leasing. In a study of three villages in Uttar Pradesh, Srivastava (1989, 1997) found that paddy was leased out seasonally on a widespread basis in western Uttar Pradesh to landless households who were expected to provide labor and one-fourth of the cost of material inputs, but the fields were plowed with the landowners' tractors or plows. Landless households had recourse to very little alternative employment other than employment on leased land, even though the returns to labor were lower than the prevailing wage level. The study noted that through seasonal leasing landowners were able to sidestep downwardly rigid wage levels, keep supervision costs low, and use nonmarketed labor in tenant households. On the

---

4. The highest proportions of marginal lessees, that is, those owning less than 0.5 ha, are in Bihar (78.5 percent), Kerala (76.9 percent), West Bengal (76.5 percent), Tamil Nadu (68.2 percent), Assam (68.1 percent), and Orissa (63.2 percent).

other hand, tenants were reduced to the status of piece-rated laborers, with the stipulation that they share production risks. There were similar seasonal leases for other, usually labor-intensive, crops in the region (e.g., onions, potatoes, and sugarcane). Seasonal leases have also been reported in other parts of the country (Bharadwaj and Das 1975; Chadha and Bhaumik 1992; Harris 1993; Khasnabis 1995).

To sum up, despite significant changes, lease relationships with land-poor households leasing in from other households continue to be the principal feature of tenancy in India. There are only a few states where land-rich households have a sizable presence as lessees due to the observed "reverse tenancy" (small lessor–large lessee). These include primarily Punjab and Haryana, where capitalism has made deep inroads into agriculture. Both macro surveys, such as the NSS, and micro studies attest to the emergence of a class of well-to-do tenants whose terms and conditions of lease are often different from those of the poorer tenants.[5] This phenomenon has gathered strength in recent years and has undoubtedly contributed to the steady increase in the concentration of operational holdings. With increasing capital, labor, and transaction costs, resident landowners have been able to increase their input and rental shares, which has also resulted in shorter leases (often for a single season). We also notice a considerable heterogeneity of lease relationships both within and between states: (1) small lessees leasing in on a crop share basis are significant in the eastern states and in Tamil Nadu (southern India), (2) the extent of leasing on a cash rent basis in Punjab and Haryana is very high among medium to large farmers, and (3) cash and fixed rent tenancies and leasing in by medium to large cultivators is also important in dry-land areas of the country.

The fact that the form of tenancy has been subject to change with the increasing penetration of capitalism into agriculture is irrefutable, and the emergence of the phenomenon of reverse tenancy is clearly an important aspect of this change. However, in the country as a whole, and specifically in several large regions, the typical lessee continues to be the small landless cultivator, and a large number of landless and poor peasants continue to lease in small plots of land under conditions of severe underemployment and pressure on land.

The Landholding Structure

With nearly three-fourth of the rural population dependent on agriculture for employment and income, the distribution of land among the various sections acquires immense importance. The landholding structure not only determines

---

5. Studies (Khasnabis and Chakravarty 1982; Bhalla 1983; Srivastava 1989; Swain 1999) find a (1) a predominance of traditional tenancy relations in poor agrarian regions, (2) transitional situations with the emergence of well-to-do tenants, and (3) a predominance of capitalist tenants among medium to large cultivators.

the way in which the rural workers make their livelihoods but also influences the production organization of agriculture.

Farm Size and the Distribution of Holdings in Rural India

The average area owned and operated is an important indicator of structural change in agriculture that has a bearing on the nature of technological change and income distribution. The long-term trend in developed agrarian economies of the West and some Asian countries has been movement toward larger but fewer farms (Hallam 1991). In India, however, the general trend has been in the opposite direction. With stagnation or slow expansion in agricultural land and a steady increase in the number of rural households, there has been a significant downward shift in farm size. The obvious result has been a decrease in the average area owned, from 1.94 ha in 1953–54 to 1.18 ha in 1991–92. The average area operated at the all-India level is generally higher than the average area owned in all the years under study. Over time, the average size of operational units has decreased, from 3.0 ha in 1953–54 to 2.3 ha in 1970–71, and further, quite sharply, to 1.4 ha in 1995–96 (Table 4.2).

A striking feature of the size distribution of ownership holdings in India is the predominance of submarginal (0.005–0.400 ha), marginal (0.400–1.000 ha), and small (1.000–2.000 ha) holdings. Submarginal and marginal holdings together accounted for about 44 percent of the total operational holdings in the country in 1961, which increased to around 62 percent in 1995–96, indicating a significant trend toward marginalization of operational holdings over time.

From Table 4.2 it is clear that the high number of marginal farms is not matched by their share in operated area, which was only 17 percent in 1995–96. On the other hand, farms of 10 ha or more, and those in the 4 to 10 ha category, operated roughly 15 and 25 percent of the total area, although they accounted for only 1 and 6 percent of the total number of farms, respectively. Similarly, semi-medium-sized holdings of 2 to 4 ha, which formed nearly 12 percent of the number of farms, operated about 24 percent of the total area.

The percentage of landless households steadily declined, from 23.1 percent in 1953–54 to 11.7 percent in 1961–62 and 9.6 percent in 1971. But thereafter the ratio marginally increased, to 11.3 percent in 1981, and that level remained stable in 1991. The upward trend in the incidence of landlessness during the 1970s and the lack of decline during the 1980s at the all-India level, coinciding with technological change in agriculture, was indeed a significant departure from the steady decline during the 1950s and 1960s.

The Trend in Land Concentration: Owned and Operated Land

Figure 4.1 presents the concentration (or Gini) ratio for owned and operated area at the all-India level. There was a decline in the concentration in ownership of land during the 1950s. The ratio has shown small changes thereafter, with a small decline in the 1960s and a small increase during the 1980s.

TABLE 4.2 Structure of operational landholdings in India for selected years

Category (ha)	Number (million)			
	1970–71	1980–81	1990–91	1995–96
Submarginal and marginal (below 1.00)	35.7	50.1	63.4	71.2
	(50.6)	(56.4)	(59.4)	(61.6)
Small (1.00 to 1.99)	13.4	16.1	20.1	21.7
	(19.1)	(18.1)	(18.8)	(18.7)
Semimedium (2.00 to 3.99)	10.7	12.4	13.9	14.3
	(15.2)	(14)	(13.1)	(12.3)
Medium (4.00 to 9.99)	7.9	8.1	7.6	7.1
	(11.3)	(9.1)	(7.1)	(6.1)
Large (10.00 and above)	2.8	2.2	1.6	1.4
	(3.9)	(2.4)	(1.6)	(1.2)
Total	70.5	88.9	106.6	115.6

SOURCE: Datanet India Pvt. Ltd. (2006), data for 2003.

NOTE: Data in parentheses show the share (as a percentage) in the total for a particular year.

FIGURE 4.1 Concentration ratios of owned and operated land in India

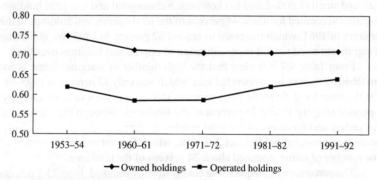

SOURCE: India, Ministry of Statistics and Program Implementation, various years.

The analysis of statewise concentration in land ownership (Sharma 1994; Chadha, Sen, and Sharma 2003) shows that the decline during the 1950s, in the initial phase of land reforms, was shared by all states. During the 1960s, the decline was moderate and confined to nine states, with only three states (Gujarat, Punjab, and Uttar Pradesh) showing sharp increases in land ownership concentration. The 1970s and 1980s, which coincided with technological change in Indian agriculture, showed a more widespread increase in the concentration of land ownership, with increases in the Gini measure in 9 out of 17 states during this period. However, agriculturally advanced states like Punjab, Haryana, and Uttar Pradesh were not a part of this group. In fact, the prominent ones among

	Operated area (m ha)				Average size of operational holdings (ha)		
1970–71	1980–81	1990–91	1995–96	1970–71	1980–81	1990–91	1995–96
14.5	19.7	24.9	28.1	0.41	0.39	0.39	0.4
(9)	(12)	(15.1)	(17.2)				
9.3	23.2	28.8	30.7	1.4	1.4	1.4	1.4
(11.9)	(14.1)	(17.4)	(18.8)				
30	34.6	38.4	38.9	2.8	2.8	2.8	2.7
(18.4)	(21.2)	(23.2)	(23.8)				
48.2	48.5	44.7	41.4	6.1	6.	5.9	5.8
(29.8)	(29.6)	(27)	(25.3)				
50.1	37.7	28.7	24.2	18.1	17.4	17.3	17.2
(30.9)	(23)	(17.3)	(14.8)				
162.1	*163.8*	*165.5*	*163.4*	*2.23*	*1.18*	*1.16*	*1.14*

them were states where agricultural modernization had made smaller inroads (Assam, Bihar, Jammu and Kashmir, Karnataka, Madhya Pradesh, Maharashtra, Orissa, and West Bengal). This is likely to have happened due to the diverse impact of land ceiling legislation, demographic factors, and the land market in different states.

The distribution of operated area happens to be less unequal than owned area at all points in time because smaller holdings predominate as lessees. At the all-India level, the Gini ratio for operational holdings declined during the 1950s and remained stable during the 1960s. However, during the 1970s and 1980s, there was a significant and steady increase in the concentration ratio of operated area. The Gini ratio increased from 0.587 in 1971 to 0.624 in 1981 and further to 0.641 in 1991. The concentration in operated area thus increased at a faster rate during the 1970s, followed by the 1980s, which coincided with technological change in Indian agriculture and the changes in tenancy patterns observed earlier.

At the state level, the concentration in operated land declined in all states during the 1950s and in a majority of the states during the 1960s. However, there was a marked increase in concentration in a large majority of the states during the 1970s and 1980s (only Andhra Pradesh and Rajasthan showed a small decline over these two decades).

Chadha, Sen, and Sharma (2003) note that over the period of about four decades (1953–92), the base of the pyramid had become much wider. At the same time, small and marginal holdings improved their share in area in some states (Bihar, Kerala, Uttar Pradesh, Tamil Nadu, and West Bengal), while in others (Andhra Pradesh, Gujarat, Karnataka, Madhya Pradesh, Maharashtra, and Punjab) the increase in the area share of medium holdings was the most pronounced. Thus, medium holdings emerged stronger in practically all states except Kerala and Jammu and Kashmir.

Land Size and Resource Use, Technology Adoption and Efficiency

The emerging pattern of landholdings analyzed earlier has definite implications for input use, technology, and economic efficiency in agriculture. Therefore, we present an overview of these issues in the context of the nature of the agrarian (and institutional) changes in India.

Farm Size and Productivity

Several studies based on data for the mid-1950s and the 1960s concluded that there was an inverse relationship between farm size and output per acre of gross cropped area, thus indicating higher productivity of small farms compared with large farms (Sen 1962; Khusro 1964; Mazumdar 1965; Paglin 1965; C. H. H. Rao 1967).

While most of the first generation studies were based on grouped data and therefore open to the criticism of group aggregation bias, several studies later worked with disaggregated data. Using farm-level data, Rudra (1968a,b) contended that although the inverse relationship was seen in some areas, it could not be accepted as a rule for Indian agriculture. C. H. H. Rao (1967) found that productivity remained constant over holding sizes in the villages examined, indicating that holding size has no effect on productivity. But Saini (1969, 1971) and Rani (1971) worked with farm-level disaggregated data and found that an inverse relationship between farm size and productivity held in most of the cases they studied.

Ghose (1979) used data for West Bengal and Punjab to estimate the relationship between farm size and productivity for farms under different types of production organization. When all farms were considered together, an inverse relationship between farm size and output per acre of net sown area was found for earlier years in most cases, although it was not always significant. Bardhan (1973) looked at the experience of Andhra Pradesh, Orissa, Madhya Pradesh, Tamil Nadu, Punjab, and Uttar Pradesh. The coefficients were negative and significant for paddy in Andhra Pradesh and Uttar Pradesh, while in other cases the coefficients were negative but statistically insignificant. However, both these authors found a positive coefficient for Punjab in 1967–68.

In all but a few cases, these studies relating farm size to productivity covered the years prior to the green revolution. Some researchers had expressed the view that technological progress, involving the introduction of chemical fertilizers, labor-saving machinery, and modern irrigation equipment, was likely to erode the basis of superiority of small-scale agriculture, and some of the studies cited earlier corroborated this view. Ghose (1979), in particular, had observed that in Punjab, where considerable technological change took place between 1955–57 and 1968–69, the relationship between farm size and land productivity had changed from negative to positive. In a comparative study of regions of Punjab based on 1970 data, Chadha (1978) observed that the inverse relationship between farm size and productivity tended to disappear in areas in which a shift to higher capital intensity had occurred on large farms. In areas where capital expansion in relation to labor input was still at a comparatively low level, the inverse relationship still held. For a later year (1974–75), and for an advanced region of Punjab, Bhalla and Chadha (1982) made similar observations, noting that large farmers had gained an edge due to the introduction of a new rice technology in whose use the smaller farmers were not up to par. Outside Punjab, Thorat (1993), in a comparative study of technologically advanced and less advanced regions of Maharashtra, arrived at an identical conclusion for technologically advanced irrigated regions and some crops. However, Chattopadhyay and Sengupta (1997) found that in West Bengal, in a more recent year (1989–90), the inverse relationship between farm size and productivity for paddy continued to hold in both agriculturally developed and less developed regions.

Farm Size, Input Use, and Modern Technology

The relationship between pattern of input use and farm size has been used to explain the observed relationship between farm size and productivity. Explanations that link input use to the inverse relationship can be grouped into "quality-based explanations" and "intensity-based explanations." The former imply that small farms use better-quality human labor (more family labor than hired labor), cultivate agricultural land of superior quality, provide better management, and enjoy a higher impact from indivisible factors (such as bullock power). Among the intensity-based explanations, the greater use of human and animal labor, current inputs (such as manure and chemical fertilizer), and irrigation; the intensity of cultivation; and the greater allocation of cropped area to high-value or cash crops have figured quite prominently. However, studies also show that some of these features have undergone a change since the onset of the green revolution, especially with respect to some of the inputs in technically progressive agriculture.

It has been observed that the high level of output per acre on small farms is really a function of the greater input of human labor, with other factors varying more or less in the same proportion as human labor (Mazumdar 1965). Studies for the 1950s and 1960s found a statistically significant inverse relationship between farm size and labor use per acre (C. H. H. Rao 1967; Bardhan 1973; Bharadwaj 1974; Ghose 1979).

Apart from the greater use of human labor, the high cropping intensity has been attributed to a high level of irrigation (Sanyal 1969; Rani 1971; Ghose 1979; Thorat 1993). However, in the highly irrigated regions the relationship tended to be neutral, while in the case of privately owned well irrigation, a bias was observed in favor of large farms in some studies (Chadha 1978; Thorat 1993).

Studies have also analyzed the difference in the use of material inputs such as manure, fertilizer, and capital services from traditional as well as modern implements and machinery, including bullocks, from the 1960s through the 1980s. For the 1960s, Ghose (1979) found an inverse relationship of manure and fertilizer per acre to farm size for the districts of West Bengal and Punjab, but in the case of Punjab, for 1968–69 a significant positive relationship was observed for all farms. Similarly Thorat (1993) observed higher expenditure and use of manure and chemical fertilizer on the small farms engaged in less developed dryland agriculture in the early 1980s. A few studies also found an inverse relationship between farm size and total input cost (including imputed costs) for the 1960s (A. P. Rao 1967; Rani 1971). Similar results were obtained for less developed dryland agriculture during the late 1970s (Thorat 1993).

Since the mid-1960s, significant changes have occurred in the nature of technology, which now consists of biochemical and mechanical inputs and is essentially capital intensive. Because the new technology requires more working and fixed capital and the large farmers have better command over owned and borrowed financial resources, they are likely to be better placed than the small farms with respect to the use of these new inputs. Some of the evidence for the 1970s and 1980s in regions that came under the influence of new agricultural technology showed that the small farmers lost their edge in the use of new inputs such as chemical fertilizer, pesticide, and modern capital services (Chadha 1978; Bhalla and Chadha 1982; Thorat 1993). Small farmers, whose resource base and capacity to borrow from formal credit institutions are smaller, were found to be in a relatively weak position in the use of new technology (Thorat 1990, 1994).

Recent Evidence

Because technology and the pattern of its diffusion has been changing over time, many of the issues we have described need continuous reexamination in the light of emerging evidence. In this regard, Sen and Bhatia (2003) have analyzed data on the cost of cultivation, and their study finds that paddy cultivation in Andhra Pradesh for 1995–96 showed an inverse relationship between farm size and both use of family and total labor and use of chemical fertilizer per hectare. However, there was no consistent pattern in the use of machine labor, while irrigation costs per hectare increased with farm size. Yield per hectare showed little variation in the size classes up to 6 ha but was higher in the largest size class (6 ha and above). In the case of sugarcane, while the input pattern was found to be similar, output per hectare was found to be higher on small farms.

Data for *jowar* cultivation for the same year (1995–96) in Maharashtra also showed an inverse relationship with farm size in the use of total labor and fertilizer (machine labor and irrigation costs were negligible), and yield per hectare did not show any systematic relationship with farm size. In the case of irrigated sugarcane, the amount of total human labor was highest in the small- and medium-size holdings. The use of machine labor was lowest in the smallest size category (up to 1 ha), followed by the largest size category (6 ha or more), while fertilizer use per hectare was also the lowest in the largest size category. Yield per hectare did not show a systematic relationship with size, although it was the lowest in the largest size category.

In the case of wheat cultivation in Rajasthan (1992–93), the use of all inputs was greater on small farms than on medium and large farms, but there was no significant trend in the yield per hectare. Data for Punjab in 1995–96 and Rajasthan in 1992–93 showed higher cropping intensity on smaller holdings. Because large farms enjoy some advantages due to a higher volume of resources and some scale advantages in ownership of assets, the study also examined the total farm economy for Punjab (1995–96), Rajasthan (1992–93), and Tamil Nadu (1995–96). In the case of Punjab, the study found that the use of inputs such as seeds, fertilizers, and machine labor increased with farm size, but total labor and family labor showed an inverse relationship. However, gross returns per hectare as well as gross margins did not vary systematically with size of holding. Thus, the Punjab data did not provide any evidence of a significant relationship between overall productivity per hectare and size of holdings.

In the case of Rajasthan, it was observed that overall input use was higher for all major inputs on small farms (costs paid out per hectare were also higher), and this resulted in higher gross output per hectare (80 percent higher in the smallest category compared to the largest). In Tamil Nadu, while total human and animal labor showed an inverse relationship with size of holding, the use of machine labor did not vary systematically with size, and some of the major inputs, such as fertilizers and hired human labor, increased with size of holding. The gross income per cropped hectare did not show a systematic relationship with size.

On the whole, therefore, with the increasing importance of nonlabor inputs into production, the earlier observed inverse relationship is much less evident. In most of the states, the spread of irrigation through bore wells, which made irrigation less human labor–intensive, also weakened the inverse relationship between use of irrigation and farm size. However, use of fertilizer, a divisible modern input, often continues to show an inverse relationship with size for many crops and for the crop economy as a whole. Thus, the small farmers do not appear to be facing significant scale disadvantages in the use of modern inputs, although because of resource constraints, large farmers in Punjab and Tamil Nadu devote a larger area to resource-intensive crops. The study also provides evidence that small farmers do not face significant price disadvantages, although they do face higher costs on indivisible fixed inputs.

Land Reforms and Rural Poverty

The influence of landholding structure, the "proletariatization" of households, and tenure status on rural poverty is of great significance and has been analyzed in a number of studies (Bardhan 1985; Parthasarthy 1987; Shergill 1989; Sharma 1995). However, these studies do not relate changes in agrarian structure to land reforms. Moreover, linking the results of these studies to the possible impact of land reform–led changes is also difficult because they do not capture the linkage and effect of the former with agricultural growth, employment in the farm and nonfarm sectors, wages, and other variables. These interlinkages have to be taken into account, because ignoring these features leads to biased estimates of poverty (van de Walle 1985; Bell and Rich 1994).

There are major problems in tracing the dynamic impacts of both agrarian structure and land reforms on agricultural growth. It has been argued that patterns of agricultural growth in India continue to have some correspondence with patterns of agrarian structure inherited from the colonial period (Bagchi 1976; Bharadwaj 1982; Mearns 1999).

Further, in all but a few states the major impacts of land reform were felt during the 1950s and 1960s, a period during which the base of land ownership expanded, concentration levels were mitigated, and tenancy declined sharply. But the impacts of these changes affected a wide range of variables with different lags.

Recent studies in states such as West Bengal, which have experienced modest but relatively rapid land reforms over different periods, link the rapid human development and decline in poverty experienced by these states to the land reforms. In West Bengal, land reforms may have contributed to a high rate of agricultural growth and reduced poverty through improved access to technology and inputs; high levels of investment in tanks, bore wells, and pump sets; "repeasantization"; and pressure on wages (Boyce 1987; Kohli 1987; Lieten 2003). Banerjee, Gertler, and Ghatak (2002) have carefully estimated the effect of tenancy reform (Operation Barga) on agricultural productivity. They hypothesize that tenancy reforms would improve tenure security and bargaining power and reduce the disincentive to effort and investment, thereby increasing productivity. Their model, based on district disaggregated results for tenancy reform, attributes 28 percent of the increased agricultural productivity in West Bengal to reform. Lieten (2003) has emphasized the stress in West Bengal on "inclusive land reform," that is, changes in production relations supplemented by improved provision of and access to inputs and "appropriate" technology, and creation of pro-poor institutions. Similarly, studies on the determinants of poverty in India over several decades associate the rapid reduction in poverty experienced by states such as Kerala with favorable initial conditions created by land reform through its impact on landlessness, rural wages, and participatory development fostering high levels of social development (Lieten 1982; Ravallion and Datt 1996; Ramchandran 1997).

Another recent study (Besley and Burgess 2000) has tested the relationship between land reforms, poverty reduction, and growth in India. The study finds a robust relationship between land reform and poverty reduction, but this is primarily related to the impact of land reform on contractual relationships rather than land redistribution.[6] The data cover the period 1958–92. The land reform variable is the (lagged) cumulative total of the various types of land reform legislation enacted since independence. The estimation of reduced form equation shows that land reform legislation had a significant impact on rural poverty as well as the rural-urban poverty difference within the states. Further, the results were driven by tenancy reforms and the abolition of intermediaries, while land ceiling legislation and consolidation had a negligible effect. Land reforms are also shown to have had an impact on rural wages, thereby affecting those sections of the poor who rely on wages rather than cultivation. The relationship to agricultural growth per capita is ambiguous, with tenancy reforms showing a negative impact and consolidation a positive impact. The greatest impact of land reform on poverty occurred in states that had high levels of initial inequality in land distribution.

In summary, the evidence from India provides support for the positive impact of land reforms on rural poverty (World Bank 1997c; Mearns 1999).

Future Directions in Land Reform

As discussed earlier, land reforms in India have led to the regulation of land markets in the form of land ceilings, tenancy regulation, rent control, and the creation of property rights in favor of the "tillers of the soil" and the land-poor. The content and scope of land reform has come under sharper scrutiny in the period of economic liberalization, because land reforms imply abridgements of extant property rights as well as market regulation. In the following sections we consider the future direction of land reform policy in the light of the analysis presented in the preceding sections.

Agricultural Land Ceilings

There is continuing debate on whether the present land ceilings should be raised, lowered, or left unchanged. While agricultural land ceilings in India were set high

---

6. One of the limitations acknowledged in the study is that the frequency of land reform legislation is used as a variable, which does not allow for the direction of legislation or for the level of its implementation. The legislation to abolish intermediaries is not seen as redistributive, although it had the greatest redistributive impact among the land reform measures undertaken in the post-independence period.

by Asian standards, technological changes and the rising capital intensity of agriculture as well as the need for investments in agricultural support argue for either raising or abolishing the ceilings. The empirical literature that we have examined suggests a weakening of the inverse size-productivity relationship, although it has not yet generally demonstrated a positive relationship either. However, because small farms continue to be labor-using and capital-saving, there is no case for raising the ceiling limit at present, while vigorous steps have to be taken to ensure that small farms are able to take advantage of technological changes.

At the same time, there is considerable scope for improved implementation of existing ceiling laws by plugging the loopholes, unearthing fake transfers with the help of grassroots organizations, and expediting decisions in cases under litigation by creating special benches in high courts or by constituting land tribunals under Article 323-B of the Indian Constitution. States have to ensure that when surplus land is allotted, mutations are effected in the land records, land is physically demarcated, and possession is handed over. Computerization of land records would help in the unearthing of fake transactions.

Tenancy Reform

Tenancy reform is viewed as a major redistributive as well as growth-inducing measure. There are three main issues relating to tenancy reforms: (1) the current restrictions on leasing out, (2) the regulation of and ceilings on rents, and (3) the right of resumption of land given to landlords and, conversely, the accrual of rights to tenants to hold or own the land.

While most states severely restrict leasing, there are states where it is permitted with or without restrictions (Table 4.1). In a majority of these states, the landlord's right to resume land is curtailed and/or subject to restrictions.

In the eastern states, where traditional tenancy relations are still significant, considerable political commitment and grassroots support are required for the successful implementation of tenancy reform. In other areas, where land markets are better developed and ground rents are high, the leasing out of land by small lessors is a viable strategy. Lessor-lessee relations are also far more compatible with the growth of investment and technological change. In such situations, the requirements of growth and equity may be better served by liberalizing the lease markets. We noted earlier that the ban on tenancies and the restriction on resumption of land by landlords have made leases more insecure, while the great diversity in rental forms has made regulation of rents even more difficult. On both counts, the needs of the poor would be better served if tenancy was legalized for all marginal and small landowners, subject to the land ceilings in operation, and the determination of rent left to market forces, subject to some realistic ceiling, which may be decided on a state-to-state basis. The state should also insist on secure long-term tenures and deal seriously with the landowners opting for short tenures.

On the question of the right of resumption, we have noted that different states treat the issue differently. Given that both lessors and lessees now belong to different classes, states may need to follow a differentiated policy with respect to marginal and small cultivators on the one hand and medium and large cultivators on the other, restricting the latter's right to resumption on a small number of grounds, such as self-cultivation and absence of alternative sources of income.

Land Records

The implementation of land reforms requires the maintenance and regular updating of land records, which have been woefully inadequate and poorly managed in several parts of the country. Since 1988–89, the central government has started schemes for the creation and maintenance of land records in areas where these were nonexistent, and for their computerization in order to facilitate maintenance and transparency. This continues to be a major policy issue. The central government's scheme for the computerization of land records is now operative in all districts, except where there are no land records (e.g., in the northeast), and it has also been decentralized to the lower administrative levels (the *tahsil* or *taluka*). The scheme has made good progress in a number of states, and the plan for strengthening revenue administration and updating land records is also operative in all districts. Therefore, the way forward is to continue supporting these efforts.

Reforms in the Land Market

With appropriate institutional reform, the land sales market can itself become an instrument for facilitating the transfer of land to agriculturally dynamic and land-poor households. Studies show that land transactions have facilitated the transfer of land from larger to smaller landowners in most parts of the country, including Punjab and Haryana (Mearns 1999). The land sales market is very sluggish in poor agrarian regions, in contrast to areas with developed capitalist agriculture, such as Punjab and Haryana (Srivastava 2000). This is a result of imperfections in the land market due to high transaction costs and imperfect credit markets (Mearns 1999). Investment in land is also uneven, which puts it beyond the reach of poor households, while large landowners fear low value realization. Compounded further by constraints on leasing, there is low intensity of use of the land market, with land simply lying fallow in the hands of absentee landowners.

Steps could be taken to facilitate the transfer of land to small and marginal landowners through the provision of long-term credit or assistance through the existing antipoverty programs, such as the Department of Rural Development's Swarnajayanti Gram Swarozgar Yojana. Furthermore, collaboration between nongovernmental organizations and the National Scheduled Caste and Tribe Finance Corporation in Andhra Pradesh, with the former identifying available land and the latter purchasing it at market prices and transferring it to the poor on long-term credit (India, Planning Commission, 2003, 308–10), is an initiative that could be replicated in other states.

Women and Land

In the past, the focus of creating new land institutions has been on promoting equity and growth between households, with land ownership and management continuing to be vested in males. Although a very large proportion of rural women are cultivators, they continue to be land- and assetless, because hardly any attention has been given to legal and other institutional impediments to the acquisition of land. Further, a significant proportion of farming households are headed by women due to male migration, death, or desertion or for other reasons. In such cases, absence of secure titles could impede incentive, investment, or access to inputs and credit (Agarwal 2003). This gender gap has important implications for equity and participatory development as well as for growth and efficiency.

The obstacles to women's ownership of land have been extensively highlighted (Agarwal 1994) in official documents (Working Group on Women's Rights 1996). Many of the states have responded by taking measures to improve women's access to land and landed property, but serious anomalies persist.[7]

In the matter of giving women a permanent stake in land distributed through government programs, the sixth five-year plan (1980–85) recommended that states give joint title to husband and wife in the transfer of assets such as land and home sites through government programs. The National Perspective Plan for Women (1998–2000) further recommended that the allotment of government wastelands, government land and surplus ceiling land, village common land, developed home sites, and tenements should invariably be done in the woman's name or under the joint names of the husband and wife. It is clear, therefore, that despite the limited progress made, there is still a long way to go in the direction indicated by these government initiatives.

Tribal Peoples and Land

India's tribal population is concentrated in the states of Bihar, Gujarat, Maharashtra, Madhya Pradesh, Orissa, Andhra Pradesh, Rajasthan, and West Bengal, apart from the northeastern region. The economy of the tribal communities continues to be land-based, with agriculture forming the mainstay of tribal life. However, the tribal land base has been steadily shrinking and is increasingly

---

7. States like Uttar Pradesh, Haryana, Jammu and Kashmir, Delhi, and Punjab are apparently yet to take adequate steps to provide constitutional or legal safeguards to women with respect to their access to land. In these states, the succession rules relating to agricultural land are different from personal laws affecting the devolution of all other property. Land devolves to male lineal descendants, and widows and daughters inherit only in the absence of male heirs.

alienated in the wake of nontribal migration into the tribal areas, leading to the "pauperization" of tribal people, rendering their situation, which is extremely vulnerable even at the best of times due to their comparatively higher levels of poverty and illiteracy, even more precarious.

Many states with a large tribal population have enacted laws prohibiting the alienation of tribal land, but legal loopholes and lack of effective political and administrative will continue to push tribal peoples toward assetless destitution. Studies initiated by the Department of Rural Development in 1997–98 (India, Planning Commission, 1999) paint a grim picture, confirming that massive alienation of tribal lands continues in tribal regions in all parts of the country.

Not only would restoration of alienated land require tough laws and an empathetic administration, but the problem would need to be addressed simultaneously along with other persistent tribal issues such as indebtedness, declining access to forest products, displacement, and ineffective implementation for tribal areas of the Panchayat (Extension to the Scheduled Areas) Act of 1996, which grants autonomy and control over local resources to tribal communities. Simultaneously, programs need to be started on a priority basis to generate employment and income and extend microcredit for self-employment ventures and consumption credit when no work opportunities are available. Special packages of poverty alleviation programs combined with basic minimum services should reach these areas through effective intersectoral coordination at the implementation level.

Common Property Resources

With land reform, all uncultivated lands including forests became vested with the state and were made available for grazing and other common purposes, and such lands are therefore part of the common property resources (CPRs). However, due to encroachments and the resultant decay of community management systems, the quantity, quality, and productivity of land-based CPRs available to the villagers have declined substantially over the years (Chambers, Saxena, and Shah 1989).

Increased policy attention to land-based and forest CPRs is warranted in the future, because such areas still play an important role in the life and economy of rural people. In villages of intensive cultivation, the CPRs are of marginal importance, but in arid, semiarid, and hilly regions, CPRs meet a significant proportion of the fuelwood and fodder requirements of poor households, besides contributing to food requirements and income (Jodha 1986, 1990)[8] and fulfilling environmental functions (Khare 1993).

---

8. According to the 54th NSS round (NSSO 1999), which made the first attempt to provide comprehensive estimates of CPRs use, 44.2 percent of rural households collect fuelwood from CPRs, 29.2 percent use CPRs for livestock rearing, and 12.7 percent use them for collection of

Although between 1952 and 1980, an average 154,571 ha per year of forest land was converted to nonforest use (mostly irrigation and power dams) and agriculture (Shyam 1993, 24), the process of further deforestation has been halted since the late 1980s. One reason has been the impact of the rise of green sentiments in the late 1980s, which gives primacy to environmental functions of forests and to satisfying the subsistence needs of the forest dwellers. This policy has called for a decentralized and participatory system of forest management, which could resurrect community interest and stakes in protecting the forests (NSSO 1999).[9]

By the mid-1970s, it became clear that if the people's demand for fuelwood and fodder were not met it would be impossible to save even productive forests. The response was a program of social forestry for the afforestation of common lands carried out by the Forest Department. The program was not very successful due to poor management and the failure to define, establish, and publicize rights to the trees and the procedures for marketing and allocating benefits, which led to indifference on the part of the local communities.

Another major problem was the degradation of common lands due to the lack of control of rainwater run-off. An integrated and participatory approach is most appropriate and has been highlighted by the new guidelines of the Hanumantha Rao Committee (1994), which aim at decentralized participatory planning and implementation of watershed development programs.

Building the capacity of grassroots organizations in planning, monitoring, implementation, and marketing should be pursued in the future. Further, the interface of the watershed associations or committees with the *panchayati raj* institutions requires strengthening through the transfer of funds to the village bodies and user groups and by making the latter accountable to the former. Where *panchayat*s represent several villages, single village organizations should be created as subunits of the *panchayat*s so that the land in question pertains to one village only. Because cultivable wastelands in many states have already been settled in favor of the poor, special projects should be undertaken to make such lands productive.

Internal Factors in Community Mobilization

There is a strong rationale for accepting community-based management of commons, provided collective action is possible. There is strong evidence that

---

fodder. Another 4.6 percent gather leaves and 3.2 percent collect fruits and roots from the CPRs. In value terms, the annual collection of fuelwood, fodder, and other items per household amounted to Rs. 693, with Rs. 777 being the highest for rural labor households with significant interstate variations.

9. With traditional community control and management, access to tree products has generally been fairly equitable. To take what may be a typical example in a hill village, Silpar, Almora District (Uttar Pradesh), an informal *panchayat* has been in existence for the past 18 years for protection of trees on common land (Tripathi 1987, 132–34).

social cohesion promotes such action, but there are sharply polarized views on whether such cohesion is likely to occur in Indian villages.[10]

Local collective action has been undermined in the past 30 years by a number of political and economic processes (Bardhan 1993).[11] The overall result of these processes has often been to forestall local action; a way out of this situation is "co-management," that is, cooperative management arrangements between state and local organizations in which states assign group rights to specific resources, establish overall guidelines for intergroup interactions, and help to create more positive environments for the operation of local organizations (Swallow and Bromley 1994, 5).

Conclusion

Agricultural land in India is overwhelmingly privately owned and operated, with total holdings numbering more than 115 million in 1995–96. More than 80 percent of the holdings are in the small and marginal categories, that is, holdings of less than 2 ha each.

The implementation of land reform policies aimed at equity and growth has been patchy across states, its success hinging on political will as well as the capacity for collective action of the people. While land reforms have led to the expansion in the base of owner-cultivators, technological and other changes have led to significant shifts in the agrarian structure. Where new technology has taken root, agriculture is generally more capital intensive, thereby transforming the old relationships. These changes, along with the new ethos of liberalization, have led to a questioning of the economic grounds of land reform. Further, land reforms that presuppose collective action by the poor also appear to have become less politically feasible with the expansion of the land-owning

---

10. According to Eckholm (1979), rigid stratification of village society inhibits the development of institutions representing a common will, while grossly unequal land tenure and access to markets ensure that only a powerful minority gains in the name of the community. Bandyopadhyay, Shiva, and Sharatchandra (1983), however, dispute that social and economic inequalities have hindered the possibility of community ownership, participation, and control in India. Management of village commons has been a historical reality for two reasons. First, whereas private resources in India have been governed by individualistic and class-dominated norms, there have been communally shared norms related to community resources. Second, the self-sufficient nature of the traditional village economy guided the exploitation of common resources through a system of self-control. The authors therefore conclude that there are no structural barriers to achieving community participation in forestry projects. Many environmentalists support this point of view (Agarwal and Narain 1990).

11. Village societies have become heterogeneous, and market forces have commercialized the erstwhile subsistence economies, integrating them with urban and national economies. Participatory politics erodes the traditional authority structures, and modernization improves the options of both exit and expression for the common people. Many rural communities in developing countries are in a difficult transition period, with traditional institutions on the decline while new self-governing institutions are yet to be born.

class as well as attachment to land and property rights. While these changes make the old agenda of land reform less politically feasible, the economic grounds of such reform also require fresh reconsideration.

Our analysis does not support a relaxation of agricultural land ceilings, but calls for a greater liberalization of the tenancy market, with safeguards for small lessees or lessors and discouragement of absentee landowners. We have also argued that the government should change gender-nonegalitarian land laws and foster landownership among women. This chapter also argues that the legal and implementation framework is still biased against tribal peoples and that this is one of the main factors leading to their pauperization.

We have shown that the management of forests and village commons, unlike that of cultivated lands, should lie with the community. This is now recognized by the government, but in practice, many of the administrative and socioeconomic dynamics are still not conducive to community management of these resources, and there are still a large number of lessons to be learned from past successes and failures.

5 The Basic Health Protection System in Rural China

LING ZHU

Despite the enormous success of market-oriented reforms in China, there is no denying that these reforms have also led to a widening of rural-urban gaps, increasing regional disparities, and income inequalities adding to poverty. Individuals and households are now at greater risk and subject to uncertainties that cannot be mitigated by the existing informal protection systems. The process of restructuring the social protection system in response to the socioeconomic transition lags behind marketization that proceeds unhindered. As a result, those outside the formal security systems, save those in the high-income group, have become more vulnerable to economic forces.

The growing health vulnerability of the rural people is becoming increasingly apparent, and although a booming medical market has emerged during the transition, medical services and drug markets remain far from well regulated. Corruption is rampant in the process of drug procurement, leading to costlier medicines and poorer access to health services. The vicious circle of poverty and illness has evoked wide public concern and calls for prompt policy intervention.

This chapter focuses on the health insecurity problems faced by the rural people of China during the country's current socioeconomic transition. I first introduce the changes in the basic healthcare system and financing and review the socioeconomic impacts of the current transition, drawing on macro-level information. Next I identify groups vulnerable to health risks through household livelihood analyses. This part of the chapter also draws heavily from sample data on the use of medical services to identify residual insecurity under the existing health risk–pooling systems. I end with a discussion of the necessary policy interventions, looking at the Indian experiences related to these issues.

The Healthcare System and Financing

Tracking the Changes

As early as the mid-1960s, a three-tier (county, township, and village) health service network had the responsibility of providing both medical treatment and healthcare in rural China. In the highly centralized planning system, public health programs sponsored by the government could be implemented rather smoothly in the countryside through this network. Rural health workers, widely known as "barefoot doctors," played a major role in providing easy and quick access to primary healthcare for the rural population. These rural health workers received work points from their respective production teams and received cash from the villagers for the inexpensive medicines.

The so-called cooperative healthcare system operating in most parts of China at this time was the grassroots public health service system closely associated with the functioning of the commune system (Zhu 2002a). The government retained firm control over medicine production and sale so as to guarantee reliable and inexpensive supply. These institutional factors and strong government financial support for public health made a decisive contribution to the improvement of rural health conditions despite the overall low level of health services.

Since the early 1980s, China's rural healthcare system has gone through far-reaching reforms. Government was the prime mover in this case, reining in the market to tackle the problems of public health financing and contain healthcare costs. Pursuing financial decentralization, higher government levels often delegated the responsibility of healthcare financing to the lower levels, which were in financial difficulties and likely to leave the responsibility to healthcare institutions. This actually meant that the problem was left to the market. Such a policy orientation became visible as early as in 1985 when the healthcare reform program was announced (China, State Council, 1985).[1] This policy document neither tried to encourage government authorities at various levels to increase their investment in public health, nor did it find a way to rein in medical costs. Instead, it allowed medical institutions to collect fees at will to deal with the shortfall in government financing.

As a result of financial decentralization, the three-tier health service network in rural China was challenged by the decline of public investment. One of the manifestations was the notable decline of the share of public health expenditure in total expenditures (China, Ministry of Public Health, 2002b). The share of public health spending declined from 2.5 percent in 1980 to 1.7 percent in 2000. The cooperative healthcare system virtually disappeared following the collapse of the People's Commune System, and the overwhelming majority of village health clinics were privatized. Subsidies for public health services at and above township levels were reduced and rural health services were commer-

---

1. This policy document considers severe shortage of investment in public health, low medical fees, and the financial loss of medical institutions the main reasons for the slow development of health enterprises. Further, strict government regulations are regarded as not conducive to stimulating private investment. The document therefore encourages collectives and individuals to set up medical institutions and allow existing medical institutions to increase user fees and charge labor and cost recovery fees for preventive and supervisory services.

FIGURE 5.1 Expenses and per capita net income of average rural households in China, 1995 and 2000

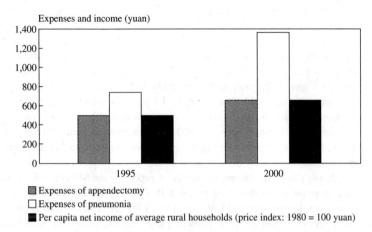

Expenses and income (yuan)

■ Expenses of appendectomy
□ Expenses of pneumonia
■ Per capita net income of average rural households (price index: 1980 = 100 yuan)

SOURCE: Editorial Committee of Health Yearbook (2001, 474 and 501).

cialized,[2] but the lack of well-functioning medical services and drug markets as well as corruption in drug procurement resulted in cost increases. For example, the cost of in-hospital treatment for appendicitis increased by 37.2 percent in 2000 compared to what it was in 1995, and the cost of in-hospital treatment for pneumonia increased by 83.2 percent, at a time when the net per capita income of rural households increased by just 25.9 percent (Figure 5.1).

These changes resulted in a turnaround from the prereform policy, which had effectively combined basic biomedical intervention and public healthcare (Wilson 1992). In order to reverse such a trend, the Chinese government has been making efforts to reestablish the cooperative healthcare system and at the same time carrying out experimentation regarding various forms of health risk–pooling system in different regions at varying development levels, making investments in upgrading public healthcare facilities, and addressing the problems of healthcare and drug markets. However, the trend has not yet been reversed, partly because the intervention is far from adequate.

The Impact of the Changes: Growing Inequality and Vulnerability

The impact of changes in healthcare financing on the health risk vulnerability of rural people has not been directly discernible in the overall health outcomes

---

2. According to an investigation I conducted in Nong'an and Yongji counties of Jilin province in November 2001, the government no longer provided subsidies to township hospitals, and subsidies were being provided to county hospitals only for their investment program.

because such outcomes are also influenced by other factors, such as nutrition, clothing, housing, jobs, education, living environment, behavior and lifestyle, and so on (Fuchs 2000). Nevertheless, one can feel the impacts in the following areas:

1. *Increasing medical costs borne mainly by patients.* In the 1980s, the total health expenditure in China was 3 percent of its gross domestic product (GDP). Figure 5.2 shows that in the early 1990s, health spending was in the range of 100–200 billion yuan, or 4.1 percent of GDP, and increased to more than 400 billion yuan, or 5.1 percent of GDP, in 1999 (Editorial Committee of Health Yearbook 2001). The increase in healthcare expenditure (in nominal terms) during these years was mainly and directly borne by patients.

2. *Declining use of healthcare resources.* A report by the Ministry of Public Health pointed out that "compared with 1990, in 1998 the average patients per doctor declined from 1683 to 1178; the utilization of hospital beds declined from 80 to 60 percent"; and "insufficient health resources co-exist with their wasteful use" (China, Ministry of Public Health, 1999, 188 and 190).

3. *A widening rural-urban gap in health resource allocation.* The urban population, especially the unemployed and their families, have also suffered from the market orientation of health services, although investment in healthcare by both central and local governments was concentrated in the cities. Social medical insurance and social aid systems were developed mostly for the cities. Under these conditions, healthcare services have been biased against the rural population. By the end of the 1990s, rural dwellers accounted for more than 70 percent of the total population in China, but rural healthcare expenditure accounted for only about 20 percent of the total government expenditure on healthcare (China, Ministry of Public Health, 1999).

4. *A notable reduction of access to medical services by rural people.* The state health service survey organized by the Ministry of Public Health found that in 1993, 58.8 percent of the rural patients needing hospitalization did not go to a hospital because of personal economic difficulties. In 1998, this percentage increased to 65.3 percent (China, Ministry of Public Health, 1999).

5. *Aggravation of the vicious circle of poverty and illness.* According to one calculation, poor households accounted for 7.2 percent of the total rural households in 1998,[3] whereas the nonpoor households falling into the category of poor households due to medical expenses accounted for 3.3 per-

---

3. The rural poverty line set by the Office of the Leading Group for Poverty Alleviation, under the State Council, was 625 yuan per capita annual net income at the end of the twentieth century. The exchange rate is 8 yuan for a dollar.

FIGURE 5.2 Total health expenditures in China, 1990s

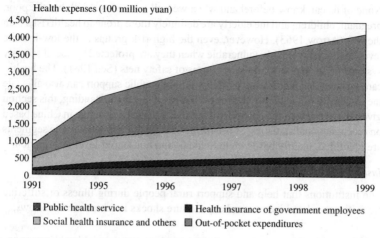

SOURCE: Editorial Committee of Health Yearbook (2001).

cent of the total households. This means that due to family medical expenditure, more people slipped into poverty and the poverty rate went up to 10.5 percent (Liu, Rao, and Hu 2001).

6. *Reduction of preventive health service at the grassroots level.* This problem exists despite the fact that the government has neither given up its management role in public health (China, Ministry of Public Health, 2002a) nor forgotten to insist that village clinics continue to take the responsibility of epidemic prevention, maternity and childcare, and family planning.[4] The government's document of healthcare reform announced in 1985 stipulated that any institution or individual could run village clinics if the village provided appropriate subsidies for the labor input by rural doctors or health workers in the area of public health work. In the poor areas, local governments were also required to provide assistance and subsidies for such activities (China, State Council, 1985). These requirements, however, were too difficult to be met in the economically less developed areas. As a result, in most rural regions, especially the poor ones, preventive services either remain deficient in terms of service supply or are starting to charge fees. This makes it more difficult for the poor to obtain preventive services, creating greater health risk vulnerability among them.

---

4. Since the beginning of the reforms, the National People Representatives have passed 9 laws, the State Council announced or rectified 25 administrative regulations, and public health authorities promulgated over 400 departmental rules concerning healthcare issues.

Identifying Rural Health Insecurity

None of us can know beforehand when we will fall seriously ill, but the poor, pregnant, children, and the elderly are definitely more prone to health risks than the rest (Arrow 1963). However, even the high-risk groups at the low-income level are not unavoidably vulnerable when they are protected by social security systems or are supported by other forms of safety nets (Sen 1981). The health-care services that increase accessibility through public support can also alleviate the insecurity of the high-risk groups. Based on this understanding, this section gives an overview of the portfolio of the social security coverage in China based on recent national statistics. Subsequently, the health risk–vulnerable segments are identified, mainly based on individual- and household-level information.

Institutions of Rural Health Security

The institutions that help and support rural people during illness or suffering from illness-related income and expenditure shocks in China are as follows:

1. Formal health insurance systems, including commercial health insurance programs, social health insurance programs, and community-based cooperative medical insurance schemes (effectively functioning only in a few well-off counties).
2. Health relief and assistance, including:
   - Medical relief in case the major income earners fall seriously ill (cases found within the rural health project financed by the World Bank [1997b] covering a number of poor counties in southern Shaanxi province).
   - Social assistance with cash transfers to the aged confronting catastrophic illness or injuries (cases recorded in Shaoxing townships of Zhejiang province).
   - Subsidized maternity services to women of poor households (cases found by the rural health project financed by the Chinese Poverty Alleviation Foundation for Lijiang county, Yunnan province).
3. Selective health service provision with budgetary subsidies for rural health education schemes and targeted preventive health plans, including prenatal and maternal care and immunization for children below age seven.
4. Informal risk pooling among family members, relatives, friends, and neighbors.

The formal Chinese social protection system for rural people, however well established it may have been in the past, is currently extremely limited in coverage. Health relief and assistance have functioned only in a few developed regions. In those poor areas where health promotion projects were carried out with the aid of poverty reduction funds, the assistance was available only for the duration of the projects.

The budgetary subsidies allocated to rural health education and targeted preventive health plans are often not sufficient to support the full operation of the programs. For example, the immunization plan was designed to be free of charges for children under the age of seven, but the central government disbursed funds for the vaccine and left the payment for services to be met by the local governments, the majority of which have not paid the cost due to either unwillingness or inability. The parents have to pay at least 1–3 yuan for every shot of vaccine, so some of the rural poor cannot afford to have their children participate fully in the program. Due to the financial and geographical constraints to accessing reproductive healthcare, around 40 percent of pregnant women from poor rural households did not receive prenatal care.

With regard to health insurance programs, people covered by health insurance schemes in China accounted for only 27 percent of the total population in 1998, with the coverage rate at 55.9 percent and 12.7 percent for urban and rural people, respectively (China, Ministry of Public Health, 1999). The elderly with declining earning abilities belong to a high–health risk group, with the coverage of their pension schemes determining their ability to cope with increasing medical expenditures (Li 2003). The coverage of pension schemes in 2001 was estimated at 29.5 percent for urban dwellers and 7.5 percent for the rural (NBS 2003). Thus, a considerable proportion of the population is not covered by the two most important schemes in both the urban and the rural sectors. The uncovered portion is substantially larger for the rural group than the urban segment (Figures 5.3 and 5.4).

FIGURE 5.3 Health insurance coverage in China, 1998

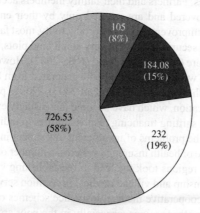

■ Urban uncovered   □ Urban covered   ▨ Rural uncovered   ■ Rural covered

SOURCE: China, Ministry of Health (1998); NBS, *China Statistical Yearbook,* 1999.

FIGURE 5.4 Pension system coverage in China, 2001

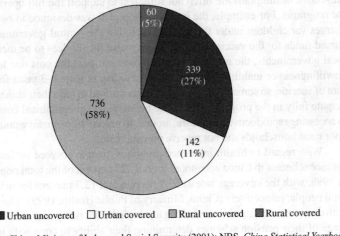

■ Urban uncovered □ Urban covered ▨ Rural uncovered ■ Rural covered

SOURCES: China, Ministry of Labor and Social Security (2001); NBS, *China Statistical Yearbook*, 2002.

Because the average rural income is lower than the urban and poverty in most part of the countryside is more severe than in urban areas, rural people are more vulnerable to health threats. The insurance schemes covering urban people are essentially related to the labor force employed in the formal economy and are similar to those in other developing countries. The rural people covered by the two formal social support systems are primarily those working in rural industries and services. Farmers and their family members account for the major portion of the uncovered and are secured only by their entitlement to land. Thanks to the great improvement in land productivity, most farming households have achieved food security even with very small land plots, measuring on average only 0.6 hectare (ha) per household (NBS 2002). However, the deficit of the basic needs that were met by the income generated from land-related activities is growing with marketization (H. Fan 2003). This is particularly true of healthcare and education, which have become increasingly expensive since the government started shifting financing responsibilities to individuals.

To overcome the problems of insufficient investment in public health and the limited coverage of health insurance systems, a number of counties or cities in the eastern rural regions took the lead in reestablishing village public clinics, integrating township and village medical prevention services, and creating community-based cooperative medical insurance schemes or social health insurance systems. In other regions, especially in the poor areas, similar efforts rarely produced successful results (Zhu 2002a). The majority of rural people have to rely on informal systems to protect themselves against health-related risks, even though it is widely understood that the informal mechanisms of social security, such as mutual assistance via family ties, friends, neighbors, and rotating saving groups, are unable to provide adequate protection and support to rural people in the context of increasing marketization (Platteau 1991).

Health-Risk Groups and Their Use of Medical Services

The characteristics of rural health insecurity can be more precisely presented with descriptive statistics derived from a sample survey I conducted.[5] In a total of 1,989 sample households (7,900 people), those covered by the cooperative medical programs accounted for 11.8 percent (Table 5.1), while schoolchildren aged 8–16 (nearly 13 percent of the sample population) are insured for accidents and hospitalization. These two categories may have some overlaps in terms of participation by the sample population, because the benefit packages of the two are very different. The findings underline the fact that the majority of rural people remain health-insecure.

Figures 5.5–5.8 show the incidence of sickness in the two weeks prior to the survey and the choices that the patients made in dealing with it. Figures 5.5 and 5.6 show that the poor suffered from a higher incidence of sickness. About 70 percent of the people who fell ill and visited a doctor chose to obtain medical treatment from the local village clinics, which generally receive nothing from government budgets. There was also a remarkable number of patients from both the poor and the nonpoor groups who bought medicine on their own for self-treatment. This practice apparently helps to reduce the cost of medical treatment, but it carries health risks that cannot be ignored. To buy and take medicines without a doctor's examination and prescription may well result in incorrect and indiscriminate use. This is even more risky for those who do not have much knowledge, a concern borne out by the fact that fewer than 30 percent of the heads of the poor households in my sample said they had received health education services, compared to 35–41 percent in the nonpoor category.

About 10 percent of the total sample reported being ill, with the sickness incidence of females at 12.6 percent, 3 percentage points higher than the sickness incidence of males. Roughly 28 percent of the ill included those over the age of 64, while preschool children under the age of 7 accounted for 13.3 percent. The group of schoolchildren between the ages of 8 and 16 had the lowest share, 5.2 percent. Ironically, only this age group is covered by commercial insurance, which is available due to a campaign launched by insurance companies throughout the school system. The companies ruled out the group over the age of 60 by requiring much higher premiums for them than for the other age groups,

---

5. I organized the sample survey in 1999–2000 in collaboration with colleagues from the Research Center for Rural Economic Policies under the Ministry of Agriculture, China. The survey included 2,500 households in 34 villages, 34 counties, and 6 provinces (Guangdong, Jiangsu, Hebei, Jilin, Sichuan, and Gansu) in 1999.

TABLE 5.1 Mean household assets possessed by the poor and the nonpoor

Asset	Total sample $n = 1,989$	Low-income $n = 266$	Middle-income $n = 671$	High-income $n = 1,052$
Human capital				
Household size (persons)	3.91	4.19	4.3	3.6
	(1.7)	(1.6)	(1.7)	(1.6)
Labor ratio (Number of	77%	54%	63%	81%
persons working/	(55.0)	(26.8)	(26.8)	(68.0)
household size)				
Years of schooling of	6.63	5.63	6.50	6.97
household head	(2.2)	(2.3)	(2.7)	(2.0)
Natural capital				
Area cultivated (mu per	6.19	6.84	6.59	5.77
household)[a]	(7.4)	(5.7)	(5.0)	(8.8)
Area contracted[b]	3.89	3.34	4.69	3.51
	(4.3)	(3.8)	(4.2)	(4.4)
Financial capital				
Bank savings and cash at	9,654	1,538	3,654	15,534
end of the year	(25,776)	(3,411)	(6,531)	(34,201)
Bonds and other capital	34	0	8	59
	(859)	(0)	(193)	(1,170)
Physical capital				
Value of production assets	6,118	2,877	3,608	8,539
	(29,081)	(6,781)	(7,392)	(39,251)
Value of nonproduction	23,381	8,767	13,249	33,538
assets	(41,135)	(8,671)	(15,179)	(53,028)
Health insurance coverage (%)	11.80	6.80	7.50	15.80

SOURCE: Author's survey.

NOTES: In this table, the poor are the low-income group with annual per capita net income below 1,000 yuan, the nonpoor earn more than 1,000 yuan, and the middle-income earn 1,000–2,000 yuan. The figures in parentheses are standard deviations.

[a]15 mu = 1 ha.

[b]Area that a household received from the process of land distribution in its village.

thereby inducing the majority of those who most require commercial insurance to give up buying it.

Residual Health Insecurity

Residual health insecurity can be generally defined as the situation of an individual or a group of people who are outside the coverage of health security institutions. For well-targeted policy intervention, it is crucial to identify the residual insecurities at both the country and the regional levels because there

FIGURE 5.5 Types of health service providers chosen by the Chinese nonpoor and average expenses

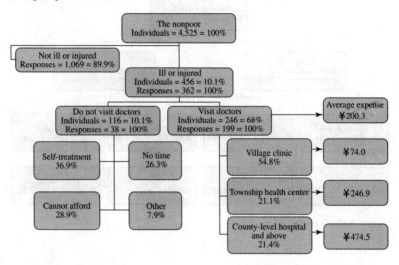

SOURCE: Author's survey.

FIGURE 5.6 Types of health service providers chosen by the Chinese poor and average expenses

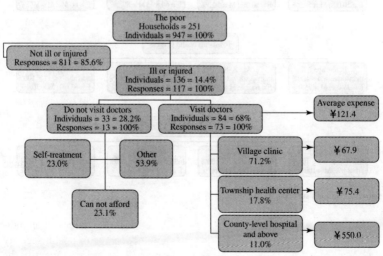

SOURCE: Author's survey.

FIGURE 5.7 Reasons for not visiting doctors in China, by gender

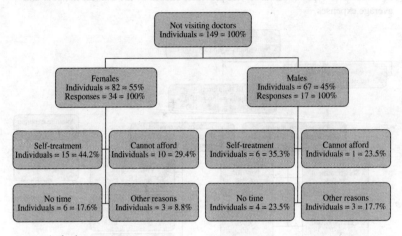

SOURCE: Author's survey.

FIGURE 5.8 Types of health service providers chosen in China, by age and gender

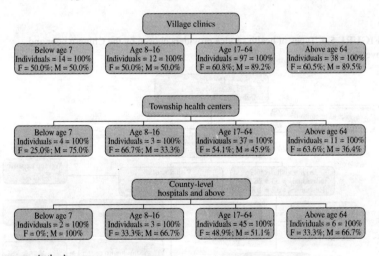

SOURCE: Author's survey.

are significant differences in security institutions between countries and regions. Groups in rural China living under conditions of residual health insecurity
can be identified as follows:

1. Those excluded by social health insurance schemes and/or by commercial
   insurance programs.
2. Within these groups, those outside community-based cooperative health
   insurance programs and those covered by the cooperative programs whose
   medical expenses exceed the limit of the benefit packages offered by the
   cooperatives.
3. Those who are eligible to receive subsidized provision of targeted healthcare services but for various reasons are not covered.
4. Among those who are covered neither by any of the insurance programs nor
   by targeted health plans, the poor, the elderly, and major income earners
   suffering from serious sickness but lacking access to relief or assistance.

The categories listed can be ranked according to the degree of insecurity,
and a visual picture is presented in Figure 5.9. However, it must be pointed out
that rural migrants are working in urban areas without health protection under
the urban security institutions. Although they are better off in terms of income
in the city than in their home villages, most of them have to face greater health
risks and more expensive medical services due to the institutional barriers against
rural-urban migration. The migrants play multiple social and economic roles,

FIGURE 5.9 Rural groups in China who are vulnerable healthwise, by severity of
insecurity

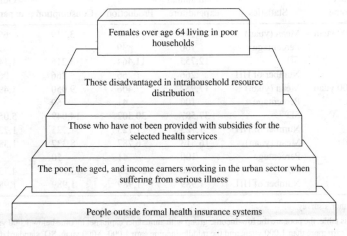

Females over age 64 living in poor
households

Those disadvantaged in intrahousehold resource
distribution

Those who have not been provided with subsidies for the
selected health services

The poor, the aged, and income earners working in the urban sector when
suffering from serious illness

People outside formal health insurance systems

SOURCE: Author's survey.

NOTE: Vulnerability is least severe for the group at the bottom of the figure and most severe for the
group at the top.

because they are the major income earners for their rural families, while in the city they belong to the most vulnerable group of the society.

Among the rural residents falling in the aforementioned categories, those who have less control over household assets; weak family, kinship, and community ties; and low income-generating capacity are regarded as the residual health-insecure in relation to the informal institutions. The most vulnerable in the insecure groups are those who are most disadvantaged in intrahousehold resource distribution. Because of the survey limitations, the data set cannot shed light on the informal risk-pooling arrangements between the sample households and the intrahousehold resource distribution among individuals. Nevertheless, it can be used to describe the economic characteristics of the health risk–vulnerable groups through household livelihood analyses.

Tables 5.1–5.3 compare the poor and nonpoor sample households in my survey with regard to (1) assets and (2) composition of consumption and total expenditures. Apparently the nonpoor households have fewer members, but they enjoy wider labor ratios. The heads of the nonpoor families received higher levels of formal education than the heads of the poorer households. This implies that the nonpoor households are able to put more labor force into income-generating activities.

The nonpoor owned a much larger amount of financial and physical assets, which partly reflects their access to more remunerative nonfarming activities. Given that all village households are eligible only for usufruct land rights and

TABLE 5.2 Composition of household expenditures of the poor and the nonpoor

Per capita net annual income	Statistics	Total annual expenditure	Production	Consumption	Other expenses
Below 1,000 yuan (poor)	Mean (yuan)	7,190	2,775	3,719	696
	Percentage	100	39	52	10
	SD	12,753	11,464	3,216	1,141
	Number of HH	266	266	266	266
Above 1,000 yuan (nonpoor)	Mean (yuan)	17,952	7,406	9,050	1,495
	Percentage	100	41	50	8
	SD	37,587	30,302	14,049	5,058
	Number of HH	1,723	1,723	1,723	1,723
Total sample	Mean (yuan)	16,513	6,787	8,337	1,388
	Percentage	100	41	50	8
	SD	35,480	28,554	13,253	4,733
	Number of HH	1,989	1,989	1,989	1,989

SOURCE: Author's survey.

NOTES: In this table, the poor are the low-income group with annual per capita net income below 1,000 yuan, the nonpoor earn more than 1,000 yuan, and the middle-income earn 1,000–2,000 yuan. SD, standard deviation; HH, households.

TABLE 5.3 Household consumption expenditures of the poor and the nonpoor

Per capita net annual income	Statistics	Total annual consumption expenditures	Food	Health	Education	Other expenditures
Below 1,000 yuan	Mean (yuan)	3,719	2,094	178	239	1,208
	Percentage	100	56	5	6	32
	SD	3216	1220	451	608	2453
	Number of HH	266	266	266	266	266
Above 1000 yuan	Mean (yuan)	9,050	3,910	432	692	4,017
	Percentage	100	43	5	8	44
	SD	14049	3223	1786	1489	12264
	Number of HH	1,723	1,723	1,723	1,723	1,723
Total sample	Mean (yuan)	8,337	3,667	398	631	3,641
	Percentage	100	44	4.7	7.6	43.7
	SD	13253	3095	1672	1412	11490
	Number of HH	1,989	1,989	1,989	1,989	1,989

SOURCE: Author's survey.

NOTES: SD, standard deviation; HH, households.

that land is by law unmarketable, the possession of financial and physical capital is indicative of substantial differences in wealth between households. The value of productive and nonproductive assets of the poor adds up to 11,644 yuan, which is equivalent to about 40 percent of the average asset value of a sample household (Table 5.1). Household assets can be used to cope with economic risks, but the assets of the majority of the sample households are far from sufficient to deal with income shocks resulting from catastrophic illnesses. This is particularly true in the case of the poor. For instance, hospitalization because of cancer cost a patient in rural areas about 5,092 yuan on average in 1998. The cost of hospitalization would be double in urban areas (China, Ministry of Public Health, 1999). This happened to be equivalent to half of the total value of assets of the poor in the survey sample.

The health vulnerability problems of the poor can be further identified by the following features of the subsistence economy that largely characterize poor areas:

1. Consumption had considerably more weight than production in total household expenditures, constituting 50 percent of total expenditure compared to 41 percent. The proportion of consumption in total expenditure of poor households was larger than that of the average household, although the poor spent a noticeably smaller amount on consumption in absolute terms that accounted for about 45 percent of the average (Table 5.2).

2. The poor households were under very tight budget constraints in meeting their basic nonfood needs because their food expenditure already took 56 percent of their total consumption (Table 5.3). While the shares of health and education in the total consumption of the poor did not differ very much from those of the nonpoor, the nonpoor actually spent as much as 2.4 and 2.9 times what the poor spent, respectively, on health and education.

In terms of health resource distribution within a poor household, the sample results showed that under financial constraints household members were generally ranked in the following order of priority: major income earners, children, and the elderly. At each level the male usually ranked better than the female due to traditional gender inequality. In extended families, frequently the elderly of over 60 years would prefer to renounce medical treatment for themselves and use the resources so saved to pay for the healthcare of their children and grandchildren. During the current socioeconomic transition, the majority of extended families were separated into nuclear families, leading to a rapid increase in the number of "empty-nest families" with only an old couple or a single elderly person. In our sample, there were 75 empty-nest families with their household heads aged over 60. Such households accounted for 3.8 percent of the total sample households, with one-third falling in the poor category. Because most rural residents were not covered by pension schemes, the livelihood of the elderly in poor households became noticeably insecure. The aging couples without working capacities were supported by their children for food and other basic necessities, while the children cultivated the land plots of the parents. The village committees took care of the aged without children in the same way. However, constrained by the lack of cash income, the elderly people in poor areas often confronted difficulties in accessing medical treatment while ill.

This information indicates that all rural groups without formal social security coverage tend to become more vulnerable when access to preventive and curative medical services deteriorates because of changes in healthcare financing. Among these, the poor, elderly, women, and preschool children are at greater risk. The elderly in poor households were the most vulnerable among all groups owing to deficiencies in both public and family support for their healthcare.

Options for Policy Intervention

We have seen that market reforms in the health sector and lack of sufficient government intervention in health service and insurance cannot overcome the difficulty of financing and cost control. The market-oriented transition leads to low efficiency in resource allocation and use, resulting in the increasing inequality of the poor and their reduced capability to access healthcare services. It has also increased the vulnerability of the already vulnerable, those who were not covered by social protection mechanisms. These problems were revealed during the recent outbreak of severe acute respiratory syndrome (SARS), which encouraged the government and the public to make greater efforts to restrict this tendency in the health sector.

Currently the government still uses a few instruments employed under the planned economy to control the health sector, those that resulted in serious price distortions and caused the public hospitals to become monopolies. For example, the authorities set the ceilings for pharmaceutical prices high enough to leave remarkably huge margins for rent-seeking activities by those who are involved in the process of delivering drugs from producers to final consumers (patients). Also, the services of doctors are so undervalued in the administrative price system that this undervaluation is an incentive for the hospitals and doctors to compensate for it by providing patients with excessive treatments and drugs. The administrative barriers erected by the health authorities against the entry of private hospitals have allowed public hospitals in most counties and cities to function as monopolies, making it virtually impossible for farmers to see doctors and seek even the low-quality yet high-cost medical services (Bureau of Health in Shuyang County 2004). This implies that "market failure" and "government failure" have coexisted in China's health sector during the period of the economic transition. Indeed, recommendations of government intervention should include demands for further reforms of the health systems by way of changing the governance and functioning of health authorities.

Based on this understanding, it is suggested that the rural health protection system be restructured systematically to meet the basic health needs of the rural population. The provision of health security depends not as much on the demand or the supply of health resources as on the political decision of the members of the entire society (Kornai and Eggleston 2003). Achieving basic health security for all rural people will require joint efforts by government at different levels as well as by village communities, households, and nongovernmental organizations (NGOs).

Improving Planned Immunization Programs

The first priority in restructuring the basic health protection system is to improve and extend the rural immunization programs. It is financially feasible for the central government to inject additional funds into preventive institutions targeting children so that the programs can be implemented free of charge. Here China should learn from the experience of India, where free immunization has been provided for many years.[6] China shares many characteristics with India, such as a huge population and a similar level of development. This also implies that the decision whether to assume the necessary costs of immunization services is as much a matter of fiscal capacity as of political will.

---

6. Information about India's experience in public healthcare and its innovative insurance programs for informal workers was acquired from training programs in which I participated in Gujarat and Kerala, India, in February–March 2003.

Because the Chinese government did not pay fees to the service providers in the planned immunization programs and financed only the production and distribution of the vaccines, they collected fees from the parents of the children covered. This situation has substantially changed in the developed regions since the outbreak of SARS. For example, the local governments at the county level in Zhejiang province have given township hospitals a public heath service fund for implementing preventive activities, including immunization programs. The size of a fund corresponds to the number of the residents living in a township. A poor county, for instance Chunan county, annually receives a transfer from the provincial government of 15 yuan per capita. In this way, free immunization services are realized in Zhejiang province. This experience provides a means for the central government to extend the free immunization services by taking the responsibility of the transfers to the poor counties located in the less developed provinces, the western regions in particular.

Investing in Village Clinics

At the village level, healthcare services most frequently used by rural residents, especially the poor, are provided by private doctors or health institutions (Filmer, Hammer, and Pritchett 1997; Gertler and Hammer 1997; Zhu 2002c). In China today, the services that village health stations regularly provide consist of disease prevention, public health intervention, and basic medical services. But health stations are hardly able to cover the costs of services, such as disease prevention and public health intervention. In the small- and medium-sized villages, the stations are usually unable to achieve economies of scale in the provision of basic medical services. This implies that market failure can occur in the provision of health services at the village level, and therefore public support is needed. The welfare of rural health risk–vulnerable groups can improve substantially if the government prioritizes its financial support to village clinics. The Indian government has already implemented such policies. For example, health workers in village clinics were paid salaries by the government in the state of Gujarat. A feasible step for China is to adapt the Indian practice to local conditions with special emphasis on providing strong incentives for village health workers to improve the quality of service.

The experiences in rural Changshu of Jiangsu province in financing and managing its village health stations also serve as a valuable model for the central government. Cases from the rural areas around Changshu city suggest that the following are necessary if the stations are to provide sufficient services of reliable quality at reasonable prices. First, the county government, township government, and village committees must invest in village health stations with both physical and human capital. Second, local health authorities must provide management and supervision for village health stations. Third, the township government and village committee must rationalize incentive mechanisms following the changing socioeconomic framework to affect the behavior of health workers. And finally, villagers must take an active part in health financing. The village committees and the township and county governments in less developed regions certainly need fiscal transfers from the upper-level governments to support the health service providers in villages, following the Indian or Changshu model or using their own institutional innovations.

In any case, there are three aspects worth noting. First, health workers should be paid an amount sufficient to serve as an incentive for them to provide villagers with the best possible services in health education and disease prevention. Second, the prereform tradition of using budgetary resources to finance periodic training for village health workers should be restored. Most training courses are now funded by the trainees themselves. As a result, village health workers have reduced their demand for basic training courses in poor areas because they cannot afford them. Third, under the framework of the cooperative medical system, an incentive structure should be designed to stimulate health operators to offer villagers inexpensive and reliable medical services. The remuneration of the health professionals—that is, the provision of a basic salary plus a registration fee charged in the village clinics of well-developed regions— can be integrated with a monitoring system by a public health regulatory institution at the township level to ensure the transparency of medical costs.

Linking Social and Commercial Insurance Programs

Prior to the SARS pandemic, government intervention, including such interventions as the experiments with community-based cooperative health insurance programs, achieved only limited success in well-developed regions and little in the medium- and less-developed regions. It has been found that the sustainability of social medical insurance or healthcare cooperatives in the more developed regions depends on a relatively high average rural income, the willingness of farmers to take a more decisive stance in avoiding health risks, the efficient provision of healthcare services, the reliable management of insurance funds, and social mobilization, along with government involvement and financial support. These are all important preconditions (Wei 2003), but unfortunately most of them are lacking in large parts of rural China. Moreover, the community-based cooperative health insurance system faced two kinds of difficulties: (1) the risk pool is so small that it is not capable of sharing risks of catastrophic diseases without running a deficit, and (2) management costs are high.

To overcome these difficulties, a new type of rural cooperative health insurance program designed to cope with risks of catastrophic illness was launched in the fourth quarter of 2003. This system is, in essence, a quasi-social medical insurance system. The central government has provided unprecedentedly strong institutional support and financial subsidies to provinces trying the system in the central and western parts of the country. The minimum funding raised is 30 yuan per rural resident per year, which is to be shared equally among the central government, the local government, and farmer households participating in the program. The money raised is mainly used to subsidize farmers and their family members when they are hospitalized. The risk pool of the new program is county-based, and a management system was established corresponding to the administrative hierarchy within a county. Apparently the design of the new system is based on the insurance principle whereby healthy groups and infirm groups share disaster risks, with the prerequisite of the broadest possible participation of the rural population.

Health insurance coverage for rural people has been rapidly scaled up based on government intervention with strong administrative powers since the end of the SARS outbreak. Up to the end of 2005, 678 counties, amounting to nearly one-third of the rural counties, were approved to undertake the new program. Some 179 million rural residents, who made up 75.7 percent of the rural population in the experimental counties, participated (China, Statistical Information Center, Ministry of Health, 2006).

According to studies that I conducted in Wuxing county in Zhejiang province, one of the factors affecting the farmers' willingness to participate in the program was that only inpatients amounting to about 3 percent of the participants in a year were eligible to receive partial reimbursement of their medical expenses because the program covers mainly the risks of catastrophic illness. Using the fund to compensate outpatients for 15–20 percent of their medical fees immediately enlarged the proportion of the beneficiaries to 52.4 percent in a year. This is because most Chinese farmers do not have enough to spare financially. If they have to pay the insurance premiums but the probability of receiving benefits is low, they are less likely to participate. For similar economic reasons, the low-income groups in the rural areas often do not see a doctor when they have minor diseases, and by delaying treatment they increase the likelihood that minor diseases will develop into major ones. So the positive effect of using the cooperative medical fund to reimburse a small portion of medical fees is that it encourages farmer families to increase their health budgets and use more medical services.

However, the use of the fund in this way not only complicated reimbursement but also increased management costs. If the amount of funds raised remains unchanged, it would inevitably lead to lower compensation for medical expenses incurred due to catastrophic illness. This is what is actually happening in all of the experimental counties, including the rich areas. A possible solution to this is to establish linkages between the commercial and social health insurance programs. Besides channeling a small portion of the fund to the medical account of the individual households in the experimental counties, it will also help to channel a portion of the fund in a county to pay a premium to the commercial insurance companies operating across the county as an additional health insurance program sharing the risks of catastrophic illness among all the participants.

The local government of Jiangyin county in Jiangsu province has set up a partnership between the government and a commercial insurance company to manage the rural cooperative health insurance program. The practice of Indian production cooperatives and NGOs in linking informal and formal insurance programs can be a good point of reference. For example, the Malabar Regional Cooperative Milk Producers Union in Kerala implemented its Mediclaim Insurance program in conjunction with Oriental and New India Assurance Companies. The farmers who were members of the union paid premiums of Rs. 130 per annum in full and were entitled to receive the benefit of hospitalization treatment costing up to Rs. 15,000 per year.[7] Acting as a facilitator, the union organized the farmers and reached a contract with the commercial insurance company. In this way, the two contractors benefited from the organizational advantages of each side. By means of such a group insurance arrangement the commercial insurance company won the enlargement of its pool of participants. And the individual farmers obtained access to the formal insurance program that the commercial insurance companies usually refuse to offer them due to high transaction costs.

Health Relief and Health Pensions

Toward the end of 2003, the Chinese central government earmarked 300 million yuan a year for use as medical relief to households enjoying the "five guarantees" and to poor farmer families with catastrophic illnesses.[8] In addition, the government requested that the provincial governments allocate fiscal resources for the same purpose. The policymakers anticipated that both the new rural cooperative health insurance program and health relief programs could help the poor break the vicious circle of poverty and illness. Nevertheless, under the principle of making a minimum payment out of one's own pocket and a co-payment to meet medical expenses over the minimum, the poor often use fewer medical services than the nonpoor. Therefore, the health relief fund has been used in three ways. First, it has subsidized the poor for paying premiums to cooperative health insurance programs as a form of health relief. Without such subsidies, either the poor households would be excluded from insurance programs or the programs could not be implemented in the first place in villages and poor areas. Second, it is transferred to the insurance fund for sharing the minimum payment and co-payment of the poor to enable them to access medical services with a higher proportion of reimbursement than the nonpoor are eligible for. Third, a part of the fund is directly transferred to the poor households suffering from economic crises due to the catastrophic illness of their members. According to rough statistics, the fund was used to pay the insurance premiums of a total of 8.68 million poor people, while those who received direct transfers from

---

7. The exchange rate was about Rs. 50 to a U.S. dollar in India during February–March 2003.

8. The five guarantees are guarantees of the supply of food, clothing, medical care, housing, and burial expenses.

the health relief fund amounted to 2.44 million people to the end of 2005 (China, Ministry of Civil Affairs, 2006).

There are two major problems in the ongoing health relief program. One is that the amount of the fiscal resources pooled into the health relief fund in a county is periodically fixed, but the number of those who are needy and eligible for relief and the amount of subsidies paid to a specific beneficiary fluctuate because of the uncertainty in the incidence and severity of diseases. Therefore, a person with the same income and similar diseases can receive different amounts from the fund in different years because of the lack of standardization of health relief. This problem will be solved in the near future when the health risks of low-income groups, including the poor, are better estimated and the resources available for the relief increase.

The other problem is that the mode and the time of delivering the relief have not matched the emergent needs of the poor, often reaching them after the misfortune has occurred, as in the case of illness affecting a family member. This problem can be avoided with the introduction of publicly financed coupons or special accounts with which the poor will be able to visit doctors or be hospitalized. The system of providing relief through medical coupons has been practiced in the city of Shanghai since the beginning of reforms of state-owned enterprises, allowing even the unemployed to purchase basic healthcare services. This is supported by the experience of the county government in Yuexi, a poor county in Anhui province, in delivering medical assistance to five guarantees households. The county government annually injects 100 yuan per capita for the five guarantees households into a specific account to meet their medical expenses. Under this system, the members of these households are exempted from users' fees when they see doctors within the county, while the hospitals acquire transfers from the specific account as well as from the cooperative insurance fund after the delivery of services.

Though a majority of the five guarantees households are made up of the elderly, there is a need for specific social assistance and relief programs targeting the rural elderly. One policy option would be to set up a pension scheme starting with the health component, encouraging rural residents to save during their working years so that the accumulated pension funds can be used to meet their basic healthcare needs after they retire. During my field studies, I learned that most elderly people tried their best to save for this purpose and wished to be exempted from the interest tax levied on their small savings. Thus, the health pension program can be operated as a supplement to family and community care services aimed at meeting the basic needs of the elderly for food, clothing, shelter, and so on. The welfare funds of Kerala have similar institutional design; the labor unions in different informal sectors collect small amounts of savings from member workers. Those who make contributions are eligible for a certain amount from the fund for specific needs (Kannan 2002).

A Health Insurance Program for Rural Migrants

At present, the insurance plans are operated locally and are far from adequate to promote and protect labor mobility to the extent required by industrialization and urbanization. A basic health insurance program with universal coverage is certainly the right solution. Yet, for a large country like China with 1.3 billion people living in a dual society, to establish a sustainable universal social health insurance system will no doubt require tremendous efforts in terms of social mobilization and organizational work. Change may gradually begin with a health insurance program for rural migrants, because they form a strong link between the rural and urban societies and face greater health vulnerability than other working people in China.

Most migrants are the breadwinners for their families in the villages. A national sample survey by the State Statistics Bureau shows that around 118 million rural people left their home villages to work in cities and towns in 2004. Those commuting between provinces every year made up 51 percent of them (Cai and Gu 2006). A majority of migrants engage in unskilled work in environs that are bad for their health, such as noisy or dusty working spaces where they are exposed to poisonous materials and other dangers related to industrial sectors. At the same time, their employment is less stable and their wages on average lower than those of workers with permanent urban residential registration. The low human capital of the migrants, such as the low level of their educational backgrounds and their lack of occupational training, which leads them to take unskilled and low-paying jobs, could also be attributed to discrimination in the past. But the social protection systems in cities almost exclusively benefit the permanent urban residents, especially the permanent employees. Though the rural cooperative health insurance program has covered those migrants, their medical expenses in cities are much higher than in their home counties. This implies that the rural sector has to share a part of the disease burden that the urban sector ought to shoulder because the migrants contribute their labor to the latter. In other words, the transfer of the disease burden to the rural sector implies that low-income groups subsidize the better off and that the poor pay more.

One way to avoid this is to integrate the rural migrants into the urban social health insurance program. In reality, the barriers to migrant participation arise from two factors. On the one hand, the urban program requires a high premium that neither migrant workers nor their employers are willing to pay (Meng and Yuan 2006). On the other hand, a large number of the local governments in the urban sector have not been willing to extend health insurance coverage to migrants, mainly due to financial difficulties.

One innovative model is found in Shenzhen city, where about 6 million rural migrants work in factories. In 2005, the city government started to implement a healthcare program targeting the rural migrants. Each enterprise pays

8 yuan per worker per month into the insurance fund, while each worker contributes 4 yuan. The participating workers are eligible to receive reimbursement of around 50 percent of both outpatient and inpatient medical expenses. The ceiling on one's annual reimbursement amounts to 60,000 yuan. To the end of 2005, there were 5,500 participating enterprises, and the participating workers numbered 1.24 million people (Meng and Yuan 2006). Another model has been in operation in Zhangjiagang city in Jiangsu province since 2004. The local government administers an area covering 854,000 people. Nearly 80 percent of the permanent residents are registered as rural people. In addition, over 200,000 rural migrants from outside of Zhangjiagang work in the nonagricultural sector. From a field study in 2005 I found that migrants working in factories were integrated into the local rural cooperative health insurance program. They were treated equally in terms of premium payments, government subsidies, and reimbursement arrangements.

From my interviews with migrant workers, I can conclude that the health protection programs established for rural migrants will not only contribute to public health security and economic security, but also promote nationwide labor mobility, leading to the narrowing of urban-rural and regional disparities. This would serve as a crucial step in developing socioeconomic policies to aid the integration of Chinese society, currently marked by a wide chasm between the cities and the countryside.

PART III

Investments in Rural Areas, Technology, and Irrigation

In Chapters 6–10, the third part of the book, the comparison between China and India is extended to the three thematic areas of rural public investments, agricultural research and technology, and water resources and irrigation. Both countries began to invest in agriculture and rural areas in the 1950s, as witnessed by the emphasis put on irrigation by Prime Minister Jawaharlal Nehru at the beginning of India's economic planning and the massive public works endeavors under the collectives in China. It is highly unlikely that India would have been able to reap the same returns from the green revolution in the absence of past government expenditures on irrigation or that China could have experienced the same rates of economic and agricultural growth and poverty reduction without extensive investments in the countryside. It is therefore argued that, as in the cases of human capital and land, better initial infrastructure endowments in irrigation and agricultural research as well as power and road networks at the outset of reforms can lead to faster growth and poverty alleviation through improved growth in agricultural production, wages, nonfarm employment, and migration.

The chapters in this part of the book, in particular Chapter 6, which focuses on rural public investments, aim to test this hypothesis by first presenting information on trends, determinants, and impacts of public investments in agriculture as well as rural education, health, infrastructure, and technology and then examining the evidence related to the contribution of rural public investment to economic growth and poverty reduction. More important, the focus is on how different types of investment, for example, that in agricultural research and development (R&D), infrastructure, or education, might have different impacts and thus different marginal returns and which type of investments had the greatest impacts on rural growth and poverty reduction. These chapters assess the implications of different investment options as well as the future priorities for public investment and offer policy options for reforming current institutions, policies, and allocations in rural public investment to ensure the maximum effectiveness of government spending.

Chapters 7 and 8, focusing on agricultural research and technology, review the evolution of agricultural research systems in China and India and dwell in some detail on the organizational structure, funding, and human resource aspects. They describe the major policy issues related to agricultural R&D and identify several areas for future reform of the current systems. It is clear that the advent of liberalization and market reforms put new pressures on the research systems of both countries. Demand factors ended the public monopoly of agricultural research and made it more market-oriented, efficient, and accountable. Further, against the backdrop of increased diversification of agriculture, it is questionable whether the focus on traditional crops is still warranted or if public-sponsored research should instead diversify away from grains to include high-value commodities such as livestock and horticultural produce.

The R&D reforms implemented in recent years included, among others, changes in funding mechanisms; the commercialization of research products by the public research institutes; the promotion of biotechnology, specifically genetically modified seed varieties; and the improvement of the intellectual property rights regime under the World Trade Organization. The different policy changes are explored with a view to determining their effect on research funding, efficiency, and private sector involvement in agricultural research. While privatization of agricultural R&D is viewed as a critical means to improve the efficiency of agricultural research, the challenges it involves are also significant and need careful consideration.

Chapters 9 and 10, covering water resources and irrigation, assess current water resources and policies and their relation to food production. The water sectors of both China and India are examined to address questions as well as compare and contrast the climatic conditions and their implications for agriculture, water storage capacity, irrigated area and agricultural productivity, share of agriculture in water consumption, efficiency in agricultural water use, and food production from irrigated agriculture in the two countries. These issues are investigated within a contemporary context as well as from a futuristic perspective through projections up to year 2025.

These chapters also examine irrigation reforms implemented so far, along with areas for future reforms to address the challenges of making water use more equitable and efficient. One of the distinguishing features of water resources in China and India is in effect their extremely disproportionate distribution. Southern China receives nearly half of China's runoff, while northern China experiences severe water scarcity, which poses a major constraint to agricultural as well as industrial development. Similarly, India's northern and eastern states are endowed with more abundant water resources than are the southern states.

The other challenge of the water sector in the two countries is inefficient water use, notwithstanding which the scarcity in some regions is related to factors such as poor management of existing irrigation systems, lack of clear ownership of water resources, and the low water use charges justified by a prevailing welfare rather than market approach to water pricing. To boost water efficiency, it is clear that the best advice is to give greater emphasis to improving the management of current water systems and promoting participatory approaches by providing incentives to managers or involving user groups, as opposed to implementing traditional methods such as large projects for interbasin water transfers and dams, for which returns from investments are no longer as great as in the past given their social and environmental implications.

Finally, another key challenge is the reform of institutions providing investments and input services. Investments in agricultural R&D, irrigation, and so on cannot be effective if there are institutional failures related to politicization and lack of transparency and accountability of the public agencies that are in charge of providing the investments and infrastructure services to agriculture and rural areas.

6 Public Investment, Growth, and Poverty Reduction: A Comparative Analysis of India and China

SHENGGEN FAN AND SUKHADEO K. THORAT

Both China and India have achieved great success in dramatically reducing poverty over the past several decades. With more than 500 million people lifted above the poverty line, these two countries contributed to a major share of the global decline in poverty incidence (Chen and Ravallion 2004). This achievement can be attributed to many factors, including policy and institutional reforms and trade and market liberalization. Public investments, particularly those in human and physical capital, science, and technology, have also been used by the governments of China and India as ways to stimulate economic growth and to promote poverty reduction in these two countries (Fan 1991; Fan and Pardey 1997; Fan, Hazell, and Thorat 2000; Fan, Zhang, and Zhang 2004). Without these investments, rapid growth and poverty reduction would not have been possible. These investments in rural areas, where the majority of the poor reside, played a particularly important role in reducing poverty. However, there are still a large number of poor, and the governments in both countries have committed to allocate more resources to eliminate the remaining poverty.[1] But how to target these public resources in order to maximize its poverty reduction impact is still a much-debated subject. For this purpose, information on relative returns to various types of public expenditures can help the governments better target their limited resources to achieve the twin goals of economic growth and poverty alleviation.

The objectives of this chapter are to review and compare the evidence on the effects of public investment on agricultural growth and poverty reduction in China and India and to draw lessons on how the Chinese and Indian governments can use public investment to achieve their stated social objectives. Our review and comparison were mainly drawn from Fan, Hazell, and Thorat (1999) and Fan, Zhang, and Zhang (2004).

---

1. For example, the Chinese government has made the development of rural areas one of the top priorities in the eleventh five-year plan (2006–10) by increasing the public resources given to rural areas and agriculture. The Indian government has also promised to allocate more budget support to agriculture and pro-poor programs such as a rural employment guarantee scheme.

These two nations share some common features but differ in other respects. Both are large countries and coincidentally underwent substantial political and economic changes about the same time—at the beginning of the 1950s. India gained its independence in 1947 and initiated the experiment of planned economic development with its first five-year plan in 1951. Following the 1949 communist revolution, China embarked on a new economic development path at the outset of the 1950s. Both countries have also experienced profound political and economic reforms for the past several decades since then.

However, there are at least three crucial differences between China and India that need to be recognized. First, following independence India adopted a mixed economic system characterized by the presence of both public and private sectors. Agriculture, which employs a major portion of the workforce and the population, is based on the principle that land belongs to the private domain. Similarly, a large portion of the industrial sector has been in private hands. Thus, only a few critical industries along with a large number of primary services, such as education and healthcare, and infrastructure, such as irrigation, roads, and power, are the responsibility of the state. China, on the other hand, embarked on a new economic development path by adopting a socialist economic framework characterized by much greater ownership and control by the state over agricultural and industrial resources, at least until recently.

Second, while the Indian state has pursued economic development and public investment policies within the framework of political democracy, where investment priorities need to go through many rounds of consultation and consensus building, China operated in a political framework that gives the state relatively more freedom in deciding its investment priorities. Thus, compared to India, China has been functioning with a reasonable degree of state control in terms of raising and allocating financial resources for public investment.

Third, China initiated the process of economic development with greater equality than India in terms of people's access to income sources (land and nonland capital assets) and services to meet their social needs (education and healthcare). In these critical areas, the Indian population could derive only relatively limited benefits from these measures, resulting in greater inequality relative to their Chinese counterparts with regard to access to land and nonland capital assets, as well as to basic services like education and healthcare. Only recently did access to education, healthcare, and other social services become less equal (Kanbur and Zhang 2003). All these similarities and disparities between China and India have had different impacts on the patterns of government spending, and therefore have led to different growth paths and poverty reduction outcomes in the two countries.

Government Spending

Both countries have experienced erratic patterns in their total government spending as well as their spending earmarked for agriculture and rural areas (Tables 6.1

TABLE 6.1 Government spending in India, 1965–2000

	Total	Rural development	Agriculture	Education	Health	Welfare	Irrigation	Roads	Power
Spending, billion rupees, 1993 prices									
1965	230.1	7.5	14.4	32.6	16.5	3.7	27.1	7.0	3.5
1970	272.5	—	15.4	54.4	23.4	4.3	28.6	8.6	3.9
1975	370.3	9.6	56.7	72.7	31.9	—	47.1	19.8	5.0
1980	536.2	17.5	83.8	94.3	47.5	13.7	60.8	33.8	10.7
1985	759.5	47.3	75.5	138.9	59.9	21.2	84.0	35.4	9.1
1990	1,054.9	67.1	89.0	207.5	63.0	25.0	94.9	45.9	24.1
1995	1,294.5	60.4	86.6	233.7	55.7	28.3	110.3	52.8	54.0
2000	2,085.8	88.7	273.8	394.7	79.6	37.8	70.4	61.4	44.7
Annual growth rate (%)									
1965–70	3.45	—	1.37	10.76	7.27	3.52	1.08	4.19	2.19
1970–80	7.00	—	18.45	5.65	7.34	12.19	7.85	14.72	10.64
1980–90	7.00	14.39	0.61	8.21	2.87	6.18	4.56	3.09	8.41
1990–2000	7.05	2.82	11.90	6.64	2.37	4.20	-2.95	2.95	6.40

SOURCE: Fan, Thorat, and Rao (2004).

NOTE: —, data unavailable.

TABLE 6.2 Public investment in rural China, 1953–2000

Year	R&D	Irrigation	Education	Roads	Power	Communication
Spending, million 1990 yuan						
1953	17	177	2,584	194	3	18
1960	770	5,291	6,314	510	78	193
1970	657	3,416	3,060	536	287	156
1978	1,145	8,566	7,526	682	1,046	298
1980	1,295	7,457	10,660	693	988	237
1990	1,625	7,164	25,006	1,113	4,968	1,078
2000	3,147	43,299	47,925	6,814	21,316	20,377
Annual growth rate (%)						
1953–78	19.1	17.5	4.6	5.4	26.8	12.4
1978–90	3.0	−1.5	10.5	4.2	13.9	11.3
1990–2000	6.8	19.7	6.7	19.9	15.7	34.2
1953–2000	11.7	12.4	6.4	7.9	20.4	16.2

SOURCES: NBS, *China Fixed Asset Investment Yearbook,* various years; NBS, *China Education Yearbook,* various years; NBS, *China Electronical Power Yearbook,* various years; NBS, *China Science and Technology Yearbook,* various years; NBS, *China Statistical Yearbook,* various years; NBS, *China Transportation Yearbook,* various years; NBS, *China Water Conservancy Yearbook,* various years.

and 6.2).[2] China and India dramatically increased their investments in agriculture from the 1950s to the 1980s, with the aim of solving their food security problems. But both countries reduced their spending in agriculture in either relative (in the case of China) or absolute (in the case of India) terms in the 1990s in response to macroeconomic reforms. Since the beginning of the new millennium, both countries have begun to allocate more resources to the agricultural sector and rural areas.

In the early years of economic planning in the 1950s and 1960s, public investment in agriculture accounted for almost half of the total investment in rural areas of India (Fan, Thorat, and Rao 2004). Government spending in agriculture increased at a per annum rate of 1.4 percent from 1965 to 1970, compared with 18 percent per annum from 1970 to 1990. Thus, public spending in agriculture grew 10 times faster during the 1970s than it did in the 1960s. During the 1980s, however, public spending in agriculture grew very little, a trend that continued to the mid-1990s. The second half of the 1990s saw a dramatic increase in government spending in agriculture. On the other hand, the government spending on rural development, which includes integrated rural development and antipoverty programs, has shown a trend completely opposite to that of agricultural spending. In the 1980s, these programs increased at more

---

2. The data used in this chapter are from Fan, Hazell, and Thorat (1999) and Fan, Zhang, and Zhang (2002) if other sources are not specified.

than 14 percent per annum and stagnated in the 1990s. Irrigation spending grew steadily in the 1960s, 1970s, and 1980s. But in the 1990s, government spending in irrigation declined by almost 3 percent per year. Government spending on general infrastructure (roads and power), education, and health has experienced steady growth over the past several decades.

The spending priorities of the Indian government have changed dramatically over the past several decades. In 1965 the top priorities of government spending were education (14 percent), irrigation (12 percent), health (7 percent), and agriculture (6 percent). In 2000 they were education and agriculture. Health spending has been reduced, to less than 4 percent in 2000 from 7–8 percent in the 1960s. Shares of other spending, including that on roads, power, rural development, and welfare, remained roughly the same.

In China, much as in India, over the past several decades government spending in rural areas experienced dramatic changes (Table 6.2). Right after the foundation of the country in 1949, China's investment in agricultural research was minimal, but grew rapidly in the 1950s. The growth in the 1960s was relatively slight due to the three-year natural disaster (1959–61) and the Cultural Revolution (1966–76). Agricultural research investment increased steadily during the 1970s, but slowed during the 1980s, increasing by only 23 percentage points during the entire 10-year period. In the 1990s, agricultural research expenditures began to rise again, largely due to government efforts to boost grain production through science and technology.

The Chinese government gave top priority to irrigation immediately after 1949. In 1953, the amount the government spent on irrigation was 10 times larger than the amount spent on agricultural research. Investment in irrigation continued to increase until 1966. Under the commune system, it was relatively easy for the government to mobilize large numbers of rural laborers on large irrigation projects. As a result, more than 10 million hectares (ha) of land was brought under irrigation during that period (Fan, Zhang, and Zhang 2002). From 1976 to 1995, investment in irrigation increased very little; it even declined between 1976 and 1989. During this period, there was no increase in irrigated areas in Chinese agriculture production. By 1989, irrigation investment was only 44 percent of the 1976 level. In response to the grain shortfall and heavy imports in 1995, the government increased its investment in irrigation sharply from 1997 to 1999. But further expansion would be difficult because of the competing industrial and residential uses of water. As a result, the returns to investment in irrigation may decline in the future.

The educational level of the Chinese population was one of the lowest in the world four decades ago. In 1956, less than one-half of primary- and secondary-aged children were enrolled in school. Since 1978, though, China has promoted an education policy that requires all children to attend school for at least nine years to finish both the primary and junior high school programs. But the policy was never seriously implemented, particularly in rural areas. In 1986, an education law requiring nine years of education was formally issued. By 2000, the enrollment ratio of school-aged children had risen to over 98 percent, and the percentage of primary schoolchildren entering junior high school to 85 percent in rural China.

Consequently, Chinese labor quality has improved substantially over the past two decades, with a decline of the illiteracy rate of agricultural labor from 28 percent in 1985 to less than 10 percent in 2004. This improved human capital in rural areas provided a great opportunity for farmers to use modern farming technology and to engage in nonfarm activities in both rural township enterprises and urban industrial centers.

Despite these successes, the Chinese government's investment in education is still not sufficient. In terms of expenditures, the government has spent roughly 2.6 percent of the total national GDP on education, which is lower than the percentage spent in most developing countries with exceptions such as Bangladesh, Indonesia, and Myanmar. In particular, many of the poor were not reached by the government efforts.

For the past several decades, China has given higher priority to electricity than road development in its investment portfolio. Investment in power has increased 90-fold. The percentage of villages that have access to electricity was 98 percent in 1998, and more than 97 percent of the households had electricity connections. For most of the years before 1980, growth in government investment in telecommunication was very slow, increasing from 166 million yuan (measured in 1990 prices) in 1953 to only 738 million yuan in 1980. However, large-scale development occurred in the past several years, when the number of rural telephone sets increased from 3.4 million in 1992 to 51.7 million in 2000. This was largely a result of both public and private investments in the sector. From 1989 to 2000, public investment in telecommunication alone increased more than 20-fold.

More recently, rural education spending accounted for 33 percent of total expenditures in rural areas of China in 2000. Irrigation ranked next, accounting for 30 percent. Investment in rural infrastructure amounted to about 33 percent of total government spending in rural areas, with 15 percent for power, 5 percent for roads, and 14 percent for telecommunications. Agricultural research accounted for only a small fraction (2.2 percent) of total government investment in rural areas.

Public Investment and Poverty Linkages: A Conceptual Framework

There have been many attempts to measure the impact of public investment on growth and on rural poverty reduction. A significant feature in the literature on public investment and rural poverty is that most of the previous studies have considered only one type of government spending (or investment).[3] This approach makes it difficult to compare the relative returns to different types of investments in terms of both growth and poverty reduction. Moreover, most of these empirical studies used a single equation approach. There are at least four disadvantages associated with this method. First, many poverty determinants, such as income, production or productivity growth, prices, wages, and nonfarm employment, are generated from the same economic process as rural poverty. In other words, these variables are also endogenous variables, and ignoring this characteristic leads to biased estimates of poverty effects. Second, certain economic variables affect poverty through multiple channels. For example, improved rural infrastructure not only will reduce rural poverty through improved agricultural productivity but also will affect rural poverty through improved wages and nonfarm employment. It is very difficult to capture these different effects in a single equation approach. Third, including only one type of public investment in estimating poverty reduction will lead to an upward bias on the impact of that particular investment. Finally, with the single equation approach it is difficult to rank the effects of different types of investment on both growth and poverty reduction.

In order to systematically assess the impact of different types of public investment on both agricultural growth and poverty reduction, several studies conducted at the International Food Policy Research Institute have tried to simultaneously estimate econometric systems that consist of many equations using pooled time series and cross-regional data. These studies differ from previous ones in several aspects. First, most types of public investment and expenditure are included in the assessment to avoid biased estimates of returns when only a single type of investment (e.g., agricultural research) is considered and to compare and rank returns of various types of investment. Second, the model has the ability to identify different channels through which government investments impact growth, inequality, and poverty. Understanding these different effects provides useful policy insights to improve the effectiveness of governments' poverty alleviation strategies. And finally, the model permits calculation of economic returns measured by the number of poor people raised above the poverty line for additional units of expenditure on different items.

More specifically, the model consists of a poverty determination equation, an agricultural production function, a rural wage equation, a rural nonfarm

---

3. For example, Alston et al. (2000) reviewed case studies on the returns to agricultural R&D investments. Almost none of these studies considered other investments, such as investments in infrastructure, irrigation, and rural education. Similarly, there is a large amount of empirical evidence that returns to education are high (Psacharapoulos 1994) and that there is a strong causal relationship between infrastructure investments and economic growth (Canning and Bennathan 2000). But very seldom did these studies include other types of investments.

employment equation, and a set of public investment stock equations that are functions of past government spending. Rural poverty is modeled as a function of growth in agricultural production, changes in rural wages, growth in rural nonfarm employment, and changes in agricultural prices.

Agricultural production is modeled as a function of conventional inputs such as labor, land, fertilizer, machinery, and public investment variables such as the use of high-yielding seed varieties, public irrigation, roads, electrification, and education.

Rural wages and nonfarm employment are modeled as functions of growth in agricultural production as well as public investment variables. Numerous studies have shown the important linkage between agricultural and nonagricultural growth. Ignoring the effect of public investment on rural poverty through this linkage could lead to underestimation of the poverty reduction effects of government investment in agriculture. A similar downward estimation bias could arise from overlooking the impact of improved infrastructure and education on wages and employment.

Finally, public investment variables are modeled as functions of past government spending. Through the equation systems we have described, the marginal return to different types of government spending in terms of their growth and poverty reduction effects can be derived by taking the first derivatives of poverty and production functions with respect to government spending.[4]

The Impact of Public Investment on Growth and Poverty Reduction

Fan, Hazell, and Thorat (2000) used the system of econometric equations described in the previous section to identify the relative roles of different types of government spending in agricultural growth and rural poverty reduction in India. The authors relied on state-level data for 1970 to 1993 to conduct their analysis. The results from the model show that additional government expenditures on roads have the largest impact on poverty reduction as well as a significant impact on productivity growth (Table 6.3). Additional government spending on agricultural research and extension has the second-largest effect on rural poverty and the largest impact on agricultural productivity growth. The third largest impact on rural poverty reduction arises from additional government spending on education, largely as a result of the increases in nonfarm employment and rural wages that it induces.

Additional irrigation investment has the third-largest impact on growth in agricultural productivity but has only a small impact on rural poverty reduction, even after allowing for trickle-down benefits. Additional government spending on rural and community development, including integrated rural development

---

4. For more information on the specifications of these equations, see Fan, Zhang, and Zhang (2004) and Fan, Hazell, and Thorat (2000).

TABLE 6.3 India state-level analysis of returns to rural government spending, 1993

Areas of spending	Returns in rupees per rupee spending	Number of poor lifted out of poverty per million rupees of spending
R&D	13.45	84.5
Irrigation	1.36	9.7
Roads	5.31	123.8
Education	1.39	41.0
Power	0.26	3.8
Soil and water conservation	0.96	22.6
Health	0.84	25.5
Antipoverty programs	1.09	17.8

SOURCE: Fan, Hazell, and Thorat (2000).

programs, contributes to reduction in rural poverty, but its impact is smaller than those of expenditures on roads, agricultural R&D, and education. Additional government expenditures on soil and water conservation and on health have no impact on productivity growth, and their poverty effects through employment generation and wage increase are also small.

In another study, Fan and Hazell (1999) attempted to estimate the returns of various categories of public investment in different regions of India, including irrigated regions and two types of rain-fed regions (Table 6.4). For every type of investment (particularly in roads, canal irrigation, electricity, and education), the highest marginal impact on agricultural production and poverty alleviation occurs in the high-potential or low-potential rain-fed areas, while that in irrigated land ranks second or last. Moreover, many types of investment in the low-potential rain-fed lands yield some of the highest production returns, and all spending except that on education has the largest impacts on poverty. These results strongly support the hypothesis that more investment should now be channeled to the less-favored areas of India. They also imply that the lower marginal impact of irrigation, power, and other expenditures in the aggregate-level analysis (observed in the two studies discussed previously) is presumably due to the lower return in the highly irrigated regions, where the optimal effect has already been reached and therefore any additional investment would not yield higher returns. Conversely, in the rain-fed regions where the level of irrigation and power is low, additional spending on these types of infrastructure and on other supplementary inputs would generate much higher returns.

Turning to China, Fan, Zhang, and Zhang (2004) adopted a simultaneous equations model to estimate the effects of different types of government expenditure using provincial-level data for 1970–2000. An important feature of the results in Table 6.5 is that all production-enhancing investments reduce poverty while at the same time increasing agricultural and nonagricultural GDP.

TABLE 6.4 India district-level analysis of marginal returns to rural public investments, 1993

Investment	Irrigated areas	High-potential rain-fed areas	Low-potential rain-fed areas
	Production return in rupees per unit of investment		
HYV (ha)	63	243	688
Roads (km)	100,598	6,451	136,173
Canal irrigation (ha)	938	3,310	1,434
Private irrigation (ha)	1,000	(2,213)	4,559
Electrification (ha)	(546)	96	1,274
Education (worker)	(360)	571	102
	Number of poor lifted out of poverty per unit of investment		
HYV (ha)	0.00	0.02	0.05
Roads (km)	1.57	3.50	9.51
Canal irrigation (ha)	0.01	0.23	0.09
Private irrigation (ha)	0.01	(0.15)	0.30
Electrification (ha)	0.01	0.07	0.10
Education (worker)	0.01	0.23	0.01

SOURCE: Fan and Hazell (2000).

NOTE: The numbers in parentheses are negative, but most of them are not statistically significant.

However, there are sizable differences in production gains and poverty reduction among the various expenditure items and across regions. For the country as a whole, government expenditure on education had the largest impact in reducing poverty. In addition, it yielded the largest return to nonfarm GDP and overall rural GDP and the second-largest return to agricultural GDP. Therefore, investing more in education is the dominant "win-win" strategy. For every 10,000 yuan invested, some 12 people are brought out of poverty.

Investment in agricultural R&D had the second-largest impact on poverty, and its impact on agricultural GDP ranked first. Agricultural R&D is thus another very feasible investment. Government expenditure on rural infrastructure also made large contributions to poverty reduction. These impacts were realized through growth in both agricultural and nonagricultural production. Among the three infrastructure variables considered, the impact of roads is particularly large. For every 10,000 yuan invested, more than 6 poor people (6.6) are lifted above the poverty line. Roads thus rank third in poverty reduction impact, after education and R&D. In terms of impact on growth, for every yuan invested in roads, 6.57 yuan in rural GDP is produced, only slightly less than the return

TABLE 6.5 Returns to public investment in China, 2000 (yuan per yuan expenditure)

	Coastal states	Central states	Western states	Average
Returns to total rural GDP				
R&D	5.54	6.63	10.19	6.75
Irrigation	1.62	1.11	2.13	1.45
Roads	8.34	6.90	3.39	6.57
Education	11.98	8.72	4.76	8.96
Electricity	3.78	2.82	1.63	2.89
Telephones	4.09	4.60	3.81	4.22
Returns to agricultural GDP				
R&D	5.54	6.63	10.19	6.75
Irrigation	1.62	1.11	2.13	1.45
Roads	1.62	1.74	1.73	1.69
Education	2.18	2.06	2.33	2.17
Electricity	0.81	0.78	0.88	0.82
Telephones	1.25	1.75	2.49	1.63
Returns to nonfarm GDP				
Roads	6.71	5.16	1.66	4.88
Education	9.80	6.66	2.43	6.79
Electricity	2.96	2.04	0.75	2.07
Telephones	2.85	2.85	1.32	2.59
Returns to poverty reduction				
R&D	3.72	12.96	24.03	10.74
Irrigation	1.08	2.16	5.02	2.31
Roads	2.68	8.38	10.03	6.63
Education	5.03	13.90	18.93	11.88
Electricity	2.04	5.71	7.78	4.85
Telephones	1.99	8.10	13.94	6.17
Poverty loans	3.70	3.57	2.40	3.03

SOURCE: Fan, Zhang, and Zhang (2004).

to education investment. This stems from high returns to nonagricultural GDP, which has the second-largest return at 4.88 yuan for every yuan invested.

Investment in rural telephony yielded favorable returns to both agricultural and nonagricultural GDP, and the impact on rural poverty was similar to that of road investments.

Although electricity investment showed low returns to both agricultural and nonagricultural GDP, its poverty reduction impact is significant. For every 10,000 yuan invested, almost five people were brought out of poverty. This is because access to electricity is essential to the expansion of nonfarm employment.

For the nation as a whole, irrigation investment had relatively little impact on rural poverty reduction, although its economic returns were still positive.

This is because irrigation affects poverty reduction solely through improved agricultural productivity.

One striking result of our study is the very small and statistically insignificant impact of government poverty alleviation loans. For every 10,000 yuan invested, more than three people are brought out of poverty.

The analysis was also disaggregated into three different regions.[5] Regional variation is large in the marginal returns to government spending in both GDP growth and poverty reduction. In terms of poverty reduction effects, all kinds of investment had high returns in the western region. For example, for every 10,000 yuan invested in agricultural R&D, education, roads, telecommunications, and electricity, the numbers of poor lifted out of poverty were 24, 19, 10, 14, and 8, respectively. These effects are 6.4, 3.7, 3.7, 7.0, and 3.8 times higher than in the coastal areas. Even for irrigation, every 10,000 yuan of additional investment was sufficient to bring five people out of poverty, four times more than in the coastal areas.

With respect to returns to growth in agriculture, most investments had the largest returns in the western areas. On the other hand, most government expenditures had their largest impact on rural nonfarm GDP in the coastal areas.

Lessons from Experience

The case studies reviewed on China and India show that public investments in rural areas have contributed significantly to agricultural growth and rural poverty reduction. Without these investments, agricultural growth and national economic growth would have been much slower, and there would be greater rural poverty in both countries. There are lessons the two countries can draw from each other's experience with respect to the impacts of public investment on poverty alleviation.

Factors Affecting Poverty Reduction

The different rates of poverty reduction in China and India are due to the following factors:

1. *There have been different growth rates in agricultural productivity, agricultural wages, and nonfarm employment.* For instance, agricultural GDP grew by more than 4 percent per annum in China from 1978 to 2002, compared with 2.9 percent per annum in India from 1981–82 to 2002–3. More-

---

5. The coastal region includes the following provinces: Hebei, Liaoning, Shandong, Jiangsu, Zhejiang, Fujian, Guangdong, and Guangxi. The central region comprises Shanxi, Inner Mongolia, Anhui, Jiangxi, Henan, Hubei, and Hunan. The remaining provinces are classified as the western region. Tibet is excluded due to the lack of data. Beijing, Shanghai, and Tianjin are excluded because of their small share of rural areas and population.

over, nonfarm employment in China has grown by more than 10 percent per annum over the past two decades, while in India it grew by only 2 percent during the same period. On the other hand, growth rates in rural regions were similar in the two countries (Fan, Thorat, and Rao 2004; Fan, Zhang, and Zhang 2004).

2. *There have also been different elasticities of poverty reduction with respect to these factors.* For given growth rates in agricultural production (or productivity), wages, and nonfarm employment, the poverty reduction impact in China is much larger than in India. These poverty reduction elasticities with respect to agricultural production, wages, and nonfarm employment amounted to 1.130, 0.560, and 0.863, respectively, in China (Fan, Zhang, and Zhang 2004), compared with 0.171, 0.185, and 0.594 in India (Fan, Hazell, and Thorat 2000).

3. *Different land distribution policies have affected the poor directly and indirectly.* In India many landless farmers are poor, while China does not have landless cultivators (see Chapter 3 of this volume). Fairly equal access to agricultural land made the poverty reduction elasticity of agricultural growth much larger in China than in India.

4. *It is also the case that increased agricultural production may result in downward pressure on agricultural (food) prices.* This downward pressure is likely to offset part of the poverty reduction effect of agricultural growth in China because farmers may be negatively affected by lower prices. In India, the landless poor may gain from lowered food prices because they are usually net buyers of food (Fan, Hazell, and Thorat 2000; Fan, Zhang, and Zhang 2004).

5. *Differences in the indirect impact of some variables in China and India also need to be recognized in order to understand the different outcomes in poverty reduction in the two countries.* Similar factors seem to have promoted agricultural productivity in both countries. In China, however, agricultural productivity does not indirectly lead to increased landlessness because the ownership of agricultural land is regulated by the state. In India, on the other hand, improvement in total factor productivity does induce landlessness and adversely impacted income distribution at least in the beginning of the green revolution. A similar difference is observed with respect to factors associated with the growth of rural nonfarm employment. In China, roads, education, rural telecommunication, and electrification have all contributed to growth in nonfarm employment. The most interesting feature, however, is the strong and positive impact of agricultural productivity on the growth of the nonfarm sector (off-farm employment elasticity with respect to agricultural productivity is 0.716). On the other hand, unlike in China, agricultural growth was less significant in inducing growth in nonfarm employment in India. Rural development programs, soil and water conservation, roads, and education matter most in the creation

of additional rural nonfarm employment in India. In all but a few regions, agricultural growth was not an important variable in the growth of non-farm employment (Fan, Hazell, and Thorat 1999).

Public Investment Priorities

Growth in agricultural productivity, the rural nonfarm sector, and rural wages, which is the main source of poverty reduction in both China and India, was in turn made possible by public investments in R&D; infrastructure such as roads, power, irrigation, and communication; education; and antipoverty programs. However, returns on public investments in terms of poverty reduction vary drastically across different types of investment.

Among the categories of investment, agricultural research, education, and rural infrastructure are found to be the three in which public spending is most effective in promoting agricultural growth and poverty reduction in both countries. This implies that there is a great deal of potential for more growth and poverty reduction if the level of public investments in these categories is raised.

Regional analyses conducted for China and India suggest that more investments in less-developed or -favored areas not only offer the largest poverty reduction per unit of spending but also lead to the highest economic returns. Thus, for the same set of investments (such as those in irrigation, power, and even R&D) in India and China, returns in highly irrigated regions seem to have reached their upper limit, whereas in less-developed areas returns are found to be higher. In the developed irrigated region, the lower level of productivity growth in the 1990s is closely associated with the lower return to irrigation and agriculture technology; therefore, there is a need both to improve the efficiency of existing irrigation projects and to expand the irrigation facilities to new areas. There is also a need for more investment in upgrading existing technology in developed regions. Irrigation should be expanded in new areas through public investment in less-favored areas such as rain-fed regions in India and in the less-endowed areas of China. This calls for the development of a clearer regional investment policy by the Chinese and Indian governments in relation to the choice of the right investment mix to be implemented in different parts of their respective countries.

Government spending on antipoverty programs has a poverty reduction impact, but this impact is targeted and narrowly focused. The impact of the antipoverty programs through agricultural growth is low, mainly due to the improper selection of the projects under public employment and self-employment. More effort is needed to better target the funds to the poor and reorient the investments toward the improvement of rural education and infrastructure. There is also a need to use public employment programs for improving the privately owned land and water resources of the small and marginal farmers. Thus, the use of antipoverty programs for the expansion of public infrastructure and public and private land and water resources will help reduce poverty not only directly but also indirectly through the promotion of agricultural growth and will thereby offer longer-run poverty reduction.

What Can China and India Learn from Each Other?

The China-India comparison offers lessons to each country about how to achieve greater poverty reduction in the future. The first lesson is that the nature of rural nonfarm enterprises matters. In China rural nonfarm employment is characterized by township and village enterprises and by the migration of farmers to urban areas to work in the service and industrial sectors. Given the nature of the work and earnings, the farmers are most likely to be out of poverty. However, in India rural nonfarm activities are performed largely in the small and informal sectors with low earning potential; therefore, even if a rural resident is engaged in these activities, he will not necessarily be out of poverty. For quite some time, therefore, the rural and urban informal sector is likely to be the main sector for the employment of small and marginal farmers and landless households. China's experience indicates that the high-productivity rural nonfarm sector can be a main source of rural poverty reduction in India.

A related aspect of China's experience is that Chinese rural enterprises began in areas where agriculture was the most advanced. In contrast, rural nonfarm growth was linked with government spending in rural infrastructure in a large part of India and less driven by agriculture-led growth. Thus, it is important for India to promote and strengthen the linkages between the farming and the rural nonfarming sectors.

The second lesson from China's experience has to do with the more widespread poverty-reducing impact of agricultural growth due to more equitable access to agricultural land. More equitable access to land has enabled farmers in China to benefit from the income gains of technological change in agriculture. Therefore, in India there is a need to improve access to agricultural land through land distribution and tenancy reform. The Chinese experience shows that land reforms in the 1950s and the introduction of the household responsibility system (which redistributed land use rights to individual farm households) led to a sharp improvement in agricultural production and productivity. Equitable land distribution also avoids the negative effects of improved agricultural terms of trade on landless farmers and marginal and small farmers, who are usually net buyers of grains.

The third lesson relates to education. Higher educational achievement levels in China and increased agricultural labor productivity give added advantages to that country compared to India. By 1997, the literacy rate of the general population and of those engaging in agricultural labor was about 90 percent in China. Consequently, the labor quality there improved substantially, which provided a greater opportunity for farmers to use modern technology and to engage in nonfarm activities in both rural township enterprises and industrial centers. This also provided more equity in rural areas. On the other hand, in India the rural literacy rate was about 59 percent in 2001, which was much lower than in China. Greater literacy over time has resulted in more poverty reduction in China than in India.

There are lessons for China, too. India's experience with respect to subsidies in agriculture provides an important lesson for China in deciding future government spending priorities. Over the past several decades, the Chinese government has implicitly heavily taxed agriculture through its central procurement and pricing system. As the economy has gradually been liberalized, these implicit taxes have been reduced, and various types of evidence have shown that China is making the transition from taxing to subsidizing agriculture. But whether and how agriculture and farmers should be supported is a hotly debated issue. India's experience clearly indicates that some direct input and output subsidies do bring loss in economic efficiency though their poverty impact is small. India's experience and efforts to rationalize subsidies in term of selected spheres and targeting probably provide useful lessons for China.

Finally, the experience of China and India also has general implications for setting right priorities for public investment and for the sequencing of such investment in other developing countries. In the first phase, investments should focus on reducing widespread poverty through broad-based economic growth extending to rural areas, while in subsequent phases more direct attention should be given to reducing poverty and income inequalities that arise and persist in reform by concentrating on investment in lagging sectors and regions, as well as on poverty at the community and household levels.

Countries like China, India, Vietnam, and Thailand have successfully completed the first phase of poverty reduction and now need to progress toward addressing regional inequities and poverty at the household level. China has traditionally favored a sectoral and regional approach to dealing with rising inequalities, for instance, in employment actions, but has recently expanded this approached to target more household and community programs. India, on the other hand, has concentrated on targeting specific sections of its population and has involved a large set of actors, including nongovernmental organizations and civil society, and it has recently expanded its employment programs, too. The experience of India shows that using a variety of programs targeted directly at specific segments of the poor can be more effective than the broader income- or area-based approaches.

Most countries of Sub-Saharan Africa are still in the first phase of poverty reduction. Investments in support of economic growth remain central to the reduction of their mass poverty. The governments of these countries have the central responsibility of forging a well-sequenced and coherent growth strategy and of determining the public investments needed. Infrastructure and agriculture are the main areas needing public investment attention. In recent years, some African governments have started to make progress. For instance, Ethiopia and Nigeria recently increased their public investments in agriculture and rural areas (World Economic Forum 2006). An improved capacity to respond to emergencies and hunger crises must complement these strategies.

7 Reforming the Agricultural Research and Intellectual Property Rights Systems of China

BONWOO KOO, PHILIP G. PARDEY,
AND KEMING QIAN

To improve performance, China began to reform its public-dominated agricultural research system in the mid-1980s. One of the major reform initiatives was to encourage the public institutions to commercialize their research achievements, and, as a consequence, the developmental firms owned by public agricultural research institutions have become increasingly concerned about intellectual property rights (IPR).

Another government initiative was to encourage the private sector and multinational companies to invest further in agricultural research and development (R&D) in China. Because the incentives for private and foreign investment in agricultural R&D are heavily influenced by a country's legislation and enforcement of IPR, the evolving status of IPR protection could substantially affect agricultural technology development in China. In recent years, public spending in agricultural R&D has increased substantially, partly due to overall improvement of the government's financial revenue.

We begin by providing a profile of the agricultural research system in China, focusing on its reforms beginning in the 1980s, the consequent emergence of nongovernmental funding institutions engaged in agricultural R&D, and their relevance to IPR protection. We next discuss the status of IPR protection in China through the case of plant variety protection and then offer some concluding remarks.

Reform of the Chinese Agricultural Research System

Before the mid-1980s, public investment was nearly the only source of funding for agricultural R&D. The Chinese agricultural research system was dominated by public research institutes affiliated with various government ministries and departments at national, provincial, and prefectural levels. Universities conducted only a few projects while private research was negligible.

The first half of this chapter draws heavily on Fan, Qian, and Zhang (2006), the second half on Koo et al. (2006). Authorship is alphabetical.

141

From the mid-1980s, the demand for increasing funding for agricultural research put pressure on government budgets, while the government was dissatisfied with the performance of the public research institutions, especially the lower than expected rates of upatke of technologies generated by these institutions. In March 1985, the Central Committee of the Chinese Communist Party called for reforms in science and technology management as proposed in the *Decision on the Reform of the Science and Technology Management System* and a similar document that was promulgated by the State Council in 1987. Since then there have been about 40 governmental decisions, regulations, and laws relating to reforms of the science and technology system. The main legislative measures taken by the government included the following:

1. Shifting the mechanism for funding research institutes, from mainly block-based core funding toward more competitive project funding arrangements.
2. Encouraging public institutes to set up development firms to commercialize their research results or technologies.
3. Rewarding individual scientists by allowing them to retain a certain proportion of the income as a salary supplement from commercializing the results of their research.
4. Drastically increase public funding to agricultural R&D to increase and maintain competitiveness of the agricultural sector.

The principal purpose of the reforms was to encourage the application of science to meet the needs of the market. The principal means for accomplishing the reforms was to change the funding system and thereby create incentives for research institutions to engage more directly with technology users and become more responsive to changing market circumstances. Direct allocation of funds by means of block grants to research institutions was largely replaced by a mixed system under which institutes sell their services in the marketplace and compete for project funds from the government. Table 7.1 indicates that the share of government funding among the income sources of the public institutes declined sharply after the beginning of reforms. More than 80 percent of the government funding in the late 1990s was competitive and project-based, compared with 100 percent of core or block funding prior to reform. State-owned or private enterprises were also encouraged to invest in agricultural R&D, but that did not happen, in part, it seems, because of poor IPR enforcement.

These changes resulted in the emergence of nongovernmental funding institutions engaged in agricultural R&D. Based on ownership and funding sources, the R&D agencies operating in China can now be categorized as (1) traditional public research institutes, (2) development firms owned by public agricultural research institutes, (3) government-owned agribusiness firms, (4) shareholding companies, and (5) multinational companies.

TABLE 7.1 Income sources of public agricultural research institutes in China, selected years (percent)

Year and level	Government	Development (sale of goods and services)[a]	Loans	Other	Total
1987					
National	86.2	12.8	0.2	0.7	100
Subnational	66.7	26.5	4.2	2.5	100
Total	*70.5*	*23.9*	*3.4*	*2.2*	*100*
1993					
National	68.1	26.2	3.4	2.3	100
Provincial	45.2	44.1	7.3	3.4	100
Prefectural	42.8	39.2	13.8	4.2	100
Total	*47.1*	*40.2*	*9.1*	*3.6*	*100*
1999					
National	52.2	45.7	2.1	0.0	100
Provincial	51.0	43.3	5.7	0.0	100
Prefectural	43.4	46.8	9.8	0.0	100
Total	*48.5*	*44.9*	*6.6*	*0.0*	*100*
2002					
National	64.0	31.4	0.6	4.0	100
Provincial	59.5	28.9	2.9	8.7	100
Prefectural	59.5	27.0	8.1	5.4	100
Total	*60.7*	*29.0*	*3.7*	*6.6*	*100*

SOURCE: China, Ministry of Agriculture, agricultural science and technology statistical materials, various years.

NOTES: The data for the national level cover Ministry of Agriculture institutes only; forestry and universities are excluded.

[a]Represents self-generated funds, largely from the sale of goods and services.

Public Sector Research Institutes

Public sector research institutes still form the backbone of the Chinese agricultural research system, despite the rapid emergence of other kinds of institutions. Agricultural research at the national level is conducted mainly within academies and institutions under the Ministry of Agriculture, complemented by research conducted by institutions under the administrative control of other ministries. The provincial agricultural academies undertake research targeted at their local circumstances, while the prefectural institutes administered by prefectural governments emphasize applied and adaptive research and development. Research at this level is important given the relatively large size of most prefectures in China. Table 7.2 summarizes the sizes and structures of the public institutes.

The Chinese agricultural research system is highly decentralized in terms of both its management and its funding. In 2002 only 12 percent of agricultural sci-

TABLE 7.2 Vertical structure of Chinese agricultural research institutes, 1989 and 2002

Category	1989				2002			
	National	Provincial	Prefectural	Total	National	Provincial	Prefectural	Total
Number of institutes	56	423	620	1,099	59	429	608	1,096
Number of staff (total)	13,590	65,124	46,562	125,276	11,641	45,086	35,662	92,349
Number of scientists and engineers	5,676	17,827	10,161	33,664	4,114	16,458	11,355	31,927
Scientists and engineers per institute	101.36	42.14	16.39	30.63	69.73	38.36	18.68	29.13
Research expenditures (million yuan, 1999 prices)	270	985	654	1,909	1,378	2,923	1,408	5,759
Research expenditure per staff (yuan, 1999 prices)	19,868	15,125	14,046	15,238	118,375	64,832	39,526	62,361
Research expenditure per scientist or engineer (yuan, 1999 prices)	47,569	55,253	64,364	56,707	334,954	177,604	123,998	180,380

SOURCE: China, Ministry of Agriculture, agricultural science and technology statistical materials, various years.

NOTE: Data pertain to the nonuniversity institutes within the Ministry of Agriculture system only.

entists and engineers (excluding university personnel) were based in national institutions. A large portion of the country's researchers (50 percent) worked in institutions administered and often largely financed at the provincial level, while the remaining 36 percent worked in prefectural institutions. There was a marked disparity in the average sizes of the institutes, ranging from 70 scientists per institute at the national level to 38 at provincial-level institutes and an average of just 19 scientists at prefectural-level institutes. The average spending per staff at the national level for 2002 was 118,375 yuan, which is 1.8 times higher than the comparable provincial figure and almost 3 times higher than the prefectural spending to staff ratio.

These data are consistent with the notion that national institutes are generally larger and better financed, focusing on pre-technology types of research with less site-specific R&D. Provincial and prefectural institutions are typically smaller in size and more involved in localized and adaptive kinds of research.

A distinctive aspect of the agricultural research system in China is that research is institutionally separated from education. The Chinese Academy of Agricultural Sciences (CAAS) falls under the administrative jurisdiction of the Ministry of Agriculture, while the provincial academies are subject to provincial oversight. Prior to 2000, key national agricultural universities were also under the jurisdiction of the Ministry of Agriculture, while provincial agricultural universities were managed by the respective provincial governments. In 2000, the management of all agricultural universities was transferred to the education system. At the national level, the three key agricultural universities, China, Nanjing, and Central, are under the jurisdiction of the Ministry of Education, while the provincial agricultural universities or colleges are the responsibility of the provincial departments of education. This contrasts sharply with the U.S. land-grant system, which involves integrated educational, research, and extension activities. Arguably, the separation of research, education, and extension has undermined efforts to develop a more integrated system for the generation and diffusion of agricultural technology throughout China.

Development Firms Owned by Public Agricultural Research Institutes

Development firms owned by public agricultural research institutes emerged after the public agricultural research system reforms that were initiated two decades ago. To date, the impact of these firms on the Chinese agricultural innovation system is mixed.

First, in the early stages these firms lacked independent legal status. In addition, the institutes' businesses were not necessarily related to their specific areas of research, but rather were developed in an opportunistic fashion, with an eye to commercial opportunities deemed likely to generate income or revenue. For example, the Institute of Taihu and the Institute of Lixiahe in Jiangsu province, both well known in China for their excellent research performance, produced mineral water and set up a plant to manufacture auto spare parts, respectively. Many CAAS institutes own restaurants, grocery stores, and commercial office complexes. A lack of capital and management skills led to low efficiency. Moreover, the research institutes were directly exposed to business risks, unprotected by arm's-length, limited-liability company structures. A typical example was the China National Rice Research Institute located in Hangzhou, which launched a business to manufacture monosodium glutamate in 1988 and lost more than 10 million yuan. The institute has been struggling with many legal battles since then.

Second, researchers are typically not well versed in extension techniques or in dealing directly with farmers on commercial terms. Those who are active and successful in their research often resent extension obligations because it takes time away from their research. Those willing to become involved in technology transfer activities often receive little or no financial reward for their efforts. The functional separation of research and extension is a problem that has yet to be fully resolved, although the commercial activities and spin-offs of many public research institutes in part substitute for this lack of formal links between extension and research.

Since the mid-1990s, based on the experience of the previous 5–10 years, many public agricultural research institutes have begun focusing their business activities on research-related industries producing such things as improved seeds, chemicals, livestock vaccines, and so on, where their research may give them a competitive edge. Increasingly, they have also structured their commercial operations as legally independent companies to minimize their exposure to business risks. A better-defined separation of operations aimed at technology generation and commercialization of technologies is beginning to develop between the mother institutes and the firms. For example, the seed company of the Institute of Vegetables and Flowers (IVF) at CAAS was established in 1990. The scientists at IVF are responsible for the development and performance testing of new varieties of vegetables and flowers. Once scientists develop new parent lines for hybrid seeds, they make these lines available to the seed company, which then holds variety demonstrations in targeted markets, produces hybrid seeds, and markets them. Since 1990, the seed company has earned more than 10 million yuan annually, and about 90 percent of the revenue has been returned to IVF, which allocates 10 percent of this income to the breeders as salary bonuses, with the rest used to cover the costs of general research projects or operations.

These spin-off companies are not only beginning to play major roles in transferring and commercializing technologies developed by the mother institutes, which was expected and encouraged by the government, but they have also generated a substantial amount of revenue to underwrite the operations of the mother institutes. In 2000, 73 companies at CAAS generated a total profit of 120.5 million yuan, complementing the 243.4 million yuan of core funding the academy received from the central government.

Agribusiness Firms Owned by Central and Local Governments

Agribusiness firms owned by central and local governments include the state-owned seed, agricultural, food, chemical, and machinery enterprises. In the previously planned economy, these companies freely accessed technologies emanating from the public agricultural research institutes. In the post-reform period, many of these institutes have sought to commercialize their own research, which has led to a greater awareness of the IPR aspects of agricultural R&D. Because it is now difficult for agribusiness companies to freely access technologies, some large, state-owned companies are forced to negotiate licenses and pay royalties or sign research contracts with the institutes or to develop their own R&D capacities.

Because of the lack of statistics, the total extent of R&D investment by state-owned agribusinesses is unknown. A case study of the Chinese seed industry found that no improved varieties were developed by companies prior to 1985. In contrast, in 1999 some 86 improved varieties were developed by these companies (including state-owned and private companies), although these accounted for less than 2 percent of the total varieties released.

Shareholding Companies

Shareholding companies based on agricultural technologies have rapidly emerged in recent years. Most of these were originally launched as development firms owned by public research institutes or agribusiness firms owned by governments. As they grew, many of them were listed on the Chinese stock market to help mobilize capital. For example, the Technology Development Company, a very successful firm formerly owned by the Hunan Academy of Agricultural Sciences, was listed in 2000 and mobilized about 700 million yuan. The national livestock and fishery companies (both previously owned by the Ministry of Agriculture) also were listed in 2000, with majority holdings retained by the government. These three companies invested several million yuan in agriculture R&D in 2000.

In that year, the central government designated 151 of the country's largest agricultural companies, most of them shareholding companies, as leading companies in agriculture. These are entitled to some preferential treatment, such as exemptions from certain taxes and ready access to low-interest loans, provided that they reinvest part of their revenue in agricultural R&D.

Multinational Companies

Technologies from multinational firms has led to rapid gains in productivity and output in many areas of China's agricultural economy. These firms may play an even larger role in the future with China's entry into the World Trade Organization (WTO). For example, modern technology has been introduced in the poultry industry through the import of parental genetic stock and breeding materials and the introduction of superior nutritional feed milling and mixing, resulting in the parallel improvement of poultry genetics (Rozelle, Pray, and Huang 1999).

However, the potential here is still largely undeveloped due to the unsecured nature of property rights in China. There are various laws and regulations to protect property rights, but enforcement is generally weak. So far, most of the plant breeding and screening research by foreign-financed firms has been on hybridized vegetables and sunflower seeds for two reasons: (1) these varieties are difficult to duplicate as long as the hybrid parents are kept confidential, and (2) these seeds were not controlled by state-owned seed companies, which enjoyed a legislative monopoly on the sale of seeds for principal food crops, especially hybrid rice and maize, whose seed quality is difficult to ensure. However, the force of this monopoly power has waned as these sales restrictions have been relaxed. Large private seed companies are now able to market seed varieties they have developed or acquired. In the agricultural chemical sector, it is still common for pesticides whose active ingredients are complex and difficult to duplicate to be illegally copied and commercialized (Rozelle, Pray, and Huang 1999).

The Challenges Ahead

Two factors will heavily influence the future of agricultural research and technology provision in China. One is how well and efficiently the public research institutions use scarce financial resources. The other is how well they mobilize more funding for R&D activities in the context of rapidly changing market conditions and increasing globalization.

The lack of sufficient resources also impacts the performance of public institutions. The lack of coordination between research, extension, and education as well as between the institutions at different levels of government and in different places results in unnecessary duplication of research effort and hampers technology transfer. Public agricultural research, extension, and education institutions in China are administratively decentralized and physically scattered, both vertically among different levels of government and horizontally in different administrative zones. In Beijing, for example, there are many institutions involved in agricultural research: CAAS, Beijing Academy of Agricultural Sciences, the National Agricultural Extension Center, Beijing Agricultural Extension Center, Chinese Agricultural University, Beijing Agricultural College, and some institutes of the Chinese Academy of Sciences and other government agencies. They are all administered and funded by different government agencies, and there is no mechanism for formal linkage and coordination among them. Many of the institutes and universities carry out duplicative research, and the extension agencies pursue their own priorities with little consultation and coordination. Public-private partnerships are set to become another coordination issue with the emergence of development firms owned by the public institutes operating alongside private agribusiness firms.

Another major problem confronting public agencies is the requirement that they provide all benefits such as salaries, housing, healthcare, and pensions to their current staff as well as their retirees. For example, there are about 40,000 CAAS retirees, equivalent to 40–50 percent of the total staff still working, who absorb a substantial amount of the resources meant for research activities.

Mobilizing private resources for research relies heavily on the extent and effectiveness of IPR protection. Generally there are three channels of funding for agricultural R&D, namely governmental, private, and foreign. Compared with rich countries' average intensity of agricultural research investment of 2 to 3 percent of agricultural GDP, the Chinese government's investment in agricultural R&D is comparatively low, accounting only for around 0.49 percent of agricultural GDP in 2002. Given the limited budgetary resources and competition from other industries, it is doubtful that the government will increase its funding for agricultural R&D to world standards, although it has promised to do so (Table 7.3). Therefore, private and foreign funding may well be the most fruitful option for bridging the gap between the demand for funding and its supply.

Intellectual Property Rights Protection

China has two official systems of IPR protection for innovation in agriculture, namely a sui generis system which protects plant varieties, and a more conventional patent system that provides protection for other types of agricultural innovations. We will concentrate our attention on the evolving nature of plant variety protection (PVP) to discern the status of the legislation and the enforcement of IPR protection more generally, cognizant of the fact that it is relatively more advanced than IPR protection in other areas of agriculture in China.

INSTITUTIONAL ASPECTS. Spurred by preparations for entry to the WTO, China began significant revision of its laws regarding patents, copyrights, trademarks, and other forms of protection for intellectual property about a decade ago, including signing various IPR conventions (Maskus and Dougherty 1998). Among the latest in a series of policy and legislative reforms affecting agriculture and agricultural R&D in China over the past several decades is the extension of IPR to include agricultural innovations.[1] China became a member state of the UPOV (the International Union for the Protection of New Varieties of Plants) Convention on April 23, 1999, after enacting its Regulations of the People's Republic of China on the Protection of New Varieties of Plants law (hereafter referred to as the PVP law) in March 1997.

China's PVP law conforms to the 1978 UPOV Convention. Like similar laws implemented elsewhere, the Chinese PVP law grants protection to varieties that are new, distinct, uniform, and stable. Holders of a PVP certificate have

---

1. Perkins (1988), Sicular (1988b), Lin (1990), and Fan, Qian, and Zhang (2006) provide perspectives on the considerable policy changes affecting Chinese agriculture, beginning with the decollectivization of farm production starting in 1978.

TABLE 7.3 Public investment in Chinese agricultural research, 1953–2002

Year	Agricultural research expenditures (million yuan per year, 1999 prices)	Number of scientists	Expenditures per scientist (yuan per year, 1999 prices)	Share of total government spending (percent)	Share of total R&D spending (percent)	Share of total government spending in agriculture (percent)	Percentage of total agricultural GDP
1953–57	130	n.a.	n.a.	n.a.	n.a.	1.49	0.07
1958–60	896	140,789	6,366	0.38	10.17	3.25	0.55
1961–65	766	102,498	7,469	0.56	10.24	3.90	0.41
1966–76	1,158	99,657	11,621	0.45	9.93	4.53	0.36
1977–85	2,429	11,621	99,657	0.56	10.34	5.24	0.44
1986–90	3,111	30,257	80,278	0.51	11.90	6.16	0.38
1991–94	3,808	53,598	58,044	0.54	14.29	6.14	0.39
1995–2000	4,667	61,876	61,545	0.53	12.06	8.42	0.34
2002	7,837	53,461	146,491	0.36	9.75	5.46	0.49

SOURCES: Fan and Pardey (1992, 1997); National Statistical Bureau, various years; and State Science and Technology Commission, various years.

NOTE: n.a., not available.

the legal right to exclude others from commercializing protected varieties for a prescribed length of time: 20 years after the date of the grant for vines, forest trees, fruit trees, and ornamental plants and 15 years for all other plants, including food, oil, and fiber crops. Exceptions to the exclusionary rights are made, however, for both breeding and other types of scientific research (breeders' exemption) and for the use of seeds saved by farmers for replanting (farmers' exemption).

Two separate administrative authorities implement China's PVP laws. The State Forestry Administration is responsible for forestry, including forest trees, bamboo, woody plants, and dry fruit trees, while the Ministry of Agriculture is responsible for all agricultural plants, including grains, vegetables, edible fungi, and grasses. On April 27, 2000, the State Forestry Administration published its first and so far only *Gazette for Protection of New Varieties of Plants (Forestry)*, which included information on 13 PVP applications for forest trees. Since then, information on applications for and grants of these PVP rights has been scattered throughout various journals and newspapers.[2] In contrast, the Ministry of Agriculture has published a *Variety Protection Gazette for Agricultural Plants* (hereafter called the PVP Gazette) on a bimonthly basis since April 1999. This study deals with the protection of agricultural plant varieties, drawing on data compiled from various issues of the Ministry of Agriculture's PVP Gazette.

Upon receiving an application, the relevant authority is required by law to complete a preliminary examination within six months. If an application is then deemed acceptable, information such as the date of application, the crop type, a description of the variety for which protection is sought, and the names of the applicants are published in the PVP Gazette. For those applications passing preliminary examination, the authority conducts a substantive examination of the distinctness, uniformity, and stability of the variety in question. The rights granted apply from the date of issuance of the PVP certificate, and, as in the case of PVP laws prevailing in many other countries, each new right pertains to a single new variety.

Administrative procedures for protecting agricultural plants are handled by the Office of Variety Protection for Agricultural Plants within the Ministry of Agriculture. In early 2002, the office had a total of 12 full-time employees handling basic assessment and administrative tasks, with 4 staff involved in preexamination activities and the rest engaged in testing and substantive examination.[3] The office devolves most of its biological evaluation to various testing centers—a main center located in Beijing and 14 other testing sites scattered throughout the main agricultural areas of China. Other procedures, such as rejection of application, denomination of new varieties, and reexamination of

---

2. By early 2002, about 190 applications had been filed for the varietal protection of forest trees, of which 48 were granted (Faji Huang, Deputy Director of the PVP Office for Forest, personal communication).

3. By way of comparison, in 2001 the PVP office of the United States employed 12 staff, including 1 commissioner, 9 examiners, and 2 support staff.

TABLE 7.4 Costs of establishing and maintaining plant variety rights in China, 1999

		U.S. dollars	
Fees	Chinese yuan	Official market exchange rate[a]	Purchasing power parity rate[b]
Costs of establishing rights			
Application fee	1,800	217	994
Examination fee	4,600	556	2,541
Costs per year of maintaining rights			
Years 1–3	1,500	181	829
Years 4–6	1,950	236	1,077
Years 7–9	2,535	306	1,401
Years 10–12	3,295	398	1,820
Years 13–15	4,283	517	2,366
Years 16–18	5,567	672	3,076
Years 19–20	7,237	874	3,998
Total maintenance fee (15 years)	40,689	4,914	22,480
Total maintenance fee (20 years)	71,864	8,679	39,704
Total costs			
Agricultural plants (15 years of protection)	47,089	5,687	26,016
Forestry (20 years of protection)	78,264	9,452	43,240

SOURCE: Koo et al. (2006).

[a]The 1999 exchange rate used here was U.S. $1 = 8.28 yuan.

[b]The 1999 purchasing power parity rate was U.S. $1 = 1.81 yuan.

applications, are handled by the ad hoc Plant Variety Reexamination Committee, which is convened by senior administrators of the Ministry of Agriculture.

Once a PVP certificate is issued, the right holder is required to pay a series of annual fees over the period of protection to maintain the rights (Table 7.4). Establishing and maintaining protection for 15 years costs the right holder 47,089 yuan or U.S. $5,687 for each plant variety right granted (excluding the administrative and other costs of submitting an application). More than 85 percent of the total fee is for maintaining the right. Establishing and maintaining PVP rights in China is costly, even by the standards of a rich country. For example, in the United States PVP fees totaled U.S. $2,450 per variety (including a U.S. $300 application fee and a U.S. $2,150 examination fee) in 1999, and there is no annual maintenance fee.[4]

Given the substantial differences in price levels between the United States and China, purchasing power parity (PPP) instead of a market exchange rate

---

4. Similarly, Brazil charges U.S. $348 to establish PVP rights and U.S. $2,609 to maintain these rights for 15 years (Koo et al. forthcoming).

provides an alternative and more realistic basis for comparing PVP costs internationally. Using PPP, the total cost of establishing and maintaining PVP rights in China for a single variety for 15 years is U.S. $26,016 in 1999 prices (Table 7.4). This is almost 5 times more than the corresponding costs when using official market exchange rates to convert currencies and more than 10 times the corresponding costs in the United States. Not enough time has passed to warrant an examination of the renewal behavior of rights holders, but the exceptionally high maintenance costs suggest that rights holders in China will maintain their rights only if significant revenue is expected from the protection in the future.

THE PATTERN OF VARIETAL PROTECTION. A total of 923 PVP applications for agricultural plants were lodged and published in the PVP Gazette through September 2003. On average, 18 applications were made monthly, but with substantial variation around the average and indications of an upward trend over time. The initial spike of 49 applications in April 1999 most likely reflects the latent demand for varietal rights for material developed prior to the implementation of the PVP law. The reported reduction in the number of applications in mid-2003 may be more apparent than real, reflecting lags between the date of application and its publication (which averaged about 6 months in our sample). Only 412 PVP rights, about 45 percent of the total of 923 applications, were granted by September 2003. About a quarter of the applications lodged in 1999 were yet to be granted as of September 2003, and some may have been rejected or withdrawn in the interim.[5] The average grant lag for applications is about 20 months from the date of application.

Based on an assessment of the early wave of PVP applications, Tong (2002) argued that the number of applications in China was limited because of a lack of appreciation of the role of property rights in a market economy, the high cost of gaining protection, the uncertain scope of protection, and the complicated and costly enforcement processes. Some of these concerns are supported by our data, others are muted by the rapid changes in the Chinese seed sector, and some are questionable. In particular, the basic premise that the initial number of PVP applications was unduly constrained by Chinese-specific factors is debatable, and the number is not out of line with the historical experience in the United States. Although there were, on average, 345 PVP applications per year in the United States during the past 10 years, there were only 121 applications per year following the passage of the U.S. Plant Variety Protection Act in 1970 (compared with 213 per year for China).

In China, plant variety rights have been sought for 23 different crops since 1999, and the number of crops for which varietal protection has been sought

---

5. By way of comparison, during the period from January 1971 to December 2002, a total of 7,386 PVP applications were made in the United States, and 4,960 certificates were granted for more than 190 crops.

TABLE 7.5 PVP applications in China, by crop, 1999–2003

Crop	First 13 months of sample[a]	Second 13 months of sample[a]	Third 13 months of sample[a]	Last 13 months of sample[a]	Total	Share of total (percent)
Food crops	*135*	*172*	*183*	*319*	*809*	*88*
Maize						
Hybrid	77	71	78	113	339	37
Nonhybrid	39	35	24	21	119	13
Rice						
Hybrid	13	26	46	130	215	23
Nonhybrid	5	17	13	22	57	6
Wheat	0	5	21	23	49	5
Soybeans	0	16	1	7	24	3
Potatoes	1	2	0	2	5	1
Sweet potatoes	0	0	0	1	1	0
Vegetable crops	*4*	*2*	*12*	*16*	*34*	*4*
Chinese cabbage	4	1	5	4	14	2
Watermelons	0	0	4	5	9	12
Tomatoes	0	1	2	3	6	1
Other vegetables[b]	0	0	1	4	5	1
Fruit crops	*0*	*2*	*10*	*7*	*19*	*2*
Pears	0	2	9	2	13	1
Peaches	0	0	0	5	5	1
Other fruit[c]	0	0	1	0	1	0
Ornamental crops[d]	*1*	*1*	*4*	*6*	*12*	*1*
Other crops	*0*	*13*	*17*	*19*	*49*	*5*
Rapeseed	0	3	11	17	31	3
Peppers	0	7	2	1	10	1
Peanuts	0	3	4	1	8	1
Total	*140*	*90*	*226*	*367*	*923*	*100*

SOURCE: Koo et al. (2006).

[a]The first 13 months of the sample were April 1999–April 2000, the second 13 months May 2000–May 2001, and the third 13 months June 2001–June 2002, the last 13 months July 2002–July 2003.

[b]These include cucumbers and wild cabbage.

[c]These include lichis.

[d]These include chrysanthemums, lilies, and tulips.

has increased over time (Table 7.5).[6] Applications were lodged for only 5 crops during the first 13 months of our sample, and for 19 crops during the last 13 months, reflecting in part the expanded number of crops eligible for protection.

Perhaps surprisingly, the preponderance of the protection sought is for hybrid, not open-pollinated, maize and rice varieties, including both the inbred lines and the final hybrid seed. The institutional arrangements for producing finished seed and the state of legal recourse for piracy may account for this apparent anomaly. The common practice in China is for research institutes or seed development firms to outsource the production of commercial quantities of seed, often to state-owned seed companies that in turn contract with individual growers to produce the seed. In these circumstances, the technology owner (that is, the seed development firm or research institute) runs the real risk of piracy or theft of its hybrid seed and even its inbred lines, so PVP certificates provide an additional legal avenue of recourse beyond that offered by contract law.

By comparison, in the United States state trade secrets laws effectively protect the theft of hybrid inbred lines. For example, in 1994 Holden Foundation Seeds was judged liable for misappropriating Pioneer Hi-Bred's inbred hybrid corn lines under the Iowa trade secrets law. It was ordered to pay Pioneer Hi-Bred International U.S. $46 million, an estimate of the profits forgone by illegal use of these inbred lines.[7] Utility patents provide an additional means of protecting inbred lines in the United States. As a consequence, the share of hybrid varieties for which plant variety protection is sought is very small in this country. Among the more than 190 crops for which PVP protection was sought during the past 30 years in the United States, open-pollinated crops accounted for the lion's share of applications. For example, soybeans accounted for 1,362 applications (18 percent) and wheat for 597 (8 percent) of the applications. Only 12 percent of the total applications were for maize varieties.

In China, the majority (69 percent) of PVP applications were filed by national, provincial, and prefectural public research institutes and universities (Table 7.6). Of these applications, more than half were made by provincial institutes, nearly one-third by prefectural institutes, 9 percent by universities, and only 2 percent by national research agencies such as CAAS. These institutional shares are roughly consistent with the corresponding shares of overall investments in agricultural research. Both publicly held seed development firms and state-owned seed companies accounted for about 11 percent of the applications, with another 16 percent made by the shareholding companies that had spun off from these firms.

---

6. In September 1999, a total of 10 species were eligible for protection. This number grew to 41 (7 major cereals, 2 oil crops, 2 roots and tubers, 11 vegetables and fruits, and 13 flowers and grasses) by September 2003.

7. *Pioneer Hi-Bred International* v. *Holden Foundation Seeds*, 35 F.3d 1226, 1240 (8th Cir. 1994).

TABLE 7.6 PVP in China, by type of applicant, 1999–2003

Type of applicant[a]	Number of applications[b]	Share of total (percent)
Public research institution		
National	19	2
Provincial	318	34
Prefectural	224	24
University	82	9
Seed development firm (by research institute)	54	6
State-owned seed company (agribusiness firm)	43	5
Shareholding company	149	16
Multinational company	5	1
Individuals	23	2
Others (foreigners)	6	1
Total	*923*	*100*

SOURCE: Koo et al. (2006).

[a]This classification structure is taken from Fan, Fang, and Zhang (2003).

[b]Joint applications (a total of 100) are assigned according to the name of the first applicant.

The demarcation between the public and private sectors in China is difficult to discern, but we estimate that 80 percent of the PVP applications are lodged by public agencies (excluding shareholding companies). This contrasts markedly with the United States where the public-sector share of PVP applications is only 15 percent. Notably, multinational companies accounted for few filings in China (two for potatoes, one for peppers, and one for an ornamental flower), a reflection of restrictive government regulations.

Table 7.7 gives more detail regarding individual applications and the crops involved. While more than 200 different applicants sought protection during the sample period, the distribution is highly skewed toward a few applicants. Just 10 institutions accounted for more than 30 percent of the total applications; 7 percent were made by the Jilin Academy of Agricultural Science (AAS), 4 percent by Jiangsu AAS, and 3 percent by Heilongjiang AAS, Laizhou AAS, and Dandong AAS. A further 18 percent of the total applications were lodged by 130 applicants, each of which filed fewer than two claims. Notably, institutions located in just five of China's 31 provinces (Sichuan, Jilin, Liaoning, Shandong, and Henan) accounted for nearly half of the total number of applications.

While there is a reasonably close correspondence between the patterns of overall R&D spending and PVP applications, the link between research and the intellectual property rights sought by an individual research institute is less clear-cut. The Jilin AAS is a relatively large provincial research institute with a total of 1,055 staff in 2000 (including 404 scientific researchers) focusing on

TABLE 7.7 PVP applications in China, by applicant and type of crop, 1999–2003

Applicant	Applications		Crop (number of applications)						
	Share (percent)	Number	Maize	Rice	Wheat	Rapeseed	Soybeans	Cabbage	Other crops[b]
Jilin AAS	7	67	50	6			11		6
Jiangsu AAS	4	34	5	17	5	1			2
Heilongjiang AAS	3	29	21	3			3		1
Laizhou AAS	3	28	21					6	
Dandong AAS	3	25	22	2					
Hunan AAS	3	24		20			1		4
Sichuan AAS	3	24	4	18	2				
Yibin ASRI	3	24		24					
Henan AAS	2	20	11		3	1		4	1
Jilin Jinong Hi-Tech Development Company	2	19	19						
Sichuan Agricultural University	2	18	6	7	5				
CAAS	2	17	2	4		3		1	7
Anhui AAS	2	16	1	9	1	2	3		
Other applicants	62	578	296	162	33	24	6	3	54
Total	100	923	458	272	49	31	24	14	75

SOURCE: Koo et al. (2006).

NOTES: Table includes data on the total number of applications lodged from April 1999 to July 2003. AAS, Academy of Agricultural Science; ASRI, Agricultural Science Research Institute.

maize and soybean research. Sichuan AAS and Jiangsu AAS are also large institutes, comparable to Jilin AAS, with 1,530 and 1,200 staff, respectively, and an emphasis on rice, cotton, and wheat research. Not surprisingly, these three institutes sought significant numbers of PVP certificates, and the crop orientation of their PVP applications aligns with their respective research emphasis. What is surprising is that some smaller research institutes, such as Laizhou AAS (a prefectural institute in Shandong province with 380 staff engaged heavily in maize breeding) and Dandong AAS (a similarly sized prefectural institute in Liaoning province), also sought varietal rights comparable in number to the larger institutes mentioned earlier. At the other extreme is CAAS, a national institute with a large staff (about 9,000, split evenly between scientists and support staff) and a research budget of about U.S. $35 million in 2001, which sought only 17 PVP certificates up to July 2003.

The prospect of topping up revenue streams appears to affect the decision of some agencies to seek PVP protection. The comparatively large number of PVP applications from financially strained agencies such as Heilongjiang AAS, Dandong AAS, and Laizhou AAS is indicative of their interest in reaping potential rewards from commercializing their technologies. Other institutes with comparatively abundant resources, such as CAAS, have made less effort to protect varieties for revenue-raising purposes. Moreover, commercial successes prior to the passage of the PVP law in 1999 may account for the application behavior of some institutes. For example, the commercial success of the "Yedan" series of hybrid maize seeds developed by Li Denghai, now president of Laizhou AAS, might have stimulated the subsequent PVP application by the institute.

Conclusion

The reform of the Chinese agricultural research system, beginning in the mid-1980s, has been characterized by a shift away from block funding toward more competitive funding of agricultural research, ostensibly to encourage public agricultural research institutes to commercialize their research achievements. As these reforms have taken hold, they have not only reduced the agricultural R&D pressure on the public purse but also appear to have stimulated the commercialization of technology generation and provision within China, which might well spur faster growth in agriculture in the future. However, striking the right balance between the nature and extent of public and private roles regarding the funding and conduct of agricultural R&D in China is an issue that still needs to be addressed. But perhaps the most fruitful achievement of the reform has been the institutional changes that have seen a large number of development firms being spawned by public research institutes. An increasing number of these firms are being privatized, either as public offerings or by being turned into shareholding companies, and they are poised to play an important role in technology improvement in China.

However, many challenges remain, the most important of which is weak legislation and enforcement related to IPR protection. Although China has joined the 1978 UPOV Convention and set up the official agencies responsible for PVP, the high cost of gaining protection and complicated and costly enforcement processes have undermined the incentives of the PVP. To encourage private and foreign investment in agricultural R&D, China still has a long way to go to enhance its PVP and other IPR protection related to agricultural innovation.

8 Agricultural Research and Technology in India: Status, Impact, and Contemporary Issues

DAYANATHA JHA AND SURESH PAL

Agricultural research and extension services not only provided the critical base for India's green revolution but hold the key to future agricultural and rural growth. This chapter will give a complete overview of the major institutions, policies, and reforms that have not only influenced Indian agricultural research in the past but will continue to do so in the future.

The first two sections review the evolution and structure of the national agricultural research system. They are followed by an overview of the financial and human resources, then a discussion of the impact of agricultural research and development (R&D) investments on growth and poverty reduction. The key priority policy areas on the future reform agenda are the focus of the final section, which is followed by the conclusion.

The Indian Agricultural Research System

The origin of formal agricultural research in India can be traced to the beginning of the twentieth century, when research laboratories for animal diseases (1895) and crops (1905) were established by the central government. Subsequently, experimental farms were established in different agroclimatic regions in each major state, and some agricultural colleges were also established. "Agricultural research, demonstration, and education" was the theme pursued by the provincial departments of agriculture (Randhawa 1979). These early efforts were unambiguously directed toward peasant and subsistence agriculture. In later years, a bias toward commercial and export crops emerged in research sponsored by the central government, though provincial research remained focused on food crops (Mohan, Jha, and Evenson 1973; Jha 2001).

The Imperial (later renamed Indian) Council of Agricultural Research (ICAR) was established in 1929 on the 1927 recommendation of the Royal

The opinions expressed in this chapter are those of the authors and do not reflect the official position of ICAR.

Commission on Agriculture to promote, guide, and coordinate agricultural research in the country. It was an autonomous body fully funded by the central government. Commodity committees were established to look after research relating to important commercial crops, and a few research institutes were created under the central Ministry of Agriculture. Though ICAR gave modest funding support, it played a coordinating and promoting role, integrating all the central and state entities.

This format persisted for nearly two decades after India achieved independence in 1947. The central ministry established a few more research institutes (focused on fisheries, potatoes, jute, dairy products, arid zones, statistics, and so on) and commodity committees (on oilseeds, areca nuts, spices, and cashews) with their own research establishments. All states established agricultural colleges (usually with zonal research responsibilities) to provide technical manpower for the newly created national extension service and an expanding research establishment.

Continuing agricultural crises, manifesting themselves in production shortfalls, imports, and rising food prices in the years following independence, prompted the government to seek external advice and help for strengthening domestic agricultural R&D capacity. The resulting joint Indo-American teams, agricultural review committees, and so on made far-reaching recommendations on agricultural research and education. Two important organizational innovations in research, including trials on farmers' fields (simple fertilizer trials) and multidisciplinary and multilocational coordinated research on maize, were undertaken. It was acknowledged that developing higher education in agriculture was essential.

Consequently, major reforms in agricultural research and education took place in the 1960s. In 1965–66 all research institutes under the central Ministry of Agriculture and various commodity boards were transferred to ICAR, which was given the responsibility to conduct research in addition to fulfilling its promoting, funding, and coordination roles. The organization became more professional as scientists assumed senior management responsibilities. At the state level, the agricultural university concept became operational, and these universities took over research being undertaken by state departments of agriculture. These departments, however, continued to hold on to mainline extension and technology transfer functions.

These research institutions helped usher in the green revolution beginning in the mid-1960s and established the pivotal role of agricultural research at both the central and the state levels. Accordingly, the coordinated research and state agricultural universities (SAUs) concepts gained widespread acceptance and adoption. For the first time, researchers moved to farmers' fields under the national demonstration programs funded by ICAR. Shortly thereafter, in 1973, another review of ICAR focused on developing a more rational personnel policy for scientists and improving linkages with the Department of Agriculture.

Necessary administrative steps were taken, such as the creation of the Department of Agricultural Research and Education (DARE) in the Ministry of Agriculture to facilitate interministerial coordination, the Agricultural Research Service to provide better incentives to researchers, and the Agricultural Scientists Recruitment Board to streamline recruitment.

These trends continued as the number of ICAR research units increased from 19 to 90 (Randhawa 1979); the number of coordinated research programs rose from a handful to more than 80; the number of agricultural universities increased to 34; and ICAR's involvement and investment in extension through training by *krishi vigyan kendras* (KVKs, farmer science centers) and frontline demonstrations grew substantially. Consequently, by the end of the 1980s the National Agricultural Research System (NARS) was one of the largest and most diverse networks of public institutions of its kind. Its contributions are well documented (Evenson, Pray, and Rosegrant 1999). Table 8.1 presents a synoptic view of this evolutionary process.

Two important points need to be highlighted. First, as ICAR assumed control of centrally sponsored research, the research portfolio was diversified considerably. Research on livestock, fisheries, horticulture, pulses, and oilseeds was strengthened, as was the research on natural resources including soils, water, genetic resources, the environment, frontier themes such as biotechnology, and so on. The 1990s posed fresh challenges in issues relating to trade, changing demand profiles, the fatigue in major cereals (rice and wheat) production and markets, sustainability, diversification, and so on, which began to gain ascendancy over the "foodgrains everywhere" paradigm. Though ICAR had the foresight to initiate relevant programs in the 1980s and 1990s, research lags, continuing rigidities in the state research system, and inadequacies in institutional and supporting processes have inhibited a green revolution kind of impact (ICAR 2000). The second point that should be stressed is that almost all the research institutes have been built on solid foundations of earlier work under coordinated projects or special projects.

Unlike the situation in many developing countries, where research has often been donor-driven and short-lived, systems growth in the core component of NARS (ICAR) has a solid foundation. Despite ICAR's exemplary record, however, since the end of the 1980s questions have been raised about research efficiency (ICAR 1988; World Bank 1990), and impact and accountability have been increasingly invoked as criteria for research evaluation. The National Agricultural Technology Project (NATP) sponsored by the World Bank in 1998 was ICAR's attempt to address some of these concerns.

The Organization of Agricultural Research

Currently, the public research system in India comprises the following at the central (ICAR) level: 90 research institutes, 89 all-India coordinated research programs, 261 KVKs, 8 trainers' training centers, 70 Institute-Village Linkage Program centers, and other frontline extension programs (ICAR, DARE, 2003). At the state level there are 34 SAUs, along with 126 zonal research stations in each agroecological zone in the country.

Figure 8.1 depicts the current organizational structure of public agricultural R&D in India. The two systems, central (ICAR) and state (SAU), are organizationally independent. Linkages are established through funding (block grants, support for coordinated research at universities, and external aided projects), participation in policymaking bodies, policy advice, support for frontline extension and professional interactions, regional coordination committees, and so on. Technology dissemination continues to be handled by the extension departments of the state governments. Very weak extension-research linkages (essentially interorganizational) continue to undermine impacts. Failure to effect any organizational innovation in extension has led to disillusionment all around, and serious discussion has begun on alternative extension approaches (India, Ministry of Agriculture, 2002). More substantively, this has forced ICAR to move further into extension, generating avoidable trade-offs. ICAR's extension budget has grown the most in recent years.

At every level in the system, governing, advisory, and management councils ensure stakeholder or peer participation, although it is ironic that with respect to several of these issues, the public systems and those of nongovernmental organizations are often out of sync, reflecting poor communication. ICAR and the SAUs need to address this hiatus through more intensive as well as wider stakeholder interaction, because the present system is obviously inadequate.

While central-level research is conducted at research institutes under ICAR, the issue of excessive control by headquarters is debated. Similarly, the zonal research stations under the SAUs are undermined by the dominant role of the central-level institutes. The issue of decentralization is linked to bureaucratic control over resources, and this has remained a stumbling block to issue-based accountability in both the central and the state systems. These systems have to grapple with "second-generation problems" relating to organizational rigidities, inefficiencies, and the difficulties of sustaining funding (Pal and Byerlee 2003).

Private sector involvement in agricultural research began in the late 1980s, picked up significantly in the 1990s, and now accounts for 12 to 15 percent of total research investments (Pal and Byerlee 2003). In some cases, private seed companies already have significant market share (Pray, Ramaswami, and Kelley 2001). Multinational companies have also entered the fray, either on their own or in partnership with national companies, amid much debate. Meanwhile, the implications of enlarging the role of the private sector in the public system are being discussed. While there is agreement over the important role of the private sector, the areas of complementarity, competition, and conflict remain gray as both the public and the government grapple with possible long-term consequences

TABLE 8.1 Evolution of central and state agricultural R&D institutions in India, pre-1950s–1990s

Time period	Areas of R&D under ICAR commodity-oriented institutes	Areas of R&D under ICAR resource-oriented institutes	State agricultural universities (SAUs)
Pre-1950s	Indian Agriculture Research Institute, New Delhi: sugarcane breeding, cotton, lac, rice, veterinary science, inland fisheries, marine fisheries, tobacco, research institutes under commodity committees		Agricultural research stations in states, agricultural colleges
1950s	Sugarcane, fisheries technology, jute and allied fiber, dairy products, potatoes	Agricultural statistics, arid zone, soil survey	Uttar Pradesh (1), Orissa, Punjab, Madhya Pradesh (1), Karnataka (1), Maharashtra (1), Maharashtra (2), Assam
1960s	Fisheries, sheep and wool, tuber crops, horticulture, jute and allied fibers technology	Soil salinity, grass and fodder	Maharashtra (3), Haryana, Tamil Nadu (1), Bihar (1), Kerala, Gujarat, West Bengal (1), Uttar Pradesh (2), Uttar Pradesh (3), Himachal Pradesh (1), Andhra Pradesh, NARP zonal research stations
1970s	Plantation crops, cotton, freshwater aquaculture, oilseeds, avian products, goats, groundnuts, subtropical horticulture, wheat	Soil and water, northeastern hills, agricultural engineering, Goa, agricultural research management, plant genetic resources, Andaman and Nicobar Islands, Almora (Hills)	

1980s	Mushrooms, pulses, buffaloes, brackish-water aquaculture, rice, citrus, spices, vegetables, cashews, horses, soybeans, cattle, coldwater fisheries, yaks, *mithun*, camels, sorghum, maize	Fish genetic resources, animal genetic resources, dryland agriculture, plant agriculture, biotechnology, postharvest engineering, cropping systems, soil, integrated pest management, agroforestry, water technology, weed control	Bihar (2), Jammu and Kashmir (1), Jammu and Kashmir (2), Himachal Pradesh (2), Karnataka (2), Madhya Pradesh (2), Tamil Nadu (2), Rajasthan (1)
1990s	Temperate horticulture, meat and meat products, arid horticulture, grapes, bananas, rapeseed and mustard, onions and garlic, poultry, medicinal and aromatic plants, oil palms, orchids	Water management, agricultural economics and policy research, biological control, animal nutrition and physiology, seed spices, women in agriculture, DNA fingerprinting, microorganisms	West Bengal (2), Manipur (4), Uttar Pradesh (5), West Bengal (3), Rajasthan (2), Maharashtra (5)

NOTE: The numbers in parentheses in the last column indicate the number of SAUs in each state.

FIGURE 8.1 Institutional structure of the public agricultural research system in India at present

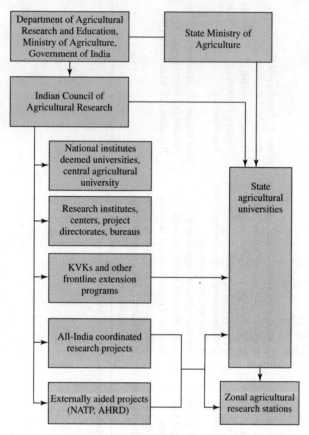

linked with issues such as intellectual property rights, World Trade Organization (WTO) membership, and environmental and public health issues.

Resources for Agricultural Research

A pro-research policy environment since the mid-1960s has undermined the need for systematic monitoring of research resources. This deficiency persists, and to date, there have been no official estimates on the level or allocation of financial or scientific manpower resources in NARS. In compliance with the financial regulations of the government, both central and state entities report expenditures under broad headings such as salaries, capital, contingent expenditures, and so on, but not in terms of research programs, and therefore very little analytical work can be done with these data. Lip service has been paid to concepts such as project- or zero-based budgeting, but implementation remains poor. Information on human resources is completely lacking, and ad hoc studies by individual researchers are the main source of such information (Evenson and Jha 1973; Rao and Muralidhar 1994; Ranjitha 1996; Pal and Byerlee 2003). Over the past decade or so, the research system has been going through a severe resource crunch, finding it difficult to maintain ongoing programs. The problem is particularly acute for the SAUs. With managers of public finance beginning to ask questions regarding the priority and probity of R&D expenditures, the system, including the extension services, is losing ground.

Financial Resources

Because all SAUs and national institutes of ICAR have the mandate to conduct both agricultural research and education and because these two types of activities are interwoven, we provide combined estimates of the government expenditure for both types of activities. Table 8.2 shows the overall trend in real government expenditures, decadal growth rates, and intensity indicators over the past 30 years.[1] There has been close to 5 percent growth in real expenditures over the past three decades. Considering the size of the country, this is impressive and bears testimony of the generally pro-research environment there.

The reorganization of NARS in the 1960s is reflected in the high rate of growth in research investments. This was the most proactive period of rejuvenation, and it spilled over to the 1980s as the research system (both ICAR and state entities) geared up to build infrastructure and confront food production challenges. There was some deceleration in the 1990s. Table 8.2 also shows that intensity indicators have improved and that research investments now represent close to 0.5 percent of the agricultural GDP (AgGDP) of the country, which is no mean achievement for a large sector that grew at more than 3 percent per annum during this period. There is a consensus on raising the rate of such investments to 1 percent over the next five years, but implementation falters on account of fiscal constraints and a creeping complacency at the policy level induced by current agricultural surpluses. For these reasons, attention is subtly shifting from more investments to greater efficiency in the tenth five-year plan (2002–7). One needs to note, however, that the modernization of research capability needs heavy investments, because tools such as biotechnology, remote sensing, space research, information technology, and so on are increasingly involved. The private sector offers opportunities, but it is a real challenge for research planners to dovetail public and private resources.

---

1. For detailed descriptions of the data and their sources, see Pal and Byerlee (2003).

TABLE 8.2 Investments in agricultural research and education in India, 1971, 1981, 1991, and 2000

Triennium ending	Research expenditure		Research intensity indicators		
	Million Rs.	Purchasing power parity, million U.S.$	Expenditure (% of AgGDP)	Expenditure per ha of net sown area (Rs.)	Expenditure per farm holding (Rs.)
1971	6,073	702	0.32	41.00	101.80
	(8.61*)		(4.74*)	(8.32*)	
1981	8,007	926	0.40	56.91	89.18
	(1.89)		(1.30)	(1.73*)	
1991	13,528	1,564	0.45	85.11	126.81
	(5.19*)		(1.73*)	(5.26*)	
2000	20,773	2,402	0.50	125.56	150.24
	(4.02*)		(0.60)	(3.06*)	
Growth rate 1971–2000	4.37*	4.37*	1.43*	4.11*	2.16*

SOURCE: Based on data in Pal and Byerlee (2003).

NOTES: The figures in parentheses are growth rates for the preceding decade. Growth rates marked with an * are statistically significant at the 1 percent level. The number of farm holdings for 2000 is an estimate. Values are expressed in 1999 constant prices.

States were the major players in the preindependence and subsequent periods, and in the early years of the green revolution they accounted for nearly 70 percent of total R&D expenditures (Table 8.3). This percentage has fallen to nearly half of the total expenditures in recent years, with funds from the central system expanding at a faster rate. Proliferation of the research agenda and inadequate capacity in any individual state to assume a national mandate prompted this trend. Now that a core capacity has been established in most areas under ICAR, and given the precarious position of state finances to sustain these long-term assets, there is a strong case for transferring funds from the central system to states incrementally.

These funds should be more objectively targeted toward state-specific research at the zonal research stations. This will reinforce the basic paradigm that applied research is best done location-specifically and implies that the central system (ICAR) will need to shed some location-specific responsibilities, such as "niche" commodities and frontline extension programs like the KVKs.

The national profile conceals considerable interstate variation in research investment. In many important states, such as Madhya Pradesh, Rajasthan, Uttar Pradesh, and West Bengal, research intensity is still meager. In fact, interstate variability in research intensity has increased over time (Table 8.4). Obviously the favorable winds that encouraged investment in the central system (ICAR) did not blow uniformly across the states. Some states may have opted for a free-

TABLE 8.3 Research and education investments in agriculture by the central and state governments in India, 1971, 1981, 1991, and 2000

Triennium ending	Research and education investment (million Rs.)		Share of states in total invesment (percent)
	Center	States	
1971	1,875	4,198	69.19
	(10.62*)	(7.94*)	
1981	3,813	4,194	52.38
	(6.81*)	(–1.32)	
1991	5,871	7,657	56.61
	(3.96*)	(6.22*)	
2000	10,291	10,483	50.46
	(4.87*)	(3.29*)	
Growth rate, 1971–2000	4.93*	4.01*	—

SOURCE: Based on data from Pal and Byerlee (2003).

NOTES: The figures in parentheses are growth rates for the preceding decade. Growth rates marked with an * are statistically significant at the 1 percent level. Values are expressed in 1999 constant prices.

TABLE 8.4 Regional variation in the intensity of agricultural R&D funding by the states of India, 1997–99

Funding as a share of AgGDP (percent)	States
<0.20	Madhya Pradesh, Rajasthan, Uttar Pradesh, West Bengal
0.21–0.30	Andhra Pradesh, Bihar, Karnataka, Orissa, Punjab
0.31—0.50	Assam, Gujarat, Haryana, Kerala, Maharashtra
>0.51	Himachal Pradesh, Tamil Nadu
Interstate variation (CV) (percent)	
1981–83	60.39
1997–99	86.10

SOURCE: Based on data from Pal and Byerlee (2003).

ride strategy, counting on spillovers. In fact, the coordinated research strategy of ICAR might have encouraged this. This hypothesis needs testing, although it must be pointed out that even without further analysis the trends substantiate the need for greater emphasis on lagging states. Pal and Singh (1997) demonstrate that the availability of public resources and the importance assigned to agriculture explain interstate variability in research intensity. Because these variables are overwhelmed by short-term sociopolitical compulsions in states, the compensatory role of central funding becomes obvious.

Scientific Manpower

Human resources is a major component of research capability that received strong emphasis during the early years. By the end of the 1980s, more than 20,000 postgraduates manned the agricultural research and education system. A research degree (Ph.D.) is now a necessary qualification for recruitment beyond the entry level. Except for the early years (when the first batch of trainers were trained in U.S. land-grant institutions), this manpower has been developed indigenously, and ICAR played a pivotal role in building this capacity in the states.

Although reliable data on scientific manpower in agriculture are not available, ICAR accounts for about a quarter of the scientists in the system. This number increased at a modest rate of 2.2 percent in the 1990s against a much higher growth rate of 4.9 percent in expenditures, reflecting the increasing costs of manpower and other components of research. The average expenditure per scientist, at 1999 prices, rose from Rs. 0.72 million in 1981 to Rs 1.11 million in 1991, and further to Rs. 1.79 million in 2001 (Figure 8.2). In the state research system, there has been stagnation or perhaps a decline in scientific manpower over the past 10–15 years. This is a more telling constraint, because it affects not only research but also agricultural education and hits teaching-research complementarity.

Qualitative Dimensions

Despite impressive investments, there were concerns in the 1990s about the quality of research. Over four-fifths of the budget in the state system is used for salaries, leaving very little for upkeep and operational needs. This obviously distorts the balance between manpower and other resources. Grants from the central system under various coordinated research programs and, recently, grants from NATP (the World Bank's National Agricultural Technology Project), barely keep the system afloat. The central system is in a better position, with ICAR able to muster more support from the central pool, although poor financial management and bureaucratic procedures impede productivity (NAAS 2002).

In human resources, qualitative deficiencies have emerged, suggesting the need for a review of the agricultural education policy. There is awareness of the deteriorating quality of higher education due to institutional inbreeding, deteriorating infrastructure, inadequate capacity in frontier areas, a growing number of vacancies, and so on. ICAR, as the coordinating body in this area, is grappling with these issues intellectually as well as substantively, but the problem is the continued dominance of the "indigenous" paradigm in its thinking. In this era of knowledge explosion and proprietary science, this paradigm accentuates the "knowledge divide" and vintage (Jha 2001). ICAR has not been able to think beyond short-term training in frontier institutions abroad, even as

FIGURE 8.2 Scientific manpower and expenditure per scientist in the Indian Council of Agricultural Research, 1981, 1991, and 2001

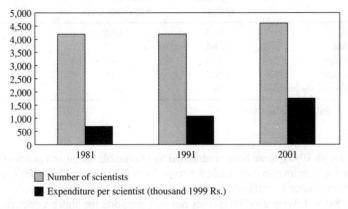

Number of scientists

Expenditure per scientist (thousand 1999 Rs.)

SOURCE: Based on data compiled from ICAR records.

countries such as Brazil and China are focusing on revitalizing their systems around graduates trained in developed countries. This clearly must change in India.

These problems are well recognized internally, and both the World Bank's NATP and Agricultural Human Resource Development projects have sought to address them. Of late, acute financial crisis has led to economizing measures in programs everywhere, including research. It is doubtful whether public funds will be available to sustain the measures initiated under the two World Bank projects, let alone implement new initiatives. As funds dwindle, such long-term priorities invariably lose out to populist programs. The crisis confronting NARS may be aggravated if corrective measures are not taken in time. What is required is a two-pronged strategy emphasizing the need to protect the priority given to agricultural R&D on the one hand and aggressive internal policies to raise research productivity on the other. The former implies better interface with policy at both central and state levels, while the latter implies the need for an internal overhaul.

The Impact of Agricultural Research

Several evaluations over the past three decades have shown the high profitability of agricultural research investments (Evenson, Pray, and Rosegrant 1999; Jha 2001; Pal and Byerlee 2003). The studies have involved analyses at several levels (aggregate, individual enterprise, national, regional, and local) and at varying levels of sophistication. Despite methodological problems (Alston, Pardey,

TABLE 8.5 Internal rate of return to research investment in India (percent)

	Aggregate analysis	Analysis of individual crops	All
Mean	75.4	69.9	71.8
Median	58.5	53.0	57.5
Minimum	46.0	6.0	6.0
Maximum	218.2	174.0	218.2
Number of studies	10	18	28

SOURCE: Pal and Byerlee (2003).

and Smith 1999), these have contributed to a favorable social and political climate for such investments. Table 8.5 reproduces Pal and Byerlee's (2003) summary of studies in India on the rate of return to such investments.

Pal and Byerlee's (2003) study not only supports the high productivity of research investments, but also highlights the fact that many research initiatives do not generate exploitable results. This should not come as a surprise, because research is an uncertain process and failures outnumber successes. Such studies have dispelled doubts that research success has been confined to a few crops and regions (mainly irrigated). Nevertheless, legitimate knowledge gaps continue to exist (both in terms of enterprises and situations); despite research investments, success has been elusive. Also, there is concern that even in the case of major crops (rice and wheat) there has been a deceleration of total factor productivity growth in recent years (Kumar et al. 2002). The studies suggest a downward slide in research productivity.

On the other hand, the evaluation methods used do not adequately capture the benefits from technical improvements such as increased stability, wider adaptation, increased shelf life, contributions to area growth and intensity through shorter-duration crop varieties, land reclamation technologies, more efficient irrigation, better resource management technologies, and so on. This results in underestimation of the impact of such improvements at the aggregate level.

Questions regarding the equity impacts of technological change have centered on regional disparities, employment, farm size, poverty, and so on. These are complex issues requiring elaborate analysis. In a multienterprise, highly diverse agriculture, it is difficult to assess the net effects. Early studies on the green revolution, for example, showed a favorable impact on employment, but current literature suggests the declining labor intensity of agriculture. Similarly, some of the regions (semiarid and eastern) deprived in the 1970s have shown better performance later. Recent studies at the aggregate level have pointed out that agricultural research is a powerful instrument not only for growth but also to combat rural and urban poverty (Fan, Hazell, and Thorat 1999; Fan 2003). On the other hand, a hypothesis has been proposed that the high capital intensity of some recently introduced technologies puts small farmers (more than 80 percent of Indian farmers) at a disadvantage, in contrast to the green revolution impact, which was largely size-neutral (Jha 2001).

The deterioration of natural resources has also been attributed to new technologies. Increasing use of chemicals, overexploitation and degradation of soil and water, and loss of biodiversity are frequently cited as examples of negative externalities that arose out of technologies of the green revolution. These have spawned a whole range of research initiatives on mitigating negative environmental externalities. At the other end, technologies for the rehabilitation of problem soils, soil and water conservation (particularly watersheds, agroforestry, zero tillage, and drip and sprinkler irrigation) have made significant positive impacts, albeit locally. In general, there has been little evaluation of crop and resource management technologies, though these have claimed considerable research resources.

Two issues need to be kept in mind. First, impacts, either positive or negative, crucially depend on the policy regime. Positive effects of a proactive output or input price regime, as well as negative externalities emanating from it, are well documented. Second, institutional inadequacies and lack of appropriate institutions often undermine the potential contributions of technologies. The government has been the major player in the institutional arena, and weaknesses here are well documented (Pal et al. 2003). It is important to make this point because policy and institutional inadequacies are often attributed to technology failure. This distorts the political and social perspectives and, in a sense, turns opinions against R&D. Lack of effective policy dialogue and interaction is emerging as a constraint confronting NARS at the policy level.

Contemporary Issues in the Indian NARS

The NARS faces several challenges, arising from both internal as well as external factors. The need to increase the efficiency of the public research system, improve the management of intellectual property, address the emerging role of the private sector in modern biotechnology research, and enhance the competitiveness of technology markets are some of the important issues highlighted in this section.

Reforming the Public Research System

While the public research system has effectively addressed the critical research needs in the past, concerns are now being raised about the efficiency of the system. Over time, ICAR has shown remarkable openness, while in sharp contrast, the SAU system has remained the same since its inception, responding only to ICAR-led (and -funded) initiatives in education and research. Both systems, however, failed to maintain their autonomous status and have surrendered autonomy and flexibility to the government bureaucracy. This and the lack of effective mechanisms to ensure the relevance, efficiency, and accountability of public-funded R&D remain the core reform issue. The focus now is on addressing this problem through the institutionalization of improved management information and research planning processes and the linking of funding with performance in a project mode.

The division of labor between ICAR and state systems continues to be hamstrung by the perception, which has lingered since the 1960s, that state research is weak and ill-equipped. The ICAR-controlled research programs grew rapidly, and the state system remained more or less static, except for the creation of a few more SAUs from the existing state infrastructure. Although the expansion of ICAR has improved research infrastructure and many ICAR programs have been implemented by SAUs, this expansion has also led to the greater centralization of agricultural research, with the result that research priority has been given to the national agenda instead of local needs. This has been further underlined by the lack of a systematic mechanism to feed regional priorities into the national agenda. It is time to seriously assess local and state research needs and the appropriate role for ICAR in addressing them. Over the past 30 years, the required infrastructure has been created with ICAR's help. Assistance should now be directed toward efficient use of this infrastructure to realize synergies between the ICAR and SAU systems.

Another issue that needs attention is improving the relevance of research by focusing research on the basis of ecological regions and production systems. At present, ICAR research is largely organized along commodity or resource lines, whereas disciplinary orientation is the rule in SAUs. The concept of eco-regional research is well accepted by the system, and both NATP and the recent review of ICAR (ICAR, DARE, 2003) have highlighted the need to narrow the ecoregional focus. However, the organizational implications of this paradigm shift need to be carefully assessed, because it will involve decentralizing research planning and dismantling current institutional and disciplinary rigidities. It can be addressed through the use of improved methods of research planning involving a participatory and bottom-up approach.

The other concern is the declining scientific productivity and quality. This is related, among other things, to distorted incentive and reward structures and the absence of effective prioritization, monitoring, and evaluation mechanisms. Quality is also related to the caliber of the institutions for human resource development in agriculture. Laxity in responding to these problems will impair the effectiveness of the system in the long term and erode its capacity to remain globally competitive in science and technology.

While poor linkages between disciplines, institutions, extension, farmers, and other stakeholders have been traditional weaknesses of the system, they have now become crucial. One of the initiatives taken to improve integration and widen stakeholder participation has been the establishment, on a pilot basis, of the Agriculture Technology Management Agency, which includes members from the research and state extension systems and from other institutions and agencies. This agency is responsible for developing research and extension plans and overseeing the implementation of extension programs at the district level.

Past R&D efforts of the public agricultural research system have been highly rewarding and over a generation have elicited popular as well as government support. This very success now threatens future support, because Indian society expects green revolution–type research and is disappointed when that is not performed. Small but significant successes go largely unheralded due to the lack of credible social and economic evaluation capacity within NARS.

Protecting Intellectual Property Rights

Protection of intellectual property rights (IPR) in agriculture was not encouraged in India. It was perceived as a threat to national food security. Agricultural chemicals and veterinary drugs, however, were protected through process patents. Today, to bring the incentives for intellectual property protection to a par with internationally accepted norms under the WTO, the scope of such protection is extended to agriculture, and a number of pieces of legislation have recently been enacted. The Patent Amendment Act (2002) allows the patenting of both processes and products and is applicable to agricultural chemicals, veterinary vaccines and drugs, food processing, and so on. Trademark, copyright, and design legislation already existed, while legislation for biodiversity, recognizing the ownership of genetic resources, and geographical indication has been enacted more recently.

The Plant Variety Protection and Farmers' Rights (PVPFR) Act (2001), providing for the protection of plant varieties through either a sui generis system or some form of patenting, has engaged public attention in the recent past. This act is considered crucial for promoting research (particularly through private investment) and overcoming critical technical constraints on access to improved cultivars. The Seed Act (1966) is also under revision. ICAR has established plant, animal, fish, and microorganism genetic resource bureaus to strengthen documentation of the wealth of indigenous life. It created senior IPR positions at its headquarters, initiated studies on indigenous technologies under NATP, and started dialogues with private sector R&D players to evolve protocols for sharing and using intellectual property.

Addressing Private R&D

The developments on protecting IPR are expected to accelerate the privatization of research. The evidence indicates that private research investment is growing rapidly, and there is an increasing tendency to protect IPR. The number of patents being filed by research organizations is growing fast (Ramanna 2002). The seed sector in particular is expanding rapidly and changing structurally.

Private seed companies are finding it more attractive to develop and sell proprietary material to capture a significant proportion of the seed market (Tripp and Pal 2000; Pray and Basant 2001).

Effective implementation of the PVPFR Act is expected to promote private plant breeding in the long run. The immediate effect would be in terms of increased access to seeds developed by transnational seed companies, which basically means that Indian farmers will have multiple choices and access to improved seed, which can have a positive effect on crop productivity. At the same time, this could create some degree of concentration in the seed market because of substantial investments made by some transnational seed companies. The provision of compulsory licensing and the presence of a strong public breeding program for developing varieties, which can be delivered by public and private seed agencies, are useful options to control monopolistic tendencies (Pal and Tripp 2002).

The provisions of the PVPFR Act regarding mandatory registration of plant varieties, farmers' right to sell unbranded seed, and the sovereign rights of the country, local communities, and farmers over genetic resources are considered somewhat detrimental to private plant breeding (SAI 2001). There could be some truth in this, but it is also true that one needs to protect genetic resources, also covered by the Biodiversity Convention, and to encourage the free flow of seed among farmers. Public ownership of genetic resources could also be used to bargain for access to proprietary technology to promote a competitive seed industry (Fischer and Byerlee 2002).

Another fear is that a seed industry dominated by the private sector may not serve resource-poor farmers in marginal areas and may raise seed prices beyond the reach of small farmers. This fear is not unrealistic, and the government should closely monitor the seed sector with an appropriate mix of measures such as laws, fiscal incentives, and the direct supply of seed to farmers.

Although a number of institutions in India were started through private initiative, private agricultural R&D still forms a peripheral part of the Indian NARS. This is despite the strong fiscal incentives in the form of complete income tax exemption for R&D expenditure and concessional duty rates on imports of equipment by an R&D organization. The situation is gradually improving with the expanding market for agricultural technologies, the easing of entry barriers, and the greater protection of intellectual property. As a result, private R&D investment has been growing at a much faster rate (7.5 percent per annum) over the past two decades, with growth much faster in the seed and food processing sectors. Most of the private investment is for R&D on pesticides, fertilizers, farm machinery, and seeds (Table 8.6).

The increasing application of biotechnology in agriculture should further fuel private R&D. The advancements on this front could be constrained by only two factors: farm realities and the credibility of IPR regulations. A large subsistence sector and a tradition of using farm-produced or -exchanged seeds may

TABLE 8.6 Private investment in agricultural research in India

Type of industry	Research expenditure (million 1995 Rs.)	Annual growth, 1985–95 (percent)	Share in state enterprises (percent)
Seed	165	13.1	0
Machinery	216	5.6	13
Fertilizer	222	-0.2	67
Pesticide	568	6.4	15
Veterinary	91	11.1	5
Sugar	83	10.2	1
Food processing	45	20.6	1
Total	801	7.5	16

SOURCE: Pray and Basant (2001).

force the nascent domestic seed sector to grow rather slowly. Inadequate documentation of domestic plant and animal wealth and knowledge on the one hand, and the populist threat of exploitation and dominance on the other, may prompt a cautious response to effective implementation of the WTO–driven IPR mechanisms, slowing down the pace of private R&D for agriculture.

One way to address this problem could be private R&D organizations' continuation of traditional methods for the protection of intellectual property, such as the use of trade secrets and technology-embedded inputs. This is particularly relevant for the dominant seed sector, where private plant breeding efforts are concentrated on hybrids and a seed company can protect parent material, that is, inbred lines. Finally, whatever may be the state of private R&D, strong public research must coexist to increase research intensity, restrict monopolistic tendencies, and therefore serve resource-poor farmers.

Making the Best Use of Biotechnology and Genetically Modified Food

Biotechnology research in ICAR was initiated in the early 1990s. The Department of Bio-Technology (DBT) of the central Ministry of Science and Technology also has programs relevant to agriculture. Research on transgenics is still nascent, although techniques such as tissue and cell culture, DNA fingerprinting, and molecular breeding have found practical application. In terms of research focus, emphasis is on tolerance to abiotic (drought-, salt-, and cold-induced) and biotic stresses, improvement of plant type, improvement of product quality and nutritive value, management of postharvest losses, and so on. Institutional response to transgenic research addresses issues relating to testing and evaluation norms.

Biosafety, human health, and environmental externalities are critical issues being carefully assessed by interministerial (biotechnology, health, environment, agriculture) groups. DBT has issued guidelines for the regulation of transgenic research, the conduct of such research, and the use of its products, genetically modified (GM) seeds, in India. The Review Committee on Genetic Manipulation of the DBT, comprising representatives from various scientific organizations, is responsible for monitoring research in transgenics and its safety-related aspects, and also for regulating import and export of transgenics. The policy is that only environmentally safe and economically viable transgenics will be recommended for release and commercial cultivation (India, DBT, 1998). The Genetic Engineering Approval Committee of the Ministry of Environment and Forest evaluates the results and recommends a transgenic variety for commercial cultivation if it qualifies under the provisions of the Environmental Protection Act (1986). The PVPFR Act also envisages protection of essentially derived varieties (primarily GM varieties) with proper guidelines for use of GM seed, for instance, the planting of "refugia" and labeling of GM seed. Both public and private sector materials pass through these time-consuming processes, but the policy stance is noncompromising.

The global debate on GM crops influenced the Indian scene as well, and it was only recently (2002) that the first GM crop, Bt (*Bacillus thuringiensis*) cotton, was approved for commercial production. Several other crops (e.g., potatoes, rapeseed, and mustard) are under advanced stages of evaluation, even as public opinion continues to be divided on GM foods. While research on edible oilseed and vegetable transgenics is ongoing, the policy on commercial use is still negative. Public expenditure on agricultural biotechnology in India was about U.S.$27 million in 2000, or 40 percent higher than that in 1990. Given the capital intensity of biotech research and the scale of commodity coverage, production environments, and research problems, this level of investment is abysmally low. There is much potential for forging linkages between the private and public sectors to enhance overall impacts. These linkages could also be useful because advances in biotechnology have blurred differences, making close linkages between general science and technology providers necessary. These public-private linkages can be fostered by putting in place an appropriate mechanism for the sharing of costs and benefits, establishing joint ventures, and management and ownership of intellectual property.

A dimension often neglected in the regulation is coherence between various acts governing an industry or sector. For instance, biotech research in India is governed by a number of pieces of legislation, notably the Seeds Act, Environmental Protection Act, PVPFR Act, Essential Commodity Act, Consumer Protection Act, and Biodiversity Act, as well as acts dealing with agricultural marketing. Coherence between these acts is essential so as not to neutralize the positive aspects of these provisions and hamper the growth of private research.

Finally, there is inadequate flow of information about new technologies to farmers (Tripp and Pal 2000). Because much of this information is a public good, public institutions and government will have to take major responsibility for providing information to farmers.

There are a number of issues to be addressed on the product side as well. A positive side of GM products, particularly those with the trait of tolerance to biotic stress, is that they may be less toxic because of less pesticide residue and thus may be preferred by consumers. Health concerns can be addressed by (1) rigorous testing for possible negative health effects, (2) education of consumers about the quality aspect of GM products, and (3) labeling of products. On the trade side, there could be a negative impact in the sense that trade in agricultural products (such as rice that is exported) may be adversely affected by the importing countries' banning cultivation and use of GM crops under the WTO's sanitary and phytosanitary provisions. So far, India has also banned the import of GM food. Oilseeds and pulses are other potential crops for which transgenics may be allowed, but there may not be any negative impact because India is a net importer for these crops. A clearer picture will emerge when most countries take a definite stand on GM products.

Concluding Remarks

The Indian NARS continues to be largely a public entity in spite of the major fiscal and legal incentives provided to attract private investment. This scenario is expected to change with the strengthening of incentives provided by the protection of intellectual property. The government and the public research system need to respond to this by developing a national innovation system that embraces all actors—researchers, extension workers, traders, institutions, and farmers—and is based on an integrated paradigm of agricultural and rural development.

Adequate capacity needs to be developed for modern biotechnology as well as for accessing and managing research in a partnership mode, particularly that emerging from several actors. This requires putting in place transparent and credible regulation mechanisms. Finally, the public research system needs to be reformed to improve its effectiveness and efficiency. The development of management information systems, decentralization of administrative authority, and closer partnerships with farming communities, the private sector, and extension departments are critical. These reforms should be carried out for both the ICAR and the SAU systems, along with increasing the flow of additional funds and the development of human resources, particularly at the state level.

9 Policy and Institutional Reforms in the Water Sector: Experiences and Lessons from China and India

RAMASWAMY R. IYER, K. V. RAJU, AND JINXIA WANG

Increasing water scarcity is one of the key challenges that must be addressed if China and India are to meet their national development objectives in the coming years. The two countries account for nearly 62 percent of the total water depletion in Asia and 36 percent in the world (Rosegrant, Cai, and Cline 2002). Shortages of water are undermining efforts to alleviate poverty and are becoming a major source of environmental concern. In many regions of these two countries, rapidly growing industry and an expanding and increasingly wealthy urban population have better access to limited water resources than farmers, threatening to curtail growth in food production.

Failure of traditional methods coupled with financial, political, socio-economic, and environmental constraints have motivated leaders in the two countries to adopt water demand management as a key strategy to combat water problems, obviously with a view to increasing water use efficiency.

In this chapter we describe the key features and experiences of China and India in terms of water policy, institutional issues, irrigation reform, and their integral relationship to food security to draw lessons and make suggestions for the future. This chapter has two parts: the first focuses on China and the second on India.

Water Resources and Irrigation Development in China

Because China's total annual rainfall occurs mostly over a couple of months, water conservation and irrigation systems have always been an integral part of its agriculture.[1] The average annual precipitation is 600–700 mm, with wide regional and seasonal variations. Precipitation is concentrated in the summer months and can vary from 2,000 mm in the south to less than 400 mm in some areas of northern China. The country has three irrigation zones: (1) the area of

---

The authors of this chapter are listed alphabetically and share equal authorship.
1. This section relies heavily on FAO Aquastat (2004) and Fan, Zhang, and Zhang (2002).

permanent irrigation where precipitation is less than 400 mm, covering the north-west and the middle section of the Huanghe River; (2) the zone most influenced by the monsoon and thus with irregular precipitation ranging between 400–1,000 mm, including the Hangh Huai Hai Plain and the northeast; and (3) the area of auxiliary irrigation in southwest China, where precipitation is more than 1,000 mm a year.

The largest expansion of irrigation took place during 1953–80, when the irrigated area increased from 16 million hectares (ha) to 45 million ha, grow-ing at a rate of almost 2.3 percent a year. By the late 1990s, it had come close to 50–55 million hectares and over 53 percent of the arable land in 1997, rising from 23.2 percent in 1953. About 70 percent of foodgrains as well as most of the cotton and other cash crops are grown on irrigated land.

Based on the scale of irrigation schemes, irrigated land is divided into large (over 20,000 ha), medium (667–20,000 ha), and small irrigation districts (un-der 667 ha). There are 173 large irrigation districts covering nearly 8.8 million ha and more than 5,300 medium districts covering 13.7 million ha. Both of these categories of scheme are run by government agencies, while the small ones are mostly managed by farmers.

Many Chinese rivers are tapped for irrigation. In China, about 1,500 rivers have basins of over 1,000 km^2. The overall mean river run-off is 2,711 km^3 per year. However, the spatial distribution of these water resources, the bulk of them concentrated in southern China, helps to explain why there are water shortages despite the endowments of large rivers and the total water supply. The Yangtze and Yellow Rivers supply 35 percent of the country's surface irrigation water through a system of dams and reservoirs that also function as flood-control units. Annual usable supplies in the two river basins doubled, and in some cases tripled, after 1949 as a result of an ambitious program of dam construction. The northern and northeastern provinces make extensive use of groundwater re-sources that are estimated at roughly 800–900 km^3.

By the late 1990s, nearly 85,000 reservoirs had been constructed, with a storage capacity of over 458 billion cubic meters (BCM). Fewer than 400 are large reservoirs with a capacity of 350 km^3 or more, while the rest are medium and small in size, with a capacity of 72 km^3 and 59 km^3 or more, respectively. Reservoirs are the main source of irrigation, accounting for nearly 31 percent of the total, followed by river diversion (28 percent), pump lifting from rivers (19 percent), and groundwater (18 percent).

Because irrigation has been a top priority since 1949, investment in irri-gation grew rapidly at 17.5 percent a year over 1953–78. Nearly 20 million ha were brought under irrigation during that period. But investment declined there-after, by 5.3 percent a year between the late 1970s and the late 1980s, with no increase in irrigated areas. In response to the grain shortfall and large imports in 1994–95, the government again increased its irrigation spending in 1996 and 1997. The northwestern region accounted for the largest increase in the 1990s, followed by the North China Plain. Despite that, irrigated area as a percentage of total land increased very little. Water use was estimated to be around 550 km³ in 2000, with domestic uses accounting for 10 percent, industrial consumption 21 percent, and agricultural use 69 percent.

Water Sector Policies and Institutions in China

Until recently, water saving and management was not a major concern of policy-makers in China. Instead, their priorities were to (1) manage the prevention of floods that have historically devastated the areas surrounding the major rivers and (2) effectively divert and exploit water resources for agricultural and industrial development. Indeed, China's success in meeting the second goal is the main reason the nation faces water shortages today.

In the past, developing water resources to increase supply was given the highest priority to meet shortages. Since the 1950s, China's government has invested more than U.S.$ 100 billion in infrastructure in developing new water resources (Wang 2000). Recently the State Council announced plans to allocate more than U.S.$ 50 billion for the construction of a project to move water from the Yangtze River Valley to north China. Despite such ambitious goals, the high cost of developing new sources of water will ensure that the volume of water that can be added to north China's water equation remains marginal. Leaders have also promoted water-saving technologies and considered whether they should use water pricing policy (Chen 2002; Rosegrant and Cai 2002) as a deterrent. Unfortunately, efforts to encourage the use of sophisticated water-saving technologies, such as drip and sprinkler irrigation, have largely failed, and the Ministry of Water Resources (MWR) has distanced itself from a policy based on water-saving technology (Zai 2002). Political considerations are keeping leaders from moving too aggressively on raising prices, at least in agriculture (Rosegrant and Cai 2002).

Instead, China's leaders have recently begun to consider water institutions and management reforms as key strategies to combat China's water problems. Despite water shortages, users in all sectors of the economy do not efficiently use the water that they are allocated. One study, for example, estimated that, due to the poor management of the canal network, only 50 percent of waters from primary canals are actually delivered to the fields (Xu 2001). There is further waste, of about 20–30 percent, of the water that actually reaches the field. Overall, only about 40 percent of the surface water allocated to agricultural production is actually used by farmers. Others have estimated even greater inefficiencies (Fang 2000). As a result, local leaders have been asked to reform the institutions that manage water among China's communities (Nian 2001; Reidinger 2002).

Water Management Institutions and Reform

Over the past 50 years, a vast and complex bureaucracy has grown up to manage water resources. The MWR formulates and implements the national water price and allocation policies and oversees water conservation investments through technical guidance to and regulatory oversight of the subnational agencies. It invests in developing the water resources from all large rivers and lakes through projects that cover more than one province. Local governments are in charge of projects within their administrative districts. Historically, investments from national funding sources have been heavily biased toward new projects, and responsibility for maintenance funds has been left to the local governments. Although much of China's water is still used by farmers in agriculture, the nation's water policy is becoming increasingly biased toward industry.

Under the 1988 Water Law, the MWR is not solely responsible for all water-related policies; other ministries influence water policy for both rural and urban areas. The diverse uses, objectives, and interests of water management agencies often result in conflicts and inefficient exploitation. For example, the MWR is in charge of agricultural water management, while the Urban Construction Bureau is in charge of urban water management. In the noncropping season, even if there is enough canal water that can be used for urban domestic and industrial uses, the bureau does not tap into it but instead explores groundwater resources. Such a management system has resulted in inefficient water allocation between rural and urban sectors as well as between surface and groundwater resources.

To get around officials from competing ministries who are working to divert as much of the scarce resource for their constituents as possible, many provinces and municipalities are promoting reforms to merge the functions of different water management units into a single authority. Although such units have different names in different places, they are most commonly called Water Affairs Bureaus (WABs or *shuiwuju*). In the most extreme cases, the WABs merge personnel, resources, and duties of the local Water Resource Bureau, the Urban Construction Commission, and the water protection division of the local Environmental Protection Bureau into a single unit.

In addition to establishing the WABs, since the late 1990s the government has also strengthened the integrated river basin management in some large river basins with serious water conflicts, such as the Yellow River Basin. However, due to the relatively high transaction costs associated with such an approach, the government is now considering the application of economic (water pricing) and market (water rights transfer) measures to realize the sustainable management of water resources.

Increasing Investment and Reversing Infrastructure Deterioration

An important aspect of China's overall water management capacity is the nature of its water recovery, storage, and delivery infrastructure. While decollectivization in the late 1970s and the early 1980s led to jumps in agricultural productivity and production, these same reforms led to ambiguous property rights over many local water delivery systems built under the people's communes, undermining the local governments' ability to invest in large infrastructure projects. The ambiguity over ownership of these systems generated weak incentives to maintain and invest in them. Moreover, transfers of investment funds from the national to local governments fell, further decreasing local governments' ability to invest in maintaining water storage and delivery infrastructure. This lack of strong incentives and ability to invest in surface water delivery infrastructure is partly responsible for the decrease in the effectiveness of surface water systems. In turn, the decline of these systems was partly behind the stagnation in grain production and rising food prices from the mid-1980s to the mid-1990s.

Decrease in irrigated area and rising food prices led to a consensus that more attention needed to be given to agriculture and generated a rebound in investment in the late 1980s. After the 1988 Water Law, investment increased from 4.9 billion yuan in 1990 to 13 billion yuan in 1995, equivalent to 3 percent of total national investment. Officials have also announced a shift in investment priorities, from new projects to renovation and maintenance of existing systems (Nyberg and Rozelle 1999).

As public investment in surface water systems waned and deliveries became more unreliable, farmers in north China began to rely more on small irrigation systems fed by groundwater. The emergence of private entrepreneurs as water suppliers has allowed many regions to maintain irrigated agricultural production even with a decline in groundwater levels. The emergence of private wells has not only led to better services but may also bring about more efficient water deliveries for on-farm water use for individual farmers. However, this does not necessarily mean that China will be able to avert a more drastic water crisis in the future.

Incentives to Reduce Farm Water Consumption

Even with an impending water crisis, farmers have hardly begun to adopt water-saving technologies or practices. The reasons for this are largely found in the nature of the incentives faced by China's farming community and other non-farm users. Until the 1970s, water was considered abundant in most parts of China and was not priced; therefore, there was no incentive for users to save water. Collectives had de facto rights over the water in their communities, whether underground or surface water (such as that of nearby lakes, rivers, or canals).

Shortly after the 1978 agricultural reforms, the central government sanctioned a system of volumetric surface water pricing. This system did not begin at once in all locations but instead was allowed to spread gradually as experience was gathered. Hence, the current structure of prices exhibits substantial variation across the country. Typically, prices are uniform for a specific end use (agriculture, industry, domestic use) in a specific province, although there are exceptions. Agricultural users pay lower prices than domestic users, who in turn pay less than industrial users.

Since the onset of the price reform for agricultural water, officials have repeatedly raised water prices in many areas, although in real terms there has not been much change. For example, in one county in Hebei province, although the nominal price of surface water per unit increased from 0.02 yuan in 1985 to 0.10 yuan in 1997, in real terms prices remained virtually unchanged at 0.023 yuan per unit.

Even if the government was committed to raising prices and charging for water on a per unit basis to encourage water savings, the fragmented and small-scale nature of China's farms poses a significant problem. It is common to have water pricing for an irrigation group at the point of entry, although farmers have little incentive to reduce their water use because they will be charged for it anyway. Indeed, there is incentive to use more than one's share of the water—the classic free rider problem. Upstream users have more opportunities to free ride at the cost of downstream users. Yet a system of volumetric pricing for individual farms would not be the most cost-effective solution given the high transaction costs associated with the measuring of water intake and collection of fees from hundreds of millions of small farms throughout China. Therefore, new and different institutions for management of water irrigation systems at the village level are regarded as more viable options, and these are examined next.

Surface Water Management Reform

Since 1990, collective water management in some surface water irrigation districts in China has been replaced by water user associations (WUAs) and contracting (Wang et al. 2003). A WUA is theoretically a farmer-based participatory organization set up to manage a village's irrigation water, and a member-elected board is supposed to be assigned the control rights over the village's water. Contracting is a system in which the village leadership establishes a contract with an individual to manage the village's canal networks. It is now the predominant form of reformed institution.

Although there are many similarities between international and Chinese experiences, the nation's water management reform strategy has taken on some unique characteristics. Above all, water officials have emphasized the role of incentives in water management reform. In many of the new reform efforts, water managers are provided with monetary rewards if they can meet certain targets, such as in water savings. Much less effort goes into encouraging participation of farmers in the management of the local irrigation system.

The prominence given to incentives is not new in the context of China's overall economic reform effort (Naughton 1995). The Household Responsibility System primarily gave incentives to farmers in crop production (Lin 1992). The fiscal reforms gave local leaders incentives to begin township and village enterprises. The grain reforms gave grain bureau personnel the incentive to commercialize commodity trading (Rozelle et al. 2000). Clearly, high-level water officials are hoping a similar set of reforms can improve China's performance in water management.

The reformed institutions have become the dominant forms of management, particularly where they were encouraged by local upper-level government officials. However, implementation has often deviated from theory because the reforms were only nominal, with a shift occurring in the institutional set-up but no incentives actually provided for water saving. Participation by farmers was low in most cases. The governing board of a WUA was the village leadership itself, so these associations differed little from collective management.

The absence of a systematic relationship between reforms and water use, however, does not mean that the reform process has failed in China. Wang et al. (2003) demonstrated that in villages located in the Yellow River Basin, where water managers were provided with strong incentives,[2] water use per hectare fell by nearly 10–20 percent when compared to the amount used in collectively managed systems, while having little or no statistical effect on agricultural production and rural incomes. The incentives also improved the efficiency of the irrigation systems since the output of major crops, with the notable exception of wheat, did not fall, leaving rural incomes unharmed.

Although negative impacts on production and farmer income were not found, in the longer run, as water management reform reaches into more water-scarce areas and seeks to continue achieving water savings in areas that have already cut back on use, there may be sharper trade-offs between water use and production and income. It could mean that some farmers who lose access to water could also suffer production and income decline. In such cases, policies such as targeted safety nets to mitigate adverse consequences should be developed.

Groundwater Management Reform

Faced with the impending reality of groundwater depletion, drops in the water table, and related environmental problems, the Chinese government has tried to implement several policies for the sustainable development of groundwater resources. The first important policy change was to adopt a system of water withdrawal permits and well licenses. In 1993, the MWR issued regulations related to permits and licenses, and most provinces began to implement the water withdrawal system in the late 1980s. The withdrawal system has performed well in urban areas. However, in rural regions, because there are too many small farmers, water management authorities face difficulties in monitoring groundwater withdrawal and digging new tubewells. According to a field survey in

---

2. Water fees collected from farmers include two elements: basic water fees associated with the fixed quantity of land in the village and volumetric water fees associated with the volume of water used. The volumetric water fees provide managers with more direct incentives, because officials agree that the water manager has to pay only the charge per cubic meter for the water that is actually used. If the actual quantity of water delivered to the village is less than the targeted quantity, the difference between the volumetric fee that is collected from the farmers, and what they pay for the water is their profit.

rural China (Wang, Huang, and Rozelle 2003), the local water bureaus focused on tubewell management given the relatively low transaction costs and more serious effects.

Charging fees was another policy change. Similar to the withdrawal permit system, this policy performed well in the urban regions. Considering the low income level of farmers, collecting fees for groundwater was not encouraged by the government but is now being considered by many local governments. Some provinces, such as Hebei, are carrying out experiments in fee collection (e.g., putting integrated circuit cards or "smart cards") in tubewells to monitor the volumes of groundwater used.

The government also encouraged reform in property rights over tubewells in rural regions. Research results show that since the early 1980s, collective ownership of tubewells has steadily been replaced by private ownership (Wang, Huang, and Rozelle 2003). At present, private tubewell ownership has become dominant in many regions. Although most private tubewells are still owned jointly by several individuals as shareholding tubewells, during the 1990s private individuals expanded their share.

The privatization of tubewells has promoted the adjustment of cropping patterns while having no adverse impact on crop yield (Wang, Huang, and Rozelle 2003). When tubewell ownership shifts from collective to private and water is more efficiently managed (Wang et al. 2003), producers are able to cultivate relatively high-valued crops, which in some cases demand greater attention of tubewell owners. These studies indicate that after privatization, farmers have expanded their sown area of water-sensitive and high-value crops, such as wheat and horticulture crops. It is perhaps because of the rising demand for horticultural produce that some private individuals have become interested in investing in tubewells.

Further, privatization of tubewells had no adverse impact on crop yields. The rising efficiency of groundwater services associated with private tubewells partly explains why agricultural production increased in the face of increasing water scarcity in the 1990s. Tubewell privatization was one of the factors that helped offset the rising water scarcity in the North China Plain.

Finally, in contrast to the concerns of some observers, the privatization of tubewells did not accelerate the fall in the groundwater table (Wang et al. 2003). While this does not imply that the rapid fall in the groundwater table is not worrying, policymakers should continue to support the privatization of tubewells in the North China Plain. Going back to collective tubewell ownership is not the answer, because land use rights were de facto privatized with the 2003 Agricultural Lease Law. Other policies on pricing and regulatory measures would be more efficient and effective in combating the fall. In fact, given the increased pressure to move into high-value crops despite increasing resource scarcity, the shift to private tubewells will continue, and, given the greater efficiency of these wells, policymakers may want to encourage the privatization process.

India: Water Resources and Irrigation Reform

We now turn our attention to India with a broad preliminary overview of the estimates of availability and future requirements for water in that country. This is followed by an overview of irrigation development, an account of the problems and weaknesses, and the reforms suggested or actually initiated. Thereafter we return to water resources and the question of how the future needs can be met against the backdrop of predictions of severe water scarcities or even a water crisis in the near future.

Water Resources: The Broad Picture

The most recent estimates of the water resources available in India are those given in the Report of the High-Level National Commission for Integrated Water Resources Development Plan (NCIWRDP) set up by the Government of India, Ministry of Water Resources, in September 1999, some of which are presented in Table 9.1.

While these figures suggest a healthy relationship between water availability and present use, there are wide variations, both temporal and spatial, in water availability. Much of the rainfall in India occurs within a period of a few months during the year, and within this period the intensity is concentrated

TABLE 9.1 National annual data on precipitation, surface water, and groundwater in India

	Billion cubic meters
Precipitation over the Indian landmass	4,000
Available surface water resources	1,953
Available groundwater resources	432
Usable surface water resources	690
Usable groundwater resources	396
Total usable water resources	1,086
Present quantum of use	Approximately 600

SOURCE: India Ministry of Water Resources (1999b).

NOTES: "Precipitation" includes rainfall and snowfall; "available surface water resources" are measured in terms of annual flows at sites close to the terminal points of the river systems; "available groundwater resources" refers to the "dynamic" quantity that can be extracted annually, taking into account the rate of annual replenishment and economic considerations; "usable water resources" refers to that part of the notionally "available" water resources that is actually available for use through impoundment or other means. (There is a view that available surface water resources of 1953 BCM includes the groundwater availability of 432 BCM, because much of the "dynamic" groundwater eventually joins surface water flows into the sea and the quantum of groundwater that independently flows into the sea is not significant. However, this view is not accepted by all.)

TABLE 9.2 Water requirements for different uses in India (cubic kilometers)

Uses	1997–98	2010 Low	High	%	2025 Low	High	%	2050 Low	High	%
Irrigation	524	543	557	78	561	611	72	628	807	68
Domestic	30	42	43	6	55	62	7	90	111	9
Industries	30	37	37	5	67	67	8	81	81	7
Power	9	18	19	3	31	33	4	63	70	6
Inland navigation	0	7	7	1	10	10	1	15	15	1
Flood control	0	0	0	0	0	0	0	0	0	0
Environment— afforestation	0	0	0	0	0	0	0	0	0	0
Environment— ecology	0	5	5	1	10	10	1	20	20	2
Evaporation loss	36	42	42	6	50	50	6	76	76	7
Total	*629*	*694*	*710*	*100*	*784*	*843*	*100*	*973*	*1,180*	*100*

SOURCE: India, Ministry of Water Resources (1999b).

within a few weeks. Spatially, there is a wide range in precipitation, from less than 200 mm (or even 100 mm) in parts of Rajasthan to 11,000 mm in Cherrapunji, in the northeastern part of the country. This has implications for water resource policy and planning. Three major studies have made the following projections of total future water requirements:

1. The Working Group (WG) of the NCIWRDP and the NCIWRDP itself have made low and high estimates of 973 to 1,180 BCM in 2050 (see Table 9.2).
2. India Water Vision (IWV) of the India Water Partnership has projected 1,027 BCM in 2025 in its "sustainable scenario" (policy changes are brought about to ensure economy in water use and long-term environmental sustainability).
3. Kanchan Chopra and Biswanath Goldar of the Institute of Economic Growth have projected 920.92 to 964.9 and 1,004.72 BCM in 2020 in their "business as usual," "sustainable," and "high growth" scenarios, respectively.[3]

All three studies predict a fragile balance between supply and demand and take a cautious but not alarmist view of the future. There are two divergent views on whether such a position is warranted. One of these, that of the NCIWRDP, goes ahead to predict an imminent crisis, while the other, that of the Center for Science and Environment, questions the prediction and argues that proper

3. For these three studies, see India, Ministry of Water Resources (1999a,b,c) (both WG and NCIWRDP) and Chopra and Goldar (2000).

water management and extensive community-based water harvesting would preclude any crisis.[4]

However, there is no disagreement on the need for economy in water use in all sectors. On the one hand, the agricultural use of water has to come down from the present level of around 80 percent of usable water resources, thereby releasing more water to meet the increasing demand from industrial, municipal, and domestic users (Table 9.2). On the other, economy, efficiency, and conservation in all uses will be imperative to restrain the growth of water demand. Here we focus on irrigation, because it is the largest use of water in India.

Irrigation Development in India

Irrigation development has been featured consistently throughout most of rural India's history. Small village-centered irrigation works for collecting and collectively managing water, and some large irrigation structures have emerged since medieval times, with the colonial era marking the beginning of an accelerated development of irrigation works throughout India. With the advent of the colonial era, control over natural resources, including water, and the management of the irrigation structures passed from the community to the state.

TANK IRRIGATION.   Surface structures that collect and store rainwater, run-off, and seepage from the surrounding areas are known as tanks or ponds. Over the centuries, locally built water storage systems (e.g., *kere* in Karnataka, *johads* in Rajasthan, and *erie* in Tamil Nadu) have served to insulate against droughts, recharged groundwater, provided crucial irrigation for crop production, functioned as sources of water for multiple uses by the village community (drinking, washing, bathing, providing water for livestock and wildlife, fishing, and cultural and ritual purposes), and played a role in the maintenance of a good natural environment. Because of these benefits, the Indian kings, *jagirdars,* religious bodies, and philanthropists built large numbers of tanks all over their domains. The tank and its surroundings used to be the common property of the village and its people.

With land reforms, beginning in the 1950s there were changes in the land ownership and use patterns, which affected the tanks negatively. As a result, the tank-irrigated area declined, while the emphasis shifted to major and medium-sized irrigation projects.[5] The share of net irrigated area under tanks declined in the country, from 17.3 percent in 1950–51 to 6.8 percent in 1990–91 (India, Ministry of Rural Areas and Employment, 1994).

IRRIGATION PROJECTS.   After India achieved independence, the government launched an ambitious program to improve agricultural production through

---

4. Paper circulated at the World Water Forum, The Hague, March 2000.

5. In India, irrigation schemes and projects are classified based on "culturable command area" (CCA) into the following categories: (1) major, with more than 10,000 ha of CCA; (2) medium, with 2,000 to 10,000 ha of CCA; and (3) minor, with below 2,000 ha of CCA.

TABLE 9.3 Number of major and medium-sized projects introduced in each of India's five-year plans

Plan period	Major	Medium-sized
First plan (1951–56)	44	169
Second plan (1956–61)	33	102
Third plan (1961–66)	32	44
Annual plan (1966–69)	11	30
Fourth plan (1969–74)	32	73
Fifth plan (1974–78)	70	300
Annual plans (1978–80)	12	52
Sixth plan (1980–85)	30	91
Seventh plan (1985–90)	12	33
Annual plans (1990–92)	1	—
Eighth plan (1992–97)	14	50
Total	*292*	*944*

SOURCE: Authors' compilation.

NOTE: —, data unavailable.

the extensive development of the irrigation infrastructure. The irrigation system in no other country but China is as extensive as it is in India. From the sixth five-year plan onward, emphasis has been placed on the completion of ongoing projects and the consolidation of gains rather than on "new starts" (Table 9.3).

However, new projects continued to be undertaken from the seventh plan onward. It was only during the eighth plan that the proposal to complete ongoing projects rather than taking up new ones (India, Planning Commission 2001b) was actualized. The ninth plan included a comprehensive irrigation development and management strategy stressing the promotion of programs for participatory irrigation management (PIM), rational pricing of irrigation water, and conjunctive use of surface water and groundwater. It especially focused on the improvement of water use efficiency by progressive reduction in conveyance and application losses. For the tenth plan (2002–7), the Planning Commission recommended a major revival of public investment in irrigation capacity and water management and suggested the Accelerated Irrigation Benefit Program as a potential means of providing resources to state governments to support ongoing projects (India, Planning Commission, 2001a).

The Present Status of Indian Irrigation

Irrigation development has varied in different zones. Some regions (the Gangetic Plains and the eastern coast) have achieved a relatively enhanced stage of development. In some developed areas, the results of overirrigation are becoming evident, with many areas in Punjab and Haryana suffering from the emergence of salinity. The incidence of "dark" blocks (i.e., blocks marked by overexploitation of groundwater) is on the increase in the north and west of the country.

Overall, the gross irrigated area (GIA) increased from about 23 million hectares (m ha) in the triennium ending (TE) 1952–53 to about 72 m ha in TE 1996–97, an increase of 2.62 percent per annum, while the net irrigated area (NIA) increased from about 21 m ha to nearly 54 m ha, an increase of 2.16 percent a year.

CANAL IRRIGATION.   In absolute terms, the net canal-irrigated area increased from about 8.61 m ha in TE 1952–53 to about 17.25 m ha in TE 1996–97, although this increase was not commensurate with the public investments in the sector. The rate of growth of the area under canal irrigation decelerated after the sixth plan despite increased investments, for the following three reasons. First, the relatively easier areas for potential canal irrigation had already been used. Second, the investment costs of the irrigation projects taken up from the seventh plan onward were much higher, which meant that investment could create only lower irrigation potential than in earlier plans. Third, adequate budgetary allocations could not be made for the major and medium-sized irrigation projects, delaying their completion. Further, while the area under canal irrigation did increase in absolute terms in almost all the states, the share of canal-irrigated area in the NIA either declined or increased marginally in the past four decades because of the significant role played by groundwater irrigation.

Many areas in the country practice traditional irrigation, usually classified in statistical tables under the heading "Other Sources," suited to the local terrain and conditions. It would be myopic to dismiss these systems as anachronistic, because they indeed have an important role. While modern knowledge and technology can be used for improving and modifying the traditional systems so as to make them more relevant to present conditions (Sengupta 1985), synthesizing modern knowledge with traditional technology could rejuvenate the development of irrigation in these areas.

TANK IRRIGATION.   Tank irrigation has gradually declined over the past 50 years, both in absolute terms and also in relation to NIA. Among the three major sources of irrigation, the tank is the only source for which this has happened. The tank-irrigated area started declining in the 1960s and has done so continuously, with some improvements in the 1990s (Figure 9.1).

Interestingly, this reduction in the area under tank irrigation happened despite the construction of thousands of new tanks during this period (Vaidyanathan 1991, 1999). Tanks are mostly concentrated in areas where other sources of irrigation are limited or absent. The worst affected because of the continuous decline in tank irrigation are the poor farmers (small and marginal) for whom an alternative source of irrigation is costly or not available.[6]

---

6. As per the estimate of all-India Report on Agricultural Census of 1990-91, tank irrigated area accounted for nearly 10 percent of the net irrigated area among marginal farmers, whereas it accounted for only 3.6 percent among large farmers.

FIGURE 9.1 Growth rate of irrigation in India from TE 1962–63 to TE 1996–97, by region and source

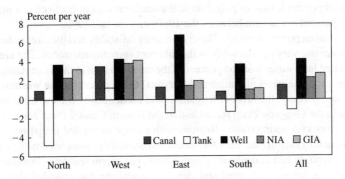

SOURCE: Authors' compilation.
NOTE: GIA, gross irrigated area; NIA, net irrigated area.

GROUNDWATER IRRIGATION.　One of the most significant developments in Indian irrigation since its independence has been groundwater irrigation predominantly owned and managed by farmers (Shah 1993). This source has come to represent around 50 percent of irrigated agriculture and 85 percent of rural drinking water.

While the groundwater-irrigated area increased to 29.81 m ha in TE 1996–97 from 6.39 m ha in TE 1952–53, its share in NIA increased from about 30 percent to about 55 percent during this period. Unlike the area under tank and canal irrigation, that under groundwater irrigation grew at a steady rate of 3–5 percent during different subperiods from the 1960s onward. The main factor in the growth of groundwater irrigation is tubewell irrigation, which grew at a high rate of 9.9 percent per annum during the period 1960–61 to 1996–97. The area under tubewell irrigation, which accounted for less than 1 percent of NIA until 1960, increased to about 33 percent in TE 1996–97. The development of rural electrification and the availability of credit at subsidized rates helped the farmers to increase the area under groundwater irrigation significantly (Vaidyanathan 1991; Shah 1993). The rapid development of groundwater helped not only the well-owning farmers but also the non-well-owning farmers through water markets (Shah and Raju 1987; Shah 1993; Narayana Murthy 1994; Saleth 1996), but this was not without problems.

REGIONAL VARIATIONS.　Between TE 1962–63 and TE 1996–97, the highest growth in the area under irrigation, whether from canals or from other sources, was registered in the western region owing to its higher irrigation potential and the level of investments made there. The growth rate of irrigation (both NIA and GIA) was very low in the southern region compared to other areas during this period. There are two reasons for this: first, most of the surface irrigation potential had been harnessed before independence in the southern region, so further growth was bound to be slow, and second, tank irrigation, which is an important source of irrigation in the southern region, declined at a rate of 1.31 percent per annum between the 1960s and the late 1990s.

AGROCLIMATIC ZONES.   Water resource availability and the circumstances of water use vary considerably in the different agroclimatic zones. The area of irrigated land varies from 64 percent of the net sown area in the Trans-Gangetic Plain zone (the states of Punjab and Haryana) to 6.3 percent in the Western Dry Region. Broadly, the level of irrigation (and consequently the use of water) is high in the Gangetic Plain region and in the Eastern Coastal Plain zone.

RAIN-FED IRRIGATION.   Regions with modest or limited irrigation development are classified as "rain-fed" areas and are usually associated with images of deprivation and underdevelopment.[7] However, recent research conducted on the divide between irrigated and rain-fed agriculture has provided some unexpected results. Fan and Hazell (2000) analyzed the productivity levels of irrigated and rain-fed districts in the country from 1970 to 1995 and reached the conclusion that investment in rain-fed areas, including many low-productivity regions, is at least as productive as in irrigated areas, and also has a much larger positive impact on poverty.

Irrigation Problems and Deficiencies

The major issues facing the dominant forms of irrigation are as follows.

CANAL IRRIGATION

- Canal irrigation efficiency in India, at 35–40 percent (India, Ministry of Water Resources, 1999b,c), is very low. While the loss from canals through seepage is partly recovered as groundwater recharge and as "return flows" farther down, this does not justify inefficient conveyance.
- Injudicious canal irrigation, overapplication of water, failure to take the groundwater table into account, and inadequate attention to drainage have led to the emergence of waterlogging and salinity in many areas, causing valuable agricultural land to go out of use. A report by a working group of the Ministry of Water Resources (India, Ministry of Water Resources, 1991) estimated the area of waterlogged land in the country to be around 2.46 m ha and that of salt-affected land to be 3.30 m ha. The reclamation of such lost lands, even where feasible, would require large investments.
- On average, the yields of irrigated agriculture in India have been relatively low in comparison to those in other countries, and inadequate attention has

---

7. The distinction between "irrigated" and "rain-fed" agriculture is somewhat misleading. The latter term includes areas meeting their agriculture water requirements largely through rainwater harvesting and watershed development as opposed to areas irrigated through canals, tubewells, and so on.

been given to increasing productivity in rain-fed areas. Even the NCI-WRDP's projections for the future seem fairly modest.[8] Higher yields, which ought to be achievable, will mean a reduction in demand for water.

- The cost of creating irrigation potential through canal projects has been steadily increasing, rising from Rs. 8,620/ha in the period of the first five-year plan (1951–56) to Rs. 29,587/ha in 1990–92 in constant 1980–81 prices (India, Ministry of Water Resources, 1997). Further, there is a persistent gap between the irrigation potential created at such cost and the extent of its use (Table 9.4).[9]

- Resource constraints, an unclear distinction between plan and nonplan, and a built-in preference for new construction over the efficient operation of existing infrastructure have together resulted in underprovisioning and neglect of maintenance. Further, irrigation water from canals is supplied to farmers at very low prices in most states, leading to the wasteful use of water. Even at the prevailing low rates, the collection of irrigation charges is poor in most states. The result is that the revenues do not even cover the operation and maintenance costs of the systems, much less make a contribution to capital-related charges or generation of resources for further investments.

- Canal irrigation in India has been marked by a number of inequities such, as "tail-end deprivation."[10] Further, with the increasing affluence of the large farmers, their money and political power start to influence policy formulation and the planning, design, location, and operation of major projects.

- Finally, most of the interstate river water disputes have arisen and could arise in the future from major canal irrigation projects. Some examples are the Ravi-Beas, Telugu Ganga, Alamatti, and Cauvery disputes.

GROUNDWATER IRRIGATION

- Overextraction of groundwater has led to depletion in some areas and to salinity ingress in coastal zones (e.g., in Gujarat). On the other hand, there

---

8. The projected average yield for irrigated foodcrops is estimated at 3 tons/ha by the year 2010 and 4 tons/ha by 2050, while for unirrigated foodcrops projections are 1.1 tons/ha by 2010 and 1.5 tons/ha by 2050.

9. "Irrigation potential" is a problematic concept given the assumptions about cropping patterns as well as watering needs and practices; nevertheless, the gap between created and used potential cannot be dismissed as unreal.

10. This term refers to the situation in which, if waters begin to rise in a reservoir and canal systems for taking them to the tail end of the system are not yet ready, the head-end farmers have plenty of water available and tend to plant water-intensive crops. This establishes a pattern of water use that cannot easily be changed at a later stage: by the time the full canal system is ready, much of the water stands preempted in the head-end areas, and there is little left for conveyance to the tail end. This is a familiar problem in most project commands.

TABLE 9.4 Irrigation potential created and used at the end of 1995–96 in India (million hectares)

Category	Ultimate	Created	Used	Gap	Actually irrigated (land use statistics)
Major or medium	58.46	32.2	27.45	4.75	
Minor (surface)	17.38	12.1	10.72	1.38	
Minor (groundwater)	64.05	44.42	40.83	3.59	
Total	*129.89*	*88.72*	*79*	*9.72*	*70.64*

SOURCE: India, Ministry of Water Resources (1999c).

is a situation of rising water tables and the emergence of waterlogging and salinity in other areas (e.g., in the Sharda Sahayak command in Uttar Pradesh).

- Water markets have emerged in the context of groundwater extraction through tubewells and bore wells, serving some useful purposes but with dangers of unsustainable extraction as well as inequitable relationships between sellers and buyers.
- It has been claimed that the solution to the previous two problems lies in regulation, but this has not been found feasible because of political factors and the legal problem of easement rights. Under the direction of the Supreme Court, the Central Groundwater Authority has been established, but it is not yet clear how it will evolve and operate, what kind of regulation it will attempt, and with what success.
- There are problems of pollution or contamination of aquifers (e.g., through fluoride, arsenic, industrial effluents, and so on).

TANK IRRIGATION

- Encroachments in the tank foreshore and along the feeder channels have reduced the supply of water to the tanks, while the accumulation of silt in tank basins or beds has reduced their water-holding capacity.
- There is a widening conflict of interests between tank-bed cultivators (including unauthorized ones) and command farmers, especially in the absence of institutional mechanisms to safeguard the interests of the resource.
- The construction of dams or reservoirs in the upper watershed or catchment area prevents the water from reaching downstream tanks. Further, the rapid development of groundwater irrigation in the tank command areas has reduced the participation of farmers in tank-related works, which has ultimately reduced the area under irrigation.
- On one hand, there has been a breakdown in village institutions because of caste and other conflicts, and community participation, which was al-

ways part and parcel of tank irrigation, has declined drastically. On the other hand, without accountability, control by the government agencies has increased, and there is an absence of accountability to or control by local communities. Political interference, compounded by poor technical capabilities in the location and construction of new tanks and their size, has hampered water regulation and the capacity of centuries-old upstream or downstream tanks in recent decades.

* The government has not paid adequate attention to the improvement of the performance of tanks, as is prominently mentioned in most of the research studies (Palanisami 1990; Vaidyanathan 1991, 1999; Palanisami and Easter 2000; Raju et al. 2003).[11]

Reforms Needed and Attempted

Over the years, many reforms including policy changes, institutional reforms, new administrative and procedural processes, new laws, and attitudinal changes have been attempted. The major ones are outlined here.

THE USE PROBLEM. At the national level, the use of irrigation potential has been 86 percent in the case of major or medium-sized irrigation projects, while for minor irrigation projects it has been 91 percent (India, Central Water Commission, 2000). However, use levels vary considerably among the various states, ranging from nearly 99 percent in some cases to significantly lower levels in others.

The underuse of surface water irrigation potential has been attributed to the delay in the construction of field channels and the establishment of distribution systems (Saleth 1996), giving rise to two serious problems, excessive conveyance losses and tail-end deprivation.[12] Deterioration in distribution infrastructure has also contributed to reduced use and increased seepage (World Bank 1999).

Notwithstanding that the gap between irrigation potential developed and that used can partly be attributed to discrepancies in the statistical data due to the multiplicity of sources and definitions of the data, the underuse of irrigation potential is a real problem.

A major move in this regard was the Command Area Development Program (CADP), which was started in 1974 to take up development works in the irrigated command areas and increase the use of created irrigated potential. By 1997, CADP covered 203 projects with a command area of about 21 m ha in 22 states. The physical progress achieved in the construction of field channels

---

11. For more on the problems of tanks, see Janakarajan (1993), Narayana Murthy (1993), Vaidyanathan (1999), Dhawan (2000), Palanisami and Easter (2000), and Raju et al. (2003).

12. It has been estimated that of the total outlet water, about 45 percent is lost through seepage by unlined field channels, while 15 percent is lost due to excessive water application, as reported by Saleth (1996).

has been very high, but in the case of rotational water distribution, it has been moderate (about 60 percent of the area covered by the field channels). CADP has not brought about significant improvements in water use efficiency or in agricultural production. Several studies have indicated that the weakest aspect of CADP is its failure to involve farmers in the program (India, Ministry of Water Resources, 1999c). On-farm development and holding or consolidation activities by the states have been hampered by the lack of appropriate legal backing for CADP.

PARTICIPATORY IRRIGATION MANAGEMENT.   If the "use gap" problem led to CADP, the failure of the major and medium-sized projects to provide satisfactory irrigation services to the farmers led to PIM programs. A growing feeling even within the government that it could not really run the huge, far-flung irrigation networks efficiently and render proper services, combined with the dissatisfaction of the farmers, led to the idea of transferring parts of the system to the farmers themselves for management. It became fashionable to talk about "farmer participation." Underlying this line of thinking in recent years has been the ideological consideration, particularly among the international financial institutions, of reducing the role of the state. By 2002, several states had initiated policy and legal reforms to encourage the formation of WUAs. This has facilitated the formation of 29,217 WUAs across several states covering 15 percent of the total net irrigated area of the country (India, Ministry of Water Resources, 2006). The proposed WUA functions include operation and management (O&M), dispute settlement, and the collection of water charges.[13]

The level of organization indicates the level at which users are expected to take an active role: water users' organizations only below the outlet level are currently found in most states, while others propose to transfer O&M responsibilities to WUAs at the distributory or minor level. The latter approach implies a somewhat greater degree of change, because it generally requires the formation of new organizations and a greater level of responsibility for farmers in O&M. However, in many cases the government does not fully withdraw, so any "farmer involvement" often becomes a supplement to that of the agency. The transfer of O&M responsibilities to joint management committees made up of farmers' representatives and government officials is also being proposed in a few states.

With regard to irrigation charges, in most states the Revenue Department or a special wing of the Irrigation Department used to collect charges from in-

---

13. The PIM programs vary considerably across states. Perhaps the most dramatic changes were proposed in Bihar, where farmers are to assume maintenance responsibility for distributory commands of up to 10,000 ha, and can retain 70 percent of the irrigation charges. Here again, a severe fiscal crisis precipitating a breakdown of the government's ability to deliver irrigation services has been responsible for the most sweeping changes (Brewer et al. 1999).

dividual farmers. Several states are now experimenting with volumetric whole-saling (i.e., bulk supply and billing by volume) of water by mid-level WUAs that assume responsibility for allocating it among their members and for collecting the charges. Because the user group pays for water by volume, it has an incentive to conserve water collectively. However, individual farmers are the ultimate water users, and this approach depends on the group's ability to motivate individuals to use water efficiently.

The success of PIM policies must ultimately be measured by the level of constructive involvement of farmers in improving the performance of irrigation systems. Pilot projects show that much can be achieved, but whether these systems can be successfully scaled up remains a question. There is a need to identify factors that tend to affect farmers' willingness to participate in irrigation systems.

PRICING OF IRRIGATION WATER.   In general, irrigation water rates (for water supplied by the state from canals) are unduly low; fees have not been fully or regularly collected and remain unrevised for years, sometimes for decades. Toward the late 1990s, there was an effort to raise water rates: Andhra Pradesh tripled its irrigation water charges in 1997, Maharashtra announced a gradually rising rate for the next five years, and many other states are contemplating similar moves. However, the overall picture during the period between 1960 and 1997 was not a reassuring one (Svendsen, Gulati, and Raju 2003).

Poor revenues from public irrigation systems created at great cost are among the many factors responsible for the severe resource constraint faced by most state governments. The result is poor maintenance of systems, leading in turn to poor revenues with hardly any resources for further investments in this sector. The Committee on the Pricing of Irrigation Water (India, Planning Commission, 1992) estimated that the total unrecovered costs for major and medium-sized irrigation projects had increased fivefold in a 10-year period, from Rs. 2,800 million in 1977–78 to Rs. 15,250 million in 1986–87. Besides, the low pricing of irrigation water encourages an extremely wasteful use of water resources.

Successive commissions and committees (namely, irrigation commissions and finance commissions) have stressed the importance of recovering at least the O&M costs if not the capital-related charges, but these have remained suggestions. The Vaidyanathan Committee on the Pricing of Irrigation Water (India, Planning Commission, 1992) recommended a two-part tariff comprising a fixed charge and a variable charge to recover the annual O&M costs and 1 percent interest on the capital cost (adjusted to remove the costs attributable to inefficiency). The objective was to move toward full cost recovery, and the change was to be brought about in three phases. Unfortunately, 10 years after the report, it remains largely unimplemented because of the lukewarm response from the state governments, despite the fact that the implementation of the recommendations would have meant more than a fivefold increase in rates, even in the first phase.

We can ask if poor farmers would be able to pay increased water charges. The short answer is that irrigation increases productivity and production, and the resulting increase in income would enable farmers to pay the water charges, which would amount to only a small fraction of the value of the output, as pointed out in the Vaidyanathan Committee's report (India, Planning Commission, 1992).

FINANCING OF PROJECTS.   The paucity of funds for new investment is forcing state and central governments to explore alternative sources of financing for developing and rehabilitating irrigation projects, such as tapping the capital of private investors through revenue-backed instruments and the mobilization of local capital through investments by farmers in the systems that serve them (Svendsen, Gulati, and Raju 2003).

Raising resources from the market through the issue of bonds was initiated with the sale of Narmada Bonds to finance the construction of a series of dams on the River Narmada in central India in the mid-1980s. Bonds were also sold to support the Upper Krishna Project in the southern state of Karnataka. Under both these schemes, secured, redeemable bonds were offered at a fixed rate of interest guaranteed by the respective state governments. The rates of interest on such bonds are very high, as high as 17.5 percent in some cases, making it a very costly source of credit. This prompts one to ask if it is proper for the government to undertake such capital- and resource-intensive projects out of the budget. This would clearly call for a very selective approach to projects and for a most stringent scrutiny with reference to certain hard criteria.

Private sector participation in irrigation financing is an idea that has been favored by both the Planning Commission and the Ministry of Water Resources. The revised National Water Policy (India, Ministry of Water Resources, 2002) advocates private sector participation in the planning, development, and management of water resources projects wherever feasible. However, there are questions as to the likelihood as well as the desirability of this course of action.

In terms of likelihood, even the most pro-business states, such as Gujarat and Maharashtra, have not been able to elicit much private sector interest in irrigation projects. State governments have not asked for expressions of interest from potential bidders, nor has any state formally declared its willingness to sell stakes in irrigation projects. In practice, private sector participation is likely to encounter several problems (Svendsen, Gulati, and Raju 2003): large investments, long gestation periods, modest or low returns, high financial risks, likely political interference in project management and water rate assessment, the political influence of farmers' lobbies, the difficulties in raising water rates and collecting them effectively, and so on. The much-advocated idea of private sector participation has hardly made any headway in power projects, and there is no basis for thinking it would be more successful in irrigation projects.

Turning to desirability, privatization can mean allowing a private entity to build dams and reservoirs on rivers or exploit surface water bodies (e.g., lakes) or an underground aquifer for commercial purposes. Even assuming that the private sector is interested in investing in such capital-intensive, long-gestation, modest-return projects, how are the environmental and social impacts going to be handled by the private entrepreneur and manager? Supply may match demand, but resource conservation may receive scant consideration; resettlement and rehabilitation aspects are likely to be given grudging attention only to the extent that resistance by those affected and public opinion compel such attention; and it is naïve to imagine that market forces will obviate conflicts or provide a magical route to their resolution.

Further, there are questions not merely of equity and sustainability but also of control over natural resources. One important question is whether allowing the domestic private sector to exploit national natural resources, particularly water, will make it difficult to deny a similar right to foreign investors in terms of the World Trade Organization regime and the principle of "national treatment" of foreign investors, and if so, whether there is a danger of India's losing control of its own natural resources. That means not that one is arguing for a dominant role for the state, but merely that the alternative to the state is not necessarily the corporate private sector.

REVIVAL OF TRADITIONAL SYSTEMS. Recently a few leading nongovernmental organizations (NGOs), in some cases supported by international donors, have made strenuous efforts to mobilize local communities into restoring the role of traditional systems such as tanks. Some state governments (e.g., those of Karnataka, Rajasthan, and Tamil Nadu) have also initiated large-scale programs to rejuvenate tanks.

However, the experience of the past few decades has been that the design and strategies used are evolved with little concern for local needs and situations, although rhetoric emphasizes community participation. Thus, tanks have not elicited much interest on the part of local communities, and tanks in many villages have lost their importance in the everyday life of the rural population. Future efforts to revive tanks need to correct this top-down approach and restore the traditional involvement of local stakeholders in tank management.

Numerous efforts are also being made to revive the old water-harvesting practices.[14] Rainwater harvesting is not merely a means of locally augmenting the availability of water but the starting point of an effort to eradicate rural poverty, generate rural employment, and reduce distress migration from rural areas to urban areas. Considering the enormous land and water resources and variability of rainfall, the calculations carried out by Agarwal, Narain, and

---

14. These include the well-known revival efforts of villagers in Ralegan Siddhi in the drought-prone Ahmednagar district of Maharashtra (under the leadership of Anna Hazare); the poor, low-rainfall villages in Alwar district of Rajasthan (under Rajendra Singh and the NGO Tarun Bharat Sangh); and the villages of Sukhomajri and Dhamala in the lower Shivalik Hills in Haryana (under the late P. R. Mishra).

Khurana (2001) show that the potential of rainwater harvesting is enormous and undeniable. So far, the initiatives undertaken have been scattered and local. What is called for is a national campaign along these lines. Prime Minister Atal Bihari Vajpayee emphasized this strongly in his address to the National Water Resources Council on April 1, 2002, while commending it for the National Water Policy of 2002.

GROUNDWATER REFORMS.   Broadly, reforms in this sector need to address the problems related to the exploitation of groundwater and equity, resource conservation, protection of quality, and environmental sustainability. Difficulties arise essentially in two interrelated contexts: the emergence of water markets and the prevailing law governing the ownership of groundwater.

Water markets for groundwater extraction through tubewells and bore wells have emerged in various forms in many regions of India and have truly been spontaneous institutional responses to emerging and variegated needs in different areas (Shah and Raju 1987; Shah 1993). At the national level, by 1993, of more than 14 million groundwater structures, fewer than 0.4 percent (50,000) were state-owned tubewells and fewer still were NGO-motivated group tubewells. In states like Uttar Pradesh, the presence of public tubewells, which dominated the groundwater scenario until the early 1960s, has long since declined to insignificance. Thus, 95 percent of the area served by groundwater in India is probably privately owned. Undoubtedly, the emergence of water markets has helped farmers who cannot afford to invest in tubewells or bore wells to buy water and practice irrigated agriculture, and they are not necessarily or always overcharged (Shah and Raju 1987; Saleth 1996).

However, groundwater "development" and the emergence of water markets are not matters for unqualified celebration. Under Indian law, the ownership of land carries with it the ownership of the groundwater under it, subject to regulation and control by the state. It has been said that "groundwater is attached, like a chattel, to land property," and thus "there is no limitation on how much groundwater a particular landowner may draw" (Chhatrapati Singh 1991). It follows, then, that only those owning land can have rights over groundwater; the landless (including communities, tribal and other, who may have been using certain natural resources for centuries) can have no such rights. This legal position makes it difficult to regulate groundwater markets and leads to inequities of various kinds: a rich farmer can install power-driven tubewells or bore wells in his land, and their operation can make dug wells in the neighborhood run dry; he can sell water so extracted to his poorer neighbors even though the water may come from a common aquifer running under their lands; and he can deplete the aquifer through excessive exploitation. So the results are not necessarily conducive to equity, to the conservation and protection of the resource, or to long-term environmental sustainability (Dubash 2002).

Following a public interest case relating to the feared depletion of groundwater, the Supreme Court mooted the establishment of a regulatory authority, and despite the doubts expressed by the Ministry of Water Resources, gave directions that resulted in the establishment of the Central Groundwater Authority (CGWA) in the late 1980s. The Ministry of Environment and Forests set it up under the provisions of the Environment (Protection) Act of 1987, but for a number of reasons the CGWA has not yet become fully operative.

The difficulty of groundwater regulation is borne out by the history of groundwater legislation at the state level. In the 1970s the central government circulated a model bill to the state governments for their consideration, and it was amended twice in later years. A few states took some action, but the general response was poor. Some degree of regulation has been attempted under the various irrigation acts in the states, but regulation largely remains in the realm of intentions.[15]

Reforms in relation to groundwater have to be twofold: (1) the legal position on the ownership of groundwater needs to change, with aquifers regarded as common pool resources to which only limited use rights (and not property rights) are conferred on individuals or institutions, and (2) water markets need to be carefully regulated with reference to equity, resource conservation, and environmental sustainability.

Water Resource Planning

Taking all water demands into account, projections of total future water requirements made by different studies are close enough to those of the availability of "usable" water, approximately 1,100 BCM (Table 9.1), to warrant concern, whether we view them as reflecting a difficult situation or a crisis. Moreover, seasonal, year-to-year, and spatial variations in rainfall could mean severe water stress in particular areas or periods. The standard response to that perception is to propose supply-side solutions in the form of large dam and reservoir and/or long-distance water transfer projects.[16] But this proposal can be highly problematic because of the following four main dilemmas.

First, there is a *money dilemma*. The NCIWRDP's rough estimates of amounts needed to complete spill-over projects were Rs. 700 billion in the tenth

---

15. The Gujarat government has an act in place for the regulation of groundwater, but it applies only to nine districts, and there is a difference of opinion as to whether it is really enforced. Maharashtra and Madhya Pradesh have statewide acts, but only for the regulation of drinking water sources. Tamil Nadu has an act applicable only to the Madras metropolitan area; for the rest of the state, a bill has been introduced. Andhra Pradesh has the act of 1996, and an ordinance of wider scope is under consideration for promulgation.

16. In its response to the Report of the World Commission on Dams (WCD) in November 2000, the Government of India brushed aside the approach and procedures recommended by the WCD as being likely to hamper developmental efforts and declared its intention of building 200 BCM of storage (i.e., many large dams and reservoirs) over 25 years. More recently, the Government of India, in response to the observations of the Supreme Court on a particular petition, announced a "mega" project for the linking of rivers and set up a task force to consider the modalities of implementing that project.

five-year plan, equivalent to 4.6 percent of overall plan outlay (Ministry of Finance, quoted in IFPRI 2004), and Rs. 1,100 billion in the eleventh plan. The actual availability of investment funds in the public sector could be no more than a small fraction of the projections made, and national private sector investment is likely to be marginal at best.

Second, there is a *market dilemma*. If engineers and administrators tend to argue for supply-side projects, "liberal" economists and officials of the multilateral financial institutions tend to argue for water markets and private sector investments. In the domestic context, the questions are how to allow limited and regulated water markets to function without inequity and injustice, without danger to the resource, and without transferring rights and control substantially away from the community. These have to be balanced by questions on how to adopt a stringent commercial approach in the context of supply for industrial use, commercial agriculture, and luxury consumption by the affluent without carrying the "commoditization" of water too far. In the international sphere, the questions are how to ensure that the few instances of international trade in water that now occur do not burgeon into a massive bulk trade in water, as in the case of oil, and how to protect the rights of the poorer countries to their own natural resources from predatory corporate giants.

Third, there is an *environmental dilemma*. If we end up putting the ecological system at risk by undertaking major interventions in nature to increase the availability of water for human use, what will eventually happen to the water? By building a series of large water projects, we may not be ensuring water security, but actually endangering the ecological system and therefore water as well.

Fourth, there is a *human dilemma*. While benefits accrue to one set of people, "social costs" are imposed on another, usually the poorer group. However, there is no reason that the people likely to be adversely affected by a project cannot in fact be treated as "partners in development" and enabled to benefit from the project, although the sad fact is that this rarely happens. A national rehabilitation policy under consideration for over 15 years has at last been adopted, but it suffers from deficiencies and needs to be revised.

Given these dilemmas, while it may not be possible to say a definitive "No" to all large water projects, we can minimize the numbers by treating them as projects of last resort. To assess whether the number of large projects can be drastically cut down requires the careful examination of (1) whether the demand for water will really be of the magnitude estimated by the NCIWRDP and (2) whether, on the supply side, there are other options.

Taking demand first, projections of future needs are generally based on current patterns of water use, with some adjustments made for improvements in efficiency and resource conservation, population growth, and urbanization. It is taken for granted that the demand for water must necessarily increase very sharply and that the needed supplies must somehow be found. That is not self-evident. If in fact water is a scarce resource and a crisis is looming on the horizon, that consciousness of scarcity and impending crisis should surely guide planning. Here there is a need to start from the recognition of finite availability and learn to live with it. With that kind of reversal of approach, the "demand" projections may undergo drastic changes.

It is noteworthy that the existing "average" urban water supply is not equitably distributed: there is minimal consumption by the poorer sections, fairly heavy use by the middle classes, and profligate use by the affluent. Instead of improving the norms for supply, it would be more appropriate to maintain or even reduce current norms and enforce economies on the middle and upper classes. Further, the demand projections will surely change if irrigation efficiency improves from the current level of 35–40 percent to say 65 or 70 percent instead of the 60 percent assumed by the NCIWRDP, and earlier than the year 2050. In industrial use of water, multiple recycling and reuse needs to be insisted upon, allowing no more than 10 percent make-up water. Strenuous efforts need to be made to promote improvements in efficiency and technological innovations in every kind of water use to maximize what we realize from each drop. With all these interventions, the demand picture will not remain the same.

Turning to the supply side, large or dam projects are not the only answer. There is a need to break free from the usual engineering conventions of defining "available water resources" in terms of flows in rivers and "usable water resources" in terms of what is stored behind a dam. What is available in nature is rainfall, not just river flows, and while storing river waters behind a dam converts "available" water into "usable" water, so do local rainwater harvesting and watershed development. If the few small success cases could be replicated wherever feasible and in the thousands across the country, they could be far more significant components of national water planning than is assumed.

Nonetheless, some large projects may still have to be undertaken, but the processes of examination and investment decisionmaking should be far more stringent, and there should be a willingness to say "No" to those projects that fail to meet the prescribed requirements.

First, environmental impact assessments (EIAs) should be made an independent professional undertaking. Also, an independent, statutory Environmental Regulatory Authority should be established under the Environment Protection Act that would (among other things) handle payments so that project proponents would not be the paymasters for EIAs. It should also be possible to ensure that the EIA agency, in each case, will be nominated by the Regulatory Authority from panels it maintains. It is of course necessary that the regulatory system neither degenerate into a rigid bureaucratic form of control nor be captured or subverted by the regulated.

Second, public hearings have now become a statutory requirement for such projects under the Environment Protection Act, but the act has not become fully effective yet. The primacy of those who are likely to be affected by a project and their claims regarding the expected benefits ought to become essential parts of water resource policy and planning.

Concluding Remarks

Bringing the twin strands of this chapter together, it is clear that heavy investment in irrigation has been the precondition for the success of the green revolution in India and has contributed to the phenomenal growth of agricultural production and productivity in China. However, as investment is not only continued but also increased over time, the marginal returns may be declining. Essentially, the implications are as follows:

- In the future, the emphasis has to shift from "water resources development" to resource management and conservation, as well as to minimization of the need for large supply-side projects. If at all necessary, such projects should be treated as projects of last resort and be better targeted to different regions (eastern India and western China, for instance).
- Irrigation reforms, including institutional reforms and the careful regulation of markets, have to be given priority with a view to realizing the maximum value per unit of water and ensuring sustainability.

10 Future Prospects for Water and Food in China and India: A Comparative Assessment

XIMING CAI AND MARK W. ROSEGRANT

China and India are the world's two largest countries in terms of total irrigated area, water withdrawals for agriculture, and cereal production, with a long history of irrigation development.

In China, the Du Jian Yan irrigation project was built 2,000 years ago and has been used since then with several rehabilitation and modification works. In modern times, major irrigation development in China has been undertaken since the 1950s, leading to an increase in irrigated area from 16 million hectares (m ha) in 1950 to 54 m ha in 1998 (Feng, Pei, and Zhang 2000). Similarly, there is evidence of water development works and irrigation in the early history of India, where a new chapter was introduced under the British hegemony after 1818 (Stone 1984). Irrigation has accounted for a large share of agricultural investment in the two countries during the past three decades (Fan, Hazell, and Thorat 1999; Fan, Zhang, and Zhang 2002).

Compared to the world average of 42 percent, 73 percent of China's current cereal production is on irrigated land, while this figure is about 57 percent in the case of India. Agricultural water depletion makes up for about 84 percent of the total water depletion in China and 90 percent in India, while total agricultural water depletion in the two countries is about 62 percent of the total water depletion in Asia and 36 percent in the world (Rosegrant, Cai, and Cline 2002). As a result of rapid pumping of groundwater, mainly for agriculture, groundwater resources have been depleted in much of north China and north and west India (Postel 1999). Today, in the major food production regions of the two countries, degradation of water sources, population growth, and competition from industrial and domestic sectors all threaten the use of water for agriculture. In terms of food production, China produces 20 percent of all cereals in the world, and India produces 10 percent. While cereal demand per capita in China is close to the world average of 315 kg, India's per capita cereal demand is only 58 percent of the world average.

Chaturvedi (2000) examined the performance of irrigation in India and concluded that the sector was in crisis, with four concerns relating to productivity, sustainability, investment focus and financial discipline, and sector management.

The assessments of irrigation in China are usually not so pessimistic and stress the relatively high productivity of irrigated agriculture (Feng, Pei, and Zhang 2000). However, the water sector in China faces similar problems, such as rapid growth of nonirrigation water demand, constraints on irrigation development, low agricultural water use efficiency, and weak irrigation management (Lohmar and Wang 2002).

It is thus interesting as well as timely to look at the possible future status of irrigation in the two countries. We begin with an assessment of the status of water and food in the two countries up to 2025 using the Global Integrated Water and Food Supply and Demand Projections model (Rosegrant, Cai, and Cline 2002). Several alternative scenarios based on policy interests in both countries are also examined. Some policy implications and lessons for water development in agriculture in China and India are provided based on the findings of the exercise.

An Assessment of Water Resources and Food Production

The analysis uses IMPACT–WATER (Appendix 10A),[1] a global integrated water and food supply and demand model developed on the basis of a long-term project being conducted at the International Food Policy Research Institute and the International Water Management Institute (Rosegrant, Cai, and Cline 2002). China and India have been studied in detail in the project, building on numerous previous national and international studies. The model divides the world into 69 spatial units, including 11 river basins in China and 13 in India (Figure 10.1), and simulates water demand and supply in domestic, industrial, livestock, and irrigation sectors and food production in each of the spatial units.

A Base-Year Assessment

Water Resources

Table 10.1 shows parameters of climate, water resources, and water uses in China and India, including the major basins. Comparing key major producing regions in both countries, it appears that climate conditions are relatively more favorable in China. While annual precipitation varies greatly over basins in both countries, the pattern of rainfall tends to follow more closely the pattern of solar radiation in the Huanghe (Yellow River) Basin as well as other basins in north China, with the coincidence of water and radiation providing conditions highly favorable to crop growth. India lacks a similarly synchronized pat-

---

1. IMPACT is an acronym for the International Model for Policy Analysis of Agricultural Commodities and Trade.

FIGURE 10.1 Major river basins in China and India

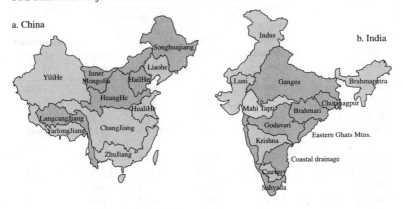

a. China

b. India

SOURCE: Rosegrant, Cai, and Cline (2002).
NOTE: Maps not made to scale.

tern of precipitation-radiation, as exemplified by the Ganges-India Basin, which produces about 40 percent of cereals in India.

"Total renewable water" (Table 10.1) refers to water that can be renewed by the natural cycling of water through the atmosphere and the earth, and "per capita renewable water" is often used as an indicator of water stress. Countries with renewable freshwater resources in the range of 1,000–1,600 m^3 per capita per year face water stress, with major problems occurring in drought years, and countries with per capita renewable water below 1,000 m^3 are severely water scarce (Engelman and LeRoy 1993). The three major basins in north China, the Huai, Huang, and Hai (the 3-H basins) have per capita renewable water below 1,000 m^3, and these basins produce 40 percent of cereals in China. In India, there are also several basins below the threshold, including Cauvery, Chotanagpur, Luni, and coastal areas. However, these basins produce only about 14 percent of cereals in India. The nationwide average per capita renewable water in China is only about one-fourth of the world average (about 8,500 m^3), while India's is slightly below one-third of the world average.

Reservoir storage of the water supply is one of the most striking disparities in water development between China and India. China has almost five times the reservoir storage of India. This difference appears to be related to the fact that groundwater pumping in India is twice that of China. In the 3-H basins in north China and several basins in India, including portions of the Indus and the Ganges, groundwater pumping reaches a high of 60 percent of recharge even at the basin scale, which results in large-scale groundwater overdraft in these basins. In India, groundwater is in a way substituting for surface water storage.

The total amount of water withdrawal and consumption is similar in China and India, and the share of agriculture in total consumption is above 85 percent

TABLE 10.1 Climate, water resources, and water uses in China and India, 1995

Region, country	Average annual precipitation (mm)	Average annual ET_0 (mm)	Renewable water		Reservation storage (km³)
			Total (km³)	Per capita (m³/p.c.)	
Huaihe	880	957	93.8	522	137
Haihe	503	1,196	42.3	470	110
Huanghe	529	1,099	71.6	526	80
China	*n.a.*	*n.a.*	*2,630.0*	*2,145*	*1,064*
Indus-India[a]	737	1,799	249.9	4,156	21
Ganges-India[a]	1,036	2,035	507.5	1,572	50
Cauvery	964	2,291	14.4	560	7
Chotanagpur	1,149	2,065	42.6	690	4
Luni River Basin	641	2,290	24.5	575	21
India	*n.a.*	*n.a.*	*2,302.0*	*2,478*	*232*

SOURCES: Compiled by the authors based on HPDGJ (1989), Qian (1991), NIHWR (1998), WRI (1998), Shiklomanov (1999), and China, Ministry of Water Resources (1990–98), for river basins in China, and ESCAP (1995) and on India, Ministry of Water Resources (1998–2000), for river basins in India.

NOTES: AGR, fraction of agricultural water consumption; ET_0, reference evapotranspiration; n.a., not applicable.

in both countries, compared to the world average of 80 percent. The ratio of water withdrawal to renewable freshwater, called the criticality ratio, shows a high degree of water use intensity. The higher the criticality ratio, the more intensive is the use of river basin water and the lower the amount of water available for instream ecosystems. Hence, at high criticality ratios, water usage by downstream users can be impaired, and during low flow periods the chance of absolute water shortages increases. There is no objective basis for selecting a threshold between low and high water stress, but the literature indicates that criticality ratios equal to or greater than 0.4 are considered "high water stress," and those greater than 0.8 are considered "very high water stress" (Alcamo, Henrichs, and Rösch 2000). By this classification, we can see that all basins in north China and several basins in India are in the high water stress or very high water stress categories, although the country-level ratio is around 25 percent in both countries.

Some parameters, particularly for agricultural water uses, are presented in Table 10.2. Livestock water consumption is only about 1 percent of total consumption in both countries. Irrigation water supply reliability (IWSR) is defined as actual water consumption over potential water consumption demanded over all irrigated crops. China's average IWSR, at 0.87, is higher than India's, at 0.81. Basin efficiency (BE), defined as beneficial irrigation water consumption over

Ground-water recharge (km³)	Ground-water pump) (km³)	Withdrawal		Consumption		Withdrawal/ renewable water	Conservation/ renewable water
		Total (km³)	AGR (%)	Total (km³)	AGR (%)		
36.5	13.3	75.6	91.9	31.7	83.2	81	34
20.7	17.6	54.5	84.3	24.3	84.6	139	57
62.7	27.8	51.0	90.5	21.0	83.9	71	29
870.0	*98.0*	*664.0*	*0.9*	*301.0*	*0.84*	*25*	*11*
25.5	29.6	149.4	99.1	83.3	93.5	60	33
171.7	80.8	237.3	89.7	128.2	85.6	47	25
13.6	3.2	10.1	92.8	5.6	88.1	70	39
8.3	1.5	7.2	21.8	3.1	14.2	17	7
5.6	5.0	45.6	99.0	23.9	87.7	186	98
376.0	*161.0*	*627.0*	*92.6*	*339.0*	*86.7*	*27*	*15*

[a]Of the total renewable water, flow from other parts of these basins covers 30, 70, and 23 percent in Brahmaputra, Indus, and Ganges, respectively, and 25 percent in India.

TABLE 10.2 Agricultural water uses in China and India, 1995 and 2025

		Irrigation consumption (km³)	Livestock consumption (km³)	IWSR	BE	Consumption per hectare (m³/ha)
1995	China	244.2	3.4	0.87	0.54	2,721
	India	321.3	2.9	0.81	0.58	5,488
2025	China	230.9	7.4	0.79	0.60	2,234
	India	331.7	8.1	0.71	0.63	4,466

SOURCE: Rosegrant, Cai, and Cline (2002).

NOTE: BE, basin efficiency; IWSR, irrigation water supply reliability.

total irrigation consumption, including losses, takes into account the reuse of return flows as well as irrigation system performance. There is a considerable difference in BE of the basins in north and south China, with higher values in north China, which is far drier than south. In India, the differences across basins are relatively small. The countrywide average in India, at 0.58, is higher than China's, at 0.54. One reason is the greater groundwater use in India, which usually results in lower distribution and conveyance loss. Groundwater has provided 35–40 percent of the total irrigation supply of water in India and 25 percent in China (Shiklomanov 1998).

TABLE 10.3 Industrial and domestic water uses in China and India, 1995 and 2025

		Industrial			Domestic			
		Con-sumption (km³)	Percent-age of total	Per thousand U.S.$ GDP (m³)	Con-sumption (km³)	Percent-age of total	Per capita per day (liters)	Total non-agriculture percentage of total
1995	China	14.6	5.0	16.0	30.1	10.4	81	15.4
	India	7.3	2.1	34.1	21.1	6.0	62	8.0
2025	China	31.1	9.5	6.82	59.4	18.1	141	27.5
	India	15.7	4.0	10.2	40.9	10.3	86	14.3

SOURCE: Rosegrant, Cai, and Cline (2002).

It is striking that irrigation water consumption per hectare of harvested irrigated land is so different in China and India, with the rate in China's basins much lower than those in India's and China's countrywide average only about half of India's. The world average irrigation water consumption is 3,850 m³/ha, about 43 percent lower than India's and 40 percent higher than China's. Is this difference caused by irrigation water use efficiency? Our conclusion is that it is not, because irrigation efficiency at the basin scale is higher in India, as shown earlier. The high level of irrigation water consumption is due to the high level of crop evaporation-transpiration and the precipitation in India's river basins, which does not coincide well with the crop water requirement. Moreover, because of the synchronized pattern of precipitation and solar energy in most of China, a large portion of irrigated crops use irrigation water only as a supplement during the drier periods.

Table 10.3 presents industrial and domestic water uses. Industrial water consumption accounts for only 5 percent of total water consumption in China and 2 percent in India, and domestic water consumption accounts for only 10 percent of total water consumption in China and 6 percent in India. More water is required per unit of GDP in India than in China: water consumption per U.S.$1,000 of GDP in India is more than double that in China. However, domestic water consumption per capita in India is 20 percent lower than that in China. Although currently industrial and domestic water uses cover a small part of the total water use in both countries, population growth and industrialization in these two developing countries will make the nonagricultural water demand increase rapidly, as we will see later.

Food Production

In 1995, the irrigated area for cereals reached 70 percent of the total irrigated area in China and 65 percent in India. The total harvested irrigated area in China

TABLE 10.4 Irrigated and rain-fed cereal area, yield, and production in China and India, 1995 and 2025

		1995		2025	
	Unit	China	India	China	India
Area irrigated	thousand ha	62,391	37,795	67,063	47,055
Yield, irrigated	kg/ha	4,225	2,653	6,027.00	3,739.00
Production, irrigated	m mt	263.61	100.26	404.18	175.94
Relative irrigated production	%	0.87	0.83	0.75	0.70
Area rain-fed	thousand ha	26,221.00	62,291.00	29,014	48,934
Yield, rain-fed	kg/ha	3,585	1,197	4,738.00	1,652.00
Production, rain-fed	m mt	94.01	74.57	137.47	80.82
Relative rain-fed production	%	0.76	0.53	0.73	0.56
Total area	thousand ha	88,613.00	100,086.00	96,077	95,989
Total yield	kg/ha	4,036	1,747	5,638.00	2,675.00
Total production	m mt	357.62	174.82	541.65	256.76
Area irrigated / total area		70.40	37.80	69.8	49.0
Production irrigated / total production		73.7	57.3	74.6	68.5
Per capita cereal	kg/person	292.0	188.0	364.0	194.0

SOURCE: Rosegrant, Cai, and Cline (2002).

(90 m ha) is 1.5 times that in India (59 m ha), and the irrigated cereal area in China (62 m ha) is 1.7 times that in India (38 m ha). Per capita irrigated land is 0.073 ha in China compared to 0.063 ha in India.

The area, yield, and production of cereals on irrigated, rain-fed, and total land are shown in Table 10.4. The irrigated cereal yield is only 17 percent higher than the rain-fed yield in China, while it is 130 percent higher in India. However, the irrigated, rain-fed, and total cereal yield in China are 1.6, 3.0, and 2.0 times those in India, respectively. For comparison, the world averages of the irrigated, rain-fed, and total cereal yield are 3,480, 2,180, and 2,580 kg/ha, respectively, which lie between the yields of China and India.

Table 10.4 also shows the relative yield for irrigated and rain-fed cereals. Relative yield is defined as actual yield over the potential yield with zero water stress. The relative irrigated yield is higher than the relative rain-fed yield in both countries; however, in China the difference is significantly smaller than that in India. There is no significant difference between irrigated relative yield in China and India, but China's irrigated cereal yield is 60 percent higher than India's. This shows that the cereal yield differences are caused by factors other than water.

As for the contribution of irrigated and rain-fed crops, in China irrigated cereals are 73 percent of the total, using 70 percent of the total cereal area, while in India they are 57 percent of the total, using 38 percent of the total cereal area. Worldwide, irrigated cereals are 42 percent of the total, using 31 percent of the total cereal area.

China produces about 20 percent of the world's cereals and India 10 percent. Per capita cereal production is 292 kg in China and 188 kg in India, compared to the world average of 314 kg. However, total cereal demand in 1995 was 375 million metric tons (m mt) in China, with 69 percent food demand and 31 percent feeding demand (food demand for livestock). Total cereal demand is 171 m mt in India, with 96 percent food demand and only 4 percent feeding demand. China imports 17 m mt, India 4 m mt. These differences are due to the high level of consumption and production of livestock products in China, which absorbs a large amount of cereal for livestock feed, while the level of meat production and consumption remains low in India.

Based on water consumption and food production, we can assess water productivity, defined here as crop production per cubic meter of water consumption, including effective rainfall and irrigation water. For rice, water productivity is 0.60 kg/m^3 in China, 0.25 kg/m^3 in India, with 0.40 kg/m^3 as the worldwide average; for nonrice cereals, water productivity is 1.00 kg/m^3 in China and 0.40 kg/m^3 in India, with 0.70 kg/m^3 the worldwide average.

A Business-as-Usual (BAU) Scenario

The starting point for the result analysis is a BAU scenario that incorporates our best estimates of the policy, investment, technological, and behavioral parameters driving the food and water sectors. In the water component, the model uses hydrologic data (precipitation, evapotranspiration, and run-off) that re-create the hydrologic regime of 1961–91 (Alcamo, Henrichs, and Rösch 2000). The results of the BAU scenario are based on the mean of 30 specified hydrologic samples for various year sequences of the hydrologic regime between 1961 and 1990.

Moderate increases are projected for water withdrawal capacity, reservoir storage, and water management efficiency, based on estimates of current investment plans and the pace of water management reform. The total water withdrawal capacity in China is projected to increase by 25 percent between 1995 and 2025, from 680 km^3 (groundwater pumping 138 km^3) in 1995 to 845 km^3 (groundwater pumping 171 km^3) in 2025, an increase of 165 km^3. The total water withdrawal capacity in India is projected to increase by 22 percent between 1995 and 2025, from 810 km^3 (groundwater pumping 237 km^3) in 1995 to 990 km^3 (groundwater pumping 255 km^3) in 2025, an increase of 180 km^3.

In China, reservoir storage for water supply is projected to increase by 15 percent or 157 km^3 over the next 25 years; a larger relative increase of reservoir storage of 58 percent is projected for India, although the absolute increase of 135 km^3 is slightly lower than China's. Both water supply capacity and reservoir storage are growing far slower than in the past decades, particularly in China, because (1) there has been a growing concern for environmental and ecological requirements, especially in the river basins in north China and north and west India, and (2) new water supplies cost much more than existing water sources (three to four times, according to World Bank 1993). In some dry basins in China, such as the Haihe, the current reservoir storage and water supply capacity is already higher than the available water source.

Increasing agricultural water use efficiency will be an important strategy in the next 30 years in both countries, because they both have low irrigation efficiency at the local level. However, local or classical irrigation efficiency often overestimates the potential of water conservation at the river basin scale because it ignores the recycling of return flow. The basin efficiency concept used in our analysis captures the potential for reducing nonbeneficial water losses. Under the BAU scenario, average basin efficiency is projected to increase from 0.54 in 1995 to 0.60 in 2025 in China and from 0.58 to 0.63 in India. This is equivalent to reducing agricultural water consumption by 26 km^3 in China (almost half of the total run-off of the Huanghe) and 34 km^3 in India (about half of the flow generated in the Indus-India).

The nonirrigation water uses, including domestic, industrial, and livestock water uses, are projected to grow rapidly (Table 10.3). The total nonirrigation water consumption in China is projected to increase from 45 km^3 in 1995 to 91 km^3 in 2025, an increase of 102 percent. The fraction of industrial and domestic water consumption is projected to increase from 15 percent in 1995 to 28 percent in 2025. The total nonirrigation water consumption in India is projected to double, from 28 km^3 in 1995 to 57 km^3 in 2025. The fraction of industrial and domestic water consumption is projected to increase from 8 percent in 1995 to 14 percent in 2025. Significant improvements in industrial water use intensity are projected, continuing recent trends. Table 10.3 also shows that from 1995 to 2025, industrial water consumption per U.S.$1,000 of GDP is projected to fall to 7 m^3 from 16 m^3 in China and to 10 m^3 from 34 m^3 in India. Domestic water consumption will increase rapidly, with per capita water consumption projected to increase from 81 liters per day (l/day) to 141 l/day in China and from 62 l/day to 86 l/day in India.

Table 10.5 shows the potential growth in irrigated and rain-fed crops, including irrigated and rain-fed area and yield for cereal crops and irrigated area for other crops, from 1995 to 2025 in China, India, and the world. For all, the area increases much more slowly than crop yields, with a decline in rain-fed cereal area projected for India. The increase in irrigated area in the two countries will account for half of the total increase of harvested irrigated area in the world, which amounts to 65.5 m ha.

Table 10.2 also shows the actual irrigation water consumption and other items projected for 2025. In China, irrigation water consumption will decline by 6 percent, from 244 km^3 in 1995 to 231 km^3 in 2025, because of the very rapid increase in nonirrigation demand, the relatively slow growth in water

TABLE 10.5 Potential growth of irrigated and rain-fed crops in China and India, 1995–2025

		China			India			World		
		1995	2025	Percentage increase	1995	2025	Percentage increase	1995	2025	Percentage increase
Cereals	Irrigated area (m ha)	64.1	69.3	8.1	38.3	48.0	25.3	222.9	249.8	13.1
	Rain-fed area (m ha)	29.5	33.5	13.6	71.7	56.0	−21.9	561.9	590.9	5.2
	Irrigated yield (kg/ha)	4,747.0	7,727.0	62.8	3,014.0	5,229.0	73.5	4,018.0	6,334.0	57.6
	Rain-fed yield (kg/ha)	4,169.0	5,640.0	35.3	1,964.0	2,554.0	30.0	3,563.0	4,961.0	39.2
Other crops	Irrigated area (m ha)	27.4	38.4	40.1	20.7	28.3	36.7	152.5	191.1	25.3
Total	Irrigated area (m ha)	91.5	107.7	17.7	59.0	76.3	29.8	375.4	440.9	17.4

SOURCE: Rosegrant, Cai, and Cline (2002).

supply, and the 11 percent decline of irrigated rice area. As a result, IWSR in most of the basins in China will decline from 1995 to 2025, particularly in the basins in north China, with the countrywide average reduced to 0.79 in 2025 from 0.87 in 1995. Irrigation water consumption per hectare of irrigated area will decline by 22 percent or 490 m³ due to the decline of the water supply and the increase in basin efficiency.

In India, irrigation water consumption will have a slight increase of 3 percent, from 321 km³ in 1995 to 332 km³ in 2025. Due to the large increase of irrigated area (25 percent), IWSR in most of the basins in India will decline from 1995 to 2025, particularly in the basins of north and west India, with the countrywide average projected to be reduced to 0.71 in 2025 from 0.81 in 1995. Irrigation water consumption per hectare of irrigated area will decline by 23 percent, or 1,020 m³.

As a result, the actual increase in irrigated area from 1995 to 2025 will be smaller than the potential (Table 10.5). In China, the total actual irrigated crop area will increase by only 15.4 percent, or 13.9 m ha, and the actual cereal irrigated area will increase by 7.5 percent, or 4.7 m ha. In India, the total actual irrigated crop area will increase by 27.0 percent, or 15.7 m ha, and the actual cereal irrigated area will increase by 24.0 percent, or 9.2 m ha. The irrigated harvested area per capita will decline by 6 percent in China from 1995 to 2025 and by 11 percent in India.

Comparing the yield and production for the realized irrigated and rain-fed area in 2025 to the figures in 1995 (Table 10.4), we can identify the following changes. The relative irrigated production (RIP, or actual irrigated production over the potential) will decline for most of the basins in both countries as a result of the fall in the IWSR (actual water consumption over potential water demand) and of the stronger effect of water stress on crop production (Figures 10.2 and 10.3).

FIGURE 10.2 Comparison of IWSR and RIP in selected basins of China and India, 1995

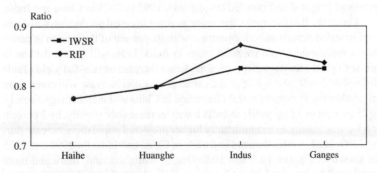

SOURCE: Cai and Rosegrant (2004).

FIGURE 10.3 Comparison of IWSR and RIP in selected basins of China and India, 2025

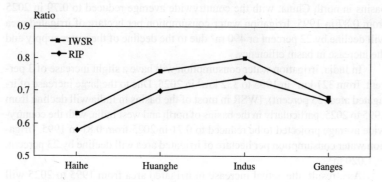

SOURCE: Cai and Rosegrant (2004).

The relative rain-fed production (RRP) is affected by two factors that contradict each other. One is the assumed improvement of rain-fed harvesting (3–5 percent higher than effective rainfall use for rain-fed crops), which will increase RRP. The other is the stronger effect of water stress on crop production, as was explained regarding irrigated production. As a result, we can see slight decreases of the RRP for river basins in China, with the countrywide average declining from 0.76 in 1995 to 0.73 in 2025, and a slight increase of the RRP in India, with the countrywide average increasing from 0.53 in 1995 to 0.56 in 2025.

In terms of the contribution of irrigated and rain-fed cereals, in China the share of irrigated cereal area and the share of irrigated cereal production will both decline slightly, while in India both will increase significantly, with the area share increasing from 37 percent in 1995 to 49 percent in 2025 and the production share increasing from 57 percent to 69 percent. Figure 10.4 shows the increases of irrigated and rain-fed cereals from 1995 to 2025 in China and India.

Under the BAU scenario, the major increase in cereal production will come from irrigated cereals in both countries, with 92 percent of the growth in cereal production coming from irrigated crops in India. India will have a decline in rain-fed cereal area, together with a moderate increase of rain-fed yield (Table 10.5). Worldwide, about half of the cereal production increase will come from irrigated crops. Per capita cereal production in China will increase significantly, by 25 percent or 72 kg, while in India it will increase only slightly, by 3 percent or 6 kg, due mainly to a significantly higher projected population increase during 2000–2025. Cereal demand and trade in China and India for 1995 and 2025 are shown in Figures 10.5 and 10.6. Due to rising demand, more and more cereals will be imported, about 7 percent of the demand in each country.

FIGURE 10.4 Cereal contribution of irrigated and rain-fed areas of China, India, and the world, 1995–2025

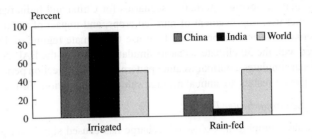

SOURCE: Rosegrant, Cai, and Cline (2002).

FIGURE 10.5 Cereal production, demand, and trade in China, 1995 and 2025

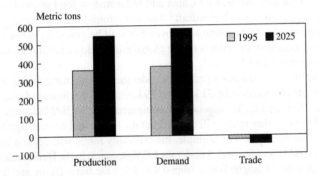

SOURCE: Rosegrant, Cai, and Cline (2002).

FIGURE 10.6 Cereal production, demand, and trade in India, 1995 and 2025

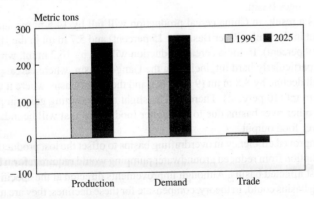

SOURCE: Rosegrant, Cai, and Cline (2002).

Alternative Scenarios

We now analyze several alternative scenarios for China and India regarding groundwater use, improvement of rain-fed crops, and impact of water prices. The alternative scenarios presented here use the climate regime of 1961–90 compared with the 30 climate scenario simulations used in the BAU scenario. This format simulates a normal weather pattern over the projection period. Specific projection results are annual average values for the period 2021–25.

Sustainable Groundwater Use

Groundwater pumping in excess of recharge has caused significant groundwater depletion in many regions, such as northern China and northern and western India. The amount of groundwater overdraft is 30 km^3 in north China, including the 3-H basins and the inland basins, and 69 km^3 in India, including the Indus and Ganges basins. Can China and India sustain food production while eliminating groundwater overdraft? The low groundwater-pumping (LGW) scenario assumes that groundwater overdraft will be gradually phased out by 2025 and examines the effects of the global elimination of groundwater overdraft, which is about 163 km^3.

The total annual water withdrawals under the LGW scenario during 2021–25 are projected to decrease by 31 km^3 and 79 km^3, or approximately 4 and 10 percent, in China and India, respectively, compared with the BAU scenario (Table 10.6). The criticality ratios will decline, but the IWSR will decline significantly in the affected basins. For example, the criticality ratios will decline from 1.6 under the BAU scenario to 1.3 under the LGW scenario in the Haihe Basin, from 1.2 to 1.0 in the Huanghe Basin, from 0.9 to 0.8 in the Indus Basin, and from 0.6 to 0.5 in the Ganges Basin. IWSR will decline from 0.61 under the BAU scenario to 0.45 under the LGW scenario in the Haihe Basin, from 0.74 to 0.54 in the Huanghe Basin, from 0.78 to 0.67 in the Indus Basin, and from 0.72 to 0.61 in the Ganges Basin.

As a result, in China cereal production will fall by 14.5 m mt, including 11 m mt in the Haihe River Basin (or 15 percent) and 5.7 m mt in the Huanghe Basin (9 percent). In India cereal production will fall by 16.2 m mt, with a few basins particularly hard hit, including the Ganges Basin, where cereal production will decline by 8.8 m mt (9 percent), and the Indus Basin, where it will fall by 4.6 m mt (10 percent). There will be slight compensating gains in production in other river basins due to the higher food prices that will be induced by the lower food output.

Improved efficiency in overdrafting basins to offset the lost production and consumption from reduced groundwater pumping would require reform beyond the most affected basins. Although improvements directed at the specific overdrafting basins could, in theory, compensate for these declines, they are unlikely to happen. For example, in the Indus Basin the 2025 BE values would need to

TABLE 10.6 Water withdrawal under BAU and LGW scenarios, 2021–25

Region or country	Water withdrawal (km³)		Water consumption (km³)	
	BAU	LGW	BAU	LGW
China	844	813	329	316
India	822	743	402	358
Developed countries	1,272	1,266	479	477
Developing countries	3,481	3,324	1,595	1,513
World	4,752	4,590	2,075	1,990

SOURCE: Rosegrant, Cai, and Cline (2002).

rise from 0.59 to 0.76 to generate enough cereal production to compensate for the reduced groundwater overdraft, and in China's Huanghe Basin the 2021–25 BE values would have to increase from 0.62 to 0.82.

In China and India, lower levels of cereal production and consumption will be accompanied by increased cereal imports. While these shortfalls will cause concern, they could very well be a worthwhile trade-off in restoring the sustainability of groundwater supplies. To compensate for the reduction in groundwater pumping, agricultural research investments should be increased to boost crop yields, and investment and policy reform, including the elimination of power subsidies for pumping, should be implemented to increase BE and encourage diversification out of irrigated cereals into crops that will give more value per unit of water. This will be particularly necessary in the hardest-hit river basins, such as the Ganges and Huanghe Basins.

Getting More Food from Rain-Fed Crops

We now present scenarios dealing with future changes in the growth and levels of investment in both irrigated and rain-fed agriculture, along with the impacts these may have on water withdrawal, water consumption, harvested area, cereal production, demand, and trade.

The low investment in infrastructure (LINV) scenario explores the impact of water supply investments on food production. Comparisons between the BAU and LINV scenarios in terms of BE, potential irrigated area, increased reservoir storage, and increased maximum allowable surface and groundwater water withdrawal (SMAWW and GMAWW) are presented in Table 10.7 for China, India, and the world. BE is projected to be lower under the LINV scenario than under the BAU scenario for all regions, which reduces beneficial crop water consumption by 10.5 km³ in China and 16.2 km³ in India. From 1995 to 2025, under the LINV scenario, reservoir storage will increase by 56 percent of the comparable increase under the BAU scenario in China and by 36 percent in India. Total water withdrawal capacity will increase by 30 percent of the comparable BAU scenario increase in China and by 35 percent in India.

The LINV scenario has significant negative impacts on water consumption, particularly on irrigation in both countries (Table 10.8). In dry basins, compared with the BAU scenario, water withdrawal will decline by 5 percent in the Haihe, 15 percent in the Huanghe, 13 percent in the Indus, and 7 percent in the Ganges River Basins under the LINV scenario. IWSR will decline from 0.61 under the BAU scenario to 0.56 under the LINV scenario in Haihe, from 0.74 to 0.61 in Huanghe, from 0.78 to 0.71 in Indus, and from 0.72 to 0.68 in Ganges.

Table 10.9 compares irrigated area, yield, production, demand, and trade for cereals in China, India, and aggregated regions under the BAU and LINV

TABLE 10.7 Basin efficiency, reservoir storage, and water withdrawal capacity under BAU and LINV scenarios, 1995–2025

Region or country	Basin efficiency (km³)		Storage increase (km³)		SMAWW increase (km³)		GMAWW increase (km³)	
	BAU	LINV	BAU	LINV	BAU	LINV	BAU	LINV
China	0.60	0.55	157.00	88.00	180.00	52.00	34.00	11.00
India	0.63	0.58	135.00	48.00	162.00	54.00	18.00	8.00
Developed countries	0.69	0.66	44.00	18.00	155.00	47.00	23.00	9.00
Developing countries	0.58	0.55	577.00	231.00	772.00	279.00	104.00	43.00
World	0.60	0.57	621.00	249.00	926.00	326.00	136.00	52.00

SOURCE: Rosegrant, Cai, and Cline (2002).

TABLE 10.8 Water withdrawal and consumption under BAU and LINV scenarios, 2021–25

Region or country	Water withdrawal (km³)		Irrigation consumption (km³)		Total consumption (km³)	
	BAU	LINV	BAU	LINV	BAU	LINV
China	844	729	233	186	329	279
India	822	742	338	299	402	359
Developed countries	1,272	1,182	278	242	479	438
Developing countries	3,481	3,044	1,216	1,013	1,596	1,374
World	4,752	4,226	1,493	1,253	2,075	1,813

SOURCE: Rosegrant, Cai, and Cline (2002).

TABLE 10.9 Irrigated cereal area, yield, production, demand, and trade under BAU and LINV scenarios, 2021–25

Region or country	Irrigated area (m ha)		Irrigated yield (mt/ha)		Irrigated production (m mt)		Increase (km³)		Cereal trade (m mt)	
	BAU	LINV	BAU	LINV	BAU	LINV	BAU	LINV	BAU	LINV
China	66.6	58.7	5.9	5.6	391.6	331.6	571.9	553.9	–42.9	–80.6
India	46.7	42.2	3.8	3.8	178.3	160.1	268.5	256.3	–8.8	–11.5
Developed countries	45.1	44.0	6.0	5.7	269.1	252.7	794.2	783.1	236.5	252.8
Developing countries	191.9	174.2	4.5	4.4	869.1	761.3	1,754.4	1,686.3	–236.0	–252.8
World	237.0	218.2	4.8	4.6	1,138.2	1,014.0	2,548.5	2,469.4	n.a.	n.a.

SOURCE: Rosegrant, Cai, and Cline (2002).

NOTE: n.a., not applicable.

scenarios in 1995 and 2021–25. Compared to the BAU scenario, irrigated cereal production in China will decline by 60 m mt or 15 percent, cereal demand will decline by 18 m mt or 3 percent, and cereal imports will increase by 37.7 m mt or 88 percent, while cereal production in India will decline by 18.2 m mt or 10 percent, demand will decline by 13.2 m mt or 5 percent, and imports will increase by 2.7 m mt or 31 percent. Irrigated production will be significantly reduced in the dry basins, including 16 percent reduction in the Haihe, 21 percent in the Huanghe, 13 percent in the Indus, and 10 percent in the Ganges Basin.

In the higher rain-fed production (HRF) scenario, two strategies to attempt compensation for the loss in irrigated production could be: (1) increasing rain-fed production through higher rain-fed yield and area growth and (2) making greater improvements in rainfall harvesting. Although irrigation is important, further expansion of rain-fed agriculture in terms of increasing crop yields through improvement in water harvesting, agricultural research, and policy reforms will be crucial to future agricultural growth.

The low investment in infrastructure but higher increase in rain-fed area and yield (LINV–HRF) scenario adds the dimension of high increases in rain-fed area and yield to the LINV scenario discussed before. To examine the potential for rain-fed production growth to compensate for the reductions in irrigated area and irrigation water supply, we assume that rain-fed area and yield will increase to levels that can almost offset the lower irrigated production and maintain essentially the same international trade prices. A larger increase is assigned to rain-fed yield than to area because of limited potential for area expansion.

The low investment in irrigation development and water supply but high increase in effective rainfall use (LINV–HIER) scenario looks at the possibility of increasing effective rainfall use to counteract the reduction of irrigated production resulting from low investment in irrigation development and water supply. Effective rainfall use will gradually increase by 10–15 percent above 1995 levels from 1995 to 2025 in those basins or countries with rainwater shortages for crop production, including river basins in northern and western China and northern and western India.

Table 10.10 shows the rain-fed yield, area, and production of cereals in China, India, and aggregated regions under the BAU, LINV–HRF, and LINV–HIER scenarios, represented as annual averages during 2021–25. The total cereal production of irrigated and rain-fed crops is also presented to show the compensation designed for the two scenarios aiming at high rain-fed production.

In China, under the LINV–HRF scenario, the rain-fed area and yield of cereals will be 7 percent and 15 percent higher, respectively, than under the BAU scenario. However, such increases will be unable to increase rain-fed production enough to offset the irrigated production decline, because the dominant share of total cereal harvested area is irrigated. The annual cereal production during 2021–25 will still be 39 m mt below that under the BAU scenario, although

TABLE 10.10 Rain-fed cereal area, yield, production, demand, and trade under BAU and HRF scenarios, 2021–25

Region or country	Rain-fed cereal area (m ha)			Rain-fed yield (mt/ha)			Rain-fed production (m mt)			Total production (m mt)			
	BAU	LINV-HRF	LINV-HIER	BAU	LINV-HRF	LINV-HIER	BAU	LINV-HRF	LINV-HIER	BAU	LINV	LINV-HRF	LINV-HIER
China	29.6	31.8	31.2	4.65	5.36	4.67	137	170	146	529.0	473.3	490.0	474.0
India	49.8	51.7	51.9	1.63	1.99	1.68	81	103	87	259.0	244.8	262.0	251.0
Developed world	196.0	198.7	44.0	3.89	4.24	3.95	762	842	822	1,031.0	1035.9	1,084.0	1,068.0
Developing world	316.1	323.4	174.2	2.08	2.36	2.18	656	763	722	1,525.0	1445.2	1,505.0	1,483.0
World	513.1	522.2	218.2	2.77	3.07	2.86	1,418	1,605	1,544	2,556.0	2481.1	2,590.0	2,551.0

SOURCE: Rosegrant, Cai, and Cline (2002).

it will be 17 m mt higher than under the LINV scenario. For particularly water-scarce basins such as the 3-H basins, the potential of using reasonably higher rain-fed area and yield to compensate for the irrigated production loss under the LINV scenario will be much less effective.

In India, under the LINV–HRF scenario the rain-fed area and yield of cereals will be 4 percent and 22 percent higher than under the BAU scenario, and such increases can increase rain-fed production enough to offset the irrigated production decline. The annual cereal production during 2021–25 will be even 3 m mt higher than under the BAU scenario and 17 m mt higher than under the LINV scenario.

Under the LINV–HIER scenario, none of the basins or countries will be able to produce enough additional food from rain-fed agriculture to compensate for the irrigated production loss from low irrigation and water supply investment. Annual cereal production during 2021–25 in China will be only slightly higher under the LINV–HIER scenario than under the LINV scenario but still 55 m mt or 10 percent lower than under the BAU scenario, while in India it will be 6.2 m mt or 2.5 percent higher than under the LINV scenario but 8.0 m mt or 3.0 percent lower than under the BAU scenario. For river basins, cereal production under the LINV–HIER scenario and compared with the BAU scenario will decline by 3 percent in the Haihe, 7 percent in the Huanghe, 13 percent in the Indus, and 7 percent in the Ganges River Basins. It is clear from these results that irrigation is critical in these basins and countries, and although water harvesting for rain-fed areas may be effective, the impacts will be limited.

Impacts of Water Prices

As in many other countries, prevailing low water prices and high subsidies for capital investment and operation and management costs threaten the financial viability of irrigation and urban water supplies in China and India, creating a particularly serious problem given the huge financial resources needed for the future. Low water prices and poor cost recovery compromise the efficient maintenance of existing water infrastructure as well as the additional investments necessary to develop future water projects. Perhaps even more fundamentally, low water prices encourage misallocation and wasteful water use in all sectors. A key motive for reforming water pricing policies is the growing competition between domestic, industrial, irrigation, and environmental uses, especially in arid or semiarid regions. If higher water prices could substantially reduce the withdrawal of water in other sectors, the savings would be available for environmental uses.

We define and analyze high water price scenarios here to explore the potential of higher water prices to achieve water conservation, balancing direct human consumptive water uses with environmental water uses in China, India, and the world. Compared with the BAU scenario, under the higher water price scenarios, water prices for agriculture, industry, and connected households are projected to increase gradually during 2000–2025. By 2025, water prices will be 2.25 times higher for industrial water use, 2.00 times higher for domestic water use, and 3.00 times higher for agricultural water use than under the BAU scenario in China and India. Based on varying levels of water use efficiency, measured as BE, and the proportion of conserved water allocated to the environment, two specific scenarios are defined, as follows:

1. Under the higher price (HP) scenario, higher water prices will be implemented with the restrictive assumption that water use efficiency will not be influenced by prices but remain the same as under the BAU scenario, and a large portion (79 percent in China and 62 percent in India) of the conserved water will be allocated to environmental uses.

2. Under the higher price, higher basin efficiency (HP–HE) scenario, higher water prices will be implemented, and a moderate elasticity of water use efficiency with respect to water prices will be assumed, so water use efficiency as a country average in 2025 will be 0.68 compared to 0.60 under the BAU scenario in China and 0.73 compared to 0.63 in India, with the portions of the conserved water allocated to environmental uses the same as under the HP scenario.

Nonirrigation consumptive water uses include industrial, domestic, and livestock water uses. Under the higher price scenarios, water demand in 2021–25 will decrease by large amounts compared with levels under the BAU scenario for China, India, and the world (Table 10.11). The total nonirrigation consumptive water use will decline by 29.3 km^3 or 29 percent in China, by 14.5 km^3 or 29 percent in India, and by 150 km^3 or 25 percent in the world.

TABLE 10.11 Consumptive water use for nonirrigated sectors under BAU and HP scenarios, 2021–25

Region or country	Domestic (km^3) BAU	Domestic (km^3) HP	Industrial (km^3) BAU	Industrial (km^3) HP	Livestock (km^3) BAU	Livestock (km^3) HP	Total nonirrigation (km^3) BAU	Total nonirrigation (km^3) HP
China	60.9	46.2	32.1	18.5	7.6	6.7	100.6	71.3
India	41.4	34.0	16	9.8	8.3	7.4	65.7	51.2
Developed countries	69.9	61.3	115.7	85.6	18.5	17.5	204.0	164.4
Developing countries	225.5	175.2	133.8	69.1	46.2	40.6	395.4	284.9
World	295.3	236.5	239.5	154.6	64.6	58.1	599.4	449.2

SOURCE: Rosegrant, Cai, and Cline (2002).

TABLE 10.12 Water withdrawal under BAU and HP scenarios, 2021–25

Region or country	Water withdrawal (km³)		Total water consumption (km³)		Agricultural water consumption (km³)	
	BAU	HP	BAU	HP	BAU	HP
China	844	676	329	329	228	206
India	822	692	402	402	336	298
Developed countries	1,272	1,080	479	479	275	265
Developing countries	3,481	2,834	1,595	1,595	1,200	1,074
World	4,752	3,913	2,075	2,075	1,476	1,339

SOURCE: Rosegrant, Cai, and Cline (2002).

Under both the HP and the HP–HE scenarios, lower levels of water withdrawal and water consumption are projected in 2021–25 than under the BAU scenario (Table 10.12). Annual water withdrawal during 2021–25 will decline by 168 km³ or 20 percent in China, 130 km³ or 16 percent in India, and 840 km³ or 18 percent in the world; annual water consumption during 2021–25 will decline by 52 km³ or 16 percent in China, 53 km³ or 13 percent in India, and 287 km³ or 14 percent in the world. The saved water in China will be close to the annual run-off of the Huanghe, and the saved water in India will be 70 percent of the run-off generated in the Indus-India Basin.

The total water consumption in 2021–25 under the HP–HE scenario will be the same as under the HP scenario, but the beneficial water consumption for irrigation will be substantially higher under the HP–HE scenario, generating significant crop production gains, as shown by IWSR under the BAU, HP, and HP–HE scenarios in Table 10.13. The beneficial water consumption for irrigation under the HP–HE scenario will be about 18.5 km³ higher than under the HP scenario in China and 30.0 km³ higher in India.

As a result, the cereal production under the HP scenario will be lower than under the BAU scenario, while the production under the HP–HE scenario will be close to that under the BAU scenario, also shown in Table 10.13, which further shows the net cereal trade in China and India. The cereal imports in both countries under the HP–HE scenario will be close to those under the BAU scenario.

For river basins, water withdrawals will drop significantly under the HP and HP–HE scenarios compared with the BAU scenario, including declines of 23 percent in the Haihe, 19 percent in the Huanghe, 20 percent in the Indus, and 15 percent in the Ganges River Basins. IWSR values will decline for all the local water-scarce basins under the HP scenario, with reductions of 0.08 to 0.13. Under the HP–HE scenario, with increases in BE in response to higher water

TABLE 10.13 IWSR, change of cereal production, and trade under BAU, HP, and HP–HE scenarios, 2021–25

Region or country	IWSR			Change of cereal production				Trade (m mt)		
			HP–ㅤ	HP		HP–HE				HP–
	BAU	HP	HE	m mt	%	m mt	%	BAU	HP	HE
China	0.77	0.69	0.77	–16.7	–4.3	–0.3	–0.1	–47.3	–56.5	–46.6
India	0.73	0.64	0.73	–10.1	–5.7	–0.2	–0.1	–10.5	–15.3	–10.7
Developed countries	0.90	0.85	0.89	–2.8	–1.0	0.3	0.1	233.9	243.4	234.7
Developing countries	0.75	0.67	0.75	–40.1	–4.6	–0.9	–0.1	–233.9	–243.4	–234.7
World	0.77	0.70	0.77	–42.9	–3.8	–0.6	–0.1	0.0	0.0	0.0

SOURCE: Rosegrant, Cai, and Cline (2002).

prices, IWSR will decline only slightly compared to the BAU scenario in the Haihe River Basin and will remain the same or increase slightly in the remaining basins. Correspondingly, shortfalls in total cereal production compared with the BAU scenario will range from 4 to 9 percent for the Haihe, Huanghe, Indus, and Ganges River Basins under the HP scenario; under the HP–HE scenario, these basins will be able to use increased efficiency to reduce or eliminate production shortfalls, with shortfall in cereal production at only 1.5 percent in the Haihe Basin and 0.5 percent in the Ganges under the HP–HE scenario compared to the BAU.

The results show that water prices are powerful tools for influencing water demand in domestic, industrial, and agricultural sectors and in determining the availability of water for the environment. Even under the worst-case scenario, where water prices will have no impact on basin efficiency, the large percentage changes in water prices will have relatively modest impacts on food production. These modest impacts will occur because the water price response is low in agriculture and the decline in irrigated production causes increases in food prices that induce more rain-fed production (and partially mitigate the fall in irrigated production). Also, in a few water-scarce regions where water use is constrained by availability rather than prices, a portion of the water released from nonagricultural uses provides additional water for irrigation.

In the more likely case that there will be at least moderate increases in BE in response to increases in agricultural water prices, beneficial water consumption for irrigation will be maintained at nearly the BAU levels, even though total consumption declines when water prices increase. Even severely water-scarce river basins such as the Huanghe and the Indus Basins will be able to compensate for water price increases and achieve water use efficiencies, irrigation reliability, and cereal production nearly equal to BAU scenario levels. The major beneficiary in the HP scenarios will be the environment. The dramatic reduction in the ratio of withdrawals to total water availability in response to price increases means there will be a significant improvement in water quality as the reuse of water declines, and the reduction in water withdrawals will provide a major increase in environmental flows.

Conclusion

We have examined the similarities and disparities between China and India in terms of water resource development and food production in both current status and future prospects. To achieve food security in the next 25 years for these highly populated countries, the infrastructure investments and water management improvements as assumed under the BAU scenario will be important. The large-scale irrigation development experienced in the past decades will not be able to continue due to financial resource limits and environmental concerns, as well as the decreasing marginal benefit (Fan, Hazell, and Thorat 1999; Fan, Zhang, and Zhang 2002). This will make management improvements at both micro and macro scales more important in the future: more attention should be given to crop breeding for rain-fed agriculture, water harvesting and minimum tillage, and investing for efficiency.

The challenge for both countries is how to implement management reforms. Considering the low level of water charges in both countries, it seems that increasing water prices will have large positive impacts in water saving in both agricultural and nonagricultural sectors and also in reservation of environmental water flows. The higher prices combined with improved water use efficiency will result in almost the same agriculture production in both countries, while a large increase in flows (about 170 km^3 less withdrawal in each of the countries) will remain in stream for environmental purposes.

However, the problems of implementing water pricing policy reform in developing countries should be noted. Most obviously, equity issues must be addressed so as to provide water to low-income households. Second, measuring and monitoring water use are costly activities, constraining water pricing where institutions and infrastructure are weak. Nevertheless, innovative water pricing systems can be designed and implemented that will have reasonable administrative costs and provide increased incentives for water conservation without reducing incomes and while possibly even enhancing the incomes of the poor. In the domestic and industrial water sectors, water price increases could be made directly, replacing existing generalized subsidies with subsidies targeted to the poor. The price incentives may include (1) direct price increases for households and industry; (2) subsidies targeted to the poor; (3) punitive irrigation water price increases; (4) design of pricing mechanisms to pay irrigators to use less water; (5) rural infrastructure investment to improve access to markets, credit, and inputs; and (6) establishment of water rights.

In countries like China and India with limited land and water for agriculture, one important prospect for food production among our assumptions is that production increase in the next 25 years will depend more on yield increase than on area increase, particularly for cereals, both irrigated and rain-fed. It will not be enough to stabilize the current crop yields by maintaining IWSR. Rather, they will have to be increased through inputs other than water, particularly in India. Although the improvement of water use efficiency and the increase of water supply capacity, particularly including rainfall harvesting from rain-fed crops, can contribute to stable crop yields, the major contribution to yield increase is expected from investment in agricultural infrastructure and agricultural research over the next 25 years (see also Fan, Hazell, and Thorat 1999). This is based on our finding that the water supply for agriculture is becoming more and more restricted due to source availability and environmental and financial constraints.

Following a BAU scenario, we find that the major increase of cereal production between 1995 and 2025 will be from irrigated cereal crops in China (76 percent) and India (92 percent). In China this will be mainly because of the larger share of irrigated crops (about 70 percent), as well as an irrigated yield increase of 60 percent. In India the irrigated area will increase by about 40 percent, while the rain-fed cereal area will decrease by 20 percent (assuming part of the rain-fed land will be converted to irrigation) and the irrigated and rain-fed yield will increase by 73 percent and 30 percent, respectively.

In terms of water productivity, or food production per unit of water consumption ("more food per drop of water"), Cai and Rosegrant (2004) argued that the major contribution comes from the increase of crop yield through investment in agricultural infrastructure and agricultural research, which is expected to have higher payoffs than investments in new irrigation. Meanwhile, large improvements in water use efficiency would significantly increase water productivity and reduce water withdrawal constraints.

India's irrigated cereal yield is much lower than China's due to factors other than water, because there is no significant difference between the relative yields (actual over potential) in the two countries. Strategies for increasing irrigated food production in India may include (1) increasing other agricultural inputs, such as fertilizer, and (2) reducing crop evapotranspiration through agronomic, hydrologic, and biotechnological studies.

India's rain-fed crop yield is particularly low due to much greater water stress compared to China. Under the BAU scenario, we do not project a large increase in the rain-fed crop yield in India but assume that a large fraction of the rain-fed land will be transformed to irrigated land following conventional practices. However, our optional scenario analysis on obtaining more food from rain-fed crops shows that India's rain-fed crops have a higher potential to increase food production through yield increases and improvements in rainfall harvesting. Drought-tolerant crops based on biotechnology will be a significant contribution (also see Pender and Hazell 2002).

The river basins in China, particularly in northern China, are highly developed. Increasing water use efficiency will be an urgent task for the country. Recent changes in investment into irrigation systems will encourage better water management, including targeting investments toward maintenance rather than new construction and establishing better management practices to encourage financial self-sufficiency. Water policy has been consolidated for integrated water resources management seeking high water use efficiency. Institutions and policy changes to encourage water conservation at the village and farm levels are being established and could have lasting impacts on water use in agriculture, including enhancing field irrigation management, raising water prices, establishing water markets (at a very initial stage), and investing in water-saving irrigation technology extension. Cropping patterns will likely adjust in response to new water management policies and more limited water delivery, even if irrigated acreage is maintained. High-value cash crops may expand in acreage in the face of water shortages, because these are often better suited to water-saving irrigation practices, bringing a higher return to water used in agriculture, and, being labor intensive, would make more productive use of China's large rural labor force. Better understanding of how these changes will affect agriculture will be a complex research topic in itself. Understanding what preconditions must be met to implement those policy reforms will assist policymakers in their decisions about sustainable development in both agriculture and water resources (Lohmar and Wang 2002). Moreover, interbasin water transfers have been conducted and will take a more important role in eliminating water stress in northern China in the future with the start of one the world's largest water transfer projects, the South–North Water Transfer Project in China (Cai and Rosegrant 2004).

During the 1980s, and especially during the 1990s, India's irrigation rapidly moved to a private provision mode. Even in Punjab and Haryana, pumps deliver over half of the irrigation water. As this ratio increases, surface irrigation systems are rapidly turning into a recharge system. This has major implications for the design of large irrigation projects. A very good example is Narmada, which has just begun providing water for irrigation and recharging groundwater. China has serious groundwater overdraft problems in the north and a large potential for groundwater use in the south. The conjunctive channel well systems that have been developed and proved to be effective in India might be a useful reference for improving the large-scale irrigation systems in China.

Appendix 10A: The Impact-Water Model

In this model, industrial water demand is dependent on GDP per capita, and demand intensity is expressed in cubic meters of water per U.S.$1,000 GDP. It also includes a technology variable that varies with time and water prices. The impact of water prices is captured through the elasticity of industrial demand with respect to water prices. Water demand is estimated based on projections of population growth, income growth, and water prices. Livestock water demand is projected as a function of livestock production and water prices.

To assess irrigation water demand, the physical demand is first estimated based on crop irrigation requirements (crop evapotranspiration minus rainfall used by crops) and irrigation water use efficiency (defined as the ratio of beneficial water consumption to total consumption). The physical water demand is then adjusted with respect to water prices using price elasticities of demand for water in irrigation. Water supply is computed based on both hydrologic processes and anthropogenic impacts. Committed flows (defined as the water that is reserved for environmental and instream uses and is thus unavailable for other uses) are treated as a predetermined constraint on the water supply, and the offstream water supply for the domestic, industrial, livestock, and irrigation sectors is determined through two steps: (1) the total water that could be depleted in each time period (month) for various offstream uses is determined, and (2) the water supply for different sectors is determined. Assuming that domestic water demand is satisfied first, followed by industrial and livestock water demand, irrigation water supply is the residual claimant, which is further allocated based on crop water requirements and profitability.

Food demand and production are calculated in a partial equilibrium model representing a competitive agricultural market for crops and livestock. Demand is a function of prices, income, and population growth. Growth in crop production is determined by crop and input prices and the rate of productivity growth. World agricultural commodity prices are determined annually at levels that clear international markets. The model makes projections for crops, area, yield, production, demand for food, feed and other uses, prices, and trade, as well as for livestock, numbers, yield, production, demand, prices, and trade.

PART IV

Market and Trade Reforms

This part of the book deals with the two current themes of agricultural marketing reforms and trade liberalization and food security. China's "mobilizing society" and the centralized Chinese polity worked together to allow relatively more effective implementation of reforms and thus gave more leeway to leaders in selecting the optimal course and pace of reforms. They chose first to create incentives and markets and then to open up markets, which proved a successful sequence based on the rates of growth and poverty reduction recorded.

By contrast, the Indian democracy was more complex; it has been described as a "debating society" (Rao 2003) and was slow, even reluctant, to reform domestic marketing policies. The fact that reforms were actually crisis driven did not give much choice to policymakers with regard to the sequencing of reforms. To tackle the country's fiscal and current account deficits, the government was somewhat bound to the path of macroeconomic and trade interventions. While it could be argued that markets did not need to be created because they were already in place in India, the persistence of a panoply of restrictions on agricultural input and output markets hindered the smooth functioning of these markets and limited the overall competitiveness of the primary sector.

China and India fostered different marketing systems and have undertaken different reforms in this area. Both countries showed considerable improvement in agricultural performance, which turned them from famine-prone countries not only into food-secure countries with rising foodgrain stocks but also into successful exporters of domestic agricultural output. The different procurement and pricing policies they followed in grains and other major agricultural commodities made vital contributions to their success in the area of food self-sufficiency. Achievement of food surpluses allowed both countries to gradually relax controls and reform the closed and highly regulated policy environments related to these policies. But there was a fundamental difference between the styles of two countries: China fully embraced a new market and export-oriented economic policy, while India hesitated on the grounds of the observed political difficulties.

Chapters 11 and 12, on agricultural marketing reforms, review the policy changes in both input and output markets and their impact on agricultural growth, farmers' income, and poverty reduction in the rural areas of the two countries. They also examine the forces behind the past interventions, the compatibility of domestic market reforms with an open economy environment, and what should be the focus of future reforms.

In China, the new economic policy implied that agricultural trade reforms were preceded by reforms of input and output markets in the domestic arena. Chapter 11 explores the major Chinese marketing reforms: the progressive liberalization of the quota procurement system for foodgrains, cotton, meat, and horticultural produce; the convergence of planned and market prices; the removal of the state monopoly in trading and the parallel removal of restrictions on private trade; and the abolition of the urban food rationing system.

In India, interventions to liberalize agricultural trade flows were not accompanied by determinant marketing reforms on the domestic front, which created imbalances in the economy. The country still retains the basic traditional closed approach to agricultural policy and the related self-sufficiency focus on foodgrains, which is no longer sustainable in the current context of increasing trade liberalization and the diversification of output toward high-value commodities. Thus Chapter 12 seeks to identify the distortions created over time by the lack of reforms in the three major traditional marketing policies: minimum support prices, the public distribution system, and input subsidies. It discusses the consequential impacts on agricultural growth and diversification, productivity, farmers' incomes, and rural poverty and highlights areas that need to be addressed.

The theme of trade liberalization and food security is explored in Chapters 13 and 14, which include discussion of the major reforms in trade policies in China and India, measures of trade distortion and their changes over time, the potential impact of liberalization on agricultural trade flows, farmers' income, and rural poverty.

To prepare for its entry to the World Trade Organization, China started liberalizing its agricultural trade in the early 1990s. Even before that, in the 1980s, significant reforms affecting agriculture, such as currency depreciation, had begun. In India, agricultural trade was opened up only in the mid-1990s with the signing of the Uruguay Round Agreement on Agriculture in 1994 as part of the overall trade liberalization.

An analysis of nominal protection coefficients for major agricultural commodities shows a gradual improvement in market access in both countries. As a result of the decline in tariffs, quantitative restrictions, licensing requirements, and other nontariff barriers, the simple applied average agricultural tariff declined to 35 percent in India as of mid-2002 and to 21 percent in China in 2001. The higher degree of openness of Chinese agriculture, determined by the more aggressive "open-door" policies pursued, particularly in the areas of foreign investment and exports, is reflected in the trade indicators, such as ratios of exports to total GDP and the share of foreign direct investment in total GDP.

What have been the effects of the new policies on trade flows in the two countries? The overall trend observed in the case of China (and expected for India with the continuation of liberalization) is that domestic output increasingly reflects the regional comparative advantages and food security is no longer bound to domestic self-sufficiency. There is greater scope for imports on the grounds of attainment of comfortable exchange reserve levels.

There are both benefits and downsides to agricultural market and trade liberalization. How does a nation manage a gradual transition from an insulated agricultural economy to a more open economy? What institutions and instruments are needed to make this transition smooth? What have been the positive and harmful effects on farmers in China and India? What are the insurance mechanisms and safety nets that need to be adopted to mitigate and counter the harmful effects? These are some of the critical issues examined in this part of the book.

11 Agricultural Marketing Reforms in China: Striking a Balance between Sequencing and Speed

BINGSHENG KE

Food and agricultural policy in China has undergone radical changes in the 25 years since the late 1970s, when the Household Responsibility System (HRS) replaced the collectives. The reforms then gradually expanded to the marketing and distribution sectors. In 1992, the 14th Party Congress explicitly declared the establishment of a socialist market system as the ultimate goal of the reform and further manifested and strengthened it at the 15th Party Congress in September 1997.

Marketing reform for agricultural commodities in China was initiated a few years after the introduction of the HRS. The most important reason for this was that agricultural reform in China started with a bottom-up approach. This was possible in the production sector with the progressive breakdown of collective farming but not in marketing, where the reform process has taken a much longer and more circuitous route. It was only after production reforms achieved great success and the deficiency in the marketing system started impeding further reforms that policymakers turned their attention to the marketing system.

Under the extremely rigid planned economic system prior to 1978, market distortions were dominant in almost all aspects of the agricultural and food chain, from farming inputs to agricultural products; from farm gate to consumer food bags; from staple food such as rice, wheat, and corn to nonstaples including meat, vegetables, fruits, and even food ingredients; and from pricing to physical distribution of the goods.

Because the whole system had been developed as a result of the shortage of food and supply of industrial raw material, it had a policy bias in favor of the urban and industrial sectors. Inputs for changing this system came from two interactive sides: changes in policy ideology and changes in production and supply conditions.

The author acknowledges the substantial, insightful, and constructive comments and suggestions as well as the editorial help received from Professor Zhong Funing of Nanjing Agricultural University.

239

We discuss first the changes in agricultural and food policy goals and then the various aspects of agricultural marketing policy changes that were implemented in both output and input markets. The next section analyzes the impact of domestic marketing reforms on agricultural performance, farmers' income, rural poverty, and consumer welfare. The final section is devoted to analyzing the interactions between marketing and trade policy reforms as well as the future reform orientation and is followed by concluding remarks on the future.

Changes in Agricultural and Food Policy Goals

Rapid and continued overall economic development has spurred changes in Chinese agricultural policy by providing favorable conditions for reform in the sector (Table 11.1). A fast-growing population with rising income requires not only an increase in food supply but also better quality and greater variety. Declining area under cultivation requires more intensive use of the existing cropland.

The increasing share of off-farm income led to weakened incentives and rising opportunity costs in farm production. The sharp decline of agriculture's share in the national economy also had far-reaching impacts on the goals and instruments of food and agriculture policy. As a result, the prevailing goals of agricultural policy in China changed significantly over time.

Industrialization

Before reforms began, agriculture was assigned an ancillary role as the major source of capital accumulation for the development of urban industries. Policymakers under the planned economy system used the obligatory delivery quotas and a ban on free marketing to hold down the prices of agricultural produce and labor costs for urban sectors. This objective was only gradually given up. Since the early 1980s, the market has been liberalized, first for fruits and vegetables and then for fishery and livestock products and oilseeds. But it was only in 2004 that delivery quotas for grains were finally abolished completely across the country and free marketing for all farm commodities, including grain, put in place.

Foreign Exchange Earnings

Agricultural products played an important role in accumulating foreign exchange reserves in the past. However, given the dramatic growth in total exports over time, the sharp decline in the share of agricultural exports, and consecutive years of trade surpluses, such earnings are no longer so important for China in food and agricultural trade policy.

Market Stability

Market stability has become a major goal in recent years. Under the old planning system, prices were completely controlled by the government and were

TABLE 1L1 Changes in the overall economy and in agriculture in China in selected years, 1980–2005

		1980	1985	1990	1995	2000	2005
Population	Million people	981	1,059	1,143	1,211	1,266	1,308
Cropland	Million ha	99.3	96.8	95.7	95	130	122
Per capita income							
Urban	Yuan	420	685	1,387	3,893	6,280	10,493
Rural	Yuan	191	398	686	1,578	2,253	3,255
Off-farm		19	70	146	483	1,117	1,400
Retail price index	1980 = 100	100	119	192	329	327	330
Total imports	Billion U.S.$	20	42.3	53.4	132.1	223.7	660.1
Total exports	Billion U.S.$	18.1	27.4	62.1	148.8	249.2	762.0
Agriculture's share of							
GDP	Percent	30.4	29.8	28.4	20.8	16.4	12.4
Employment	Percent	68.6	62.4	60.2	52.2	50.0	47
Imports	Percent	34.6	12.1	16.1	9.3	5.0	4.3
Exports	Percent	26.5	24.5	17.2	9.4	6.3	3.6
Food expenditures	Percent	61	56.7	54.7	52.3	46	43
Rural	Percent	62	58	59	50	48	46
Urban	Percent	57	52	50	39	38	37
Chemical fertilizer use	Million tons	12.7	17.8	25.9	35.9	41.5	48
Grain production	Million tons	320.6	379.1	446.2	466.6	462.2	484
Meat production	Million tons	12.1	19.3	28.6	52.6	61.3	77
Fruit production	Million tons	6.8	11.6	18.7	42.1	62.3	170
Cotton production	Million tons	2.71	4.15	4.51	4.77	4.42	5.70

SOURCE: NBS, *China Statistical Yearbook*, various years.

seldom changed, irrespective of any fluctuation in production. However, as market mechanisms play an increasingly important role in the reform process, price fluctuations have occurred frequently in response to instability in food production since the mid-1980s, creating inflation worries. As the Chinese domestic market continues to become more closely integrated with the world market, particularly following China's entry into the World Trade Organization (WTO), market stabilization considerations will become even more important for agricultural policy in the future.

Food Security and Sovereignty

Food security and sovereignty have been two dominant goals in trade policy. As food supply has burgeoned, especially since the 1990s, their importance has been reduced. Besides, the emphasis of farm production shifted from quantity to quality and variety. But these goals continue to be important as a result of the grain production shortfalls in the early years of this century, which led to a sharp price rise for all grains in 2003–4.

Farmers' Income

Since the early 1990s, increasing farmers' income has gained an importance equal to, if not greater than, that of production growth. This change in priorities resulted from the fact that the supply of all farm products has greatly improved, while the rural-urban income gap has widened continuously. In 2001, the national average per capita income of the rural population was only one-third that of urban residents. The need to improve farmers' income is not just an economic issue but also a social and political one.

Food Safety and Quality

Partly due to trade disputes between Japan and the European Union at the WTO over sanitary and phytosanitary measures of food imports from China, and partly because of the increased awareness of domestic consumers, the issue of food safety has gained a lot attention from both policymakers and the general public. A series of moves were launched nationwide to address the issue and led, for instance, to the introduction of new standards for "pollution-free" and "green" products.

Environmental Protection

Awareness of the need for environmental protection has become a new component in agricultural policy, with emphasis placed on the sustainability of natural resources. The severe flooding in the middle and lower reaches of Yangtze River in 1998 and the recurrence of sandstorms in north China have been the most important factors triggering environmental concerns in the minds of policymakers. Although environmental planning was never a priority under central planning, some efforts are now being made in soil erosion and desertification control, promotion of research on and extension of water-saving technology, and so on.[1]

Marketing Reforms for Agricultural Output

Major components of marketing reforms include policy changes regarding farmers' delivery obligations, marketing channels, pricing mechanisms, consumption rationing, and restructuring of the state marketing enterprises. Tax and/or subsidy components are inherent in those policy changes. The pace and process of marketing reforms vary significantly for farm products, which can be divided into four categories: (1) grains, mainly wheat, rice, and corn; (2) fiber, primarily cotton; (3) livestock and meat, mainly pig meat; and (4) vegetables and fruits. The reform process related to each of these four product groups is described and analyzed separately.

Grains

Grains were and still are by far the most important farm products in China. The same Chinese word, *liangshi,* is used to describe both food and grains. As a result of the overwhelming importance attached to them, grains have experienced the most swings in marketing reform and have remained the only subsector still under explicit and direct government intervention.

Table 11.2 provides an overview of the fundamental changes that occurred over time in the four key elements of the grain marketing policy, that is, the obligatory delivery quota, the monopoly status of the state marketing enterprises, the pricing mechanism, and consumption rationing. Associated with changes in these instruments are reforms in government subsidy policies including consumer, producer, and marketing subsidies.

THE OBLIGATORY DELIVERY QUOTA FOR PRODUCERS. The procurement policy was first introduced in 1953 as a result of food supply shortage and consisted of two elements: low procurement prices and compulsory delivery quotas. The purpose was to secure basic food supply for the expanding urban population at low cost so that urban salaries and industrial costs could also be kept at a low level. In the early days, the free market was still allowed to run parallel with state trading, but, as the supply situation kept deteriorating, it was gradually restricted and then completely banned.

The grain procurement quota varied over time, declining from about 57 million tons (mt) in the mid-1980s to 45 mt in the mid-1990s. In terms of its percentage of total production, it declined noticeably, from 16 percent to 11 percent, over the same time. Rice and wheat together made up three-quarters of the

---

1. Please also refer to Chapters 10 and 11 on environmental problems related to water resources.

TABLE 11.2 Overview of grain marketing policy development in China, 1950s to 2002

Policy type	1950s–1970s	Late 1970s to mid-1980s	Mid-1980s to early 1990s	Early 1990s to 1998	1998–2000	2000–2002
Delivery quota	Delivery quota	Delivery quota	Quota continued	Quota continued	Quota with new impact	Quota remained in some regions
Private trading	Banned	Gradually permitted	Permitted	State share further lowered	Banned	Allowed again
Price policy	Fixed price	Fixed price for state purchasing	Two-tier pricing	Free market price	Support price	Support price remained in some regions
Consumption ration	Ration established	Continued	Continued	Abolished	No ration	No ration
Producer subsidy	No	No	No	No	Through support price	Support price in some regions
Consumer subsidy	Through low price	Through low price	Through low price	No	No	No
Marketing subsidy	No	No	Introduced	Soaring	Continued to rise	Continued to rise

SOURCE: Author's summary.

total quota amount, and the rest was corn. The continuing decline in procurement was accompanied by additional purchase at the free market price. Purchase at the higher market price and resale at the lower state-set price for urban consumers (reverse or minus marketing margin) have traditionally been the major cause of both fiscal deficits and price subsidies.

The quota system continued, with changes in actual implication and impacts. Since the late 1990s, grain supply has exceeded demand every year, resulting in a sharp decline in market prices and large stockpiles. As a result, the central government initiated a price support policy to protect farmers from falls in income. According to the policy, farmers had the right to sell their grain to the state grain bureaus at the preset support price without quantity limitations. However, in practice, the local state-owned enterprises were often reluctant or unable to fully implement the policy due to lack of storage capacity, fear of market risk, insufficient subsidies by the state to cover the costs and risks involved, and so on. Therefore, in many places the price support and purchase guarantee applied only up to the previous amount of the delivery quota. Since 2000, about two-thirds of the provinces in the country have completely abolished the old procurement system and have relied on free markets for grain distribution. Currently, the price support continues only in some major grain-producing regions, such as Heilongjiang and Jilin provinces in northeast China.

THE STATE MARKETING MONOPOLY.   Until the late 1970s, private marketing of grain was banned, except for a short period in the mid-1960s, when free market exchange in grain occurred on a small scale, usually directly between producers and consumers.

In the late 1970s and early 1980s, the state marketing monopoly was gradually dismantled. A document issued by the State Council stipulated that purchase of grain by any organizations other than the state grain marketing enterprises was strictly prohibited. However, in less than two years, another document of the Communist Party of China turned the order upside down; multi-channel grain trading was allowed on the condition that the state procurement quotas were fulfilled first. That was seen as a breakthrough in China's grain marketing reform.

In the mid-1980s, large surpluses of all grain products occurred for the first time in China's modern history. Faced with insufficient purchasing and storage capacity, the government introduced a two-tier grain marketing system in 1985 in which state and nonstate grain marketing enterprises were allowed to coexist. In addition, two types of marketing activities, one based on the state plan and the other on the free market, were permitted to coexist within the same state grain marketing enterprises. Two prices, the administrative one for state purchases and the free market price (usually higher) for above-quota purchases, were applied at the same time.

Another important reform was the replacement of the obligatory quota delivery with contract delivery, implying that quantities were no longer preset but could be negotiated between farmers and state grain bureaus. However, in the following years, as grain production declined and supply became short, the contract system became compulsory again and thus became like the old quota system, but with a different name. Nevertheless, market trading after quota fulfillment was kept open until the late 1990s.

In 1998, a new package of grain marketing reforms was adopted due to a grain market glut resulting from consecutive years of bumper harvests as well as a decline in market price and income for farmers. This package had three elements: unlimited purchase by state marketing enterprises, a guaranteed support price, and resale at a profitable marketing margin. The aim of the first two measures was to protect farmers' interest, while the last measure was meant to prevent the state marketing enterprises from sustaining losses.

The reform was controversial from the very beginning. Without a complete monopoly, it was impossible for the state grain bureaus to achieve the third goal, resale at profitable prices. Therefore, nonstate marketing of grains was strictly banned in 1998, and only direct sale by farmers to consumers was exempted. Later experience proved that the 1998 reform was far from successful in achieving its objectives. It was impossible to close the free market, so the goal of reselling at a lucrative price level could not be achieved. This resulted in increasing pressure on the state to use budget outlays to subsidize the stockpiles in the state grain enterprises. Insufficient subsidy funding, in turn, resulted in reservation by the local state grain marketing enterprises or their refusal of unlimited purchase. Instead of declining, the deficit and the subsidy balance soared.

The unexpected strong complaints of various stakeholders and the immense subsidy pressure forced the government to modify the policy. In 1999 and 2000, some varieties of grains were excluded from the price support system. In 2000 and 2001, the coastal provinces and other grain-deficit provinces were again allowed to free the grain market. A dozen major grain-producing provinces were instructed to continue price supports to avoid extreme market fluctuations. Even in those remaining provinces, the local governments were allowed to decide the level of the support price, which in most cases was set at about the same level as the local market price.

PRICING POLICY AND PROCUREMENT.   For the state grain marketing sector, a fixed price system was practiced for a very long time at both producer and consumer levels. Once the price was set, it often remained unchanged for years, especially the retail price. The procurement price had been increased several times before the 1970s to encourage producers to sell more surplus grain to the state, and a premium of 20–30 percent was paid for the amount exceeding the quota.

There was a large price increase in 1978, when the government decided to increase the quota rate by 20 percent and the over-quota premium to 50 percent. By the late 1990s, there was actually no significant gap between the average market and quota prices (Table 11.3). The adjustment of the quota price was

TABLE 11.3 Grain prices in China, 1985–2002 (yuan/ton)

	Wheat			Corn		
	Quota price	Market price	Support price	Quota price	Market price	Support price
1985	430	466		310	370	
1986	440	517		320	450	
1987	440	576		330	500	
1988	470	705		340	570	
1989	510	979		370	780	
1990	510	896		380	690	
1991	510	795		380	600	
1992	590	776		420	630	
1993	660	810		460	730	
1994	890	1,140		690	1,010	
1995	1,080	1,690		860	1,580	
1996	1,460	1,740		1,220	1,490	
1997	1,470	1,630		1,230	1,170	
1998			1,440			1,230
1999			1,310			1,140
2000			1,140			960
2001			1,090			940
2002		1,048			1,033	

SOURCES: China, Ministry of Agriculture, *China Agricultural Development Report,* various years; China, RCRE (2002).

mostly forced by the price hike in the free market and had two goals: first, to ease the difficulties in procurement, thereby reducing the complaints of farmers, and second, to provide more incentives for grain production, although this has been debated by the academic community.

In 1998, a support price mechanism was introduced at a level significantly lower than both the quota and the market prices of the previous years and showed a clear declining trend in the four years of its operation. At present, the market price and the support price, where the practice still continues, are generally at the same low level, which is lower than a decade ago in real terms.

THE GRAIN RATIONING SYSTEM. Grain rationing was introduced as early as the obligatory delivery system in 1953. Under this system, every urban resident was entitled to receive a food coupon each month for a certain amount of foodgrains based on criteria such as age, work type, and region of residence. The grain rationing prices were frozen for 25 years, from 1965 to 1990 (Ke 1995). Marking a breakthrough in the consumer pricing policy, ration prices were increased twice, in 1991 and 1992, each time by an average of 50 percent. These were very bold steps, breaking the emotional and psychological taboo related to the lifting of grain ration prices and the unquestioned assumption that any such change would cause social instability.

The consumers' acceptance of the price hikes encouraged policymakers to finally abolish the rationing system itself. This process started in some provinces in 1993 and was completed nationwide by early 1994 (Chen 1995). Although food coupons were reintroduced in some large cities later on because of the price hikes that followed, they were basically meant to assist only the poorest.

THE GRAIN SUBSIDY POLICY.   Traditionally, urban consumers were the beneficiaries of the price subsidy policy. However, the subsidy was paid for not by the state budget, but rather by producers through the compulsory low-priced procurement up to the mid-1980s. The need for an explicit grain subsidy from the government budget first arose in the mid-1980s, when procurement prices increased sharply relative to ration prices and the state had to purchase increasing amounts of grains at the free market price. The subsidy was granted to the state grain marketing system according to the standard marketing costs and the price gap. This kind of marketing subsidy reached a very high level by the late 1990s and was a major reason for the 1998 reform.

Other related grain subsidies are provided to the state grain marketing enterprises for food security and market stabilization purposes. More specifically, two special policy measures have been implemented since the 1990s: the "special grain stock" (SGS) and the "grain risk fund" policies.

The SGS system was first introduced in 1990 to be run at both the national and the provincial levels through the newly created State Grain Reserve Bureau (China, Ministry of Agriculture, 1997). Existing state grain marketing enterprises were designated to keep a certain amount of grain in reserve as part of the SGS and were entitled to obtain some compensation from the government to cover the costs related to keeping the stock. In theory, it was supposed to operate as a buffer stock system, but in practice it did not function well because of two main problems: (1) the lack of reliability of the data kept by the state's grain enterprises on the reported grain amounts of the SGS and (2) the lack of interest by local governments in running their own stock programs due to the high costs involved, especially in surplus areas, where budgets were always tight. These problems led to difficulties in assessing the size of the stock and thus to lack of transparency in the disbursement of subsidies, with many unclear or false claims. To address these issues, in 1994 the government decided to designate some large-scale grain storage warehouses with close access to major transportation lines under the direct control of the State Grain Reserve Bureau.

Separate from the SGS system, a grain risk fund was initiated in 1994, with the central government requiring provincial governments to provide local revenues to match the fund allocated by the center. The new policy sought to provide necessary financial means for market stabilization, including the financing of the SGS regime. The risk fund was also meant to cover the costs created by the price support policy.

However, Chinese farmers did not receive any direct government subsidy and instead have until recently paid a heavy agricultural tax that was made heavier with the passing of the Rural Taxation Reform, which increase the tax burden to over 8 percent of the production value on average. This is in sharp contrast with the situation in other WTO member countries, such as the United States, the European Union, and Japan, where farmers are substantially subsidized by their governments in various ways. One policy that is gaining increasing public support is the provision of direct subsidies to farmers and the reduction and/or abolishment of the agricultural tax and fees.

Nonstaples

Generally speaking, the meat marketing policy was roughly in line with that for grain but was subject to a lower degree of state control. The reform of meat marketing also came somewhat earlier and experienced a relatively smoother path, especially after the late 1970s. An overview of the marketing policy for pigs and pork, the predominant meat in China, is presented in Table 11.4.

The pig and pig meat marketing policy in China evolved in the following stages: no direct intervention in the first half of the 1950s; intensified intervention from 1955 onward; complete control over production, marketing, and consumption after the 1960s; and gradual relaxation of controls after 1978.

A compulsory delivery system was first introduced in 1955. The market share of private trading declined sharply, from about 80 percent in 1955 to about 1 percent in 1958, as the compulsory delivery policy was tightened. For 20 years thereafter, private trading of pork meat was strictly forbidden, and the occupation of private butcher virtually disappeared. Direct sales from producers to consumers at local markets were occasionally allowed only after fulfillment of the state quota.

After reform, private trading of pigs and pork meat was first allowed and then encouraged. With the mushrooming of "free markets" on city streets, the private marketing of hogs and pork began to develop very rapidly. In 1985 the obligatory delivery of hogs was abolished and a multichannel pig and pork meat marketing system was established. Today the state-owned meat marketing companies have been restructured, and most of the remaining ones are concentrating on meat processing. The retail sector is dominated by a great number of small traders and various kinds of food chain shops, such as supermarkets.

A fixed price policy long practiced at both producer and consumer levels was abolished, first at the producer level for the purchase of hogs, because the state meat marketing companies had to be price-competitive to sustain their market share. The fixed price for consumers was maintained for several years.

TABLE 11.4 Overview of the evolution of pig and pork meat marketing policy in China, 1950s to present

Policy type	Mid-1950s	Late 1950s to mid-1960s	Mid-1960s to late 1970s	Late 1970s to mid-1980s	Mid-1980s to early 1990s	Since early 1990s
Obligatory delivery	Introduced	Strict	Continued	Continued	Abolished	No
Private trading	Allowed	Forbidden	Forbidden	Allowed	Allowed	Allowed
Price policy	Fixed price	Fixed price	Fixed price	Fixed price	Pig price freed	Meat price freed
Consumption ration	No	Introduced	Continued	Break in 1965–68	Abolished	No
Producer subsidy	No	No	Cheap feed grain	Cheap feed grain	No	No
Consumer subsidy	Low-priced meat	Low-priced meat	Low-priced meat	Low-priced meat	No	No
Marketing subsidy	—	—	—	Subsidy	Subsidy	Abolished

SOURCE: Author's compilation.

During that time, the local governments, especially in the big cities, not only set fixed prices for the local state-owned food companies, but also set price ceilings for the free market. Rising subsidies were needed to cover the losses in state meat companies, but eventually the competing pressures from nonstate sectors and the much improved income and purchasing power of the urban population led to the scrapping of the price control policy between the late 1980s and the early 1990s.

Several forms of subsidy existed in meat production, consumption, and marketing. Subsidies were given to producers, mostly in the 1970s, in the form of inexpensively priced feed and to consumers in the form of low-priced meat with coupons. Marketing subsidies were given to the state meat enterprises for a long time, but today this kind of subsidy is found only occasionally in some very large cities.

The pricing and marketing policy for vegetables and fruits was similar to that for meat, although it was less strict. In fact, fruits and vegetables led the marketing reforms of agricultural products in China, and in the early 1980s a free marketing system for fruits and vegetables had already been established.

Cotton

The marketing reform process for cotton lagged far behind that for other farm products. The marketing of cotton had previously been monopolized by quasi-state agencies, the supply and marketing cooperatives (SMCs), which covered the whole marketing chain, from procurement to processing, storage, transportation, and the allocation of cotton to textile industries. No firms except the SMCs were permitted to purchase cotton from farmers. Reform attempts were made in the mid-1980s and early 1990s, but they were not completed, and the control policy continued to dominate.

In 1996 the first cotton fair was organized to bring the suppliers (SMCs at county and provincial levels) and buyers (textile manufacturers) together. This was a fundamental change from the previous system, under which no direct negotiation between the textile firms and the suppliers was possible, with buyers having to accept their allocation. Since then, other cotton fairs have been organized.

A fixed price system was practiced at all stages, which meant that the marketing margin was also fixed. For example, the procurement price in 1997 was 14,000 yuan/ton, and the allocation price was 17,100 yuan/ton (Table 11.5). The differential was to cover the collection, packaging, and storage costs as well as the marketing profits. These prices were normally set at the beginning of the year and would not change. There were some shortcomings to this rigid pricing system. First, the fixed price could not reflect the market supply and demand situation. When it was too low, farmers lacked incentives to grow and provide sufficient cotton, causing severe shortage. When it was too high, farmers produced more than needed and the consequent excess stocks resulted in a heavy

TABLE 11.5 Cotton price trends in China, 1978–2000

	In-quota price[a] (yuan/ton)	Price premium for over-quota (%)	Weighted average (yuan/ton)
1978	2,300	0	2,300
1979	2,720	30	2,960
1980	3,000	30	3,460
1981	3,000	30	3,470
1982	3,000	30	3,560
1983	3,000	30	3,630
1984	3,400	0	3,400
1985	3,400	0	3,400
1986	3,400	0	3,400
1987	3,400	0	3,400
1988	3,800	0	3,800
1989	4,720	0	4,720
1990	6,000	0	6,000
1991	6,000	0	6,000
1992	6,000	0	6,000
1993	6,600	0	6,600
1994	10,880	0	10,880
1995	14,000	0	14,000
1996	14,000	±4[b]	13,160
1997	14,000	±4[b]	13,160
1998	13,000	±5[b]	12,350
1999[c]	7,600		7,600
2000	8,000		8,000

SOURCE: China, Ministry of Agriculture (1984); China, Ministry of Agriculture, various years, documents on adjusting cotton purchase price; China, Ministry of Agriculture (n.d.).

[a]Standard quality = 327.

[b]Officially, the allowed price change for the procurement price could go in either direction (±4 and 5 percent), but in practice all price adjustments were made downward due to oversupply.

[c]Since 1998, the price of cotton has officially been set free, although in reality it is still controlled by the dominant SMC system.

burden on the state budget. Second, because there was no seasonal price premium, farmers tended to sell their cotton as soon as possible after harvest. While textile firms attempted to minimize their stocks, the SMCs had to keep excess stocks at considerable costs, and the losses had to be covered by state subsidies.

In recent years, there have been two main changes in the allocation price charged by SMCs to cotton users. In 1996, after the introduction of direct trading through organized cotton fairs, the allocation price was allowed to fluctuate within a certain range, generally +/– 4 percent. The second pricing reform occurred in 1998, when the allocation price was liberalized but the procurement price remained fixed. This unbalanced pricing mechanism at farm and end-user levels made the relationships among different market participants more complicated.

Further, there have been changes in the procurement price levels but not in the pricing system. The policymakers wanted to keep a rational price ratio between grains and cotton because grains, especially wheat, are the major alternative crops in cotton-growing areas. A long-standing traditional assumption is that when the cotton-wheat price ratio is around 8 to 1, grain and cotton production will be in balance.

In 1999 a significant cotton marketing reform was launched in the context of a glut in the cotton markets. This entailed two changes. First, it gave completely free market access to textile firms on the condition that they have the needed physical and personnel capacity and first apply for certificates from the provincial governments. The textile firms could also commission the local SMCs to purchase and process cotton for them. Second, the price control was abolished. The government still issues a reference price, but it is not binding. In line with this liberalization process, a national cotton exchange market was established and has been in operation since 2000.

Marketing Reforms for Agricultural Inputs

The similar radical changes in the price and marketing policies for agricultural inputs have impacted agriculture both favorably and unfavorably. The important favorable developments have been the liberalization of markets and their exemption from the value-added tax. The unfavorable developments involve mainly the reduction or abolition of various subsidies to the input manufacturing industries and the associated rise in prices of some agricultural inputs.

Chemical Fertilizer

The production and distribution of chemical fertilizers was highly regulated and subsidized until the mid-1980s. The marketing of chemical fertilizers was monopolized by the SMCs until 1985, when a dual marketing system similar to that for grain marketing was introduced. Large and medium-sized manufacturers were allowed to sell a certain percentage of their production freely after fulfilling the plan target, while small fertilizer producers were permitted to trade freely. Provincial governments were urged to exert price controls, including farm-gate price ceilings for large fertilizer producers and marketing margin controls for wholesale and retailing operation of the SMCs. In the area of external trade, the subsidy system for fertilizer imports was abolished; they were exempted from tariffs.

Until the mid-1990s, the central government controlled the distribution of about 20 percent of the total fertilizer supply, and local governments regulated the rest. The marketing took place through "one major channel and two supplementary channels" (China, Ministry of Agriculture, 1997). The major channel was the SMC system, while the two supplementary ones were the marketing departments of the factories and various agricultural extension services.

The main reasons for controlling fertilizer prices and marketing were traditionally to protect farmers from low quality or false products, to ensure a timely supply, and to keep fertilizer prices at a level that did not arouse too many complaints from farmers. In view of China's WTO entry, fertilizer marketing has been further reformed since the late 1990s, and a freer system has been established under which fertilizer prices and trade activities are guided by the market mechanism, while the government focuses on quality control.

Seeds

Great efforts have been made in improving the quality and availability of seeds. To strengthen the seed breeding and production bases, the Ministry of Agriculture recently launched a Seed Program and a special fund was set up to support research work in seed breeding. In addition, seed marketing and distribution are licensed to control quality and protect the interests of farmers.

In 2002 a policy experiment was undertaken to subsidize soybean farmers. For each hectare of soybean-producing area, a seed subsidy of 150 yuan (U.S.$18) is provided to certified seed companies offering high-yielding varieties, and they in turn provide inexpensive soybean seeds to farmers. This policy measure has reduced soybean production costs, but, more important, it has encouraged farmers to adopt the same soybean variety in one region. In doing so, it has solved some long-standing problems, such as the great number of farmers in the same region producing many varieties of soybean and the failure of high-quality soybeans to earn higher prices due to the uneconomic marketing scale. This experiment proved very successful in improving soybean yield and quality in its first year of implementation. Similar measures are expected for other crops, most likely wheat and cotton.

Feed

The Chinese feed industry has developed from scratch during the past two decades. Industrial feed production has soared, from merely 2 mt in 1980 to over 50 mt in 1995, and further to 78 mt in 2002. The quality of the manufactured feed has improved gradually, and the reticence of many livestock producers, including those in the traditional sector, to purchase industrial feed has been overcome. The robust development of the feed sector was the decisive factor in increasing the share of intensive livestock-rearing systems, especially in the poultry and pig sectors.

A special administrative service, the State Office for the Feed Industry, was established to guide the development of the sector. In its early stage, in the 1980s and early 1990s, low-priced grains were provided to the feed industry, especially state-owned large-scale feed mills. In the late 1990s, the scale of the subsidy was substantially reduced, and from 1997 large-scale feed mills were granted the same preferential treatment as the state grain marketing enterprises in interregional feedgrain (mainly corn) purchases. This included low-interest loans and preferential arrangements in rail and sea transportation. In recent years, there has been no more subsidized grain for the feed mills, primarily because the market price for grains has been lower than the state-set purchase and resale prices since 1998. In 1999 and 2000, it would have been a blessing for feed mills to be able to purchase grain from the free market rather than from the state grain marketing enterprises.

Machinery

The agricultural machinery sector was placed under the market system in the very early stage of reforms. This is now one of the most highly competitive sectors, with very limited subsidies to promote the adoption of new technology. In some provinces, especially in the economically advanced coastal regions, a subsidy is provided to farmers to encourage their purchase of agricultural machines. For example, local governments in Guangdong and Jiangsu provinces cover one-third of the purchase cost of rice harvesting machines.

Water

Water is a very important input for agriculture in China, but its use has hardly been regulated so far. Despite increasing shortages in the water supply, it is available virtually free. Large investments are made in water projects of various sizes, with the most gigantic one, the Three Gorges Dam on the Yangtze River, just completed.

Governments at various levels are involved with building and maintaining irrigation systems. The funding is no problem, but the market mechanism needs to be introduced in a bigger way to better price this precious resource and increase the efficiency of its use. Some pilot programs have been implemented to explore new forms of water management. These include water cooperatives of villagers and a shareholding system for the maintenance of irrigation systems.

Impacts of Agricultural Marketing Reforms

The impacts of agricultural marketing reforms have been profound, with both producers and consumers net gainers over the long term. The policy changes have brought inevitable restructuring pains for the state marketing system, but they have also generated new opportunities to develop and grow. Moreover, agricultural marketing reforms have had spill-over effects for the overall process of reform toward market orientation, providing operational experience and confidence in the functioning of the market mechanism.

Agricultural Production Growth and Resource Use Efficiency

While the reform of the production management system, that is, the introduction of the HRS, sought to address the issue of who owns the products, the marketing reforms aimed to address the issues of what to produce and how much to produce.

As indicated in Table 11.6, agricultural production has increased substantially over the past two decades. Although it is not possible to separate the production-stimulating effects of marketing reforms from those related to changes in the land tenure system and other factors, there is no doubt that the former is an important contributing factor to the successful performance of the sector.

The impacts of reforms on production growth were particularly strong for grains in the early years of the reform process (Table 11.7). Over time, the production of other crops and meat showed much faster growth than grains, which suggests the existence of a process of restructuring toward more high-value products. This is an explicit indication of the resource-use impact of marketing reforms.

Farmers' Income Gains

Marketing reforms have significantly improved rural income over the past two decades (Figure 11.1).

TABLE 11.6 Agricultural production growth in China in selected years, 1980–2000 (million tons)

	Grain	Meat	Fruits	Oilseeds	Sugar crop	Cotton
1980	320	12.1	6.8	7.7	29.1	2.7
1985	379	19.2	11.6	15.8	51.6	4.2
1990	446	28.6	18.7	16.1	57.6	4.5
1995	467	52.6	42.2	22.5	65.4	4.8
2000	462	61.3	62.3	29.6	68.3	4.4

SOURCE: NBS, *China Statistical Yearbook,* various years.

TABLE 11.7 Changes in agricultural structure in China in selected years, 1980–2000 (percent)

	1980	1985	1990	1995	2000
Farm labor's share in total rural labor	93.6	81.9	79.3	71.8	68.4
Crops' share in total value of agricultural production	75.6	69.3	63.1	58.4	55.7
Grain area's share in total cultivated area	80.1	75.8	75.1	73.4	69.4
Pig meat's share in total meat production	94.1	85.9	78	69.4	65.8

SOURCES: China, Ministry of Agriculture, *China Agricultural Development Report,* various years, and Editing Committee of China Agricultural Yearbook, various years.

FIGURE 11.1 Income of the agricultural population in China, 1983–2001

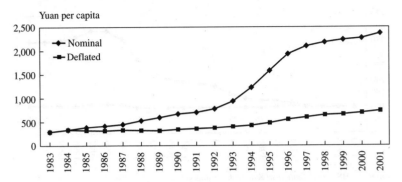

SOURCE: NBS, *China Statistical Yearbook,* 2006.
NOTE: Real income is expressed in 1980 yuan.

.The income gains have accrued in several ways. The first and most direct benefit has come from the increase in the prices obtained by farmers, especially in the early stage of the reforms (Table 11.3), leading to rapid growth in farmers' income in the late 1970s and the early 1980s. The only exception was the cotton sector, where the abolition of the fixed price system in 1999 first introduced a sharp price fall due to a huge market surplus and the SMCs' manipulation of prices through their established market power. Cotton prices recovered gradually in the following years, with strong fluctuations.

Second, benefits accrued to agricultural producers through better use of farm resources, which broadened income sources and increased returns from the same land area, especially with regard to high-value products such as fruits, vegetables, and livestock. The free market mechanism provides timely price signals to producers so they can adjust their output structure to the changes in market demand and earn more income. The structural changes would not be possible without the marketing reforms.

Third, growth of the multichannel marketing system has reduced post-harvest losses, especially in the case of perishable products such as fruits and vegetables.

Fourth, farmers have gained from marketing reforms, which increased their efficiency and narrowed the marketing margin. The benefit from reduction in the marketing margin is shared between producers and consumers. Increased competition in marketing activities has also forced the state marketing sector to improve its efficiency, which contributed to improving the marketing and overall economic environment, thereby benefiting the farmers operating in it.

FIGURE 11.2 Price index of farm production inputs in China, 1980–2001

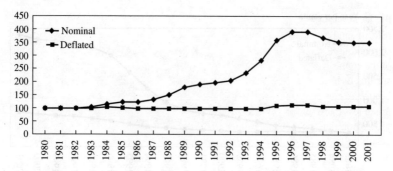

SOURCE: NBS, *China Statistical Yearbook,* various years.

Fifth, as users of farm products produced on other farms, farmers have more choices and also share the benefits of the reduced marketing margin as consumers.

Sixth, reforms in the input market benefited farmers in that they now have not only more supply channels for agricultural inputs but also access to better quality. The effects of marketing reforms have been particularly noticeable as domestic markets of farm inputs have been opened to foreign suppliers. The prices of inputs in real terms have remained largely unchanged over the past two decades, although in nominal terms they have increased by a factor of two and a half (Figure 11.2).

Last but not least, the marketing reforms have brought about profound changes in the minds of all stakeholders. Reforms have changed the nature of the government's role from a full-scale, top-down, command role to a more general guiding, facilitating, and service-providing role with greatly reduced direct interventions. The success of the marketing reforms also demands that farmers take initiatives with an entrepreneurial spirit and respect the market rules in seeking their economic interests and other goals.

Rural Poverty Reduction

The marketing reforms were also expected to have major beneficial impacts on poverty reduction, because the market mechanism theoretically allows farmers in poverty-stricken areas to better use their resources and improve their welfare through the exchange of agricultural products at more favorable price ratios with industrial goods. However, due to differences in resource bases, infra-structure, and other natural, economic, and social conditions, great variations resulted among the various regions following the implementation of reforms.

In some areas, such as the coastal regions of Zhejiang province, which were once among the poorest areas in China, with poor and limited land resources, the local people grasped the development opportunities brought about by the reforms and took the lead in developing the nonstate economy. In contrast, in some mountainous western regions that are physically isolated from other parts of the country and the market, where farmers either do not have much marketable surplus or have great difficulties in bringing their products to the outside market for reasonable returns, their income and living conditions have benefited much less from reforms. Therefore, it is clear that to benefit the poorer segments of the population, measures other than marketing reforms, such as public investment to improve infrastructure, basic education, and technical extension, need to be implemented.

An indirect aspect of the marketing reforms that should not be neglected when considering their impacts on poverty reduction is rural-urban migration. A large share of the rural migrants working in coastal regions and cities are from the poorest regions. There are over 100 million such rural migrants, who stay and work away from their home villages for at least six months per year. The earnings of those migrants have been the most important factor in the income growth of the rural population in recent years, especially for low-income regions.

Consumer Welfare Gains

Consumers benefited as much as producers from the marketing reforms, although in the early stages they often opposed the policy changes that came with price increases. To gain the support of consumers, the government provided them with direct subsidies, following the approach of "turning hidden subsidy into direct subsidy."

Consumers gained in several ways. First, they benefited from the rapid improvement in food supply. The common scene of queuing observed almost everywhere in the state shops disappeared, and the quotas and coupons also became useless in practice before they were officially abolished.

Second, together with the ever-increasing food supply, consumers also acquired freedom of choice, because the consumer-producer interaction induced by price and market mechanisms resulted in a greater range of products and improvement in the quality of all farm products.

Third, consumers benefited greatly from the decline in prices of agricultural produce. After an increase in the initial stages, agricultural prices soon fell and decreased further as production was stimulated and supply expanded rapidly. This was true with regard to almost all products. Prices for wheat and corn, for example, are now at the same level as in 1985 in nominal terms and only one-third as high in real terms. Drops in prices for off-season horticultural products are even sharper. Official statistics show that the urban population's Engle coefficient has continuously fallen, from about 60 percent in the late 1970s to 38 percent in 2001.

Domestic Marketing and Trade Policy Reform

Domestic marketing reforms and trade policy liberalization have been two major pillars of China's economic reforms in the past two decades. There have been close interactions between these two areas.

During the past 20 years, agriculture has taken the lead in domestic policy reforms, while it has often lagged behind other sectors in the area of trade policy reforms. In the pre-reform era, agricultural trade policy measures were a combination of tariffs, quantity restrictions, licensing, and state trading for both exports and imports. Exports of nongrain products were encouraged to earn foreign exchange, while grain exports were rigidly restricted to secure domestic food supply. This system remained untouched for a long time; it was only the WTO commitments that influenced trade policy in significant ways.

China's WTO commitments in market access for agricultural products apply mainly to two areas: tariff reduction, from an average level of 21.2 percent to 17 percent, and replacement of various nontariff barriers with a tariff rate quota (TRQ) system. The introduction of TRQs for grains and cotton is especially relevant to domestic grain and cotton reforms.

Table 11.8 shows that China's TRQs are very high by any standard; they are several times larger than the actual imports in the base year. The TRQs also represent a large share in domestic commercial consumption (excluding farmers' self-consumption), which really matters in terms of the market price and farmers' income and far exceeds the minimal market access of 5 percent required by the WTO rules. Because the in-quota tariff is very low, about 1 percent that for wheat, corn, rice, and cotton, the in-quota imports are almost free of tariff. The huge TRQ amounts and the nearly nil tariff protection combined mean that Chinese domestic markets for these products have become very closely

TABLE 11.8 China's TRQs, by commodity, 2002 and 2004

	Wheat	Corn	Rice	Cotton	Sugar	Wool	Oils
Million tons							
China's TRQs, 2002	8.47	5.85	3.99	0.82	1.76	0.27	5.80
China's TRQs, 2004	9.64	7.20	5.32	0.89	1.95	0.29	8.00
World trade	101.25	75.88	23.04	4.99	47.07	1.06	42.30
Base-year imports of China (1996–98)	3.89	0.23	0.44	0.35	0.85	0.20	2.52
China's TRQs as a percentage of							
World trade	10	10	23	18	4	27	19
Base-year imports	248	3,130	1,201	254	230	144	318
Consumption	8	5	3	19	22	40	50
Commercial consumption	20	8	15	19	22	40	50

SOURCES: Author's compilation based on legal documents of China's accession to the WTO, available from WTO, various years; FAO statistics; and NBS, *China Statistical Yearbook,* various years.

integrated with the world market. The challenges and pressure from the international market after China joined the WTO may have triggered—or, more precisely, accelerated—the pace of domestic marketing reforms, particularly for grains and cotton.

Under the TRQ system, continuation of the previous support price policy for grains would have led to a large volume of cheap foreign imports and the parallel accumulation of stockpiles by the state marketing enterprises. To prevent these consequences, the government accelerated the grain marketing reforms. In 2001 and 2002 it changed the price support system, which led to convergence between the support price and the market price levels and to the restriction of the amount covered by state purchase to an amount equivalent to the previous procurement quota.

Another direct impact of the trade policy changes induced by China's entry into the WTO is the reform of rural taxation. The WTO rules set ceilings and disciplines for domestic support. Experiments have been implemented in some provinces to revise the agricultural tax system in order to reduce the tax burden and control its growth. In some places, such as Shanghai and Zhejiang, local authorities have completely canceled the tax for special agricultural products.

Trade liberalization also affected the domestic transportation fee policy. Exemption from the railway construction fee was granted to soybean and maize producers in northeast China, which significantly enhanced their marketing advantage in the sale of their produce to south China.

Another development caused by the WTO discipline relates to the government's role in promoting agricultural marketing; increasingly greater attention is now being paid by the government to services, including the provision of market information, marketing facilities, technical assistance, and standards and quality control. Policy objectives have been formulated to support the development of various kinds of farmers' associations and marketing cooperatives. Favorable policy measures have been drafted to support agricultural marketing and processing enterprises, such as the so-called Dragon Head Companies, which should serve as intermediaries between the numerous small producers and the large-scale market demand to direct the small producers to produce quality products and to implement the same standards at a business scale.

Lessons from the Past and the Future Agenda

Looking Back

Reform of agricultural marketing has come a long way in China, but the process is still unfinished. Past experience and its lessons can be perceived from different angles. From a function-goal perspective, that is, by viewing marketing reforms as a means to achieve various objectives, the following observations can be made.

First, to achieve the goal of national food safety, market-oriented policies are much more efficient than rigid market controls. While marketing reforms were not the only variable that brought about change, they were a precondition that enabled full play of the other factors.

Second, to achieve the goals of increasing farm income and consumer welfare, the market system is more effective than a system with heavy direct government intervention. Even when state intervention is in the form of price support, the result from market distortion is not in the best interests of farmers. This is the lesson from the grain price support policy of 1989–2000.

Third, to achieve the objectives of efficient resource use and establishment of a rational agricultural structure, market instruments are preferable to administrative instruments that lead to market distortions. Under the old system, production structures were conceived independent of efficiency in resource use and the principle of comparative advantages was ignored.

Finally, experience has shown that achieving marketing reforms is a complicated process. Unlike the change of the land tenure system through the HRS, which was a matter confined to the agricultural sector, marketing reforms involved many stakeholders outside agriculture whose interests were challenged by the policy changes, so supplementary measures had to be introduced to address their concerns.

Looking Forward

There are several areas in which further reform efforts are needed, including some unfinished tasks in correcting market distortions and perfecting governmental functions toward the elimination of market failures.

Market distortions still exist, for instance, in the grain markets of some provinces in central and northeast China and the cotton markets in Xinjiang in the northwest. Under the current system, state grain marketing enterprises are subsidized according to the quantities of their purchases and stocks. There is a tendency to overstate those amounts, and it is very difficult for the central government to monitor them.

On the one hand, the government wants the state-owned enterprises (SOEs) to operate the same way as commercial companies in terms of efficiency and profit earnings, but on the other it asks them to fulfill some social functions (namely, provide welfare and social security) that are against market rules and usually lead to financial losses, which eventually need to be subsidized. The only way out of this dilemma is to restructure the state marketing sector and turn all SOEs into independent companies free of government intervention. To this end, three issues must be properly addressed in future reform moves: first, the need to establish a system with minimal and affordable budget requirements that provides basic financial support to farmers; second, the need to establish an efficient state reserve system with predictable and controllable budget outlays; and third, the need to find a proper solution to the problem of the huge deficits of the state grain and cotton marketing enterprises accumulated in the past 10 years. The reform of the state grain marketing firms would require a redefinition of the legal and market status of SOEs and their functions and of their relationship with the government, especially at the local level. They should be turned into fully independent enterprises that follow market rules. This reform can be realized by contracting commercial enterprises for each unit of purchase and stock keeping.

A minimal price support system should be introduced and the support price designed in such a way that only farmers in the main producing areas (that is, the lowest production cost regions) could make use of it. These farmers specialize in grain production without any alternative sources of income, and that places them in a position where they have to sell their products immediately after the harvest, which is often the prime reason they receive poor prices. A system similar to the nonrecourse loan system practiced in the United States can be established in which farmers will be able to meet their short-term financial needs and maintain their right to withdraw their products from the state support system and sell them in the free market when the market price grows higher than the support price.

To correct market failures, there is a need to look into the establishment and implementation of laws and regulations that would prevent malpractice by market participants, eliminate market manipulation, establish product standards and classifications, and enhance food safety. Measures to safeguard food safety are of utmost importance not only to protect people's health but also to enhance the competitiveness of Chinese farm products in the world market. Strict quality control is not an easy task due to the huge number of tiny smallholders, each with half a hectare of farmland on average. There are great difficulties in product traceability, especially for vegetables and fruits.

The other major area that needs deepening of reforms is public market services. Market information, particularly on prices, is of vital importance to traders and producers alike. With the rapid spread of modern information technology, the hardware of market information systems has improved significantly, but the processing and provision of the information flow need substantial government support.

Further government support is required to improve the marketing facilities. Tens of thousands of wholesale and retail markets for farm products have been set up in large cities and small towns. The physical facilities at these markets have improved substantially, but many of them are still far from meeting the standards of modern wholesale markets. The largest problem is that the fees collected are usually too high due to a lack of public investment. Many of these markets are running as commercial enterprises and not as public service establishments, which inevitably has adverse impacts on the trading of agricultural products.

These issues are critical, and addressing them should be central to the design of the agenda for future Chinese agricultural marketing reforms.

12 Market Reforms in Indian Agriculture: One Step Forward, Two Steps Back

V. S. VYAS

Agriculture is the single largest industry in India, employing nearly 58 percent of the workforce.[1] It is the largest user of land and water resources. With a growing proportion of purchased inputs it has forged strong backward linkages with industry. Similarly, with the growth of agroprocessing in recent years, its forward linkages are also becoming progressively strong. The Index of Industrial Production assigns a weight of 20 percent to agro-based industries, including textiles. The share of agriculture in international trade accounts for nearly 18 percent of the country's total external trade. Finally, the share of agricultural products in the consumers' budget, nearly 54 percent, further contributes to the importance of this sector. Thus, changes in income, production, and productivity in agriculture are vital not only to the people directly dependent on this sector but also to the entire country.[2]

At the beginning of the chapter I outline the agricultural context of India, then present an analysis of the existing agricultural policy regime followed by the impacts of this regime on growth and equity. The chapter concludes with suggestions on the directions that agricultural reforms, especially domestic marketing reforms, ought to take.

Initial Conditions

Economic policies cannot be implemented in a vacuum. The important features of Indian agriculture that have a bearing on the content and pace of reforms include the agrarian structure, the production base, the support systems available, resource use and productivity, domestic demand, and external trade envi-

---

1. The data on the role of agriculture in the Indian economy are from the following sources: WDI, *World Development Indicators,* 2001; India, Ministry of Agriculture, *Agricultural Statistics at a Glance,* 2002; CMIE (2001), National Accounts Statistics, December.

2. Unless otherwise mentioned, all data in the text of this chapter are from India, Ministry of Agriculture, *Agricultural Statistics at a Glance, 2002.*

ronment. A brief introduction to these aspects is necessary to understand the impacts of past policies as well as to suggest desirable directions for future reforms.

The Agrarian Structure

Agricultural production in India is accomplished on 105 million holdings. Nearly 72 percent are smallholdings of less than 2 hectare (ha), which accounted for nearly one-third of India's cultivated area as of 1990–91. Holdings of 10 ha and above (in the large-sized holding category) account for less than 18 percent of cultivated area. Due to demographic, legislative, and economic factors the area in smallholdings is progressively increasing and that of large holdings declining (Vyas 2002). Apart from the raising of crops, other agricultural activities, such as dairy, animal husbandry, poultry, and fishery activities, are largely pursued either as supplementary activities on small farms or independently in small-scale units (India, Planning Commission, 2002). Thus, any reform should recognize that Indian agriculture is essentially a small-scale agriculture in which large numbers of farmers have almost no marketable surplus.

The Production Base

With its continental size, India also has continental diversity in soils and climate. Around 51 percent of the total surface area of 328.7 million hectares (m ha) is the net sown area. The scope for extension of the arable land is virtually nonexistent. Even the current land base is weak and deteriorating, with nearly 57 percent of land slightly or extremely degraded. Investment in land improvement is grossly inadequate, and, as a result, little has been achieved in terms of land improvement (Chadha 2002). The same is true of water resources, which are unevenly distributed throughout the country, leading to floods in some areas and droughts in others. In many areas harnessing water resources and providing irrigation are preconditions for profitable agriculture. But achievements in irrigation are inadequate, still amounting to only about 68 percent of the irrigation potential, which is reckoned at nearly 140 m ha (India, Ministry of Finance, *Economic Survey,* 2000–2001).

Support Systems

The country has a highly developed institutional framework for agricultural research, extension, marketing, and credit. However, these institutions, heavily reliant on state support and guided by state bureaucracies, are hardly accountable to the service users. Although there are exceptions, the institutional support available to agricultural producers, especially the small farmers, is grossly inadequate. Some of the recent reform measures in agriculture, particularly in credit and marketing, sought to address the problems of support systems, but the agenda here is largely unfinished.

Resource Use and Productivity

Because land and water resources are limited, their use is intensive. Nearly 33 percent of the net cultivated area is sown more than once per year. Spurred by input subsidies, the share of purchased inputs is on the rise. The use of fertilizers, for instance, increased from 67.5 kg/ha in 1990–91 to 101.2 kg/ha in 2001–2 as net irrigated area increased from 34 percent in 1990–91 to 39 percent in 1998–99. There was also significant growth in the use of pesticides and chemicals, farm machinery, and electric power. However, there has been no corresponding increase in productivity. Overall, the improvement in yield per hectare has slowed down in recent years, with the yields of practically all crops lower than those in several other Asian countries.

Domestic Demand

The number of undernourished people in India exceeds 208 million (FAO 2001). Foodgrain production is progressing at a rate lower than population growth, yet foodgrain stocks have been rising over the past five years, clearly hinting at distributional and access bottlenecks. The country is carrying a stock of over 50 million tons, way above the buffer stock and the Public Distribution System (PDS) requirements. The main reason for slackness in the demand for cereals is rising prices, especially PDS issue prices for the poor. Inefficiencies in the PDS further exclude many potential consumers.

In the case of noncereal food crops, such as sugar and edible oils, relative stagnation in production and large year-to-year variability constrain demand. Demand for commercial crops such as cotton and other fibers is directly linked with growth of industries that use them as raw materials. With the slackness in industrial growth in recent years, domestic demand for these crops is also facing a slack. Fluctuating production and poor quality further aggravate the situation.

External Demand

Indian agriculture primarily depends on its large domestic market. A large unsaturated domestic market and low productivity, leading to poor competitiveness, constrain the external demand for agricultural produce.

The Agricultural Policy Regime

The agricultural policies in India evolved in the context of food scarcity and were influenced by a "closed economy" syndrome. They framed two basic objectives: (1) stimulating domestic food production and (2) controlling price increases in basic consumption goods. Over time, these objectives expanded to include, for instance, self-sufficiency in cereals and oilseeds in recent years. From the beginning of the planning era, in the early 1950s, foodgrain price control has been a cornerstone of the inflation strategy.

Until the late 1950s, agricultural policies and state interventions in the sector were of an ad hoc nature. It was only in the early 1960s that, faced with severe food shortages, a decision to increase the foodgrain supply by popularizing the "new technology"—high-yield varieties (HYV) of seed, chemical fertilizers, and so on—was taken and the need for a comprehensive and coherent policy highlighted.

In 1964, the Foodgrain Prices (Jha) Committee made comprehensive recommendations on different aspects of the price policy, including minimum support prices (MSPs), procurement prices, buffer stocks, the PDS, and consumer issue prices. It also suggested an institutional set-up to implement these policies, the Agricultural Prices Commission (later renamed the Commission on Agricultural Costs and Prices, or CACP), to advise the government on price policies and related issues and the Food Corporation of India (FCI) to implement these decisions. The basic framework of agricultural price policies has remained more or less intact since then, with only a few minor changes. We will briefly discuss some components of agricultural policies and how they were affected by the liberalization of agricultural marketing in the reform era.

Input Subsidies

Three major inputs, fertilizers, electric power, and irrigation water, account for the bulk of agricultural subsidies (Table 12.1). The subsidy on fertilizers was introduced in the mid–1970s to insulate domestic fertilizer prices in the face of a steep rise in international prices following the first oil crisis in 1973–74. Subsidies on power and canal water, which are borne by the states, also came into existence and grew over time because the state governments could not, or would not, recover the costs of generating these inputs and providing them to agricultural producers.

The policy on input subsidies is predicated on the premise of "cheap inputs, cheap output." Because the bulk of the consumers are poor and food and

TABLE 12.1 Major input subsidies in Indian agriculture, 1991–92 to 1995–96 (Rs. 10 million)

	Fertilizers				Canal	Total		Total subsidy as a percentage
Years	Imported	Domestic	Total	Electricity	irrigation	subsidy	AgGDP	of AgGDP
1991–92	130.0	350.0	480.0	588.9	310.9	1,379.8	16,231.7	8.50
1992–93	99.6	514.0	613.6	733.5	342.0	1,689.1	18,453.6	9.15
1993–94	60.0	380.0	440.0	896.6	388.0	1,724.6	20,632.2	8.36
1994–95	116.6	407.5	524.1	1,094.1	450.2	2,068.4	23,915.9	8.65
1995–96	193.5	430.0	623.5	1,360.6	525.3	2,509.4	25,561.3	9.82

SOURCE: Acharya and Chaudhari (2001).

agricultural commodities account for a large part of their expenditures, a cheap food policy is advocated. At the same time, it is recognized that such a policy will be ruinous for the producers unless they, too, are supported by subsidized inputs. Moreover, input subsidies are less discriminatory toward small farmers than are output subsidies, which would benefit only those who have large amounts of marketable surplus. Per hectare use of subsidized inputs such as fertilizers and irrigation is the same, if not higher, on small farms than on larger farms.

The basis of determining fertilizer subsidies has changed since 1977. Since then, the domestic producers of urea, the main fertilizer, have been allowed a retention price that is plant-specific. The measure of a fertilizer subsidy is the difference between the retention price and the price at the farm gate. Besides, the imported fertilizers are also subsidized. There is serious debate on the amount of subsidy going to inefficient fertilizer plants thanks to the retention price scheme. Several proposals have been made to bring down the amount of fertilizer subsidies, with little success.

The second major input subsidy is the subsidy on power, calculated as the difference between the cost of generation and the cost of transmission of power and the tariff charged by the state-level electricity authorities for agricultural operations. Practically all states charge lower tariffs, by one-half to one-third, for agricultural use than for domestic, commercial, or industrial use.

The third important input subsidy is that on canal water. Over time the system has been less and less able to recoup the operation and maintenance (O&M) costs, let alone provide a return on the investment. In a highly competitive political context, the states are not willing to implement the reforms suggested, which are summarized in the report of the National Commission for Integrated Water Resources Development (India, Ministry of Water Resources, 1999b).

From the figures for subsidies on fertilizers and power from India's Ministry of Finance (*Economic Survey,* various years) and estimates of the subsidies on canal irrigation from Acharya (2000a), it is clear not only that the subsidy bill for all three inputs is increasing but that it accounts for a progressively rising share in government revenues, the value of agricultural output, and GDP.

Output Pricing

India's agricultural price policy comprises four elements: (1) a minimum support price to be announced before the sowing season to assure the producers of certain commodities, mainly cereals, that the state will purchase all the quantities offered for sale should the market price fall below the MSP in the postharvest period with higher production, thereby providing an incentive to adopt new technologies; (2) a procurement price at which the government agency would procure foodgrains from the producers; (3) a buffer stock to cushion the country from any large shortfall in domestic production of foodgrains; and (4) the PDS, which will distribute procured foodgrains to the poorest at an issue price lower than the prevailing market price.

This policy structure was introduced in the mid-1960s during the period of food shortages and served well the overarching objective of closing the gap between domestic foodgrain demand and production. It was an integrated system suited to a food shortage economy that aimed at food security on the one hand and at sharing gains in productivity between the producers and the consumers on the other.

Over time, the system developed certain discrepancies. The distinction between the MSP and procurement prices was eliminated, and the state agreed to purchase *all* commodities offered for sale by the producers, for which the MSP was announced. A second set of distortions arose from the method of determining the MSP, which is now synonymous with procurement prices. Although CACP claims that several factors, including border prices, domestic demand, prices of competitive crops, agriculture's terms of trade, and so on, are taken into consideration, the cost of production has emerged as the main determining factor. Distortions of this figure are aggravated as the definition of the cost of production is enlarged to include not only the paid-out costs on purchased items, which are more like variable costs, but also the imputed value of several owned and fixed factors (for instance, owned land, owned capital, and family labor). Further, the list of commodities for which the MSP is announced has been progressively enlarged to include 24 items. There is actual procurement of much fewer commodities, and mainly in the surplus states, which erodes the credibility of the government. In recent years the actual prices announced by the government for most of the commodities have been even higher than those recommended by CACP.

Because the other plank of the policy, the PDS issue prices, are related to the MSP, there have been only two options available to policymakers of late due to rising MSPs: (1) raise the issue prices and/or (2) increase the level of food subsidies. Fiscal "discipline" coupled with a resource crunch has put the entire burden on the first option. The situation was further aggravated in 1997, when a decision was taken to divide those who were benefiting from the PDS into two categories, households below the poverty line (BPL) and households above the poverty line (APL). Foodgrain prices for the APL were brought closer to, and in many instances above, market prices. With the attendant complications of this division on an already inefficient PDS, this move drove most households outside the PDS. The net result was huge foodgrain stocks with the FCI, the principal operating arm for agricultural price policy.

Removal of Restrictions on Agricultural Marketing

Many of the features of domestic marketing policies were introduced with the objective of protecting farmers' or consumers' interests. Underlying many of the acts and regulations was a deep suspicion about the "exploitative" role of middlemen. In these changed circumstances, many of the pieces of legislation are proving dysfunctional, among which the most pernicious is the "zoning" provision whereby sale of foodgrains outside a zone was prohibited. The purpose was to "bottle up" the surplus region and facilitate state purchase of grains at a previously announced procurement price. In effect, zoning led to "balkanization" (i.e., excessive fragmentation) of the domestic market. Recent reforms include the abolition of zones, spurring the slow but sure growth of a huge unified market of continental size.

The provision allowing the sale and purchase of farm produce only in regulated markets was another example of misplaced concern for the producers' welfare. Many states promulgated agricultural produce marketing acts and established "regulated markets." This reform, introduced to regularize marketing and protect small producers from manipulation by traders, is now proving a constraint on the farmers. Similarly, the Essential Commodities Act was introduced to protect consumers during times of acute scarcity, especially in food products, but is now a hindrance to organized marketing and increased private trade. Both these measures, and several others such as the levy on rice millers or sugar producers, have lost their relevance now and are counterproductive.

Some of the more onerous pieces of legislation, such as that on zoning, have been removed and several others relaxed. For example, by a recent order the government has removed all restrictions on the purchase, stocking, and movement of specified commodities, which were earlier covered under the Essential Commodities Act. One of the southern states, Karnataka, has relaxed its Agricultural Produce Marketing Regulation Act and has allowed the National Dairy Development Board, an autonomous corporation, to establish and manage markets in fruits, vegetables, and flowers. Other states are following suit.

Reforms in Support Systems

An important area in which reforms are taking place is the organization and functioning of support systems that value the importance of efficient research, extension, credit, and marketing systems for small farm–dominated agriculture. Reforms in these supportive services have proceeded in two directions. First, the exclusive or even major reliance on the state for the provision of these services was relaxed, and the cooperative sector was encouraged in the marketing and credit areas more decisively than in the prereform era. The private sector has also been strengthened, not only in its traditional activities of marketing and credit but also in areas such as research (e.g., seed research) and extension (e.g., veterinary services). Second, the promotional as well as the regulatory role of the state in providing these services to agriculture has been strengthened. For example, mandatory lending of 18 percent of all advances to agriculture by financial institutions is a necessary step to provide enough credit to the small farm sector, which otherwise would have been subject to credit rationing (ECRC 2001). Similarly, creation and maintenance of one of the largest research and extension systems in the world in the public domain has been part of the public policy to strengthen agriculture and small farm producers.

However, despite very elaborate legislation, large amounts of resources, and extensive implementing machinery, not all of these policies could attain their objectives. In the next section we will examine the effects of two sets of measures—input subsidies and output pricing—on agricultural growth and equity.

An Assessment of Policy Impact

Although the outcomes of agricultural policies can be assessed from several angles, we will be looking at a few critical aspects, including growth and diversification of agricultural production, factor productivity and farmers' incomes, rural poverty, and private trade. Admittedly, it is difficult to isolate the impact of any one policy on agricultural production, producers, consumers, or traders, because several developments in the domestic as well as the international spheres are taking place simultaneously. Besides, it is difficult to segregate short-term outcomes from the underlying trends. Nevertheless, some rough assessments can be made. The following review is confined to the experience of the past two decades.

Growth and Diversification

Two interesting trends can be observed in the growth rates of agricultural production since the 1980s. On the one hand, the rate of growth of both food and nonfood crops decelerated in the 1990s compared to the 1980s, from 3.19 percent to 1.73 percent per year. On the other, growth in production of plantation crops, horticultural crops, milk, and fish was generally higher in the 1990s compared to the 1980s (Table 12.2). By the 1990s, production of major food crops, especially wheat, had plateaued in the states of Punjab and Haryana, where procurement is the greatest. It may be noted that wheat and rice are major beneficiaries of the MSP system. Faster growth in noncereal food commodities was a response to the secular rise in income and the consequent changes in demand (Vyas 2002). Administered prices did not contribute to the diversification of agricultural activities.

Growth in Productivity

Total factor productivity (TFP) is the correct measure of impact on production, but there are serious methodological problems in estimating TFP in agriculture. Studies are few; the two best-known ones are those by Dholakia (1997) and Fan, Hazell, and Thorat (1999), which estimate a rise in TFP from the mid-1980s to the mid-1990s of around 2.5 percent per year.[3] This was a period that witnessed

---

3. The study by Dholakia, an extension of an earlier study (Dholakia and Dholakia 1993), compares TFP in the prereform years 1960–61 through 1985–86 with the postreform years 1985–86 through 1995–96. The author estimates TFP for the first period at 0.59 and for the later period at 2.45. In Fan, Zhang, and Zhang (2002) the index of TFP for 1985–86 is 128.48 (with 1970–71 = 100), and that for 1994–95 is 151.80.

TABLE 12.2 Annual compound growth of crops, area, production, and productivity in India, 1980–81 to 2000–2001 (percent)

Crop	1980–81 to 1989–90			1990–91 to 2000–2001		
	Area	Production	Yield	Area	Production	Yield
Rice and wheat	0.43	3.59	3.15	0.84	2.27	1.42
Rice	0.41	3.62	3.19	0.63	1.79	1.16
Wheat	0.47	3.57	3.10	1.21	3.04	1.81
Coarse cereals	-1.34	0.40	1.62	-1.84	0.06	1.65
Pulses	-0.09	1.52	1.61	-1.02	-0.58	0.27
Total foodgrains	*-0.23*	*2.85*	*2.74*	*-0.20*	*1.66*	*1.34*
Nonfood crops	1.12	3.77	2.31	0.84	1.86	0.59
Oilseeds	-1.51	5.20	2.43	0.44	0.66	0.61
Sugarcane	1.44	2.70	1.24	1.72	2.62	0.89
Cotton	-1.25	2.80	4.10	2.21	0.92	-1.26
All crops	*0.10*	*3.19*	*2.56*	*0.08*	*1.73*	*1.02*

SOURCE: India, Ministry of Finance, *Economic Survey,* 2001–2.

a more or less uninterrupted run of good monsoon rains, except for 1986–87. In other words, weather was one of the explanations for the favorable TFP. There are no studies of TFP in Indian agriculture for the second half of the 1990s.

A simpler alternative would be to study the input-output relationship. The figures given by national accounts on inputs, mainly the purchased inputs, and outputs of agriculture in constant and current prices suggest that the input-output relationship remained more or less stable from 1993–94 to 1999–2000 (Figure 12.1). Input data in this case do not include the contribution of land and labor.

There has been a clear deceleration in the productivity of land. The annual compound growth of yield per ha decreased from 2.56 from 1980–81 to 1989–90 to 1.02 percent per year from 1990–91 to 2000–2001 (India, Ministry of Finance, *Economic Survey,* 2002). It is important to note that in the context of the overall slowdown in per hectare yield for all crops taken together, deceleration in the rate of growth of yield was sharper in the case of rice and wheat, crops that received all the policy attention under the MSP regime.

Agricultural Incomes

The income of agricultural producers is determined by total production on one hand and by the prices paid and received on the other. The ratio of the last two prices, defined as barter terms of trade, is bedeviled by several conceptual problems as well as difficulties in measurement. Despite these limitations, there is enough evidence to suggest that barter terms of trade during the 1990s moved in favor of agriculture (for detailed statewise, cropwise estimates of terms of trade,

FIGURE 12.1 The value of Indian output and input at 1993–94 prices

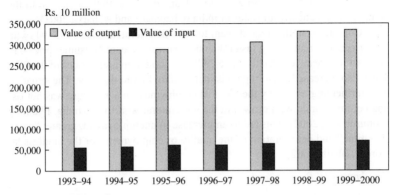

SOURCE: India, CSO, various years.

see Acharya 2000b). MSPs announced by the government played a positive role in improving agriculture's terms of trade. Equally important was the "deprotection" of industry and proper alignment of the exchange rate during this period.

As agricultural production improved, the income terms of trade also improved. From all indications, the incomes of the agricultural producers went up in the 1990s. According to one estimate, the index of farmers' income, with 1981–82 as the base year, increased from 137.3 in 1990–91 to 143.6 in 1997–98 (Misra 2004). But improvement in agricultural income was neither spread uniformly in all regions nor accrued to all categories of agricultural producers, with important wheat- and rice-growing states (especially Punjab, Haryana, and Andhra Pradesh) benefiting the most.

The Impact on Poverty

According to official estimates, the rural poverty ratio declined from 39.1 percent in 1987–88 to 37.3 percent in 1993–94 and further to 27.1 percent in 1999–2000. Although the comparability of the poverty figures is disputed for the years 1993–94 and 1999–2000, a steep fall in rural poverty during this period is indisputable.

Rural poverty is largely concentrated among the landless laborers and the marginal and small farmers (Chaudhari and Acharya 2001). However, there is no conclusive way to prove that the improvement of income at the sector level also made a dent on these segments of the rural poor. On the positive side were the falling prices of cereals in real terms, at least until 1993–94 (Zhou, Liu, and Perera 2001). Because the poor spend a large part of their consumption expenditures on cereals, they should have benefited from this decline in prices. Further, to the extent that the poor are able to take advantage of the PDS, they have gained in real terms, because the issue prices of the PDS were lower than the market prices. Data based on the 1993–94 NSS (National Sample Survey) suggest that the poor were taking greater advantage of the PDS compared to the nonpoor in practically all states in India (Chaudhari and Acharya 2001).

Conditions in this regard seem to have deteriorated since 1993–94, with the prices of cereals rising faster than the general index of consumer prices. In the past few years, especially since 2000, the foodgrain issue prices of the PDS have also increased, entailing a distinct welfare loss to the poor. The situation was further aggravated by the fact that employment in agriculture was not rising commensurate with growth in the agricultural workforce (India, Planning Commission, 2002). This led to an increase in unemployment, greater "casualization," and deterioration of the quality of employment for the landless laborers (Bhalla 2002).

The Impact on Private Trade

India has a fairly well-developed market structure, although there are imperfect monopsonic and monopolistic markets for coarse cereals and "minor" crops in the remote and inaccessible areas. The agricultural policies pursued in the country, instead of strengthening private trade, contributed to making them less effective. The virtual monopoly of the FCI in the procurement of rice and wheat in the surplus regions limited the scope for private trade. The high procurement prices led to high wholesale prices, which were rising faster than the retail prices and thus squeezing the margin of the retail traders. Large stocks with the FCI posed a threat to private traders and created uncertainty on the supply side. Periodic releases from FCI stocks at subsidized prices had a further depressing effect on private trade (Chand 2002).

To conclude, the agricultural policies directly or indirectly resulted in the improvement of agricultural incomes, mainly due to the favorable terms of trade rather than an improvement in productivity. The impacts of these policies on the rural poor, the landless, and the marginal farmers, as well as on the environment for private trade, especially for the retail trade, appear to have been negative.

Lacunae and Gaps

If the reforms in agriculture did not yield the desired results, it was due partly to the speed and partly to the nature of the reforms (Vyas 2001). In the sequence of reforms, agriculture was given low priority. The major reasons for a hesitant approach to agricultural reforms were the overwhelming concern for food security and the "closed economy" approach to policymaking. It was not considered prudent to depend on foreign sources for foodgrains, partly because of the bitter memory of the food shortages in the country and partly because of the dependence of a large portion of workforce on grain production for their livelihood. The "scarcity syndrome" had influenced policymaking in agriculture from the beginning, and these considerations continue to exert a strong influence. This also explains the more than enthusiastic response to the technology centering on HYV seeds, which became the dominant paradigm for agricultural policy in the country in the 1960s and 1970s. The policy regime based on input subsidies and MSP–procurement–PDS was put in place to provide incentives for self-sufficiency in food production and at the same time protect the vulnerable sections of the population from any sharp rise in market prices. Both these objectives were fulfilled to a large extent, albeit with several distortions that make this policy package dysfunctional.

Input Subsidies

The main justification for the policy of input subsidies was that it would enhance production and productivity and make subsidies useless. This has not happened because, even as the use of subsidized inputs is spreading, productivity growth is decelerating. So productivity considerations are no longer a valid rationale because the effects have been just the opposite. Subsidizing certain fertilizers led to the excess of chemicals in the soil and to environmental decay in some areas. The irrigation subsidy resulted in excessive use of water and to waterlogging and salinity. Cheap power encouraged indiscriminate use of power in lifting water, thus leading to unsustainable exploitation of groundwater. Subsidized inputs of water made farmers indifferent to the need to economize on its use.

The implicit justification for subsidizing inputs is to give income support to agricultural producers because output prices are kept deliberately low. In the first place, administered prices and subsidies are not the correct vehicles to transfer income because they create and strengthen political lobbies. In any event, because the output prices are continuously increasing, subsidizing inputs has lost its rationale even on the basis of income considerations. Rather, input subsidies have created larger income inequalities. In particular, subsidized irrigation discriminates against the dry areas. Even within the irrigated areas, farmers using canal water for irrigation are favored, while those using groundwater irrigation are discriminated against. Part of the subsidies are going to inefficient input producers (fertilizer plants) and suppliers (canal authorities and electricity boards) who have vested interests in perpetuating subsidies and concealing inefficiencies in the production and supply of inputs.

The share of subsidized inputs increases with growth in production, leading to a vicious circle in which the greater the production, the higher the subsidies. Subsidies also take away the incentive for improving productivity, because they provide an easier way to augment incomes. The worst consequence of these subsidies is that they are "crowding out" investment in research and rural infrastructure. Fiscal constraints of the central government as well as the states make sure that the huge outflow of resources for subsidies is at the cost of investment in agriculture and rural areas. The share of public investment in agriculture is on the slide, and its harmful effects are compounded because private investment is not able to compensate for the decline in public investment.

Minimum Support Prices

Much greater distortions have been introduced by the MSP regime, for which different justifications have been provided. In recent times, the dominant rationale has been the assurance of "fair" income for producers, that is, producers with marketable surpluses.

Administered prices are an inefficient way to transfer income. In this case, income is determined by the coverage of crops under MSP and the regions and farms that produce and market these crops. The MSP regime has favored some regions at the cost of others. Even in the favored regions, it has been beneficial in proportion to the marketed surplus of the commodities, thus increasing regional as well as interfarm inequality. A negative effect has been the increase in the prices of foodgrains for the poor farmers as well as the PDS subscribers because of higher issue prices. More important, these policies have clouded the main function of prices as signals for resource allocation. Although CACP claims that it takes into account the prospective demand for various commodities when fixing the MSP, in practice this has amounted to protection of the incomes of the cereal producers, notwithstanding the declining demand for these crops. The policy has led to huge foodgrain stocks, which are difficult to dispose of, and prioritizing cereals and few other crops as key to food security has gotten in the way of diversification of agriculture. Besides, there is no evidence to suggest that the productivity in the crops covered by MSPs has increased. The main benefit of the MSP regime, when it is properly implemented, has been its salutary effect on the market-induced price risks for producers of certain crops in certain regions. The key issue, therefore, is the need to look for more efficient ways of protecting farmers from severe price fluctuations without introducing distortions and inequity in the system.

It is indeed a strange situation. The surplus farmers and their spokespersons are asking for and actually receiving progressively increasing input subsidies and higher procurement prices on the grounds of rising costs of production, while the attempts to curtail subsidies are mainly directed at raising the issue prices of the grains released through the PDS. The net result is that the expected off-take from the PDS is declining and the stocks are rising at an unsustainable level. The time has come to seriously think about dismantling the "high-cost, high-subsidy" regime, which is not only not contributing to the increase in productivity but also eating into the vital parts of the agricultural economy by diverting resources from rural investment.

The Way Ahead

My introductory remarks suggested four major handicaps faced by Indian agriculture, including the preponderance of low-value agriculture, the low cost-benefit ratio, the inefficient use of natural resources, and excessive government interventions and deterioration in the self-help institutions. Future policy initiatives and reforms must address these interrelated problems in Indian agriculture, which must be transformed into a high-value, efficient enterprise that ensures judicious use of land and water resources with strong institutional underpinnings. These objectives have to be achieved in the context of a small farm agriculture functioning in a democratic, multiparty political system. It would be simplistic to assume that the problems of growth and equity could be resolved by policy initiatives alone. Nevertheless, economic policies have an important role, and if used judiciously can supplement or support technological and institutional developments. We will focus on three major areas in which reforms are urgently needed: (1) policy on input subsidies; (2) policies addressed to MSP, procurement, and the PDS; and (3) measures for liberalizing the market.

Input Subsidies

A policy of subsidizing inputs can be justified under the following conditions:

- If the introduction of a new input warrants the sharing of risks by the state.
- If the use of subsidized inputs ensures continuous increase in productivity that is shared by both producers and consumers.
- When subsidizing inputs is the only way to transfer income to poor producers.
- In the case of heavily traded products, where trading partners are resorting to overt or covert subsidization and there is no other means of redress.

Close scrutiny of the functioning of the farm subsidy regime suggests that none of the arguments for input subsidization apply today. Modern inputs such as fertilizers or electric power have been used for decades now, so one rationale for subsidies, that is, providing encouragement to adopt a new technology, has become irrelevant. The available evidence suggests that the phase of improvement in productivity and its sharing between the producers and consumers is already over. Productivity growth is decelerating, and the real prices of foodgrains are growing faster than the index of consumer prices. If it is true that some of the trading partners, particularly the OECD (Organisation for Economic Cooperation and Development) countries, are discriminating against the developing countries' exports, the solution is to build coalitions of similarly placed economies and strengthen the WTO dispute mechanism.

A beginning could be made by dismantling the fertilizer subsidy. No reform in fertilizer pricing is possible without reforms at the industry level. Among various suggestions for reforming this sector, those offered by the Expenditure Commission, which recommended replacement of the existing retention price system in a phased manner, are more practical. As expected, these suggestions have not found favor with the fertilizer industry or with the government, which is unwilling to face the powerful farm lobby clamoring for increases in the farm gate prices once the fertilizer subsidy is eliminated.

There is a growing consensus on removing subsidies after reforming the power sector. Moves include unbundling and corporatizing state electricity boards, setting up regulatory commissions, privatizing electricity distribution in some parts of the country, and removing cross-subsidization in a phased manner. A number of states have started acting on these measures, but so far perceptible results are not forthcoming (Kannan and Pillai 2002). The Achilles' heel of power reform is the inefficiency of power generation along with huge transmission losses. Unless these are remedied, it would be difficult to remove power subsidies for agricultural purposes, no matter how strong the case for removal of subsidies.

While there have been some thoughts on removing fertilizer and power subsidies but not much action, the removal of subsidies on canal water has not attracted any serious attention from policymakers. Like other subsidized inputs, canal water is also managed in a grossly inefficient way. The need to strengthen the administration and systems for water delivery has been emphasized by several authorities, the latest of which was the National Commission for Integrated Water Resources Development, headed by S. R. Hashim. In some states attempts are being made to resolve the problem by organizing water users' associations and entrusting them with the responsibility of O&M as well as the collection of water fees. The involvement of consumers in both water and power distribution is a promising approach.

A determined move needs to be made to dismantle the subsidy regime in agriculture, because the Indian system has grown addicted to subsidies. Also, the states rather than the central government must take the lead role in the case of irrigation and power subsidies. Action is needed to enable a "retreat without disarray." None of the suggestions that follow will be easy to implement, but continuing with the same regime will make future tasks even more difficult.

Agricultural Price Policy

The objectives of Indian price policies have been multiple and often conflicting. Following are some considerations for forging a new price policy regime.

- A modified MSP may need to continue as assurance against recouping the variable costs of production and the imputed value of family labor. It should be restricted to a few important commodities, including crops for which technological breakthroughs are imminent and those grown in high-risk environments. In these cases, MSPs should be treated as a transient measure to be used until India is able to evolve a viable crop insurance and/or forward trade program. Action in both these directions should be accelerated.

- The objective of risk minimization should be achieved by first declaring a price band with upper and lower limits beyond which there should be state intervention. A certain percentage, say 20 percent above or below the moving average of prices of a selected commodity for the past seven years, could be taken as the band's boundaries. If the prices go above or below, states should organize open market operations by buying or selling grains in the domestic as well as foreign markets. Such an operation should be mounted in conjunction with fiscal, monetary, and trade measures.

- Given the magnitude of procurement operations to keep public stocks and meet PDS requirements, as well as difficulties in obtaining required quantities of foodgrains on short notice from the international market, keeping a "buffer stock" in foreign exchange is not an efficient solution (Chand 2002). In view of the huge transport and storage costs entailed in a centralized operation for a country as large and diverse as India, the PDS should be made a primary responsibility of the states. In fact, states should be put in charge of public distribution, and functions should be delegated further to the lower tiers of the *Panchayati Raj* system.[4] In order to encourage this development, the central government should pass on the money saved from the centralized operations of procurement and public distribution to the states. Further, the food credit facilities should also be made available to the states. FCI might curtail its procurement operations to the limit of the buffer stocks and facilitate the interstate and international marketing operations of state-level agencies.[5]

- There should be greater coordination between the pricing and trade policies. The current spectacle of export of certain commodities at one point of time and import of the same commodities at a loss (to meet domestic demand) only after a few months will be repeated more often if trade and pricing policies are not coordinated properly.

- CACP should take a more comprehensive view of the agricultural economy of the country and the developments taking place at the international level and should advise the government accordingly.

Apart from drastic reforms in input pricing, MSPs, procurement, and PDS policies, there are other irritants that need to be removed to complete the reform agenda in agriculture (India, Planning Commission, 2001a). These would include amending the Essential Commodities Act to make it an emergency provision for a limited period of time, enacting a central measure to ban controls

---

4. A *Panchayati Raj* is the grassroots unit of government in a decentralized form of government.

5. The High Power Foodgrains (Sen) Committee endorses the idea of decentralization of procurement and PDS operations at the state level, but gives the FCI a pivotal role. By contrast, we have proposed that the primary role be assigned to the states, with the FCI playing a facilitating role, except in the maintenance of the buffer stock.

on movement between states, phasing out all levies and monopoly purchases, removing licensing and control measures and dereserving agro-based and food processing industries, meeting domestic shortages by means of adequate imports rather than by imposing export controls, decontrolling sugar and also removing it from the PDS, removing all restrictions on export of agricultural products, and removing restrictions on agricultural marketing under Agricultural Markets Regulation Acts in different states. The arbitrary levies and surcharges imposed by various states also need a closer look.

The Sequencing and Process of Reforms

Although it may be possible to build consensus on domestic market reforms among academics and even among policymakers, it would require support from a much larger section of the population to administer these reforms. This takes us into the realm of political economy.

Indian polity has three important features: it is a functioning democracy in which consensus has to be built to ensure acceptance of any major reform, it comprises multiparty states characterized by competitive politics, and it is a federal state in which agriculture comes under the purview of the constituent states. The central government as well as the several states are governed by coalitions of varied colors and hues, so reforms have to be gradual. Historical experiences of "big bang" reform processes have not been very reassuring.

Another factor impinging on the success of reforms is that past policies have created groups with vested interests who may feel threatened by radical changes. Clearly, reform cannot be achieved by state decree, and its success will hinge on building alliances and educating people, especially opinion makers, and forging alliances with those who are likely to benefit from the changes.

Much depends on the sequencing of reforms. Before attempting to correct a major market distortion introduced by input subsidies, the elimination of inefficiency in production and delivery of inputs and services have to be ensured. In a situation in which a large part of fertilizer production is accomplished by inefficient producers protected by a regime of "retention prices," the case for reduction of the fertilizer subsidies given to the agricultural producers is considerably weakened. Similarly, a heavily staffed power sector notorious for large transmission losses would find it difficult to present a convincing case for elimination of power subsidies. The same would be true for cost recovery for irrigation water, where again a bloated bureaucracy and inefficiencies in conveyance inhibit any move to raise water rates. Therefore, a case for eliminating subsidies on inputs will become more convincing if a beginning is made toward reforming the input-supplying institutions and arrangements.

In the case of MSPs, an alternative safety valve in terms of crop insurance and/or forward marketing has to be put in place to build a convincing case for progressively dismantling the present regime. Apart from the "rent" element in the present system of support prices, MSPs do provide a cushion against market-induced risks to the agricultural producers, at least to foodgrains producers. A superior alternative means to minimize risks should be a precursor of any major reform in this area.

Decentralization of the PDS is heavily constrained by the budgetary position of the states, and the least the central government should do is to transfer all subsidies, overt and covert, entailed in the present centralized system to the states. This together with the continuation of a buffer stock by the central government and assurance that it will be the "lender of last resort" would allay the fears of the states about taking up this additional responsibility.

Reforms in agriculture, as in other economic spheres, should also have positive connotations. Apart from ensuring efficiency gains to the economy, they should directly and explicitly benefit those who have been denied the fruits of development. In the Indian context, the small and marginal farmers are one such important group. With proper institutional support, a larger number of them can be made viable. This would require reforms in the institutions dealing with research, extension, credit, and marketing, and such reforms should be designed to be congruent with their recipient systems. Reform in the supportive institutions is as important as market reforms.

Summary and Conclusion

The time has come to take a serious look at the scope, instruments, and institutions of Indian agricultural pricing policy. The main ingredients of a market reform agenda in agriculture should include the following:

- Establishing the principle of cost recovery in agricultural inputs and phasing out input subsidies by placing a "cap" on existing subsidies while announcing a time-bound program of phasing out and assuring the efficient operation of input-supplying agencies.
- Thoroughly revising the agricultural price support system by curtailing the scope of MSPs to the protection of variable costs for a few commodities in selected regions, and placing a greater emphasis on crop insurance and forward markets.
- Carrying out procurement operations on commercial lines by decentralizing and debureaucratizing the FCI and involving the states and the lower tiers of *Panchayati Raj* institutions in the public distribution of foodgrains.
- Dovetailing price and trade policies in an effective manner.
- Accelerating the process of liberalization in agricultural marketing and removing bureaucratic hurdles.

I have suggested that the success of reforms will largely depend on the process and sequencing of those reforms. Keeping in view the ground realities in India, the approach has to be driven by consensus rather than relying on state fiat. The benefits of reforms have to be established and superior alternatives provided before dismantling the current regime of high input subsidies and high MSPs. Finally, the disadvantaged segments of agricultural producers—the small farmers, of whom a large number are potentially viable—should be supported by institutions responsible for research, extension, credit, and marketing to enable them to benefit from economic reforms.

13 Gains from Trade Reform: The Likely Impact of China's WTO Accession on Its Agriculture

JIKUN HUANG AND SCOTT ROZELLE

Decollectivization, price increases, and the relaxation of local trade restrictions on most agricultural products were the main drivers for the take-off of China's agricultural economy from 1978 to 1984. Although agricultural growth decelerated after 1985 following the one-time efficiency gains from decollectivization, the country has still enjoyed agricultural growth rates that have outpaced its rise in population. In fact, expanding supplies and increased liberalization have pushed real agricultural prices to their lowest levels in history (Park et al. 2002). Still, new opportunities in the off-farm sectors have allowed farm families to shift part of their household labor out of agriculture and into higher-paying off-farm jobs. However, even though China's record in the rural economy is stellar, there are still large numbers of people—over 100 million, according to World Bank (2000a) estimates—who are poor and vulnerable to even relatively minor income shocks. Agriculture was at the center of discussion of China's entry into the World Trade Organization (WTO), partly because of its vulnerability and partly due to its importance in the political economy of a number of developed nations. However, despite being a central concern for China's policymakers as well as the negotiators from other countries, the likely shifts in China's future agricultural policy and its impacts are not clear to all. Debates in this area remain unresolved, with some arguing that the impact of China's joining the WTO on its agriculture will be extensive, adversely affecting hundreds of millions of farmers (Li, Zhai, and Wang 1999; Carter and Estrin 2001). Others believe that, despite some severe effects in specific areas, the overall impact on agriculture will be modest (Anderson and Peng 1998). In part, the confusion about the ultimate impact of WTO membership can be traced to a general lack of understanding of the policy changes that may be induced by China's WTO accession (Martin 2001). The lack of clarity of the debate can also be traced to a lack of understanding of the fundamental facts about the nature of distortions in China's agriculture on the eve of its entry into the WTO.

The authors thank research assistants Yuping Xie and Min Chang.

283

The objective of our chapter is to contribute to the empirically based literature on the likely effects of China's accession to the WTO on its agriculture. We begin with a brief review of reform in the trade policy and its impacts. Next we present an estimation of remaining distortions in the agricultural sector and discuss how these distortions should be expected to change as China implements its WTO obligations and gains access (or not) to the promises made to it. This is followed by an examination of the WTO effects away from the border, the transmission of price shocks throughout the economy, and the impact of China's WTO accession on certain groups of farmers in different regions. The conclusion discusses the implications of our findings.

Major Reforms in Trade-Related Policies

Exchange Rate Policy

Before economic reform, China adopted a state-monopolized unified system of foreign exchange management to support the nation's import substitution industrialization strategy (Lardy 1995). In 1979, with the implementation of economic reform, China introduced the foreign exchange retention system, under which enterprises and local governments were able to retain a certain proportion of the exchange that they earned through exports. In 1988, additional reforms were made, one of which allowed local governments and enterprises to control and use all the foreign exchange they earned as long as they complied with state regulations. While the implications were wide-ranging, the policy shifts provided strong incentives for local leaders to encourage exports.

From the 1980s until the early 1990s, exchange rate management was controlled by a two-tier foreign exchange rate system. The official rate was set by policy, and another rate was set by a swap center where those units with extra foreign currency could exchange it with those units that needed additional allotments. The foreign exchange rate in the swap center was based mostly on supply and demand forces. The swap rate was about 20 percent higher than the official rate in the mid-1980s and 75 percent higher in the late 1980s. When China's leaders devalued the official rate by more than 40 percent in the early 1990s, the gap between the swap and officials rates fell to 25 percent.

Then, in 1994, China unified the official exchange rate and the swap market exchange rate and adopted a single-currency, managed exchange rate system that was supposed to be managed at a rate consistent with supply and demand. As a result, the exchange rate was effectively devalued from the official exchange rate of 5.76 yuan per U.S. dollar in 1993 to the managed floating market exchange rate of 8.61 yuan per U.S. dollar in 1994, a steep one-step devaluation of more than 50 percent. In December 1996, after the currency stabilized at that rate, the yuan became convertible on China's current account. From 1979 to the mid-1990s, the real exchange rate depreciated by about 400 percent (IMF 2002).

Since 1996, the black market or unofficial secondary markets for foreign exchange have moved closely with the official exchange rates and stayed remarkably constant.

The impacts of the devaluation of its currency on China's trade are substantial. Foreign reserves rose from U.S.$28.6 billion in 1990 to $73.6 billion in 1995 and reached $166.5 billion by 2000 (China, Ministry of Foreign Trade and Economic Cooperation, 2002). Since 1996, China has been the second largest foreign reserve holder (just behind Japan) in the world. The country's agricultural trade (both imports and exports) nearly tripled from 1980 to 1995 and continued to grow after 1995 (China, Ministry of Foreign Trade and Economic Cooperation, 1990, 2002). Exports have risen faster than imports.

Trade Policy

The changes in the exchange rate system occurred at the same time that China began to liberalize its international trading system. Moves to relax the rights of access to import and export markets were matched by actions to reduce the taxes that had been assessed at the border since the mid-1980s, particularly in the 1990s. The simple average agricultural import tariff fell from 42.2 percent in 1992 to 23.6 percent in 1998 and to 21 percent in 2001 (China, Ministry of Foreign Trade and Economic Cooperation, 1999, 2002). In its WTO accession, China agreed to further lower the agricultural tariff to 17 percent by 2004.

Despite the real, and in some areas rapid, reforms, the control of a set of commodities considered of national strategic importance, such as rice, wheat, and maize, remains with policymakers to a much larger extent (Huang and Rozelle 2002b). Although the import tariff rate has been low, prior to WTO accession China's leaders did not allow the import of grain except by those agencies and enterprises that hold licenses and import quotas. When traders bring in grain specified within the quota, the tariff rate is only about 3 percent, while the tariff rate for grain brought in above quota has been as high as 114 percent. No above-quota grain has entered China, however, because in the case of grain trade, imports have to be arranged by state traders. For the entire reform period, China National Cereals, Oils, and Foodstuffs Import and Export Corporation (COFCO) has been the nation's single-desk state trading company for grain and edible oils.

However, COFCO itself has undergone a series of reforms. Specifically, since the late 1990s officials have tried to streamline importing procedures by commercializing COFCO and decanalizing the trade of a number of commodities. For example, soybeans have been completely liberalized, with a single tariff management scheme. The effective tariff rate on soybean imports has been only 3 percent since 1999. For the trade of rice, wheat, and maize managed under the tariff rate quota (TRQ) regime, WTO obligations not only forced COFCO to gradually phase out its monopoly power but were instrumental in the introduction of competition in grain trade among domestic SOEs (state-owned enterprises). For example, in the case of rice and maize, the Jilin Grain Group Import and Export Company (JGIEC), a provincial level of STE (state trading enterprise) established in April 2001, has taken over the import and export responsibilities of COFCO for most maize and rice exports from northeast China. The establishment of JGIEC marked an end of the complete monopoly of COFCO in China's grain trade. Moreover, within the COFCO network (COFCO has branches in each province and in key municipalities), competition has been introduced. Better incentives were given to managers and branch officials to increase their attention to the activities that affect profitability. Also, an agency system has been imposed to implement a payment-for-services policy.

China also has had a policy to subsidize certain agricultural commodities from time to time. For example, it used export subsidies in the years prior to its WTO accession to increase exports of two commodities, maize (about 30 percent of freight on board, or FOB) and cotton (10 percent of FOB). But China has committed to phase out its export subsidies after joining the WTO.

Trade-Related Policies

China has effectively used its taxation policy to protect its agriculture. Based on production cost data, we estimate the average agricultural tax at about 6 percent at farm gate.[1] For traders who purchase agricultural products from farmers and resell them at a downstream wholesale market, the value added tax (VAT) is then assessed, but the trader owes only the tax on the amount of the marketing margin, or the difference between the procurement price and the sale price. Recent fieldwork for a grain study found that the marketing margins are between 1 and 10 percent. Taking an average of 5 percent, the tax rate on domestic agricultural goods after the farm gate is less than 1 percent (5 percent of 17 percent = 0.85 percent). Some scholars in China have also pointed out that because part of the value of agricultural commodity production uses inputs on which the VAT has been assessed, the "real" tax rate on agricultural commodities is actually higher. This adds 2 to 4 percentage points (15 percent VAT times the share of the inputs that were taxed—about 10 to 30 percent— depending on the commodity, the technology, and the region of production). Adding all these together with the total tax at the farm level results in a total agricultural tax of about 10 percent (6 percent + 3 percent + 1 percent). National regulations require imported goods that are not for immediate reexport to be assessed for the VAT. Although there are varying rates, the typical VAT ranges from 13 to 17 percent. Therefore, the current tax system can provide some of China's farmers with up to 7 percent protection.

---

1. Using production cost data, we estimate that the crop sector was taxed at about 3 percent of total output values for sugar, 4 percent for cotton, 4.5 percent for grain and oil crops, and 5–10 percent for horticultural crops at the farm level in 2001. Using shares of outputs as weights to estimate the average tax rate, we get a rate of about 6 percent for the agricultural tax at the farm gate. Some scholars argue that these figures might overestimate the agricultural tax, because part of this tax is on land.

China has been using a tax rebate policy for its exports. The rebate rates range from 13 percent to 17 percent for nearly all commodities exported, including agricultural products. Prior to its accession to the WTO, China had subsidized maize and cotton exports. China has also been providing substantial subsidies to the state grain bureau for domestic grain procurement and marketing since the mid-1990s (Nyberg and Rozelle 1999). Because many of the gains from traditional trade reforms have been realized, Huang and Rozelle (2002b) show that gains from the nontraditional sources of trade liberalization or protection may be as important as those that come from traditional trade reform.

After China joined the WTO at the end of 2001, a bold reform policy on the grain sector was proposed to completely liberalize the domestic grain marketing system and phase out the planned government grain procurement regime. Under this reform, the savings of billions of yuan that have been used to subsidize the state grain bureau's grain procurement will be used to pay direct subsidies to farmers under an income transfer program, which signals a historical turning point of China's agricultural policy in moving from taxing to subsidizing regimes. This reform was first implemented in Auhui province in 2002 and expanded to Jilin, Henan, Hubei, Hunan, Jiangsu, and Zhejiang in 2003. It was expected that within two to three years, the direct income transfer program would be implemented throughout China—and it has been.

Impacts of Trade and Trade-Related Policy Reforms

The experience of China's agricultural tariff and foreign exchange policies illustrates the dramatic changes that China has experienced in the past two decades. In the late 1970s and early 1980s, the domestic wholesale prices of China's four major commodities, converted at the official exchange rate, all far exceeded the world prices (measured at China's border and presented in Table 13.1). However, over the next two decades, the protection rate on rice became negative and that on wheat, maize, and soybeans fell to around 20–30 percent.

Falling protection and changes in international trade and domestic marketing policies have resulted in dramatically shifting trade patterns. Disaggregated, crop-specific trade trends show that exports and imports are increasingly moving in a direction that is more consistent with China's comparative advantage. For example, the proportion of grain exports, which was around 20 percent of total agricultural exports in the 1990s, is less than half of what it was in the early 1980s (Huang and Chen 1999). By the late 1990s, horticultural products and animal and aquatic products accounted for about 80 percent of agricultural exports. These trends are even more evident when reorganizing the trade data, grouping them on the basis of factor intensity (Table 13.2).

The net exports of land-intensive bulk commodities, such as grains, oilseeds, and sugar crops, have fallen, while exports of higher-valued, more labor-intensive products, such as horticultural and animal (including aquaculture) products have risen.

TABLE 13.1 Changes in the NPRs of China's major agricultural commodities, 1978–2001

	Rice	Wheat	Maize	Soybeans
1978–79	10	89	92	40
1980–84	9	58	46	44
1985–89	−4	52	37	39
1990–94	−7	30	12	26
1995–99	−7	22	26	26
2000–2001	−2	18	26	19

SOURCE: Authors' calculations.

NOTE: Border prices are average prices of exports (rice and sometimes maize) or imports (wheat, soybeans, and sometimes maize) for the varieties that are comparable with domestic grains. Official exchange rates are used in the case of border prices.

TABLE 13.2 China's agricultural trade, by factor intensity, 1985–97

Year	Land-intensive products		Labor-intensive products		Labor- or capital-intensive products	
	Value (U.S.$ million)	Share (percent)	Value (U.S.$ million)	Share (percent)	Value (U.S.$ million)	Share (percent)
			Agricultural exports			
1985	2,119	36.4	2,199	37.8	1,497	25.7
1990	1,689	17.7	4,971	52.1	2,881	30.2
1995	875	6.0	7,095	48.4	6,704	45.7
1997	2,158	14.1	6,538	42.6	6,642	43.3
			Agricultural imports			
1985	1,072	43.8	680	27.8	695	28.4
1990	4,032	71.9	642	11.5	935	16.7
1995	6,575	54.5	3,278	27.2	2,216	18.4
1997	4,644	47.3	2,179	22.2	2,987	30.5

SOURCE: Huang and Chen (1999).

From this discussion, three things become clear. First, distortions have declined significantly in the past 20 years. The current episode of policy reform that has accompanied China's accession to the WTO should therefore be considered an extension of past efforts. Second, much of the fall in protection has come from the decentralization of authority and the relaxing of licensing procedures for some crops (e.g., moving oil and oilseed imports away from state trading firms), devaluation of domestic currency, reduction of the scope of nontariff barriers, relaxation of real tariff rates at the border, and changing quotas

(Huang and Chen 1999). Third, China's agricultural policy has entered a new era, shifting from taxing agriculture to subsidizing farmers. While the policy has widely gained support from both central and local governments, concerns have also been raised about the efficiency of public spending and the sustainability of the income transfer program.

Estimates of Remaining Distortions

We now estimate a new set of nominal protection rates (NPRs) in an attempt to overcome some of the previous problems of researchers. We conducted a set of interviews and surveys with the stated goal of precisely identifying the differences in prices at a precise point of time and a particular location between an imported good on one side of the border (outside China) and a domestic good of identical quality on the other side (inside China). We also sought to identify the same price gap between exportable domestic goods as they leave the country and the same goods from other countries that are being traded in international markets. The enumeration team was in the field for more than three months during 2001, from August to November, visiting seven port cities (Guangzhou, Shenzhen, Ningbo, Shanghai, Lianyungang, Qinghuangdao, and Dalian) and two other more inland cities, Beijing and Changchun. In each port, a number of "sampling frames" were used to select a sample of domestic traders, importers and exporters, wholesalers, grain and oilseed users, trade regulators, agents, and other grain and fiber officials. In total, more than 100 people were interviewed, with fewer than 10 percent refusing to be interviewed.

The results of our analysis illustrate the problems with the conventional method that attempts to come up with a single rate of protection for a commodity impacted by China's WTO accession. We use wheat as an example to demonstrate the importance of estimating precise NPRs for agricultural commodities with a large variation in their quality. Table 13.3 shows that it is difficult to provide one single NPR for wheat in China.

The average trader reported that if a ton of Canadian Number 3 hard white wheat was brought in and auctioned off in October 2001, the competitive bid price would have been 20.5 percent higher than the international price on a c.i.f. (cost, including insurance and freight) basis. Hence, based on this price gap, one would have to assume that China's protection price is high and that, if it were to open its markets completely, wheat prices would plummet and import volumes soar.

However, traders were quick to point out that they did not think that, even with open markets, China's wheat price would fall anywhere close to 50 percent. According to our interviews, the market for wheat of the quality needed for baking, the main use for hard white wheat from North America, is actually relatively small in China, at most only several million metric tons (m mt). We were also told that few users in China outside those who demanded flour for

TABLE 13.3 Disaggregated NPRs for selected grains in China, October 2001

Variety or quality	Comparable domestic price		Border prices (U.S.$/ton)		NPR (percent)
	Yuan/ton	U.S.$/ton	c.i.f.	f.o.b.	
Rice (weighted average)					−3
Thai jasmine rice	3,690	446	380		17
High-quality Japonica	2,930	354		398	−11
Medium-quality Indica	1,519	184		185	−0.5
Wheat (weighted average)					12
U.S. DNS	2,350	284	190		49
Canadian No. 3	1,800	218	181		20
Australian soft	1,625	196	175		12
U.S. hard red	1,550	187	169		11
U.K.	1,350	163	145		12
China high-quality	1,350	163	145		12
China medium-quality	1,250	151	140		8
China low-quality	1,100	133	133		−0.1
Soybeans Common variety	1,950	236	205		15
Maize Common variety	1,150	139		105	32

SOURCE: Authors' survey.

NOTE: The estimated official exchange rate used is 8.28 yuan per U.S.$ as of October 2001.

making cakes, pastries, and high-quality breads would use this type of wheat and that only a small group of farmers and processors inside China could supply it. If this is the case, it would mean that even in a world that was free of any trade restrictions, imports would come into China until demand was fulfilled and the domestic price for that variety fell to international levels. With few domestic suppliers of this high-quality wheat and with little or no substitution of the baking-quality wheat for other domestic uses, there would be only a small price impact on most domestic producers.

While not as extreme as the case for North American baking-quality wheat, traders reported that there were arbitrage possibilities in other markets (Table 13.3). With a remarkable degree of consistency, they reported that the c.i.f. price of medium-quality wheat imports from Australia, England, and the Pacific Northwest of the United States (hard red) was 10 percent lower than the price that they believed the same wheat would command in China's domestic market. The interviewees believed that the market for this wheat, used for more common bread, less expensive pastries, industrial uses, and high-quality noodles, accounted for around 10 to 15 percent of China's wheat demand. However, there was more production of it in China than of the highest-quality baking wheat. In fact, in 2001, domestic producers supplied most of the wheat of this quality to this segment of China's wheat market. In China's domestic market, however, this wheat was considered high-quality Chinese wheat. Interestingly, we found evidence that medium-quality wheat on international markets is the same as the high-quality wheat supplied by China's farmers. When we asked our interviewees how much *loss* a trader would incur if China's high-quality wheat were sold on international markets, our survey found the loss estimated at 10 percent. This was almost the same as the premium importers would make from bringing in medium-quality grain from the international market.

Finally, although there have been no imports of low- (or lower-medium-) quality wheat from international markets, it appears as if China's medium-quality wheat, by far the biggest part of China's production (estimated to be more than 60 percent), is only marginally protected (Table 13.3). Our survey found that traders believed if China's medium-quality wheat was sold on the international market in late 2001, it would sell at a discount of about 8 percent. Because this wheat is the largest part of China's wheat crop, the persistent price gap would mean there would be imports of wheat after China's WTO accession. The effect, however, appears to be less than 10 percent. China's lowest-quality wheat (about 10 to 15 percent of its harvest) is at the world's price for feed wheat. Similar differences in the size of the price gap among varieties of a single grain are found for rice, though not for soybeans and maize, which are more homogeneous products.

Although there are differences among major individual agricultural commodities, weighting them by the shares of sown area (for crops) and production (for meats), a set of aggregate NPRs can be created (Table 13.3). Wheat, for example, has an NPR of 12 percent when the individual NPRs for different types of wheat are weighted by shares for their area. On average, the prices of all varieties of domestically produced wheat sold in the domestic markets of China's major port (and inland) cities are 12 percent above the average c.i.f. prices of all types of imported wheat varieties. Rice, on the other hand, is implicitly taxed by 3 percent. The aggregate figures, although helpful, are less interesting and provide much less insight about the groups of farmers in specific areas producing specific varieties that will be hurt or helped if trade liberalization reduces the distortions.

However, to the extent that certain commodities have fewer intracrop quality differences, the aggregate measures have more inherent interest. For example, maize and soybeans as well as cotton and sugar have far fewer quality differences among varieties than do rice and wheat. This is partly due to the fact that maize and soybeans are rarely consumed directly, as are rice and wheat, which makes the latter more sensitive to human tastes and preferences. Instead, maize and soybeans are mostly used as feed or are processed. As a consequence, in our analysis we examine aggregate crop NPRs only for maize, soybeans, cotton, and sugar.[2]

Our findings show that not only do significantly positive rates of protection exist for a number of China's major field crops, but they even vary across the nation and according to China's status as a net importer or exporter. According to exporters, maize prices were, on average, more than 30 percent above world prices. In other words, traders would have lost more than 30 percent of the value of their shipments had the government not paid them a subsidy. Protection rates differed when maize was considered as an import. For example, traders in the northeast told our survey team that if they were not exporting and foreign maize were to come into China, the importer could make 21 percent. Our interviews in south China, however, found that the price gap between imported maize at c.i.f. prices and maize being traded in the domestic market in and around Guangzhou was more than 30 to 40 percent. Aggregated across areas on the basis of their meat consumption shares, we estimate that China's maize NPR was 32 percent in 2001 (Table 13.4).

Interviewees also reported that, despite the large volumes of increase in soybean imports in recent years, there is still a difference between the c.i.f. and domestic prices in the port. The average difference between the domestic price and the international price was 15 percent. That there is a remaining price gap is remarkable given that China imported almost 15 m mt of soybeans in 2001, the official tariff is only 3 percent, and the commodity is freely traded without a license or quota allocation. On the other hand, the remaining price gap reminds us that there may be other reasons for distortions beyond tariffs and state trading, a point to which we will return shortly.

Our survey also found that cotton and sugar were fairly highly protected in October 2001 (Table 13.4). The case of cotton, however, is an example of how fast the NPR can change across time. The NPR was measured at 17 percent in October 2001, and when the team went back to do follow-up work at the end of November, the domestic price of cotton had fallen from 9,500 yuan per ton in October to less than 8,000 yuan per ton. With this fall, the NPR went to less than zero. However, later in the year, the international price of cotton also dipped, a fact that would lead to a higher NPR.

To analyze what would have happened had we not used this time- and data-intensive survey methodology, we calculated NPRs for China in 2001 using the same methodology, data sources, and assumptions that many people use for cal-

---

2. We stress that our survey was conducted the same way. In most cases, interviewees told us that there were not a lot of quality differences among maize varieties. Moreover, there was only a slight (around 2 to 3 percent) price difference related to quality between imported and domestic soybeans.

TABLE 13.4 Average NPRs for major imports and exports in China, October 2001

Major imports and exports	Domestic price (yuan per ton)	NPR (percent)
Imports		
Wheat[a]	1,250	12
Maize	1,150	32
Soybeans	1,950	15
Cotton	9,500	17
Sugar	2,612	40
Exports		
Rice[a]	1,954	−3
Pork[a]	11,442	−30
Beef[a]	13,743	−10
Poultry[a]	9,904	−17
Fresh fruits	5,472	−4

SOURCE: Authors' survey.:

[a]Average NPRs are created by summing the NPR rates of individual varieties weighted by the sown area (production) share.

culating NPRs.[3] Although the two approaches give almost the same answers for commodities such as soybeans and maize, the answers vary considerably for other commodities. For example, the national average price for wheat in 2001 reported from the Ministry of Agriculture's reporting system was 1,113 yuan per ton. The average price of imports, calculated by dividing total import value by total import quantity, was 1,393 yuan per ton. In other words, the domestic price of wheat using these sources of data about prices is 21 percent below the c.i.f. price of imports. From this standard methodology, one would come to the conclusion that wheat, rather than being protected (by 12 percent; see Table 13.3), was actually being taxed by trading policies. Yet, the main reason for generating a negative rate of protection is that China is importing almost exclusively very high-grade, baking-quality wheat, while its domestic consumers use mostly medium- and lower-quality wheat. The wrong conclusion is reached when one uses the specialty prices for imports as an international reference price for types of wheat that are less expensive and of much lower quality.

3. Generally, NPRs are computed by comparing the domestic wholesale price with the average implicit price of trade, which for the importable crop is total import value divided by total import volume and for the exportable crop is total export value divided by total export volume.

The same problem is found in the case of rice. Because China imports only high-quality jasmine rice from Thailand, the international price of rice (3,908 yuan per ton, calculated by total import value divided by total import quantity) appears to be more than 48 percent higher than the average domestic price (1,464 yuan per ton). In fact, as shown in Table 13.3, China's average price protection (tax) rate, calculated on a variety by variety basis, is almost zero (–3). Thus, exports are implicitly taxed, while imports are protected.

From this illustrative example we can see the necessity of estimating the NPRs in a more careful way for some commodities. Traditional approaches work well for commodities that are fairly homogenous in their quality characteristics (such as maize and soybeans). For wheat and rice, however, comparing average prices inside and outside of the nation can yield misleading results. Based on this example, one might conjecture that traditional estimates of NPRs for some products, such as sugar and edible oils, may be fairly reliable, while those for meat products, cotton, and horticultural crops could be misleading.

Away-from-the-Border WTO Effects

While important in determining the size of the shock at the border, the broader magnitude of the effects of the WTO agreement on China's farmers depend not only on the size of the distortion but also on the size of the area across which it will be felt. This second factor, in turn, is a function of the size and nature of China's market. There are at least three factors at play: policy safeguards (that limit market forces from fully equilibrating domestic and international prices), household responses (by which households are able to move into the production of higher-profitability commodities and away from those that experience price falls), and high transaction costs (that can serve to buffer the effects of liberalization policies on those who live in rural areas in China). Here we focus on the nature of markets. The policy safeguards and the effects of household responses are discussed by Taylor (1998) and Huang and Rozelle (2002b).

Ultimately, the distributional impacts of China's WTO membership will depend on the nature of the country's markets. If large areas of the country are isolated from coastal markets where imports land, the effects of WTO accession may be limited and should not have highly adverse impacts on the poor, who are largely located in inland areas far from major urban centers. Although being isolated from negative shocks is a plus, there is also a cost. Those living in poor, isolated areas also would not benefit from the price rises and opportunities to export. However, if there are markets that link distant regions with the coast and price changes in one part of the economy do ripple through the economy, even imports into (and exports out of) areas concentrated around a few large coastal cities could have ramifications for poor households thousands of kilometers away.

Assessing the Determination of Price and Market Integration

To assess how integrated and developed markets in rural China were in the late 1990s and 2000, we first describe the data. Then we test for integration and conduct direct tests of how well prices in different markets move together and if prices are integrated between the market town and China's villages.

Data

The data come from a unique price data set collected by China's State Market Administration Bureau. Nearly 50 sample sites in 15 of China's provinces report prices of agricultural commodities every 10 days. The prices are the average prices of transactions that day in the local rural periodic market. We examine rice, maize, and soybean prices from 1996 to 2000 (except for maize, for which data were available only through 1998). The three crops are produced and consumed in nearly every province in China. Rice price data are available for 31 markets. Because of quality differences among rice varieties in different regions of China, we look at price integration between markets within four regions, south China, the Yangtse Valley, the North China Plain and northwest China, and northeast China. For the provinces included in the sample, rice prices are available for more than 90 percent of the time periods. Prices for maize and soybeans are available for 13 and 20 markets, respectively.[4] Product homogeneity makes it possible to include a broader geographic range of buyers and sellers in a single analysis, and we are able to assess the integration of markets spread out over long distances. We compare these to results from 1988 to 1995 that were produced with the same sources of data and published in Park et al. (2002).

Integration Tests

We use cointegration statistics to test market integration. Such statistics measure the proportion of movement in one price that is transmitted to another price during the period of observation. The coefficient on the "causing" price is bound between zero and 1, where zero indicates that there is no impact on the "affected" price variable (and markets are not integrated) and 1 indicates that markets completely adjust within the period of analysis. A coefficient inside the zero to 1 interval indicates that prices adjusted only partially within the period of observation (or that markets are integrated but frictions slow down price transmission). Two markets are cointegrated if the coefficient is not different from 1 at a 5 percent level of significance.

Using the results from the early 1990s as a baseline, our current analysis shows that during the late 1990s, China's markets continued along their

---

4. Nominal prices from our data set are deflated using monthly consumer price indexes from China's National Bureau of Statistics. Deflation facilitates transaction cost comparisons across time and allows us to disregard transaction cost increases in periods associated with inflation.

TABLE 13.5 Percentage of market pairs that test positive for integration based on the Dickey Fuller test in rural China, 1989–2000

Commodity	1989–95	1996–2000
Maize	28	89
Soybeans	28	68
Japonica rice (Yellow River Valley)	25	60
Indica rice (Yangtse Valley and south China)	25	47

SOURCES: Huang and Rozelle (2002b) for the results from 1989 to 1995 for maize and rice. The results for soybeans for 1989 to 1995 and all results from 1996 to 2000 are from the authors. The rice results are for the whole country in 1989–95.

previous path of maturity and markets in China are remarkably integrated. In the late 1990s, examining the comovement of prices between pairs of markets in our sample, we see a large increase in the number of integrated markets. In the case of maize, for example, in 89 percent of the cases, prices in one market moved at the same time as those in another (Table 13.5). This was up from only 28 percent in the early 1990s. The pairs of markets for soybeans show similar increases. The integration of these markets is notable because in many cases, the markets within pairs are separated by more than 100 km.

Despite the significant progress in terms of integration, our results also show that there are pairs of markets during different years that are not integrated. For example, in one-third of the cases, Japonica rice prices moved in one market but not in another. The case of Indica rice trade is even more notable. More than half the time (and in different places), prices did not move together in China's Indica rice producing and consuming regions. One explanation for such a result is that there is some kind of institutional (policy or infrastructure or communication) breakdown that is creating China's fragmentation, as shown by Park et al. (2002). Another is that, because every province in China produces and consumes rice, if during a certain year in a certain region supply is just equal to demand, moderate price movements in another area may not necessarily induce a flow into or out of the region that is in equilibrium.

Even with the nontrivial number of cases in the late 1990s in which prices in pairs of markets did not move together, based on each of the market performance analyses, one must conclude that the impact of WTO membership on China's agriculture will be experienced across wide regions of the nation, from coastal to inland areas. However, this is only half the story. While the preceding analysis demonstrates a remarkable degree of integration between markets on the coast and those inland, such an analysis is still not sufficient to allow us to definitively conclude that many of China's villages will be affected by the shocks that hit the coast and are transmitted inland.

To draw such a conclusion, we examine the extent to which villages are integrated into regional markets, essentially testing to determine if farmers in

TABLE 13.6 Village price regression in China for soybeans, corn, and wheat, 2002

Explanatory variable	(1) Soybean price	(2) Corn price	(3) Wheat price
Distance to the nearest county market	−0.029	−0.00064	−0.0095
	(2.37)**	(−1.63)*	(3.24)**
Village-level shock to production	−0.04	0.12	0.081
	(−0.17)	(−1.34)	(−1.02)

SOURCE: Authors' calculations.
*Significant at the 10 percent level.
**Significant at the 5 percent level.

China's villages are price takers or whether villages are so isolated that prices are determined by local supply and demand. If variables that affect local supply significantly affect prices, we will assume that villages are isolated and markets are not integrated to the village level. In contrast, the local supply shock does not affect the price, villagers are price takers and markets will be taken to be integrated.[5] Our regression analysis clearly shows that markets in China are integrated down to the village level (Table 13.6).

The signs and level of significance of the coefficients on variables, such as the distance of a village from the market, demonstrate that the farther a village is from a market, the lower price the farmer receives, which is the expected result. The *t*-ratios of the coefficients of the village supply shock variables are all less than 1.35 in terms of absolute value, signifying that the crop output of the local village does not affect the local price. One implication of this result is that it is factors outside the village that are affecting the price that farmers receive, making them price takers. In other words, farmers, even in China's remote villages, are linked to the markets.

---

5. The data were collected in a randomly selected, nearly nationally representative sample of 60 villages in 6 provinces of rural China, called the China National Rural Survey (CNRS). To reflect income distribution in each province, one county was randomly selected from within each income quintile for the province, as measured by the gross value of industrial output. Two villages were randomly selected within each county. The survey teams used village rosters and our own counts to randomly choose 20 households, both those with their residency permits (*hukou*) in the village and those without. A total of 1,199 households were surveyed. The CNRS team gathered information on the production and marketing behavior of the farmers in the sample and the characteristics of each village and its relationship to the nearest regional market. Using data on the sale price and timing for each commodity, we constructed an average village price for each month in yuan per kg. From the questionnaire we also know how far the village's center is from the nearest paved road and the distance to the county market. For each crop, the respondent indicated whether it suffered a shock, recording both the incidence and the percentage by which the yield fell. Sales among farmers within a village were rare, at less than 5 percent of sales, according to our data.

Impacts of WTO Accession on Poverty

When examining the benefits or costs for certain groups of farmers, one needs only to examine the production mix and match it to see whether the prices of the products rose or fell over the period and whether farmers are moving into or out of the production of the concerned products given the nature of distortions for major agricultural products and market integration. Table 13.7 shows the sectoral shares of agricultural production for each group of farmers with different income levels in China and by region in 1999.

The data are from the China National Bureau of Statistics household income and expenditure survey and are representative of all of China in 1999. To show the difference in production structure among farmers, we first divide our entire sample of more than 67,000 households into 11 groups based on their in-

TABLE 13.7 Share of agricultural production in China, by region and income category, 1999

				Production[a]	
	Income group	Share of population (percent)	Per capita income (current yuan)	Sector I Competitive sectors (percent)	Sector II Noncompetitive sector (percent)
All China	Group 1	0.0–3.5	491	42	58
	Group 2	3.5–10.0	875	46	54
	Group 6	40.0–50.0	1,928	53	47
	Group 11	90.0–100.0	5,889	64	36
West	Group 1	0.0–3.5	356	36	64
	Group 2	3.5–10.0	592	47	53
	Group 6	40.0–50.0	1,302	56	44
	Group 11	90.0–100.0	3,961	52	48
Central	Group 1	0.0–3.5	459	40	60
	Group 2	3.5–10.0	840	47	53
	Group 6	40.0–50.0	1,785	56	44
	Group 11	90.0–100.0	4,726	65	35
East	Group 1	0.0–3.5	598	47	53
	Group 2	3.5–10.0	1,074	45	55
	Group 6	40.0–50.0	2,425	50	50
	Group 11	90.0–100.0	8,040	74	26

SOURCE: NSB (1999).

[a]Sector I includes those commodities with prices that were projected to rise when China entered the WTO (rice, vegetables, pork, beef, mutton, poultry, eggs, and fish). Sector II includes those commodities with prices that were projected to fall (wheat, maize, other coarse grains, soybeans, cotton, edible oil crops, sugar, and milk).

come for all of China as well as for each region (western, central, and eastern). Then we divide the agricultural production for each group of farmers into two sectors: Sector I (with negative NPRs in 2001) includes those commodities whose prices or production levels are expected to rise with China's WTO accession, and Sector II includes all other commodities that have positive NPRs (the noncompetitive sector) and for which prices and production levels are expected to be negatively associated with China's WTO accession.

The analysis shows that as farm households move among income categories from the poorest of the poor (Group 1) to the richest of the rich (Group 11), the share of their products that are in the competitive sector steadily increases and their share in the uncompetitive sector decreases. Likewise, even within income groups (e.g., within the poorest of the poor), the share of products in the competitive sectors rises as households move from west to central to east China. In fact, when comparing the richest farmers in the east to the poorest farmers in the west, the share of competitive products produced by the richest coastal farmers (74 percent) is more than twice that produced by the poorest western farmer (36 percent).

Therefore, we expect that not all farm households benefit or lose equally from China's accession to the WTO. The extent of benefits is reduced as farmers move from eastern to central and western China, because the production shares in the competitive sector are less than those in eastern and central China. Moreover, the relative costs of trade liberalization for western farmers are expected to be more than those for central and eastern farmers because the latter produce less (in terms of production shares) in the noncompetitive sector than do the western farmers.

Concluding Observations

Although other effects on the rural economy from other subsectors may be equally large or even larger, our study's focus on the agricultural sector shows that there will definitely be an impact from China's WTO accession. However, like other effects, those in the agricultural sector may not all be negative. Our findings, based on new methods of collecting data and coming up with NPRs, show that indeed for some crops, WTO membership will likely lead to a fall in prices and a rise in imports. Maize and cotton may therefore be the most affected. Soybeans and sugar could be significantly affected in the longer run. There are also commodities in which China has considerable comparative advantage (e.g., rice, meats, and horticultural products), and WTO membership could provide benefits to those engaged in producing these. The prospect of increased imports of feed grains (e.g., maize and soybeans) at lower prices means that livestock producers could become even more competitive.

The extent to which prices fall from rising imports or rise from rising exports in part depends on how China executes its WTO obligations. Likewise,

China's benefits are going to depend on how well her trading partners honor their commitment and provide China with better access to global markets.

We have also found that, unlike in the case of Mexico, most of China's markets appear to be well integrated into the economy. This brings both good news and bad news for poor farmers. The good news is that they can benefit from falling input prices and rising export opportunities. The bad news is that, unlike a large number of maize farmers in Mexico who were not affected by the North American Free Trade Agreement's reduction in the maize import restriction, maize farmers in large parts of China will be affected. The problem, although it may be a short-run one, is that it is this group of rural households that are most dependent on agriculture and the least flexible. As a consequence, our findings should be taken as a warning by government leaders if they are concerned about the welfare of these susceptible groups.

The analyses based on the production structure of farmers in different income categories show that the impacts of trade liberalization have strong implications for equity. Some benefit (or lose) more than others, and unfortunately, in terms of poverty alleviation and equity, the richer farmers in coastal areas will benefit more than poorer inland farmers. The main advantage of coastal farmers is that they produce more products in the competitive sector than those who live in the central and western regions. Consequently, when WTO membership results in the drop of protection of agricultural products in which China does not have a comparative advantage and in better access to foreign markets for crops in which it does, richer coastal farmers will benefit the most. Policymakers, therefore, need to take one or both of the following actions. First, they need to try to encourage farmers in poorer inland areas to shift their production decisions (where appropriate) to the more competitive sector. Second, officials may also need to take non-trade-related actions to improve the livelihood of farmers in these areas. In many areas, farmers do not have an advantage in any farming activity. In such areas policies regarding rural education and better communications and other policies that might facilitate shifts into the nonfarm sector may be the most beneficial. China's recent shift from taxing agriculture to subsidizing it might help farmers to increase income and reduce the negative shocks resulting from WTO accession in the short term. While most arguments in China have supported this new development, the policymakers might also need to consider sustainability and efficiency aspects.

Our results show the close relationship between the high degree of integration of the economy, the size of the price effect, and the fraction of the TRQ that will be imported. If China's markets are really so integrated, and leaders do not artificially delay traders' execution of TRQs, our findings suggest that the price effects may not be too large, because they will be spread across a large area of the country. However, if the price effects for a given quantity of imports are not large, the volume of imports may be larger than predicted by some, and the bindings may be more likely to take effect. We do not expect that in any circumstance imports will ever exceed the limits imposed by the TRQ.

14 Agricultural Trade Liberalization, Poverty, and Food Security: The Indian Experience

ANWARUL HODA AND C. S. C. SEKHAR

Even though the share of agriculture in India's GDP is down to a quarter (WDI 2004), the sector dominates the political scene because it provides a livelihood to a majority of the Indian population. In the 1950s and 1960s, India relied heavily on food aid to feed its growing population. In the mid-1960s, however, after a disruption in food aid supplies, India embarked on a policy of self-sufficiency in the principal food crops. With the emphasis on self-sufficiency in the basic food items and foreign exchange constraint, India gradually slid into a virtually autarkic trade policy regime. It was only after the introduction of economic reforms in the early 1990s that a beginning was made toward liberalizing agricultural trade policy.

We evaluate here the Indian experience with trade policy liberalization and examine its implications for domestic agriculture in general and poverty and food security in particular. The first section of the chapter gives an outline of the evolution of agricultural policy and growth performance since India achieved independence, and the next section traces the agricultural trade policy developments over time with an emphasis on the past decade. The following section discusses the issues related to agricultural growth, poverty, and food security, and the final section summarizes the conclusions drawn.

Indian Agriculture in the Past Five Decades

The focus of planning efforts in agriculture can be broadly divided into four phases. During the first phase (1950–64), the thrust was on investment in agricultural infrastructure, irrigation, and electricity. The major source of agricultural growth during this period was an increase in agricultural area without notable productivity gains.

During the second phase (1965–80), major food shortages in the 1960s and the politically motivated disruption in food aid supplied under the U.S. program established by Public Law 480 (the Agricultural Trade Development and Assistance Act of 1954) led to the adoption of the objective of self-sufficiency in the production of foodgrains. With the advent of new technology and high-yield varieties (HYV) of seeds (popularly called the green revolution), government efforts were concentrated on the high-potential regions in the northwest of the country that had assured irrigation. While the policy of a minimum support price (MSP) was extended in principle to several crops, actual purchase operations by government agencies were carried out only for two cereals, rice and wheat. In the case of sugarcane, the government did not make any purchases, but payment of the support price by the mills in the organized sector was enforced through law by the state governments. By protecting farmers from intraseasonal and interseasonal fluctuation in prices, price support stimulated investment in agriculture.

Input subsidies on power, fertilizers, and irrigation water, introduced with the objective of inducing the adoption of modern agricultural practices, were another major component of domestic support for agriculture. Fertilizers were supplied at a fixed retail price, in most cases below the cost of domestic production, with the government meeting the entire difference. The government adopted the policy of self-sufficiency in fertilizer production and undertook to compensate individual industrial units for their higher costs of production. Thus, in addition to subsidies for farmers there were substantial subsidies for industrial units as well. Another ambitious plan was launched during this period to boost milk production. But the strategy followed was very different from the one adopted for crops, with the focus on linking milk-producing areas with consumers in cities and suburban areas.

These policies were immensely successful, and by the end of the 1970s, India had become virtually self-sufficient in grain production. Impressive gains had also been made in the production of milk and sugar. The major source of growth during this period was an increase in productivity. However, the focus on well-endowed regions resulted in interregional disparities in growth. Throughout this period, trade in basic food items remained under severe restrictions that applied to imports as well as exports. Imports were controlled to protect farmers and conserve foreign exchange, while exports were limited for the fear that they would fuel price inflation.

Private wholesale trade in foodgrains was abolished and retail trade placed under licensing restrictions. Controls on movement and stocking of agricultural commodities across the country became a feature of the domestic marketing policy and were later instrumental in distorting private incentives in agriculture. To enable the Food Corporation of India (FCI) to achieve the foodgrains procurement targets, measures such as compulsory procurement and zonal restrictions were employed. The government also resorted to compulsory levies on sugar factories and rice mills. The FCI became the main channel for distributing foodgrains and other food items such as sugar through the fair price shops. The prices of foodgrains were kept low by means of agricultural input subsidization. The distribution responsibility of the FCI led to substantial consumer subsidies as well.

The third phase (1980–92) of agricultural planning saw the green revolution technology spreading to pockets beyond northwest India. With self-sufficiency in foodgrains achieved, attention was shifted to oilseeds and pulses, in which growth had lagged. A major policy initiative was taken in 1986 with the establishment of the Technology Mission in Oilseeds and Pulses. This period can be called the best phase of Indian agriculture, because growth was achieved along with equitable distribution of benefits. The production of foodgrains continued to rise, and that of oilseeds also made impressive progress. However, restrictive trade policies were continued, and the import policy for edible oils was squeezed even further. The policies for control of internal trade and operation of the Public Distribution System (PDS) continued during this period.

In the fourth phase (1992–2002), with the launching of economic reforms in 1991, the focus shifted to containing and curtailing the huge subsidies to agriculture, which had contributed to unsustainable fiscal deficits. However, political difficulties inhibited meaningful steps by the government, and subsidies kept mounting. In a democracy where more than two-thirds of the electorate has its roots in agriculture, reducing domestic support for farming is always a daunting task for governments. The inherent political difficulty has been compounded by the succession of coalition governments at the center since the mid-1990s. These difficulties resulted in a substantial rise in the MSPs for wheat and rice.

Traditionally the MSPs fixed by the central government were based on the recommendations of the Commission on Agricultural Costs and Prices (CACP). However, in the mid-1990s the MSP announced by the government was much more than recommended by the CACP. As a result, the price support operations caused the government to be saddled with mammoth food stocks, which rose from 19 million tons (mt) in 1991 to 46 mt in 2001, far in excess of the maximum required for food security purposes (India, Ministry of Agriculture, *Agricultural Statistics at a Glance,* 2002).

On the trade policy front, a beginning was made with the almost complete liberalization of export controls and substantial advances in the liberalization of import controls. The government also made considerable progress in dismantling internal controls on wholesale and retail trade.

So how did these initiatives impact Indian agriculture on the whole during 1951–2001? The performance was undoubtedly impressive. Foodgrain production increased from 48.1 mt to 171.6 mt, and the country turned from being a net importer to a net exporter of foodgrains (India, Ministry of Finance, *Economic Survey,* 2001–2). The net irrigated area increased from 20.8 million hectares (m ha) in 1950–51 to 57 m ha in 1998–99 (India, Ministry of Agriculture, *Agricultural Statistics at a Glance,* 2002). As a percentage of net sown area, the increase was from 11 to 35 percent. Fertilizer consumption rose from negligible quantities to 93 kg/ha. The area of paddy sown with HYV seeds grew from 0.89 m ha (3 percent of cropped area) in 1966–67 to 32.2 m ha (74 percent) in

1997–98. The corresponding increase in the case of wheat was from 0.54 m ha (4 percent) to 23 m ha (86 percent). Before the mid-1960s, increase in acreage was principally responsible for the increase in production. After the green revolution, the increase in yield was substantial and across the board for all crops.

On the negative side, the subsidies on power, fertilizer, and food grew from 1.34 to 2.54 percent of the GDP between 1983–84 and 1998–99. Subsidies to the fertilizer industry were never based on an economic rationale, and the input subsidies to agriculture, initially justified for providing a stimulus for the modernization of agriculture, ended up absorbing the funds that could have been used for public investment. As a result, the gross capital formation by the public sector in agriculture has declined sharply since 1980, from 17.7 percent in 1980–81 to 7.1 percent in 1990–91 and 5 percent in 2000–2001 (India, Ministry of Agriculture, *Agricultural Statistics at a Glance,* 2002).

Trade Policy—An Instrument of Food Security

Domestic policies to increase food production could not succeed unless they were supplemented by trade policy actions. Throughout the period from the early 1950s to the late 1990s India had an autarkic trade policy with respect to basic food items with food security given paramount priority.

Import Policy

A few years after India achieved independence, its import policy was strongly influenced by the dearth of foreign exchange for imports. Because of this constraint, India virtually banned all consumer goods, howsoever described, of industrial, agricultural, or animal origin throughout the period, until the introduction of economic reforms in 1991–92, which led to the gradual phasing out of quantitative restrictions. This ban did not apply to cereals, vegetable oils, or pulses. Pulses were the only basic food commodity that was freely permitted for import (from the late 1970s), and their import was regulated by tariffs at moderate levels. Cereals and vegetable oils were subject to quantitative restrictions administered through a state trading monopoly until the mid-1990s. Milk and milk products were prohibited on a commercial basis, and the only imports allowed were those of food aid consignments.

In the case of vegetable oils, an import trade monopoly was granted to the State Trading Corporation (STC) or its subsidiary, the Vegetable Oils Corporation, and for cereals to the FCI. These entities did not need a specific license for import transactions; they were to make such transactions on the basis of foreign exchange released by the government in its favor. It was also stipulated that imports, distribution, and pricing would be made as per the connected policy of government. State trading monopolies on imports, operating under the control and direction of the relevant ministries, meant that import of cereals and edible oils was a function of government decisionmaking, not of market forces. The government saw a number of advantages in regulating trade through state trading. On account of balance-of-payments (BOP) problems, restrictions of imports and the state trading import monopoly made it possible for the government to conduct import operations in relative secrecy. If there had been no state monopolies, one possible way of meeting import needs would have been for the government to publicly announce an import quota at the beginning of each year to enable private traders to make the imports. Given the significant quantities that India needed to import in the years of shortfall in domestic production, public announcement of annual import quotas could have sent international prices soaring in those years. A monopoly over imports helped the state to negotiate better terms with sellers abroad. Because state monopolies functioned under their close supervision, government ministries were able to exercise total control on import operations. In making an assessment of the quantum of imports, the government needed to balance the interests of consumers and producers. Total control enabled the government to fine-tune the import operations to maintain this balance.

With the 1991 economic reforms, the import policy was gradually liberalized, but the restrictions on basic food commodities took longer to be phased out. Among the items that were restricted in the prereform era, edible oils (other than coconut oil) were the first to be liberalized, in 1994. It was not until March 2002 that restrictions on milk, milk products, and cereals were phased out. These restrictions had earlier been maintained under the provisions of the General Agreement on Tariffs and Trade (GATT), and subsequently the World Trade Organization (WTO), which allowed quantitative restrictions in importing countries for BOP reasons, as an exception to the general rule prohibiting such restrictions. With the improvement in the BOP in the 1990s, there was no longer a justification for maintaining these restrictions. But there was a WTO dispute over the time frame for India to complete phasing them out, and it was not until the United States secured a WTO verdict that India finally decided to phase out these restrictions on March 31, 2002. India retained the state trading monopoly for all cereals and on coconut oil even after the liberalization. However, the import policy document states that the state trading monopolies must make purchases solely in accordance with commercial considerations, including price, quality, availability, marketability, transportation, and other conditions of purchase.

Import Duties

India had zero duties on wheat, rice, maize, and milk ever since it made a commitment within GATT in 1947 to eliminate customs tariff on these items. The duties on vegetable oils were substantial, but for the basic food items imported through state monopolies, the level of duties hardly mattered. Import transactions of these state monopolies were generally exempted from the application of duties. The mark-up in domestic sales depended on the advice of the government, and this mark-up served the same purpose as tariffs in protecting the interests of both consumers and domestic producers.

TABLE 14.1 Tariffs and bound rates on major Indian agricultural commodities as of April 1, 2002

Item description	Basic duty (percent)	Bound duty (percent)
I. Cereals and pulses		
1. Pulses	10	100
2. Wheat (other than *meslin*)	50	100
3. Maize (corn) seed	50	70
4. Maize (corn) if imported under TRQ up to an aggregate of 350,000 tons in a financial year	15	70
5. Maize (corn), if imports are not under TRQ	50	70
6. Rice in the husk	80	80
7. Husked (brown) rice; broken rice	80	80
8. Semimilled or wholly milled rice, whether or not polished	70	70
9. Millet, *jowar*	50	70
10. Sorghum	50	80
11. Other cereals (rye, barley, buckwheat, canary seed, etc.)	0	100
II. Dairy products		
1. Fresh milk and cream	35	100
2. Butter, dairy spreads, and melted butter (*ghee*)	30	40/60
3. Cheese	35	40
4. Milk powder up to 10,000 tons under TRQ	15	15
5. Milk powder (outside TRQ)	60	60
III. Plantation crops		
1. Tea	100	150
2. Coffee	100	100/150
3. Coconut, desiccated coconut	70	100
IV. Sugar	60	150
V. Edible oils (crude)		
1. Soybean oil	45	45
2. Palm oil (for manufacture of *vanaspati*, i.e., margarine)	65	300
3. Palm oil (for other than manufacture of *vanaspati*)	65	300
4. Groundnut oil	75	300
5. Sunflower	75	300
6. Coconut oil	75	300
7. Rapeseed oil	75	75
8. *Colza* or mustard oil	75	75
9. Castor oil or tung oil	75	100
10. Other oils	75	300

TABLE 14.1 *Continued*

Item description	Basic duty (percent)	Bound duty (percent)
VI. Edible oils (refined)		
1. Soybean oil	45	45
2. RBD palmolein	85	300
3. Palm oil	85	300
4. Groundnut oil	85	300
5. Sunflower oil	85	300
6. Coconut oil	85	300
7. Rapeseed oil	75	75
8. Colza or mustard oil	75	75
9. Castor oil or tung oil	85	100
10. Other oils	85	300

SOURCE: India, Ministry of Agriculture, *Agricultural Statistics at a Glance,* 2002.

After 1994, when the government decided to give up the state trading monopoly on all edible oils other than coconut oil, imports were determined mainly by tariffs. The government regulated the customs tariffs on these products fairly frequently, taking into account the balance of interest between consumers and producers. As for the other basic food items, import of pulses has been regulated through moderate levels of tariff for a long time. Milk products, however, were prohibited for commercial imports, and skimmed milk powder was imported only by way of food aid.

When it became apparent that quantitative restrictions would have to be phased out with improvement in the BOP situation, India moved in the WTO to raise the duties on the food commodities on which it had committed to eliminate tariffs in earlier GATT negotiations. In the resulting renegotiations, it succeeded in raising the duties considerably, and the renegotiated level of duty on cereals is in the range of 60–80 percent (Table 14.1). Tariffs were also raised from zero to 60 percent on skimmed milk powder and from 45 to 75 percent on rape, *colza,* and mustard oils. A feature of the renegotiated tariffs was that for the first time India had tariff rate quotas for maize, skimmed milk powder, and rape, *colza,* and mustard oils. For all these products the government moved swiftly to raise the applied level of duties to the bound level, even before the quantitative restrictions were phased out.

Export Restrictions

Besides imports, exports of basic food items were also controlled. Before the 1991 reforms, exports were permitted only for traditional tropical products such as tea, coffee, spices, cashew nuts, fruits, and so on. The export policy for 1988–91 included milk and milk products, pulses, several oilseeds (except groundnuts), and several edible oils on the list of items not allowed for exports. All cereal exports, except fine (basmati) rice, and products of the milling industry derived from them were placed under quantitative limits for exports. Fine rice could be exported subject to minimum export prices. Sugar exports were routed through the STC.

Even after the introduction of economic reforms, the government did not relinquish control on exports of food items easily. The policy for the period 1992–97 maintained licensing requirements for exports of milk, baby milk, and sterilized milk, as well as pulses and vegetable oils. Exports of butter, butter oil, milk powder, and onions could be made only through state trading monopolies. Cereal and sugar exports were generally freed from licensing, but were subjected to terms and conditions such as minimum export prices or registration requirements. The policy for the period 1997–2002 finally freed the export policy of milk, baby milk, sterilized milk, and vegetable oils. Exports of milk powder, butter, butter oil, and pulses were permitted, but only in consumer packs. However, exports of wheat, wheat products, and sugar were brought back under quantitative restrictions. For all other cereals and their flours, exports were made subject to registration or registration plus an "allocation certificate" to be issued by the Agricultural and Processed Foods Export Development Authority (APEDA). It was only during 2002–7 that almost all basic food commodities were freed from export restrictions. Restrictions now apply only to onions, exports of which are routed through designated state trading monopolies, and fine (basmati) rice, for which export sales contracts have to be registered with APEDA.

The main reasons for prohibiting exports of some basic food commodities and maintaining strict limits on others were the concern for food security and the need to make adequate levels of food available to the public at affordable prices. Quantitative restrictions, together with state trading monopolies, ensured that exports did not result in an upward pressure on prices. In the case of sugar, state trading also helped in the realization of the best prices from international markets.

Trade Flows

Table 14.2 gives a picture of the effect of the changing policies on trade flows. In the early 1960s, imports, mainly of wheat from the United States under the food aid programs, constituted a large chunk of domestic supplies, accounting for as much as 42 percent. After the government made the decision to work for self-sufficiency, import dependence rapidly declined.

Except during 1974–76, and to some extent in 1983, the contribution of grain imports to domestic availability was not more than 3 percent in any year, even in the early 1960s, at the peak of India's import dependence for foodgrains. Since then, imports have tapered off to negligible quantities.

As regards dairy products, India was importing large quantities of skimmed milk powder in the early 1960s, amounting to as much as 7 percent of domestic

TABLE 14.2 Indian imports and exports of major agricultural commodities in the past four decades

Year	Production (million tons)	Imports (million tons)	Exports (million tons)	Domestic supply (million tons)	Imports as a percentage of domestic supply	Exports as a percentage of production
Wheat						
1961	10,997,000	3,093,754	179	14,110,176	21.93	0.00
1966	10,394,000	7,794,189	1,420	18,441,412	42.26	0.01
1971	23,832,500	1,914,691	5,517	23,731,220	8.07	0.02
1981	36,312,608	585,178	3,390	36,971,380	1.58	0.01
1991	55,134,500	472	662,231	58,344,493	0.00	1.20
2000	75,574,000	13,696	1,166,531	66,165,437	0.02	1.54
Rice, milled equivalent						
1961	35,680,831	743,835	34	35,916,334	2.07	0.00
1966	30,453,224	999,958	2,415	32,113,867	3.11	0.01
1971	43,089,534	541,903	16,066	42,968,916	1.26	0.04
1981	53,281,966	52,340	969,601	54,444,901	0.10	1.82
1991	74,732,014	100,059	680,249	75,205,720	0.13	0.91
2000	86,339,147	27,726	1,543,360	82,335,586	0.03	1.79
Sugar, refined equivalent						
1961	3,028,640	28	295,652	2,050,002	0.00	9.76
1966	3,532,800	52	410,244	2,774,280	0.00	11.61
1971	3,739,800	3,431	382,645	4,028,085	0.09	10.23
1981	5,147,400	195,992	100,694	5,089,773	3.85	1.96
1991	11,859,720	2,386	169,301	10,549,395	0.02	1.43
2000	18,601,480	30,858	324,162	15,853,565	0.19	1.74
Skimmed milk						
1961	7,240,974	418,900		7,659,874	5.47	0.00
1966	7,015,917	500,587		7,516,504	6.66	0.00
1971	7,210,283	380,041		7,590,324	5.01	0.00
1981	11,983,620	465,581		12,449,201	3.74	0.00
1991	17,668,140	3,704	9,423	17,662,421	0.02	0.05
2000	32,961,060	7,237	310,679	32,657,618	0.02	0.94

(Continued)

TABLE 14.2 *Continued*

Year	Imports palm oil (million tons)	Imports of all oils (million tons)	Domestic supply of palm oil (million tons)	Domestic supply of all oils (million tons)	Palm oil imports (as a percentage of domestic supply)	Palm oil imports (as a percentage of supply of all oils)	Total imports (as a percentage of total domestic supply)
Palm oil							
1961	33,708	35,283	33,708	1,469,098	100	2.29	2.40
1966	11,095	44,507	11,095	1,539,841	100	0.72	2.89
1971	698	77,454	688	1,837,988	101	0.04	4.21
1981	557,563	1,325,606	558,856	3,284,668	100	16.97	40.36
1991	259,834	285,607	328,753	4,368,953	79	5.95	6.54
2000	3,353,111	3,986,114	3,387,646	7,881,737	99	42.54	50.57
Rape and mustard oil							
1961	399,000		—		397,804	0.00	
1966	390,000		405		389,882	0.10	
1971	615,000		71		610,180	0.01	
1981	708,000		130,422		838,286	15.56	
1991	1,600,000		2,682		1,612,837	0.17	
2000	1,823,000		49,985		1,888,434	2.65	
Soybean oil							
1961	500		1,487		1,987	74.84	
1966	1,000		33,007		34,007	97.06	
1971	1,500		76,685		78,185	98.08	
1981	32,000		637,312		684,217	93.14	
1991	386,000		21,729		420,133	5.17	
2000	795,000		582,988		1,395,645	41.77	

SOURCE: FAOSTAT, various years.

availability in some years. Much of the import volume came by way of food aid and was used to augment liquid milk supplies in the country. With the manifold increase in domestic production, food aid has become unnecessary, and commercial imports have not taken place.

Pulses have been a stable item in India's import basket of basic food commodities since the liberalization of import policy in the late 1970s. It is interesting that, compared to other basic food items, there has been a relatively smaller rise in domestic production of pulses over the past four decades, and annual import levels have been maintained at between 3 and 7 percent of domestic availability.

Due to fluctuations in domestic production, the country had to import substantial quantities of sugar in some years. During 1985–87, its import dependence was in the range of 7–11 percent, and in 1994 it rose again, to 15 percent.

Increasing reliance on imports to meet the needs of domestic consumption has been a feature of India's edible oils economy. We consider together the four main edible oils (groundnut, rapeseed and mustard, soybean, and palm oils), because they can be substituted for the medium and long terms. The import dependence of edible oils was in the range of 2–5 percent in the period 1961–75, when India was constrained by its BOP problem from adequate imports. However, with the easing of the BOP position in the late 1970s, imports increased and remained in the range of 36–47 percent during 1976–87. With the tightening of import restrictions in the following years, import dependence was reduced to 4 percent in 1993. After liberalization in 1994, it rose steadily, exceeding 50 percent in 1999 and 2000. This was despite a reasonable rise in domestic production of soybean oil. The greatest rise has been in the import of palm oil, which is not surprising on account of its lower international price compared to those of other edible oils. Imports of palm oil alone amounted to 40 percent of the total domestic supply of the four edible oils in 1999 and 2000.

How did changes in the trade policy manifest in terms of exports? Among cereals, India is a long-term exporter of basmati rice, and the export of this commodity had already risen to more than half a million tons by 1993. Concern for food security made the government hesitant to allow export of other varieties of rice. However, when nonbasmati rice was finally freed from export restrictions in 1995, exports rose to the level of almost 5 mt, or 6 percent of domestic production. In subsequent years annual exports of rice have remained in the range of 2–5 mt. For wheat, too, liberalization in the early 1990s resulted in exports' rising to the level of almost 2 mt, or 3 percent of the production, in 1996. India was a regular exporter of sugar over the 1960s and the 1970s. Sugar exports were as much as 22 percent of its domestic production in 1963 and 21 percent in 1975, but have been modest in recent years.

What conclusions can we draw from the experience of India in the use of trade policy instruments to meet food security concerns? For much of the past four decades, India has had a highly restrictive trade policy regime for basic food items. Where it was able to produce efficiently, this policy has contributed to the success of domestic policies in stimulating production. Domestic production of the main cereals, sugar, and milk rose manifold. In the case of the major cereals, India not only became self-sufficient but also managed to build a large exportable surplus. However, where it was not an efficient producer, as in the case of edible oils, restriction of imports did not result in self-sufficiency. In fact, after the liberalization of quantitative restrictions, import dependence for the four major edible oils used in the country rose steadily, from 4 percent in 1993 to more than 50 percent in 2000. By not allowing exports of wheat or rice other than basmati rice, even after higher production was achieved, the government denied the producers an opportunity to participate in the international market. When it did make the necessary changes in policy, very large exports of rice became possible on a sustained basis with no adverse impact on domestic prices. For wheat, too, the decision to liberalize exports proved to be correct. Exports and imports of sugar in the past have been a function of domestic production and the volatile international prices.

During 1965–99, self-sufficiency in all the basic food commodities was the cornerstone of the policy for achieving food security. International trade figured in the food economy on a residual basis, and imports and even exports were kept to the minimum level. Imports were tightly controlled except for pulses, and exports were not allowed at all, except in the case of high-value items such as fine rice on a sustained basis and sugar and wheat sporadically, when international prices were high. In the postreform period India has been moving cautiously toward somewhat greater reliance on international trade for achieving food security. Quantitative restrictions on both imports and exports are gone. The level of tariffs on pulses and edible oils has allowed increasing levels of imports. But in the case of cereals, milk, and milk products, the import duty has been jacked up to a level that precludes imports. Also for sugar, a very high tariff level of 100 percent has been maintained.

The WTO Agreement on Agriculture

India became a member of the WTO in 1995 and consequently became obligated under the Uruguay Agreement on Agriculture (URAA). In this section we look at whether this resulted in any change in its trade and related policies on agriculture. In terms of market access, India had to bind its tariffs on all agricultural products, and it availed itself of the flexibility granted to developing countries to bind them at ceiling levels. Except in the case of preexisting commitments, India bound its agricultural tariffs at 100 percent for primary products, 150 percent for processed products, and 300 percent for certain edible oils. The level of WTO bindings is far in excess of the applied level, and one estimate shows that the average applied rate of basic customs duty as of April 1, 2002, was 37 percent against the simple average bound tariffs of 115 percent (Hoda and Gulati 2003). India did not have to tariffy its import restrictions, because they were maintained at that time for BOP reasons, and such restrictions were exempted from the tariffication obligation.

The URAA also imposed an obligation on members to reduce domestic support if it was above the stipulated (*de minimis*) levels. The threshold for developing countries was 10 percent, separately for product-specific and non-product-specific support. In India's case, product-specific support was negative for most products and positive but below the 10 percent limit for a few products during the base period (1986–88). Its non-product-specific support was also estimated to be below the limit. Consequently, it did not have to undertake reduction commitments on domestic support. According to the latest WTO notification made by India for 1996–97 and 1997–98, the product-specific support was negative for all supported crops and below the stipulated level (1.8 percent) for non-product-specific support.

At the time of its entry into the URAA, India did not have any export subsidy programs listed for reduction in the agreement, and consequently it did not undertake any reduction commitments in this area. As a developing country it had the possibility of using subsidies to reduce the costs of marketing exports, including the costs of international transport and freight, and also of giving more favorable terms for internal transport and freight charges of export shipments. Since 2000, however, India has had recourse to these export subsidies in seeking to sell its accumulated stocks of wheat and rice in the international markets. Doubts have been expressed in the WTO on the consistency of these measures because of the extent of subsidization (Hoda and Gulati 2003).

Adherence to the URAA has not constrained India with respect to either the domestic support programs or the external trade policies related to agriculture.

Implications of Trade Liberalization for Agricultural Growth, Poverty, and Food Security

Agricultural Growth

In the prereform era, the pursuit of an autarkic and import-substituting development strategy relying on high levels of tariff and nontariff protection as well as overvalued exchange rates had resulted in diminished incentives for agriculture relative to manufacturing in India. The bias against agriculture is clear from a comparison of the nominal protection coefficients (NPCs) for the agricultural and manufacturing sectors and the movement of relative terms of trade (TOT) between the two sectors. Analyses of agricultural and manufacturing NPCs reveal that between 1981 and 1997, the average agricultural incentives were only half the incentives for manufacturing (Gulati and Pursell 2000). The anti-agricultural bias was considerably greater in the 1970s than in the 1980s and 1990s (Figure 14.1). One notable feature is the declining trend in the antiagricultural bias starting in 1981, mainly due to a steady decrease in the measured manufacturing protection and to correction of the exchange rate regime.

FIGURE 14.1 Manufacturing and agricultural NPCs in India, 1971–97

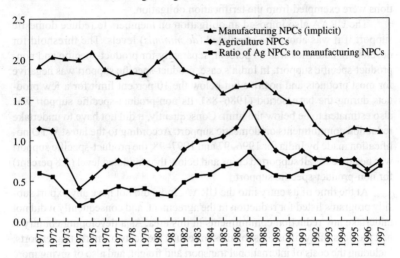

SOURCE: Gulati and Pursell (2000).

The peak tariffs on industrial products came down from 300 percent in 1991–92 to 30 percent in 2002. Similarly, in 1991–92 import controls were withdrawn on virtually all raw materials as well as intermediate and capital goods. One of the effects of the decrease in protection to the industry was an improvement in the TOT for agriculture in the 1990s (Table 14.3), which is expected to raise investment and employment in the primary sector. Equally significant would be the indirect effect of agricultural growth on rural poverty alleviation through its strong linkages with other sectors of the economy.

The index of TOT (1990–91 = 100) rose from 88.7 in 1981–82 to 101.9 in 1990–91 and further to 104.2 in 1999–2000 (India, Ministry of Agriculture, *Agricultural Statistics at a Glance,* 2001). A significant feature of this growth is that the index remained above 100 during the entire period of the 1990s. Did the improvement in the TOT translate into a higher level of private sector investment in agriculture? Evidence suggests so. The private sector gross capital formation increased from Rs. 69.5 billion (1993–94 prices) in 1981–82 to Rs. 114.2 billion in 1990–91 and to Rs. 149.3 billion in 2000–2001. The rate of growth at 2.5 percent in the 1990s was higher than the 2 percent in the 1980s.

While the improving TOT had a positive effect on private investment in agriculture, rising fiscal deficits, on the other hand, contributed to a decline in public investment. The public investment of Rs. 73.0 billion in 1980–81 fell to Rs. 50.0 billion in 1990–91 and further to Rs. 45.2 billion in 2000–2001 (India, Ministry of Agriculture, *Agricultural Statistics at a Glance,* 2002). As a result, the development of infrastructure such as irrigation, rural electrification,

TABLE 14.3 Index of terms of trade between the agricultural and nonagricultural sectors of India, 1981–82 to 1999–2000

Year	Index of prices received	Index of prices paid			Combined index	Index of terms of trade
		Final consumption	Intermediate consumption	Capital formation		
Weights	73.54	73.54	21.63	4.83	100	
1981–82	54.9	54.4	88.5	56.9	61.9	88.7
1985–86	70.4	69.5	94.3	76.4	75.2	93.4
1989–90	97.5	97.6	99.2	100.6	98.1	99.4
1990–91	112.3	112.1	104.0	108.5	110.2	101.9
1995–96	182.9	173.7	174.2	176.1	173.9	105.2
1999–2000	223.1	217.1	203.9	213.3	214.0	104.2

SOURCE: India, Ministry of Agriculture, *Agricultural Statistics at a Glance*, 2001.

NOTE: Base period: triennium ending 1990–91.

rural roads, and markets has suffered. There is broad consensus that this decline had a very adverse effect on the performance of agriculture in the country in the 1990s.

The growth rate of output of the principal crops came down from 3.19 percent per annum during the 1980s to 2.28 percent in the 1990s. This major decline in the second period is mainly attributable to the significant drop in yield growth, from 2.56 percent in the first period to 1.31 percent in the second. The cultivated area has remained virtually unchanged, and all the crop groups show a significant drop in the growth rates of both production and yield. The drop in yield growth rates is much sharper than in output. Notably, yield growth rates have fallen not only in the case of dry crops such as coarse cereals but also in the case of irrigated crops such as rice and wheat.

Poverty

In the area of poverty reduction, there are some encouraging signs. According to official estimates, rural poverty as measured by the head count ratio (HCR) showed a continual decline, from 56.4 percent in 1973–74 to 27.1 percent in 1999–2000. The highest drop in rural poverty was observed between 1993–94 and 1999–2000, from 37.3 percent to 27.1 percent. The same is true for overall poverty levels (rural and urban), which declined from 55 percent in 1973–74 to 26 percent in 1999–2000. Also for total poverty, the maximum decline was between 1993–94 and 1999–2000, from 36 to 26 percent.

The estimates of poverty in India have evoked considerable controversy on methodological grounds. Various scholars have debated the relative merits of indicators such as the HCRs and poverty gap indexes. The criteria for measuring poverty, such as consumption expenditure and nutritional adequacy, have also come under intense scrutiny vis-à-vis multidimensional criteria encompassing social indicators such as child mortality, literacy rates, female health status, and so on. The HCR, however, remains the most popular indicator of poverty, mainly because of its simplicity and communication value (Deaton and Dreze 2002). Even after adopting the HCR, there has been considerable disagreement over the true incidence of poverty in the recent past, particularly in the past decade.

There are arguments that there has been a slowdown in poverty decline (Gupta 1999; Hashim, Kashyap, and Joshi 2000; Radhakrishna 2002), and there are arguments to the contrary (Deaton and Dreze 2002; Sundaram and Tendulkar 2002). However, there is some consensus on the rising real agricultural wages (Sundaram 2001a,b; Deaton and Dreze 2002; Radhakrishna 2002). There is unanimity only on the slowdown in rural employment (Chadha and Sahu 2002; Radhakrishna 2002). The link between the observed reduction in poverty in the 1990s and relevant economic indicators remains unclear. Deaton and Dreze (2002) concluded that the pace of poverty reduction in the postreform period could have been more or less the same as in the 1980s. But this finding does not appear to be consistent with the decline in employment growth and the slowdown in real rural wages during the postreform period. Deaton and Dreze (2002) attribute the observed drop in poverty, despite the not so favorable factors, to the "density effect" or the "bunching" of poverty around the poverty line. Given such a density, even a small rise in the average per capita expenditure could cause a significant number of people to cross the poverty line. However, the density phenomenon had been noticed in the 1980s as well.

Self-Sufficiency, Food Security, and Related Issues

We have seen that India has made impressive progress in increasing the production of its basic food commodities during the past 50 years. This raises the question of whether it vindicates the policy of self-sufficiency implemented by the government. It cannot be denied that the policy of virtual closure of the domestic markets sheltered the agricultural producers from the vicissitudes of import competition, both fair and unfair, and provided price stability, which is essential for growth. Import controls were necessary for the effective functioning of price support schemes wherever they were in operation, as in the case of wheat and rice.

But a striking feature of the policy was that the price support was not generally provided at levels above the prevailing international prices. For the most part, the import prohibition maintained over the past five decades prior to reforms was policy overkill. It was justified more for conserving foreign exchange in times of severe BOP constraint than for protecting the agricultural producers. A recent study (Hoda and Gulati 2003) has shown that during 1965–2000, if allowance is made for the exchange rate misalignment, India's NPCs (under the importable hypothesis) were less than unity for all the basic food commodities except oilseeds in most years. Except for these products, the economic distortions caused by the trade barriers were not very acute.

For some oilseeds (rapeseed and copra), the NPC (under the importable hypothesis) has been consistently above unity, while for others (soybeans, groundnuts, and sunflowers), it has been below unity, at least in recent years as shown by Figure 14.2, which illustrates the NPCs for a number of key commodities. However, because edible oils are substitutable to a large degree and palm oil is the least expensive oil produced mainly outside the country, the drive toward self-sufficiency during the period 1986–94 caused huge distortions. The domestic prices of all edible oilseeds and oils rose sharply, causing hardship to consumers. When edible oil imports were liberalized in 1994, large imports of palm oil took place, and the percentage of imports of palm oil relative to the total domestic supply of the four main edible oils rose from 6 percent in 1991 to 43 percent in 2000. This happened despite the fact that domestic production of rape and mustard oil as well as soybean oil grew rapidly during the years of total protection.

The high levels of protection in India for basic food crops allowed it to deal with volatility, which is a feature of international trade in agricultural commodities, as well as the domestic support and export subsidies provided by

FIGURE 14.2 NPCs of selected commodities in India, 1965–2002

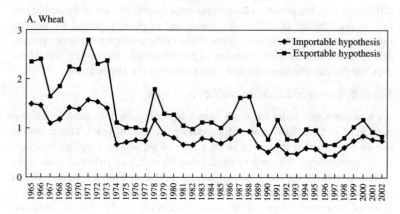

A. Wheat

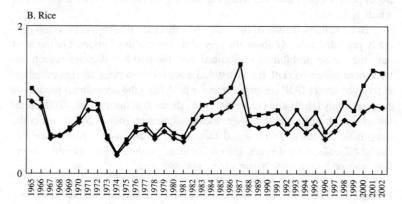

B. Rice

SOURCE: Hoda and Gulati (2007).

some industrialized countries to their farmers. Indian producers were protected against these dangers by the solid barriers of quantitative restrictions administered through state trading monopolies before liberalization in 2002. Even since the phasing out of quantitative restrictions, India has maintained tariffs on many of the principal food crops at levels that effectively kept imports out.

In India, a substantial segment (56.8 percent)[1] of the population depends on agriculture for income and employment, and the government has to take into

---

1. This figure refers to 1995–97 and includes farmers as well the landless or nearly landless laborers deriving sustenance from agricultural activities.

FIGURE 14.2 *Continued*

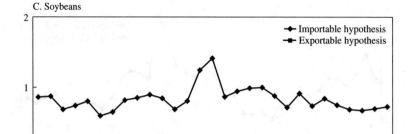

C. Soybeans

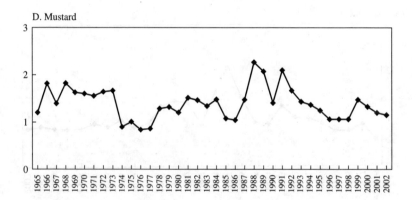

D. Mustard

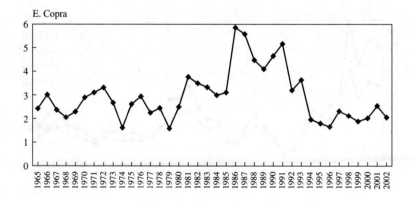

E. Copra

FIGURE 14.2 *Continued*

F. Groundnuts

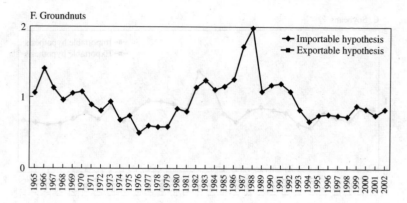

G. Sunflowers

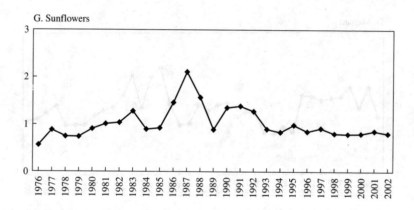

H. Sugar

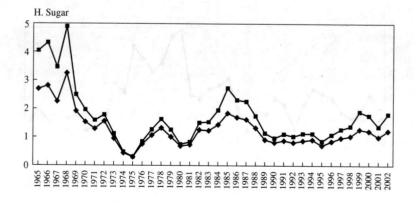

FIGURE 14.2 *Continued*

I. Cotton

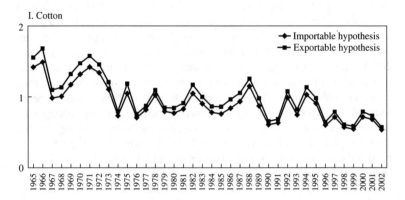

account their interests as well. According to recent estimates, the incidence of rural poverty has been coming down, but the HCR of the poor was still 26.8 percent in 1999–2000. States in which agricultural progress has been made, such as Punjab, Haryana, Kerala, and Andhra Pradesh, had HCRs in the range of 6–10 percent. However, in the less advanced states of Assam, Bihar, Orissa, and Uttar Pradesh it was in the range of 31–47 percent. While consumers, particularly those in urban areas, will gain from unshackled trade liberalization, the rural poor will be adversely affected. When it concerns the livelihood of millions of people and when alternative opportunities for their redeployment are not readily available, a decision to liberalize agriculture cannot be made simply on the basis of net social welfare.

Clearly, limits have to be set to the level of protection. On average, the urban population spent as much as 48 percent of their household income on food in 1999–2000 (India, Ministry of Agriculture, *Agricultural Statistics at a Glance,* 2002). The figure for rural areas was even higher, at 59 percent. In protecting the livelihood of one section of the population, an intolerable burden cannot be imposed on another. A balance needs to be struck between the interests of producers and consumers. Moderate levels of tariff protection would be sufficient in normal times to strike this balance. But for the tariff levels to be dropped to moderate levels, additional mechanisms would be needed, in national and international laws, to deal with the twin perils just mentioned. A special agricultural safeguard mechanism is already receiving attention in the negotiations on agriculture in the Doha Round of the WTO. In the same negotiations an attempt is being made to obtain substantial reductions in domestic support and market access barriers and elimination of export subsidies. Success in these negotiations is a precondition for India to bring down its own tariffs in agricultural products to moderate levels.

The Indian experience on export policy for basic food items is also instructive. Exports of rice, wheat, and even skimmed milk have risen impressively since liberalization. Export trade liberalization is expected to bring gains not only for farmers but also for agricultural laborers through wage and employment increases resulting from increased exports (Gulati and Narayanan 2002b). In the past, the government was inhibited from taking action toward the liberalization of food commodity exports by the fear of domestic price rises. However, with plentiful domestic supplies these fears have proved to be unfounded. When a stop-go policy is followed for exports, critical shortages and unacceptable price increases may take place at times, but when a long-term policy is followed, as has been the case for fine rice, production is expected to expand and take care of the increased export demand. Exports in such a situation should have no adverse impact on the domestic prices.

What then are the implications of trade liberalization for food security? Food security was defined at the 1996 Food Summit at Rome as when all people, at all times, have physical and economic access to sufficient, safe, and nutritious food to meet their dietary needs and food preferences for an active and healthy life. While this definition raises a number of issues, the two main components of food security are physical availability at the national level and economic access at the household level. Self-sufficiency as a prerequisite for food security is fast losing its appeal, and there is growing consensus across the world that greater reliance must be placed on imports with respect to commodities in which a country does not have a comparative advantage. A few industrialized economies are keeping up their fight to maintain uneconomic agricultural production under the pretence of nontrade concerns. While the rich taxpayers and consumers in those economies can perhaps afford to pay the price of agricultural protectionism, low-income countries cannot. India has already moved away from the single-minded pursuit of self-sufficiency, at least with respect to two major food items, namely pulses and edible oils.

Physical availability implies that sufficient publicly held buffer stocks are available at all times to satisfy consumer needs in the country and that the government has established norms for maintenance of minimum buffer-stocks of the main foodgrains at different times of the year. In India, the FCI has recently been holding stocks with volumes in the range of 42.2–61.7 mt, far in excess of the norm of 15.8–24.3 mt. While there has been no problem with physical availability—in fact, there has been a glut in domestic supplies of foodgrains in the recent past—government programs to provide economic access to food are still evolving. The government established a vast network of fair price shops to supply foodgrains and sugar to the entire population at subsidized prices. It was only in 1997 that the government moved toward targeting the indigent segments of the population for subsidized supplies. Although eligibility to receive supplies remained universal, the central grain issue price was differentiated based on whether families were below the poverty line (BPL) or above the poverty line (APL). The issue price for BPL households was fixed at 50 percent of the "economic cost" and that for APL households at 90 percent of the economic cost.[2] Later, in 2000 and 2001, when the offtake from the PDS declined, the government reduced both the APL and BPL prices, the former quite drastically, and launched a number of food and nutrition programs targeted at the poor, also to address the surplus in the buffer stocks.

Conclusion

India has made impressive progress in increasing its agricultural production in the past 50 years, but the success cannot be ascribed to the policy of self-sufficiency in the main food crops and the virtual prohibition of imports that was maintained during most of the period. There is evidence that in most of these products India was highly competitive and import controls were needed more to conserve foreign exchange than to protect domestic farmers. Where India was not competitive, as in the case of edible oils, the choking off of imports in the mid-1990s did not lead to growth of domestic production commensurate with consumption needs, and as soon as import barriers were lowered, very large imports took place.

The twin strategies of input subsidies and minimum price support initially proved effective in boosting agricultural production. However, when the support prices were increased in the 1990s to very high levels, there was massive growth in subsidies to carry out the price support operations and maintain the public distribution system. Food and agricultural subsidies have contributed to increasing the fiscal deficit and crowded out public investment in agriculture. As a consequence, the growth rates in the yield and output of the principal crops started registering a serious decline.

Political difficulties have inhibited serious reform in the agricultural sector, although a beginning has been made in the area of domestic marketing policy by abolishing controls on wholesale and retail trade.

As for food security in India, with huge food stocks accumulated in recent years one can say that the requirement of physical availability has been fully met at present, though economic access has not been provided to all segments of the population. In recent years, the government has taken steps to expand food supplies at concessional prices to the indigent and other needy segments of the population. Consolidation of these schemes will result in providing economic access to food, which is an essential component of food security.

For a low-income country like India, self-sufficiency in food cannot be justified from the point of view of food security. While protection of agriculture

---

2. The economic cost includes the costs of foodgrains, procurement incidentals, and the distribution while excluding the cost of carrying buffer stocks.

may be necessary for the bulk of the population that depends on the sector for its livelihood, the cost of protection must be taken into account. Therefore, there seems to be justification for moderate levels of protection. For the levels of agricultural protection to be further reduced, an agreement needs to be reached with industrialized countries to sharply reduce their subsidies. Safeguards must also be provided to protect domestic producers against volatility in international prices.

Agriculture has benefited from measures such as correction of exchange rates and reduction in industrial protection since the initiation of the 1991 reforms. There has been continuous improvement in the TOT of agriculture vis-à-vis the nonagricultural sector over the past two decades, and to some extent this has been reflected by an increase in private investments in agriculture. There is also some evidence of a decline in rural poverty, although there is a lack of consensus on whether the rate of decrease has improved since economic reforms were introduced.

The focus of future reform efforts in India should be, on the domestic front, on reducing subsidies, moderating price support, and stepping up public investment in rural infrastructure, thereby raising agricultural growth and diversification in a cost-effective way. This would make India's farm products competitive and strengthen effective food security by expanding rural employment and reducing poverty through the development of the rural nonfarm sector.

PART V

Rural Diversification and Vertical Integration

This part of the book, which includes Chapters 15–19, analyses the relationship between market-based reforms in agriculture, the development of the rural non-farm (RNF) sector, and diversification of the rural economy in India and China. Rural diversification has been a fundamental source of growth and improvement in rural livelihoods since it allowed the rural population to switch from low-productivity jobs in farming to more productive nonfarm activities and, within farming, from producing grains and other inexpensive basic staples to producing higher-value-added commodities. By creating a freer economic environment for private players, market-oriented reforms and relaxation of government interventions promoted gradual rural diversification, characterized by the shift of resources within and among sectors in search of higher returns.

The unfolding of this process is clearer in the case of China, where the different market-oriented incentive reforms, including the decollectivization of agricultural production and the progressive reduction in the scope of the central planning and quota procurement system as well as the opening up of trade flows, led to the reorientation of production to better reflect the regional comparative advantages. The higher growth in agriculture resulting from the market reforms also fueled the rapid industrialization of rural areas and the development of the nonfarm sector by generating higher demand for nonfarm goods and a surplus of resources to invest in nonfarm production.

The diversification of Indian agriculture also benefited from market reforms and a decrease in the scope of government restrictions. This led to improvement in the terms of trade for agriculture and to consequent improvement in the investment climate in the sector. In addition, the increase in income per capita produced by reform-induced growth changed consumption patterns by increasing demand for high-value agricultural products. But India benefited from this process to a more limited extent than China because the bulk of these new measures were carried out in nonagricultural sectors, with the exception of trade reforms in agriculture, which improved the agricultural export environment. Indian agriculture remains under a cap of rigid government interventions in procurement, price support, and subsidy policies. Liberalization in these areas would greatly benefit diversification and the rural economy.

Chapters 15 and 16 outline the experience in the two countries related to the development of the RNF sector, analyze the policies and institutions that have promoted or hindered the development of the sector, and examine the roles of migration, rural infrastructure, human capital, and agricultural growth in promoting rural industries and services. The RNF contribution to the rural economy through agricultural and nonagricultural linkages is also examined. The way this sector shaped up in the two countries contributed in a major way to their different growth outcomes.

Chapters 17 and 18 focus on the nature and determinants of diversification as well as the ramifications for the production portfolio, the consumption basket, and the linkages between the farmers' plow and the consumers' plate. There are implications not only for the crop, livestock, fishery, and forestry subsectors, but also within the subsectors.

Following the rising per capita incomes during the 1980s and 1990s, the consumption patterns in India and China are gradually shifting to include more high-value agricultural products such as livestock and fishery products, fruits, and vegetables. This has encouraged producers to diversify their production mix, although the process has been somewhat slower in India than in China due to the lack of adequate infrastructure as well as the restrictive institutional and policy environment, which do not allow for faster vertical integration between farmers, processors, and consumers—the "farm–firm–fork" linkage. Of late, India has recognized the immense potential of the RNF sector.

While high-value agricultural products hold good potential for the growth of the food processing industry and the retail sector, they also entail different processing and marketing arrangements due to their perishable nature. Therefore, the integration of the chain of activities from production to marketing and consumption—from "plow to plate"—acquires special relevance. It is in this context that the role of new institutional arrangements, such as contract farming and cooperatives, in promoting vertical integration is examined.

A similarity between the two countries in the diversification of the cropping sector is that it particularly benefited small farmers who are efficient in the production of high-value crops because production is labor-intensive. The development of the high-value product sector significantly contributed to improving the incomes of small cultivators given its lucrative nature as well as its quick and constant returns. Because the production of high-value commodities suits the smallholders who dominate Chinese and Indian agriculture, diversification has emerged as a promising strategy for income and employment generation and for making smallholding agriculture more viable. However, high market risks and transaction costs due to various infrastructural and informational shortcomings can hinder growth, as evidenced in Chapter 19, a case study of tomato farmers in Nanjing, China. The need to reduce risks and transaction costs makes the case for further improvement of vertical integration an imperative one.

15 China's Nonfarm Sector Development: Implications for Rural Off-Farm Employment and Rural Development

LINXIU ZHANG, SCOTT ROZELLE, JIKUN HUANG, AND ALAN DE BRAUW

Postreform, agriculture has made important but declining contributions to China's national economic development in terms of GDP share and employment. Before 1980, agriculture contributed more than 30 percent of China's GDP and half of its export earnings. These shares fell below 20 percent by the early 1990s (Huang and Chen 1999). Agriculture employed 81 percent of the country's labor in 1970, but only 50 percent in 1996.

Rural industrialization has played a vital role in generating employment for rural labor and in raising agricultural labor productivity and farmers' income. Most important, rural enterprises employed 35 percent of the rural labor that works off the farm. In addition to formal wage-earning jobs in rural areas, part of the rural labor force, which rose from 8 percent in 1990 to 13 percent in 2000 (de Brauw et al. 2002), also works in the self-employed sector. It is claimed that off-farm employment has been the most important activity that has contributed to increased household incomes in recent years.

The major objective of this chapter is to discuss the development of the rural nonfarm sector in the past two decades and its implications for rural labor markets and the rural economy in China. Based on national statistics and household survey data collected in late 2000, linkages were found between agricultural and nonagricultural growth and between nonagricultural growth and labor market development. Data support the view that China's nonfarm sector has experienced fast growth in the past two decades since reform. This also resulted in a significant increase in off-farm employment of the rural labor force. Most of the increase has been driven by young migrants and women, especially those in the youngest bracket. The off-farm employment rate in poor areas is also catching up, despite the fact that these areas are still far behind the developed areas.

This chapter will first review the evolution of nonfarm enterprises or township and village enterprises (TVEs), focusing on the post-1978 years. Next we examine linkages between off-farm development and labor movement. Using household survey data, we empirically analyze rural off-farm employment in the past 20 years and discuss its implications for increases in rural household income and rural development. We then seek to identify the determinants of off-farm participation through a multivariate regression model. Some discussions on policy options in promoting rural labor market development are presented in the last section.

Development of Rural Township and Village Enterprises

The fast expansion of China's rural nonfarm sector is reflected in the rapid growth of TVEs in the past 20 years. Until the 1970s, these were initially engaged mainly in providing inputs and technical and other support services to the primary sector. In the second stage, in the 1980s, they expanded their production base toward the provision of goods and services not directly related to agriculture. Following the reforms of 1979, the number of TVEs increased from about 1.5 million in 1978 to more than 23 million by 1996 (Table 15.1) and now play an important role in China's rural economy. Although the total number of TVEs has decreased since 1996, this decline was compensated by the continued increase in the value added. The gross output value of rural industries and services in real terms increased at an annual rate of 23.5 percent between 1978 and 1995. By 1996, TVEs accounted for about three-quarters of rural gross output values and about 40 percent of China's export earnings (NBS 1996). Their share in GDP rose significantly from less than 4 percent in the 1970s to more than 30 percent by 1999. TVEs have dominated the export sector throughout the 1990s (NBS 2001). In the late 1990s, they accounted for almost 50 percent of industrial value added.

The development of TVEs in rural areas has maintained momentum by absorbing surplus rural labor, and the sector employed 135.1 million rural laborers in 1996, 4.8 times more than in 1978 and an increase of more than 6 million annually. While absorbing labor surpluses, TVE development in rural China raises farmers' incomes, promotes rural urbanization and market development, and stimulates structural changes in the rural economy.

The evolution of the TVEs in rural China has not been smooth, though policy reforms have played an important role in setting them up and encouraging their development. Rural industry in the early 1950s was primarily staffed by farmers holding part-time jobs in commercialized handicraft industries. Many of these workshops were quite small because their technology or work organization offered no economies of scale. Reforms during the commune era (1958–78) organized the workshops and individual handicraft workers into a large number of communes, brigades, and team enterprises. Local governments and others arranged many profitable business deals during this period, including production of building materials and some farm inputs, subcontracting of various sorts from urban industry, and some simple agricultural output processing.

The post-1978 reforms drastically altered the operation of the commune-run enterprise system. The monopolistic and monopsonistic powers of state-

TABLE 15.1 Number and value added of TVEs in China, 1978–99

Year	Value added (billion yuan)	No. of TVEs (million)
1978		1.52
1979		1.48
1980		1.43
1985		12.23
1990	250.4	18.50
1991	297.2	
1992	448.5	
1993	800.7	
1994	1092.8	
1995	1459.5	22.03
1996	1765.9	23.36
1997	2074.0	20.00
1998	2218.6	
1999	2488.3	20.90

SOURCES: Lu (2001) for figures on value added. NBS, *Chinese Statistical Yearbook,* various years; China, Ministry of Agriculture, *China Rural Statistical Yearbook,* various years, and *China Township and Village Enterprises Yearbook,* various years, for data on the number of TVEs.

owned enterprises (SOEs) deteriorated as urban economic opportunities became more accessible to TVEs. With central government recognition of individual and private enterprises in 1984, employment in cooperative and private enterprises expanded by 34.2 million between 1984 and 1990.

Characterized by labor intensity and flexibility to respond to changing market conditions, TVEs have responded to China's growing demand for a greater variety of consumer products by employing surplus labor in rural areas. TVE development has been closely linked to the growth of urban industry, especially in the early stages as TVEs subcontracted production from large urban industries, hired retired urban technicians (either directly or indirectly), and purchased retired equipment. Asset transfers from urban industry, including retired equipment, accounted for 35 to 45 percent of new TVE assets between 1978 and 1984.

However, since the fast growth of TVEs in the 1980s, their significance has been declining in terms of its contribution to the whole economy and its capacity to absorb rural surplus labor force. One could argue, of course, that improved environments in urban areas and greater population mobility between rural and urban areas had led to the movement of resources to rural TVEs. However, with increased competition and improved regulatory controls over marketing and quality standards, the limitations of collective ownership of rural TVEs started to show, which were mainly the lack of management incentives and unclear ownership rights.

At the same time, strong growth of rural enterprises in the private sector from the 1980s and early 1990s provided a dynamic source of new growth in the rural economy. Before the mid-1980s, most rural TVEs were collectively owned. The dominant model was the "Sunan model" (southern Jiangsu model), comprising over 90 percent of existing enterprises. The owners were mainly township or village collectives. The second most prevalent variety, the "Wenzhou model," was privately owned. While the central leadership abhorred such models, these became significant when the growth of collectively owned enterprises stagnated due to unclear ownership and low economic efficiency. The early 1990s were marked by a swift move to privatize rural TVEs.

By the end of the 1990s, the local officials were seriously trying to privatize rural industries. Almost 90 percent of local government-owned firms had transferred their shares to the private sector partially or completely by 1999, giving complete control to the new managers. Moreover, many of the privatization moves created new firms that were more efficient than the ones they replaced (Li and Rozelle 2000). After that, private rural enterprises became the dominant rural industrial force.

As a consequence, in 1997 the share of private nonfarm enterprises in the overall value added of the rural nonfarm sector was 51 percent, and their employment share was 72 percent (Lu 2001). By 1999, private and cooperative rural firms accounted for more than 95 percent of total rural enterprises and employed over 75.6 million laborers, accounting for 60 percent of the total rural nonfarm employment, and experienced fast growth in terms of total numbers, total asset holdings, and share of employment and value added. One of the factors that has contributed to the significant development of rural private firms has been the improvement of the policy environment in that the government has recognized their importance and role as an integral part of the rural industry. Thus, the policy environment that used to be biased against rural industrialization and TVEs in favor of urban SOEs gradually improved through a relaxing of constraints in areas such as access to credit services and marketing.

Linkages between Off-Farm Development and Labor Movement

Consistent with the economic development experience in other nations, China's modernization has triggered a massive transfer of rural labor into industry and services. The shift of labor from agriculture to nonagricultural sectors took place primarily in two ways: by the absorption of labor force into rural TVEs and by movement of massive numbers of people into the off-farm sector in the cities. Previous studies have shown that migration is important for many of China's rural workers looking for more lucrative off-farm employment. The volume of migrant workers has reached up to 20 percent of the population in some urban areas.

China's migration experience is shaped by urban and rural institutions unique to its current economic environment. In urban areas, the household registration system (*hukou*) effectively prevented massive rural-to-urban migration during the prereform period and continues to affect it today. Before the reforms, state-controlled employment, housing, and food markets denied rural households basic goods and services when they moved into cities. Today, government monopolization of labor, housing, and food markets has been relaxed, although residual state influence in the urban economy still denies most rural-to-urban migrants access to the well-paid jobs, comfortable living arrangements, and basic social services that urban registered households enjoy. Remaining restrictions affect the wages and lengths of stay of rural migrants. Zhang (2004) reports that lack of an integrated service system for both migrants and urban residents has made the opportunity costs of migrants living in cities much higher than those of urban residents. Thus, this group of people is much more vulnerable to any shocks and risks encountered. Often they become the victims of government interventions in the names of social stability and urban worker protection. Although official data do not reveal this fact, this study found that during the first stage of SOE reform some cities sent many rural migrants home and replaced them in their job positions with laid-off urban workers. Thus, migrants' job security is weaker than that of urban workers.

The emergence of rural industry also distinguishes China's development and has given rural workers an alternative to migrating into cities. This was especially evidenced in the early reform period. Between 1978 and 1990, the share of rural industrial employment in total rural employment increased from 9 to 22 percent. Most such increase was due to increased employment opportunities created by rural TVE sectors. Of course, from a regional perspective, this was not balanced development. For example, rural industrial output and employment have grown rapidly since the reforms, and by 1995 the sector employed over 100 million workers. Most of the development, however, has occurred in the coastal provinces (Rozelle 1996b), while inland rural areas still rely on agriculture and do not enjoy the high incomes of their more industrialized coastal counterparts. Factors contributing to such regional differences have included differentiated regional economic development policies (e.g., special economic zones) and the historical relationship between people living in coastal regions and their overseas kin. By creating direct overseas technological and information linkages, the overseas Chinese had provided much-needed assistance in developing the commodity market. At the same time, foreign direct investment also helped promote industrial development in coastal regions.

While growth in rural industry initially provided off-farm employment opportunities primarily for local residents (Meng 2000), the continuing success of rural enterprises has begun to open up local labor and managerial markets. Since the beginning of the reform era, the rural industrial sector has faced fewer regulations than its urban counterpart. Despite having relatively more freedom in the 1980s, collective enterprises still favored local workers. The rise of private enterprise in the rural economy and competitive pressures (Naughton 1995) have induced local leaders to offer contracts with more autonomy for the managers of collective firms, an action that has freed managers to hire with fewer restrictions.

Rural Labor Markets and Their Implications for Household Income

In this section we use data from a sample survey to show how the rural TVE development and the national industrial development facilitated rural off-farm employment and migration and contributed to the increase of household incomes.

Survey Methodology and Data

The data for our study (the China National Rural Survey or CNRS) were collected in a randomly selected, almost nationally representative sample of 60 villages in six provinces of rural China.[1] To accurately reflect varying income distributions within each province, one county was randomly selected from each income quintile for the province, as measured by the gross value of industrial output. Two villages were randomly selected in each county. The survey teams used village rosters and our own counts of households to randomly choose 20 households, both with and without residency permits (*hukou*) in the village. A total of 1,199 households were surveyed.

The CNRS project team gathered detailed information on household demographic characteristics, wealth, agricultural production, nonfarm activities, and investment. Several parts of the survey were designed to tell us about the household's migration decisions as well as its participation in other labor market activities over time. For roughly half of the households surveyed (610 out of 1,199), a 20-year employment history form was completed for each family member and each child of the household head (even when a person was no longer considered a "household member"). For each year between 1981 and 2000, the questionnaire tracked each individual's participation in off-farm employment, the main type of off-farm work performed, the place of residence while working (within or outside the village), the location of the off-farm employment, and whether each individual was self-employed or wage earning.[2]

---

1. The provinces surveyed were Hebei, Liaoning, Shaanxi, Zhejiang, Hubei, and Sichuan. The data collection effort involved students from the Center for Chinese Agricultural Policy, Renmin University, and from China Agricultural University and was led by Loren Brandt of the University of Toronto, Scott Rozelle of the University of California, and Linxiu Zhang of the Center for Chinese Agricultural Policy, Chinese Academy of Sciences.

2. Enumerators attempted to seek the employment histories from the individuals themselves. If a household member was not present, the respondent (who was almost always the household head or the spouse of the household head) answered. Extensive pretesting found that the data are fairly accurate. In addition, we conducted a practical test to see whether a respondent bias problem exists in the employment history part of our data. We replicated the analysis after excluding observations on individuals we did not interview directly, and found that the results of our analysis did not change.

Using the employment history data, off-farm workers were divided into four types: migrant wage earners (henceforth migrants), self-employed migrants, local wage earners, and local self-employed. Migrants were identified as men or women with off-farm jobs who did not live in the household while working. Local wage earners were individuals who had off-farm employment, were not self-employed, and lived at home while they worked. All respondents who reported being self-employed off the farm were so categorized. Each household member was also asked about the extent of his or her participation in the household on-farm activities in each year. A household labor force measure was created by aggregating all individuals in the household above age 16 who indicated that they were either working or searching for employment in each year. People over 16 who indicated that they were retired, unable to work for health-related reasons, or enrolled full time in school were not included in the total labor force.

The Evolution of China's Rural Labor Market

Consistent with previous findings of other national studies of rural off-farm employment, the CNRS data show that the off-farm labor force expanded steadily between 1981 and 2000. The data indicate that the proportion of the rural labor force that found some off-farm employment increased from around 16 percent in 1981 to 43 percent by 2000 (Table 15.2).

By assuming that neighboring provinces similar to those surveyed have identical rates of off-farm labor participation, we estimated that off-farm rural employment in China had risen from fewer than 40 million farmers in 1981 to more than 200 million in 2000, a growth in off-farm employment of more than 150 million during the reform era. Though it is not conclusive evidence,

TABLE 15. 2 Labor participation rate in China, by employment type, 1981–2000

Employment type	1981	1985	1990	1995	2000
Off-farm employment[a]	16	18	23	32	43
Of which work is					
Full time	6	6	8	14	20
Part time—1[b]	3	4	5	5	7
Part time—2[c]	7	8	11	13	17
Farm only	81	78	72	63	48
Idle or unemployed	4	4	4	6	8
Total labor force percentage	100	100	100	100	100

SOURCE: Authors' survey.

[a]The differences between total off-farm employment and the sum of components are due to rounding.
[b]Part time—1 refers to those who work off-farm on a seasonal basis.
[c]Part time—2 refers those who work on-farm and off-farm at the same time.

such a large increase in labor flow could indicate that China's labor market is functioning well. Although these estimates are based on a relatively small sample, they demonstrate the consistency of our data with much larger national studies by the China National Bureau of Statistics (NBS 1996) and our own 1995 national village survey. For example, the CNRS estimates that the off-farm employment rate was 31 percent in 1995, which exactly matches the NBS estimate of the nonfarm labor force (31 percent) and is consistent with the 1995 community questionnaire-based estimates of rural off-farm employment at 34 percent (Rozelle et al. 1999).[3]

By disaggregating China's labor trends, our data also demonstrate that labor markets are providing more than just off-farm income to rural residents and are developing in a way consistent with modernization trends (Chenery and Syrquin 1975). Trends by employment type clearly show that the target destination of workers over the past 20 years has shifted from rural to urban. In 1981, most rural individuals (nearly 85 percent) spent their time farming. Individuals who worked off the farm were almost three times more likely to live at home and work in or close to the village (7 percent were local self-employed; 4.2 percent were local wage earners) than to work outside of the village and live away from home (fewer than 1 percent were self-employed migrants; fewer than 4 percent were migrants). By 2000, almost as many off-farm workers were living away from home (more than 85 percent in cities or suburban villages of major metropolitan areas) as in the village. Migrants composed both the largest and the fastest-growing component of the rural labor force.

According to data from our previous work (Rozelle et al. 1999) and the work of others (e.g., Solinger 1999), migrants have also been venturing farther from home over the past 20 years, a trend that has continued in recent years. In 1990, over 70 percent of migrants worked within their own provinces and just under 30 percent went out of their provinces in search of work. By 2000, almost 40 percent of migrants left their provinces for jobs, most of them workers under 30 years of age.

The labor movement contours created from the off-farm employment histories of workers of different ages amplify these trends and demonstrate one of the most striking characteristics of China's changing employment patterns: the shift toward the domination of off-farm employment by younger workers (Figure 15.1). Workers in all age categories participated at similar rates (18 to

---

3. Our data are also consistent with the estimates of NBS in the late 1980s and with Parish's study (Parish, Zhe, and Li 1995) in the early 1990s. For example, our data set estimates that 20 percent of the rural labor force worked off-farm in 1988, which nearly agrees with the NBS estimate of 21 percent for that year. Our 1993 labor force participation rate, 29 percent, is only 3 percentage points higher than the best guess made by Parish, Zhe, and Li (1995) in their national study, a difference that, in part, can be explained by Parish's slightly broader definition of off-farm labor.

FIGURE 15.1 Comparison of off-farm labor participation rates in China, by age cohorts, 1990 and 2000

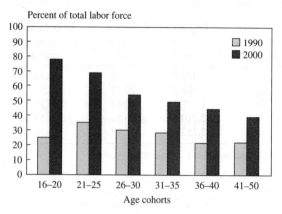

SOURCE: Authors' calculations.

19 percent) in 1981. In 1990, participation rates of all age groups similarly fell to a range of 20.5–33.6 percent.

One decade after the onset of the reforms, there was no clear progression when moving from the oldest to the youngest groups. By 2000, however, the rise in the off-farm participation rates of younger workers had accelerated relative to those of older ones, and a distinct ranking appeared from the youngest cohort to the oldest. In 2000, young workers in the 16- to 20-year-old category participated at rates more than three times (75.8 percent) those of 16- to 20-year-olds in 1990s (23.7 percent). Those in the 21- to 25-year-old and 26- to 30-year-old groups doubled the off-farm participation rates of their 1990 counterparts. In contrast, older workers, while still increasing their participation rates (by 17 percentage points), worked off the farm at less than half the rate (only 37.6 percent) of those in the 16- to 20-year-old category. The work behavior of younger workers also illustrates their increasing specialization in the off-farm sector. In 1990, for example, of those in the younger groups who had off-farm jobs, more than half spent time (either part time or during the busy season) working on the farm, while by 2000 fewer than one-third of the youngest cohort spent any time in agriculture.[4]

---

4. In addition, women in the age categories between 21 and 25 and between 26 and 30 also have a higher probability of not being in the labor force at all. In our entire sample, 8 percent of the sample are neither working nor searching for a job; more than 10 percent of women between 21 and 30 fall into this category. However, in almost all cases this is explained by the fact that they have children who are two years old or younger.

TABLE 15.3 China's off-farm employment and per capita net income and its composition, 1985–2000

Year	Percentage of off-farm employment	Per capita net income (yuan)	Wage income (percent)	Family property and business income (percent)	Transfer income (percent)
1985	18	397.6	18.15	74.44	7.41
1990	21	686.31	20.22	75.56	4.22
1995	28	1,577.74	22.42	71.35	6.23
1999	30	2,210.34	28.51	65.53	5.96
2000	32	2,253.42	31.17	63.34	5.50

SOURCES: NBS, *Chinese Statistical Yearbook*, various years.

Off-Farm Employment and Rural Household Income

Two significant and successful features of rural economic development in the past two decades have been the overall increase in rural household income and changes in income composition. An increase in off-farm employment has contributed the most to both. Using provincial-level data, Table 15.3 shows the relationship between the level of off-farm employment and how rural per capita income has changed over time in terms of both level and composition. There has been an overall increase in the level and share of wage income in the past two decades. There is also a clear positive relationship between the percentage of off-farm employment and the level of per capita income.

Our household survey data also show the same relationship (Table 15.4). Households with at least one member working off-farm would earn more than twice the level of income on a per capita basis of households without any member working off the farm. This was especially true for the poor areas in the sample.

Determinants of Off-Farm Participation

Further facilitation of labor movement between rural and urban sectors requires an understanding of the factors that contributed to the increase in off-farm participation.[5] Using an econometric model (a multivariate regression), we identified factors that constrained or promoted rural migration. A detailed description of the model is included in Appendix 15A at the end of this chapter.

Findings from the previous section and the labor supply literature seem to indicate that aspects particularly affecting off-farm participation rates are age,

---

5. This section is drawn from de Brauw et al. (2002).

TABLE 15.4 Per capita income in China and households with and without labor force working off-farm, 2000 (yuan)

Province	All households	Households with no labor working off-farm	Households with labor working off-farm
Hebei	2,075.2	1,812.6	2,481.2
Shaanxi	2,436.0	1,505.2	4,297.7
Liaoning	2,581.4	2,060.9	3,454.8
Zhejiang	6,241.0	2,977.5	8,321.1
Sichuan	1,808.1	1,353.7	2,670.9
Hubei	2,921.1	2,198.1	3,658.8
All in sample	*3,010.9*	*1,901.9*	*4,502.6*

SOURCE: Authors' survey.

NOTE: Data are mean values.

human capital (measured in terms of years of education or whether a person received any professional training), wealth (measured as the value of durable goods owned and the amount of land held), size of the household labor force, and the average amount of off-farm experience that an individual's household members have had.

Based on the model results, we can state that in almost all respects, the multivariate regression analyses perform well.[6] For example, the findings show that the size of the household labor force increases participation in the wage earning sectors (Table 15.5). Moreover, education is shown to increase an individual's participation in off-farm labor markets and increasingly so over time.

Most important, the results clearly demonstrate that the findings in the descriptive results hold up to multivariate analysis of migration.[7] In the 1980s, males were more than 12 times as likely to participate in migration as females. By the 1990s, males were only 3.2 times as likely (regression 1).

Hence, in the same way shown in the descriptive statistics, although men still participate in migrant labor markets at rates far higher than women, the employment access gap has narrowed considerably over time.

When the sample is divided into men and women, we see that most of the same factors affect participation in the migrant labor force, although the

---

6. The R-square measures of goodness of fit of OLS versions of the equations all exceed 0.90. Most of the coefficients of the basic variables in the models have the expected signs and are highly significant. The coefficient in the regression using wheat plots is positive (which is consistent with the rest of the findings) but not significant (Table 15.5 and 15.6).

7. For instance, although, according to the coefficient on the base gender indicator variable (regression 1), male participation in migration (holding all else constant) was 610 percent (or 6.1 times) higher than female participation, by the 1990s the relative difference was only 57 percent (see the coefficient on the interaction term—regression 1). A similar story is told by comparing the coefficients on the gender indicator variables in regressions 2 and 3.

TABLE 15.5 Conditional fixed-effects logit estimators explaining the change in participation of individuals in migration in rural China, 1980s–1990s

	Dependent variable		
Explanatory variables	(Regression 1) Migration	(Regression 2) Migration 1980–90	(Regression 3) Migration 1990–2000
Age	0.94	0.94	0.92
	(14.53)**	(13.43)**	(30.26)**
Gender (1 = male)	6.10	12.87	3.23
	(16.55)**	(20.58)**	(21.76)**
Years of education	1.10	1.06	1.17
	(7.07)**	(5.55)**	(17.35)**
Skill training (1 = yes)	2.37	1.87	1.58
	(9.43)**	(21.85)**	(8.13)**
Average household experience	1.55	1.64	1.16
	(17.51)**	(27.84)**	(15.77)**
Size of household labor force	1.16	1.17	1.28
	(6.83)**	(7.93)**	(18.07)**
Total land area, 2000	0.98	0.99	0.99
	(3.58)**	(1.33)	(3.82)**
Value of durables, 2000	1.00	1.00	1.00
	(1.44)	(0.95)	(3.16)**
Age* 1990s dummy	0.99		
	(3.20)**		
Gender* 1990s dummy	0.57		
	(4.74)**		
Education* 1990s dummy	1.08		
	(4.96)**		
Training* 1990s dummy	0.64		
	(4.22)**		
Experience* 1990s dummy	0.74		
	(11.66)**		
Labor force* 1990s dummy	1.13		
	(5.21)**		
Land area* 1990s dummy	1.01		
	(1.83)		
Durables* 1990s dummy	1.00		
	(1.85)		
Time trend	1.09		
	(11.80)**		
Year dummies		Included	Included

SOURCE: Authors' survey.

NOTES: The coefficients reported are odds ratios; asymptotic z statistics are in parentheses. Odds ratios can be interpreted as the additional probability of an event if there is an additional unit of the explanatory variable, *ceteris paribus*. 34,257 observations were used in column 2, 12,623 observations in column 3, and 21,631 in column 4. The 1990s dummy variable is 1 for all years between 1990 and 2000 and zero otherwise. The odds ratios for the interacted variables should be interpreted as multiplicative. Column 3 includes only data from 1981 to 1990, and column 4 includes only data from 1990 to 2000 (1990 was included in both regressions as the base year).

** indicates significance at the 5 percent level; * indicates significance at the 10 percent level.

magnitudes of the impacts differ (Table 15.6). For example, both younger women and men work more than do those with more years of formal education and training. However, the differences between the coefficients in the regressions in the women's and men's equations show that both the age effect and the education effect are even more pronounced for women. Moreover, these effects are increasing over time. The propensity for younger women with higher levels of education to find migrant jobs has risen over time. Such findings support calls by academics and policymakers to increase the education opportunities for young women (Nyberg and Rozelle 1999).

Summary and Conclusion

To understand the effect of the development of the rural nonfarm sector and China's labor market on the welfare of rural households and individual groups (e.g., women) during reforms, we first documented the rapid growth of TVEs after the controls on them were eased and individual and private enterprises were recognized in the 1980s. Then we looked into how such development has been linked with the emergence of China's rural labor market during the reform period. Specifically, we found that the rapid rise in employment that began in the 1980s and the early 1990s continued even during the late 1990s, a time when some feared that macroeconomic conditions might keep rural residents on the farm or drive them back to the farm. Our disaggregation of labor market trends also shows that labor markets are clearly acting in a way consistent with an economy that is in transition from being dominated by agriculture to being characterized by the rising presence of other forms of production. Labor markets have allowed migration to become the most important form of off-farm activity and have become increasingly dominated by younger workers who are specializing in off-farm work.

Assuming that participation in nonfarm labor markets, higher wages, and increased income raises the welfare of households, evidence shows that the level of off-farm employment participation is positively related to the level of household per capita income. Both the macro-level data (provincial) and micro-level information (households) indicate that as the percentage of rural labor working off the farm increases, household per capita income increases as well, especially in poor areas.

The econometric analysis shows that although the labor market has been increasingly providing equal opportunities to men and women, the migration participation rate is still much higher for men than for women. Besides factors such as household labor resources and household assets, human capital as a mix of education and skills has played a crucial role in ensuring off-farm participation.

To conclude, the nature of China's growth has led to fast-growing labor markets. Policies that help this growth to strengthen must be continued (e.g., higher spending on rural education). The government should also play an active

TABLE 15.6 Conditional fixed-effects logit estimators explaining the change in participation of individuals in migration in rural China, 1980s–1990s

Explanatory variables	Dependent variable (participation in migration)	
	(Regression 4) Women only	(Regression 5) Men only
Age	0.89	0.95
	(7.27)**	(12.02)**
Years of education	1.17	1.11
	(3.66)**	(7.41)**
Skill training (1 = yes)	2.10	2.21
	(2.52)**	(7.99)**
Average household experience	1.68	1.61
	(7.77)**	(16.34)**
Size of household labor force	1.24	1.18
	(3.43)**	(6.53)**
Total land area, 2000	0.92	0.98
	(2.47)**	(3.11)**
Value of durables, 2000	1.00	1.00
	(0.69)	(2.05)**
Age* 1990s dummy	0.97	0.99
	(2.29)**	(2.82)**
Education* 1990s dummy	1.13	1.03
	(2.72)**	(1.95)
Training* 1990s dummy	0.53	0.70
	(2.02)**	(3.06)**
Experience* 1990s dummy	0.69	0.72
	(5.49)**	(11.12)**
Labor force* 1990s dummy	1.09	1.11
	(1.36)	(3.84)**
Land area* 1990s dummy	1.05	1.01
	(1.64)	(1.43)
Durables* 1990s dummy	1.00	1.00
	(1.64)	(2.00)**
Time trend	1.18	1.05
	(10.64)**	(6.24)**
N	16,625	16,929

NOTES: The coefficients reported are odds ratios; asymptotic z statistics are in parentheses. Odds ratios can be interpreted as the additional probability of an event if there is an additional unit of the explanatory variable, *ceteris paribus*. The 1990s dummy variable is 1 for all years between 1990 and 2000 and zero otherwise. The odds ratios for the interacted variables should be interpreted as multiplicative. Column 2 includes data only from 1981 to 1990, and column 3 includes only data from 1990 to 2000 (1990 was included in both regressions as the base year).

** indicates significance at the 5 percent level; * indicates significance at the 10 percent level.

role in ensuring that women become even more active in off-farm labor markets to prevent the gap in intergender income from widening as well as to narrow it.

Appendix 15A: Multivariate Regression

To explain the determinants of different types of off-farm employment among individuals in the sample villages and to examine the increased participation of women after considering multivariate effects, a fixed-effects conditional logit estimator is used that is similar to that developed by McFadden (1974).[8] In each year, t, an individual, i, from a village, v, chooses to participate in migration or not, and this choice maximizes the individual's expected utility, given a vector of individual, household, and community characteristics, X_{ivt}. If we define an indicator variable, y_i, that is 1 when individual i participates in the migrant labor market and is zero otherwise, we can estimate the effects of the variables contained in X on the individual's labor market participation decision by estimating

$$y_{ivt} = f(X_{ivt}\beta + \mu_v) + \varepsilon_{ivt}, \tag{1}$$

where β represents a vector of parameters that corresponds to the effects of the individual and household characteristics on participating in each economic activity and μ_v is a village-level intercept.[9]

To test the effect of labor market development on the participation of women, we specify a dummy variable that is 1 if the individual is male and zero if female. In a regression in which we include all observations from the 1980s and 1990s (regression 1), the gender indicator variable is interacted with a period dummy variable that is 1 if the year of observation was in the 1990s and zero if it was in the 1980s. In two other regressions, we include only a gender dummy. In one (regression 2), we use only the data for the 1980s; in the other (regression 3) we use only the data for the 1990s. The increased participation of women in the labor force is measured in two ways: by the coefficient on the interaction term in regression 1 and by comparing the magnitudes of the coefficients of the gender variable in regressions 2 and 3. In regressions 4 and 5 we use the gender variable to divide the sample into male and female in order to examine how different factors affected the participation of each gender in the 1980s and the 1990s. In all of our regression models, we include the rest of the variables in X_{ivt} measured at the individual and household levels to explain participation in the migrant labor force. Based in part on our observations and in part on the labor supply literature, we hypothesize that each person's age in year t affected his or her participation rate. We further hypothesize that human capital measures, including years of education and whether one received any

---

8. This appendix is drawn from de Brauw et al. (2002).

9. ε_{ivt} is assumed to be independent and identically distributed across observations according to the Weibull distribution.

training (either in a formal apprenticeship program or in a formal training program) positively affect participation rates if labor markets are working relatively efficiently. At the household level, we include two variables that control for wealth (the value of durable goods owned and the amount of land held), the size of the household labor force in year *t,* and the average amount of "off-farm experience" that a household had in year *t,* defined as the sum, back to 1981, of the total number of years in which each member of a person's household worked in the off-farm sector. In order to avoid endogeneity, we lag the variable in our regression analysis.

Finally, we include a time trend. All variables in all equations are time-varying by year except for the measures of wealth, land size, and the value of the household's durable goods. In the first set of regressions, which include observations for all of our sample years, these variables are set at their 2000 levels and act as shifters.

In most of our estimations, we use data on 2,297 individuals from 610 different households that were employed in either the on-farm or the off-farm sector or in both at some time during 1981–2000. Because some individuals entered the labor force during this period and others stopped working, we do not have a full panel of the 45,940 observations; rather, we have 34,257 observations in total. We dropped villages in the rare case in which there was zero participation in a particular type of employment. For example, in the case of one village, none of the individuals in the sample household migrated during the sample period. These households could not be included in the migration equation because there was no variation within the village for the left-hand side of equation 1, making the village fixed effect perfectly correlated with the dependent variable for that village. As a result, 33,214 observations from 59 villages were used to explain migration participation, and 33,198 observations from 59 villages were used to explain participation in self-employment.

16 The Rural Nonfarm Sector in the Indian Economy: Growth, Challenges, and Future Direction

G. K. CHADHA

In recent years, the necessity of expanding the network of nonfarm activities has gained great policy significance in the developing world; what was once considered a passive side route to employment growth is today advocated as the central plank of rural development. Indeed, in peasant economies, typically characterized by demographic pressures and an ever-increasing imbalance between the amount of land and the number of people, agriculture alone cannot provide the ultimate solution to rural underemployment and poverty (Bhalla, Chadha, and Sharma 1986; Chadha 1994). A developing economy must steadily reduce its dependence on agriculture and expand its nonfarm sectors to facilitate the transfer of workforce out of agriculture in the long run.

A number of theoretical arguments support the case for rural nonfarm (RNF) development: a planned strategy of RNF development may prevent many rural people from migrating to urban centers (Islam 1987); rural industrialization has significant spin-off effects on agricultural development that, in turn, stimulate further expansion of RNF activities; income distribution is much less unequal in areas with a wide network of RNF employment avenues (Bhalla and Chadha 1983; Chadha 1989); a wide network of nonfarm activities can make a real dent in rural poverty (Chadha 1994); RNF activities bring substantial employment and earning benefits to rural female workers (Rosegrant and Hazell 2000, 89; Haggblade, Hazell, and Reardon 2002, 10); and the labor and local resource–intensive rural industrialization policies fit in well with the industrial location strategies being followed by multinational and national enterprises alike for a wide range of products of light industry (Saith 1992, 7).

Rural India, characterized as it is by population pressures, an ever-declining land to man ratio, small and fragmented holdings, highly inequitable land distribution structures, and so on, presents an obvious case for RNF development. The employment problem has continued to be the Achilles' heel of the Indian economy, partly due to the failure of the modern industrial sector to absorb the expanding number of surplus agricultural workers and partly because agriculture cannot take on more working hands on an indefinite basis. It is extremely

343

doubtful whether institutional reforms for enhanced labor absorption in agriculture, especially the creation of an egalitarian land distribution structure, are easy policy options for India. Besides, the consistently declining employment elasticity of India's aggregate agricultural output, from 0.54 in 1972–78 to 0.49 in 1977–83 and further to 0.36 in 1983–88, signals technological difficulties in moving toward employment expansion (Bhalla 1994, 131). Such difficulties are likely to increase, especially in regions involved in external trade of agricultural items, and can be averted by an increased reliance on the RNF sector. Studies show that a much higher percentage of the landless and marginal farming households pursue nonfarm activities and that the expanding network of nonfarm jobs has a salutary effect on the highly inequitable distribution of incomes arising out of land cultivation alone (Bhalla and Chadha 1983, Chapter 4; Chadha 1994, Chapter 8; Rosegrant and Hazell 2000, 89–91).

In India, the need to diversify the rural economic base was felt as early as the 1960s. The rural workforce engaged in agriculture continued to decline steadily, while the proportion of those engaged in RNF activities expanded until the reforms. The new regime threw up a mixture of challenges and opportunities; some nonfarm activities declined, while others, such as those related to the nonrural domestic market or external trade, received a boost. The employment effects on the RNF sector have not been the same for rural male and female job seekers and workers. In this chapter I will unravel the contrasts between the 1990s and the 1980s and focus on the specific weaknesses of rural job aspirants that, unless remedied through effective policy interventions, will not take them very far in the coming years. The years from 1983 to 1993–94 are taken, for notional convenience, to roughly cover the prereform decade and 1993–94 to 1999–2000 the postreform period. The latter period is not long enough to reflect any decisive impact of economic reforms, because many things were yet evolving, yet I believe the period indicates the directions in which rural employment in general and nonfarm employment in particular may move in the future.

We begin with a look at the changing size and composition of India's RNF sector and then at the share of female workers in RNF employment. Next we discuss productivity levels in the RNF sector as proxied by rural industry. Then we deal with the relationship between RNF activities and rural poverty, and finally we look at some concluding observations.

The Size and Composition of the RNF Sector

Conventionally, all activities other than agriculture and its associated enterprises are treated as nonfarm activities. One can measure the size of the RNF sector in two ways: by the volume of income generated in rural net domestic product and by the volume of employment in the rural job market.

The Income Volume of the RNF Sector

In the Indian statistical system, estimates of net domestic product (NDP) are not derived separately for rural and urban areas. Nonetheless, based on a set of less than fully satisfying assumptions, the Central Statistical Organization has computed NDP estimates for various sectors of the rural economy for four years (1970–71, 1980–81, 1993–94, and 1999–2000). Table 16.1 presents such estimates of rural NDP.

A few interesting features stand out. First, the share of agriculture in NDP declined rather markedly during the 1970s and the 1980s. From 1993–94, the decline has slowed down. Looking at the process of structural transformation from the opposite angle, the share of RNF sector in rural NDP has been continuously increasing, from 27.63 percent in 1970–71 to 35.64 percent in 1980–81, to 43.00 percent in 1993–94, and to 45.59 percent in 1999–2000. Thus, the pace of expansion was markedly faster during the 1970s and 1980s and sluggish since 1993–94, indicating the adverse impact of the reforms on the sector.

Second, as expected, the share of rural NDP originating in manufacturing did register substantial expansion during the 1970s, but halted thereafter and has remained unchanged during the postreform years. Among the nonfarm sectors, community, social, and personal services; construction; transport, storage, and communications; banking and insurance; and utilities have increased their visibility over time, while the share of real estate, ownership of dwellings, and business services in rural NDP has consistently been on the decline. The only RNF sector that did well until the beginning of 1990s and suffered a slight setback thereafter was trade, hotels, and restaurants.

Third, there has not been much reshuffling among the major RNF sectors. The top four nonfarm sectors during 1999–2000 were community, social, and personal services; manufacturing; trade, hotels, and restaurants; and construction, while in 1970–71 they were community, social, and personal services; real estate, ownership of dwellings, and business services; manufacturing; and construction. So structurally, the RNF sector remained the same for all those years. The more recent years have witnessed a higher degree of structural slackness; the coefficient of rank correlation between each nonfarm segment's share in rural NDP during 1993–94 and 1999–2000 is as high as 0.99.

Finally, rural India's nonfarm economy is well spread over different sectors, and the internal composition of each RNF sector is what it should ideally be in a populous developing agrarian economy. For example, within manufacturing the registered segment is heavier than its unregistered counterpart, although it is the other way around for employment. In trade, hotels, and restaurants, the lion's share is occupied by trade; under transport, storage, and communications, the dominant position is occupied by road transport, which has its own logic in the context of rural–urban–rural movement of goods and human

TABLE 16.1 Distribution of rural NDP among the farm and nonfarm sectors in India, 1970–71 to 1999–2000 (percent)

Industry	Sectoral distribution of rural NDP				Rural areas' share in sectoral NDP		
	1970–71	1980–81	1993–94	1999–2000	1970–71	1980–81	1999–2000
1. Agriculture	72.37	64.36	57.00	54.41	96.23	94.89	94.04
2. Mining and quarrying	0.86	1.24	2.59	2.39	61.01	54.75	65.76
3. Manufacturing	5.87	9.16	8.16	8.13	25.79	31.84	29.58
a. Registered	2.88	3.15	5.22	5.13	23.74	20.37	30.05
b. Unregistered	2.99	6.01	2.94	3.00	28.13	45.18	28.81
4. Utilities	0.37	0.56	0.88	1.34	39.81	40.02	40.37
5. Construction	3.47	4.05	4.61	4.99	43.22	45.62	39.12
6. Trade, hotels, and restaurants	2.72	6.68	7.77	6.94	18.18	30.34	22.82
a. Trade			7.41	6.63			23.22
b. Hotels and restaurants			0.36	0.31			16.81
7. Transport, storage, and communication	1.26	1.32	3.41	4.17	22.81	22.99	34.39
a. Railways	0.51	0.25	0.61	0.47	26.36	29.52	33.83
b. Other transport	0.44	0.67	1.95	2.67	16.13	17.84	32.48
c. Storage		0.03	0.05	0.04			26.35
d. Communication	0.31	0.37	0.80	0.99	35.82	16.67	41.80
8. Banking and insurance	0.54	0.81	1.73	1.97	19.31	15.70	14.48
9. Real estate and business services	6.18	4.55	4.26	3.16	48.41	49.88	29.32
a. Real estate		*	0.00	0.01		*	6.91
b. Owner of dwelling		4.53	4.15	2.90		51.12	35.44
c. Business services		0.02	0.11	0.25		9.32	9.94
10. Community, social, and personal services	6.36	7.27	9.59	12.50	39.80	39.08	41.70
a. Public administration and defense	3.01	2.80	4.13	5.41	42.20	34.28	40.34
b. Other services	3.35	4.47	5.46	7.09	37.86	42.85	42.80
11. Total RNF sector	27.63	35.64	43.00	45.59	32.43	34.97	31.64
12. NDP	100.00	100.00	100.00	100.00	62.35	58.91	49.52

SOURCES: India, CSO (2000, 202–3).

NOTE: Blank cells indicate that data are not available; * indicates that data are included in 9c.

beings. Under real estate, ownership of dwellings, and business services, ownership of dwellings is the dominant activity. And finally, under community, social, and personal services, the network is well balanced between public administration and defense services and others such as education, medical services, and community services.

Farm and Nonfarm Income Linkages

The literature points to the level of agricultural development as the main determinant of the size and composition of the rural nonfarm sector. If local agriculture is growing and stable, the network of nonfarm activities expands and helps increase the employment and earning levels, which in turn makes a noticeable dent in rural poverty (Hazell and Haggblade 1991, 515). But the converse is also true, and even the staunchest advocates of agriculture-led growth theories visualize an important role for the RNF sector in stimulating agricultural growth through intersectoral linkages (Mellor 1976, Chap. VII). A two-way relationship between the farm and nonfarm sectors is a historical reality that has existed in varying form and content in most economies of the world. In India's case, too, the two-way causal relationship was clearly discernible when the Granger Causality Test was applied to state-level data on net state domestic product, originating in the primary, secondary, and tertiary sectors during the 1980s and the 1990s (Gujarati 1995, 620–23).

Indian agriculture has promoted the RNF sector in three ways. First, an increase in farm incomes stimulates demand for a wide variety of consumer goods, some of which might be produced by the local nonfarm economy. Second, a growing agriculture sector demands production inputs either produced or distributed by local nonfarm enterprises. Third, rising agricultural productivity and wages raise the opportunity cost of labor in RNF activities, inducing a shift from very labor-intensive, low-return activities to activities that require more skill and a higher level of investment and provide a higher level of return (Hazell and Haggblade 1991, 519).

Looking at the changing structure of rural economic activities and consumer expenditure patterns in the 1980s and the 1990s, one can conclude that since the beginning of the 1980s the proportion of purchased agricultural inputs has been rising consistently, agricultural production and marketing have been increasingly linked to a variety of secondary and tertiary sector activities, and the rural consumption basket has reflected a steadily diversifying demand for goods and services.

The rising quantum of agricultural output has lent dynamism to agro-based industrialization besides encompassing a growing network of construction, trade, transport, storage, communication, finance, and a host of other service activities. The tremendous changes in the rural consumption baskets brought about by rising levels of incomes and urbanization have also been contributing to an expanding network of consumer goods industries in the rural areas (India,

TABLE 16.2 Sectoral distribution of the "usual (principal + subsidiary) status" workers in India, by gender, 1983–2000 (percent)

Sector description	Male				Female			
	1983	1987–88	1993–94	1999–2000	1983	1987–88	1993–94	1999–2000
Primary sector	77.5	74.5	74.1	71.4	87.5	84.7	86.2	85.3
Mining and quarrying	0.6	0.7	0.7	0.6	0.3	0.4	0.4	0.3
Manufacturing	7.0	7.4	7.0	7.3	6.4	6.9	7.0	7.6
Utilities	0.2	0.3	0.2	0.2	0.1	0.1	0.1	0.0
Construction	2.2	3.7	3.2	4.5	0.7	2.7	0.9	1.1
Secondary sector	10.0	12.1	11.2	12.6	8.7	10.0	8.4	9.0
Trade, hotels, and restaurants	4.4	5.1	5.5	6.8	1.9	2.1	2.1	2.0
Transport, storage, and communication	1.7	2.0	2.2	3.2	0.1	0.1	0.1	0.1
Services	6.1	6.2	7.0	6.2	2.8	3.0	3.4	3.6
Tertiary sector	12.5	13.4	14.7	16.2	4.8	5.3	5.6	5.7
All nonagricultural	22.5	25.5	25.9	28.6	13.5	15.3	13.8	14.7

SOURCES: Vaidyanathan (1986), Visaria and Minhas (1991), and India, Ministry of Statistics and Program Implementation (NSSO data) (1990a, 99; 1997, 33 and 82–86; and 2001, A182–A194).

NOTES: See Appendix 16A for a discussion of the meaning of "usual status." Blank cells indicate that data are not available.

Ministry of Statistics and Program Implementation, 2000, 64–65). These changes prove that growth of the nonfarm sector is linked to agricultural growth.

The Employment Volume of the RNF Sector

Table 16.2, based on National Sample Survey estimates, gives a 17-year history of the sectoral distribution of rural workers. The proportion of rural male workers engaged in the primary sector has steadily declined, from 77.5 percent in 1983 to 74.6 percent in 1987–88 and to 71.4 in 1999–2000. On the other hand, the proportion of their employment in the secondary and tertiary sectors has risen, from 22.5 percent in 1983 to 28.6 percent in 1999–2000. By contrast, the rural female workers' dependence on primary sector employment witnessed a steady decline until 1987–88, thereafter remaining more or less constant at 85–86 percent. Consequently, their employment in the secondary sector rose from a mere 8.7 percent in 1983 to 10 percent in 1987–88, after which it showed a mild decline. Finally, not more than 5–6 percent of female workers were ever employed in the tertiary sector. The employment base of rural female workers remains heavily tagged with agriculture. Even as late as 1999–2000, not more than 14–15 percent of them could be absorbed into nonfarm activities.

One clear departure of the 1990s was thus a substantial slowdown of the process of weaning away rural male workers from agriculture, and its complete halt, if not a reversal, in the case of rural female workers. The sluggish pace of rural workers' shift to nonagricultural sectors witnessed after economic reform clearly signals their relative inability to access these jobs, perhaps because of the low level of their human capital. The infirmities are far more pronounced in the case of rural female workers, because they have to compete not only with their male counterparts from the rural areas but also with their "more qualified" sisters in the urban areas.

THE CASUALIZATION OF EMPLOYMENT.   An examination of the changing mode of rural farm and nonfarm employment between 1983 and 1999–2000 reveals the high incidence of casualization among rural workers and its rise over time (Table 16.3).[1] The male-female contrasts are striking enough to invite a special emphasis, while the extremely low share in regular salaried jobs of rural workers (e.g., 9.0 percent in 1999–2000 against 36.1 percent in casual labor for rural males and only 3.3 percent against 39.5 percent in casual labor for rural females) tells the story of their relative vulnerability. The very high values on the index of casualization confirm numerous disadvantages, such as low wage rates, irregularity and uncertainty of employment, and uncongenial work conditions of rural workers in general and of females in particular.

Self-employment dominates in agriculture as well as nonfarm sectors.

---

1. For a discussion of the ways employment is classified in India, see Appendix 16A at the end of this chapter.

TABLE 16.3 Composition of the "usual (principal + subsidiary) status" rural workers in India, by activity and gender, 1983–2000

Gender	Sector of employment	Self-employment (%)			Regular employees (%)			Casual labor (%)			Index of casualization		
		1983	1993–94	1999–2000	1983	1993–94	1999–2000	1983	1993–94	1999–2000	1983	1993–94	1999–2000
Male	Agriculture	62.7	60.7	58.4	4.3	1.9	1.8	33.0	37.4	39.8	767	1,968	2,211
	Secondary		38.3	37.3		18.3	17.9		43.4	44.8		237	250
	Tertiary		55.6	52.9		34.5	34.2		9.9	12.9		29	38
	Total nonfarm	*50.2*	*48.2*	*46.1*	*30.8*	*27.7*	*27.0*	*19.0*	*24.1*	*26.9*	*62*	*87*	*100*
	Total employment	59.9	57.6	54.9	10.2	8.5	9.0	29.9	34.0	36.1	293	400	401
Female	Agriculture	54.3	58.5	56.5	1.3	0.7	0.8	44.4	40.8	42.7	3,415	5,829	5,338
	Secondary		59.3	66.7		7.4	7.4		33.3	25.9		450	350
	Tertiary		61.1	52.9		27.8	35.3		11.1	11.8		40	33
	Total nonfarm	*53.7*	*60.0*	*61.4*	*18.4*	*15.6*	*18.2*	*27.9*	*24.4*	*20.4*	*152*	*156*	*112*
	Total employment	54.2	58.7	57.2	3.6	2.7	3.3	42.2	38.6	39.5	1,172	1,430	1,197
Total	Agriculture	59.8	59.7	57.7	3.3	1.4	1.3	36.9	38.9	41.0	1,118	2,779	3,154
	Secondary		44.2	44.7		16.3	14.9		39.5	40.4		242	271
	Tertiary		56.9	52.9		33.3	33.3		9.8	13.8		41	41
	Total nonfarm	*50.9*	*51.0*	*49.0*	*28.1*	*25.5*	*24.5*	*20.9*	*23.5*	*26.5*	*74*	*92*	*108*
	Total employment	58.0	57.9	55.6	8.1	6.5	6.7	33.9	35.6	37.7	419	548	563

SOURCES: India, Ministry of Statistics and Program Implementation (1988, S132–S134; 1997, A112–A114; and 2001, 75).

NOTES: See Appendix 16A for a discussion of the meaning of "usual status." The index of casualization shows the number of casual wage earners for every 100 regular salaried jobs. Blank cells indicate that data are not available.

While regular salaried jobs are almost conspicuous by their absence in the primary sector for both categories of workers, they are available to a fairly sizable proportion of laborers in nonagricultural activities, especially to rural males. Accordingly, the structure of nonfarm employment seems much more favorable, especially to male workers, to the extent that casual wage employment does not encompass more than one-fourth of them; nearly three-fourths of them are either self-employed or working in a wide variety of nonfarm jobs.

THE STATE- AND SECTORWISE DISTRIBUTION OF WORKERS. The process of structural transformation of the rural workforce that tilted in favor of non-agricultural jobs during the decade preceding reforms, for both rural male and female workers, was reversed in some states or slowed down in others. In a few states, a noticeable shift from agriculture continued during the postreform years (India, Ministry of Statistics and Program Implementation, 1990b). In as many as 15 of the 17 states, no fewer than two-thirds of the rural workers were employed in agriculture as late as 1999–2000. In 10 states, their share in agricultural employment continued to exceed 75 percent; in 5 of them, their share exceeded 80 percent. It was in only 5 states (i.e., Kerala, West Bengal, Tamil Nadu, Assam, and Haryana) that rural nonfarm employment exceeded 30 percent. Despite the steady structural transformation in the rural economy during the 1980s and 1990s, the level of nonfarm employment available to rural households was limited, especially for rural female workers.

In the majority of states, the level of rural employment in manufacturing has been very low. During 1999–2000, in as many as 10 major states, not more than 5–6 percent of rural workers were engaged in manufacturing. States with 10 percent or more rural workers engaged in this sector were West Bengal, Kerala, and Tamil Nadu. This was mainly because a very large proportion of female workers in these states are traditionally engaged in a variety of rural handicrafts, typically based on local craftsmanship.

Employment in construction does not seem to have picked up in many parts of rural India. In 11 states, the percentage of rural workers engaged in diverse types of construction activities did not go beyond 2–3 percent. It was only in Kerala, Rajasthan, Jammu-Kashmir, Himachal Pradesh, Punjab, and Haryana that this proportion increased during the 1980s and 1990s.

Trade, transport, storage, and communications and community, social, and personal services are the two major subaggregates under the service sector that present a contrasting picture. While the proportion of rural workers engaged in trade, transport, storage, and communications witnessed varying degrees of increase in practically all 17 states, the proportion of those engaged in community, social, and personal services went down during the postreform years in 11 states. There was a decline even in states (e.g., Punjab, Haryana, Kerala, West Bengal, and Tamil Nadu) that managed to expand their rural nonfarm economic base during the postreform years. Therefore, this was clearly a case of a shift in demand for such services from rural to urban areas.

Finally, evidence does not support the commonly held perception that manufacturing always dominates the rural nonfarm economy (Table 16.2). In 12 states, the service sector is larger than manufacturing alone or even larger than the total of the secondary sector from the point of view of rural nonfarm employment. Therefore, it is clear that the expansion of a wide variety of services rather than manufacturing and/or construction has been contributing most substantially to rural nonfarm employment.

Regional Clusters in RNF Development

It may be instructive to look at the changing clusters of regions in terms of low, medium, and high levels of rural nonfarm development (Table 16.4). Notionally, a rate of nonfarm employment of less than 20 percent for rural workers is taken as a surrogate for a low level of nonfarm development. Similarly, a rate of nonfarm employment ranging between 20 and 25 percent represents a medium level of nonfarm development, while a rate of more than 25 percent indicates a high level of nonfarm development.

In 1983, 12 states were operating at a low level of nonfarm development, 2 were at a medium level, and only 3 operated at a high level. Interestingly enough, the cluster at the low level of nonfarm development had very wide internal variations, ranging from 10 percent to 20 percent. After a decade, the situation had changed considerably; in 1993–94, only 7 were operating at the low level, 5 at the medium level, and the remaining 5 at the high level. Most of the states reached this position through substantial improvement in their rural nonfarm employment base.

The situation changed further during the post-1993 years. During 1999–2000, 5 states were languishing at the low level of nonfarm development (Gujarat, Madhya Pradesh, Maharashtra, Karnataka, and Bihar). However, 2 states (Jammu-Kashmir and Assam) moved from the medium to the high level of nonfarm development, with 1 (Himachal Pradesh) moving straight from the low to the high level of development, and 5 states (Punjab, Haryana, Tamil Nadu, West Bengal, and Kerala) moved ahead within the cluster of high-level nonfarm development, testifying to the overall improvement of the nonfarm employment base in rural India.

Finally, by and large, each state witnessed some improvement in its base of rural nonfarm employment, first between 1983 and 1993–94, and then between 1993–94 and 1999–2000, as reflected in Table 16.4.

The Share of Female Workers in RNF Employment

In a majority of the states, the most visible presence of the rural female workers has been discernible in agriculture (India, Ministry of Statistics and Program

TABLE 16.4 Clusters of Indian states in terms of low, medium, and high proportions of rural nonfarm employment, 1983–2000 (percentages of workers engaged in nonfarm activities)

	1983		1993–94		1999–2000	
Up to 20.0% (low)	Madhya Pradesh	9.7	Madhya Pradesh	10.1	Madhya Pradesh	12.8
	Himachal Pradesh	12.4	Bihar	15.8	Maharashtra	17.2
	Rajasthan	13.3	Maharashtra	17.4	Karnataka	17.8
	Maharashtra	14.2	Karnataka	18.1	Bihar	19.3
	Gujarat	14.8	Orissa	19.0	Gujarat	19.6
	Karnataka	15.5	Himachal Pradesh	19.8		
	Bihar	16.4	Uttar Pradesh	20.0		
	Punjab	17.4				
	Uttar Pradesh	17.7				
	Andhra Pradesh	19.7				
	Jammu and Kashmir	19.8				
	Assam	20.0				
20.01 to 25.0% (medium)	Orissa	20.8	Rajasthan	20.2	Andhra Pradesh	21.2
	Haryana	22.3	Andhra Pradesh	20.7	Orissa	21.4
			Assam	21.2	Rajasthan	22.1
			Gujarat	21.3	Uttar Pradesh	23.6
			Jammu and Kashmir	24.4		
>25.01% (high)	Tamil Nadu	25.1	Punjab	25.4	Himachal Pradesh	25.2
	West Bengal	26.3	Haryana	28.1	Jammu and Kashmir	27.0
	Kerala	36.9	Tamil Nadu	29.6	Punjab	27.1
			West Bengal	36.4	Haryana	30.2
			Kerala	43.9	Tamil Nadu	31.7
					Assam	32.3
					West Bengal	37.0
					Kerala	51.2

SOURCES: India, Ministry of Statistics and Program Implementation (1988, S132–S134; 1997, A112–A114; and 2001, 75).

Implementation, 1990b).[2] Female workers have also had a formidable presence in manufacturing and construction under the secondary sector and in community, social, and personal services and trade under the tertiary sector. Other sectors, such as utilities; transport, storage, and communications; finance, insurance, and real estate; and so on, have been offering them only marginal employment support, but these are not the major employment sectors in the rural economy. In overall terms, therefore, no fewer than one-fifth to one-fourth of rural nonfarm jobs have been filled by rural female workers.

That rural manufacturing has typically been a major absorber of rural female workers is both good and bad news. It is cheering because employment in rural manufacturing is expected to save women the drudgery of agricultural chores and bring them somewhat higher earnings. However, the bad news is that their share of employment in rural manufacturing declined by varying magnitudes in the post-1993 years in as many as nine states and remained practically unchanged in two others. Moreover, their involvement was great in household-type self-employing ventures, such as own-account manufacturing enterprises, which operate at a low level of technology, suffer low and fluctuating levels of productivity, cater largely to the local market, and are now under threat of liquidation due to the current increasingly open and fiercely competitive regime. For many female workers, employment in rural manufacturing reflects more distress and less choice. But this does not negate the importance of education, training, and skills for rural workers who wish to switch to nonagricultural jobs, primarily to education- and skill-intensive branches of manufacturing.

The temporal changes in the female share of employment in community, social, and personal services have also not been good news. After 1993, their share of employment suffered a varying degree of setbacks in as many as eight states and remained more or less unchanged in another two states. Only in Bihar, Himachal Pradesh, Kerala, Madhya Pradesh, Punjab, and Uttar Pradesh did their share of employment look up, by varying margins. In 1999–2000, Andhra Pradesh, Karnataka, Kerala, Punjab, Tamil Nadu, and West Bengal were the only states where more than one-fourth of rural employment in community, social, and personal services went to the rural females. Most of these states had steadily expanded their rural nonfarm base, and by 1999–2000 they had succeeded in joining the cluster of states with a high level of development (Table 16.4). Thus empirical evidence, albeit sketchy and tentative, supports the view that the share of females employed in the dominant segment of the tertiary sector, namely community, social, and personal services, is guided by the level of nonfarm development itself.

---

2. At the all-India level, as of 1999–2000 the share of the rural female workforce was 38.9 percent in agriculture and 21.5 percent in nonagricultural activities. Of the nonagricultural activities, 33.3 percent of rural female laborers were in manufacturing; 11.5 percent in construction; 15.3 percent in trade; 1.6 percent in transport, storage, and communication; and 25.3 percent in community, social, and personal services.

Perhaps the issue of the association between the share of female employment and the level of nonfarm development needs to be analyzed at the level of total nonfarm employment rather than at the level of individual economic activities or sectors.

Productivity Levels

The RNF sector is a mix of assorted production and service activities characterized by sharp variations in employment levels and composition, technology, scale of production, product quality, market coverage, and so on. We next consider manufacturing as a RNF sector and look at its productivity profile for three definite reasons: (1) it is a major sector of the rural nonfarm economy, (2) no other nonfarm sector has as much information available for three points of time as does unorganized rural manufacturing, and (3) many alarming signals are already being sounded about the future of small rural industry (Dubashi 2000, 10). We look into the productivity levels for each of the following three layers of the unorganized segment (Chadha and Gulati 2003, 58): tiny enterprises (own-account manufacturing enterprises or OAMEs), middle-level enterprises (nondirectory manufacturing establishments or NDMEs), and top-level enterprises (directory manufacturing establishments or DMEs).[3] To comprehend the locational handicaps under which the rural manufacturing units operate, rural-urban productivity differentials are given for each of the three groups of enterprises. Table 16.5 looks at real productivity levels per worker for 1984–85, 1994–95, and 2000–2001.

First, rural productivity has been considerably lower than urban productivity in all three categories of manufacturing enterprises, both agro-based and non-agro-based. In other words, rural enterprises suffer substantial production losses, irrespective of their scale of operation, due to the sheer fact of their rural location. The rural-urban gaps are most astounding with respect to the availability of sewerage, telephone, fax, and computer services, which by any objective reckoning are now the minimum essentials for a modern production outfit. Such gaps are no less glaring in terms of the educational and technical backgrounds and training of the entrepreneurs. Also, the relatively greater neglect of rural industrial enterprises by public agencies that provide institutional services, such as market intelligence and information, product design, industrial training, and finance services, is more than apparent (Chadha 2001, 105).

Second, in the group of tiny enterprises (OAMEs), the disadvantage of rural units is more pronounced among the non-agro-based enterprises than among the agro-based. Generically, the non-agro-based industries (those manufacturing chemical and rubber products, nonmetallic mineral products, basic metal

---

3. For a discussion of these categories of enterprise, see Appendix 16A.

TABLE 16.5 Productivity per worker in unorganized manufacturing, by location, enterprise type, and semiaggregate industrial category in India, 1984–85 to 2000–2001 (Rs. at 1981–82 prices)

Firm categories[a]	1984–85			1994–95			2000–2001		
	Rural	Urban	Rural to urban ratio	Rural	Urban	Rural to urban ratio	Rural	Urban	Rural to urban ratio
1. Own-account manufacturing (OAME)									
Agro-based	1,502	2,704	0.6	1,447	2,913	0.5	2,227	3,835	0.6
Non-agro-based	1,780	4,618	0.4	1,995	6,155	0.3	2,612	5,359	0.5
All industries	1,554	3,139	0.5	1,761	4,119	0.4	2,549	4,235	0.6
2. Nondirectory manufacturing (NDME)									
Agro-based	3,279	6,599	0.5	3,699	6,758	0.5	4,821	8,161	0.6
Non-agro-based	3,133	9,643	0.3	4,232	7,185	0.6	7,423	1,0739	0.7
All industries	3,227	7,579	0.4	3,974	6,943	0.6	5,542	9,090	0.6
3. Directory manufacturing (DME)									
Agro-based	2,650	7,426	0.4	3,798	8,048	0.5	4,805	10,395	0.5
Non-agro-based	3,173	10,837	0.3	5,981	12,220	0.5	7,405	13,449	0.6
All industries	2,839	8,778	0.3	4,310	9,285	0.5	6,156	11,043	0.6
4. Total unorganized manufacturing									
Agro-based	1,741	4,675	0.4	1,874	5,339	0.4	2,626	6,525	0.4
Non-agro-based	2,065	7,915	0.3	2,717	8,225	0.3	4,493	9,792	0.5
All industries	1,802	5,673	0.3	2,227	6,392	0.3	3,227	7,427	0.4
5. DME to OAME ratio									
Agro-based industries	1.8	2.7		2.6	2.8		2.2	2.7	
Non-agro-based industries	1.8	2.3		3.0	2.0		2.8	2.5	
All industries	1.8	2.8		2.4	2.3		2.4	2.6	

SOURCES: NSS Report No. 363, June 1989; Report No. 433, August 1998; and unit-level data for 2000–2001 on CD-ROM, supplied by NSSO (National Sample Survey Organization), New Delhi.

[a]For a more detailed description of each firm category, see Appendix 16A at the end of this chapter.

products, machine tools, electrical machinery, transport equipment, etc.) demand more capital and higher levels of skill and training. It is therefore the inadequacy or absence of infrastructural and institutional support that inflicts productivity losses on rural enterprises. The institutional bias against the rural nonfarm sector as a whole must cease. OAMEs overwhelmingly dominate the unorganized sector, most markedly in the rural areas, and the dismally low productivity standards of such enterprises determine the productivity levels in the rural industrial sector as a whole.

Third, during the post-1994 years, the rural-urban productivity gaps have narrowed, in both agro-based and non-agro-based industries, for each of the three groups of manufacturing enterprises. Despite the post-reform record of productivity improvement, the locational disadvantage of the rural units remained high in 2000–2001, primarily because their productivity levels were substantially lower in 1994–95. Conversely, during the post-reform years, the relative position of the rural manufacturing enterprises has not worsened.

Fourth, substantial diseconomies of scale are discernible for each category of manufacturing, among both rural and urban enterprises. Taking the ratio of the productivity of DMEs to that of OAMEs as a surrogate for such diseconomies, we discover a relatively better post-1994 record for rural enterprises, among both the agro-based and the non-agro-based industries. For both categories of manufacturing, the ratio has declined in the rural areas, while it has increased or remained the same in the urban areas. This means that in the urban areas the tiniest of the manufacturing units have not been able to move closer to the productivity levels of their bigger counterparts, while in the rural areas they have registered some success.¯

The RNF Sector and Poverty

The impact of RNF development on rural poverty has been the subject of intense debate (Mitra 1993, 466; Chadha 1994, 191–215). At the household level, numerous studies show that a fairly large proportion of the rural landless, marginal, and small cultivating households are involved in a wide variety of nonfarm activities; this adds substantially to their limited earnings from agricultural wages and/or farming and helps many of them to stave off poverty (Bhalla and Chadha 1983, 88–101; Corner 1986, 51–54; Saith 1992, 3–5; Chadha 1994, 206–8). If such households were to depend on agricultural income alone, the incidence of poverty among them would be substantially higher (Chadha 1994, 193).

However, some analysts make a distinction between distress-driven nonfarm expansion and market-driven nonfarm expansion (Vaidyanathan 1986, A144–A146; Chadha 1996, 1). The regions thus stand divided into two groups. In one group, agriculture is growing, productivity levels are high, agricultural output per rural dweller is high, and consequently, through a chain of forward and backward linkages, a variety of local nonfarm activities are enhanced. In the other group, agricultural growth is sluggish and erratic, productivity levels are low, per capita agricultural output is low, and many of the rural people hunt for any nonfarm job, locally in the village or in the nearby urban and semi-urban centers, that can sustain them on a day-to-day basis. Overall, therefore, the level of rural poverty in any state depends on the combined effect of the pace of agricultural development and the nature and spread of nonfarm activities.

Table 16.6 shows the statewise picture of rural poverty for 1983, 1993–94, and 1999–2000 in relation to the level of agricultural development (for which the surrogate is agricultural production per rural dweller) and RNF development. RNF development is characterized quantitatively, by the percentage of rural workers engaged in nonfarm activities, and qualitatively, by the level of productivity per worker in rural industry.

A few interesting facts need to be underlined. Given the usual limitations of state-level cross-section data, no significant (negative) correlation between rural poverty and RNF development emerges for any of the three points of time (Table 16.6).[4] This upholds the contention that in some states the sheer proliferation of rural nonfarm employment may not make a dent in rural poverty if the agricultural base is weak and the movement into the nonfarm sector is a distress-driven phenomenon. On the other hand, there are states where a low level of rural poverty goes hand in hand with a medium to high level of RNF activity as well as agricultural development. Finally, there are states where the level of rural poverty is high partly because their agricultural productivity is low and the RNF sector is weak. In sum, RNF development, for which the surrogate is the percentage of rural workers engaged in nonfarm activities, does not show its impact on rural poverty alleviation in all cases.

If RNF development is proxied by a more refined and qualitatively superior indicator, say the level of productivity per worker in rural industry, its poverty alleviation impact comes up neat and clean.[5] This lends considerable support to the point that a mere switch of rural workers from agriculture to nonfarm activities may not relieve many of the rural households of their poverty; the productivity levels of the nonfarm activities to which they migrate are a more decisive factor.

In plain terms, RNF activity can make a contribution to poverty alleviation if and only if the workers shift from low-productivity to higher-productivity jobs. In an oblique sense, many of the state-sponsored poverty alleviation schemes that encourage rural households to undertake a variety of self-employing

---

4. The values of the coefficients of rank correlation between the rural poverty ratio and the percentage of rural nonfarm workers are 0.22 for 1983, –0.43 for 1993–94, and –0.28 for 1999–2000.

5. The values of the coefficients of rank correlation between the rural poverty ratio and productivity per worker in rural industry are –0.68 for 1983, –0.48 for 1993–94, and –0.76 for 1999–2000; each coefficient is significant at the 0.01 level.

TABLE 16.6 Rural poverty, agricultural development, and rural nonfarm employment in India, by state, 1983–2001

State	Percentage of rural population in poverty			Per capita net state domestic product from agriculture (Rs. at 1980–81 prices)			% rural nonfarm workers			Productivity per worker in rural industry[a]		
	1983	1993–94	1999–2000	1983–84	1993–94	1999–2000	1983	1993–94	1999–2000	1984–85	1994–95	2000–2001
Andhra Pradesh	26.5	15.9	11.1	998	1,049	1,083	19.7	20.7	21.2	2,530	2,412	3,455
Assam	42.6	45.0	40.0	748	772	802	20.0	21.2	32.3	2,665	2,418	2,776
Bihar	64.4	58.2	44.3	585	484	425	16.4	15.8	19.3	3,091	2,449	3,748
Gujarat	29.8	22.2	13.2	1,349	989	914	14.8	21.3	19.6	7,200	6,403	8,116
Haryana	20.6	28.0	8.3	1,650	2,083	2,121	22.3	28.1	30.2	7,033	8,192	7,788
Himachal Pradesh	17.0	30.3	7.9	930	931	1,037	12.4	19.8	25.2	5,014	3,151	6,162
Jammu and Kashmir	26.0	30.3	4.0	1,048	872	895	19.8	24.4	27.0	3,809	3,034	6,007
Karnataka	36.3	29.9	17.4	1,053	1,314	1,462	15.5	18.1	17.8	2,755	2,925	4,171
Kerala	39.0	25.8	9.4	633	930	924	36.9	43.9	51.2	3,673	3,522	5,504
Madhya Pradesh	48.9	40.6	37.1	1,036	1,128	1,072	9.7	10.1	12.8	3,134	4,223	3,086
Maharashtra	45.2	37.9	23.7	1,060	1,438	1,441	14.2	17.4	17.2	4,909	6,928	7,415
Orissa	67.5	49.7	48.0	808	492	461	20.8	19.0	21.4	1,272	1,013	1,584
Punjab	13.2	12.0	6.4	1,975	2,799	2,961	17.4	25.4	27.1	6,672	6,816	8,685
Rajasthan	33.5	26.5	13.7	1,122	955	1,100	13.3	20.2	22.1	2,704	4,555	5,910
Tamil Nadu	54.0	32.5	20.6	651	994	1,055	25.1	29.6	31.7	2,452	4,534	5,091
Uttar Pradesh	46.5	42.3	31.2	852	870	880	17.7	20.0	23.6	19,22	3,117	3,762
West Bengal	63.1	40.8	31.9	852	1,085	1,359	26.3	36.4	37.0	2,529	2,557	3,848

SOURCES: India, Ministry of Statistics and Program Implementation (1990a, 1997, 2001); NSS Report No. 363, June 1989; Report No. 433, August 1998 and unit level data for 2000–2001 on CD-ROM, supplied by NSSO (National Sample Survey Organization), New Delhi. India, Ministry of Finance, *Economic Survey*, various years; and net state domestic product data obtained on floppies from India, CSO (Central Statistical Organization), New Delhi.

[a]Productivity per worker in rural industry is the gross value added at constant 1981–82 prices divided by the total workers in the unorganized manufacturing sector.

nonfarm activities have had a limited impact primarily because the "new enterprises" could not show a significant improvement in productivity.

Further, agricultural development continues to make a decisive dent in rural poverty.[6] This should caution RNF promoters against dismissing the poverty alleviation capability of agriculture. Agriculture still contributes nearly 55.0 percent of rural NDP, and any breakthrough here in productivity per worker is bound to have an effect on rural poverty, most ostensibly because no fewer than three-fourths of rural workers are still engaged in this sector. The primacy of agriculture cannot be dismissed for many more years to come.

Concluding Remarks

In recent years, the RNF scenario in India has not been encouraging. It has presented a mixture of achievements and setbacks across production and service sectors, individual states, and male and female workers. In our assessment, the overall situation during the postreform period compared with the prereform period is cause for concern. This concluding section sketches out the major trends on the RNF front during the 1980s and 1990s and poses a few policy questions for public debate and further research.

1. As in most other developing economies, in India the RNF sector consists of a wide array of activities that provide livelihood to a sizable segment of the landless households and supplementary employment and earnings to a fairly large proportion of submarginal and marginal cultivating households. Part of the reduction in rural poverty can also be attributed to the availability of nonfarm employment and earnings to the landless or the nearly landless and to underprivileged segments of the rural society.

2. The RNF sector holds great significance for India's rural economy due to its expanding contribution to income generation. Intersector reshufflings and adjustments, perhaps extending their sway over the rural economy that was itself becoming integrated with the rest of the market-driven economy, contributed to the structural changes in the RNF economy. By the close of the 1990s, like its urban counterpart, the rural economy was finding its moorings under the dictates of a competitive market system.

3. Farm incomes played a significant role in promoting the expansion of nonfarm incomes during the 1980s. During the 1990s, linkages between the farm and the nonfarm sectors became stronger, partly because the demand for purchased agricultural inputs was increasing steadily during the 1980s

---

6. The values of the coefficients of rank correlation between rural poverty and agricultural production per capita are –0.67 for 1983, –0.55 for 1993–94, and –0.44 for 1999–2000; all are significant at the 0.05 or 0.10 level.

and 1990s and partly because the consumption basket of rural households has been tilting in favor of nonfood and processed food items, promoting the expansion of local nonfarm activities.

4. Employment in India's RNF sector has been expanding over time. Rural India's excessive dependence on agriculture as a source of livelihood has decreased, and its employment base has seen a modest degree of diversification. This process slowed down in the 1990s, after reform, with the brunt of the impact falling on rural female workers.

5. The nonfarm employment base of many states witnessed some increase, first during the 1980s and then during the 1990s, yet the base could not exceed 25 percent in more than 8 of the 17 major states.

6. There is a marked difference in the mode of employment between the agriculture sector and the nonagricultural sector. Self-employment dominates in the farm sector as well as the nonfarm sector, for both rural male and female workers. Further, while regular salaried jobs are nearly conspicuous by their absence in agriculture, such jobs constitute a fairly large proportion of employment in the nonfarm sector, especially for rural male workers. In relative terms, access to tertiary sector jobs is more widely spread than is access to secondary sector jobs. Furthermore, casual wage labor constitutes around 40 percent of agricultural employment, making up about one-fourth of nonfarm employment for rural male workers and nearly one-fifth for rural female workers. Finally, there is a clear tendency for the casualization of employment to increase over time, not only in agriculture but also in the RNF sector; rural male workers suffer more from this handicap.

7. Productivity levels are generally low in most of the rural nonfarm activities compared with the urban, with marked variations even among the rural enterprises. The urban-rural productivity gaps are indeed the widest among the tiniest of the rural manufacturing enterprises, the OAMEs.

8. Interregional variations in labor productivity have tended to widen in recent years. To the extent that the level of labor productivity is a surrogate for the quality of nonfarm employment, different regions have registered varying levels of improvement in their RNF development. In recent years the orientation of credit and public investment flows has been moving away from rural areas (Chadha 2002, 33), and tiny and small-scale nonfarm activities have been exposed to harsher institutional dispensations in agriculturally backward areas. All this, combined with the usual policy of fiscal compression exercised by a number of states during the 1990s, does not bode well for the RNF sector. Policy correction is urgently needed.

9. Rural infrastructure, population growth, and education play a significant role in promoting the RNF sector. The role of infrastructure and education became more pervasive as we moved into the 1990s. Clearly, in the coming years, means of transport and communication, power, and finance are going to be critically important in strengthening the productivity levels of

rural nonfarm activities and lending them the competitive edge they need in the emerging free market dispensations.

10. RNF development plays a significant role in alleviating rural poverty. However, it is the quality of nonfarm employment rather than its sheer expansion that makes the decisive impact. A number of government-sponsored poverty alleviation schemes, largely in the vein of promoting nonfarm enterprises, need critical scrutiny in terms of their potential for productivity improvement. Because agriculture's primacy in rural poverty alleviation is undeniable from the point of view of its share in rural NDP and rural employment, improvement in agricultural productivity would of course contribute to rural poverty alleviation.

To conclude, India's postreform experience provides hints as to the nature of the changes that the country's market-driven economy would brook in the days ahead. As a medium-term strategy, the states must strive to strengthen their agricultural base by reversing the recent trend of downswings in investment. The crucial role that public investment has to play in strengthening the infrastructure and other supporting institutions, which seems to have receded to low levels of government priority, must be reemphasized with the utmost stress. This is an inescapable conclusion, partly because more than 70 percent of the rural workforce is still absorbed by agriculture in a preponderant majority of states and partly because it is this very sector that has the potential to absorb the employment setbacks that may emerge in other sectors when the country proceeds further into the new economic regime (Chadha and Sahu 2002, 2026). Most important, this study clearly shows that productivity levels in agriculture play an extremely crucial role in alleviating rural poverty. For healthy growth of the RNF sector, agricultural growth is an essential prerequisite. A concrete reorientation and reversal of investment priorities in favor of agriculture is bound to help the RNF sector as well.

Appendix 16A: Data, Definitions, and Concepts

This chapter draws on diverse sources of data, chief among them the National Sample Survey (NSS) reports. The NSS reports are especially useful for gauging the rural-urban and male-female contrasts in employment in all major sectors of the Indian economy. The other sources of data are the National Accounts Statistics, Population Census Reports, statistical sourcebooks of the central and state governments, and data published in individual research writings. A number of comments about the NSS data, especially their relevance and adequacy to answer questions on rural nonfarm employment, are in order.

1. The time profile for employment cannot go very far back, because temporally comparable data started pouring in only after 1972–73. Specific to

our requirements, temporally comparable NSS data on farm and nonfarm components of employment are available only for seven points of time: the 27th round (October 1972–September 1973), the 32nd round (July 1977–June 1978), the 38th round (January–December 1983), the 43rd round (July 1987–June 1988), the 50th round (July 1993–June 1994), and the 55th round (July 1999–June 2000). To avoid a jumble of statistics, I have chosen to report data for three points of time—1983, 1993–94, and 1999–2000—to capture the employment situation before and after the 1991–92 economic reforms. As noted earlier, the period 1983 to 1993–94 is taken as a proxy for the prereform decade, and the period between 1993–94 and 1999–2000 proxies the postreform developments.

For unorganized manufacturing, I draw on the NSS data for three points of time: the 40th round (July 1984–June 1985), the 51st round (July 1994–June 1995), and the 56th round (July 2000–June 2001). Data for 2000–2001 are extracted from the household-level data on CD-ROM.

2. Most of my analysis uses "usual status" data. The status of activity in which a person has spent relatively more of the 365 days preceding the date of survey is considered the person's "principal usual status" activity. A person categorized as a nonworker who pursued some economic activity in a subsidiary capacity is called a "subsidiary status worker." These two groups, principal status workers and subsidiary status workers, together constitute "all workers" according to the "usual (principal + subsidiary) status" classification. In most cases, principal and subsidiary status estimates are combined to present the most comprehensive picture on employment.

3. While the NSS data show what percentage of the rural workforce was engaged in different gainful activities or what share of rural workers in the total workforce was in each production sector, they provide no direct information as to whether a particular source of employment was in a rural, semiurban, or urban area. In India, all places with a population of less than 5,000, a population density not exceeding 400 persons per square kilometer, at least 75 percent of the male working population engaged in agriculture are defined as rural areas (India, Office of the Registrar General and Census Commissioner, 1991, 7). The employment estimates for the rural households are thus free of locational specificities. In a way, this fit remarkably well with my objective inasmuch as under the forthcoming economic regimes, rural job aspirants would not seek employment only in the rural areas.

4. In the Indian NSS reports, employment is characterized as "self-employed," "regular salaried jobs," or "casual labor." People who operate their own farm or nonfarm enterprises or are independently engaged in a profession on their own account or under a partnership are deemed self-employed. Employees working on others' farms or at nonfarm enterprises on a regular basis (i.e., not on the basis of daily or periodic renewal of a work contract)

are defined as "regular salaried workers." Finally, those who are casually engaged on others' farms or at nonfarm enterprises and earn wages according to the terms of a daily or periodic work contract are classified as "casual laborers."

5. In the Indian system of classification of business enterprises, an enterprise owned and operated without the help of any hired worker, employed on a fairly regular basis, is described as an "own-account manufacturing enterprise" (OAME). An enterprise run with the assistance of at least one hired worker, employed on a fairly regular basis, is called an "establishment." An establishment that employs a total of not more than five workers is known as a "nondirectory manufacturing establishment" (NDME), while one employing a total of six or more workers is categorized as a "directory manufacturing establishment" (DME). A directory establishment that employs 10 or more workers and uses power or one that employs 20 or more workers without using power is considered an "organized manufacturing enterprise" (OME).

17 Diversification: Implications for Rural Growth in China

FUNING ZHONG AND JING ZHU

Reforms revitalized the Chinese primary economy in an unprecedented manner. The GDP generated from primary industry increased from 101.8 billion yuan in 1978 to 1,460.9 billion yuan in 2001 (NBS 2002).[1] This represents an annual growth rate of 12.28 percent in nominal terms, or 4.66 percent in real terms,[2] in 23 years compared with the annual growth rates of 4.28 percent and 2.05 percent, in nominal and real terms, respectively, recorded during the prereform period of 1952–78.

Farmers' livelihood has improved by a much larger proportion than has growth in agriculture, largely due to the development of the township and village enterprises (TVEs) and other nonfarm activities, including work in nonagricultural sectors away from home. The per capita net annual income of rural households increased from 133.6 yuan in 1978 to 2,366.4 yuan in 2001, or by 13.3 percent per year in nominal terms and 7.3 percent per year in real terms in 23 years (NBS 2002). Following the continuing growth in net income, the Engle coefficient dropped from 67.7 percent in 1978 to 47.7 percent in 2001 in rural areas, indicating a very significant improvement in the Chinese farmer's daily life (Table 17.1).

Many studies attribute the great achievement in Chinese agriculture and farmers' livelihood since 1978 to institutional reforms, especially the introduction of the Household Responsibility System or HRS (Lin 1988), along with significant success in agricultural sciences and extension (Fan 2000) and increased application of modern inputs. The role of TVEs is also well recognized. Combined with remittance from earnings obtained in nonagricultural sectors away from home, TVEs have provided an increasingly larger share of farmers' net income, especially since the mid-1980s. As a result, the annual rural per capita income earned from secondary and tertiary industries increased from 69.4 yuan in 1985 to 1066.4 yuan in 2001, or from 17.5 percent to 45.1 percent of the total in 16 years (NBS 2002).

---

1. In Chinese statistics, "primary industry" is equivalent to the agricultural sector.
2. Or "comparative prices," as indicated in the *Chinese Statistical Yearbook*.

TABLE 17.1 Per capita net annual income and Engle coefficient of rural households in China, 1978–2001

Year	Per capital net annual income of rural households		Engle coefficient of rural households (percent)
	Value (current yuan)	Index (1978 = 100)	
1978	133.6	100.0	67.7
1980	191.3	139.0	61.8
1985	397.6	268.9	57.8
1990	686.3	311.2	58.8
1995	1577.7	383.7	58.6
2000	2253.4	483.5	49.1
2001	2366.4	503.8	47.7

SOURCE: NBS, *China Statistical Yearbook,* 2002.

However, the importance of diversification in Chinese agriculture has not been fully understood, and its contribution to agricultural growth and farmers' income has not been fully estimated and documented. At the early stage of development, producers tended to concentrate on an increase of production of the same products with increased application of modern inputs, and scientists tended to develop new varieties and techniques to be applied to the same products, mainly grain crops. At this stage, growth in agricultural production came from productivity gains resulting from technology advances and application of modern inputs in the same production lines. However, following rapid growth in agriculture and reform of the economic system, producers are able to pursue higher economic returns from reallocation of their production resources, partly in response to changing demand, and scientists are able to respond to such a shift in production by developing new varieties and techniques for alternative crops. At this stage, diversification appears to be another major contributor to growth in agriculture and farmers' income. While in the short run diversification may rely on available technology, to fully realize its potential over the longer run diversification will require development of new technology, probably used in altogether different production activities. Therefore, agricultural research and development (R&D) as well as increasing use of modern inputs are essential to create new opportunities for diversification and to capture the benefits of diversification.

In this study we attempt to document the diversification process in China. In the first section we set the context by reviewing the main drivers of agricultural growth. We then examine diversification in both agriculture and the rural economy and develop an equation to estimate the contribution of diversification to economic growth in the past two decades. The effect of diversification on farmers' income then analyzed, with the future perspectives of diversification outlined in the final section.

Major Contributors to the Growth in Chinese Agriculture

Agricultural GDP in China grew at a rate of more than 2 percent in real terms over a 26-year period prior to reform. This record is quite significant when compared to those of other countries. It can be attributed to factors such as land reform, heavy government and collective investment in irrigation and land improvement, high levels of public investment in agricultural R&D, and increasing uses of modern inputs, among others.

The land reform in the early 1950s provided some 300 million farmers (more than 60 percent of the rural population) with 46.7 million hectares of arable land (about half of the total arable land) without any payment and simply abolished the annual rent of roughly 35 million tons of grain, or 20–25 percent of the total output. This dramatic institutional change greatly induced the production incentives in Chinese agriculture and provided the first push to agricultural growth at that time (Carter and Zhong 1988).

Continuous efforts in irrigation and land improvement were two other important factors that contributed to Chinese agricultural growth. Du Jian Yan, a famous water control system, has served a large agricultural area for more than 2,200 years and still functions very effectively today. Since the mid-1950s, the collective farming system, though it proved inefficient in many aspects, provided a useful vehicle for mobilizing rural resources, especially labor, in constructing and maintaining water projects. The huge annual investment from farmers in surface water systems and then in tubewell irrigation, combined with government investment in major water control projects that were the largest component of public investment in agriculture, improved production conditions in Chinese agriculture significantly. The continued investment in basic production infrastructure contributed not only to long-term growth, but also to less fluctuation in annual output.

Technology advancement in Chinese agriculture was also quite impressive during the 1960s and 1970s. Chinese semidwarf and dwarf varieties provided high yields equivalent to those produced in India during the green revolution, followed by breeding and commercialization of hybrid rice, which was an even more significant achievement. China's agricultural extension system was quite efficient during the communal era, because it allowed all those high-yielding varieties to spread rapidly over the whole country together with various new techniques and farming practices.

Application of chemical fertilizers and pesticides, unknown to most Chinese farmers in the 1950s, dramatically increased after the early 1960s. By the late 1970s, the level of application of agricultural chemicals in China was well above the world average. The use of farm machinery also increased very fast under the agricultural mechanization movement. Many farm machines, such as hand tractors, were specifically designed and produced for small-scale agriculture, and they greatly helped farmers in expanding production.

All these factors contributed to the 2 percent annual growth in Chinese agriculture that was seen for over three decades. Although the potentials of these factors were not fully realized due to some institutional constraints, they actually provided a solid base for faster growth in the near future.

Growth in agriculture and farmers' income prior to reform was relatively slow compared with what was achieved afterward. This has been generally attributed to two important institutional factors that prevented Chinese agriculture from fully capturing the growth potentials provided by the available technology and inputs: the disincentive in collective farming under the communal system and the inefficiency in resource allocation under rigid central planning. The production incentives have been further depressed by the low procurement prices administered, which have been used to "tax" agriculture and support rapid industrialization. The introduction of the HRS greatly stimulated farmers' incentives in production. Along with technology advances and the increasing use of modern inputs, it has brought remarkable increases in yield, that is, productivity gains. At the same time, the reform of product and factor markets has significantly reduced government intervention, providing farmers with increasing autonomous power in decisionmaking, and has resulted in improved efficiency in resource allocation (Carter, Zhong, and Cai 1996). Because the real agricultural GDP has increased roughly twice as fast as the weighted yield since 1978, diversification is likely to have contributed more than half of the growth in Chinese agriculture during the reform period (Zhong and Zhu 2000). If the incomes earned from nonagricultural sectors are included, the contribution of diversification to the improvement in farmers' livelihood is likely to have been even greater. In addition, because the fundamental problems in Chinese agriculture are small farm size and excess labor supply, diversification provides a partial solution to these problems by shifting resources to more labor-intensive production and creating new job opportunities in nonfarm sectors.

Following its entry to the World Trade Organization (WTO), China is likely to undertake a series of structural adjustments to fulfill her commitments. As a result, the gap between the domestic prices of agricultural produce and those prevailing in the world market will be narrowed. Because the WTO rules prohibit some of the traditional policy tools, such as the use of price subsidies in supporting agriculture, diversification will be even more important in the future growth of Chinese agriculture and farmers' income.

Diversification in the Agricultural Sector

No matter how we view the reforms today, they were not planned in advance of December 1978 and probably were not intended to be as comprehensive and long lasting as they have turned out to be. A common understanding was that the past development strategy, which was intended to speed up industrialization through mobilizing all available resources at the cost of current consumption, could not be continued any further due to the continuous decline in production incentives and the consequent continuous drop in productivity and efficiency. Therefore, reform was started in the rural areas and could be characterized as a significant and continuing reduction in the government interventions imposed on the agricultural sector.

On the incentive side, the government began the reform with raising the procurement prices of 18 major farm products by 24.8 percent on average within one year and encouraging the reinstitution of close linkages between material rewards and working efforts, known as various "responsibility systems" within the communal system. At the beginning of reform, the "Da Baogan" or "Baogan Daohu," later known as the HRS, was not allowed, but it was secretly adopted by farmers in one village in Anhui province in 1978. Even as late as the end of 1980, the government insisted on some degree of collective farming and permitted the HRS to be adopted only under special conditions. However, the adoption of the HRS was soon to be encouraged by the government, and it had become the dominant form of farming organization in China by 1984, leading to the termination of the communal system. Because Chinese agriculture exhibited extraordinary growth from 1978 to 1984 and the growth rate slowed down afterwards, many researchers concluded that the introduction of the HRS was the main reason for the changing growth pattern in Chinese agriculture.

However, the reform policies on the allocation efficiency side should not be ignored or underestimated. The government first gave more autonomy in decisionmaking to production brigades and teams under the communal system by making most of the production plans guidelines rather than compulsory. It then reduced procurement quotas for both types and quantities of production and encouraged the establishment and expansion of the so-called specialized production of cash crops and production activities in noncropping sectors. Free and long-distance private trade in grain was also legalized and encouraged after fulfillment of the quota obligations. The market-oriented reforms went further: the urban food rationing system was formally abolished in the early 1990s, edible oil procurement was stopped at about the same time, and government intervention in grain and cotton marketing was reduced to a minimum level in the late 1990s.

The main interest of this study is to explicitly demonstrate the effects of resource allocation improvement, which is certainly attributable to the market reforms, on the rapid growth and development in Chinese agriculture and the improvement of farmers' income during the past two decades. Table 17.2 shows that although the output of cropping sector increases by more than 170 percent in real terms in 23 years, indicating a remarkable 4.44 percent rate of annual growth over more than two decades, other sectors have grown even faster.

Animal production increased by almost 670 percent during the same period, while fishery production increased by 1,244.7 percent. The annual growth rates have been 9.28 percent and 11.96 percent, respectively, for the two sectors.

TABLE 17.2 Shares of gross output value of farming, forestry, animal husbandry, and fishery and related indices in China, 1978–2001

Year	Shares of gross output value of farming, forestry, animal husbandry, and fishery (percent)					Indexes of gross output of farming, forestry, animal husbandry, and fishery (1978 = 100)				
	Total	Farming	Forestry	Animal husbandry	Fishery	Total	Farming	Forestry	Animal husbandry	Fishery
1978	100.0	80.0	3.4	15.0	1.6	100.0	100.0	100.0	100.0	100.0
1980	100.0	75.6	4.2	18.4	1.7	109.0	106.7	113.8	122.6	104.0
1985	100.0	69.2	5.2	22.1	3.5	160.7	145.3	176.1	203.0	185.2
1990	100.0	64.7	4.3	25.7	5.4	202.6	170.4	179.2	281.4	348.9
1991	100.0	63.1	4.5	26.5	5.9	210.1	171.9	193.6	306.2	373.2
1992	100.0	61.5	4.7	27.1	6.8	223.5	179.1	208.5	331.1	430.4
1993	100.0	60.1	4.5	27.4	8.0	241.0	188.4	225.1	369.1	572.1
1994	100.0	58.2	3.9	29.7	8.2	261.7	194.5	245.2	430.8	686.5
1995	100.0	58.4	3.5	29.7	8.4	290.2	209.8	257.4	494.5	819.7
1996	100.0	60.6	3.5	26.9	9.0	317.5	226.2	272.1	550.9	934.5
1997	100.0	58.2	3.4	28.7	9.6	338.8	236.4	281.1	606.5	1041.9
1998	100.0	58.0	3.5	28.6	9.9	359.1	247.9	289.2	651.4	1133.6
1999	100.0	57.5	3.6	28.5	10.3	376.0	258.6	298.5	684.4	1215.3
2000	100.0	55.7	3.8	29.7	10.9	389.5	262.2	314.6	724.3	1294.3
2001	100.0	55.2	3.6	30.4	10.8	405.9	271.7	312.4	769.9	1344.7

SOURCE: Calculated from data in NBS, *China Statistical Yearbook*, 1991 and 2002.

NOTE: Shares are calculated at current prices, while the indexes are calculated at comparable prices.

Large amounts of resources have flown from cropping to other sectors, and such structural changes have brought higher rates of growth in agriculture as a whole.

The cropping sector, dominated by grain production for a long time, has been the largest in Chinese agriculture. However, following the faster growth in other sectors during the reform era, the structure of Chinese agriculture has changed dramatically.

The share of the cropping sector declined from 80 percent to just over 55 percent in 23 years, while that of animal and fishery production increased from 15 percent and 1.6 percent to 30.4 percent and 10.8 percent, respectively, in the same period (Table 17.2). Because cropping was the dominant and least profitable agricultural sector before the reform, faster growth in other sectors resulted not only in significant structural changes in agriculture itself but also in significant improvements in resource allocation efficiency and farmers' income. The structural adjustment is likely to be just as significant within each of the sectors as among them. For example, during the period under discussion, the weighted yield per unit of sown area increased by roughly 2 percent per year and the output value of the cropping sector increased by 4.44 percent in real terms, while the total sown area was virtually unchanged. By measuring yield in real terms, we have ruled out the effect of price change over time, so the difference between the two growth rates we have given can be explained only by the change in crop mix that resulted from shifting production from grain to cash crops and from low-quality, low-value varieties to high-quality, high-value ones. Such sectoral structural changes appear to be more significant in animal and fishery production, because their products are more market-oriented and profitable due to changing and growing patterns of consumers' demand.

Diversification of the Rural Economy

When the Rural People's Commune was established in 1958, it was designed as a self-sufficient community in all aspects, including production, consumption, education, healthcare, and other social functions. Small-scale enterprises in the rural areas were highly encouraged by the government as an essential component of the self-sufficiency of the People's Commune. They were established and run by the commune and/or production brigades and thus named commune and brigade enterprises (CBEs). CBEs were mainly engaged in producing farm inputs, processing farm products, and providing technical services to agricultural production.

However, as a logical consequence, they expanded both in scale and into other more profitable sectors. During the Great Leap Forward, which happened at the same time, some of the CBEs even tried to produce steel and iron, as well as other producer goods not directly related to agriculture. However, the growth of CBEs was more or less restricted by the overall development policy.

The development of the CBEs was greatly influenced by the changes in the national economic and political environment. After the famine of the early 1960s, the government put grain production on the priority list. Accordingly, most, if not all, available resources had to be allocated to it , and all CBEs were supposed to directly serve agriculture. The development of CBEs beyond the purpose of directly serving local agriculture was considered contradictory to the overall development strategy, which required mobilization of all available resources for fast growth in the state-run heavy industry.

When the Cultural Revolution broke out in the mid-1960s, the production of most state-owned enterprises (SOEs) in the urban areas was disrupted or even curtailed. In some areas, such as southern Jiangsu province, CBEs benefited from the chaos in the nearby urban areas. Many technicians and skilled workers who were sent back to their original home villages at that time contributed to their expansion. Many CBEs even changed their production lines and went into urban consumer goods markets because the supply from SOEs was interrupted. They were also able to obtain some important industrial inputs through nonofficial channels unavailable to them in the past, because the functioning of the planning system was also disturbed. Because CBEs had already become important players in the local economy in some areas, local governments supported them, even if the policy set at upper levels restricted the development of CBEs. Nevertheless, CBEs were able to grow further only in some limited areas due to the overall development strategy and the associated policy environment.

The reform sought to boost agricultural production to provide the nation with an increased supply of consumer goods. The development of CBEs (renamed TVEs after 1985) was encouraged by the government as an effective tool to provide additional income to farmers and additional investment funds to the local rural community. This policy objective was clearly reflected in the slogan "Yi Gong Bu Nong" (subsidizing agriculture with income from industry) and stipulated in the Township and Village Enterprise Management Law passed by the Standing Committee of the National People's Congress.

The gradual advance of the reform in the urban-industrial sectors and in the planning system itself brought two significant changes to the development of TVEs after the mid-1980s. On the one hand, the adoption of the "double-track" pricing system in input markets provided TVEs with better market access. On the other, the reform carried out in SOEs enhanced their competitiveness and advantages based on production scale, technology, and productivity, leading to the bankruptcies of many TVEs in the late 1980s and early 1990s and to the restructuring of these enterprises afterwards. Table 17.3 presents some major development indicators of TVEs during 1978–2001.

Although these statistics are not considered highly accurate and should be used with caution, the trend they present is clear and impressive. The number of TVEs increased at an annual rate of 12 percent, while the number of employees, total sales, and total wage payrolls rose at 6.8 percent, 27.1 percent,

TABLE 17.3 Major development indicators of TVEs in China, 1978–2001

Year	Number of TVEs (millions)	Number of employees (millions)	Total sales (billion yuan)	Total wage payroll (billion yuan)
1978	1.5	28.3	43.2	8.7
1980	1.4	30.0	59.6	11.9
1985	12.2	69.8	256.1	47.2
1990	18.5	92.7	861.4	112.9
1995	22.0	128.6	5,729.9	438.1
2000	20.8	128.2	10,783.4	706.0
2001	21.2	130.9	11,658.5	773.2

SOURCES: China, Ministry of Agriculture, *China Township and Village Enterprises Yearbook,* various years; NBS, *China Statistical Yearbook,* various years.

and 21.1 percent, respectively. These data suggest that although the growth in the numbers of TVEs and their employees has more or less leveled since 1990, the total sales and wage payroll continued to increase, at 26.7 percent and 19.1 percent per year, respectively. While the TVEs' capacity to absorb rural surplus laborers has been reduced to a large extent, they continue to provide additional income to farmers.

The development of other nonfarm activities followed the same pattern as that of CBEs or TVEs. When the commune was a closed, self-sufficient community and its main task was providing farm products, especially grain, at the lowest prices to the other sectors of the nation, all nonfarm economic activities, such as handicrafts and commerce, and even country fairs, were highly restricted. At the same time, migration of laborers was prohibited in order to retain the surplus and inexpensive labor in agriculture. After the reform started in 1978, "sideline" production was highly encouraged for the same reason as was the development of TVEs: providing farmers with additional income in order to cross-subsidize agriculture. All types of small private businesses, including shops and street peddlers as well as handicraft, transportation, construction, and manufacturing businesses, emerged and grew very quickly. The number of out-migrated rural laborers reached over 100 million, working in the urban industrial and commercial sectors as well as in TVEs in the coastal areas.

Table 17.4 indicates that while the number of rural laborers working in the traditional agricultural sector increased slightly during the 23-year period we are considering, those working in the industrial sectors increased 3.5 times during the same time period, and more and more rural laborers were working in other nonagricultural sectors as well.

In the 16 years from 1985 to 2001 (for which statistics are available), while rural laborers working in agriculture and industry increased by 8 percent and 56.7 percent, respectively, those employed in other sectors increased much faster, by 150 to 200 percent. As a result, the share of rural laborers working in

TABLE 17.4 Rural labor force at year end in China, by sector, 1978–2001 (million people)

Year	Farming, forestry, animal husbandry, and fishery	Industry	Construction	Transport, storage, postal, and communication services	Wholesale, retail trade, and catering services	Other nonagricultural trades
1978	284.6					
1980	298.1	16.3				
1985	303.5	27.4	11.3	4.3	4.6	19.5
1990	333.4	32.3	15.3	6.3	6.9	25.9
1991	341.9	32.7	15.3	6.6	7.2	27.3
1992	340.4	34.7	16.6	7.1	8.1	31.2
1993	332.6	36.6	18.9	8.0	9.5	37.0
1994	326.9	38.5	20.6	9.1	10.8	40.6
1995	323.4	39.7	22.0	9.8	11.7	43.8
1996	322.6	40.2	23.0	10.3	12.6	44.2
1997	324.3	40.3	23.7	10.6	13.8	46.8
1998	326.3	39.3	24.5	10.9	14.6	48.7
1999	329.2	39.5	25.3	11.2	15.8	48.0
2000	328.0	41.1	26.9	11.7	17.5	54.4
2001	324.5	43.0	28.0	12.1	18.6	56.1

SOURCE: NBS, *China Statistical Yearbook*, 2002.

agriculture declined from about 82 percent of the population in 1985 to 67 percent in 2001, while that in nonagricultural sectors increased from 18 percent to 33 percent.

These rural employment statistics do not include rural laborers employed by enterprises at town or township and higher levels. Because those enterprises hire a total of more than 40 million workers and most of them are usually farmers or classified as rural residents,[3] the share of rural laborers working in nonagricultural sectors is likely to be underestimated by about 10 percent. Therefore, after more than 20 years of reform and the associated diversification in the rural economy, about 200 million rural laborers, or more than 40 percent of the total, have engaged primarily in nonfarm activities. Some of them have been employed outside their home villages and their jobs may have no direct connection with agriculture at all. Even so, they still make a contribution to agriculture in various ways: leaving land and other resources to those who remain in agriculture, sending money back to their families and/or relatives, bringing back financial and human capital, establishing networks connecting home villages with the outside world, and so on. The overall significance of diversification is far beyond that of pure economic gains; it has contributed greatly to the complete development of the Chinese rural society.

The Contribution of Diversification to Rural Economic Growth

The contribution of structural adjustment to the cropping sector is estimated as the first step, based on which the contribution of intra- and intersector adjustment to agricultural growth is calculated or inferred. This contribution may be estimated by decomposing the gross output value (GOV) of the sector, which is the sum of the products of sown areas, yields per unit of sown area, and prices of the outputs:

$$GOV = \Sigma(area \times yield \times price). \tag{1}$$

The growth in yields is attributable to increasing application of inputs, technology improvement, and all other factors leading to higher productivity. The changes in nominal prices may result from various factors, such as the change in government policies in the case of administered procurement and the change in supply and demand in free market cases. If we want to estimate the relative contributions of area, yield, and price to GOV over time, equation 1 may be transferred into index form:

$$Ind_{gov} = Ind_{area} \times Ind_{yield} \times Ind_{price}, \tag{2}$$

---

3. Some of them may have recently obtained "urban resident" status as towns have expanded and/or the definition of resident status has changed.

where Ind_{gov} is the index of the GOV measured at comparable (or constant) prices, Ind_{area} is the index of total sown areas, Ind_{yield} is the index of weighted yield per unit of sown areas, and Ind_{price} is the index of the weighted price.

This means that the growth of GOV is the product of the growth of the area, the weighted yield, and the weighted price. However, there is a difference between equations 1 and 2. In equation 1, price is measured for each specific crop, so any change in its value reflects a change in the nominal price for that crop. The weighted price in equation 2 is measured based on specific prices as well as weights, that a change in its value may not necessarily reflect any change in any specific price. Rather, it may just indicate a change in the weights. Therefore, if equation 2 is measured at comparable (or constant) prices for all crops, a change in Ind_{price} no longer represents a change in the price of any specific crop or the general price level; its changing value simply represents a structural change in the crop mix. It implies that if farmers substitute high-value crops for low-price ones and hence sown areas are shifted among crops, the calculated weighted average price may increase, while in fact the prices of all crops remained the same. In this case, the increase in the weighted average price is implied or can be calculated even though it is not shown directly in any statistics. However, because the GOV in comparable prices, sown area, and yield data are available, it is possible to calculate the implied weighted average prices, and the change in such prices over time can be taken as an indicator of structural change in the cropping sector.

The indexes of the GOV at comparable prices are published in the *China Statistical Yearbook* (Table 17.2), and those of sown areas and yields can be calculated from respective statistics contained in the same yearbook.[4] Therefore, the indexes of the implied weighted price can be calculated by modifying equation 2 as follows:

$$Ind_{price} = Ind_{gov} / (Ind_{area} \times Ind_{yield}). \tag{3}$$

Three-year moving averages are used in this study to reduce the effects of weather and other random disturbances. If the 1978–80 averages are taken as the respective data for the base year of 1979, the index of the GOV in the cropping sector is calculated as 2.556 in 2000 (the 1999–2001 average over the 1978–80 average), those of the total sown area and weighted yield are calculated as 1.053 and 1.647, respectively.[5] Substituting those indexes into equation 3 results in the following:

$$Ind_{price} = 2.556/(1.053 \times 1.647) = 1.474.$$

4. Vegetables and fruits are not taken into consideration in the calculation for data consistency. However, sown areas of all other crops that are used to calculate indexes of areas and yields accounted for 80 to 90 percent of the total over time and thus can be taken as good proxies of the total.

5. The weights are 1978–80 sown area shares.

The results suggest that while the total sown area and weighted yield increased by 5.3 percent and 64.7 percent, respectively, in the 21 years under consideration, the implied weighted price was able to increase by a remarkable 47.4 percent, basically due to the structural adjustment in the cropping sector. Accordingly, the annual growth rates are calculated as 0.25, 2.40, and 1.86 percent for the total sown areas, weighted yield, and implied weighted price, respectively, while that for the GOV is 4.57 percent. If the relative shares of the contributions to the GOV are further calculated, they are likely to be 5.5, 53.2, and 41.3 percent for the increases in the total sown area, weighted yield, and implied weighted price, respectively.

One may argue that the contribution of yield growth might be underestimated and that of structural change overestimated. The yields of high-value varieties are usually lower compared with those of low-value, low-quality ones. Therefore, when farmers shift their production to high-value crops, the recorded yields for one crop or one category of crops go down, though actually there are no yield losses for any specific variety or crop. In this case, the same yields recorded in statistics may imply actual increases in the yields of the high-value varieties, or in some other crops in the same category, and any increase in the yield statistics may imply a higher rate of growth in reality. This argument is certainly valid. However, there are no appropriate data to estimate such changes in yield statistics, so we will just keep this in mind and make reference to the calculated contribution of structural change with caution.

From the calculation performed earlier, we can conclude that structural adjustment contributed about 40 percent to the total growth in the cropping sector during the reform era. Certainly, structural adjustment requires increases in input applications, improved technology, innovation in institutional arrangements, and so on. However, without structural adjustment, the contributions of all these factors may not materialize as efficiency gains in resource allocation, in which case they may lead only to productivity gains.

The problem with estimation of the contributions made by other sectors, such as forestry, animal husbandry, and fishery, is that their growth cannot be broken down by applying the above calculation. Therefore, a simple logic inference is used in the following analysis. As generally recognized, cropping was not only a dominant sector in Chinese agriculture but also the least profitable and slowest growing in the past. Therefore, it can be expected that if farmers were given autonomous decisionmaking power, they would shift their resources from cropping to other sectors. As a result, other sectors and agriculture as a whole would grow faster than would cropping. If we further assume that other sectors may have grown at the same rate as cropping without such adjustment, then the difference between the growth rates of cropping and agriculture as a whole can be taken as the contribution of reallocation of resources among sectors, that is, efficiency gains from intersectoral resource allocation.

However, as in the cropping sector, efficiency gains are likely to be found within each of the other sectors, because adjustment is also likely to occur within each sector. Lacking appropriate analytical tools, it is even more difficult to measure such intrasector efficiency gains resulting from structural adjustment. So it is simply assumed here that the contribution of structural adjustment within each sector is the same as that in cropping; that is, about 40 percent of the growth in each sector is attributable to intrasector structural adjustment.

Based on these assumptions, the overall contribution of structural adjustment to the growth of agriculture as a whole can be summed up as follows:

$$Con_t(\%) = Con_b(\%) + Con_c(\%) \times Con_i(\%), \tag{4}$$

where Con_t is the share of contribution to the growth of agriculture made by overall structural adjustment, Con_b is the share of contribution to the growth of agriculture made by intersector structural adjustment, Con_c is the share of contribution to the growth of agriculture made by all sectors (based on the growth of the cropping sector) without intersector structural adjustment, and Con_i is the share of contribution to the growth of each sector made by intrasector structural adjustment.

Agriculture as a whole increased by 273.7 percent, while cropping increased by 155.6 percent in 21 years if we use the same three-year moving averages. If the difference between the two is taken as the contribution of intersector structural adjustment, it was roughly 43 percent of the total, and the remaining 57 percent of total growth was contributed by growth in each sector. Again, of the remaining 57 percent of total growth, about 41 percent was contributed by intrasector structural adjustment. Therefore, the overall contribution of structural adjustment can be calculated as

$$Con_t = 43\% + 57\% \times 41\% = 43\% + 23\% = 66\%.$$

This indicates that the overall structural adjustment has contributed 66 percent to the total growth of agriculture as a whole, of which reallocation of resources among sectors was responsible for two-thirds and the rest for one-third, by means of intrasector structural adjustment.

It is hard to accurately measure the contribution of the fast growth in the nonagricultural sectors. Nevertheless, developments in three areas should not be ignored. The first is the development of TVEs. In 1978, the total annual sales of TVEs (then known as CBEs) were 43.2 billion yuan, roughly equal to 31 percent of the GOV of agriculture including cropping, forestry, animal husbandry, and fishery. However, this total increased to 11,658.5 billion yuan by 2001, equivalent to 4.5 times the GOV. If the total annual sales of TVEs had increased at the same pace as the GOV of agriculture, it would have been only 811.6 billion yuan in 2001, or only 7 percent of what was actually reached, and the difference would be 10,846.9 billion yuan.

The second development that contributed to the fast growth in the nonagricultural sectors is the growth in small-scale private business in nonagricultural sectors in the rural areas. As shown in Table 17.5, of the per capita

TABLE 17.5 Per capita net annual income of rural households in China, 1985–2001 (yuan)

Source of income	1985	1990	1995	2000	2001
Net income, by source	*397.6*	*686.3*	*1,577.7*	*2,253.4*	*2,366.4*
Wages income	72.2	138.8	353.7	702.3	771.9
Net income from household Business	295.9	518.6	1,125.8	1,427.3	1,459.6
Farming	202.1	344.6	799.4	833.9	863.6
Forestry	6.2	7.5	13.5	22.4	22.1
Animal husbandry	51.9	96.8	127.8	207.4	211.9
Fishery	3.6	7.1	15.7	26.9	28.9
Industry	2.2	9.2	13.6	52.7	54.6
Construction	7.4	12.2	34.5	46.7	45.4
Transport, postal, and telecommunication services	8.5	13.5	27.8	63.6	63.2
Wholesale and retail and catering	6.1	12.7	34.3	78.5	78.8
Social services	3.3	6.6	17.2	28.1	30.1
Culture, education, and healthcare				6.9	7.6
Other	4.7	8.5	41.9	60.1	53.4
Transfer income and property income	29.5	28.9	98.2	123.8	134.9
Grouped by type of income					
Productive income	367.7	657.4	1,479.5	2,129.6	2,231.6
Primary industry	298.3	510.9	996.5	1,125.3	1,165.2
Secondary industry	29.5	70.7	287.2	488.9	532.6
Tertiary industry	39.9	75.8	195.7	515.4	533.8
Nonproductive income	29.9	28.9	98.3	123.8	134.8

SOURCE: NBS, *China Statistical Yearbook,* 2002.

NOTE: Values are in current prices, and indexes are in comparable (or constant) prices.

net annual income from household businesses, income from the agricultural sectors was 263.8 yuan in 1985, or 89 percent of the total. Although it increased to 1,126.6 yuan in 2001, its share in the total declined to 77 percent, and the income from the nonagricultural sectors increased from 32.2 yuan in 1985 to 333.1 yuan in 2001. If the income from the nonagricultural sectors had increased at the same rate as that from agriculture, it would have been only 160 yuan in 2001, with a difference of 173 yuan per capita and a total of 137.6 billion yuan in the rural areas. Because the total revenue from household businesses is 60 percent greater than the net income, the total gains, in total sales equivalent, from faster growth in the nonagricultural sectors was thought likely to be 220 billion yuan in 2001.

The third development that contributed to growth in the nonagricultural sectors is the increasing number of outgoing laborers who have found temporary or permanent jobs outside their home villages. They may not have added output to the rural economy directly, but they have certainly contributed indirectly in many ways: the money they remitted went to financing agriculture at home, the skills and entrepreneurship acquired from outside were employed to start their own businesses at home, and the land they left behind brought about efficiency gains due to economies of scale.

The findings of the approach we have used should be interpreted carefully. In addition to the possible underestimation of contributions from productivity gains, that is underestimation of yield growth, mentioned earlier, efficiency itself should be viewed as partly relying on some factors normally contributing to productivity. Although we attempt to distinguish efficiency gains from productivity gains by breaking down output values, the contribution of R&D and the increasing use of modern inputs to efficiency gains should be kept in mind. We are trying to analyze efficiency gains resulting from diversification over more than two decades, not a once-for-all reallocation of resources based on fixed available technology. As mentioned earlier, in the long run, diversification will be available only when R&D creates new opportunities and inputs are accessible.

The approach used here breaks down sources of growth in agriculture into two broad categories: productivity and efficiency gains. Both need public and private inputs in R&D, one to increase the yield or productivity of existing crops or forms of production and the other to develop and extend new ones. Both also need institutional changes, one to improve production incentives and the other to facilitate reallocation of resources. Following decades of development, especially after China's accession to the WTO, efficiency gains will be more and more important for future growth. The development of agricultural R&D should fully reflect this trend and provide farmers with better opportunities to further diversify and reallocate their resources.

The Contribution of Diversification to Farmers' Income

Chinese farmers' income increased very rapidly during the reform era. Per capita net annual income increased from 134 yuan in 1978 to 2,366 yuan in 2001, almost 17 times in 23 years in nominal terms, or over 4 times in real terms. Compared with the increase in nominal terms, from 57 yuan in 1952 to 134 yuan in 1978 in the 26 years before the reform era, it was a very significant achievement. The growth in farmers' income resulted from both productivity and efficiency gains, that is, increases in the sources and diversification of income sources.

Restricted by the available data, the discussion here refers to farmers' income by source from 1985. The per capita net annual income of rural households increased from 398 yuan in 1985 to 2,366 yuan in 2001, or by 495 percent in 16 years, and a large percentage of these increases can be attributed to diversification. Without faster growth in incomes from the nonagricultural sectors, or conversely, if these incomes grew at the same rates as those in agriculture, farmers' net income would have increased by only 290 percent in the 16-year period in nominal terms (87.4 percent in real terms), which, albeit remarkable in international comparisons, is much less than the 495 percent actually scored (Table 17.5).

In household businesses, the income from farming increased by 327 percent during the 16 years, while that from animal husbandry and fishery increased by 308 percent and 704 percent, respectively. Thus, income from farming has been more or less constant since the mid-1990s, and all increases in incomes from household businesses thereafter have come from other sectors.

As a result of changes in the structure of total net income, the share of income from agriculture, or primary industry, declined from 75 percent in 1985 to 49.2 percent in 2001, while that from secondary and tertiary industries increased from 7.4 percent and 10 percent in 1985 to 22.5 percent and 22.6 percent in 2001, respectively (Table 17.6).

If the incomes from household businesses in farming, forestry, animal husbandry, and fishery are taken as a subgroup, the share from farming within this group declined from 83.5 percent in 1995 to 76.7 percent in 2001, while those from forestry, animal husbandry, and fishery increased from 1.5, 13.4, and 1.6 percent to 1.9, 18.9, and 2.5 percent, respectively, during those years.

If net incomes from all other sources had increased at the same speed as that from farming, which increased from 202 yuan in 1985 to 864 yuan in 2001, per capita net income would have been 1,699 yuan in 2001, almost 30 percent less than was actually earned by rural households. Therefore, it is likely that more than a half of farmers' net income today has resulted from diversification or reallocation of resources in the past 20 years or so.

Conclusion and Future Perspectives

We have used the term *diversification* here broadly to include both changes in the crop mix and structural adjustments in the economy. However, due to the dominance of cropping, especially grain production, in agriculture and the whole rural economy, any significant reallocation of resources could be defined as both structural adjustment and diversification. Instead of making a precise distinction between the two terms, we just use the simple meaning of diversification.

The improvement in resource allocation through rural diversification is likely to have had various causes, including:

1. Relaxation of controls on agricultural production and marketing, which permitted a shifting of resources to more profitable sectors and/or products.

TABLE 17.6 Composition of per capita net annual income of rural households in China, 1985–2001 (percent)

Source of income	1985	1990	1995	2000	2001
Net income, by source					
Wages income	18.1	20.2	22.4	31.2	32.6
Net income from household business	74.4	75.6	71.4	63.3	61.7
Farming	50.8	50.2	50.7	37.0	36.5
Forestry	1.5	1.1	0.9	1.0	0.9
Animal husbandry	13.1	14.1	8.1	9.2	9.0
Fishery	0.9	1.0	1.0	1.2	1.2
Industry	0.5	1.3	0.9	2.3	2.3
Construction	1.9	1.8	2.2	2.1	1.9
Transport, postal, and telecommunication services	2.1	2.0	1.8	2.8	2.7
Wholesale and retail trade and catering	1.5	1.8	2.2	3.5	3.3
Social services	0.8	1.0	1.1	1.2	1.3
Culture, education, and healthcare	0.0	0.0	0.0	0.3	0.3
Other	1.2	1.2	2.7	2.7	2.3
Transfer income and property income	7.4	4.2	6.2	5.5	5.7
Grouped by type of income					
Productive income	92.5	95.8	93.8	94.5	94.3
Primary industry	75.0	74.4	63.2	49.9	49.2
Secondary industry	7.4	10.3	18.2	21.7	22.5
Tertiary industry	10.0	11.0	12.4	22.9	22.6
Nonproductive income	7.5	4.2	6.2	5.5	5.7

SOURCE: Calculated from data in NBS, *China Statistical Yearbook,* 2002.

NOTE: Values are in current prices, and indexes are in comparable (or constant) prices.

2. Reduction and/or removal of barriers to interregional marketing, which permitted specialization in production, use of economies of scale, and cost reduction.
3. Reduction of the control on input markets, especially the labor market, which permitted better use of rural surplus laborers.
4. Changes in consumer demand, especially for farm products, which provided farmers further opportunities to shift their resources to high-value products.

In general, the market-oriented reforms of the past two decades first permitted and then stimulated rural diversification. They have brought about some fundamental changes in political, economic, and social institutions and made profit seeking and better use of comparative regional advantages possible. They have also encouraged fast growth of consumer purchasing power and the demand for high-value products.

Diversification has also reduced fluctuations in Chinese agricultural production, especially in the past two decades, by spreading risk among various types of production in any region and on each farm. The actual diversification has been accompanied by a continuing reallocation of production from relatively less suitable areas to where comparative advantages exist, after the abolition of centrally set production plans. Therefore, while grain output declined by 10 percent between 1999 and 2001, agricultural GDP was still able to increase by 5 percent during this two-year period.

China's WTO accession is likely to put heavy pressure on the country's agriculture, especially bulk commodity production. However, it may also provide it with greater opportunities to further adjust resource allocation on broader grounds through enlarged markets and higher incomes. In addition, the WTO commitments may help to further deepen the market-oriented reforms, eliminating most or all the remaining barriers to interregional trade. If accompanied by interregional trade, specialization in agricultural production may improve not only the efficiency of resource allocation and farmers' income but also the competitiveness of Chinese farm products in the world market (Zhong, Xu, and Fu 2001).

Several important policy measures are essential to realize the potential gains in rural diversification, among them furthering the market-oriented reforms and increasing and better allocating public investments in infrastructure, research and extension, information, and so on. Market-oriented reforms enable farmers to allocate their resources more efficiently, while public investments in infrastructure, research and extension, and information facilitate shifts of resources and provide new and better opportunities for structural adjustment. Above all, the creation of nonfarm job opportunities on a large scale will permit diversification of the employment of the abundant workforce to the desired level. This will require that China make the fast development of labor-intensive industries a top policy priority and coordinate various policy measures, such as technology innovation, institutional reform, public spending, and so on, to ensure its implementation. It is also essential to further reform the labor market. Only a functioning nationwide integrated labor market could facilitate reallocation of the rural workforce on a scale of millions.

Like the efficiency gains generated from other sources, those from diversification may not be distributed evenly among regions and groups of farmers. However, any development in the labor market will provide improved mobility to the rural workforce and better opportunity for them to share in the benefits of development. Therefore, labor market reform will be very important not only to fully use the workforce and better facilitate diversification and efficiency gains, but also to reduce income inequality.

18 From Plate to Plow: Agricultural Diversification in India

P. K. JOSHI AND ASHOK GULATI

The sustained growth of India's GDP at 5 to 6 percent per annum and of its per capita income at about 3.5 percent per annum over the past two decades has brought about major changes in consumption patterns across the country. Preference is shifting from basic staples toward high-value agriculture such as fruits, vegetables, and dairy, poultry, and fishery products. The dietary mix and flavor are changing fast on the plates and palates of Indian consumers.

Interestingly, this change is happening not only in the upper-income brackets of the Indian population but even below the so-called poverty line. For example, the National Sample Survey Organization (NSSO) estimates that the per capita consumption of cereals by people below the poverty line declined by 10 percent over the period 1983 to 1999–2000. On the other hand, their consumption of milk increased by 30 percent, of vegetables by 50 percent, of fruits by 63 percent, and of meat, eggs, and fish by 100 percent over the same period (Table 18.1). These percentage changes in the consumption of high-value agricultural products in the poorest segments of the population point to a silent revolution.

This revolution is also reflected in the rapidly rising exports of high-value agriculture, especially fruits and fish, during the past two decades (Figure 18.1). Given the perishable and high-value nature of these commodities, the growth in their export has strong implications not only for producers but for financiers, processors, exporters, and the retail chain industry, too. It also has repercussions for the institutional innovations that are emerging to link the plate to the plow—efforts to link changing consumer preferences and rising exports of high-value agriculture to the production decisions of the growers.

What could be driving this silent revolution? Besides rising incomes, changes in relative prices between cereals and high-value agricultural products, increasing urbanization and infrastructure, and more open trade policies are behind this changing scene (Kumar and Mathur 1996; Joshi et al. 2002; Kumar and Mruthyunjaya 2002).

Changing relative prices are resulting from a mix of technology impacts as well as changing demand pressures. While the green revolution (wheat and

384

TABLE 18.1 Annual per capita consumption of various commodities in India, by income group and urbanization of setting, 1983 and 1999–2000 (kilograms)

	1983				1999–2000			
	Lower-income group	Upper-income group	Rural	Urban	Lower-income group	Upper-income group	Rural	Urban
Cereals	147.1	194.3	181.5	141.7	132.4	154.6	157.3	131.1
Pulses	7.6	17.7	11.1	12.4	6.9	16.6	11.2	14.7
Edible oils	2.6	7.3	3.5	6.1	4.6	13.7	8.4	13.3
Vegetables	36.0	65.2	46.0	50.9	53.9	90.8	74.3	79.1
Fruits	1.6	6.4	2.8	46.2	4.2	18.2	9.6	35.6
Milk	15.7	89.7	37.0	55.5	20.5	117.2	63.3	90.7
Meat, eggs, and fish	1.9	4.8	3.9	1.4	3.8	10.6	6.7	9.5

SOURCE: Kumar and Mruthyunjaya (2002).

FIGURE 18.1 Indian exports of nontraditional crops, 1980s and 1990s

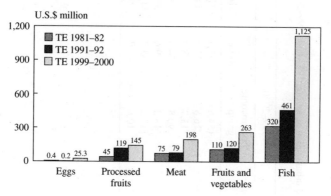

SOURCE: Joshi et al. (2002).

rice) technology was running out of steam in the 1980s, technological and marketing boosts were given to dairy products, fruits, vegetables, poultry, fish, and
so on. Thus, this high-value segment of agriculture, within and outside the crop
sector, started increasing its share. Sizable changes took place within the crop sector, with the share of foodgrains, the hallmark of food security, giving way to
high-value nonfoodgrains. From the triennium ending (TE) 1981–82 to TE
1998–99, the share of foodgrains in the value of the output of the crop sector
fell from 48 percent to 40 percent, while in terms of area it fell from 70 percent
to 65 percent over the same period (Joshi et al. 2002).

By the end of the 1990s, surpluses of cereals and storage costs were rising
rapidly and putting greater pressure on the farming community and policymakers to explore possibilities for a more remunerative and viable alternative
production mix. Diversification of agriculture in favor of noncereals and high-
value commodities such as fruits, vegetables, milk, meat, eggs, fish, and so on
continues to offer such an alternative. These commodities are also emerging as
promising sources of income augmentation, employment generation, poverty
alleviation, and export promotion (Jha 1996; Chand 1996; Vyas 1996; Delgado
and Siamwalla 1999; Ryan and Spencer 2001; Joshi et al. 2002).

Therefore, it is important to diagnose the production-consumption linkages
in the context of agricultural diversification. This requires identification of the
driving forces that alter the production portfolio and the consumption basket.

It is important to understand how the production portfolio is being transformed in response to changes in the consumption basket, in a scenario where
smallholders dominate Indian agriculture and the majority of consumers live in
rural areas. The available evidence shows that the primary production centers
of high-value commodities are largely concentrated with smallholders. There

is also evidence to show that small farm holders are relatively more efficient in producing these commodities (Jha 2001). Unfortunately, due to their tiny amounts of marketable surplus and lack of access to appropriate markets and information, their transaction costs are too high. This does not permit them to take full advantage of the changing scenario in domestic consumption patterns and rising exports of high-value products. Therefore, it is imperative to establish strong and cost-effective linkages between plow and plate and to examine the role of innovative institutional arrangements for integrating production and consumption.

In the first section of this chapter, we trace the nature of agricultural diversification in some detail, then examine what is driving that trend. Thereafter we probe consumption patterns and review the types of institutional arrangements that are emerging between growers and processors or exporters in some selected segments of Indian agriculture. In the final section we highlight some policy implications.

Agricultural Diversification in India

Our Approach

We make a shift from the usual definitions of agricultural diversification to a definition that emphasizes movement of resources from a low-value commodity mix (mainly foodgrains) to a high-value commodity mix (vegetables, fruits, livestock, fishery products, and so on).[1] The information we use is collated from three ongoing studies on (1) constraints and opportunities related to agricultural diversification in south Asia, (2) diversification in food baskets, and (3) innovative institutions for accelerating diversification on small farms. Our analysis covers the decades of the 1980s and 1990s. A comparison between the two decades is expected to provide some useful insight into the implications of economic reform for agricultural diversification and the consumption basket.

The Nature, Speed, and Determinants of Diversification

Those promoting agricultural diversification in India are gradually choosing to emphasize high-value crops and livestock activities that augment incomes rather than resorting to a coping strategy to manage risk and uncertainty. Crops, livestock, fisheries, and forestry constitute the core subsectors of agriculture. The crop subsector is the principal source of income in agriculture, followed by the livestock sector (Joshi et al. 2002). There is strong synergy in the crop and livestock subsectors, which are complementary to one another. The fishery subsector is prominent in the coastal areas, forestry in the hilly regions.

---

1. The usual definitions are (1) shift of resources from farm to nonfarm activities and (2) use of resources in a larger mix of diverse and complementary activities within agriculture.

The share of the crop subsector in the agricultural GDP marginally declined during the 1980s (from about 76.25 percent in TE 1981–82 to 73.65 percent in TE 1990–91), then slowly recovered during the 1990s (rising to 74.91 percent in TE 1998–99) (Joshi et al. 2002). This happened due to the normal monsoon rains during most of the 1990s and the greater emphasis on and higher level of production of horticultural crops. On the other hand, there was an increase in the share of the livestock subsector during the 1980s, from about 18 percent in TE 1981–82 to 23 percent in TE 1990–91. Later, though the value of livestock during the 1990s nearly doubled, its share in the sector remained stagnant at 23 percent. This was because the value of the larger crop subsector increased relatively higher than that of the livestock subsector and hence masked the latter's performance. The same was true for the fishery subsector, the value of which swelled by about 50 percent during the 1990s, though its share in agricultural GDP declined marginally, to about 1 percent in TE 1998–99 from 1.35 percent in TE 1990–91.

DIVERSIFICATION WITHIN THE CROP SUBSECTOR.   The trends show that non-foodgrain crops have gradually replaced foodgrain crops, with the area of the former increasing from about 30 percent of the total crop area in TE 1981–82 to 35 percent in TE 1998–99. This trend was more pronounced in terms of value—from about 52 percent to 60 percent (Joshi et al. 2002). Coarse cereals were mainly replaced by nonfoodgrain crops such as oilseeds, fruits, vegetables, spices, and sugarcane.

Cereals continued to dominate the foodgrain crops and accounted for more than half (53 percent) of the gross cropped area in TE 1999–2000, compared to 59 percent in TE 1981–82. Crop diversity within the cereal sector declined during the past two decades, much faster during the 1990s than in the 1980s. The sown area and production of rice, wheat, and maize increased, while the sown area of barley, millet, and sorghum decreased rapidly. The expansion of the area sown in wheat and rice was mainly on account of the availability and large-scale adoption of remunerative and stable technologies as well as favorable and assured government policies on the prices and procurement of these crops. Maize, on the other hand, emerged as an important crop mainly to meet the requirements of the booming poultry sector. The availability of improved maize hybrids, the flexibility of the maize growing season, and the diverse uses of maize were responsible for its area expansion. The crop is also finding niches in nontraditional areas (e.g., the southern part of India) and seasons (e.g., there is now winter maize). Noncereals, including pulses, were gradually moving toward nontraditional areas, too, and silently increasing.

A swift diversification of agriculture was noted in favor of oilseeds, vegetables, and fruits. Oilseed production jumped remarkably, from 18 million tons (mt) in TE 1981–82 to 30 mt in TE 1991–92, and touched 40 mt in TE 1999–2000. The annual compound growth rate of oilseed production was quite impressive, at 5.35 percent during the 1980s, which slowed down to 2.31 percent in the 1990s (Table 18.2). The sown area and production of the majority of oilseed crops increased substantially during 1980s, while in the 1990s only soybeans, coconuts, rapeseed, and seed cotton gained in area, and groundnuts, sunflower seed, and linseed lost. The remarkable success in oilseeds was a result of the Technology Mission on Oilseeds (TMO) launched by the Indian government in 1986 to meet domestic demand and control imports of edible oils. The mission encompasses a blend of improved technologies and favorable policies to augment production. Despite the acclaimed success of oilseed production, the country is not globally competitive in the edible oils sector and faces a severe threat to its domestic oilseed producers, so the tariffs on edible oils had to be raised from 15 percent to more than 70 percent during recent years. Sustaining the success of the TMO will depend on how well technical efficiencies can be increased at the production and processing levels.

During the past two decades, the sown area and production of vegetables increased considerably, with the subsector diversifying toward new areas, new crops, and new seasons. India is the second-largest producer of vegetables, next to China. Output grew at an annual rate of 2.53 percent during the 1980s, then slowed to 1.99 percent per annum in the 1990s. Yield increase contributed significantly to higher levels of production in the 1980s, while area expansion was important in the 1990s. The vegetables sector is becoming strong in the urban peripheries and emerging as an important source of income augmentation for small farm holders in water-scarce regions due to the massive subsidies extended by the government on water-saving devices (e.g., sprinkler and drip systems). In addition, the watershed programs gave high priority to vegetable production to enhance the efficiency of conservation of the scarce water in the rain-fed areas.

Fruit production (both fresh and dry) is gaining importance. Production grew at an annual rate of 6.3 percent during the 1990s, rising from about 3 percent in the previous decade (Table 18.2). A large share (approximately 60–65 percent) of increased fruit production in both decades was realized through productivity gains. Indian *desheri* and *alfonso* mangos have an excellent export market. Mango production increased by 67 percent in the 1990s, as did the production of bananas, oranges, grapes, apples, papayas, and pineapples. Dry fruits and spices also gained over the past two decades. Higher fruit production was a result of the changing diet of the high-income group and, on the supply side, of the government's initiatives in food processing. During the mid-1980s, a new ministry on food processing was set up to strengthen agroprocessing, reduce postharvest losses, and enhance value addition. Private sector participation in fruit processing is growing, though slowly.

In summary, during the 1980s, oilseeds, fruits, and vegetables performed impressively in all regions of India. While the TMO resorted to high levels of protection to encourage the expansion of oilseed production, the government opted for the establishment of the National Horticultural Board in 1984 to promote the integrated development of horticulture by coordinating, stimulating,

TABLE 18.2 Temporal changes in area and annual compound growth rates of area, production, and yield of major commodity groups in India, 1981–82 to 1999–2000

Commodity group	Average area (in thousands of hectares) in triennium ending			Annual compound growth rates (percent)					
				1981–90			1991–2000		
	1981–82	1991–92	1999–2000	Area	Output	Yield	Area	Output	Yield
Cereals	104,350	102,279	101,190	−0.20	3.32	3.53	0.20	2.22	2.01
Pulses	22,780	23,817	23,442	0.08	2.50	2.42	0.08	0.66	0.58
Oilseeds	26,675	33,004	37,471	1.79	5.35	3.50	0.94	2.31	1.36
Vegetables	5,064	5,738	6,767	0.41	2.53	1.09	1.48	1.99	−0.50
Fruits	2,239	2,638	3,567	1.04	2.98	1.92	2.38	6.30	3.83
Spices	1,627	1,848	2,142	1.45	5.13	3.64	0.55	2.73	2.17
Fiber crops	1,354	777	800	−7.43	0.53	8.61	0.87	0.91	0.04
Dry fruits	646	766	1,030	1.59	3.87	2.24	3.87	4.52	0.63
Miscellaneous	11,762	13,470	14,084	1.39			0.59		

SOURCE: Joshi et al. (2002).

NOTE: Blank cells indicate that data are unavailable.

and sustaining the production and processing of fruits and vegetables. To further promote the horticulture sector for domestic and global markets, adequate attention must be given to the development of infrastructure and effective quality control.

DIVERSIFICATION WITHIN THE LIVESTOCK SUBSECTOR. The livestock subsector is also growing rapidly. Its share in the total value of agricultural output is progressively rising (Birthal and Parthasarathy 2002). Milk accounted for around 68 percent of the total value of livestock products during the past two decades (Joshi et al. 2002). The remaining 32 percent of livestock products is distributed over several items, such as meat, poultry, wool, and so on. Milk production more than doubled, from 33 mt to 71 mt over TE 1981–82 to TE 1998–99, with an annual compound growth rate of about 4.62 percent. The growth rate of milk production was much higher, at 5.23 percent in the 1980s than in the 1990s (3.46 percent). Such a breakthrough was aided by the Operation Flood Program, which was launched to accelerate the progress and rapid development of the dairy sector.

The meat and poultry subsectors registered good performance, increasing from a low of 0.80 mt in TE 1982–83 to 2.73 mt in TE 1991–92 and finally to 4.41 mt in TE 1998–99, with an annual compound growth rate of about 5.81 percent in the 1980s vis-à-vis 3.90 percent in the 1990s. Meat's share in the value of livestock grew from 6.6 percent in 1982–83 to 8.4 percent in 1989–99 (Birthal and Parthasarathy 2002). The large increase in meat production over the 1980s was due partly to the severe drought in 1987 in most parts of the country. An acute shortage of green and dry fodder forced the disposal of less productive animals at a large scale. Poultry, too, flourished during the 1980s, with its share in the value of livestock rising from 7.8 to 9.6 percent between 1982–83 and 1998–99 (Birthal and Parthasarathy 2002). The share of poultry and goat meat in the total value of meat production went up from 66 percent to 77 percent. Similarly, egg production increased by 8.46 percent annually in the 1980s as against 4.60 percent annually in the 1990s. Unlike the dairy sector, the poultry sector grew with the help of the private sector, which controls roughly 80 percent of total production.

The future of the livestock sector is quite promising, because it still has a huge potential to raise the production, consumption, and export of different livestock commodities. Meat production, for instance, is mostly confined to the unorganized sector and is just waiting for modern slaughter facilities and the development of cold chains to take off in a big way.

DIVERSIFICATION WITHIN THE FISHERY SUBSECTOR. The fishery subsector has seen a gradual shift from marine to inland fisheries. Traditionally, marine fisheries, accounting for more than 75 percent of the total production in 1960–61, used to dominate fish production. In recognition of the importance and potential of the fish sector in the inland areas, a greater impetus was accorded to inland fisheries. The share of marine fisheries in the sector's total production fell to about 54 percent in TE 1999–2000, while that of inland fisheries rose to about 46 percent, from less than 25 percent in 1960–61. The annual compound growth rate of inland fisheries was higher, at 6.54 percent, in the 1990s than in the 1980s, when it was at 5.27 percent. Marine fish production, which performed poorly during the 1980s (0.12 percent), improved afterward (2.53 percent). The potential of inland fisheries is still higher, with well-spread locations of rivers, canals, and reservoirs.

The higher rate of growth in inland fisheries is mainly attributed to the overwhelming progress in aquaculture, in both fresh and brackish waters. The share of culture fisheries in the inland sector has gone up, from about 43 percent in 1984–85 to a high level of about 84 percent in 1994–95 (Kumar, Joshi, and Birthal 2001). The bulk of the growth in culture fisheries has come from freshwater aquaculture (Krishnan and Birthal 2000). There is good scope to expand the production of culture and other products in brackish-water areas, because only 10 percent of the available brackish-water areas (12 million ha) had been exploited by 1995–96 (IASRI 2001). The expansion of inland fisheries has also led to some negative externalities related to the degradation of arable lands due to salinity.

The remarkable progress in fisheries was the outcome of a well-knit strategy to augment production, enhance exports, and overcome the poverty of fishermen. Several production- and development-oriented programs were implemented in both marine and inland areas by the freshwater aquaculture, integrated coastal aquaculture, coastal marine fisheries, and fish farmers' development agencies established in freshwater areas and the brackish-water fish farmers' development agencies in brackish-water areas. For better infrastructure facilities, fisheries industrial estates were developed by grouping the fishing villages.

The future of the fisheries sector is bright with the opening up of the economy. There is a promising export market for both marine and inland fish and aquaculture products. In this context, sanitary and phytosanitary issues gain importance. There is a need to focus on quality control, modernize the crafts used in marine areas, and use the full potential of the inland fisheries.

Determinants of Crop Diversification

Several forces influence the nature and speed of agricultural diversification from staple food to high-value commodities. Earlier evidence suggests that the process of diversification out of staple food production is triggered by rapid technological change in agricultural production, improved rural infrastructure, and diversification in food demand patterns (Pingali and Rosegrant 1995). These are broadly classified as demand- and supply-side forces. The hypothesis in this study is that demand-side forces, including per capita income and urbanization, and supply-side forces, including infrastructure (markets and roads), technology (relative profitability and risk in different commodities), resource endowments (water and labor), and socioeconomic variables (pressure on land and literacy rate), influence agricultural diversification.

The generalized least squares (GLS) technique with a fixed-effect model is applied to examine how different forces have influenced crop diversification in India. The analysis is based on the pooling of cross-section and time-series information from major states (19 out of 28) in India for the period from 1980–81 to 1998–99.[2] The GLS technique eliminates the effect of heteroscedasticity that arises due to cross-section data and the autocorrelation that results from time-series data. The following model is used to examine the determinants of diversification:

$$D_c = f(tech, infr, prof, know, dema, rain).$$

The variables are defined as follows. The dependent variable, D_c is defined in two ways: (1) as the Simpson index of diversity in the crop sector (SID_c) and (2) as the index of the output values of horticultural commodities at constant prices, with 1980–81 used as the base year. The results for the latter were found to be statistically superior (Joshi et al. 2002) and are therefore used for discussion.

The independent variables are broadly grouped as follows: (1) technology related (*tech*), (2) infrastructure related (*infr*), (3) profitability related (*prof*), (4) resources and information related (*know*), (5) demand-side related (*dema*), and (6) climate related (*rain*). To capture their effect, a few proxy variables are used. For technology (*tech*), these include proportion of area sown in high-yielding varieties of foodgrain crops (percent), fertilizer use (kg per ha), proportion of gross irrigated area to gross cultivated area (percent), mechanization (number of tractors per 1,000 ha). For infrastructure (*infr*), the proxy variables are market density (number of markets per 1,000 ha of gross cropped area) and road length (square km per 1,000 ha of gross cropped area). The relative profitability of high-value enterprises with cereals and other crops is the proxy for the profitability-related variables (*prof*). Average size of landholding (ha) and the proportion of small landholders in total holdings are used as proxies for available resources and rural literacy (percent) for information-related variables (*know*). Urbanization (percent urban population) and per capita income (rupees per person) are used in the model as demand-side variables (*dema*). Annual rainfall (mm) is used to define the climate-related variable (*rain*) in the model.

Different combinations of independent variables have been tried to arrive at the best-fit equations. Both linear and double-log equations have been used and the best ones selected.

The study covers two decades divided into two periods—1980–81 to 1989–90 and 1990–91 to 1999–2000—for two reasons. First, historical evidence shows that the impact of the green revolution gradually faded during the 1980s.

---

2. Nineteen states in the country are categorized as major and the remaining nine states as small on the basis of geographical area, production, and population size.

TABLE 18.3 Determinants of diversification in favor of horticultural commodities in India, 1980–81 to 1999–2000 (double-log estimates of generalized least squares)

Explanatory variables	Dependent variable: Index of gross value of horticultural commodities at 1980–81 prices		
	Equation 1	Equation 2	Equation 3
Irrigation	−0.4575*** (0.0614)	−0.4697*** (0.0607)	−0.5073*** (0.0564)
Relative profitability	0.3549*** (0.04450)	0.3329*** (0.0411)	0.3152*** (0.0441)
Roads	0.2873*** (0.0664)	0.2843*** (0.0665)	—
Markets	0.1261* (0.0710)	0.1870*** (0.0528)	—
Rural literacy	−0.7976*** (0.1458)	−0.8415*** (0.1419)	−0.5497*** (0.1389)
Small landholders	1.1964*** (0.2283)	1.2016*** (0.2285)	1.6043*** (0.2002)
Urbanization	0.1840 (0.1438)	—	0.3050*** (0.1094)
Income	0.4892*** (0.0668)	0.5082*** (0.0652)	0.4671*** (0.0686)
Rainfall	−0.0583 (0.0422)	−0.0712* (0.0411)	−0.0949** (0.425)
Time dummy: 1981–90 = 0; 1991–99 = 1	0.8944*** (0.0700)	0.8839*** (0.0696)	0.8960*** (0.0722)
R-square	0.7735	0.7722	0.7572
Adjusted R-square	0.7642	0.7637	0.7490
F-statistic	82.82***	90.00***	91.40***

NOTES: The figures in parentheses are standard errors of the respective coefficients.

*** Significant at the 1 percent level.

** Significant at the 5 percent level.

* Significant at the 10 percent level.

Second, the process of economic reforms started in the early 1990s, and India bound itself to the World Trade Organization commitments, which will impact agriculture. The data for the study were collected from various published sources, especially the national statistical bulletins (CMIE 2001).

To examine the forces influencing diversification in favor of high-value commodities, explanatory variables related to infrastructure development, technology adoption, relative profitability, resource endowments, and demand-side factors including urbanization and income level were studied. The double-log estimates of generalized least squares are given in Table 18.3.

To capture the effect of infrastructure development, two important variables, namely markets and roads, were included in the model. Both variables yield positive and significant influence on the diversification of the crop sector. Obviously, better markets and road networks induce diversification in favor of horticulture, because they result in low marketing costs and easy and quick disposal of commodities. They also reduce the risk of postharvest losses of perishable commodities.

Although technology was defined by area sown in high-yielding varieties of cereals, irrigated area, and extent of mechanization, irrigated area turned out to be the most significant and represented the technological advancement in the region. The regression coefficient of this variable shows a negative relationship with diversification, which means that crop diversification in favor of horticultural commodities is declining with increasing irrigated area.

This suggests that crop diversification is more pronounced in rain-fed areas, which are deprived of technological advancement in terms of irrigation. These areas are characterized by low levels of resource endowment but with abundant labor force and were bypassed during the green revolution.

The regression coefficient is significant and positive, because obviously the higher profit of horticultural commodities would induce farmers to diversify in their favor. The relative profitability of fruits is more than 8 times higher than that of cereals, while the corresponding figure for vegetables is 4.8. However, while high profits from horticultural crops encourage their cultivation, price and yield instability limit widespread cultivation. The high price variability of fruits and vegetables is due to poor vertical linkages between production, marketing, and processing. This calls for the development of appropriate institutional arrangements for minimizing the price uncertainty, and more rigorous work needs to be done in this area.

There is a positive relationship between the growth of horticultural commodities and the proportion of smallholders. This indicates that diversification in favor of horticultural products is mostly confined to the smallholders because it is labor intensive and generates a regular flow of income. However, absence of appropriate markets and increase in supply may adversely affect the prices and opportunities for higher income (Joshi et al. 2002).

Rainfall is another variable included in the model to assess the effect of climate on crop diversification. This variable is negative and highly significant, indicating that crop diversification is limited to higher-rainfall areas. Obviously, high-rainfall areas specialize in rice, while farmers in medium- and low-rainfall areas lean toward diversification to increase their income and minimize their risk. Demand-side factors such as urbanization and per capita income also have a positive and significant impact on crop diversification.

Our discussion suggests that assured markets and a good road network could stimulate agricultural diversification in favor of high-value crops because they help maximize profits and minimize the uncertainty of output prices. Encouraging appropriate institutional arrangements for better markets through cooperatives or contract farming would go a long way toward strengthening farm-firm linkages. The role of technology also cannot be ignored. The high-yielding and more stable genotypes of fruits and vegetables need to be propagated by the development of a strong seed sector.

Diversification of Dietary Patterns

There are apprehensions that a shift in the crop portfolio from foodgrain to nonfoodgrain commodities may lead to an imbalance in dietary patterns and adversely affect food security from the nutritional point of view. However, the high-yielding nature of foodgrain crops has in fact improved availability, and production trends reveal that the per capita daily availability of foodgrains increased from 448.56 grams in TE 1981–82 to 475.4 grams in TE 1999–2000. Similarly, the per capita daily availability of milk increased substantially, from 128 grams in 1980–81 to 214 grams in 1999–2000 (India, Ministry of Agriculture, *Agricultural Statistics at a Glance,* 2002).

Income levels of consumers and urbanization are two important forces that influence dietary consumption patterns as well. Earlier studies have shown that diversification is strongly determined by these two demand forces (Joshi et al. 2002). As income increased and urbanization grew, diversification moved in favor of high-value commodities. Evidence from the consumption basket shows similar patterns across all income brackets.[3]

Consumption Patterns and Income

The level of per capita consumption of all commodities is higher in the upper-income group than in the lower-income group (Table 18.1). Consumption of fruits, vegetables, milk, meat, eggs, and fish has increased in all the groups. Even in the lower-income group, consumption of these commodities has increased markedly. On the other hand, consumption of cereals declined during the past two decades in all income groups,[4] though the pace of decline of cereal consumption was faster in the upper-income group. For example, per capita consumption of cereals in the upper-income group declined from 194.3 kg in 1983 to 154.6 kg in 1999–2000. The corresponding figures for the lower-income group were 147 kg and 132 kg. Contrary to the trend for cereals, the per capita consumption of vegetables increased from 36 kg in 1983 to about 54 kg in 1999–2000, an increase of about 50 percent. Similarly, consumption of meat, eggs, and fish doubled, from 1.9 kg in 1983 to 3.8 kg in 1999–2000.

The bottom income group, however, consumed smaller quantities of high-value commodities, although their consumption of these commodities also increased. This is an indication that the consumption baskets of poor as well as rich consumers have changed, shifting in favor of noncereals. The diversification of consumption patterns was a combined result of three different forces: (1) income effect, (2) price effect, and (3) changes in tastes and preferences.

---

3. Those below the poverty line were classified as the lower (or bottom) income group, those above the poverty line but below 150 percent of the poverty line as the middle-income group, and those above 150 percent of the poverty line as the upper-income group.

4. This may be one of the reasons for the growing buffer stock of foodgrains in the late 1990s.

The fall in the relative prices of these commodities also contributed to the increase in their consumption (Kumar and Mruthyunjaya 2002).

Consumption Patterns and Urbanization

Another important factor that determines consumption patterns is urbanization. Earlier studies have shown that urbanization has strongly influenced the diversification of agricultural production. The urbanization-induced production of high-value commodities is rapidly increasing in the periurban areas (Parthasarthy et al. 2002). The level of consumption of high-value commodities, namely fruits, vegetables, milk, meat, eggs, and fish, has been much higher in the urban areas than in the rural areas. The share of cereals, pulses, and edible oils in total expenditures increased from 41 percent in 1983 to 51 percent in 1999–2000 in the urban areas. In rural areas their share in expenditures declined from 69 percent in 1983 to 61 percent in 1999–2000. The share of fruits, vegetables, milk, meat, eggs, and fish in total expenditures increased from 41 percent in 1983 to 49 percent in 1999–2000 in the urban areas. The corresponding increase in the rural areas was from 31 to 39 percent.

Per capita consumption of cereals has declined in both urban and rural areas, with the decline steeper in the latter. On the other hand, per capita consumption of milk, vegetables, meat, eggs, and fish increased sharply in both rural and urban areas. Per capita consumption of all commodities except cereals was higher in urban areas than in rural areas. The shift in consumption patterns in favor of high-value commodities did not have any adverse effect on calorie intake. Per capita calorie intake increased marginally in rural areas, from 2,205 in 1983 to 2,332 in 1999–2000, while the corresponding increase was quite substantial in urban areas, from 1,972 in 1983 to 2,440 in 1999–2000.

In sum, the evidence we have presented reveals that income and urbanization are influencing the diversification of dietary patterns in favor of nonfoodgrain commodities and therefore toward the diversification of agricultural production. A more favorable environment for diversification toward high-value commodities will not only ease the pressure of storing huge surpluses of rice and wheat but also accelerate the growth of the agricultural sector and agricultural incomes.

Integration of Consumption and Production

Although the demand for noncereal commodities is growing fast, farmers, the majority of whom are smallholders, are constrained by high transaction costs resulting from (1) lack of access to markets, (2) limited marketable surplus, and (3) the perishable nature of their products. Due to the rising demand for high-value commodities, different forms of production-market integration are slowly emerging in the food supply chain. These include (1) spot or open market transactions, (2) agricultural cooperatives, and (3) contract farming. The features of these modes of integration are now briefly discussed.

The Spot Market

Spot or open market transactions are traditional and common in developing countries where the level of market uncertainty is high. In this model, the prices are determined by the demand and supply of the commodity under transaction. In India, the concept of spot or open markets has been initiated in some states where producers and consumers transact business without any middlemen. Ryat Bazaar in Karnataka and Apana Bazaar in Andhra Pradesh are examples of spot or open markets for fruits and vegetables. These markets provide a forum in which producers can deal directly with consumers. However, the uncertainty of prices during excess supply periods and high transport costs still persist.

The Cooperative Model

The agricultural cooperative model has overcome the problems of spot markets. In this model a group of producers with common interests own and manage production and/or marketing to take advantage of economies of scale. Cooperatives enhance the bargaining power of the producers in input and output markets, and by integrating input and output markets, they tend to reduce transaction costs. In India, one of the most successful models of a cooperative is in the dairy sector, where the breakthrough is ascribed to the implementation of the Operation Flood Program through the National Dairy Development Board (NDDB), which developed a cooperative for procuring and marketing milk and milk products. Encouraged by the success of dairy cooperatives, the NDDB has diversified its product portfolio in recent years to include fruits, vegetables, oilseeds, and plantation crops, which are sold in cooperatives developed along the lines of dairy cooperatives. In 1985, the NDDB started under the banner of SAFAL to meet the growing demand for fruits and vegetables of the Delhi metropolitan area. This is one of the largest public sector undertakings in the marketing of fresh fruits and vegetables in the world. In 1996, the company established an ultramodern 100 percent export-oriented fruit processing unit in Mumbai. At present, there are 75 associations throughout the country with a membership of 15,000 growers selling about 200 tons of fruits and vegetables every day through its 275 retail outlets in and around Delhi. This model has most benefited the smallholders in remote areas where markets for fruits and vegetables were previously absent.

Contract Farming

The contract farming model is relatively new in India. In this model, farmers are contracted to produce the commodity desired by a firm. The firm controls the production process without owning or operating the farms, while the farms are assured procurement of the output at remunerative prices. India is witnessing a silent revolution in this form of mutually beneficial integration of farm, firm, and consumer.

One successful example of contract farming is the multinational company Nestlé India Limited. Nestlé entered into the dairy business in 1961 by collecting a mere 540 kg of milk from 180 farmers in four villages and setting up a milk plant at Moga in Punjab (National Dairy Development Board 2002). By 2002 the milk collection had grown to over 650 thousand kg/day from about 90,000 farmers in about 1,600 villages in Moga and the adjoining districts of Ferozpur, Faridkot, Muktsar, and Ludhiana in Punjab. The company's success resulted from developing effective backward and forward linkages. Most of the milk comes from the small dairy producers. The company provides free veterinary aid and extension, breeding services, information on fodder production techniques, and so on for quality production.

Another successful example of the integration of production and marketing is witnessed in the poultry sector. The poultry industry grew mainly due to the strong integration of poultry producers and firms. Several poultry firms have entered into contract farming for the production, marketing, processing, and export of eggs and broiler chickens. The most important ones are Saguna Hatcheries Limited and Venkateshwara Hatcheries Limited (VHL). The latter is the leading firm in the poultry sector and has been in operation since 1971. Initially the firm was engaged in the breeding of chicks, the production of vaccines, and their sale to poultry producers. Since the early 1990s, VHL has ventured into contract broiler farming in the major poultry-producing states of Andhra Pradesh, Karnataka, and Maharashtra. VHL has its own poultry breeding farm, feed plant, vaccine manufacturing unit, and research laboratory and has developed innovative approaches to reduce transaction costs and enhance production efficiency. The consequence of contract farming in the poultry sector has been a marked increase in the production of eggs and broilers in these states.

To sum up, the integration of production and marketing is critical for high-value commodities, because they are perishable and their markets are restricted. To expand the scale of production, integrating production and marketing through cooperatives or contract farming seems to be a prerequisite.

Conclusion

India's agricultural production portfolio is gradually diversifying in favor of high-value commodities. In particular, the production of horticultural commodities, milk, meat, fish, and eggs has shown a remarkable increase during the past two decades. These commodities are well suited to the needs as well as the resources of small farm holders. Therefore, strengthening the horticulture, livestock, and fisheries subsectors would benefit them and significantly contribute to enhancing farm income, offering employment opportunities in rural areas, and meeting the food and nutritional needs of small farm holders.

The consumption basket is also diversifying in favor of high-value commodities in both rural and urban areas and across both rich and poor consumers. In the absence of appropriate integration of production, markets, and consumption, the potential of high-value commodities is yet to be fully exploited. Strengthening the integration of these three areas would promote the production of high-value commodities because of their growing demand.

To cater to the demand for these commodities in metropolitan cities, a few innovative institutional arrangements are gradually emerging in the form of cooperatives and contract farming, which benefit producers, firms, and consumers. Establishing strong farm-firm linkages strengthened both types of entities and gave them the opportunity to benefit from the expanding domestic and international markets. These kinds of arrangements need to be replicated so that more small farm holders can share the benefits of the growing markets for high-value commodities. This will have several macro-level benefits, including food management and diversification of agriculture.

In terms of policy implications, the following points are worth noting. First, greater attention needs to be given to the nongrain economy in terms of research and development (R&D) expenditure and investment in marketing, storage, and processing facilities. Although the share of the nongrain component in the total value of agriculture is already more than half, that component does not receive commensurate attention and resources. This distortion needs to be corrected.

Second, India has constrained its own potential by not changing the restrictive laws toward the development of a high-value chain in agriculture. Giving preference to cooperatives or public sector firms in the past restricted the entry of big players into the private sector. This needs to change if a revolution in the value addition process is to be unleashed. All legal impediments that restrict the entry of big private sector entities into marketing, storage, and processing facilities need to be lifted. Further, retail chain stores with foreign direct investments (FDIs) are still not permitted in accord with the recommendation of the latest government task force on FDIs.

Third, to ensure an efficient basis in the value addition process, it is necessary to withdraw the preferential treatment given to cooperatives and public sector concerns, often in the form of corporate tax exemptions, subsidized finance, and so on. This preferential treatment often drives out private sector investments. Further, major investments in retail chain stores, processing, and storage facilities would emerge if the legal environment was cleaned up and the private sector was provided with a level playing field vis-à-vis cooperatives and public sector concerns.

Fourth, it is essential to facilitate the emergence of vertical integration between farmers, processors, and retailers (farm–firm–fork linkages) in high-value agriculture. India must graduate from producing raw commodities to adding value and developing brand equity. A major role needs to be played by the private sector, the sooner the better, although it is disheartening to see that it took 10 years to delicense the dairy and sugar industries. Many others in agro-processing are still waiting for delicensing, including those involved in the processing of groundnuts and mustard oilseeds, which are reserved for small-scale industries. To ensure food safety, laws need to be duly enforced and sanitary and phytosanitary standards adopted, and it would be desirable to promote large processing facilities with state-of-the-art technology.

All these policy changes are basically in line with the emerging demand-pull forces, and therefore are likely to be more sustainable. But they need to be supplemented by some policy changes on the supply side, too. First, the land-lease market should be freed and smaller cultivators helped to increase the sizes of their operational holdings. They are efficient producers, but their transaction costs need to be cut if Indian agriculture is to remain competitive internationally.

Second, investments will have to be stepped up in basic infrastructure, such as roads and power, where the private sector is still reluctant to enter. Government programs on highways and rural roads are laudable, but reform in the power sector is another story altogether. Major institutional and price reforms are required in the power sector to plug the leakages, raise efficiency, and generate surpluses to plow back into investments. The cold storage chain, often talked about as an important form of infrastructure for high-value agriculture, cannot be developed without reforming the power sector in rural areas.

Third, the level of R&D expenditure in India, at less than 0.5 percent of agricultural GDP, is way below the 1 percent level in most developing countries. In biotechnology research, the record is even worse. The country is losing out on a revolution in biotechnology that is waiting in the wings. If the government does not have ample resources for this, the private sector could be invited in on a large scale. For this purpose, the government should put in place for biosafety appropriate regulatory institutions that are transparent and time bound.

Fourth, the Indian agricultural credit scene is contradictory: commercial banks are saddled with excess liquidity, while farmers are still relying on informal sources of finance for almost 45 percent of their requirements and at much higher rates of interest than are offered by the commercial banks. High-value agriculture needs higher amounts of working capital and also has higher risks. While schemes like the *kisan* credit cards (Gulati and Narayanan 2002a) are a step in the right direction,[5] facilitating credit through processors, input dealers, and others who are vertically integrated with the farmers for the provi-

---

5. Under this scheme, established by the government in 1998–99, farmers are eligible for production credit in the amount of Rs. 5,000 or more issued against a *kisan* card, which is valid for three years but subject to an annual review. Credit limits are fixed depending on need related to crop production, operational holdings, cropping pattern, and scale of finance. By January 2001, over 13.4 million *kisan* cards had been issued to farmers by cooperatives and regional rural banks.

sion of critical inputs or for processing their produce could increase the credit flow to agriculture greatly. These dealers or processors could act as nonbanking financial intermediaries, able to obtain refinancing from the banking sector with a margin to cover the risk of default. Such a scheme could bring about a revolution in the financing of agriculture, provided the government facilitates the entry of such nonbanking financial institutions and frees up interest rates.

19 Transaction Costs and Marketing Chain Efficiency: The Case of Tomatoes in Nanjing City

RUERD RUBEN, HUALIANG LU, AND ERNO KUIPER

Supply chains and procurement regimes for fresh vegetables in Southeast Asia are subject to profound and rapid changes. Although a major share of the produce is still sold at wet markets, urban retail networks are increasingly shifting to delivery arrangements with wholesalers and preferred suppliers. Changes in consumer preferences for quality, safety, and convenience also lead to a search for more and better-integrated supply chains. Local and international supermarkets respond to these changing shopping habits by developing direct relationships with selected producers and traders. Improving the efficiency of delivery channels could in turn provide incentives for upgrading product quality. These business networks have to establish new trust relationships that modify traditional *quanxi* practices.[1]

Transaction costs in local markets can seriously constrain efficiency. The costs of gathering information, searching for and mobilizing production factors, monitoring quality, and transporting the produce tend to raise pure production costs and could reduce the incentives for better input application (Williamson 1986; Gabre-Madhin 2001). Consequently, farmers will be reluctant to make the required investments to improve product quality. Lower transaction costs would encourage farmers to produce for the market and raise family income. Thus, lower transaction costs are useful for enhancing productivity and quality that could lead to higher farmer income and better resource management practices (North 1990). Traditional relationships between buyers and sellers based on social networks (*quanxi*) might be useful to facilitate information exchange but could also seriously hinder the dynamic performance of supply networks (Zhang and Li 2003).

Tomato producers in Nanjing can choose between different marketing outlets. Their produce can be sold at a local stall, delivered to traders on the wet market, or sold through the local wholesale market. Farmers can choose to sell

---

1. The literal meaning of *quan* is "close ties" or "critical conjuncture," while *xi* means "fasten ties."

their whole harvest or a share of their vegetable produce. Delivery conditions and quality demands tend to differ widely among these outlets, giving rise to various transaction costs relating to transportation of the product, the search for trading partners, negotiation on an acceptable selling price, and control of product quality. The three types of market outlet serve different market segments: in local markets farmers directly provide fresh products to rural villages, (semi-) urban wet markets are important retail outlets served by local traders, and wholesalers deliver to long-distance traders and supermarkets. Producer prices tend to be the highest at the local market, while the prices paid by traders and on the wholesale market are 10–35 percent lower. These price margins can be partly attributed to quality differences, because consumers are usually keen on fresh produce from the wet markets.

Through the case of tomato marketing in Nanjing, we show here how resource endowments and household characteristics influence market channel choice. We assess the performance of each type of market outlet, using a disaggregated analysis of different categories of transaction costs. Differences in prices and sold quantities are used as major indicators for supply chain efficiency. These are estimated as a hedonic process relying on Heckman's two-stage procedure (Hobbs 1997; Escobal 1999; Hualiang 2003). Finally, prices and volumes of trade are related to the transaction costs faced within each type of marketing channel. This chapter provides an opportunity to understand differences in product quality and input intensity as a function of the transaction costs met by different types of producers.

Older studies on the technological and policy strategies feasible for improving land use practices have focused on the application of better production and crop management practices (AVDRC 1998; Li et al. 1998) or on incentives to fan farmers' interest in improved production methods (Scott 1995; Hueth et al. 1999). Far less attention has been given to the options for improving coordination and trustful relationships among agents within the marketing chain as an alternative strategy for price support and quality upgrading. Reduction of transaction costs throughout the chain could indeed help control *ex ante* and *ex post* information problems and other uncertainties that hinder farmers' adoption of improved production methods (Calabresi 1969; Hobbs 1997). Consequently, with shorter search and negotiation periods and foreknowledge of prices, local farmers will be more inclined to make the investments necessary for better production practices.

We begin with a discussion of the development of tomato production and the organization of the tomato marketing system in Nanjing, which is followed by an analysis of the determinants of market channel choice to determine the importance and marginal effects of farm household characteristics such as age, gender, education, household size, assets, and distance to markets. Next we apply a hedonic price model for attributing the differences in sales prices and volumes of tomato sales to four specific categories of transaction costs: information, negotiation, monitoring, and transportation. Then we discuss the differences in transaction costs at different market outlets. The impacts of transaction costs on product quality are assessed next, and then we add some concluding notes.

Tomato Production and Marketing in Nanjing

Nanjing city is the capital of Jiangsu province. It covers an area of 6,600 km^2 and has 5.5 million inhabitants. Nanjing is one of the most important agricultural centers in the lower reaches of the Yangtze River due to its notable seasonal differences, warm and humid climate, and long frost-free periods, which encourage the production of horticulture crops. Vegetable production in Nanjing has a long history. After the 1979 reforms in China, the vegetable circulation system in Nanjing also liberalized, changing rapidly from a sellers' market into a buyers' market.

Vegetable production in Nanjing has grown very well in recent years. Between 1998 and 2001, the cultivated area in vegetables increased from 53,700 hectares (ha) to 110,100 ha, representing an annual growth rate of 27 percent. Vegetable production reached 2,480 million tons in 2001 and output value 2,318 million yuan. During those four years, production and output value recorded a 23 percent growth rate per year (Table 19.1).

With the liberalization of the marketing regime, Nanjing vegetable markets became far more competitive (Ahmadi-Esfahani and Stanmore 1997). Today, the vegetable marketing chain includes large-scale wholesale markets located in net consumption and net production areas, retail markets (mainly wet markets), and local or foreign supermarkets. Traders and transporters play an active role in all these markets. Baiyunting and Zijinshan wholesale markets serve as the main places for vegetable wholesale activities in Nanjing. These wholesale markets are mainly responsible for the supply of vegetables to Nanjing and the nearby cities in Jiangsu province, and even for Shanghai.

The wet markets, including indoor and open-air markets, are spread throughout Nanjing and represent the most important retail outlets. Ninety

TABLE 19.1 Development of vegetable production in Nanjing city, 1998–2001

Year	Area (thousand ha)	Output (million tons)	Value (million yuan)
1998	53.7	1,339.0	1,240.0
1999	69.5	1,648.0	1,647.0
2000	104.7	2,125.0	2,076.0
2001	110.1	2,479.5	2,318.0
Growth rate (percent)	27.0	22.8	23.2

SOURCE: China, Nanjing Agricultural and Forestry Bureau (2002).

percent of the vegetables in Nanjing are sold through these markets. Some 50 different vegetable varieties are sold. Supermarkets are a relatively new development, offering guaranteed sanitary conditions and introducing relatively new and luxury varieties as well as conveniently prepacked and processed vegetables. There are about 10 large supermarket chains present in Nanjing, accounting for less than 5 percent of the vegetables sold.

The technologies used for tomato production are still rather traditional, although some new technologies have been introduced recently. In Maqun township, farmers use small shelters for tomato production to enable early harvesting and obtain a higher market price. Small quantities of pesticides are used in tomato production to reduce the incidence of wild grasses, although most farmers use organic manure. Farmers find it difficult to access good-quality seed.

We collected data from a random sample of 86 farm households in Maqun township of Qixia district in Nanjing, where all farmers have been producing tomatoes for more than 20 years. Their average age is 50 years, because most young people prefer nonfarm activities in the nearby urban area. The farmers rely on three different marketing channels:

1. Direct sales to consumers, either through a stall at the wet market or through bilateral exchange ($N = 46$).[2]
2. Sales transactions with traders who purchase the produce at the stall or deliver it to local institutions, called Dui trade ($N = 20$).
3. Delivery to the local wholesale market ($N = 20$).

Direct sale is considered the most convenient outlet for resource-poor farmers without any means of transportation. The wet market is usually far from the production area, and most farmers have only a bicycle. Female sellers face more difficulty in transporting tomatoes to the wet market. Usually females have more time and bargaining power and can therefore negotiate better prices with traders at the wholesale market, where often more time is needed before buyer and seller reach an acceptable agreement. About 30 percent of the respondents possessed a fixed stall at the wet market. Most of them sold their tomatoes directly to consumers, but some also sold part of the produce to traders. The stall fee for selling at the wet markets was relatively expensive (5–10 yuan/day), but ownership of market stalls facilitates more permanent relations with traders. The stall fees, which are high when compared to the volume of transactions, can be a prohibitive entry cost. Because not all farmers produce enough vegetables to deliver daily, only a few are able to maintain a fixed stall. Consequently, retailers today occupy a large number of the stalls. Farmers who are engaged in wholesale transactions maintain this channel as an exclusive outlet.

---

2. N indicates the number of the different types of market included in our sample.

TABLE 19.2 Tomato production and exchange characteristics in Nanjing city, 2002

Marketing chains	Average tomato area		Average farm size		Distance to market		Average yield		Average price	
	Mu	SD	*Mu*	SD	Km/min	Min	Kg/*mu*	SD	Yuan/kg	SD
Direct sale	0.66	0.53	2.5	1.06	10.8	58.0	3508.3	2225.3	1.18	0.14
Sale to trader	0.71	0.6	2.5	0.89	12.0	58.5	3803.5	2907.4	1.08	0.11
Wholesale	0.78	1.31	3	2.17	2.3	20.5	3056.5	2514.5	0.76	0.97
Total	0.7	0.78	2.6	1.37	9.2	49.4	3461.4	2457.7	1.06	0.15

SOURCE: Authors' survey of the Nanjing vegetable marketing chain.
NOTE: SD, standard deviation.

Tomato fields in Maqun township are dispersed and small in size (Table 19.2). Most farmers posses about 2.5 *mu* (0.17 ha) of farmland and cultivate several vegetable varieties so they can harvest during the whole year, earning regular income streams for their daily needs and insuring themselves against various risks.

The average tomato cultivation area is about 0.7 *mu* (0.05 ha). Producers linked to the wholesale market have slightly larger farms but are less specialized in tomato production, while farmers selling at the farm gate or to traders devote about a quarter of their field to tomatoes. Tomato yields are significantly higher for farmers engaged in direct sales and sales to traders. Prices are significantly different for the three tomato marketing chains. The price the farmers receive from direct sale is the highest (1.18 yuan/kg), while prices received from traders or at the wholesale markets are 8 and 35 percent below the direct sales price.

The three types of market outlet differ in access and price conditions. The average distance to the market is about 9 km. The wholesale market is located nearby, while the wet market is farther away. Different negotiation procedures are common to each of the marketing chains. Direct sellers have the shortest negotiation time. Consumers buying tomatoes at the wet market care more about quality and less about price, while farmers operating at the wet market are usually better informed about market prices. Traders operating at the wholesale market offer lower prices because they buy large quantities. The wholesale market is a buyers' market where prices tend to be depressed and the negotiation time that much longer. Another difference in the marketing process accrues from the time and space available for transactions. Due to long travel times and the small transaction size of each consumer, farmers usually need the most time (up to 8 hours) for the wet market, while for the wholesale market they need only 2.5 hours a day for all transactions.

Market Outlet Choice

The selection of appropriate marketing outlets for different types of producers is supposed to be largely dependent on the household and farm characteristics that determine the production scale and the quality of the output. Availability and technical qualifications of the labor force, distance to the market, and access to means of transportation and market stalls are important for timely delivery of high-quality produce. Farmers mention higher price and less friction as major reasons for direct selling at the wet market, while lower risk and larger volume are considered the main advantages of the wholesale market. A fixed stall at the wet market shortens negotiation time and raises the price received, and having one's own means of transport could reduce marketing time and permit larger sales.

We used a multinomial logit model to capture the effects of farm household characteristics and resource endowment on their choice of different tomato marketing chains (Cramer 1991). The model is specified as follows:

$$P(MC_{ji}) = \frac{\exp(\beta_j' x_i)}{\sum\limits_{j=0}^{2}\exp(\beta_j' x_i)},$$

where

i represents the ith farmer ($i = 1, 2, \ldots , 86$);

j represents different marketing chains, $j = 0$ for sale to traders at the wet market, $j = 1$ for direct sale to consumers at the wet market, and $j = 2$ for sale to traders at the wholesale market;

P represents the probability that tomato marketing chain j will be chosen by farmer i;

MC_{ji} means that tomato marketing chain j is chosen by farmer i; and

x_i represents farm household characteristics (age, gender, education, family size, means of transport, market stall, market distance).

To find the marginal effect, δ, of a given attribute x on the probability of a household's choosing marketing chain j, a vector of partial derivatives of the probabilities to the attributes can be specified as

$$\delta_j = \frac{\partial P(MC_{ji})}{\partial x} = P(MC_{ji})[\beta_j - \sum\limits_{j=0}^{2} P(MC_{ji})(\beta_j)].$$

The effects of farm household characteristics and resource endowments on the choice of direct sale to consumers or to wholesalers (compared to the trader outlet) are reported in Table 19.3. We find a negative relationship between family size and direct sales to consumers at the wet market. This means that

TABLE 19.3 Determinants of tomato marketing chain choice in Nanjing city, 2002

Variable	Direct sale Coefficient (SE)		Wholesale Coefficient (SE)	
Constant	4.3493	(2.8005)	1.7469	(4.4549)
Gender of household head	−0.7467	(0.6891)	−2.3592*	(1.2232)
Age of household head	−0.0227	(0.0396)	0.0891	(0.0827)
Education of household head (years)	0.0053	(0.0918)	0.0835	(0.1590)
Total number in farm household	−0.5034**	(0.2389)	−0.1357	(0.3564)
Own transportation (value >1,000 yuan)	−0.5525	(0.8665)	5.2572*	(2.7578)
Fixed stall at wet market	1.3103*	(0.6697)	−3.0878**	(1.5209)
Distance to the market	−0.0262	(0.0427)	−1.4485**	(0.5717)

Number of observations	86		Chi square	75.6197
Log likelihood function	−49.3172		Degrees of freedom	14
Restricted log likelihood	−87.1271		Significance level	0.0000

SOURCE: Authors' survey of the Nanjing vegetable marketing chain.
NOTES: SE, standard error.
** Significant at the 5 percent level.
* Significant at the 10 percent level.

larger families will not choose to sell at the wet market, probably because their household income tends to be more diversified through the engagement of other family members in off-farm employment. These households have less time available for the wet market and prefer to rely on wholesalers due to the time saved.

Farmers with a fixed stall sell their tomatoes almost exclusively at the wet market and mostly to consumers directly, because paying the rent for the stall is an investment that reduces their options.

Transactions on the wholesale market are mostly conducted by females and are more likely to be conducted by households with their own means of transportation and when the wholesale market is closer. Farmers using the wholesale market outlet produce tomatoes on a larger scale and thus cannot rely on the wet market.

Marketing channel choice is also related to the production system's characteristics. Farmers relying on the wholesale market outlet tend to cultivate larger areas and use more fertilizers in tomato production. Given their yields, they prefer selling on a larger scale, even at a lower price.

Transaction Costs in Tomato Chains

Marketing of tomatoes is a complex process that involves various types of transaction costs. Depending on the outlet choice, costs are incurred for transporting the produce, visiting different traders to know the ruling price, negotiating the price, and maintaining regular contacts with traders to monitor the market. The level and composition of these transaction costs determine the efficiency of the tomato chain.

Following Escobal (1999), we used an indirect procedure for quantifying the observable attributes of transaction costs. Two possible transactions (T^1 and T^2) are considered. The one with lower transaction costs (TC) will occur as follows:

$$T^*T^1, \text{ if } TC^1 < TC^2, \text{ or } = T^2, \text{ if } TC^1 \geq TC^2. \qquad (1)$$

Although TC^1 and TC^2 are not directly observable, it is enough to observe vector X, which represents observable attributes that affect transaction costs:

$$TC^1 = \beta_1 X + \varepsilon_1 \; TC^2 = \beta_2 X + \varepsilon_2. \qquad (2)$$

Empirically, the probability of observing T^1 would be equivalent to

$$prob(TC^1 < TC^2) = prob(\varepsilon_1 - \varepsilon_2 < (\beta_2 - \beta_1)X). \qquad (3)$$

Transaction costs decide which rural households will participate in what kind of market. The degree of risk aversion and profit maximization determines the choice of the marketing chain. Different transaction costs between market chains can help to explain their preference. If p is the effective price that determines production and consumption decisions, each household faces the following conditions:

supply of product, or $\qquad\qquad\qquad\qquad\qquad q = q(p, z^q),$ (4)

demand for product in market j, or $\qquad\qquad c^j = c^j(p^j, z^{dj}),$ (5)

idiosyncratic transmission of prices in market j, or $p^{sj} = p^{sj}(z^{pj})$, and (6)

transaction costs in market j, or $\qquad\qquad TC^j = TC^j(z^{ij}),$ (7)

where z^q, z^{dj}, z^{pj}, and z^{ij} are exogenous variables that affect supply, demand, sales price, and transaction costs, respectively. Thus, for the retailers of a product in market j, the effective price at the level of each household would be

$$p^j = p^{sj}(z^{pj}) - TC^j(z^{ij}). \qquad (8)$$

The condition of being a retailer of agricultural product in market j would be

$$q \lfloor p^{sj}(z^{pj}) - TC^j(z^{ij}), z^q \rfloor \; \chi \lfloor p^{sj}(z^{pj}) - TCuj(z^{ij}), z^{dj} \rfloor > 0$$
$$\text{or } I(z^q, z^{dj}, z^{pj}, z^{ij}) > 0. \qquad (9)$$

The model can be estimated using the following *probit* equation:

$$prob(\text{net seller in market } j) = prob[I(z^q, z^{dj}, z^{pj}, z^{ij}) > 0]. \qquad (10)$$

This model can make an estimation based on a probit or logit specification, depending on whether we are dealing with two or more destinations. A two-limit

Tobit model can also be used to estimate the participation of a trader in sales in each market as the base and take into account that the endogenous variables are between 0 and 1.

After estimating the model in equation 10, the reduced form of the equation of supply conditioned on the selected strategy can be derived as follows:

$$q = q(p, z^q | prob \, [\text{net seller in market } j]). \tag{11}$$

The estimation of equation 11 equals the estimation in two stages, where the inverse Mills ratio (IMR) is introduced to take into account the endogenous nature of the decision (sell to consumer directly at the wet market or also at other markets).

A hedonic price procedure is used to associate transaction costs to the effective price each farm household receives (Rosen 1974). Hence, the average price can be defined as a function of hedonic prices, which is simply the mathematical relationship between the prices received by this added value and the characteristics of the transaction associated with the product. This is

$$p_j = h(z_{1j}, z_{2j}, z_{3j}, \ldots, z_{kj} | prob \, [\text{net seller in market } j]), \tag{12}$$

where p_j is the average price obtained by the jth farm household for the vegetable sale $z_{1j}, z_{2j}, z_{3j}, \ldots, z_{kj}$ represents the vector of characteristics associated with the transactions completed by the farm household.

Heckman's (1979) two-stage procedure is applied to this estimation to avoid selectivity bias in the marketing chain choice strategy. At the first stage, a probit analysis is used to determine the probability of a farm household's choosing a certain marketing chain. Thereafter, the IMR is calculated, representing the conditional probability of the household's choosing this marketing outlet. At the second stage, the IMR is taken as an explanatory variable to control for selectivity bias. A significant coefficient for the IMR indicates that the differences registered in received prices depend on the marketing strategy adopted.

We used a composite of various indicators to disentangle the effects of different components of transaction costs on differences in sales prices and volumes sold. The four categories of transaction costs included are as follows:

1. Transportation costs, depending on distance, time, road conditions, and availability of one's own transport.
2. Information costs, depending on the number of visits before selling the produce and the sources of access to market information.
3. Negotiation costs, related to the number of visits required to reach agreement on the selling price.
4. Monitoring costs, related to the number of years that the farmer has been engaged with the trader or consumer.

TABLE 19.4 Determinants of tomato direct sales in Nanjing city, 2002 (probit estimate)

Explanatory variables	Coefficient	Standard error
Constant	0.7866	(1.057)
Gender of household head (male = 1)	−0.4625	(0.074)
Age of household head (years)	0.0174	(0.019)
Total tomato area (*mu*)	0.1018	(0.271)
Using chemical fertilizers? (Yes = 1)	0.6341*	(0.368)
Average distance to sale point (km)	0.0225	(0.024)
Negotiation time to reach a price (number of visits)	−1.1528**	(0.227)
Number of observations	86	
Adjusted R squared	0.44	

SOURCE: Authors' survey of the Nanjing tomato marketing chain.
** Significant at the 5 percent level.
* Significant at the 10 percent level.

Appendix 19A reports the descriptive statistics of the data on tomato production and sale in Nanjing city.

Table 19.4 reports the results of a probit model estimated using equation 10. This will serve as the basis for both the supply and price equations.

We find a negative relationship between the negotiation time required to reach agreement on the price for farmers choosing to sell their tomatoes directly on the wet market. This means that when farmers want to economize on negotiation costs they prefer the direct marketing channel. There is also a positive relationship between chemical fertilizer use and farmers' choosing the wet market. This indicates reliance on more input-intensive practices that guarantee better tomato quality.

Tables 19.5 and 19.6 summarize the estimation results of equations 11 and 12. The supply equation can be interpreted as a reduced form of the model. In both equations, the IMR is significant, indicating that there are relevant differences in prices and sales volumes depending on the marketing outlets selected by farmers. Hence, the prices received and volumes traded by the farmers are significantly different in each of the marketing supply chains. The price and sale volumes are thus not only dependent on farm household characteristics, but also influenced by transaction costs.

The sales price is positively influenced by the age of the household head, the number of years the farmer has known the traders (related to monitoring and negotiation costs), and the average time needed to reach the market (related to transport costs). The use of fertilizers is not directly reflected in a higher sales price, nor does the possession of a fixed stall at the wet market automatically improve the price received. This is already an indication that differences in trans-

TABLE 19.5 Determinants of tomato sales price in Nanjing city, 2002 (ordinary least squares estimation of sales price)

Explanatory variables	Coefficient	Standard error
Constant	1.304***	(0.107)
Inverse Mills ratio	0.160***	(0.035)
Age of household head (years)	0.004**	(0.002)
Using fertilizer? (Yes = 1)	−0.075**	(0.036)
Fixed stall at the wet market? (Yes = 1)	−0.070*	(0.038)
Number of years producing tomatoes (years)	−0.005**	(0.002)
Total tomato production (kg)	−0.00001*	(0.000)
Access to information from trader? (Yes = 1)	−0.085**	(0.042)
Number of years having known the trader (year)	0.053**	(0.027)
Average time to reach the market (minutes)	0.002***	(0.0006)
Price below the market average level? (Yes = 1)	−0.372***	(0.035)
Ratio of marketing effectiveness	−0.004***	(0.001)
Inverse Mills ratio * price below the market average price	−0.149**	(0.061)
Number of observations	86	
Adjusted R squared	0.768	

SOURCE: Authors' survey of the Nanjing vegetable marketing chain.

NOTES: Ratio of marketing effectiveness = number of traders with transactions / number of trader contacts.

*** Significant at the 1 percent level.

** Significant at the 5 percent level.

* Significant at the 10 percent level.

action costs might be more important than price differences. The number of years a household is involved in tomato production and the total tomato volume together work to depress the price.

The traded volume is positively influenced by the education level of the household head, the total area of tomato production, and the number of traders who buy from the same farmer (related to monitoring and negotiation costs). More tomato trade takes place when a long-term relationship between the farmer and the trader exists (related to monitoring and negotiation costs) and when better road conditions (related to transport cost) are available. Scarcity of market information has a negative effect on the amount sold to the market. The percentage not sold (produce remaining after market closure) and the percentage of product denial (due to inferior quality performance) also reduce the total traded volume.

Disaggregation of Transaction Costs

We distinguished earlier between different types of transaction costs related to the activities of transport, information search, monitoring, and negotiation. For

TABLE 19.6 Determinants of tomato sales volume in Nanjing city, 2002 (ordinary least squares estimation of sales volume)

Explanatory variables	Coefficient	Standard error
Constant	−76.42	(241.88)
Inverse Mills ratio	303.11**	(129.54)
Education level of household head (years)	43.76**	(16.93)
Total area of tomatoes (*mu*)	1587.64***	(101.90)
Number of traders to whom farmers sell	71.58**	(27.21)
Number of years knowing the trader (years)	303.06***	(110.64)
Average condition of road (good = 1)	713.05***	(220.87)
Percentage not sold	−26.28**	(10.98)
Percentage of waste	−43.39**	(17.91)
Total volume × average distance to market	0.02***	(0.002)
Condition of road × average distance to market	−63.13***	(12.44)
Price below average market price × ratio of marketing effectiveness	−17.20***	(5.58)

Number of observations	86	
Adjusted R squared	0.915	

SOURCE: Authors' survey of the Nanjing vegetable marketing chain.

NOTES: Ratio of marketing effectiveness = number of traders with transactions / number of trader contacts.

*** Significant at the 1 percent level.

** Significant at the 5 percent level.

each of the market outlets, the structure of transaction costs reveals the efforts made in delivering the produce, finding the appropriate trade partners, reaching an acceptable price agreement, and controlling the product standards. The further disaggregation of the transaction costs, using estimations presented in Tables 19.5 and 19.6 as a base, will enable us to identify the reductions in sales price and traded volumes attributable to these specific operations.

Figure 19.1 shows the discounts in the price farmers received due to the transaction costs incurred, which suggest that prices could have been, on average, 26 percent higher if farmers had not incurred any transaction costs. Transactions based on direct sales face the largest price discount. Negotiation costs are higher for direct sales, whereas sales to traders and at the wholesale market incur more information costs.

The most important transaction costs are associated with information and negotiation procedures, which account for about 20 percent and 16 percent of the total price discount, respectively. Due to the limited development of local organizations and information networks, farmers face major difficulties in receiving adequate services and market information. Hence, they can obtain this

FIGURE 19.1 Effects of transaction costs on tomato prices in Nanjing city, 2002

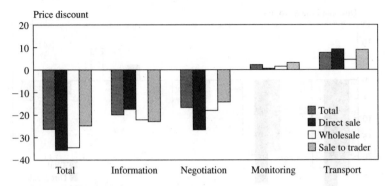

SOURCE: Authors' compilation based on survey data.

information only by making frequent visits to traders or maintaining intensive contacts with neighbors. Maintaining a fixed stall at the wet market clearly reduces information costs but raises fixed investments. Farmers with a stall need to sell all their tomatoes during a short period and therefore face higher negotiation costs that tend to reduce their margin.

Monitoring and transportation costs appear to have a positive effect on the price received. The positive effect of monitoring costs is surprising, but perhaps explained by the fact that farmers had already made the effort to establish long-term relationships with traders, resulting in a higher current price that compensates for the previously incurred costs. Such long-term relations are more commonly associated with sales to traders and wholesalers. Transport costs usually reduce the price, but this depends as much on the competitive conditions. Prices paid at the wet markets for direct sales or for transactions with traders are substantially higher than those at the wholesale market. Therefore, higher transport costs are more than compensated by the higher prices that are received in distant markets, encouraging farmers to travel a long distance to get a better price.

In summary, we see that the direct marketing chain faces the highest negotiation cost, while sales to traders and wholesalers have the most information costs. Farmers who sell their tomatoes at the wet market have to negotiate the price with each individual customer, and although each transaction may be short, the time involved for all transactions would add up to a high total cost. Farmers selling their tomatoes to traders at the wet market or wholesale market have to collect more information about the marketing situation to be able to deal with the traders, which greatly increases their information costs and results in a larger price discount.

FIGURE 19.2 Effects of transaction costs on tomato volumes in Nanjing city, 2002

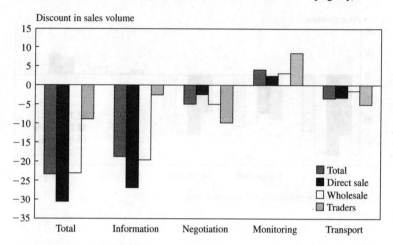

SOURCE: Authors' compilation based on survey data.

The analysis of the impact of transaction costs on the sales volume is based on the supply function (Table 19.6). The total quantity sold could have been nearly 24 percent higher if transaction costs had not been incurred (Figure 19.2).

Information costs are by far the most important factor affecting sales volume. This is again related to the limited development of commercial organizations and market facilities. Negotiation and transportation costs represent up to 15 percent of the volume discount. Monitoring costs have a positive effect on sales volume. Information costs strongly reduce the sales volume, because the usual large fluctuations at the wet market require farmers to collect information frequently. Negotiation and transportation costs are the most important costs affecting the sales volume in sales to traders. Marketing through traders involves traveling a longer distance to reach the wet market, and consequently more time is required to sell all the produce. Monitoring costs had a positive effect on sales volume in the study. This may again be related to the trust involved in more permanent trading relationships.

In summary, direct marketing involves most transaction costs and thus results in high discounts in the sales volume, while sales to traders meet with the lowest transaction costs. Information costs are most important in discounting sales volume within the direct and wholesale channels, while negotiation costs are most relevant for marketing transactions with traders.

The aggregate effect of transaction costs on sales value (Figure 19.3) reveals that estimated sales value was on average 44 percent lower due to transaction costs and that farmers involved in direct sales are the most affected. Informa-

FIGURE 19.3 Effects of transaction costs on tomato sales value in Nanjing city, 2002

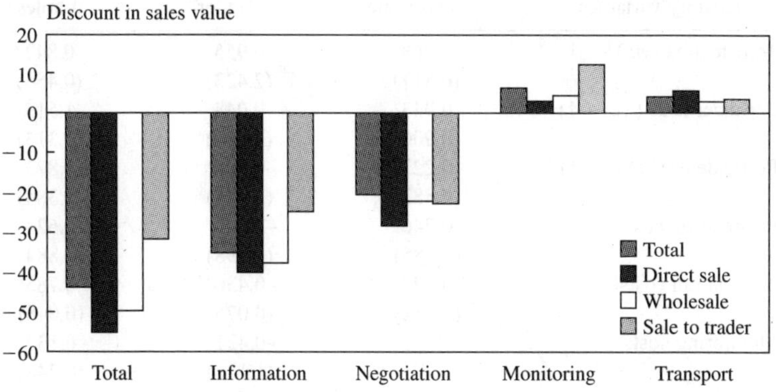

Discount in sales value

Legend:
- Total
- Direct sale
- Wholesale
- Sale to trader

Categories: Total, Information, Negotiation, Monitoring, Transport

SOURCE: Authors' compilation based on survey data.

tion costs proved to be the most important category, followed by negotiation costs. Information and negotiation costs have a strong negative effect on tomato sales values; the former affect both price and volume, whereas the latter affect price. Nearly all transaction costs have the strongest effects on the direct marketing chain, with the sole exception of transportation costs, which tend to be lower for this channel.

Transaction Costs and Quality Performance

Transaction cost analysis can also be used to identify how market and institutional reforms could contribute to improved resource management or quality upgrading. A reduction in transaction costs could provide important incentives for the intensification of resource use in vegetable production (Ruben, Wesselink, and Saenz 2001).

Intensification of resource use could lead to higher yields and better vegetable quality. Tomato yield and color tend to be positively influenced by fertilizer application, while reduced pesticide use enhances quality but may lead to preharvest losses. Consumers at the wet market are usually more concerned about quality and are willing to pay a higher price for higher-quality produce. Efforts to cover inferior quality through postharvest pesticide applications could lead to product denial. Farmers care most about pesticide use if they want to sell tomatoes at the wet market, because direct consumers are generally more concerned about tomato quality.

The impact of different transaction costs on tomato quality is assessed with an ordinary least squares regression analysis and presented in Table 19.7.

TABLE 19.7 Factors influencing tomato quality in Nanjing city, 2002

Explanatory variables	Direct sale	Trader	Wholesale
Tomato area (*mu*)	−1.268	0.955	−0.842*
	(0.817)	(2.423)	(0.455)
Fertilizer use? (Yes = 1)	0.943	−0.048	1.515
	(0.900)	(3.290)	(1.313)
Pesticide use? (Yes = 1)	−0.223	−6.580*	−1.873
	(0.882)	(3.058)	(1.384)
Information costs	−0.746	−3.320	−0.624
	(0.785)	(6.398)	(0.884)
Negotiation costs	−0.597***	−0.436***	−0.785***
	(0.032)	(0.075)	(0.048)
Monitoring costs	—	−0.421	−0.137
		(1.118)	(0.748)
Transport costs	−0.005	−0.006	0.091**
	(0.012)	(0.051)	(0.042)
Adjusted R squared	0.899	0.683	0.964

SOURCE: Authors' survey of the Nanjing vegetable marketing chain.
*** Significant at the 1 percent level.
** Significant at the 5 percent level.
* Significant at the 10 percent level.

Nearly all kinds of transaction costs have a strong negative effect on quality performance (measured as product denial). If more time is required to find the appropriate trading partners and negotiate an acceptable price, bargaining power is affected and selectivity regarding tomato quality will increase. A 1 percent reduction in negotiation costs could lead to an improvement of quality by 4–8 percent. Transport costs hardly influence tomato quality on the wet market, whereas rapid and timely delivery is highly appreciated at the wholesale market. Even though this market is closer than the wet market, inferior-quality tomatoes are sometimes not even sold at the wet market. Consequently, the percentage of tomato denial is substantially lower for the wholesale market.

The greatest margins for quality improvement through better negotiation are available at the wholesale market. This is precisely the market segment where local supermarkets today purchase the major share of their vegetables, usually in bulk volumes delivered by medium- and large-scale producers. These suppliers tend to rely more on pesticides to reduce labor costs for manual pest and disease control. Once farmers are involved in direct trade, they are more inclined to reduce pesticide applications, because this leads to higher negotiation costs at the market, given the increased risk of product denial when traders or consumers recognize the pesticides and classify the produce in a lower category.

Negotiation costs also have a significant negative impact on fertilizer use, especially in the direct sales channel. Negotiations regarding the delivery conditions between farmers and traders or consumers are more complex when transactions are conducted for smaller quantities and at an irregular frequency. If these negotiation costs can be reduced, farmers may become more inclined to apply the required amounts of fertilizers in order to achieve high tomato quality.

Conclusion

The empirical results of our study reveal that transaction costs in the sample area are almost 27 percent of sale price, 23 percent of sales volume, and up to 44 percent of sales value. Direct sales to consumers incur the highest transaction costs but are nevertheless the preferred marketing regime for most tomato producers and consumers. Several factors explain this.

First, farmers operating at wet markets can traditionally rely on a wide network of personal relations with customers who are able to directly verify the origin of the produce and its quality characteristics. This provides farmers involved in direct sales a comparative advantage that is reflected in substantially lower information and monitoring costs for price determination and quality control. However, given the large number of relatively small transactions, information costs are high with respect to the traded volume.

Second, the current market situation for vegetables is rapidly shifting toward complete liberalization. Private small-scale vegetable production received an early stimulus in Chinese agrarian policies during the "start-to-develop" period (1949–58), when farmers were allowed to sell their produce freely in the local markets. However, during the period of strict economic planning (1959–81), only state-owned companies were entitled to trade in vegetables. With the introduction of the Household Responsibility System in the early 1980s, vegetable production substantially increased. In addition, aspects of quality, variety development, greenhouse production, and improved technologies for disease control received major attention. From 1985 onward, the Vegetable Basket Project, which aimed at improving the vegetable circulation regime, was implemented. During the 1990s, vegetable production further expanded due to the favorable market prices of horticultural crops compared to cereals. Consumption increased at an even higher rate, although the vegetable market is gradually shifting from a sellers' to a buyers' market. Consequently, consumers have a larger choice between different market outlets and are in a better position to select the quality they require.

Third, transactions with traders, wholesalers, and supermarkets suffer from higher transaction costs relating to price information and quality monitoring, but compare favorably with the direct sales channel in negotiation costs and traded volumes. The expected growing importance of supermarkets in vegetable retail—now representing less than 5 percent of the tomato market—will probably lead to greater attention to the product quality, timely delivery, and longer shelf life of vegetable products. Also, preferred-supplier arrangements may be made with a selective group of larger producers to reduce information costs. These arrangements could include detailed provisions regarding seed material, required fertilizer and pesticide applications (with regular inspection), and delivery dates for specified amounts and qualities of products at a fixed price.

The economic transition in the Chinese vegetable markets calls for accompanying adjustments in market integration. Information and negotiation costs represent a major share of all transaction costs and can be reduced only when improved market information systems are put in place. The lack of price transparency and the exclusive reliance on personal trust can seriously hamper fluid transactions (Sternquist and Chen 2006). When product quality, safety and health attributes, freshness, frequency of delivery, and convenience become more important criteria, we may expect consumers to demand more reliable product standards and transparent tracking and tracing regimes. Reducing these information barriers and costs only within social networks and through *quanxi* relations is unlikely to lead to more transparent markets. The alternative of developing vegetable auctions can be explored to reduce negotiation costs.

Policies and incentives for quality improvement in tomato supply chains may focus on reducing transaction costs as a feasible strategy for optimizing production systems and enforcing product and process standards. Because the product quality (and safety) of vegetables are highly sensitive to negotiation costs, labeling and certification of products will certainly lead to more stringent production procedures. Increasing market competition, improved transparency of market conditions, and institutional and market reforms will further spur quality upgrading.

Appendix 19A: Supplementary Table

TABLE 19A.1 Descriptive statistics on tomato production and sale in Nanjing city, 2002

Variable	Direct sale	Trader	Wholesale	Sign difference
Farm household characteristics				
Gender of household head	0.56	0.75	0.40	2.56*
	(0.50)	(0.44)	(0.50)	
Age of household head	50.93	52.1	47.4	1.36
	(9.39)	(8.06)	(11.4)	
Education of household head	7.11	6.85	6.50	0.17
	(3.30)	(4.59)	(4.46)	
Family size	*3.48*	*4.30*	4.05	2.88*
	(1.17)	(1.49)	(1.70)	

Variable	Direct sale	Trader	Wholesale	Sign difference
Means of transport	0.17	0.25	0.30	0.69
	(0.38)	(0.44)	(0.47)	
Fixed stall	*0.48*	*0.20*	0	9.79***
	(0.51)	(0.41)	(0)	
Time to market (minutes)	*58.0*	58.5	*20.5*	13.17***
	(34.8)	(26.1)	(8.09)	
Distance to market (km)	*10.85*	12.00	*2.30*	12.90***
	(8.39)	(6.42)	(1.08)	
Production characteristics				
Tomato area (*mu*)	0.66	0.71	0.78	0.15
	(0.53)	(0.60)	(1.31)	
Tomato production (kg)	2310.87	2996.75	2368.75	0.21
	(1922.47)	(2395.99)	(2694.50)	
Chemical fertilizers	0.63	0.65	0.55	0.25
	(0.49)	(0.49)	(0.51)	
Pesticides	0.63	0.65	0.50	0.60
	(0.49)	(0.49)	(0.52)	
Years producing tomatoes	18.82	19.85	16.5	1.05
	(7.42)	(8.53)	(7.04)	
Waste or nonsale (percent)	11.99	14.37	11.20	0.90
	(8.04)	(8.76)	(6.89)	
Product denial (percent)	18.46	*23.10*	*15.01*	2.01*
	(12.81)	(15.91)	(8.80)	
Transaction costs				
Number of trader contacts	*0*	*14.45*	16.55	92.58***
	(0)	(6.88)	(8.66)	
Years having known trader	*0*	*0.65*	0.20	7.70***
	(0)	(1.18)	(0.52)	
Number of traders with transactions	0	*5.30*	*4.10*	58.08***
	(0)	(3.61)	(2.29)	
Information from trader	*0.30*	*0.95*	0.95	31.80***
	(0.47)	(0.22)	(0.22)	
Price below market price	*0.41*	*0.05*	*0.8*	15.26***
	(0.50)	(0.22)	(0.41)	
Negotiation time	*1.13*	*2.30*	2.65	27.62***
(number of visits)	(0.65)	(1.17)	(0.88)	

SOURCE: Authors' survey of the Nanjing vegetable marketing chain.

NOTES: Coefficients in italics have significantly different means.

*** Significant at the 1 percent level.

* Significant at the 10 percent level.

PART VI

Poverty Alleviation Programs and Safety Nets

This section of the book—consisting of Chapters 20 and 21—studies and compares the experience of China and India in antipoverty programs (APPs), which are still considered critical safety nets for the poor and disadvantaged. India has had a longer experience as well as a greater variety of such programs. Yet, compared to other types of public investments, government spending on antipoverty programs has had the lowest impact on poverty reduction (Fan, Hazell, and Thorat 2000; Fan, Zhang, and Zhang 2002). This is because, despite good intent, the programs suffered in practice from leakages, poor design, inaccurate targeting of the poor, misappropriation of funds, political interference, and implementation problems.

We have seen earlier that growth has been crucial in reducing poverty in the two countries. But their experiences also show the limits of growth in eradicating poverty, because large sections of the population remain trapped in poverty. In both countries, growth in the primary sector, which is still dominant in the rural economy and employment, is vital for poverty alleviation. But growth and increasing liberalization have brought their share of problems as well, one of which is widening income disparities, and direct attacks in the form of well-designed APPs can be judiciously used to redistribute the gains from economic growth. What has been the record of China and India in targeted poverty programs? Both countries implemented direct APPs, but poverty strategies developed in different ways in the two countries. In India, during the green revolution era, rapid agricultural growth led to a dramatic reduction in rural poverty through the trickle-down effect, but the trend stagnated from the late 1980s. Thus, in the 1990s, a new emphasis was placed on APPs, and new schemes were adopted in rural areas to mitigate the adverse impacts of liberalization on the poor. These programs have differed in their effects on poverty reduction.

Since the mid-1980s, China has also introduced various direct APPs through state development funds and government antipoverty credits and loans. Prior to 1984, social welfare and relief funds were mainly used to subsidize poor families, and there was no formal strategy. From 1984 to 1995, the government pursued the strategy of "regional targeting," which aimed to alleviate poverty by developing the regional or local economies. This effectively wiped out large-scale poverty by developing poor areas, although it brought little benefit to the extremely poor in the poorest areas. The poor were thus increasingly concentrated in remote regions with limited access to roads and other infrastructure, making it difficult for the benefits from the development of the local economy to trickle down to them. After 1996, the government altered its strategy to one of targeting poor households directly.

Many researchers and policymakers are increasingly concerned about the effectiveness of the APPs in these countries, where poverty affects millions. Are self-targeting schemes such as rural public works, age- and other vulnerability-based plans, such as those for indigent women, children, and the elderly, more pro-poor than nontargeted food programs (such as the Public Distribution System in India)? Are decentralized participatory schemes more effective than centralized ones? How have the governments in India and China improved their targeting of the poor? How can the poorest benefit from development in general and from APPs in particular? The following two chapters address these questions and draw valuable lessons from the rich experience of the two counties that can be used to develop a more effective strategy for poverty alleviation.

20 Poverty Alleviation in China: Successes and Lessons

LINXIU ZHANG, SCOTT ROZELLE, AND JIKUN HUANG

Over the past two decades, China has grown impressively, contributing to a dramatic improvement in the living standard of its population. Rapid growth has also brought about a sharp rise in the rural per capita income and a significant reduction in the number of poor people, a fact widely recognized both at home and abroad. In China though, poverty is primarily a rural phenomenon.

While most agree with the scope of the fall in poverty, the reasons for this decline are less appreciated. The importance of understanding the determinants of the success in poverty reduction and its links with economic growth in poor rural areas has to go beyond academic interest, because there are still, depending on different estimates, 30–100 million people, if not more, living below the nation's poverty line. Even the pace of poverty reduction has slackened recently. A series of policy and institutional reforms have frequently been counted among the major driving forces that contributed to the remarkable poverty reduction in China. The success of these changes, especially in the early reform period, has definitely resulted in significant economic growth, but the nation's antipoverty programs should receive some credit, too. That is important to ensure that lessons from the programs are taken into consideration in the design and improvement of future policy to fight poverty.

We start with a review and assessment of China's antipoverty strategy, programs, and other relevant policies. Next we look at the lessons that can be learned with regard to the role of antipoverty programs as well as other broadbased economic development and public investment policies for alleviating poverty. The following section is devoted to the challenges facing China in terms of poverty reduction, including improving the targeting of antipoverty programs, building institutional and human capacity in rural areas, providing social services for the rural poor and rural migrants, and moderating the negative impacts of World Trade Organization (WTO) adjustments on the poor. The final section has some concluding remarks.

Government Poverty Reduction Programs

Before 1986: Emergency Relief

Until the mid-1980s, China did not have an explicit national policy on poverty alleviation, although the government gave some special attention to rural poverty problems (Rozelle, Zhang, and Huang 1999). Some communes in poor areas were allowed to decollectivize earlier than in other areas (as early as the late 1970s), and the central government had already subsidized poor areas through direct budgetary transfers (Park, Wang, and Wu 1998), subsidized grain sales, and other assistance to farmers in need. However, with fiscal decentralization and increasing scarcity of budgetary resources, these forms of support were reduced over time (Rozelle, Zhang, and Huang 1999).

During this period the leading antipoverty strategy was made up of institutional, land, market, and employment system reforms. Land reforms stimulated greater interest of farmers in production, while market reforms led to widespread increases in specialization, yields, and income (Weersink and Rozelle 1997). These changes helped many rural people to escape poverty, especially those in central and coastal China, who had been hurt most by the grain-first policies because they lived in areas not well suited to grain production (Lardy 1983). By the end of 1985, the number of poor had gone down from over 250 million before 1978 to 125 million, that is, from 30.7 percent to 14.8 percent of the total rural population.

China's nationwide poverty alleviation program did not start officially until 1986, when the government recognized two facts. First, although economic reforms brought about significant changes and improvements in society, income disparity had increasingly become a cause for concern (reflected by the Gini coefficients presented in Figure 20.1). Second, the high rate of economic growth did not reach the extreme poor, who lived in remote areas untouched by

FIGURE 20.1 Income inequality in China, 1978–95

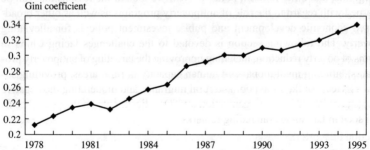

SOURCE: Authors' elaboration based on NBS, *China Statistical Yearbook,* various years.

markets. In general, China's poverty alleviation program can be divided into three stages, which we will now explain.

The First Nationwide Poverty Reduction Program

The National Plan for Poverty Reduction was initiated in 1986. With the financial and political committees established by the government, regional targeting was one of the many policies adopted for poverty alleviation. The government approached poverty targeting by identifying counties with low per capita income. A county was identified as poor if its 1985 average rural per capita income fell below 300, 200, or 150 yuan, depending on location and political factors, such as the presence of large minority populations. Antipoverty efforts might well have benefited from a narrowing down of the government's targeting criteria from counties to townships or smaller units.

The 8-7 Poverty Reduction Plan

Following numerous targeting complaints, a new targeting operation was undertaken in the early 1990s by revising the poverty line and adjusting the designation of poor counties. Some counties "graduated" and others were added, resulting in the inclusion of a total of 592 counties in the poverty program. The new poverty reduction plan, named the 8-7 Plan, which was adopted in 1994 and focused on the designated 592 poor counties, established the objective of lifting the remaining 80 million rural poor above the official poverty line during the seven-year plan period (1994–2000). An integrated area development approach was adopted, and the plan provided for (1) giving assistance to poor households in the form of improvements in agricultural and livestock production and access to off-farm employment, (2) extending road infrastructure and electricity to most or all townships and improving access to safe drinking water for most poor villages, and (3) providing access to universal primary education and basic preventive and curative healthcare.

Beginning in 1986, the national and provincial lists of poor counties were the central focus of China's poverty reduction efforts. Central government expenditures on poverty reduction were concentrated in these designated poor counties. The annual expenditures ranged between U.S.$1 billion and U.S.$1.5 billion equivalent from 1984 to 1996 (Table 20.1). They increased to U.S.$2 billion in 1998 and were estimated to have exceeded U.S.$3 billion in 2000. The expenditures comprised state poverty alleviation loans (52 percent) channeled through the Agricultural Development Bank of China (ADBC) at subsidized interest rates of below 3 percent, grants from the Ministry of Finance (17 percent), Food-for-Work funds (26 percent), and others (5 percent). This is a clear demonstration of the seriousness of the government's efforts to address poverty reduction on a priority basis.

The major criticisms of the implementation of the 8-7 Plan relate to targeting and supervision. First, the plan covered only the 592 designated poor

TABLE 20.1 Investment in China's poor areas, 1986–97 (100 million yuan)

Year	Subsidized credit		Food for work		Development fund		Total	
	Nominal	Actual	Nominal	Actual	Nominal	Actual	Nominal	Actual
1986	23	22	8	7	10	9	41	39
1987	23	21	8	7	10	9	41	37
1988	29	22	2	2	10	8	41	31
1989	30	19	2	1	10	6	42	27
1990	30	18	7	4	10	6	47	28
1991	35	21	38	23	10	6	83	49
1992	41	23	36	20	10	6	67	49
1993	35	17	51	25	11	5	87	48
1994	45	18	61	25	11	4	117	47
1995	48	17	61	11	9	3	118	30
1996	57	18	31	10	13	4	101	32
1997	87	28	31	10	28	9	146	45
Total	483	244	336	145	142	75	931	462

SOURCE: Huang, Ma, and Rozelle (1998).

NOTE: Real values are at 1985 prices.

counties, where only around 50 percent of the rural poor were located, thus effectively excluding half of the poor residing in other counties (not counting the urban poor). Second, the bulk of the poverty alleviation loan funds were channeled by the ADBC to local enterprises, including township and village enterprises (TVEs), which were chosen for their potential to generate high returns, but had very little to do with poverty reduction. Low repayment rates on the loans by the TVEs compounded the problem. Also, the ADBC encountered significant difficulties in directing loans to poor households. This led the government to experiment with microfinance programs during the latter half of the 1990s, and they also encountered some initial difficulties. Little is known about the use of the Finance Ministry grants for the poverty alleviation program. The Food-for-Work Program suffered from the same targeting problems as the overall plan (UNDP, LGPA, and World Bank 2000).

New Antipoverty Policy Initiatives

In response to the recommendations of various poverty studies and in view of the circumstances within the country (e.g., structural constraints to further poverty reduction through economic growth alone, deteriorating targeting, relative low efficiency of poverty fund use, etc.), the government held a national poverty conference in late May 2001. The conference was held to review past poverty alleviation experiences and formulate a new strategy called the Rural China Poverty Alleviation and Development Plan—2001 to 2010. This plan set out the following objectives and premises: (1) the basic needs of the extreme poor should be met by year 2010, (2) the basic production conditions of the poor areas would need to be further improved, (3) comprehensive skill training would be necessary to improve human capital development in poor areas, and (4) emphasis needed to be placed on the improvement of basic infrastructure in poor areas.

A major shift reflected in the plan is to give provincial governments more autonomy in dealing with poverty alleviation funds and resources. Counties are still to be used as a unit for targeting, but each province is expected to receive more authority and resources to cover a wider range of smaller poor communities, such as villages and households. About 30 percent of the resources would be used outside the targeted counties and directed to poor villages and households. There will be a new set of criteria for the selection of poor counties and poor villages.[1]

The key features and goals of intervention outlined in the new plan include (1) emphasizing crop and livestock production with market orientation, (2) improving the quality of commodity and information services, (3) achieving both environmental and economic sustainability, (4) improving the basic living and production conditions of the poor areas by ensuring wider implementation of nine-year compulsory education in poor areas and the availability of basic health services in most villages by the year 2010, (5) using new science and technology in the process of poverty reduction, (6) improving human capital development by offering more training and education to poor people, (7) facilitating voluntary migration, and (8) encouraging voluntary resettlement of dwellers from extremely poor areas.

Several measures were adopted to ensure the smooth implementation of the Poverty Alleviation and Development Plan—2001 to 2010. They included (1) increasing financial support, (2) improving the efficiency of management of poverty funds as well as intensifying the auditing and monitoring of their use, (3) increasing subsidized loans, (4) linking poverty initiatives with the Great West Development Program, (5) mobilizing civil society to join poverty alleviation forces, and (6) encouraging and collaborating with international agencies.

Government Support

Since the adoption of the national poverty alleviation program, Chinese governments at both the central and local levels have diverted significant amounts of funds to the designated impoverished counties in the form of grant funds, subsidized loans, and projects. While the overall funds allocated to poverty

---

1. The county selection criteria are poverty incidence (with the poverty line at 625 yuan), per capita net income, and per capita financial revenue. The village selection criteria are cash income, grain output, housing conditions, access to roads, access to electricity, availability of drinking water, women's illnesses, and children dropping out of school.

alleviation have increased during the new phase, subsidized loans have become its most important component.

In 2001, the central government budgeted 10 billion yuan as poverty alleviation funds, an increase of 0.5 billion yuan from the year 2000. At the same time, local governments budgeted 4 billion yuan as a core budget, an increase of 0.6 billion from the previous year. In addition, an annual budget of 6 billion yuan was used in food-for-work programs. According to statistics, between 2000 and 2002 the central government invested 18 billion yuan, while local governments' core funding was 11 billion yuan, amounting to a total of 29 billion yuan allocated to food-for-work programs. The amount of subsidized loans also increased significantly in recent years. In 1995, subsidized loans were 4.6 billion yuan and accounted for 46.2 percent of poverty funds, while in 1996 subsidized loans increased to 5.5 billion yuan and accounted for 50.9 percent of the total funds; in 1997 the share increased to 55 percent and further rose to more than 60 percent in 1999 (NSB, *Poverty Monitoring Report of Rural China,* 2002). Other types of poverty alleviation efforts, such as resettlement schemes and both South-North and East-West collaborations, have also intensified.

China recently published its White Paper on Rural Poverty Alleviation (People's Daily 2001). The report recognized the poverty alleviation efforts and the successes of all sectors of society for the past 20 years. At the same time, it indicated the future direction of the new poverty alleviation efforts. In recognizing the increasing difficulties in the poverty alleviation process, China has paid special attention to ethnic and minority groups, the disabled population, and women groups. In recognizing the challenges ahead, the country is committed to making continuous efforts and putting poverty alleviation on top of the priority list in the development process. It is noteworthy that women have been listed, for the first time, as one of the target groups for the new century. Furthermore, emphasizing sustainable development has been one major step forward in the process of poverty alleviation.

Institutional Support

To ensure the successful implementation of the national poverty program, the State Council's Leading Group Office for Poverty Reduction (LGPR) was established in 1986 to provide greater coherence to the poverty reduction efforts of various agencies and to facilitate economic development in poor areas. The LGPR members include the related government line ministries, commissions, banks, federations, and committees, with the different agencies specializing on poverty alleviation activities linked to their specific areas of concern.

While the LGPR and its executing agency, the Poor Area Development Office (PADO), are the principal advocates for the rural poor, most poor provinces, prefectures, and counties have also established leading groups and PADOs along the lines of the central model. The central LGPR provides the overall framework and coordination for the poverty reduction efforts. However, it is not directly involved in the implementation of poverty reduction projects, except for some small programs. Instead, implementation of most of the organized poverty reduction efforts is carried out by sectoral line agencies (for instance, rural roads under the Food-for-Work program are implemented by the local staff of the Transportation Bureau).

Successes and Lessons

A reduction in poverty on the scale witnessed in China in the past 20 years is unprecedented in the history of development. Estimated along China's official poverty lines, the number of China's rural poor decreased dramatically, from 260 million in 1978 to 128 million in 1984 (Figure 20.2).

After slowing down in the late 1980s, the rapid fall in the poverty head-count continued in the 1990s, declining to 42 million in 1998 and about 30 million in 2001, with an annual reduction of 10.4 million. The incidence of rural poverty (the poor as a proportion of the rural population) also decreased sharply during this period, falling from 32.9 percent in 1978 to 15.1 percent in 1984 and further to 3.2 percent in 2001.

Poverty estimates based on the U.S.$1 per day measure (in terms of pur-chasing power parity) developed by the World Bank indicate that there were substantially greater numbers of poor in absolute terms in all years. Still, the trend of both headcount and incidence confirms the remarkable decline in poverty in China. Even if the international standard of U.S.$1 per day is used, the reduction of China's poverty rate from 31.3 percent in 1990 to 11.5 percent in 1998 is remarkable. Comparatively, using the same poverty line, the inci-dence of poverty in South Asia declined gradually, from 45 percent in 1987 to 40 percent in 1998, while in Africa the decline was marginal, from 46.6 percent in 1987 to 46.3 percent in 1998 (World Bank 2001).

FIGURE 20.2 Number of rural poor in China, 1978–97

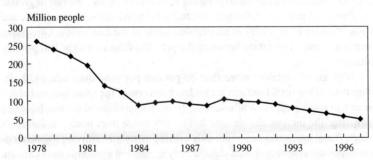

SOURCE: Authors' elaboration based on NBS, *China Statistical Yearbook*, various years.

Other significant improvements were also made in basic infrastructure, drinking water facilities, human capital development, and so on. The educational status among rural people has seen remarkable progress in China due to government spending in rural education in the past several years. Between 1992 and 2000, the number of illiterates per 1,000 rural people declined from 204.0 to 82.5 on average. However, this improvement has been unevenly shared across regions, and the low education levels of people in remote, mountainous, marginal, and western poverty-stricken regions remain a cause for concern.

There was also remarkable nutritional improvement in rural China in the 1990s, as indicated by the evident improvement of child nutrition, which is a sensitive nutritional indicator. Between 1990 and 1998, the incidence of being underweight among children five years of age and younger declined from 22 to 12.6 percent in rural China, while the incidence of stunted growth went down from 41.4 to 22 percent. This trend was partly driven by the rapid socioeconomic development in China during this period (Chang et al. 2000) and, most important, by various poverty alleviation and other special programs. Income, another important indicator of welfare, has also been on the rise in both rural and urban China over the past two decades, though with variations.

Despite the achievements to date, scholars both inside and outside China believe there is scope for improvement in terms of the poverty reduction policy itself and the efficiency of resource use.

General Economic Development

The success of China's economic reform is obvious and well recognized. From the data presented in Table 20.2 it is clear that while the relative importance of agriculture in the national economy has been declining, there has been an overall increase in total agricultural value added and in total output.

The development of the rural sector is also reflected in the diversification of the economic structure. The continuous increase in per capita income has been a significant phenomenon of the rural economy since the late 1970s. During the prereform period, per capita income increased by only 0.6 percent per year. However, during the initial period of reforms (1978–84), the rate of growth was about 3.2 percent. Although this trend declined between the 1980s and 1990s (Rozelle et al. 1999), it accelerated again in the late 1990s. Obviously, there is a causal correlation between the growth of the economy and poverty reduction.

With growth rates of more than 30 percent per year since late 1979, development of the rural nonfarm sector has been one of the main factors behind the rise in rural income. While income from the agricultural sectors has been stagnating, the incremental income has mainly come from nonagricultural activities. Rural industrialization not only created many off-farm employment opportunities but also contributed significantly to national economic development and foreign trade. In 1999, for example, the total value added from this sector

TABLE 20.2 Major indicators of China's agricultural and rural economy, 1983–99

Year	Share of agriculture in GDP (percent)	Share of total labor force engaged in farming (percent)	Agricultural value added (billion yuan)	Total output of grain crops (million tons)	Per capita net income (yuan)
1983	33.9	67.1	19.6	38.7	309.8
1985	29.8	62.4	25.4	37.9	397.6
1990	28.4	60.2	50.2	43.5	686.3
1992	23.6	58.6	57.4	44.3	784.0
1995	20.8	52.2	119.9	46.7	1,577.7
1996	20.4	50.5	138.4	50.5	1,926.1
1997	18.3	49.9	144.7	49.4	2,090.1
1998	18.0	49.8	145.6	51.2	2,162.0
1999	17.6	50.1	144.6	50.8	2,210.3

SOURCE: China, Ministry of Agriculture, *China Agricultural Development Report*, 2000.

NOTE: All values are in current prices.

accounted for more than 27 percent of national total GDP, and exports accounted for nearly 35 percent (NBS, Poverty Monitoring Report of Rural China, 2001).

Government Investment Policy

Earlier, in Chapter 6 of this book, we saw the impact of government public expenditure on economic growth and poverty alleviation in China. The results show that government spending on production-enhancing investments, such as agricultural research and development (R&D), irrigation, rural education, and infrastructure (including roads, electricity, and communication) all contributed not only to agricultural growth but also to reduction in rural poverty and inequality. Other studies (Rozelle, Zhang, and Huang 1999; Fan, Zhang, and Zhang 2002) generally show that appropriate investments matter for growth and poverty reduction. Investments centered on education and agricultural R&D and those that could get into the hands of rural farmers have positive growth and poverty impacts. Most important, investments that create an economic environment that can foster entrepreneurship, off-farm employment, and labor movement—such as those focused on increasing human capital—have a significant impact on poverty reduction. The weak correlation between investment in poverty alleviation schemes and actual poverty reduction shows that there may be ways to increase the effectiveness of this type of investment, because the loan component accounts for the lion's share of the governmental poverty alleviation expenditures.

Government Poverty Alleviation Programs

Poverty alleviation efforts have intensified, both institutionally and financially, since the government made poverty alleviation a high priority. Since 1986, after the national poverty alleviation program was established, nearly 4 billion yuan (in 1985 constant prices) have been allocated yearly to poverty alleviation purposes through subsidized loans, food-for-work programs, or grant funds. This money was channeled only to the nationally designated poor counties (Zhang, Rozelle, and Huang 2000). In the earlier stage, provinces also allocated substantial amounts of funds to locally designated poor counties. The question, however, is this: Did such an effort have a significant impact on poverty alleviation in China?

Studies that have been carried out by scholars in the area of poverty policy assessment (Huang, Ma, and Rozelle 1998; Park, Wang, and Wu 1998; Rozelle, Zhang, and Huang 1999; Fan, Zhang, and Zhang 2002) have come to the general conclusion that poverty targeting was not satisfactory and poverty investment has not been effective in terms of reducing poverty. This does not mean, though, that the government's efforts have not been effective at all. Some studies conclude that if projects are well designed and targeted, they do pay off. One such example is the Food-for-Work Program (Zhu and Zhongyi 1996).

The Food-for-Work Program (FWP) has always been a major component of poverty alleviation programs in rural China. This type of poverty project not only improves local conditions in poor areas, but also makes direct contributions to increased household income. Based on the calculations of the National Bureau of Statistics (NBS), each billion yuan of the FWP fund can generate 50 million mandays of work (*Poverty Monitoring Report of Rural China*, 2002). If the government allocates 6 billion yuan to the scheme every year, a total of 0.3 billion days of work will be generated. Thus, farmers will receive direct payment of 1.2 billion yuan.

Improving conditions for rural education has also been an important activity in poverty alleviation. In total, the central government budgeted 3.9 billion yuan, with 7.7 billion from local core funding, to implement the poor areas' Compulsory Education Program between 1995 and 2000. This program was designed to be used in the government-designated poor areas to upgrade or build schools, pay tuition for poor children, provipde books, and so on. The program has benefited more than 852 counties in the past six years.

Other special programs directly targeting women, children, and minorities have also made significant progress.

Future Challenges

Despite the evident successes to date, there are still more than 100 million rural poor based on the international poverty line, and in most cases the remaining poverty is both severe and relatively intractable. In the past, the broad incidence of poverty made it possible to achieve substantial reductions through general economic growth and broadly targeted programs. At present, the majority of the rural poor are concentrated in resource-deficient areas and comprise entire communities located mostly in upland sections of the northern, northwestern, and southwestern provinces of China. The poorest households are typically those further disadvantaged by high dependency ratios, ill health, and other difficulties. Minorities and the disabled are known to represent a highly disproportionate share of the poor. Gender inequality, reflected by the lower rate of female participation in education and the higher female infant mortality rate, is also widely observed in these poor areas. Both income and human poverty need to be addressed simultaneously in poverty alleviation programs in the future. The provision of social security for the urban poor, the elderly, and migrants from rural areas is another challenging issue that has emerged out of the social and economic transition following reforms.

The Chinese government is strongly committed to poverty reduction, as revealed in official documents such as the 8-7 Plan and the more recent White Paper on Poverty Alleviation. The strategies adopted by the Chinese government range from setting up special poverty alleviation offices at different governmental levels and well-funded national antipoverty programs to the implementation of multidimensional, multiministerial poverty alleviation schemes. However, the past poverty alleviation efforts have not been without problems affecting the efficiency of use of poverty funds. These problems are reviewed in the following sections.

Targeting Poverty

Poverty targeting in China has gone through a number of major shifts in the past 20 years. Since the early 1980s, the poverty policy has shifted in emphasis from household to enterprise and from agriculture to industry. Unfortunately, many loans were given to TVEs or county-owned enterprises, which increased the local revenue base for local governments but did not greatly benefit poor households. China's poverty alleviation efforts are now intensively targeting those poor areas based on the nationally designated 592 poorest counties. However, the poor counties and villages selected for the poverty programs missed some of the poor and even some of the very poor. Although the 1994 redesignation rectified part of the problem, many beneficiaries were still left out, and the targeting criteria adopted were not satisfactory because many of the urban poor and the poor in nonpoor areas were not considered.

Building Institutional and Human Capacity

Why the poor remain poor relates to a complex set of factors, but poor communities generally lack community development, healthy functional institutions, and natural and human capital resources. The shift in focus from welfare funds to economic and human development reflects the government's recognition of the importance of capacity building in poverty alleviation. However, limited efforts have been made to carry out comprehensive antipoverty programs that not only provide financial support to vulnerable areas but also help the local community to improve institutional arrangements and empower human capital.

Rural education and rural educational conditions have been left far behind their urban counterparts. Given the fact that investment in rural education has yielded by far the highest returns in terms of both rural economic growth and poverty alleviation, rural education should be placed at the top of the government's investment priority list.

Fostering Stakeholder Participation

Poverty alleviation programs should be designed according to the needs of the poor, because involving and mobilizing them would make the schemes more effective. To this end, a participatory approach is most effective. In the past, most of China's poverty alleviation programs were implemented using a top-down approach, and, as a result, the poor were usually passive players and achievements consequently limited.

Nongovernmental organizations (NGOs) also have an important role to play in the poverty alleviation effort. Compared with government antipoverty agencies, NGOs can do better in terms of reaching the grassroots, targeting, innovating, and achieving depth as well as breadth of reform. Qu (2002) quotes a research finding that during the period of the 8-7 Plan, NGO efforts accounted for 20–35 percent of poverty reduction (measured as the proportion of total antipoverty inputs from NGOs). Only 47 percent of the government poverty loans reached poor rural households, and the loan repayment rate was 50 percent, while more than 90 percent of poverty loans managed by NGOs were repaid. By 1998, there were a total of 165,000 NGOs in China, with 21 percent of them working in poverty alleviation and rural development. However, the NGOs are faced with financial constraints as well as heavy dependence on the government. These issues need to be addressed for them to contribute fully to poverty reduction.

Providing Social Services for the Rural Poor and Migrants

An issue long discussed is that Chinese farmers have been suffering from discriminatory social services in such areas as healthcare, housing benefits, education, and so on. One of the positive features of the old collective system was that rural residents could at least enjoy collective medical services. However, there has been a reversal in this trend since the early 1990s, partially indicating the deterioration of basic public health services. In a recent empirical study, Zhang (2003), using data collected in six nationally designated poor counties, found that nutrition and health status affect the productivity of poor rural households significantly. This implies that, given the vital role played by investments in nutrition and health for poverty alleviation, the government should step up funding in these areas to pursue further poverty reduction.

Poverty in the countryside is associated with poor access to information, technology, extension, and infrastructure. Investment in social services has proved a high-return activity and an effective measure for reducing poverty.

Therefore, antipoverty plans need to pay greater attention to providing social services in rural areas.

Migration also helps in alleviating rural poverty. However, given the current employment and welfare systems in China, it is difficult for rural people to permanently reside in urban areas. Nonetheless, many rural people go to work in cities and urban areas, and the lack of adequate support systems makes their lives more difficult than are those of urban residents. The welfare of rural migrant workers needs to be addressed.

Recognizing the Dynamic Linkages between Poverty and the Environment

The relationship between poverty and environment is increasingly gaining recognition at both policy and community levels and is particularly relevant to the present situation in rural China. The clusters of poor people are closely linked to a depleted or resource-poor natural environment. Observers have conceptualized the link between rural poverty and environment as a downward spiral associated with population growth and inadequate resource management. Alternatively, the economic marginalization of the poor is seen as leading to their migration to even more environmentally fragile lands. This simplistic model has sometimes led to policies that reduce poverty at the expense of the environment, or vice versa (UNDP and EU 1999). This also poses challenges to the government on how to deal with the "critical triangle" of development objectives: how to promote agricultural growth, take care of poor people in rural and resource-poor areas, and ensure the sustainable use of natural resources at the same time (Vosti and Reardon 1997).

Although the Chinese government has come to view poverty alleviation as one of its major policy priorities, environmental protection is another parallel goal. China, with support from international organizations, has worked hard to tackle environmental problems in the past by making heavy investments in programs such as soil and water conservation and terracing projects as well as through legislation and institutional empowerment (e.g., upgrading the Environmental Protection Bureau). Significant achievements have been made, but China is still facing obvious and serious challenges of environmental decay such as land degradation, desertification, soil erosion, deforestation, water shortage and pollution, loss of biodiversity, and so on. Deforestation and grassland degradation are at present regarded as the most significant and serious environmental problems in China. These can be the consequences of economic development and may ultimately threaten the livelihood of people who live in a fragile environment and are heavily dependent on natural resources.

With the recognition of the importance of the linkages between poverty and environment, many government initiatives, such as the Great Western Development Program and the New Rural Poverty Reduction and Development Plan, have connected environmental protection and poverty alleviation as twin policy objectives. Other large operations of this type, such as the newly launched program under the PRC-GEF-ADB (People's Republic of China, Global Environmental Facility, and Asian Development Bank) partnership on land degradation in dryland ecosystems, are under way through domestic and international efforts.

Moderating the Negative Impacts of WTO Accession

China's accession to the WTO is set to have huge impacts on China's economy, especially the rural economy and the rural poor (Zhu 2002b). In rural China, the primary livelihood of many poverty-stricken households hinges on agriculture, one of the sectors that will bear the negative impacts associated with China's accession to the WTO. Given that agricultural production by poor farmers is still at a subsistence rather than a commercial level, it is less likely that these farmers could escape poverty by improving their farming conditions. Previous studies have already shown that being underemployed or employed with meager payment is one of the major factors that leads to or aggravates poverty in rural China. In these circumstances, governments at both central and local levels should simultaneously integrate antipoverty and employment promotion into their policy formation, and the latter should be given the highest priority in China's new 10-year antipoverty strategic plan. If the government wishes to promote the employment of poor rural laborers, efforts must be made to help build human capital by providing education, healthcare, and nourishment as well as financial resources to improve labor mobility.

It cannot be denied that agricultural extension or training projects in government antipoverty programs help to build the human capital of the rural poor in the project sites. However, the technological assistance provided by these programs is usually too crop- or livestock-specific to enable timely and adequate adaptation to the changing market. Thus, a fundamental way to help the rural poor in the long run would be to provide them not only with technical knowledge but also with broader skills in reading, interpreting, and responding to the changes in markets.

Compared to education and labor mobility, the importance of health has been neglected. Zhu (Chapter 5) quotes an unpublished report by the Ministry of Health, which points out that in 1998, nearly 22 percent of rural households plunged abruptly into poverty because of illness or injuries of household members. She also quotes Dreze and Sen (1989), who say that the rapid economic growth recorded by China since reform could be attributed, to a large extent, to the progress that had been made in basic education and health services prior to reform.

Concluding Remarks

It is still too early to assess the impact of the new poverty alleviation policies, but the multiscale and multidimensional nature of poverty has been recognized and well understood, as reflected in the approaches adopted during the current stage of policymaking. Although China still has a long way to go to alleviate its remaining poverty, it can continue to make an important contribution to the world by providing positive examples of poverty reduction combined with sustainable development.

21 Antipoverty Programs in India: Are They Pro-Poor?

KIRIT PARIKH, S. MAHENDRA DEV,
AND ABUSALEH SHARIFF

Poverty alleviation has been one of the guiding principles of the Indian planning process, and the country has done reasonably well in reducing poverty in
the past three decades. The vital role of economic growth in providing more
employment and income avenues to the population is unquestionable. Equally
important is the role played by direct antipoverty programs in the process of
poverty alleviation.

The success of Indian antipoverty policies is reflected in the decline of the
combined rural and urban poverty ratio from 54.9 percent in 1973–74 to 27.5 percent in 2004–5 (Table 21.1).[1] Specifically, rural poverty declined from 56.5
percent to 28.3 percent. In the postreform period, rural poverty declined from
37.3 percent in 1993–94 to 28.3 percent in 2004–5. In absolute terms, the number
of rural poor declined from about 244 million in 1993–94 to 221 million in 2004–5.
Despite this noteworthy performance, as of 2004–5, India was still home to nearly
302 million poor (221 million rural poor and 81 million urban poor).

The existing literature shows that variables such as agricultural output, inflation rates, relative food prices, nonagricultural employment, government's
development expenditure, infrastructure, and human development are important determinants of rural poverty (Datt and Ravallion 1997). The importance
of these factors, however, varied over different periods; green revolution–led
agricultural growth emerged as the major factor leading to poverty decline in
the 1970s, whereas rural nonfarm employment and public expenditure in rural
areas, including antipoverty programs, were key factors in the 1980s (Sen 1996).
The higher rate of economic growth was the major determinant of poverty reduction in the 1990s.

Direct antipoverty programs such as self-employment and wage employment programs provided by central and state governments have been partly
responsible for the decrease in poverty in India. The central government, in par-

---

1. We have not included the poverty ratio for 1999–2000, as the data are not strictly comparable with those from other NSS rounds.

2. Deaton and Dreze (2002) provide alternative estimates of poverty ratios. According to
them, the rate of decline in poverty was similar in the 1990s to that in the 1980s.

TABLE 21.1 Official estimates of the incidence of poverty in India, 1973–74 to 2004–5

Year	Poverty ratio (percent)			Number of poor (million)		
	Rural	Urban	Combined	Rural	Urban	Combined
1973–74	56.45	49.0	54.9	261.3	60.0	321.3
1977–78	53.1	45.2	51.3	264.3	64.6	328.9
1983	45.7	40.8	44.5	252.0	70.9	322.9
1987–88	39.1	38.2	38.9	231.9	75.2	307.1
1993–94	37.3	32.4	36.0	244.0	76.3	320.3
2004–5	28.3	25.7	27.5	220.9	80.8	301.7

SOURCES: India, Ministry of Finance, *Economic Survey,* 2002–3, for the period 1973–74 to 1993–94; India, Planning Commission (2007).

ticular, has been spending a lot of money on its own programs, reaching 1 percent of the GDP in the late 1990s. Considerable amounts also came from banks in the form of credit and loans.

The objective of this chapter is to review India's experience with antipoverty programs and highlight its lessons to help shape a more effective strategy for poverty reduction. We begin with an overview of direct antipoverty programs. The second section assesses the effectiveness of these schemes and presents the results of an applied general equilibrium model on side-effects, opportunity costs, and dynamic consequences of antipoverty plans under alternative policy scenarios. The next section discusses the lessons learned and strategies needed to design poverty reduction programs more effectively, and it is followed by some concluding remarks.

Overview of the Major Direct Antipoverty Programs

The Evolution of the Approach Used

PRE-1970. The first antipoverty initiative after India achieved independence in 1947 was the Community Development Program, started in 1952 to promote integrated development with the cooperation of the people and the convergence of technical knowledge in various fields at the local level. Another initiative was the abolition of intermediary institutions and systems of landholding such as Zamindari, Jagirdari, and so on. This effort was followed by attempts to put in place a comprehensive policy of land reforms. The third initiative was the emphasis during the third five-year plan (1960–65) on foodgrain production through the introduction of new technology, which led to the agricultural production boom known as the green revolution, which lasted from the mid-1960s until the end of the 1980s. Although the achievements of many of these efforts were significant, the final impact of these initiatives on poverty was far from satisfactory. For instance, despite the abolition of intermediary systems of land tenure, land reform is still an ongoing process and has not yielded the desired results in terms of either growth or social justice. Even the success of the green revolution was limited to specific areas and crops.

THE 1970s.   During this period there was a general rethinking of the policies and approaches that are effective in fighting poverty. The need for a direct approach to targeting the poor, as opposed to indirect benefits through agricultural growth and institutional reforms, was finally realized during the fourth five-year plan (1969–74). The 1970s were a significant decade in this context, because many new programs were tried in rural areas, including the Rural Work Programs (RWP), the Drought Prone Areas Program, the Desert Development Programs, and programs for small and marginal farmers (e.g., those of the Small Farmers Development Agency, the Marginal Farmers and Agricultural Laborers Agency, etc.).

THE 1980s.   Since the 1980s there has been a proliferation of centrally sponsored poverty alleviation programs, with allocations increasing in every five-year plan. Self-employment and wage employment programs, such as the Integrated Rural Development Program, the National Rural Employment Programs, and the Rural Landless Employment Generation Program, were introduced. And the Public Distribution System (PDS) and nutrition programs spread to rural areas.

THE 1990s: THE REFORM PERIOD.   With the introduction of economic liberalization policies in 1991–92, the role of safety nets in poverty alleviation became much more important. Until that time, the PDS was considered the largest safety net to mitigate any adverse impact on the poor due to stabilization and structural adjustment policies. Large amounts of funds had also been allocated for wage employment programs.

But since the mid-1990s, there has been more emphasis on human development and physical infrastructure. The importance of health and education, roads, communications, electricity, and housing in raising the living standard of the poor was recognized, particularly in the latter half of the 1990s, and the traditional antipoverty programs received much less attention in the central budgets during 1998–2001 (see Appendix 21A for more information on current antipoverty schemes). Conversely, expenditures on infrastructure, including roads, increased significantly in the late 1990s (Fan, Hazell, and Thorat 1999).

The Scope and Magnitude of the Programs

The major programs for the poor and vulnerable groups in India over the past two decades can be broadly divided into the categories covered in the following four subsections.

SELF-EMPLOYMENT PROGRAMS.   In such programs, the focus is on the provision of productive assets to households in the target group or on the provision of credit meant to finance the purchase of such assets. These programs could also have a third focus, that is, training and skill creation schemes, which would improve a household's ability to generate self-employment subsequently. Credit provides the financial resources necessary to complement the labor resources of the poor for undertaking a variety of productive activities. Microcredit, one of the main programs among self-employment schemes, often has the dual objective of alleviating poverty and empowering poor women.

The Integrated Rural Development Program (IRDP) was the first major self-employment program started in the late 1970s; it was first started as a pilot project and then was applied nationwide in 1980. The program aimed at providing assistance to beneficiaries in the form of bank credit and government subsidies to help them in acquiring sustainable income-generating assets. The target group of the program consisted of families below the poverty line in rural areas, including the landless, small and marginal farmers, agricultural laborers, rural artisans, and so on.

In order to strengthen the IRDP, there were a few allied subprograms. Training of Rural Youth for Self-Employment (TRYSEM), established in 1979, was intended to take care of the training requirement of the people who were selected and assisted under the IRDP. Focusing on poor rural women, the Development of Women and Children in Rural Areas (DWCRA) scheme was started in 1982–83.

In terms of achievements, more than 54 million families had benefited under the IRDP as of March 1999 since the inception of the program. The total credit mobilized during this period was Rs. 22.5 billion, and the total investment, including subsidies, was Rs. 33.9 billion. Similarly, under TRYSEM 4.6 million youths had been trained from 1980–81 to 1998–99. A total of 273,000 groups with 4.1 million women members were formed under the DWCRA scheme from 1982–83 to 1998–99, with expenditures of up to Rs. 4,225 million.

A committee constituted by the Planning Commission reviewed the IRDP and its subprograms along with wage employment programs in 1997. It recommended a single self-employment program for the rural poor and suggested that efforts be made to move away from individual beneficiary approaches, with an expressed preference for group activities and a cluster approach. Swarnajayanti Gram Swarozgar Yojana was accordingly launched in April 1999 as a single self-employment program in place of the earlier programs (for more on this program see Appendix 21A).

WAGE EMPLOYMENT PROGRAMS.   India has a long experience of experimenting with labor-intensive public works. After it achieved independence in 1947, many central government–sponsored schemes were launched, beginning with the Rural Manpower program in 1960. The Employment Guarantee Scheme (EGS) of Maharashtra has received acclaim from several sources and is a particularly interesting example because of its unprecedented feature of guaranteed rural employment, which made it a model for other states in India.[3] At the national level, Jawahar Rojgar Yojana (JRY) and the Employment Assurance Scheme (EAS) are the important programs in rural areas.[4] In implementing JRY, an important role was enviaged for the *panchayats* (local councils), with funds given directly to them.

In terms of persondays of employment created, India's rural public works programs are the largest in the world. JRY, which has a significant share in total social sector expenditures, reached around 1 billion persondays in recent years. Around Rs. 350 billion were spent on JRY from 1989–90 to 2000–2001, and it was restructured in 1999 and renamed Jawahar Gram Samridhi Yojana (JGSY).

THE PUBLIC DISTRIBUTION SYSTEM AND NUTRITION PROGRAMS.   The PDS is a significant instrument for improving food security at the household level in India. It ensures the availability of essential commodities such as rice, wheat, edible oils, and kerosene at below-market prices through a network of outlets or fair price shops. The origins of the Indian PDS can be traced back to the Second World War and the Bengal Famine of 1943, when the colonial government felt the need to develop a food policy for the country. Over the years the system expanded enormously in terms of area covered, volume of foodgrains handled, and costs involved. With a network of more than 462,000 fair price shops distributing commodities worth more than Rs. 300 billion annually to about 160 million families, the PDS in India is perhaps the largest distribution network of its kind in the world.

Interestingly, the PDS was actually launched as an instrument of price stabilization and operated as one for the first few decades. Until the late 1970s, the PDS was mainly restricted to urban areas and food-deficient regions. The main emphasis was on price stabilization and providing an alternative channel for private trade. Since the sixth five-year plan (1980–85), however, the welfare aspect of the PDS has gained importance. Coverage under the PDS spread to rural areas in many states in the 1980s. The access to the system was universal until 1997, when the government decided to rationalize and restructure the PDS into the Targeted PDS (TPDS) and issued special cards to families below the poverty line (BPL). A separate higher issue price was fixed for people above the poverty line (APL). In 1999, the BPL ration cards numbered 73 million while there were 118.6 million APL cards. Until the introduction of the TPDS, the criteria for allocations were not explicitly stated, and a series of considerations, including the historical allocation patterns, foodgrain availability, and prices in various states, determined the statewise allocations of grains by the gov-

---

3. The EGS is commended by the United Nations Development Program's Human Development Report (1993) as one of the largest public works programs in the developing world.

4. The National Rural Employment Program and the Rural Landless Employment Guarantee Program were in operation in the 1980s.

ernment from the central pool. There was no correlation between incidence of poverty and allocation and off-take of grains until the introduction of the TPDS.

Apart from poverty, malnutrition among children and women is severe in India. The Integrated Child Development Services (ICDS), initiated in 1975, is the main system for providing nutrition to children under six years of age and to pregnant and lactating women and is perhaps the largest of all food supplementation programs in the world.

Since 1990–91, the ICDS has used World Bank assistance to expand in selected states.[5] The ICDS is a centrally sponsored endeavor in which the center bears the cost of maintaining the infrastructure, while the states fund the expenditures on the food component. The central government expenditure on the expanded scheme increased from Rs. 15.4 million in 1975–76 to Rs. 10,000 million in 2000–2001.

SOCIAL SECURITY PROGRAMS. The National Social Assistance Program (NSAP), introduced in 1995, was the first-ever social security system in India. It represents a significant step toward the fulfillment of the Directive Principles in Articles 41 and 42 of the Constitution. It introduced a National Policy for Social Assistance to provide for poor households in the case of old age, death of the primary breadwinner, and maternity. The program accordingly had three components, namely the National Old Age Pension Scheme (NOAPS), the National Family Benefit Scheme (NFBS), and the National Maternity Benefit Scheme (NMBS).

The NSAP supplements the efforts of state governments to ensure minimum national levels of well-being. The central assistance is not meant to displace the states' own expenditures on social protection schemes.

GENDER-SPECIFIC PROGRAMS. Gender inequality does not automatically decline with the progress of economic growth, as is clear from the Gender Related Development Index and Gender Empowerment Measures used in the United Nations Development Program's Human Development Reports. Even when economic growth has a positive influence on the status of women, for instance, by expanding female employment opportunities or literacy rates, this impact tends to be slow and indirect. Therefore, devising and implementing gender-specific antipoverty programs are necessary to bring about radical and rapid social change.

The major gender-specific antipoverty programs in India include (1) Support to Training and Employment, launched in 1987 to upgrade the skills of poor and assetless women with a view to securing employment on a sustainable

---

5. WB–ICDS Project I (1991–97) covered 301 projects in the states of Andhra Pradesh and Orissa, while WB–ICDS Project II (1997–2002) covered 454 projects in Bihar and Madhya Pradesh. WB–ICDS Project III (1998–2004) started 461 projects in Andhra Pradesh, Kerala, Madhya Pradesh, Maharashtra, Rajasthan, and Uttar Pradesh.

basis in traditional sectors; (2) Training-cum-Employment-cum-Production Centers, particularly funded by the Norwegian Agency for International Development Cooperation to train women with a view to securing employment on a sustainable basis in nontraditional trade production; (3) the Socio-Economic Program implemented by the Central Social Welfare Board to provide work and wages to needy women such as widows and the destitute, deserted, and handicapped; (4) Condensed Courses of Education and Vocational Training, for adult women who discontinued their studies; (5) Balika Samridhi Yojana, to encourage the enrollment and retention of girls in schools; (6) the Rashtriya Mahila Kosh, to meet the credit needs of poor women, and Mahila Samridhi Yojana (MSY), which aims to promote saving habits among women; (7) Indira Mahila Yojana, for empowerment of women, with which MSY has merged; and (8) the ICDS discussed earlier. The most ambitious and nationwide development program undertaken for women's development is the DWCRA scheme discussed earlier.

The Effectiveness of Antipoverty Programs

This section looks at the effectiveness of some of the major antipoverty projects in terms of their impact on the poor, their targeting, and their cost-effectiveness.

The Self-Employment Program: The IRDP

The results of the last (1996) evaluation revealed that 14.8 percent of the beneficiaries assisted under the IRDP would have crossed the revised poverty line of Rs. 11,000 at 1991–92 prices. It shows that in terms of crossing the poverty line, the program had limited impact. The recovery performance was also poor, at 41 percent as of March 1996. The program had a negative impact on the health of the financial institutions due to the increasing proportion of nonperforming assets and defaults in loan repayments.

Researchers, scholars, various national institutions, and international organizations have extensively evaluated the IRDP. According to Dreze (1990), "(1) even if IRDP were flawlessly implemented, we could not expect this program to bring about the kind of radical reduction of rural poverty in India that is often claimed or expected to be produced; (2) in large parts of India (with some important exceptions such as West Bengal) the selection of IRDP beneficiaries is at best indiscriminate and at worst biased against the poor; and (3) we have no solid evidence on the actual effects that IRDP has on the living standards of the participating households." Instead of the IRDP, Dreze advocates a serious program of employment generation, preferably in the form of an employment guarantee scheme with legal status.

Leakages, misappropriation of funds, violation of program guidelines, selection of the nonpoor as target groups, absence of proper maintenance of accounts, and poor quality of assets are some of the problems mentioned by various studies regarding the IRDP.

Wage Employment Programs

EMPLOYMENT AND INCOME BENEFITS. The latest concurrent evaluation of JRY relating to the year 1993–94 found that JRY workers received, on average, 11.06 days of employment from *panchayat* JRY works during the reference period, the 30 days preceding the date of the survey (or 133 days per year). In some poorer states, such as Madhya Pradesh and Orissa, JRY workers received fewer than 10 days per month.

According to the evaluation, the average daily wage rate was Rs. 33.36 (Rs. 30.54 cash + Rs. 2.82 in foodgrains). On average, a JRY worker at the all-India level earned Rs. 369 during the 30 days preceding the date of the survey. Because the poverty line was an income of Rs. 917 per month per family, a JRY worker earned, on average, 40 percent of the poverty line threshold. Thus, JRY seems to be contributing substantial income to the families working under the scheme.

JRY TARGETING. The concurrent evaluation for 1993–94 shows that 82 percent of the JRY workers had an annual family income of less than the revised poverty line. Therefore, for the most part, the workers who were provided employment belonged to the poorer segments of the population, although there were significant variations in the coverage of the poor under the JRY across states. The Indian experience also shows that the public works programs are more useful during drought years. For instance, the incidence of poverty did not increase in a drought year like 1987–88 mainly because of the purchasing power created by the massive employment programs in the drought-affected states (e.g., Gujarat and Rajasthan).

The Impact of the Employment Guarantee Scheme on Poverty

An evaluation of the EGS in Maharashtra shows that the program reduced unemployment in the state; increased the incomes of many participating households, acted as an insurance mechanism, had an impact on agricultural growth and wages, made the rural poor a political force, and had considerable impact on the empowerment of women (Dev 1996). Although it must be noted that the EGS alone cannot lead to poverty alleviation, and it may not have a significant impact on poverty in terms of headcount ratio, it nevertheless positively impacts the intensity of poverty, with the result that the gap between the extremely poor and the poor has been narrowing in recent times.

The Contribution of the JRY and the EAS to Rural Employment

Since both the JRY and the EAS are major programs that provide rural employment, it is useful to consider their contribution to rural employment creation by examining the two schemes together. The total employment generated by these two programs in 1998–99 benefited 4.4 million people. Given that the size of the total labor force is over 300 million and assuming that the segment of the rural poor is about 30 percent of the rural labor force, these employment schemes touch about 4.5 percent of the rural workforce. This is still small, but considering the scale of unemployment in rural areas (around 7 percent), it can make a significant difference. One can therefore conclude that the schemes do help to contain the level of unemployment in a significant way.

The PDS and Nutrition Programs

THE PDS. The PDS has been effective during severe drought years, such as 1979–80 and 1987–88 (Tendulkar and Jain 1993), and in transferring food-grains from surplus regions to a few deficit ones such as the state of Kerala. But the present system of public distribution has many problems: (1) it is benefiting the poor only marginally (Parikh 1994), (2) in some areas the poor have to pay higher market prices in the presence of the PDS (Radhakrishna and Indrakant 1987), (3) there has been a considerable decline in the consumer share in food subsidies due to the high costs of procurement and carrying costs, and (4) there are leakages to the open market (Ahluwalia 1993) and inefficiency in the Food Corporation of India (India, Ministry of Industry, 1991). A study conducted by Tata Economic Consultancy Services also found that there has been significant diversion of PDS commodities from the system.

The overall impact of the PDS on the poor seems to be less than assumed. According to Parikh (1994), "The cost effectiveness of reaching the poorest 20 percent of households through PDS cereals is very small. For every rupee spent less than 22 paise reach the poor in all states, except in Goa, Daman and Diu where 28 paise reach the poor. This is not to suggest that PDS does not benefit the poor at all, but only to emphasize that this support is provided at high cost." A study by Radhakrishna, Indrakant, and Ravi (1997) concludes that the "potential benefits from the PDS to the poor could not be realized cost-effectively due to weak targeting and leakages. The cost of income transfer was high mainly because the program was open-ended and never targeted." The study also says that approaches other than quantity rationing, including self-targeting and food stamps, need to be considered in order to deliver food transfers to the needy in a cost-effective manner (Ramaswamy 2002). Poor states have not benefited much, and the relationship between poverty and PDS off-take is weak across most states.

The income gains through the PDS formed about 0.7 percent of the total monthly per capita expenditure in rural areas and 0.5 percent in urban areas at the all-India level in 1999–2000 (Dev et al. 2004). As compared to 1986–87, the income gain of the rural poor in 1999–2000 had more than doubled (1.98 percent over 0.97 percent), which means that there was an improvement in returns to the rural poor from the PDS between the mid-1980s and the late 1990s (Dev et al. 2004). On the other hand, there was a marginal reduction in the income gain of the urban poor, from 1.3 percent of monthly per capita consumption in 1986–87 to 1.29 percent in 1999–2000.

At the all-India level, rural poverty decline due to income transfer was 0.61 percent in 1986–87 (Dev et al. 2004). However, in 1999–2000 the decline in poverty was 1.27 percent. In other words, the PDS had a greater positive impact on rural poverty. This does not take away from the fact that the general impact of the PDS on poverty is much less in proportion to the large amount of the food subsidies given.

THE ICDS. The World Bank and the Indian government reviewed the ICDS program in 1997 and found that though ICDS services were much in demand, there were problems in delivery, quality, and coordination. The program might be improving food security at the household level, but it has failed to effectively address the issue of prevention, detection, and management of undernourished children and mothers. It was also found that (1) eligible children in the 6- to 24-months age group and pregnant and lactating women did not go to the *anganwadi,* nor did they receive food supplements; (2) the available food was shared among 3- to 5-year-old children irrespective of their nutritional status; (3) there was no focused attention on the management of severely undernourished children; (4) no attempt was made to provide ready mixes that could be given to 6- to 24-month-old children 3–4 times a day, nor did nutrition education focus on meeting these children's needs; (5) the childcare education of mothers was poor or nonexistent; and (6) there were gaps in workers' training, supervision, and community support (India, Planning Commission, 2000).

Social Security Programs

Despite some initial troubles, the NSAP has proved a popular program. In 2000–2001, Rs. 4.8 billion was spent on the NOAPS (the old-age pension scheme), and Rs. 2.0 billion was spent on the NFBS (the family benefit scheme). Around 5.1 million people benefited from the NOAPS in the same year.

The NSAP was evaluated by the Operations Research Group three years after its implementation. The study was taken up in eight states (Andhra Pradesh, Bihar, Gujarat, Kerala, Madhya Pradesh, Maharashtra, Orissa, and West Bengal). It revealed low levels of physical achievement for all three schemes in the first two years of implementation. However, in the third year, achievement under the NOAPS had surpassed the targets in most of the states, whereas achievement under both the NFBS and the NMBS (targeting needy mothers) continued to be low. The program appeared to have been well targeted, largely reaching scheduled castes or scheduled tribes and women. The coverage of women was found to be 40– 60 percent in the NOAPS and 40–50 percent in the NFBS. Lack of awareness about the program and a complicated, bureaucratic registration procedure are major problems. The evaluation revealed that the use of benefits in income-generating activities was negligible, and there had been cases of corruption in the implementation of the program. Most NMBS beneficiaries reported having received the benefits only after delivering their babies. There is therefore a need to create awareness of the scheme among the target segment so that claims will be made well in time. The procedures for all the schemes under the NSAP need to be simplified and made more transparent so that they are more beneficiary-friendly.

Gender-Based Programs

Among the programs for women, group-based microcredit programs such as the DWCRA scheme and self-help groups are doing well. It was found that these groups had a perceptible impact on empowerment and poverty alleviation, particularly in states such as Andhra Pradesh. The additional income accruing to the members from the activities undertaken under the DWCRA scheme varied, on average, between Rs. 10 and Rs. 30 per day. Though gender poverty did not decline significantly, food security improved marginally. These group-based activities enabled the nearly poor to cross the poverty line. In many cases, the quality of employment improved as a result of shifts from wage employment to self-employment. Women took up nonfarm activities (i.e., in services and small businesses) and ventured into nontraditional tasks and enterprises. Further, there were noneconomic impacts of the groups on literacy, health, housing, and empowerment, with moderate improvement in the role of women in family decisionmaking. Some of the participants contested local elections. However, the participation of the poorest of the poor in the existing self-help groups remained low.

The Targeting and Cost-Effectiveness of Some Antipoverty Programs

TARGETING.   The main objective of poverty alleviation programs is to directly help the poor to improve their economic and social conditions. It has been shown that self-targeting schemes such as rural public works score better than income-based targeting (Ravallion and Datt 1995). A comparison of public works programs and the IRDP (self-employment program) in Maharashtra suggests that public works are much better targeted, while income-based measures do not ensure better targeting.

In recent years, comparisons have been made between the EGS and the PDS (Table 21.2). Although transfer efficiency is higher under the PDS than in the EGS, the benefit-cost ratio in the PDS is probably only half that in the employment programs because of better targeting in employment programs. However, the coverage is much wider under the PDS (Dev 1996), while employment programs are expected to be better targeted at the nonpoor than is the PDS. The EGS is also considered superior to the PDS in view of its secondary benefits, such as asset creation, an increase in agricultural wages, and serving as an insurance mechanism against unemployment during slack agricultural season (Parikh 1994).

Regarding credit-based self-employment programs, group lending is more successful in targeting than individual lending. In general, the government-run programs are less successful in targeting compared to NGO- and community-

TABLE 21.2 Comparison of the cost-effectiveness of India's Employment Guarantee Schemes and Public Distribution System (percent)

	EGS	PDS
1. Budgetary cost	100[a]	100[b]
2. Overheads	50[c]	37[d]
3. Leakages	10[e]	35[f]
4. Gross benefit $(1 - 2 - 3)$[g]	40	28
5. Participation cost	16[h]	Neg[i]
6. Net benefit $(4 - 5)$[j] (i.e., transfer efficiency)	24	28
7. Targeting efficiency (coverage of poor)	0.9	0.4
8. Final transfer to poor (6×7)[k] (benefit-cost ratio)	21.6	11.2

SOURCE: Adopted from Guhan (1994).

[a]Aggregate cost of creating one personday of employment.

[b]Cost of food subsidy.

[c]Administrative overhead and nonlabor expenditures.

[d]Distribution overhead, such as freight, storage, other costs, and interest, with 57 percent of 65 percent reaching consumers.

[e]Underpayment of wages.

[f]Lost in transit and at point of sale.

[g]Budgetary cost minus overheads minus leakages.

[h]Forgone earnings.

[i]Negligible, assuming that forgone earnings are not significant due to waiting time and costs of transport to retail shops.

[j]Gross benefit minus participation cost.

[k]Net benefit times targeting efficiency.

based programs. Targeting by age, gender, and other vulnerabilities (e.g., as is done in nutrition programs, programs for children and women, and programs for the elderly, widows, and the handicapped) is also successful in identifying targeted groups. Decentralized programs (e.g., those provided through *panchayats*) are also more effective in targeting compared to centralized programs. Maternal and child nutrition schemes appear to be better targeted than most other programs, presumably because targeting women and children requires less administrative effort.

FINANCIAL VIABILITY AND COST-EFFECTIVENESS. As a result of government budget cuts, there has been more emphasis on the cost-effectiveness and self-sufficiency of funds. Programs with budgetary support are not sustainable over the longer run, and even if they are sustained, the opportunity costs of those funds could be quite high. A comparison of some antipoverty programs in India shows that employment programs fare better than food transfer programs in terms of cost-effectiveness (Table 21.3).

TABLE 21.3 Cost per rupee of income transferred by various antipoverty programs in India, 1993–94

Scheme	Rs.
Andhra Rice Scheme	6.35
Public Distribution System	5.37
Jawahar Rojgar Yojana	2.28
Maharashtra EGS	1.85
Integrated Child Development Services	1.80

SOURCES: Radhakrishna, Indrakant, and Ravi (1997) for PDS, Andhra Rice Scheme, and ICDS; Dev (1996) for JRY and EGS.

The PDS and Andhra Rice Scheme emerge as very expensive, because it costs Rs. 5.37 and Rs. 6.35, respectively, to transfer Rs. 1 to the poor under these schemes. Employment programs such as the JRY and the EGS are better largely because of their potential for self-targeting. The ICDS is the least expensive of all in terms of cost per rupee of income transfer, thus implying that self-targeting under the ICDS is the most cost-effective of that among the schemes considered.

The analysis in this section shows that public works wage employment programs such as the EGS, JRY, and EAS certainly appear to be more pro-poor than programs such as the IRDP and PDS. The PDS covers the maximum number of people but at a high cost. A comparison of the impact of the PDS on the poor over time shows that the income gain and poverty impact in rural areas improved in 1999–2000 over 1986–87, but the impact on poverty was still marginal relative to the funds spent on the program.

Counterfactuals Using an Applied General Equilibrium Model

While most antipoverty programs benefit some of the poor, with each we are left with the question of how cost-effective the particular program is. Would the poor have been better off if the money spent had been dropped from a helicopter as the goods offered by relief operations are? This is a serious issue, because most antipoverty programs have legitimate and unavoidable implementation costs. Leakages and inefficiency increase these costs. Further, targeting the benefits only to the poor is often difficult and involves large transaction costs. Thus, one also needs to examine the cost-effectiveness of alternative antipoverty programs. Could the money have been spent differently to give more benefit to the poor? There is also the question of the side-effects of policies: for instance, if food prices are raised, poor farmers may benefit, but the urban poor may lose. If the government distributes free food by importing it, food prices would fall and consumers would gain, but poor farmers could get hurt. Equally important are the long-term or dynamic consequences of a policy. An antipoverty program competes with other uses of resources, and if it reduces public investments it could lower the growth rate to the detriment of the future incomes of the poor. It is therefore important to examine the opportunity costs of resources used in antipoverty programs and their long-term consequences.

We will use a general equilibrium model of India, with empirically estimated parameters that are appropriate for examining such counterfactual questions. We will generate alternative policy scenarios and compare the results with those of a reference scenario to identify the policy impact. We examine three types of policy: (1) direct transfer of income in cash or in kind, (2) employment generation, and (3) pricing policies such as output price support.

The model used is the Agriculture, Growth, and Redistribution of Income Model developed by Narayana, Parikh, and Srinivasan (1991). We will not present the methodology and the tables relating to simulation results here,[6] but instead give a summary of the results for the above policies. This model is not a forecasting model; all the scenarios including the reference scenario are counterfactual simulations.

FREE DISTRIBUTION OF FOOD.   A massive redistributive program giving 100 kg of wheat to households free of charge, financed through substantially higher taxes, results in a substantial reduction of 99 million persons in 2000 from a reference level of 164 million in 1980 in the poorest class in rural areas (Parikh, Dev, and Shariff 2003). Their average energy intake and equivalent incomes improve as well. Such a redistributive program is welfare-improving even when it is financed without raising taxes, but it involves a substantial cost in terms of forgone investments and growth.

EMPLOYMENT GENERATION.   In the well-designed, -executed, and -targeted RWP (Rural Works Programs), not only do the rural poor improve their welfare substantially but the economy grows a little faster because of the additional investment through rural work, provided that the resources needed for the RWP are raised through additional taxation. However, the additional tax effort needed initially is substantial; in 1980 an additional 6 percent of GDP had to be raised as income taxes over the reference value of 2 percent. But with the economy growing, the additional tax effort required declined substantially and was reduced to around 1 percent of GDP by the year 2000 as opposed to the reference value of 7 percent. In this case, if foreign aid in the form of grants is available for a limited period, poverty alleviation through the RWP can be initiated without straining the fiscal capacity of the government. Without foreign aid and without a rise in taxes, a RWP financed through a reduction in investment could decrease real GDP in year 2000 by a marginal 4.6 percent relative to the reference run, while GDP is higher by 3.5 percent in the scenario with tax-financed RWP. Thus the sacrifice in growth is modest, while the favorable impact on the welfare of the poor is unchanged. Further social welfare comparison using the

---

6. For these aspects of the model see Parikh, Dev, and Shariff (2003).

Bailey-Willig criterion (Parikh, Dev, and Shariff 2003) shows that such a RWP (tax-funded) is superior to a free food policy that costs just as much.[7] Finally, if the investment component of the RWP is inefficient, and a 50 percent leakage occurs, the welfare of the poor is roughly halved compared to a well-designed, -executed, and -targeted RWP also financed by taxation.

OUTPUT PRICE SUPPORT. The cross-sectional impact of the price hike in terms of distribution of the number of poor, income, and welfare is instructive. There is a significant population increase in the poorer classes, in both rural and urban areas. A Willig-Bailey comparison (Parikh, Dev, and Shariff 2003) of the two (urban and rural) income distributions under the assumptions of Pareto principle, anonymity, and aversion to regressive transfers clearly indicates that with higher minimum support prices (MSPs) there is a significant worsening of the welfare of 80 percent of the population in rural areas and of all urban dwellers. Further, the welfare loss is in general larger for the urban population than for the rural population across classes and over time. The welfare loss is in general regressive in the sense that the lower classes seem to lose more than the upper classes. Only the top 20 percent of the rural population experiences welfare increases in the third year. It should be emphasized that the rural population received part of their income from nonagricultural activities. Thus, the decline in nonagricultural output adversely affects the income of the rural population, which to some extent neutralizes the gains from the increase in agricultural prices. The top quintile of the rural population has a larger marketable surplus of wheat and rice, and they also receive a relatively larger share of nonagricultural income.

To summarize, the counterfactual simulations show the following:

- When untargeted income redistribution programs financed by raising taxes can be carried out without any transaction costs, they can increase aggregate social welfare. Whether or not a significant increase in taxes is possible is a separate issue.
- When such redistribution is financed by reducing investment, it involves significant costs in terms of forgone growth. Even then the welfare of the rural population improves.
- An employment program is an attractive antipoverty program because it is self-targeting and leads to a substantially larger increase in the welfare of the poor relative to an untargeted income transfer, with comparable gov-

---

7. The Willig and Bailey (1981) approach takes into account changes in both the population proportions and equivalent incomes across classes and allows comparison of alternative income distributions under the assumptions of the Pareto principle, as well as anonymity and aversion to regressive transfers. These authors compare the average per capita equivalent incomes of bottom X percent of the population for all X from 0 to 100. When one policy scenario shows higher equivalent incomes for all values of X, we can say that it represents a superior welfare situation.

ernment outlay. Employment programs are more efficient even when they involve leakages and generate worthless assets.

• The policy of MSPs introduced to protect farm income can lead to a decrease in the welfare of the farmers themselves if prices are set too high. This is an example of a perverse dynamic consequence of an antipoverty program.

These counterfactual simulations demonstrate that the efficiency of antipoverty programs and their dynamic consequences matter. When these are neglected, antipoverty programs can even be antipoor.

Lessons and Strategies to Increase the Effectiveness of Antipoverty Programs

Some Lessons

TARGETING.   Successful targeting seems to be crucial for the success of the programs. One of the main problems of the PDS is leakage, while programs such as public works are relatively successful because of their self-targeting nature. The involvement of *panchayats* and civil society at the village level would help identify the right beneficiaries.

IMPACT ON THE SEVERITY OF POVERTY.   Some of the poverty alleviation programs might not have allowed the poor to actually cross the poverty line, but they reduced the severity of poverty.

ECONOMIC GROWTH AND THE NEED FOR LINKAGES WITH SECTORAL PROGRAMS.   A low rate of growth of the economy, particularly in agriculture, can act as a constraint on the success of the programs. It is therefore necessary to recast the employment programs to make them more effective not only in meeting the short-term objective of providing temporary work but also in building up the productive capacity of individuals or areas so that employment is on a more sustainable basis (Nayyar 1996). Public works programs should not be relief programs (Hirway and Terhal 1994), but instead should create assets, which can provide sustainable, productive employment in the future.

The most glaring weakness of the expenditures made every year in public works is that they are not conceived in the framework of an overall development plan of an area. Rao (1992) discusses the lack of integration of employment generation schemes such as JRY with development programs in India. Some novel experiments can also be tried for effective use of these programs at the local level. For instance, one can try public work schemes, such as those successfully tried in Zimbabwe, in which government provides only the casual wage costs, requiring the community to mobilize its own resources for nonwage expenses.

MINIMUM AND MARKET WAGE RATES.   Areas to be covered by the wage employment programs need careful attention. Such programs are not relevant and appropriate in localities where the market wage exceeds the minimum wage. If there is no demand for employment at the minimum wage rate of the wage employment programs, the program could simply be discarded in that locality, leaving more resources available for poorer localities.

USE OF FUNDS.   Studies (Rajaraman 2001, 2004) focusing on some major schemes of the Ministry of Rural Development for 2000–2001 (e.g., the EAS and its successor, JGSY) found that the use rates of poverty funds for most of the schemes were less than 50 percent of the amount allocated for the first six months. This is especially surprising "since the first six months of the fiscal year from April encompass the agricultural slack season, when the demand for rural employment should be at its peak" (Rajaraman 2001, 20). The use rates at the end of the year, however, are much higher, "suggesting hasty, wasteful utilization in the second half of the fiscal year" (Rajaraman 2001, 20). Underuse of funds seems to be higher in the poorer states, implying that although these schemes are meant to alleviate poverty, the better-off states use them more efficiently than the poor states.

THE GROUP APPROACH TO MICROCREDIT FOR WOMEN.   The earlier IRDP approach of giving credit to individuals has not been successful. The group approach is working reasonably well. This approach has improved the social mobilization and empowerment of women.

PUBLIC INVESTMENT IN INFRASTRUCTURE.   Using econometric methods, Fan, Hazell, and Thorat (1999) examine the impact of government expenditures in rural areas. Their results show that investments in rural roads and agricultural research and development have the greatest impact among all types of government spending, including antipoverty funds, which makes a strong case for increasing public investment in rural infrastructure in India.

Challenges Ahead

The major criticism of the government antipoverty programs relates to the lack of people's participation. The current approach seems to be still excessively technocratic and top-down in implementation. There is a need to involve *panchayats,* NGOs, self-help groups, and community organizations to strengthen the poverty reduction programs.

STRENGTHENING THE PANCHAYATIT RAJ.   Under the 73rd and 74th Amendments to the Indian Constitution, people at the village level are now empowered to exercise their rights and manage their own developmental activities through participation in the local government. This reform opens up space for potentially effective and creative local development efforts with built-in mechanisms for accountability.

STRENGTHENING VOLUNTARY ORGANIZATIONS.   Wherever local voluntary organizations have shown interest and have been involved, the effectiveness of government-sponsored antipoverty programs has improved. Moreover, the activities of the government at the local level should be transparent, and the people should have the right to demand and receive information on funding and other activities. In this regard, through their advocacy and disclosure practices, voluntary organizations can make the *panchayats* more accountable. NGOs can also facilitate the social mobilization of people, in particular women. Given their well-documented effectiveness, self-help (e.g., microcredit) groups can be made responsible for the implementation of some of the special employment programs, such as that of the DWCRA scheme.

HUMAN DEVELOPMENT.   India has made good economic progress in the past 50 years, and its poverty ratio has halved. However, it must be remembered that economic growth and development are only the means; social development is the end. From this point of view, India has a long way to go, with about half of the population still illiterate and with a high level of gender bias, relatively low life expectancy at birth (64 years according to WDI 2004), high levels of undernutrition and anemia, and lack of adequate safe drinking water. Also, the Human Development Index figures of Indian states show a high disparity.

There are a number of challenges to be met in improving the country's human development parameters to match international levels. The primary challenge emerges from the way the parameters and indexes are defined in India. For example, literacy, unemployment, sources of safe potable water, institutional delivery, and so on are defined at rudimentary levels.[8] This is also the case with regard to the poverty line, which is an amount barely adequate to purchase a small basket of food items to furnish 2,200 to 2,400 kilocalories of energy. This cut-off point is far lower than even the benchmark of U.S.$1 a day used by international governmental agencies. In the case of employment, given the high incidence of poverty, the poor are forced to take up low-productivity and often menial jobs and are reported as employed even though their income from these occupations cannot lift them out of poverty.

THE STATUS OF SCHEDULED CASTES AND SCHEDULED TRIBES.   It is well known that for historical and cultural reasons people identified as scheduled castes and scheduled tribes are highly deprived. Despite the constitutional guarantees that their interests will be protected through positive affirmative action, one cannot find a measurable change for the better in relative terms among these communities over a period of more than five decades. Similar problems exist with respect to regional- or state-level imbalances, which is a formidable challenge.

ACCESS TO LAND.   Given the importance of access to assets for poverty reduction, land reforms should be part of the agenda for poverty alleviation. Tenancy reforms, prevention of alienation of tribal lands, and land rights for women are important in this context.

---

8. For instance, literacy in India is defined in terms of an individual's ability to write his or her own name in any of the recognized languages. The definition does not set standards for assessment of the quality of education or literacy.

LIVELIHOOD STRATEGIES FOR SELF-EMPLOYMENT.   The poorest of the poor are often left out of the existing microcredit groups, a situation that needs to be corrected. Repayment schedules are not suitable for the most disadvantaged, and thus they should be reconsidered to make them more pro-poor. Other initiatives such as improvement of skills, development of other asset bases, and interventions in commodity markets are needed, because credit alone is not enough to address the problems of the self-employed poor. Another challenge is to make the existing self-help groups sustainable over time. Poor economic growth and existing class relations put hurdles in the way of the relatively better off among the poor who are trying to improve their well-being. The process of empowering women cannot be sustained unless their livelihood concerns are aptly addressed. There is a need to undertake viable economic activities that can improve incomes much faster.

IMPROVING THE DELIVERY SYSTEMS THROUGH PEOPLE'S PARTICIPATION. The success of the antipoverty programs ultimately depends on the capability of the delivery systems to absorb and use the funds in a cost-effective and scrupulous manner. An effective delivery system has to ensure people's participation at various stages of the formulation and implementation of the programs, transparency in the operation of the schemes, and adequate monitoring.

THE PRIVATE SECTOR AND CIVIL SOCIETY.   The government has to take the lead role in providing supplementary employment, but it cannot provide for everything, and thus the problem of poverty cannot be solved by government intervention alone. Also, excessive centralization of program design and implementation has curtailed the initiative of the people. Therefore, in its strategic planning of antipoverty programs the government should aim at creating an enabling framework, setting objectives, committing resources, and promoting capacity building and social mobilization with a view to putting the management of certain activities into the hands of the people and their organizations.

Concluding Observations

Both economic growth and direct poverty alleviation programs helped reduce poverty in India. This chapter shows that in terms of targeting, wage employment programs (rural public works) are more pro-poor than are programs such as the IRDP or the PDS. Nutrition programs and social security programs are also better targeted to the beneficiaries. These programs have helped in reducing the depth and severity of poverty in the country, although they may not have helped many more people to cross the poverty line. But the opportunity costs and cost-effectiveness of such programs need to be looked into. Our simulations with applied general equilibrium showed that rural public works are better than free food distribution. If the poverty alleviation programs are not effectively implemented, they can be antipoor in terms of opportunity costs.

In India there has been an increasing policy emphasis on improving antipoverty schemes in recent years. According to the Task Force on Employment Opportunities (2001), wage employment programs can play a very useful role in providing supplementary employment to vulnerable segments of the population, especially in seasonal lean periods, which are common in agriculture, and in the absence of an extensive system of social security.[9] They can also act as a social safety net to help people deal with situations of exceptional distress, such as droughts. Wage employment programs should be focused as much as possible on maximizing the developmental impact on rural areas through the creation of durable assets in terms of economic and social infrastructure. The experience in self-employment programs is mixed at best: there are some outstandingly successful examples of self-help groups involving women, but the general experience with the IRDP has not been very encouraging.

The Special Group on Targeting Ten Million Employment Opportunities per Year suggested that of the proposed 50 million job opportunities to be generated over the period of the 10th five-year plan, nearly 20 million should come from specific employment generation programs and 30 million from growth buoyancy.[10] There is a need to launch specific employment-generating programs in some areas where aggregate growth has had little impact. It is clear that direct poverty alleviation programs are going to stay whether they are supplementary or able to create large amounts of employment. Substantial funds are allocated for these programs; therefore, they have to be implemented effectively.

This chapter has discussed strategies needed to strengthen Indian antipoverty programs. Economic growth and public investment in infrastructure in areas such as health and education are important for sustaining these schemes. Yet agricultural growth still holds the key to poverty alleviation in the Indian context, and thus it is necessary to reorient the antipoverty programs so that they can contribute more efficiently to the creation of rural assets, both private and community.

Appendix 21A: Major Employment Generation and Poverty Alleviation Programs in India

Following are nine of the more significant programs for employment and poverty reduction in India. Some but not all are discussed in this chapter.

1. *Swaranjayanti Gram Swarozgar Yojana (SGSY)*. SGSY became operative on April 1, 1999, as a result of the amalgamation of programs such as the

---

9. Montek Ahluwalia is the chairman of the task force.
10. S. P. Gupta is the chairman of the study group.

Integrated Rural Development Program, Development of Women and Children in Rural Areas, Training of Rural Youth for Self-Employment, the Million Wells Scheme, and others into a single self-employment program. It aims to promote microenterprises and form the rural poor into self-help groups (SHGs).[11] This scheme covers all aspects of self-employment, such as organization into SHGs, capacity building, training, planning of activity clusters, infrastructure development, obtaining financial assistance through bank credit, subsidy and marketing support, and so on. It is being implemented as a centrally sponsored scheme on a cost-sharing ratio of 75 to 25 between the central government and the states.

2. *Jawahar Gram Samridhi Yojana (JGSY)*. JGSY was formed in April 1999 by restructuring the Jawahar Rozgar Yojana and is being implemented as a centrally sponsored scheme on a cost-sharing ratio of 75 to 25 between the central government and the states. The program is implemented by Gram Panchayats, and works that result in the creation of durable productive community assets are taken up. The secondary objective, however, is generation of wage employment for the rural unemployed poor.

3. *The Employment Assurance Scheme (EAS)*. The EAS was started in October 1993 for implementation in 1,778 identified backward Panchayat Samitis of 257 districts situated in drought-prone areas, desert areas, tribal areas, and hill areas in which the revamped Public Distribution System was in operation. It was subsequently expanded by 1997–98 to all the 5,448 rural Panchayat Samitis of the country. It was restructured in 1999–2000 to make it a single wage employment program and implemented as a centrally sponsored scheme on a cost-sharing ratio of 75 to 25 between the central government and the states.

4. *The Food-for-Work Program (FWP)*. The FWP was initially launched in February 2001 for five months and was further extended. The program augments food security through wage employment in the drought-affected rural areas of the eight states of Gujarat, Chattisgarh, Himachal Pradesh, Madhya Pradesh, Maharashtra, Orissa, Rajasthan, and Uttaranchal. The central government makes an appropriate quantity of foodgrains available free of cost to each of the drought-affected states under the program. Wages owed by the state government can be paid partly in kind (up to 5 kg of foodgrains per manday) and partly in cash. The workers are paid the balance of their wages in cash so that they are assured of the notified minimum wages. This program was extended to March 31, 2002, for notified "natural calamity affected districts."

5. *Sampoorna Grameen Rozgar Yojana (SGRY)*. Launched in September 2001, SGRY aims to provide wage employment in rural areas along with food

---

11. The source for this section is India, Ministry of Finance, *Economic Survey,* 2001–2.

security and to create durable community, social, and economic assets. The scheme is being implemented on a cost-sharing ratio of 75 to 25 between the central government and the states. The ongoing Employment Assurance Scheme and Jawahar Gram Samridhi Yojana would subsequently be fully integrated within the scheme as of April 2002.

6. *The National Social Assistance Program (NSAP)*. The NSAP was introduced in August 1995 as a 100 percent centrally sponsored scheme for providing social assistance benefits to poor households affected by old age, death of the primary breadwinner, and maternity. The program has three components: the National Old Age Pension Scheme, the National Family Benefit Scheme, and the National Maternity Benefit Scheme.

7. *Annapurna.* This scheme went into effect in April 2000 as a 100 percent centrally sponsored scheme. It aims at providing food security to meet the requirements of those senior citizens who, although eligible under the National Old Age Pension Scheme, are not receiving pensions. Foodgrains are provided to the beneficiaries at subsidized rates of Rs. 2 per kg of wheat and Rs. 3 per kg of rice. The scheme is operational in 25 states and 5 Union Territories. More than 608,000 families have been identified, and they receive the benefits of the scheme.

8. *Krishi Shramik Samajik Suraksha Yojana.* This scheme was launched in July 2001 to provide social security benefits to agricultural laborers for hire in the age group from 18 to 60 years.

9. *The Swarna Jayanti Shahri Rozgar Yojana (SJSRY).* The Urban Self-Employment Program and the Urban Wage Employment Program are two special schemes of the SJSRY, initiated in December 1997, which replaced various programs operated earlier for urban poverty alleviation. The SJSRY is funded on a 75 to 25 cost-sharing basis by the central government and the states. During 2001–2, an allocation of Rs. 168 crore was provided for various components of this program.

PART VII

Lessons Learned and Future Directions

This part of the book consists of the last chapter, which brings together the findings of the preceding chapters in a way that can be comprehended as an experience of growth and the lessons that can be learned out of this experience. The main lessons from the Chinese and Indian reform experiences are drawn and future challenges highlighted in the hope that it will be of service not only to the two countries in their continuing journey down the path of reform but also to other developing countries that are striving for a better future for themselves and their people.

22 Synthesis: Lessons and Challenges

SHENGGEN FAN, ASHOK GULATI,
AND SARA DALAFI

China and India have achieved enormous successes in promoting their economic growth for the past two decades. The rapid rise of these, the two most populous countries in the world, has led to the sudden increase of total world wealth in a short period of time. This rise has no precedent in history. However, there is still a large gap between these two countries and more developed countries of the world in terms of many development indicators. Their per capita income, even measured in terms of more comparable measures such as purchasing power parity, is still a small fraction of that of many advanced countries. Their social development indicators, such as literacy rate, infant mortality rate, access to safe and clean drinking water, access to social services, and many environmental indicators lag far behind the world average. Both countries still have a long way to go to reduce the number of their poor—a total of 300 million.

Therefore, continued rapid economic growth is needed to further improve the social development indicators of China and India and to reduce the poverty in those countries. But such growth is also necessary for their stability, because their citizens are expecting continued high rates of growth regardless of their different political and economic systems. If their high growth rates cannot be maintained, social unrest or even breakdown of the existing social, political, and economic systems will inevitably occur. Both countries are also facing gigantic challenges in maintaining their current growth rates and in the meantime improving their various development indicators.

Continuing on the path of reform, both China and India have to learn from their own failures and successes as well as the other's. To this end, both need to set their economies firmly on the path of faster yet more efficient, equitable, and sustainable growth. Here we summarize the main lessons that have emerged from the review of the reforms made so far from various chapters of this book and underline the key challenges in the way of further change. The first section provides a synthesis of the lessons learned, and the second presents a review of the major challenges that lie ahead. Finally we offer some brief concluding remarks.

Lessons Learned

Here we discuss the factors that provide the similarities as well as the disparities between the reform experiences of China and India. Such an analysis yields
some common lessons from the reform measures adopted so far, including those
that are still works in progress.

To Reduce Poverty Faster, Begin with Agriculture Reforms

From the trend in the growth rates of agriculture and the incidence of poverty
in the pre- and postreform periods in China, it is clear that the acceleration in
agricultural growth during 1978–2002 (4.6 percent a year as opposed to 2.5
percent a year over 1966–77) was the primary factor influencing the sharp drop
in the number of poor in that country, from 33 percent of the population in 1978
to 3 percent in 2001 (NBS 2002). The better part of this decline occurred in
the first reform phase, 1978–84, when agricultural GDP jumped to 7.1 percent
a year and rural poverty dropped from 33 percent to 15 percent (NBS 2002). In
India, the most rapid poverty reduction occurred from the late 1960s to the late
1980s. This was the period of the so-called green revolution, and the rate of
agricultural growth was high due to the use of modern technologies and the
strong policy support given to agriculture. In contrast to the situation in China,
agriculture was *not* a major factor behind poverty reduction in India during the
era of reforms. In fact, farm growth fluctuated and remained around the same
levels as in the 1980s, if not marginally lower. From 1991 to 2003, agricultural
GDP grew at a rate of 2.7 percent a year compared to 2.9 percent a year between 1980 and 1990 (India, CSO, 2004). Agricultural growth did rise immediately after reforms began in 1991, at a rate 4.1 percent a year, and continued
until 1997 before dipping again to 2 percent. However, this higher growth rate
for six years did not have a noticeable impact on rural poverty, which reduced
only slightly, from 37.4 percent in 1990–91 to 35.7 percent in 1997.[1] That is
partly because agriculture growth was induced in India not by reforms that directly affect the farm sector, but primarily by interventions outside agriculture,
including currency depreciation and reduction of protection in industry, leading
to an improvement of the terms of trade for agriculture.

By making agriculture, the sector that gave the majority of the people their
livelihood, the starting point of market-oriented reforms, China could ensure
the widespread distribution of gains and build consensus and political support
for the continuation of reforms. Reform of incentives resulted in greater returns
to the farmers and in more efficient resource allocation, which in turn strengthened the domestic production base and made it more competitive. Besides,
prosperity in agriculture favored the development of a dynamic rural nonfarm

---

1. The first data are from the 46th National Sample Survey (NSS) round, July 1990–June
1991, and the second from the 53rd NSS round, January–December 1997 (IFPRI 2004).

(RNF) sector, which is regarded as one of the main reasons for the rapid poverty reduction in China because it provided additional sources of income outside farming (Fan, Zhang, and Zhang 2002). The rapid development of the RNF sector also encouraged the government to expand the scope of policy changes and put pressure on the urban economy to reform as well, because nonfarm enterprises in rural areas had become more competitive than the state-owned enterprises (SOEs). Reforms of the SOEs in turn triggered macroeconomic reforms, opening up the economy further.

The comfortable domestic food supply achieved through the various incentive reforms ensured a critical level of grain production before liberalization could begin and allowed Chinese policymakers to abandon the old agricultural policy framework geared toward self-sufficiency in foodgrains (Vyas and Ke 2004). The procurement system was dismantled everywhere except for the main grain-producing regions, and the food rationing system was abolished in the early 1990s. As a result, private agricultural trade is now flourishing.

In India, reforms were actually prompted by macro imbalances and thus started with macroeconomic and nonagricultural reforms. These led to impressive rates of economic growth in the 1990s, but, because they were limited to the nonagricultural sectors, did not have as significant an impact on poverty as in China. Policy changes related to agriculture were carried out much later, and even then were only partial. India continues state food procurement and distribution, mainly because these are seen as forms of affirmative action for over two-thirds of the population, including the poorest, who are dependent on agriculture and the rural economy for their livelihood.

Make Reforms Gradually and Carefully

The Chinese policymakers first created the incentives and institutions required by the market economy and then, in the mid-1980s, they began to slowly open up markets (Chapter 11) by withdrawing central planning and reducing the scope of procurement while expanding the role of private trade and markets. Studies show that the impact on growth of incentive reforms of land use rights, agricultural production management through the Household Responsibility System, and rising procurement prices during 1978–84 was larger than that of the market liberalization reforms made after 1984 (Lin 1992; Fan, Zhang, and Zhang 2004). Ke (Chapter 11) felt this was because incentive reforms in China aided the gradual emergence of markets, which kept at bay the negative effects of the sudden collapse of the old central planning system in the absence of market-based allocative mechanisms, as experienced in other transitional countries.

It is not that the Chinese policymakers had planned this sequence meticulously; rather, it evolved out of a "trial-and-error" approach to implementing reforms. The adoption of new measures through experimentation rather than a predetermined blueprint increased the likelihood of the success of reforms, because it implied a "learning-by-doing" approach or, in the words of Deng

Xiaoping, one of "crossing the river while feeling the rocks" (Chow 2002). This was peculiar to the Chinese reform process, in which the government made sure that each new policy was field-tested at length and determined to be successful in selected experimental districts before it could be applied nationwide and the next measure introduced (Chen, Wang, and Davis 1999).

In the case of India, agricultural trade reforms were a point of departure in agricultural policy. It can be argued that this sequence was a natural choice for India because it had a much larger scope for the role of markets than China. But, as has been pointed out in earlier chapters, the incentive structure of Indian agriculture was highly distorted at the outset of reforms; the sector was, and still is, burdened with excessive regulations on private trading and most market activities. There is an enormous potential for growth only if these constraints are removed.

In India, the liberalization of agricultural trade policies created a series of imbalances by preceding incentive and market reforms in the domestic arena. Lowered protection against a backdrop of low international prices increased imports, although in the case of wheat there was already excess supply from domestic production induced by a high MSP. While broad-based economic and trade reforms resulted in the new export orientation of the sector and improved the incentive framework of agriculture, they also left the sector more exposed to international competition because of persisting constraints to productivity improvement in the domestic front.[2] As a result, India is now focusing on marketing reforms and the removal of regulatory constraints, at least in some of the states.

Initial Conditions Matter

In 1970 the likelihood that an Indian child would die before age five was twice that for a Chinese child. Life expectancy was 49 years in India against China's 62 years, and 70 percent of India's rural population was illiterate as opposed to 49 percent of China's (WDI 2003). One important reason for China's edge over India in health and education was the collective system, whereby the government provided these basic amenities free. In China, rural electrification had made headway in the prereform years; rural electricity consumption grew at a rate of 27 percent a year over 1953–80 as opposed to 10 percent a year over 1980–90, and government investment in power grew at a rate of 27 percent a year during 1953–78 (Fan, Zhang, and Zhang 2002). Egalitarian access to land was ensured by the land distribution and tenure system, which also performed a crucial welfare function by limiting the number of the landless, providing the bulk of the rural population with subsistence, and helping to widely distribute

---

2. See Elbehri, Hertel, and Martin (2003) for a case study on the impacts of trade liberalization in the cotton sector.

the benefits of agricultural price and market reform. The resultant improvements in efficiency and productivity were major triggers to poverty reduction in China.

In India, on the other hand, land reforms to make the agrarian structure more equitable were not as successful and left a relatively larger number of landless agricultural laborers exposed to the harsh impact of unemployment and underemployment. In the power sector, too, although public investments were substantial, an annual growth rate of 12 percent during 1981–90 (Fan, Thorat, and Rao 2004) was not as high as in China, and thus rural electrification and even the establishment of telecommunications connections proceeded more slowly in the Indian villages. This slow pace severely affected the growth of agro-processing and cold storage in India's rural nonfarm sector. The levels of processing remain abysmal even now, with over 80 percent of fruit and vegetables produced going to waste, and the government is currently designing policies to encourage this sector.

Thus, the relatively more favorable initial conditions in China help explain why, despite the private and economic restrictions imposed on the Chinese rural population, the country could achieve sustained growth even before reform (NBS 2003).[3] However, China could not fully realize the benefits of the physical and social infrastructure available in the prereform period because of lack of incentives under the commune system. Once economic reforms were introduced, they released the latent energy in the system, resulting in a very high rate of growth and a rapid reduction in poverty after the 1970s (Rao 2003).

Both countries recorded a slowdown in meeting their health and education goals after reforms began (Rao 2003). In India this was primarily due to the fiscal disciplines imposed by the macroeconomic crisis, while market-oriented reforms in China introduced the concept of profit in the management of social services. In China this implied a progressive privatization of supply agencies, a decline in government subsidies, and an increase in education and health costs, which caused more school dropouts and rising health vulnerability (Rao 2003). In devising mechanisms to address the risks involved in increased privatization of social services, China could perhaps learn from India's long experience of a vast system of government safety nets and welfare programs for the rural population.

With regard to land, both countries have high population-land ratios, but distribution is less skewed in China than in India, and landlessness is virtually absent. As in the case of education and health, in China equal access to land was a product of the egalitarianism inherent in the collective era, which played a vital role in minimizing risks and ensuring the availability of means of minimum subsistence. In India, replication of the Chinese agrarian system is not politically

---

3. Between 1952 and 1977, Chinese agricultural GDP increased at a rate of about 2.3 percent a year.

feasible, so marginal and landless farmers will require a strong social protection system provided through well-targeted social security and employment policies (Srivastava and Yao 2004). Effective social protection measures will also be required in China, where land distribution is likely to become skewed and more concentrated following the adoption of the new agricultural lease law, which enables farmers to transfer lease rights.

Both China and India—especially China—are characterized by the predominance of small farms (smaller than 2 ha), which has implications for rural employment (Srivastava and Yao 2004). China's experience shows that small farms support more intensive use of family labor resources, while in India owners of holdings larger than 2 ha, who account for less than 20 percent of total landholdings but over 60 percent of cultivated area, often lack the incentive to practice labor-intensive cultivation (Srivastava and Yao 2004). Therefore, reforms are required to optimize land use and eliminate distortions such as the concealed tenancy in Indian land markets. Land leasing is restricted in India, affecting private investment as well as the scope for consolidation of small-holdings into larger and more efficient operational holdings (Landes and Gulati 2003). However, given the high population-land ratio, India's approach to deregulation is naturally cautious, allowing a minimum set of safeguards (for example, liberalizing leasing within ceilings) to prevent absentee landlordism and an increase in landlessness (Chapter 4; Haque and Sirohi 1986).

Focus on Public Investments, Technology, and Irrigation

In China, the correlation between the initial conditions and postreform achievements in poverty reduction and growth makes a convincing case for stepping up government investments in rural infrastructure and social services. In India, on the other hand, the decline in rural public investment as a result of fiscal profligacy and rising subsidies on fertilizers, power, water, and price support is regarded as a primary cause of slower growth after 1997. Because both these countries have budget pressures and are unlikely to be able to increase public investments significantly, they would just have to invest the available resources more efficiently. Returns to public investments vary drastically across different types of investment and regions even within the same country. This implies a great potential for achieving more growth and less poverty even with the same amount of investment, assuming public resources can be allocated optimally on the basis of reliable information on the marginal returns of different types of government spending. Studies have found that spending on agricultural research, education, and rural roads is the most effective for promoting agricultural growth and poverty reduction (Chapter 6; Fan, Hazell, and Thorat 1999).

Then again, both countries will find it tough to expand their cultivable land and water resources, so yield-based farm growth will become important and will call for increased agricultural research and technology development. Agricultural research and development (R&D) takes place in both the public and the private sectors, but managing public versus private R&D can be tricky. China promoted the development of the public business sector through the commercialization of technologies by public research institutes (Chapter 7), but this often led to duplication of research and overlap of efforts with SOEs. The Chinese experience can provide valuable lessons in this sector for other countries in transition.

The improved intellectual property rights (IPR) regime under the World Trade Organization (WTO) stimulated private research and patenting activity in both countries (Chapter 7; Pal 2004). However, weak implementation of IPR in the two countries and the high costs of maintaining patents in China are obstacles to the entry of private players. The Chinese experience also shows that protection of plant varieties can help improve resource generation by the poorer public research institutes, because the number of IPR applications filed was effectively higher for resource-poor institutions than for better-funded national institutes. In terms of increasing the scope for private research, India's case indicates that the IPR regime is more effective if complemented by favorable policies in the areas of tax, investment, and input imports (Pal 2004).

Private agricultural R&D provides both opportunities and challenges. Significant opportunities can arise for public-private partnerships in the areas of funding, research, and extension (Pal 2004). However, policymakers need to be aware that the private sector tends to privilege higher-value crops and concentrate on areas where agriculture is already advanced (Pal 2004). Given agriculture R&D's potential to reduce poverty in marginal regions, public research spending should target poorer farmers in less favored environments such as India's semiarid tropics and rain-fed areas and China's poor western regions.

In the water sector of each country, government spending in irrigation effectively promoted growth and poverty reduction, but the marginal returns of such spending have decreased over time (Chapter 6). Indeed, studies have shown that investments in rain-fed areas have had high marginal returns for agricultural growth and poverty reduction (Chapter 6; Fan, Hazell, and Thorat 1999). Major investments in harvesting rainwater by means of watersheds, through public-private partnerships, may help usher in a "multicolored revolution" (not just a "green" one) in agriculture (Chapter 9).

In both countries, water use efficiency can be vastly improved through institutional and management reforms of existing water systems. India's experience with water users' associations (WUAs) in some states, participatory watershed schemes, and community-based rain harvesting can provide a good learning experience (Chapter 9; Rao 2002). The transfer of the management of these systems to user groups was more successful in India, although the coverage of irrigated areas by these user associations remains low in India compared to other Southeast Asian countries (Rao 2002). Insufficient administrative and political will to devolve management powers to the local WUAs and inadequate infrastructure for building capacity inhibited the involvement of farmers in India (Rao 2000). On the other hand, the Chinese experience shows that reforms aimed at giving incentives to irrigation system managers to improve use efficiency had a positive effect on crop yields, groundwater tables, and cereal production (Wang et al. 2003). The question is whether the strategy of transforming water bureaucrats into managers is possible in India.

Providing the right incentives to farmers is crucial to promoting water saving. Low water prices and profligate power subsidies for operating tubewells have encouraged wasteful use of water and depletion of groundwater resources. Ambiguous water use rights following decollectivization in China and laws linking water rights to land ownership in India also led to inefficiencies (Chapter 9). These included the emergence over time of unfair water markets where rich landholders with modern water extraction technology profited from selling water to poorer cultivators (Chapter 9).

Increasing water use charges may not be feasible in the short to medium term without changes in the institutional set-up. In India, irrigation is affected by realpolitik in that free electricity for pumping water is offered for political rent-seeking. In both countries, given the booming numbers of private tubewell owners and the weak institutions and infrastructure that make monitoring of water withdrawals and revenue collection difficult,[4] the impact of reforms such as withdrawal permit systems and volumetric charging can only be limited (Wang, Huang, and Rozelle 2003; Shah, Scott, and Buechler 2004). Improved crop yields can also lead to more efficient use of scarce water resources in agriculture. For that, inputs other than water, such as credit and agricultural research on water-saving and yield-improving technologies, need to be deployed (Chapter 10). This is particularly true in India, where both irrigated and rain-fed crop yields are lower than those in China (Chapter 10). In both countries, this may also call for trade and price policies favorable to high-value, less water-intensive crops. In India, technological innovations to improve yields seem more feasible in the short and medium terms than management reforms for improving water use efficiency, given the political and institutional constraints (Rao 2002).

Reform Incentives before Opening Markets and Trade

China's experience with marketing reforms holds valuable lessons for other transitional economies. Farm support policies lose their rationale when there is an oversupply of food and agricultural trade is free and open. India's minimum price supports (MSPs) and input subsidies were intended to encourage the adoption of new technologies and fuel growth, but they turned into inefficient and costly income-support interventions encouraging the buildup of vested interests because they were not abolished after their aim was realized. China could learn from this experience and seek to encourage agricultural growth in the fu-

---

4. There were nearly 20 million private tubewell owners in India as of 2003 and 3.5 million in China as of 1997.

ture yet avoid the large, inefficient Indian subsidies. This issue is important because India has recently introduced a costly direct transfer program for rural areas and also because late, increasing government support to agriculture and rural areas is finding many takers among scholars and government officials alike.

Despite limited reforms in agricultural marketing in India, the impact of policy changes has slowed down because state governments are reluctant to implement them (Landes and Gulati 2003). In addition, a host of outdated domestic regulations, such as those of the Agricultural Produce Marketing Committee, regulation of agricultural produce market sales, restrictive land laws, and license requirements for food processing units, continue to weaken the environment for agribusiness and private sector involvement in agricultural marketing, which could boost employment and efficiency (Landes and Gulati 2003). Against the backdrop of increasing, diversified food demand and the opening up of agricultural trade, legal and regulatory reform remains critical given its capacity to directly impact the sector adjusting to the changing environment. Given that smallholder agriculture is predominant in both countries, farmers could be excessively penalized because they do not possess sufficient capital and information to manage the risks inherent in agricultural activities (Chapter 12). While China and India are reconsidering the current forms of agricultural and input subsidies, they should also put in place well-targeted and innovative cost-effective crop insurance policies to protect farmers vulnerable to drastic supply and price shocks. Such shocks can only intensify as trade policies are further liberalized. In India, the abolition of restrictions on trading on the futures markets in major agricultural commodities is a step in this direction.

One other important area for reform is the strengthening of the network of support services to small farmers related to information, credit, and extension (Chapter 12). India is ahead of China in these areas, especially in the institutional infrastructure of rural credit and marketing. The Indian experience shows that smallholder agriculture needs strong institutional support in these areas to grow and prosper (Vyas and Ke 2004).

With regard to broad trade liberalization, both countries made progress in reducing protection levels. Still, India's weighted average tariff, at 29 percent, is double that of China, at 16 percent (Ahluwalia 2002). India was able to sustain its current growth rate with lower inflows of foreign direct investment (FDI) and relatively less export orientation than in China. But if it is to attain the target of 8 percent GDP growth (Ahluwalia 2002), it needs to further reform the FDI climate in view of its potential to transfer know-how, managerial skills, and new technologies. China can offer valuable lessons in this area.

The inevitable restructuring and adjustments involved in opening up agricultural trade flows will produce both winners and losers. Domestic producers of crops in which each country lacks comparative advantage (for example, edible oils in the case of India and wheat and maize for China) are likely to suffer increasingly from the falling prices resulting from higher levels of imports

(Chapter 13). They will also be negatively affected when pressure is placed on the governments to reduce their support for inefficient national producers. Broad-based structural adjustments in the economy may depress rural incomes, increase opportunities in manufacturing as well as services primarily located in urban areas, and widen rural-urban inequality. These intersectoral adjustments will progressively shrink the size of the primary sector, which will release additional unskilled labor into the labor markets.

The rural population in each country will gain if it is able to shift to more profitable off-farm occupations (Chapter 15). Here, investment in rural education can help farmers move out of traditional occupations. It will also be important to increase investments in rural R&D and infrastructure to enhance productivity. These investments fall under the WTO "green box" and are therefore exempted from reduction commitments, although their positive impact will be realized over the longer run. On the positive side, WTO membership can provide the much-needed external pressure to improve efficiency and implement reforms in tradable inputs such as seeds, fertilizers, farm machinery, and pesticides, where markets are inefficient due to either government intervention or lack of infrastructure. It can also highlight the facilitating role of the government in the provision of services such as providing information and technical assistance, making marketing facilities available, and establishing standards and quality control regulations. Finally, WTO membership also offers the two countries an opportunity to join hands and create a third force of countries besides the giant European Union and the United States in negotiations within the framework of the Uruguay Round Agreement on Agriculture.

Promote Rural Diversification and Vertical Integration

A major shift in farm production toward nonfoodgrain products such as livestock, fishery, and horticulture products has been well under way in China and India since the 1980s. In China, achievement of food self-sufficiency and the extraordinary growth in basic grain production by the late 1970s immensely helped diversification. This is because food surpluses provided the government with enough leeway to feed the increasing population and relax controls on the foodgrain sector (Vyas and Ke 2004). China gradually abandoned the policies biased in favor of rice and wheat, such as the food rationing system for urban areas and the mandatory levy quotas, which encouraged farmers to diversify production. Developing countries affected by chronic food shortages can learn from this experience. In contrast, steadily growing MSPs in India artificially increased the production of major cereals, discouraging diversification toward nongrain commodities (Zhong and Joshi 2004).

A comparison of the shares of government expenditure to the pace of growth in output in different agricultural subsectors of the two countries indicates that despite high rates of growth, some high-value products (such as livestock and horticulture products) are underfunded relative to traditional food crops (Pal 2004). Policymakers must encourage higher levels of investment in research to boost yields and expand cultivation given the export potential of these crops, the positive impact on smallholders, and growing domestic demand.

Postreform, rising per capita income, influencing food consumption patterns, has been a major driver of diversification into nonfood crops. Without vertical integration between production, processing, and marketing—that is, between "plate and plough"—the potential for growth inherent in the diversification process may remain underexploited (Chapter 18). Vertical integration reduces risks by providing assured markets, cuts transactions costs, and helps improve quality standards and food safety. In both countries, new and innovative institutional arrangements have emerged, promoting the development of new products, and these need to be strengthened. India's successful experiments with contract farming, which helped cut risk, promote the production and export of high-value foods, and raise the income and level of employment of smallholders, can be valuable for China. On the other hand, the experience of growth in the retail food chains and supermarkets in China in recent years could benefit India, where restrictions on FDI and infrastructure bottlenecks are limiting progress (Zhong and Joshi 2004).

In smallholder-dominated farming, diversification has important implications for poverty reduction. Not only is the labor-intensive nature of the production of high-value products well suited to the small farm economy, but there is also great potential for employment creation in agroprocessing and retail chains. Strengthening vertical integration through innovative institutional arrangements without tackling the other major obstacles faced by small farmers would not be effective in reducing poverty. In fact, India's case shows how institutional deficiencies such as weak enforcement of contracts and the high transaction costs faced by small cultivators often prompt agrofirms to deal directly with large farmers (Srivastava and Yao 2004).

Acceleration of diversification in favor of small farmers is also hindered by lack of access to markets, technology, and information; poor rural infrastructure; and inadequate marketing facilities. Future reforms need to address these issues through increased investments in basic rural infrastructure and marketing facilities such as cold storage chains. Finally, small cultivators often lack sufficient marketable surplus. Nor can they raise production at will due to their lack of access to technology and financial services. Well-targeted government support services are needed in credit markets and extension services designed specifically for smallholders.

Looking away from crops, as the Chinese experience has amply demonstrated, the evolution of a dynamic rural nonfarm sector offers great potential for rural diversification. Rapid growth of rural enterprises in China is one of the most striking differentiators between the reform processes of the two countries, especially because township and village enterprises (TVEs) provided increasing numbers of jobs outside agriculture by diversifying and expanding the sources of household income. Agricultural growth and favorable demand conditions were critical to the development of the RNF sector in China because, after 1978, reforms triggered a surge in demand from prospering rural areas for TVE products (Bhalla, Chadha, and Zhang 2004). TVEs also benefited from the close connection with dynamic urban markets established since the early stages of their development (Bhalla, Chadha, and Zhang 2004). The connection with urban markets brought TVEs in competition with SOEs and stimulated the latter to increase their productivity and unit scale (ILO 1998).[5] In India, however, farm output growth rates decelerated, dampening demand as well as farm and nonfarm employment.

India's nonfarm economy produces low-profit services of the informal sector primarily for the rural markets and is dominated by tiny own-account family-operated units. These are characterized by low productivity brought about by their poor technological base and by policies aimed at protecting rural employment by reserving certain activities for small units (Chapter 16). The limited growth of RNF job opportunities is also related to the poorly educated rural labor force (Chapter 16). This is a challenge that will increasingly confront both China and India as they adjust to greater market and trade liberalization leading to economic restructuring and the replacement of traditional and low-productivity jobs by new and more productive occupations requiring more educated laborers. Thus, spending on rural education will be crucial.

The role of nonfarm employment is expected to become increasingly significant as the average size of farms becomes smaller. Small farms may be efficient in terms of land productivity but not in labor productivity, which is more closely linked to farmers' income. Greater off-farm opportunities and migration to urban areas are required to increase average farm size, labor productivity, and farmers' income.

Establish Well-Targeted Antipoverty Programs and Safety Nets

The role of antipoverty programs (APPs) and safety nets in poverty alleviation was brought into sharp focus in the 1990s to address the negative impact of liberal policies on income distribution (Chapter 21; Parikh, Dev, and Shariff 2004). The need for fiscal stabilization in India meant the reduction in transfers to the states and in capital expenditures on rural infrastructure (Jha 2000), to counterbalance which the government stepped up funding for several existing APPs

---

5. TVEs' size varies considerably by both province and ownership. In some of the more developed provinces, such as Jiangsu, the smaller TVEs employ fewer than 100 people, while the largest one employs more than 15,000 workers. Generally, township-owned enterprises are relatively large and village-owned and collectively owned ones are smaller. For instance, construction TVEs employ, on average, 86 workers in township-run enterprises and 36 in village-run enterprises. In garment and leather goods TVEs, employees number, on average, 108 in township-run enterprises and 52 in village industries (personal communication, Peter Hazell, IFPRI).

and created new ones (Jha 2000). In China, the government was strongly committed to addressing the poverty problem, and government initiatives, as announced in official plans and government conferences starting in the mid-1990s, were revived (Chapter 20).

Poverty funds and programs have documented shortfalls and inefficiencies in terms of targeting and cost-effectiveness, but their significant contribution to limiting the severity and the extent of poverty is inescapable (Chapter 20). There are still more than 300 million rural poor in China and India (more than 100 million in China and more than 200 million in India), based on the international standard of U.S.$1 a day. In China, the bulk of the rural poor are primarily in the remote, mountainous, or natural resource–poor western provinces (Fan 2004). In India, they are concentrated in the eastern (Bihar, Orissa, and West Bengal), central (Madhya Pradesh), and northern (Uttar Pradesh) states, where the level of rural poverty is higher than the all-India average of 24 percent as of 1999–2000 (IFPRI 2004).

Radical redistributive measures such as land reforms are relatively impractical in India due to their potential for social conflict, while public investments take a long time to translate into employment and economic growth. Compared to these, APPs are a more agile instrument in the short run, provided their shortcomings are removed.[6] Poor design, targeting, and implementation and fund misuse are key causes of ineffective APPs. To improve targeting, one lesson that China may draw from the experience of India is to use a greater variety of targeted programs directed to specific sections of the poor as opposed to its own traditional, broader income- or area-based approaches. Self-targeting schemes such as rural public works and plans targeting women, children, and the elderly are more pro-poor, because identification of the beneficiaries is easier, faster, and less costly.

To strengthen the impact of APPs, decentralized and participatory approaches are more effective than top-down strategies because they involve a greater variety of agents—nongovernmental organizations (NGOs), civil society, and international aid organizations—in the fight against poverty besides the government. India is a good point of reference in this respect, because the extensive participation of *panchayats* and civil society at various stages of the formulation and implementation of the programs ensures the tailoring of programs to local needs, thereby improving their impact and effectiveness.

Work on the Right Institutions, Regulations, and Political Governance

In both countries there was political will to carry out reforms, but in practice outcomes were shaped by the different patterns of governance. India is a "debating

---

6. Jha (2001) provides a comprehensive analysis of the financial, regulatory, and political ways to improve the effectiveness of poverty reduction programs.

society" (IFPRI 2004) in which political differences are expressed freely. Policy-making is exposed to the pressure of various interest groups, and there are long debates before decisions are made. The lengthy bureaucratic procedures, intended to ensure checks and balances in the system, often delay decisionmaking and implementation. This exercise is compatible with the needs of a free and dynamic polity but in practice is a key reason for the slow pace of India's economic reforms.

China, on the other hand, is a "mobilizing society" in which decisions are made faster and state power is backed by mass mobilization (IFPRI 2004). As a result, implementation of decisions is more effective, although the lack of more elaborate debate on major reforms can sometimes lead to disastrous actions, as in the case of the Great Leap Forward in 1958 and the Cultural Revolution of 1966–76. Interestingly, as China's economic system opens up further and its prosperity increases, it will become harder and harder to reconcile the centralized political set-up with the more liberal economic system. Indeed, this is one of the most important challenges before China today (Prabhu, Kathel, and Dev 2004).

However, in China the ideology-induced commitment to build an equitable society in the prereform years created a strong political will to provide the population with nearly universal access to basic healthcare and education services, while the administrative set-up of the communes proved an effective mechanism of resource mobilization and service delivery. Although similar administrative machinery is not replicable in the Indian context, that country can still try to strengthen the initial conditions in terms of rural electrification, roads, access to education and healthcare services, and so on.

A critical factor in explaining dissimilar reform outcomes in China and India is the difference at the level of reform implementation, which is shaped by their different institutional, regulatory, and political settings. Investments in rural infrastructure and other key public services are crucial, but it is equally critical to develop suitable institutional arrangements for their delivery. Major failures in public provision notwithstanding, the government continues to be the major supplier of infrastructure services in both countries (Herath and Gulati 2003). Input suppliers such as the state electricity boards (SEBs) in India and the SOEs (including grain bureaus) in China do not function efficiently due to the lack of transparency and accountability. Instead of the required 3 percent return on investment, SEBs have recorded negative returns since 1981. By 2000–2001, their returns were a negative 27 percent after subsidies (Gulati and Narayanan 2003). In the case of power and water, underpricing of user fees does not allow recovery of costs sufficient even to meet the costs of operation and maintenance, and this leads to deterioration in the quality of water and power services to farmers. Strengthening public institutions that provide public goods and services and making them cost-efficient can lead to both fiscal sustainability and long-term growth. These goals can be achieved in different ways, such as privatization, unbundling, decentralization, and contracting (Herath and Gulati 2003).[7] Effective public institutions also require an adequate supply of trained and motivated personnel and investments in training to increase the supply.

Another reason for slower implementation of reforms in India relates to the regulatory environment and the enforcement bureaucracy there. Although streamlining the regulatory apparatus through delicensing has begun, much inefficiency remains. Several private investment decisions still require government approval, entailing lengthy procedures encouraging corruption.

During the reform years China relaxed regulations on mobility between rural and urban areas, which promoted the development of the nonfarm sector and abetted economic migration. Recently it has also started to relax the complex system controlling broad-based personal mobility, removing state interference in private life and creating a more mobile and open social environment in tune with the freer economic setting (The Economist 2003b).[8] One bit of fallout from these changes is the faster issue of passports and visas.

Finally, a key factor in the effective implementation of reforms in China was the ability of the leadership to set both clear objectives and time frames for transition to the reformed regime (Ahluwalia 2002), which was no doubt helped by the centralization of decisionmaking, which minimizes dissent. In the context of a highly pluralist society like that of India, consent is more difficult to achieve, so neither clear objectives nor time frames for transition can be set. This has been the case, for instance, in phasing out subsidies, tariff reduction, price increases for economic services, and so on (Ahluwalia 2002). There is also a tendency toward populist policymaking in India, as is clear in the case of subsidies, which, although acknowledged as inefficient and iniquitous, have been tough to remove or minimize (Ahluwalia 2002). This slows the pace of

---

7. With privatization, firms have a stronger incentive to build and run infrastructure industries effectively and at low cost. Unbundling in sectors such as the power, irrigation, telecommunications, and roads sectors involves the separation of activities such as generation, distribution, retailing, and other activities that can be subjected to competition. Decentralization can be an effective alternative to monopolistic utilities when the benefits of an infrastructure service are mostly local and there is little scope for economies of scale such as those found in water supply, road maintenance, and urban transit. Besides, recent technological innovations are gradually eliminating the need to centralize infrastructure and reducing the need for services to be provided by monopolistic utilities. An added advantage is the participation of the users who have stronger incentives than bureaucrats to run and maintain community infrastructures efficiently. In another option, private firms can be contracted to build and maintain schools, health centers, roads, and the like. Establishment of partnerships between the public, private, and NGO sectors through contracting arrangements can be much more cost-effective and may offer better possibilities for involving local people and communities.

8. In recent years some cities, including Beijing, were allowed to relax the "*danwei*" system of permits, a government-controlled work unit to which urban citizens had to apply for permission to receive housing, wedding licenses, passports, and so on. The decline of the *danwei* system is a consequence of the restructuring of the SOEs during the reform years.

change in the short and medium terms. Although democracy and participation have intrinsic value and are not mere instruments of development, the role of democracy in enhancing or hampering economic change and poverty reduction remains a complex subject for development research. Comparisons of China and India on these broad political matters may produce a fascinating set of insights in the coming years.

Future Challenges

Although both China and India have made remarkable progress in terms of growth and poverty reduction, much remains to be done given the sizable share of their populations still living in poverty. The two countries are confronted with three formidable challenges: accelerating growth, improving efficiency, and ensuring that growth is equitable, sustainable, and environmentally friendly.

Accelerating Growth

There are three major sources of rural growth that can further push the two countries' production frontiers in the future. The first is agricultural research and technology, which can increase crop yields. Although average yields in China are double those in India, there is still potential to increase them in the poorer western provinces (Chapter 10). The same is the case in India, where the highly irrigated areas of Punjab and Haryana show average yields of 5–6 tons/ha as opposed to 2 tons/ha in the eastern states, which have yet to benefit from the green revolution. Future agricultural growth will rely heavily on yield improvement because of increasing population pressure on land and the lack of scope to bring more land under cultivation. Research focus needs to be reoriented toward rain-fed regions for their higher returns relative to irrigated areas. New breakthroughs in biotechnology (such as genetically modified organisms) are vital. So is the establishment of regulatory bodies in charge of creating and enforcing biosafety standards and regulations for the new technology. These are critical preconditions for the effective use of R&D spending in this sector.

The second source of rural growth is broader government investment in rural areas. This applies particularly to education and rural infrastructure such as roads, because these are the two areas, besides agricultural research, in which both countries have shown the highest returns. Higher literacy rates as a result of increased spending on education will encourage the adoption of new technology and, in turn, improvement in agricultural productivity as well as occupations in nonfarm sectors. Investment in rural infrastructure will boost productivity and foster both farm and nonfarm diversification by reducing transaction costs, favoring market integration, and strengthening urban and rural linkages. A study by the International Food Policy Research Institute on pro-poor infrastructure that sought to estimate the effects of different types of roads on growth and poverty reduction in China found that the marginal returns from investments in lower-quality roads (mostly rural roads) are more than four times higher than those from high-quality roads (Fan and Chan-Kang 2005b). In India, another sector in which public spending is expected to translate into higher growth is irrigation. The country's potential of gross irrigated area is 140 million ha, while the actual irrigated area is only around 90 million ha. What needs to be determined now is the direction of the resources: should it be toward improving the management of existing water systems through watershed development and user groups or toward the expansion of irrigation systems through new projects. Similar inefficiencies need to be corrected in the power sector, where the states are now losing nearly 1 percent of their GDP due to a whopping 35–50 percent distribution loss rather than 10–15 percent at the most (Ahluwalia 2002).

The third source of future rural growth is high-value agriculture and vertical integration through contract farming. Diversification from low-value foodgrains to high-value commodities needs to be encouraged because horticulture, livestock, and fishery products provide high returns and are labor-intensive in nature. Such products also have the potential to generate employment in agroprocessing and retail chains. In both countries, but more so in India, the challenge is how to reorient the policy environment, which continues to be tied to wheat and rice, toward perishable and high-value products that would entail the establishment of new institutions and marketing facilities. Further, diversification should not be restricted to farming alone, because rural income enhancement requires growth in nonfarm employment (Chapter 17). In India, this calls for overcoming infrastructure bottlenecks, which severely affect the development of rural industries and services, and increasing human capital through education for the poor. To respond to the increased competitiveness due to globalization, the rural TVEs in China need to gear up in terms of management and technical efficiency. The reform of macropolicies aimed at enhancing access to credit and specialized firm services, which are less favorable to labor-intensive enterprises, is an additional challenge.

Promoting Efficient Growth

An increase in total factor productivity is conducive to higher levels of growth and is a challenging goal in itself. Such an increase will come from three sources. First, funds are needed for productive investments. Inefficient agricultural subsidies need to be phased out to free up such funds. This is more the case in India, where subsidies are about five to six times higher than investments in rural areas (Gulati and Narayanan 2003). The issue here is to eliminate inefficient support without creating political turmoil. The second source is a strong institutional environment of agricultural policies, a precondition for making the provision of public investments and services more efficient and pro-poor. The third source is the economic integration of global markets in India and China as a follow-up to the economic integration of local markets in the two countries. Further opening up the two economies would involve a host of reforms on various fronts—in investment; access to foreign inputs, technology, and managerial skills; reduction in price gaps between domestic and world markets; improvement of quality and safety standards—all of which would lead to structural improvements in efficiency.

This increase in productivity needs to be accompanied by increased bilateral and multilateral trade. The trade relations between China and India are currently much below their potential, especially in agricultural products (Agrawal and Sahoo 2003). Similarly, cooperation under the WTO can help change policies in developed countries that adversely affect producers in China and India (von Braun 2003). Such cooperation is necessary because of the major commonality between the two economies, where agriculture is still the major single source of employment. The other rationale comes from the potential benefits of international trade. If the efforts of developing countries—under the leadership of India and China, and perhaps of Brazil—to improve trade liberalization are successful, the WTO can improve export and employment prospects in the labor-intensive production of the horticulture, livestock, and fishery sectors. These are areas in which China and India have comparative advantage (Lin 2003; Sharma 2003).[9] WTO membership can also accelerate the growth of employment in labor-intensive industries, facilitating the shift of rural workforce out of agriculture (Lin 2003).

Ensuring Equitable Growth

Neither in China nor in India has reform-induced growth benefited all and/or benefited people equally. Inequality as measured by the Gini coefficient rose sharply, from 0.21 in 1978 to 0.46 in 2000, in China (Fan and Chan-Kang 2003), more than doubling in the past 25 years. This placed China among the highly unequal economies of the world, marking a great paradox for one of the most

---

9. Against this background, the visit of India's Prime Minister Shri Atal Bihari Vajpayee to China in June 2003 and the common stance adopted by the two countries along with Brazil on the occasion of the WTO negotiations in Cancún in November 2003 were positive developments showing the willingness of both countries to take steps to bring their positions closer for their mutual benefit as well as in the interest of the developing world at large. During the official visit of Prime Minister Bihari Vajpayee to Beijing, a number of initiatives were proposed with a view to adopting a common stance in the WTO in areas such as investment policy, dispute settlement, and trade-related aspects of intellectual property rights. The Chinese and Indian leaders agreed to call a meeting of the Joint Economic Group by the end of 2003 and to establish an Indo-China Business Forum. They also decided to boost bilateral trade up to U.S.$5 billion by 2005. To this end, they decided to reopen the route through the post of Nathu La in the bordering region of Sikkim. Another promising step was the recent establishment of an Indo-China Study Group by the Indian government in 2004 to explore concrete ways to intensify economic cooperation and analyze the merit of establishing a free trade area between India and China. The April 2005 visit to New Delhi by the China's Premier Wen Jiabao and the signing of various agreements has further strengthened the possibility of establishing long-term as well as mutually beneficial economic relations between the two countries.

egalitarian societies (WDI 2003).[10] Inequality worsened between rural and urban areas and among regions as well as different age groups. The average rural income was 60 percent of urban income in 1984, but declined to 33 percent in 2002. The per capita GDP in Shanghai was 10 times higher than that in the southwestern province of Guizhou (Fan and Chan-Kang 2003). New graduates employed in joint ventures with foreign businesses and working in cutting-edge sectors of the new economy earn up to five times more than their parents with fewer educational opportunities or those employed in the SOEs (Fan and Heerink 2004). Regional inequality increased because of the preferential policies implemented in eastern China in the areas of infrastructure, TVEs, export-oriented enterprises, and foreign investment, all of which led to higher rates of productivity growth in that region. Institutional reforms aimed at dismantling the commune system increased urban-rural inequality because they scrapped the mechanisms for the egalitarian distribution of resources (e.g., food, land, education, and healthcare services) embedded in the communes. The rural-urban gap was accentuated by failure to eliminate the prereform urban policy bias. In several areas, such as labor mobility, housing, welfare, inflation subsidies, and investment credits to the urban sector, policies continue to be more favorable to urban dwellers, thus perpetuating the rural-urban divide.

Between 1978 and 1993, employment grew by 2.5 percent per annum in China, but dropped to just over 1 percent per annum between 1993 and 2004.[11] The share of agriculture in total employment also declined, from 70 percent in 1978 to 50 percent in 1996. This is partly because of the demise of TVEs, but mainly because of a very slow relocation of farm labor because of controlled migration policies and a very high capital-output ratio in industry. This slow shift of labor out of agriculture has been responsible for a low rate of per capita rural income growth, eventually leading to a wide rural-urban income disparity.

In India, the reform process was accompanied by rising income inequality as well, although it was less marked than in China. The World Bank found the Gini coefficient in India to be 0.33 in 2000 (WDI 2004). The milder impact in India is explained by that country's cautious approach to liberalization and by the partial reforms. Labor legislation still offers considerable guarantees to workers, shielding their jobs from adverse business cycles in manufacturing (Jha 2000). One of the reasons for the rise in inequality was the concentration

---

10. In terms of inequality, China joined the ranks of Thailand (0.43), Russia (0.45), and Latin American countries such as Venezuela (0.49) and Peru (0.46). China's Gini coefficient is higher than that of Germany (0.38) and the United States (0.40), but is still lower than that of Brazil (0.606), Nicaragua (0.603), and Namibia (0.70), the countries with the highest levels of income inequality as of the late 1990s. The honor of being more egalitarian economies rests at present with the northern European countries, the Scandinavian countries, and Japan, all with Gini coefficients of around 0.25 throughout the 1990s.

11. China's pattern of growth is provided by Kujis and Wang (2006).

of new growth in the service sector, which enormously benefited skilled workers and specialized factors of production and was not shared with the bulk of the workforce employed in agriculture (Jha 2000). In addition, reforms in investments and industrial policies were conducive to greater opportunities to earn capital income rather than wage income (Jha 2000).

Even if worsening inequality in the two countries is viewed as a natural corollary of the growth process, addressing this issue is critical for social stability, equity, and even future growth. This calls for a mix of effective redistributive mechanisms such as targeted fiscal transfers, safety nets, and public investments for less advantaged groups and areas. In China, the 11th five-year plan has adopted a goal of "construction of the new socialist countryside" by increasing productivity.

Promoting Sustainable Growth and Protecting the Environment

It is widely agreed that China's remarkable growth has been resource-intensive in recent years, drawing heavily on physical capital, energy, and natural resources (Kujis and Wang 2006). There will be heavier demands on natural resources in the future due to the imperative of increasing growth, and even the high savings rate is expected to plateau. Coupled with slowing employment growth, especially in the agricultural sector, leading to a decline in productivity, these factors have given rise to several concerns about the quality and sustainability of China's growth. The high degree of favor shown to industry and investment resulted, in effect, in the subsidization of agriculture in terms of input prices, which in turn encouraged a noneconomic and nonsustainable use of energy and primary commodities as well as degradation of the environment.

The challenge of sustainable growth relates in particular to the four aspects of energy consumption, water resource use, environmental degradation, and financial sustainability. Demographic issues, especially the rise in the number of aged people in China in the future and its implications for the economy, are important concerns, although this study does not deal with these issues directly and in detail.

Economic and population growth have together helped to lift energy consumption in India and China to the fastest-growing rates in the world in the past two decades. It is feared that this frantic pace will continue and may even accelerate. However, such fast growth in energy consumption may not be sustainable in the future due to its fiscal and environmental implications.

China's energy consumption accounts for approximately 53 percent of East Asia's total, excluding that of Japan. The country's energy consumption grew by 130 percent from 1980 to 2001, when China became second in the world, behind the United States, in both total energy consumption (9.8 percent of the world's total) and carbon emissions (12.7 percent of the total). In 2002, China was the third-largest consumer of oil products, following the United States and Japan, with total demand of 5.26 million barrels per day (bpd) and net imports of 1.87 million bpd. China's oil demand is projected to reach 10.9 million bpd by 2025, with net imports of 7.5 million, making it a major player in the world oil market. India's energy consumption grew by 208 percent between 1980 and 2001, and India ranks fifth after Germany, Japan, China, and the United States. India's oil use was 2 million bpd in 2002, of which 1.2 million bpd are net imports.

Despite government efforts to mitigate pollution, both countries suffer from major energy-related environmental problems. Heavy reliance on coal (which supplies more than 50 percent of the energy needs in both countries) has meant that carbon emissions are rising fast. A 1998 report by the WHO indicates that 7 of the 10 most polluted cities in the world are located in China, owing primarily to coal combustion. China accounts for 12.7 percent of the world's carbon emissions (832 million metric tons or m mt) and India for 3.8 percent of the total (251 m mt), which is lower than Japan's 4.8 percent (316 m mt) and the United States' 24 percent (1,565 m mt). Between 1990 and 2001, China's and India's carbon emissions increased by an astonishing 111 percent and 61 percent, respectively. Their carbon emissions are expected to continue to increase throughout the decade, offsetting the planned reduction in carbon and greenhouse gases (GHGs) under the Kyoto Protocol. Both China and India are "non–Annex I countries" under the United Nations Framework Convention on Climate Change, meaning they are not obligated to comply with the Kyoto Protocol mandating reduction requirements in the emissions of carbon GHGs because of the high priority placed on their economic development. In the case of China, doubts have been raised about whether its current growth pattern, which is energy-intensive and trade-led, especially in manufacturing, can be supported in the long run. This also implies that future growth in the agricultural sector should be energy-efficient and that the agricultural sector soon needs to develop innovative ways to provide renewable energy for the manufacturing and service sectors. It also requires more actively promoting the job-creating service sector, removing barriers to labor mobility, and decreasing subsidies to manufacturing and investment therein. The 11th five-year plan takes these factors into consideration and signals a change to more balanced growth, with more attention to the environment and income distribution. However, the plan's targeted reduction in the energy intensity of the economy by over 20 percent over the next five years may be too ambitious to achieve easily (World Bank 2006).

Sustainable use of water resources is another major challenge in the environmental context of economic growth. Water use in agriculture is highly inefficient in China and India (Chapter 10) because of policies treating inexpensive water and power supply as welfare measures (Meinzen-Dick, Raju, and Gulati 2000). Booming groundwater irrigation in China following the tubewell privatization wave in the 1990s, like underpricing and in some cases the provision of free power in India, caused problems of groundwater depletion and lowering of water tables and thus needs policy attention. Similarly, providing inexpensive water for irrigation and fertilizers in India will lead to further waste of scarce water resources and aggravate the problems of waterlogging and salinity of land if it is not addressed soon. In addition, as development progresses, domestic and industrial uses will increase dramatically and compete with the primary sector for scarce water resources. Against this backdrop, China and India have to seek to reduce water use without affecting food production and farmers' incomes (Chapter 9).

Although increasing water charges is expected to have a positive influence on water conservation and the environment without compromising food production, implementation of such a policy remains a great challenge in China and India. Implementing an increase in prices without parallel improvement in the institutional shortcomings of supplying agencies will prove difficult. In China, an increase in water prices may be carried out administratively overnight, but the welfare effects on poorer farmers will be no less painful than in India in the absence of adequate safeguards.

The challenge of financial sustainability applies in India, particularly to the budget deficit. As a result of reforms, the problems of double-digit inflation and shortages of foreign exchange were brought under control in India (Srinivasan and Tendulkar 2003; IMF 2004).[12] However, the budget deficit, one of the major triggers of the macroeconomic reforms in 1991, remains alarmingly high. After declining to 7 percent of GDP right after the 1991–93 reforms, the consolidated budget deficit has climbed back to the prereform level of 9 percent (India, Ministry of Finance, *Economic Survey,* 2001–2). This is regarded as one of the prime reasons that economic growth slowed down after 1996–97 and why, overall, Indian GDP growth during the postreform period was not very different from that in the 1980s. Although the growth rate climbed back to 8 percent levels in 2005, sustaining it calls for cutting expenditures, particularly subsidies, and improving revenue collection by both the tax system and input suppliers such as SEBs and Water Canal Authorities (India, Ministry of Finance, *Economic Survey,* 2001–2), which can incidentally increase the pool of resources available for productive public investment. Of late, the savings rate has inched up to 29 percent, bringing India closer to China, where the savings rate hovered around 35–40 percent throughout the reform period (WDI 2004). One encouraging development has been the passage of the Fiscal Responsibility and Budget Management Act, which mandates the elimination of the government's revenue deficit by 2009.

China has so far managed to maintain the fiscal deficit of the central government at 3–4 percent of GDP (NBS 2003). The imbalance in the sectoral com-

---

12. In 1990–91 inflation was 11.6 percent, and foreign exchange was $1.5 billion. By 2000–2001 inflation was brought down to 3.8 percent, and by October 2004 foreign reserves had jumped to $120 billion.

position of GDP growth—between the contributions of industry and services to GDP growth—has narrowed after a recent revision. Compared to what was seen as a disproportionate 53 percent, industry's share in GDP is now 47 percent. And the service sector has gained, from 32 percent according to the old accounting system to a little over 40 percent. China's high investment and savings rates, which have major contributions from government and SOEs, are also expected to moderate in the future, even though the economy has been booming in recent years (Kujis 2005). But the banking system and the exchange rate regime require serious reform, considering the need to conform to WTO requirements and rules. However, even agriculture's contribution to GDP is down, from 15 percent to only 12.5 percent now. The revaluing does not change the causes of concern much, though, because the differential between productivities in agriculture and in other sectors continues to grow.

Concluding Remarks

A number of factors help to explain the differences in growth between China and India during the reform era: the initial conditions, the sequencing and pace of reforms, and the political system, institutions, and regulatory environment. Yet special mention must be made of the fact that China and India achieved remarkable development and growth even though aid as a percentage of GDP in the two countries remained low. This is in direct contrast to the situations in most other developing countries and regions, where the amount of aid is much higher, while development and poverty reduction lag far behind. This is an important lesson for developing and developed countries, multilateral agencies, and local NGOs and groups. It questions the very basis of current policy prescriptions that accompany aid packages, not only raising issues related to the efficiency and effectiveness of external aid but also, conversely, revealing the extraordinary and often underestimated capacity of national initiatives and policy actions to turn—and in fact halt—the tide of poverty.

Both countries still face tremendous challenges on the path to further prosperity. Continued growth is a must, owing to pressure from growing populations and the need for jobs for them. It is also a condition for a more stable society. Given the high expectations of their citizens, the lack of growth or even slower growth could lead to unrest in both countries. The limited natural resource base can be a critical constraint to growth. The future economic growth of both countries increasingly depends on imports of energy, for which future prospects are uncertain. Both countries are also among those most severely affected by water shortages.

Consequently, future growth must be based on higher efficiency and will require China and India to invest in science and new technologies to harness their energy and water, optimize their economic structures for allocative efficiency, and reform their fiscal, financial, banking, and insurance systems. Both countries must also pursue more pro-poor growth, which is not only a development objective in itself but also a precondition for future growth in the long term.

China and India can both gain tremendously by learning from each other, because both have a long way to go. The dragon is breathing competitive fire over a large part of the world, and the elephant is ambling briskly, but both need to address their weaknesses and build on their strengths in order to achieve their national goals and fulfill the aspirations of their people. The lessons learned from the experiences of China and India will also help other developing countries and provide direction in the global fight against hunger and poverty.

References

Acharya, S. S. 2000a. Domestic agricultural marketing policies. In *Indian agricultural policy at the cross road,* ed. S. S. Acharya and D. P. Chaudhari. Jaipur, India: Rawat.

———. 2000b. Terms of trade for the agricultural sector. In *Indian agricultural policy at the cross road,* ed. S. S. Acharya and D. P. Chaudhari. Jaipur, India: Rawat.

Agarwal, Anil, and Sunita Narain. 1990. Strategies for the involvement of the landless and women in afforestation: Five case studies from India. A Technical Cooperation Report, World Employment Program, International Labor Office (ILO), Geneva.

Agarwal, Anil, Sunita Narain, and Indira Khurana, eds. 2001. *Making water everybody's business: Practice and policy of water harvesting.* New Delhi: Center for Science and Environment.

Agarwal, Bina. 1994. *A field of one's own: Gender and land rights in South Asia.* Cambridge, England: Cambridge University Press.

———. 2003. Gender and land rights revisited: Exploring new perspectives via the state, family and the market. *Journal of Agrarian Change* 3 (1–2): 184–224.

Agrawal, Pradeep, and Pravakar Sahoo. 2003. China's accession to WTO: Implications for China and India. *Economic and Political Weekly,* June 21.

Ahluwalia, Deepak. 1993. Public distribution of food in India. *Food Policy* 18 (1): 34–54.

Ahluwalia, Montek S. 2002. Economic reforms in India since 1991: Has gradualism worked? *Journal of Economic Perspectives* 16 (3): 67–88.

Ahmadi-Esfahani, F. Z., and R. G. Stanmore. 1997. Demand for vegetables in a Chinese wholesale market. *Agribusiness* 13: 549–559.

Alcamo, J., T. Henrichs, and T. Rösch. 2000. World water in 2025: Global modeling and scenario analysis for the world commission on water for the 21st century. Kassel World Water Series Report 2. Kassel, Germany: Center for Environmental Systems Research, University of Kassel.

Alston, J. M., P. G. Pardey, and V. J. Smith, eds. 1999. *Paying for agricultural productivity.* Baltimore: The Johns Hopkins University Press.

Alston, J. M., C. Chan-Kang, M. Marra, P. Pardey, and T. Wyatt. 2000. A meta-analysis of rates of return to agricultural R&D: Ex-pede Herculem? Environment and Production Technology Division Research Report 113. Washington, D.C.: International Food Policy Research Institute.

Amin, S. 1982. Small peasant commodity production and rural indebtedness: The culture of sugarcane in Eastern Uttar Pradesh, 1880–1920. In *Subaltern Studies,* Vol. 1, ed. R. Guha. New Delhi: Oxford University Press.

Anderson, K., and C. Y. Peng. 1998. Feeding and fueling China in the 21st century. *World Development* 26 (8): 1413–1429.

Appu, P. S. 1996. *Land reforms in India: A survey of policy legislation and implementation.* New Delhi: Vikas.

Arrow, K. J. 1963. Uncertainty and the welfare economics of medical care. *American Economic Review* 8 (5): 141–149.

AVDRC (Asian Vegetable Research and Development Center). 1998. *Improvement and stabilization of year-round vegetable supplies.* Taiwan: Asian Vegetable Research and Development Center.

Bagchi, A. K. 1976. Reflections on the pattern of regional growth in India during the period of the British rule. In *Bengal past and present* (Calcutta), January–June.

Bandopadhyay, D. 1986. Land reforms in India: An analysis. *Economic and Political Weekly* 21 (25–26).

Bandyopadhyay, J., V. Shiva, and H. C. Sharatchandra. 1983. The challenge of social forestry. In *Towards a new policy,* ed. Walter Fernandes and Sharad Kulkarni. New Delhi: Indian Social Institute.

Banerjee, Abhijit V., Paul J. Gertler, and Maitreesh Ghatak. 2002. Empowerment and efficiency: Tenancy reform in West Bengal. *Journal of Political Economy* 110 (2): 239–280.

Bardhan, Pranab K. 1973. Size, productivity, and returns to scale: An analysis of farm-level data in Indian agriculture. *Journal of Political Economy* 81 (6).

———. 1985. Poverty and trickle down in rural India: A quantitative analysis. In *Agricultural change and rural poverty: Variations on a theme,* ed. John Mellor and Gunvant Desai. Baltimore: The Johns Hopkins University Press.

———. 1993. Managing the village commons. *Journal of Economic Perspectives* 7 (4): 87–92.

Bauhoff, Sebastian, and Yang Yao. 2002. The Guizhou experiment and agricultural investment. Working paper, China Center for Economic Research, Beijing University, Beijing.

Becker, Jasper. 1996. *Hungry ghosts: Mao's secret famine.* New York: Free Press.

Bell, C., and R. Rich. 1994. Rural poverty and aggregate agricultural performance in post-Independence India. *Oxford Bulletin of Economics and Statistics* 56 (May): 111–133.

Besley, Timothy. 1995. Property rights and investment incentives: Theory and evidence from Ghana. *Journal of Political Economy* 103 (5): 903–937.

Besley, Timothy, and R. Burgess. 2000. Land reform, poverty reduction and growth: Evidence from India. *Quarterly Journal of Economics* 115 (2): 389–430.

Bhalla, G. S., and G. K. Chadha. 1982. Green Revolution and the small peasant: A study of income distribution in Indian agriculture. *Economic and Political Weekly,* May 15.

———. 1983. *The Green Revolution and the small peasant.* New Delhi: Concept.

Bhalla, G. S., G. K. Chadah, and R. K. Sharma. 1986. Structural and institutional set up of rural Punjab in the year 2000: The implication of population growth and distribution. CSRD/JNU Occasional Paper, Jawaharlal Nehru University, New Delhi.

Bhalla, Sheila. 1983. Tenancy today: New factors in the determination of mode and level of rent payments for agricultural land. *Economic and Political Weekly* 18 (19–21): 832–854.

————. 1994. Globalisation, growth and employment. In *World economy in transition—An Indian perspective,* ed. G. S. Bhalla and Manmohan Agarwal. New Delhi: Har-Anand.

————. 2002. Behind poverty: The qualitative deterioration of employment prospects for rural Indians. In *Sustainable agriculture, poverty and food security,* ed. S. S. Acharya, Surjit Singh, and Vidya Sagar, Vol. 2. Jaipur, India: Rawat.

Bhalla, Sheila, G. K. Chadha, and Linxiu Zhang. 2004. The rural non-farm sector in India and China: An overview. Paper presented at the Jawaharlal Nehru University (JNU)–International Food Policy Research Institute (IFPRI) International Conference of the Dragon and the Elephant, Beijing, November 11–12. Washington, D.C.: International Food Policy Research Institute.

Bhalla, Surjit. 2003. *Imagine there's no country: Poverty, inequality, and growth in the era of globalization.* New Delhi: Penguin.

Bharadwaj, K. 1974. Notes on farm size and productivity. *Economic and Political Weekly,* March.

————. 1982. Regional differentiation in India: A note. *Economic and Political Weekly,* April, 605–614.

Bharadwaj, K., and P. K. Das. 1975. Tenurial conditions and mode of exploitation: A study of some villages in Orissa. *Economic and Political Weekly,* February, 221–224, and *Review of Agriculture,* June, A49–A55.

Binswanger, Hans, and Klaus Deininger. 1995. World Bank land policy: Evolution and current challenges. In *Agriculture in liberalizing economies: Changing roles for governments: Proceedings of the Fourteenth Agricultural Sector Symposium,* ed. D. Umali-Deininger and C. Maguire. Washington, D.C.: World Bank.

Birthal, Pratap S., and R. P. Parthasarathy, eds. 2002. *Technology options for sustainable livestock production in India.* New Delhi and Patancheru, Andhra Pradesh: National Center for Agricultural Economics and Policy Research and International Crops Research Institute for the Semi-Arid Tropics.

Bo, Yibo. 1992. *Reflections on some important historical events* (in Chinese). Beijing: Renmin.

Boyce, J. 1987. *Agrarian impasse in Bengal: Institutional constraints to technological change.* Oxford: Oxford University Press.

Brada, J. C., and A. C. King. 1993. Is private farming more efficient than socialized agriculture? *Economica* 60 (237): 41–56.

Brandt, Loren. 2003. The usefulness of corruptible elections. Working paper, Department of Economics, University of Toronto, Toronto.

Brewer, J., S. Kolavalli, A. H. Kalro, G. Naik, S. Ramnarayan, K. V. Raju, and R. Sakthivadivel. 1999. *Irrigation management transfer: Policies and processes.* New Delhi: Oxford and IBH Publications.

Bruce, John, Migot-Adholla, J., and Atherton J. 1995. When should land rights be formalized? Issues in the phrasing of property system reforms. In *Agriculture in liberalizing economies: Changing roles for governments: Proceedings of the Fourteenth Agricultural Sector Symposium,* ed. D. Umali-Deininger and C. Maguire. Washington, D.C.: World Bank.

Buchanan, James. 1993. *Property as a guarantor of liberty.* Brookfield, Vt.: E. Elgar.

Bureau of Health in Shuyang County. 2004. Weisheng gaige wenjian huibian (A compilation of health reforms). In *Zhongguo renkou yu laodong wenti bao gao* no. 7

(Reports on China's population and labor no. 7) (2006), ed. F. Cai and Gu. Beijing: Shehui Kexue Wenxian Chubanshe (Social Sciences Literature Press).

Burgess, Robin. 2003. *Access to land and hunger: Opening the black box in China.* London: London School of Economics. Available at <http://econ.lse.ac.uk/staff/rburgess/wp/land3.pdf> (accessed February 2004).

Cai, F., and B. Gu, eds. 2006. Zhongguo renkou yu laodong wenti bao gao no. 7 (Reports on China's population and labor no. 7). Beijing: Shehui Kexue Wenxian Chubanshe (Social Sciences Literature Press).

Cai, X., and M. W. Rosegrant. 2004. Optional water development strategies for the Yellow River Basin: Balancing agricultural and ecological water demands. *Water Resources Research* 40 (4), DOI: 10.1029/2003 WR002488.

Calabresi, G. 1969. Transaction costs, resource allocation and liability rules: A comment. *Journal of Law and Economics* 11: 67–73.

Canning, D., and E. Bennathan. 2000. The social rate of return on infrastructure investments. Policy Research Working Paper 2390. Washington, D.C.: World Bank.

Carter, C. A., and A. Estrin. 2001. China's trade integration and impacts on factor markets. Mimeo, University of California, Davis.

Carter, Colin A., and Funing Zhong. 1988. *China's grain production and trade.* Boulder, Colo.: Westview.

Carter, Colin A., Funing Zhong, and Fang Cai. 1996. *China's ongoing agricultural reform.* San Francisco: 1990 Institute.

Carter, Michael, and Yang Yao. 1999a. Specialization without regret: Land investment and agricultural productivity in an industrializing economy. World Bank Policy Research Working Paper 2202. Washington, D.C.: World Bank.

———. 1999b. Market versus administrative reallocation of agricultural land in a period of rapid industrialization. World Bank Policy Research Working Paper 2203. Washington, D.C.: World Bank.

Chadha, G. K. 1978. Farm size and productivity revisited: Some notes from recent experience of Punjab. *Economic and Political Weekly* 13 (39).

———. 1989. Agricultural growth and rural non-farm activities: An analysis of Indian experience. In *Rural industrialization and non-farm activities of Asian farmers,* ed. Yang-Boo Choe and Fu-Chen Lo. Kuala Lumpur: Asian and Pacific Development Center (APDC).

———. 1994. *Employment, earnings and poverty: A study of rural India and Indonesia.* New Delhi: Sage.

———. 1996. The industrialization strategy and growth of rural industry in India. ILO/SAAT Working Paper, June. New Delhi: South Asia Multidisciplinary Advisory Team / International Labour Organization.

———. 2001. Rural industry in India and China: Exchanging technological and institutional lessons. CSRD-SSS/JNU paper. Mimeo, Jawaharlal Nehru University, New Delhi.

———. 2002. Indian agriculture in the new millennium: Human response to technical challenges. Presidential address to the 62nd Annual Conference, Indian Society of Agriculture Economics, December, New Delhi.

Chadha, G. K., and S. K. Bhaumik. 1992. Changing tenancy relations in West Bengal: Popular notions, grassroot realities. *Economic and Political Weekly,* May 9.

Chadha, G. K., and A. Gulati. 2003. Performance of agro-based industry in India: Analyzing post-reform advances and reverses. Mimeo, International Food Policy Research Institute, Washington, D.C.

Chadha G. K., and P. P. Sahu. 2002. Post-reform setbacks in rural employment: Issues that need further scrutiny. *Economic and Political Weekly,* May 25.

Chadha, G. K., S. Sen, and H. R. Sharma. 2003. *Land resources. State of Indian farmers: A millennium study,* Vol. 2. New Delhi: Academic Foundation, under arrangement with Department of Agriculture and Cooperation, Ministry of Agriculture, Government of India.

Chambers, Robert, N. C. Saxena, and Tushaar Shah. 1989. *To the hands of the poor: Water and trees.* New Delhi: Oxford and IBH Publications; London: Intermediate Technology Publications.

Chand, Ramesh. 1996. Diversification through high value crops in western Himalayan region: Evidence from Himachal Pradesh. *Indian Journal of Agricultural Economics* 41 (4): 652–663.

———. 2002. Government interventions in foodgrain markets in the new context. Policy Paper 19. New Delhi: National Center for Agricultural Economics and Policy Research.

Chandra Bipan, Mridula Mukherjee, and Aditya Mukherjee. 2000. *India after independence, 1947–2000.* Calcutta: Penguin.

Chang, Gene, and James Wen. 1998. Food availability versus consumption efficiency: Causes of the Chinese famine. *China Economic Review* 9 (2): 157–165.

Chang, Suying, Fu Zhenying, Wu He, and Chunming Chen. 2000. Current situation and trend of child growth in China. *Journal of Hygiene Research* 29 (5): 270–275.

Chattopadhyay, M., and A. Sengupta. 1997. Farm size and productivity: A new look at the old debate. *Economic and Political Weekly,* December 27.

Chaturvedi, M. C. 2000. Water for food and rural development: Developing countries. *Water International* 25 (1): 40–53.

Chaudhari D. P., and S. S. Acharya. 2001. Poverty and equity issues in Indian agriculture. In *Indian agricultural policy at the cross road,* ed. S. S. Acharya and D. P. Chaudhari. Jaipur, India: Rawat.

Chayanov, Alexander. 1966 (1925). *Peasant farm organization.* Homewood, Ill.: Irwin.

Chen, Fu, Liming Wang, and John Davis. 1999. *Land reform in rural China since the mid-1980s.* Rome: Sustainable Development Department of the Food and Agriculture Organization (FAO). Available at <www.fao.org/WAICENT/FAOINFO/SUSTDEV/LTdirect/LTan0031.htm> (accessed March 2004).

Chen, L. 2002. Revolutionary measures: Water saving irrigation. Speech given at the National Water Saving Workshop held by the Ministry of Water Resources, Beijing, April 16.

Chen, S., and M. Ravallion. 2004. How have the world's poorest fared since the early 1980s? *World Bank Research Observer* 19 (1): 141–169.

Chen, Xiwen. 1995. On the current grain supply, demand and prices in China. *Chinese Rural Economy* 1.

Chenery, Hollis, and Moises Syrquin. 1975. *Patterns of development, 1950–1970.* London: Oxford University Press.

Cheng, Chen. 1961. *Land reform in Taiwan.* Taiwan: China Publishing.

China, Ministry of Agriculture. 1984. Agricultural economic data, 1949–1983. Beijing. Internal document.

————. 1989. *Forty years of China's rural areas.* Beijing: Zhongyuan Farmers' Publishing House.

————. 1997. *China agricultural development in 1992–1997.* Beijing: Agricultural Publishing House of China.

————. Various years. Agricultural science and technology statistical materials. Beijing.

————. Various years. *China agricultural development report.* Beijing: Agricultural Publishing House of China.

————. Various years. *China rural statistical yearbook.* Beijing: Agricultural Publishing House of China.

————. Various years. *China township and village enterprises yearbook.* Beijing: Agricultural Publishing House of China.

————. Various years. Documents on adjusting cotton purchase price, 1984, 1988, 1989, 1990, 1993, 1994, 1995, 1998. Beijing. Internal documents.

————. n.d. Survey data of the cotton purchase price. Beijing. Internal data.

China, Ministry of Civil Affairs. 2006. Nongcun yiliao jiuzhu gongzuo de qingkuang (Information about the performance of rural medical relief program). Working report, March. Beijing: Ministry of Civil Affairs.

China, Ministry of Foreign Trade and Economic Cooperation. 1990, 1999, and 2002. *Foreign trade and economic yearbook of China.* Beijing: China Statistical Press.

China, Ministry of Public Health. 1998. The second national health survey. Beijing. Internal report.

————. 1999. Research of the state health services—Analytical report of the second state health service survey, 1998 (in Chinese). Beijing.

————. 2002a. *Collection of frequently used health regulations and rules* (in Chinese). Management Bureau of the State Chinese Medicine. Beijing: Law Press.

————. 2002b. National health expenditure in various periods. In *2001 China health statistics abstract.* Beijing: Health Statistical and Information Center of the Ministry of Public Health. Available at <www.moh.gov.cn/statistics/digest01>.

China, Ministry of Labor and Social Security. 2001. Labor and social security development statistics report. Beijing. Internal report.

China, Ministry of Water Resources. 1990–1998. *China's water resources annual book.* Beijing: China Water Resources and Hydropower Press.

China, Nanjing Agricultural and Forestry Bureau. 2002. Statistical yearbook. Nanjing.

China, Research Center for Rural Economy (RCRE). 2002. Nationwide agricultural monthly price survey system. Beijing. Internal data.

China, State Council. 1985. The State Council notice on the report by the Ministry of Public Health on reform policies concerning health work (in Chinese). Notice by the State Council, April 25. Available at <www. jkcj.yeah.net>.

China, Statistical Information Center, Ministry of Health. 2006. 2005 Nian zhongguo weisheng shiye fazhan qingkuang tongji gongbao (Statistical bulletin on development of health sector in China in 2005), issued April 25. Available at <www.moh.gov.cn/uploadfile/200642584823110.doc> (accessed May 1).

China Daily. 2004. Agricultural tax to be phased out in 5 years. Available at <www.chinadaily.com.cn/english/doc/2004-09/11/content_373647.htm> (accessed October 2004).

Chopra, Kanchan, and B. N. Goldar. 2000. Sustainable development framework for India: The case of water resources. Report prepared for the project Sustainable Development Framework for India at United Nations University, Tokyo. New Delhi: Institute of Economic Growth.

Chopra, R. N. 1981. *Evolution of food policy in India*. New Delhi: Macmillan India.

Chow, C. Gregory. 2002. *China's economic transformation*. Malden, Mass.: Blackwell.

Chowdhury, B. 1964. Growth of commercial agriculture in Bengal (1757–1900). In *Indian studies past and present, 1963–64*. Calcutta: Scholarly Publications.

Corner, Lorraine. 1986. The prospects for off-farm employment as an anti-poverty strategy among Malaysian paddy farm households: Macro and micro views. In *Off-farm employment in the development of rural Asia*, ed. R. T. Shand. Canberra: Australian National University (ANU).

Datanet India Pvt. Ltd. 2006. Indiastat.com. Available at <www.indiastat.com>.

Datt, G., and M. Ravallion. 1997. Why have some states performed better than others at reducing poverty? Food Consumption and Nutrition Division (FCND) Discussion Paper 26. Washington, D.C.: International Food Policy Research Institute.

Deaton, A. 2003. Adjusted Indian poverty estimates for 1999–2000. *Economic and Political Weekly* 38 (4).

Deaton, Angus, and Jean Dreze. 2002. Poverty and inequality in India—A re-examination. *Economic and Political Weekly*, September 7.

de Brauw, Alan, Jikun Huang, Scott Rozelle, Linxiu Zhang, and Yigang Zhang. 2002. The evolution of China's rural labor markets during the reforms. *Journal of Comparative Economics* 30 (2): 329–353.

Delgado, C. L., and A. Siamwalla. 1999. Rural economy and farm income diversification in developing countries. In *Food security, diversification and resource management: Refocusing the role of agriculture*, ed. G. H. Peters and Joachim von Braun. Proceedings of the twenty-third International Conference of Agricultural Economists. Brookfield, Vt.: Ashgate.

Desai, Meghnad. 2003. India and China: An essay in comparative political economy. Paper presented at the IMF (International Monetary Fund) Conference, New Delhi, November.

Dev, S. Mahendra. 1996. Experience of India's (Maharashtra) Employment Guarantee Scheme (EGS): Lesson for development policy. *Development Policy Review* 14 (3).

Dev, S. Mahendra, C. Ravi, Brinda Viswanathan, Ashok Gulati, and Sangamitra Ramachander. 2004. Economic liberalization, targeted programmes and household food security: A case study of India. IFPRI Discussion Paper 68, May. Washington, D.C.: International Food Policy Research Institute.

Dhawan, B. D. 1996a. Price and non-price factors in agricultural investments. *Economics and Political Weekly*, June 22.

———. 1996b. Relationship between public and private investments in Indian agriculture with special reference to public canals. *Indian Journal of Agricultural Economics* 51 (1–2).

———. 2000. *Studies in traditional and modern irrigated agriculture*. New Delhi: Commonwealth.

Dholakia, B. H. 1997. Impact of economic liberalisation on the growth of Indian agriculture. In *Agricultural development paradigm for the 9th plan under new economic environment*, ed. Bhupat M. Desai. New Delhi: Oxford and IBH Publications.

Dholakia, R. H., and B. H. Dholakia. 1993. Growth of total factor productivity in Indian agriculture. *Indian Economic Review* 28 (1): 25–40.

Dong, Xiao-Yuan. 1996. Two-tier land tenure system and sustained economic growth in post-1978 rural China. *World Development* 24 (5): 915–928.

Dong, Xiao-Yuan, and Gregory Dow. 1993. Does free exit reduce shirking in production teams? *Journal of Comparative Economics* 17 (2): 473–484.

Dreze, Jean. 1990. Poverty in India and the IRDP delusion. *Economic and Political Weekly* 25 (39).

Dreze, Jean, and Amartya Sen. 1989. *Hunger and public action.* Oxford, England: Clarendon.

Dubash, Navroz. 2002. *Tubewell capitalism.* New Delhi: Oxford University Press.

Dubashi, Jay. 2000. Is the finance minister painting an overly optimistic picture of the economy? *Sunday Times* (New Delhi), October 22.

Dutt, R. P. 1970. *India today.* Calcutta: Manisha.

Eckholm, Eric. 1979. *Planting for the future: Forestry for human needs.* Washington, D.C.: Worldwatch Institute.

Economist, The. 2003a. Two systems, one grand rivalry: Special report on India and China. *The Economist,* June 21–27, 21–23.

———. 2003b. Danwei people become citizens. *The Economist,* September 6–12.

———. 2003c. Rich man, poor man. *The Economist,* September 27–October 4.

ECRC (Expert Committee on Rural Credit). 2001. Report submitted to the National Bank for Agriculture and Rural Development (NABARD). New Delhi.

Editing Committee of China Agricultural Yearbook. Various years. *China agricultural yearbook.* Beijing: Agricultural Publishing House of China.

Editorial Committee of Health Yearbook. 2001. *China health yearbook* (in Chinese). Beijing: People's Health Press.

Elbehri, Aziz, Thomas Hertel, and Will Martin. 2003. Estimating the impact of WTO and domestic reforms on the Indian cotton and textile sectors: A general-equilibrium approach. *Review of Development Economics* 7 (3): 343–359.

Engelman, R., and P. LeRoy. 1993. Sustaining water: Population and the future of renewable water supplies. Washington, D.C.: Population Action International.

ESCAP (United Nations Economic and Social Commission for Asia and the Pacific). 1995. *Guidebook to water resources, use and management in Asia and the Pacific.* Water Resources Series 74. New York: United Nations.

Escobal, J. A. 1999. Transaction costs in Peruvian agriculture: An initial approximation to their measurement and impact. Research Report GRADE. Lima, Peru: Grupo de Análisis para el Desarrollo.

Evenson, R. E., and D. Jha. 1973. The contribution of agricultural research system to agricultural production in India. *Indian Journal of Agricultural Economics* 28 (4): 212–230.

Evenson, R. E., C. Pray, and M. W. Rosegrant. 1999. Agricultural research and productivity growth in India. Research Report 109. Washington, D.C.: International Food Policy Research Institute.

Fan, Hua. 2003. Farmers' ability of payment and willingness to pay the rural health cooperative insurance. Ph.D. dissertation, Chinese Academy of Social Sciences, Beijing.

Fan, Shenggen. 2000. Research investment and the economic returns to Chinese agricultural research. *Journal of Productivity Analysis* 14 (2): 163–182.

———. 2004. Rural development strategy in Western China under WTO. Paper prepared for the annual conference of the Chinese Economist Society, Frontier and Development Strategy of Agricultural Economics, Hangzhou, China, June 25–27.

Fan, Shenggen, and Connie Chan-Kang. 2003. Regional inequality in China: Its measures, sources and strategies to reduce it. Paper presented at the international seminar Economic Transition and Sustainable Agricultural Development in the East Asia, Jiangsu Conference Center, Nanjing, October 20–22.

———. 2005a. National and international agricultural research and rural poverty: The case of rice in India and China. *Agricultural Economics* 33 (3): 369–379.

———. 2005b. Road development, economic growth and poverty reduction in China. Research Report, International Food Policy Research Institute, Washington, D.C.

Fan, Shenggen, and Peter Hazell. 2000. Should developing countries invest more in less-favored areas? An empirical analysis of rural India. *Economic and Political Weekly,* April 22.

Fan, Shenggen, and Nico Heerink. 2004. Emerging issues and IFPRI research priorities in China. Paper presented at the seminar Emerging Issues and IFPRI Research Priorities in China. Washington, D.C., International Food Policy Research Institute, March 4.

Fan, S., and P. G. Pardey. 1992. Agricultural research in China: Its impact and institutional development. International Service for National Agricultural Research, The Hague.

———. 1997. Research, productivity, and output growth in Chinese agriculture. *Journal of Development Economics* 53 (1): 115–137.

Fan, Shenggen, and Xiaobo Zhang. 2002. Production and productivity growth in Chinese agriculture: New national and regional measures. *Economic Development and Cultural Change* 50 (4): 819–838.

Fan, Shenggen, Peter Hazell, and Sukhadeo Thorat. 1999. Linkages between government spending, growth, and poverty in rural India. IFPRI Research Report 110. Washington, D.C.: International Food Policy Research Institute.

———. 2000. Government spending, agricultural growth and poverty in rural India. *American Journal of Agricultural Economics* 82 (4).

Fan, Shenggen, Keming Qian, and Xiaobo Zhang. 2006. China: An unfinished reform agenda. In *Agricultural R&D in developing countries: Too little too late?,* ed. J. M Alston, P. G. Pardey, and R. R. Piggot. Washington, D.C: International Food Policy Research Institute.

Fan, Shenggen, Sukhadeo Thorat, and Neetha Rao. 2004. Investment, subsidies, and pro-poor growth in rural India, revised version. Mimeo, Department for International Development (DFID), London.

Fan, Shenggen, Linxiu Zhang, and Xiaobo Zhang. 2002. Growth, inequality and poverty in rural China: The role of public investments. IFPRI Research Report 125. Washington, D.C.: International Food Policy Research Institute.

———. 2004. Reform, investment and poverty in rural China. *Economic Development and Cultural Change* 52 (2): 395–421.

Fang, S. 2000. Combined with allocating and controlling local water resources to save water. *Journal of China Water Resources* 439: 38–39.

FAO (Food and Agricultural Organization). 2001. *The state of food insecurity in the world*. Rome: United Nations Food and Agricultural Organization.

FAO Aquastat. 2004. FAO's information system on water and agriculture. China Country Report. Available at <www.fao.org/ag/agl/aglw/aquastat/countries/china/index.stm> (accessed February).

FAOSTAT. Various years. Agricultural statistics database. Web-based subscription. Washington, D.C.: International Food Policy Research Institute. <http://faostat.fao.org/>.

Feder, Gershon. 1985. The relation between farm size and farm productivity. *Journal of Development Economics* 18 (2–3): 297–313.

Feder, Gershon, Tongroj Onchan, Yongyuth Chalamwong, and Chiura Hongladarom. 1988. *Land policies and farm productivity in Thailand*. Baltimore: The Johns Hopkins University Press.

Feng, Guangzhi, Yuansheng Pei, and Hansong Zhang. 2000. Irrigation development and food safety in China. Policy paper, Ministry of Water Resources, Beijing.

Filmer, D., J. Hammer, and L. Pritchett. 1997. Health policy in poor countries: Weak links in the chain. World Bank paper. Available at <www.worldbank.org/html/dec/Publications/Workpapers/WPS1800series/wps1874/wps1874.pdf> (accessed December 15, 2003).

Fischer, K., and D. Byerlee. 2002. Managing intellectual property and income generation in public research organizations. In *Agricultural research policy in an era of privatisation*, ed. D. Byerlee and R. G. Echeverria. New York: Commonwealth Agricultural Bureau International.

Fuchs, Victor R. 2000. *Who shall live? Heath, economics, and social choice* (in Chinese), trans. Luo Han, Jiao Yan, and Zhu Xueqin. Shanghai: Shanghai People's Press.

Gabre-Madhin, E. Z. 2001. Market institutions, transaction costs, and social capital in the Ethiopian grain market. IFPRI Research Report 124. Washington, D.C.: International Food Policy Research Institute.

Gertler, P. J., and J. S. Hammer. 1997. Strategies for pricing publicly provided health services. World Bank paper. Available at <www.worldbank.org/html/dec/Publications/Workpapers/WPS1700series/wps1762/wps1762.pdf> (accessed December 12, 2003).

Ghose, A. K. 1979. Farm size and land productivity in Indian agriculture: A reappraisal. *Journal of Development Studies* 16 (1): 27–49.

Guhan, S. 1994. Social security options for developing countries. *International Labour Review* 133. Geneva: International Labor Organization.

Gujarati, D. N. 1995. *Basic econometrics*. New York: McGraw-Hill.

Gulati, Ashok. 2000. Trade, WTO and food security: Emerging issues and options. Paper presented at the XXIV Conference of the International Association of Agricultural Economists, Berlin, August 13–19.

————. 2003. Unsung heroes of Indian agriculture. Paper, International Food Policy Research Institute, Washington, D.C.

Gulati, Ashok, and Seema Bathla. 2002. Capital formation in Indian agriculture: Trends, composition and implications for growth. Occasional Paper 24, National Bank for Agriculture and Rural Development, Mumbai.

Gulati, Ashok, and Tim Kelley. 1999. *Trade liberalization and Indian agriculture—Cropping pattern changes and efficiency gains in semi-arid tropics.* New Delhi: Oxford University Press.

Gulati, Ashok, and Kathleen Mullen. 2003. Responding to policy reforms: Indian agriculture during the 1990s and after. Paper prepared at Stanford University, July. Mimeo, International Food Policy Research Institute, Washington, D.C.

Gulati, Ashok, and Sudha Narayanan. 2002a. Fertilizers and power subsidies in India. In *Indian agriculture in the changing environment,* ed. Raj Kapila and Uma Kapila. Ghaziabad, India: Academic Foundation.

———. 2002b. Rice trade liberalization and poverty. Markets, Trade, and Institutions Division Discussion Paper 51. Washington, D.C.: International Food Policy Research Institute.

———. 2003. *The subsidy syndrome in Indian agriculture.* New Delhi: Oxford University Press.

Gulati, A., and Gary Pursell. 2000. Trade policies, incentives and resource allocation in Indian agriculture. Mimeo, World Bank, Washington, D.C.

Gulati, A., Gary Pursell, and Kathleen Mullen. 2003. Indian agriculture since the reforms: Performance, policy environment, and incentives. World Bank Working Paper, May. Washington, D.C.: World Bank.

Guo L., S. Rozelle, and L. Brandt. 1998. Tenure, land rights, and farmer investment incentives in China. *Agricultural Economics* 18 (1).

Gupta, S. P. 1999. Trickle down theory revisited: The role of employment and poverty. V. B. Singh Memorial Lecture, 41st Labor Economic Conference, IGIDR (Indira Gandhi Institute of Development Research), Mumbai.

Haggblade, Steven, Peter Hazell, and Thomas Reardon. 2002. Strategies for stimulating poverty-alleviating growth in the rural non-farm economy in developing countries. Paper prepared for the World Bank. Mimeo, International Food Policy Research Institute, Washington, D.C.

Hallam, A. 1991. Economies of size and scale in agriculture: An interpretative view of empirical measurement. *Review of Agricultural Economics* 13: 155–171.

Haque, T., and A. S. Sirohi. 1986. *Agrarian reforms and institutional change in India.* New Delhi: Concept Publishing.

Harris, J. 1993. What is happening to rural West Bengal? *Economic and Political Weekly* 28 (24).

Hashim S. R., S. P. Kashyap, and S. N. Joshi. 2000. Agriculture and rural development. Paper presented at the UNU/IAS (United Nations University, Institute of Advanced Studies) second project review meeting on India's Sustainable Development Framework, Tokyo, May 26 and 27.

Hayami, Yujiro. 1997. *Development economics.* New York: Oxford University Press.

Hazell, Peter B. R., and Steven Haggblade. 1991. Rural-urban growth linkages in India. *Indian Journal of Agricultural Economics* 46 (4): 515–529.

He, Xuefeng. 2003. *The new rural China.* Nanjing, China: Guangxi Normal University Press.

Heckman, J. 1979. Sample selection bias as a specification error. *Econometrica* 47 (1): 153–161.

Herath, Gamini, and Ashok Gulati. 2003. Public institutions: The case of infrastructure. In *Public expenditures, growth and poverty in developing countries: Issues, methods and findings*. Final Synthesis Report on Public Expenditures and the Poor. Washington, D.C.: International Food Policy Research Institute.

Hirway, I., and P. Terhal. 1994. *Towards employment guarantee in India*. New Delhi: Sage.

Hobbs, J. 1997. Measuring the importance of transaction costs in cattle marketing. *American Journal of Agricultural Economics* 79 (4): 1083–1095.

Hoda, Anwarul, and Ashok Gulati. 2007. *WTO negotiations on agriculture and developing countries*. Baltimore: The Johns Hopkins University Press.

HPDGJ (Hydropower Planning and Design General Institute). 1989. *China's water resources and uses*. Beijing: China Water Resources and Hydropower Press.

Hualiang, Lu. 2003. Tomato marketing supply chain: Choice, efficiency and transaction costs analysis. A case study in Nanjing City, Jiangsu Province, P. R. China. M.S. thesis, Wageningen University, The Netherlands.

Huang, Jikun, and C. Chen. 1999. *Effects of trade liberalization on agriculture in China: Commodity and local agricultural studies*. Bogor, Indonesia: United Nations ESCAP (Economic and Social Commission for Asia and the Pacific)—CGPRT (Coarse Grains, Pulses, Roots and Tuber Crops) Center.

Huang, Jikun, and Scott Rozelle. 2002a. Trade reform, WTO and China's food economy in the 21st century. CCAP working paper, Center for Chinese Agricultural Policy (CCAP), Beijing, China.

———. 2002b. Market distortions and the impact of WTO on China's rural economy. Working paper, University of California, Davis.

———. 2003. Trade reforms and the likely impacts of China's WTO accession on its agriculture. Revised version of a paper presented at the international Jawaharlal Nehru University (JNU)–IFPRI conference, New Delhi, March 25–26.

Huang, Jikun, Hengyun Ma, and Scott Rozelle. 1998. Rural poverty and policy in China. *Reforms* 4: 72–83.

Huang, Jikun, Mark Rosegrant, and Scott Rozelle. 1999. Public investment, technological change, and agricultural growth in China. Working Paper, Food Research Institute, Stanford University, Stanford, Calif.

Hueth, B., E. Ligon, S. Wolf, and S. Wu. 1999. Incentive instruments in fruit and vegetable contracts: Input control, monitoring, measuring and price risk. *Review of Agricultural Economics* 21 (2): 374–389.

IASRI (Indian Agricultural Statistics Research Institute). 2001. *Agricultural research data book 2001*. New Delhi: Indian Agricultural Statistics Research Institute.

ICAR (Indian Council of Agricultural Research). 1988. *Report of the ICAR Review Committee*. New Delhi: Indian Council of Agricultural Research.

———. 2000. *Vision 2020*. New Delhi: Indian Council of Agricultural Research.

ICAR, DARE (Indian Council of Agricultural Research, Department of Agricultural Research and Education). 2003. *Annual report*. New Delhi: Department of Agricultural Research and Education, Ministry of Agriculture, Government of India.

ILO (International Labor Organization). 1998. China: Promoting safety and health in township and village enterprises. Report of the ILO East Asia Multidisciplinary Advisory Team, the ILO Regional Office for the Asia and the Pacific, Bangkok. Available at <www.ilo.org/public/english/region/asro/bangkok/asiaosh/country/china/tradeuni/chinatss.htm#Development> (accessed May 18, 2004).

IMF (International Monetary Fund). 2002–2004. *IMF's statistical database*. Washington, D.C.: International Food Policy Research Institute.

———. Various years. International financial statistics browser. <www.imfstatistics.org/imf/>.

India, Central Water Commission (CWS). 2000. *Water and related statistics*. New Delhi: Central Water Commission, Government of India.

India, CSO (Central Statistical Organization). 2004. Macroeconomic aggregates at constant (1993–94) prices, 1950–51 to 2002–03. Ministry of Statistics and Program Implementation. Available at <mospi.nic.in/3_macro_agg_const.pdf> (accessed March).

———. Various years. Annual survey of industries. New Delhi.

———. Various years. *National accounts statistics*. New Delhi: Ministry of Statistics and Program Implementation, Government of India.

———. n.d. Net domestic product by economic activity in rural/urban areas 1999–2000. Available at <http://mospi.nic.in>.

India, DBT (Department of Bio-Technology). 1998. *Revised guidelines for research in transgenic plants and guidelines for toxicity and allergenicity evaluation of transgenic seeds, plants and plant parts*. New Delhi: Ministry of Science and Technology.

India, Ministry of Agriculture. 2002. Policy framework for agricultural extension, Extension Division. New Delhi: Ministry of Agriculture, Government of India.

———. Various years. *Agricultural statistics at a glance*. New Delhi: Agricultural Statistics Division, Directorate of Economics and Statistics, Department of Agriculture and Cooperation.

———. Various years. *All-India report on agricultural census*. New Delhi.

India, Ministry of Finance. Various years. *Economic survey*. Economic Division. New Delhi: Government of India Press.

India, Ministry of Industry. 1991. *Report on the operations of the Food Corporation of India*. New Delhi: Bureau of Industrial Costs and Prices.

India, Ministry of Rural Areas and Employment. 1994. Guidelines for watershed development. New Delhi: Ministry of Rural Areas and Employment, Government of India.

India, Ministry of Rural Development. 2003. *Annual report 2002–03*. New Delhi: Ministry of Rural Development, Government of India.

India, Ministry of Statistics and Program Implementation. 1988. *Sarvekshana*, Vol. 11, No. 4, Issue No. 35, April. New Delhi: National Sample Survey Organization (NSSO).

———. 1989. Tables with notes on survey of unorganised manufacture: Non-directory establishments and own-account enterprises, July 1984–June 1985, Part 1, All-India. NSS Report 363/1. New Delhi: National Sample Survey Organization (NSSO).

———. 1990a. Results of the fourth quinquennial survey on employment and unemployment (all-India). NSS (National Sample Survey) 43rd round, July 1987–June 1988. *Sarvekshana*, Special Number, September. New Delhi: National Sample Survey Organization (NSSO).

———. 1990b. *Sarvekshana*, Special Number, Vol. 14, Nos. 1 and 2, July–December. New Delhi: National Sample Survey Organization (NSSO).

————. 1997. Employment and unemployment. NSS (National Sample Survey) 50th round, July 1993–June 1994. NSS Report 409. New Delhi: National Sample Survey Organization (NSSO).

————. 1998. Unorganised manufacturing sector in India: Its size, employment and some key estimates, July 1994–June 1995. NSS Reports 433–435. New Delhi: National Sample Survey Organization (NSSO).

————. 2000. Level and pattern of consumer expenditure in India 1999–2000. NSS Report 457 (55/10/3). New Delhi: National Sample Survey Organization (NSSO).

————. 2001. Employment and unemployment situation in India, 1999–2000. NSS 55th round, July 1999–June 2000. NSS Report 458 (55/10/2). New Delhi: National Sample Survey Organization (NSSO).

————. 2002. Unorganised manufacturing sector in 2000–01. NSS Report 477. New Delhi: National Sample Survey Organization (NSSO).

————. Various years. Operational land holdings in India: Salient features. NSS (National Sample Survey) 8th, 16th, 26th, 37th, 48th Rounds. New Delhi: National Sample Survey Organization (NSSO).

India, Ministry of Water Resources. 1990–1998. *Annual report.* New Delhi: Ministry of Water Resources, Government of India.

————. 1991. Waterlogging, soil salinity, alkalinity. Report of the Working Group on Problem Identification in Irrigated Areas with Suggested Remedial Measures. New Delhi: Ministry of Water Resources, Government of India.

————. 1997. Report of the Working Group on Participatory Irrigation Management for the Ninth Plan. New Delhi: Ministry of Water Resources, Government of India.

————. 1999a. Integrated water resources development—A plan for action. Report of the National Commission on Integrated Water Resources Development Plan. New Delhi: Ministry of Water Resources, Government of India.

————. 1999b. Report of the National Commission for Integrated Water Resources Development (Chairman, S. R. Haqshim), Vol. 1. New Delhi: Ministry of Water Resources, Government of India.

————. 1999c. Report of the Working Group on Perspective of Water Requirements (National Commission on Integrated Water Resources Development Plan). New Delhi: Ministry of Water Resources, Government of India.

————. 2002. *National water policy 2002.* New Delhi: Ministry of Water Resources, Government of India.

————. 2006. Report of the Working Group on Participatory Irrigation Management Programs for the XI Five Year Plan. New Delhi: Ministry of Water Resources, Government of India.

India, Office of the Registrar General and Census Commissioner. 1991. Provisional population totals: Rural-urban distribution. *Census of India 1991*, Paper 2. New Delhi: Office of the Registrar General and Census Commissioner, Government of India.

India, Planning Commission. 1992. Report of the Committee on the Pricing of Irrigation Water. New Delhi: Planning Commission, Government of India.

————. 1999. *Ninth five year plan,* Vols. 1 and 2. New Delhi: Planning Commission, Government of India.

————. 2000. Mid-term appraisal of ninth 5-year plan, 1997–2002. New Delhi: Planning Commission, Government of India.

————. 2001a. Draft approach paper to the tenth five-year plan (2002–2007). New Delhi: Planning Commission, Government of India.

————. 2001b. *Eighth five-year plan.* New Delhi: Planning Commission, Government of India. Available at <www.planningcommission.nic.in/plans/planrel/fiveyr/default.html>.

————. 2002. Report of the Special Group on Targeting Ten Million Employment Opportunities per Year over the Tenth Plan Period. New Delhi: Planning Commission, Government of India.

————. 2003. *Tenth five year plan (2002–2007),* Vols. 1–3. New Delhi: Planning Commission, Government of India.

————. 2007. Poverty estimates for 2004–05. Available at <planningcommission.nic.in/news/prmar07.pdf>.

India, RBI (Reserve Bank of India). 2003. Sectorwise GDP until 2000–01. In *Handbook of statistics on the Indian economy.* Available at <www.rbi.org.in/sec7/36946.doc> (accessed March 2004).

————. 2006. *Handbook of statistics on Indian economy.* Available at <www.rbi.org.in/scripts/AnnualPublications.aspx?head=Handbook%20of%20Statistics%20on%20Indian%20Economy>.

Institute of Human Development. 2002. Dynamics of poverty, employment and human development in Bihar. Report of a study sponsored by NABARD (National Bank of Agriculture and Rural Development). New Delhi: National Bank of Agriculture and Rural Development (NABARD).

Islam, Rizwanul. 1987. *Rural industrialization and employment in Asia.* New Delhi: International Labor Organization / Asian Regional Team for Employment Promotion (ILO/ARTEP).

Jacoby, Hanan, Guo Li, and Scott Rozelle. 2003. Hazards of expropriation: Tenure insecurity and investment in rural China. *American Economic Review* 92 (5): 1420–1447.

Janakarajan, S. 1993. Economic and social implication of groundwater irrigation: Some evidence from South India. *Indian Journal of Agricultural Economics* 48 (1): 65–75.

Jha, Dayanath. 1996. Rapporteur's report on diversification of agriculture and food security in the context of new economic policy. *Indian Journal of Agricultural Economics* 51 (4): 829–832.

————. 2001. Agricultural research and small farms. *Indian Journal of Agriculture Economics* 56 (1): 1–23.

Jha, P. K. 1997. *Agricultural labor in India.* New Delhi: Vikas.

Jha, Raghbendra. 2000. Reducing poverty and inequality in India: Has liberalization helped? WIDER Working Paper 204. Helsinki, Finland: World Institute for Development Economic Research (WIDER), United Nations University.

————. 2001. *Rural poverty in India: Structure, determinants and suggestions for policy reform.* Canberra: Australian National University. Available at <rspas.anu.edu.au/papers/asarc/jha_2002_07.pdf> (accessed January 2003).

Jodha, N. S. 1986. Common property resources and rural poor in dry regions of India. *Economic and Political Weekly,* July 5.

————. 1990. Rural common property resources: Contributions and crisis. *Economic and Political Weekly* 25 (26): A65–A78.

Johnson, D. Gale. 1995. China's rural and agricultural reforms in perspective. Working paper, Department of Economics, University of Chicago, Chicago.

Joshi, P. K., Ashok Gulati, P. S. Birthal, and L. Tewari. 2002. Agricultural diversification in South Asia. Paper presented at the workshop Agricultural Diversification in South Asia, Paro, Bhutan, November 21–23.

Kanbur, R., and X. Zhang. 2005. Spatial inequality in education and health care. *China Economic Review* 16 (2): 189–204.

Kannan, K. P. 2002. The welfare fund model of social security for informal sector workers—The Kerala experience. Working Paper 332. Trivandrum, India: Center for Development Studies.

Kannan, K. P., and N. Vijayamohanan Pillai. 2002. *Plight of the power sector in India.* Thriuvanantpuram, India: Center for Development Studies.

Ke, Bingsheng. 1995. *Grain market and policy in China.* Beijing: Agricultural Publishing House of China.

Khare, Arvind. 1993. Marketing of social forestry products—Issues, strategies and priorities. Paper written for the M. P. World Bank Re-appraisal Mission, Bhopal, India.

Khasnabis, R. C. 1995. Empowering people: Panchayats and rural development in West Bengal. In *Tenurial conditions in West Bengal—Continuity and change.* Report of IDPAD (Indo-Dutch Program for Alternatives in Development) Project 3.2.1. Calcutta: IDPAD.

Khasnabis, R. C., and J. Chakravarty. 1982. Tenancy, credit and agrarian backwardness: Results of a field survey. *Economic and Political Weekly,* March, A21–A32.

Khusro, A. M. 1964. Return to scale in Indian agriculture. *Indian Journal of Agricultural Economics* 19 (3–4): 51–80.

Kohli, Atul. 1987. *The state and poverty in India: The politics of reform.* Bombay: Orient Longman.

Koo, Bonwoo, Philip G. Pardey, Keming Qian, and Yi Zhang. 2006. An option perspective on generating and maintaining plant variety rights in China. *Agricultural Economics* 35: 35–48.

Koo, B., P. G. Pardey, E. Castelo-Magalhães, and C. Wetzel. Forthcoming. Protecting and licensing biological innovations: Crop-related research in Brazil. Discussion Paper. Washington, D.C.: International Food Policy Research Institute.

Kornai, J., and K. Eggleston. 2003. *Welfare, choice and solidarity in transition—Reforming the health sector in Eastern Europe.* Chinese edition. Beijing: Zhongxin Press.

Krishnan, M., and P. S. Birthal, eds. 2000. *Aquaculture in India: Retrospect and prospect.* New Delhi: National Center for Agricultural Economics and Policy Research.

Kujis, Louis. 2005. Investment and savings in China. World Bank Policy Research Working Paper 3633. Washington, D.C.: World Bank.

Kujis, Louis, and Tao Wang. 2006. China's pattern of growth: Moving to sustainability and reducing inequality. *China and World Economy* 14 (1).

Kumar, Anjani, P. K. Joshi, and P. S. Birthal. 2001. Fisheries sector in India: An overview of performance, policies and programs. Paper presented at the international workshop Strategies and Options for Increasing and Sustaining Fisheries Production to Benefit Poor Households in Asia, August 20–25, World Fish Center (ICLARM), Penang, Malaysia.

Kumar, P., and V. S. Mathur. 1996. Structural changes in the demand for food in India. *Indian Journal of Agricultural Economics* 51 (4): 664–673.

Kumar, P., and Mruthyunjaya. 2002. Long term changes in food basket in India. Paper presented at the workshop Agricultural Diversification in South Asia, Paro, Bhutan, November 21–23.

Kumar, Praduman, D. Jha, A. Kumar, M. K. Chaudhary, R. K. Grover, R. K. Singh, R. K. P. Singh, A. Mitra, P. K. Joshi, A. Singh, P. S. Badal, S. Mittal, and J. Ali. 2002. Economic analysis of total factor productivity in crop sector in the Indo-Gangetic Plains of India by district and region. Agriculture Economic Research Report 2. New Delhi: IARI (Indian Agricultural Research Institute)—NCAP (National Center for Agricultural Economics and Policy Research).

Kung, James. 1993. Transaction costs and peasants' choice of institutions: Did the right to exit really solve the free rider problem in Chinese collective agriculture? *Journal of Comparative Economics* 17 (2): 485–503.

———. 1994. Egalitarianism, subsistence provision, and work incentives in China's agricultural collectives. *World Development* 22 (2): 175–187.

———. 2002. Off-farm labor markets and the emergence of land rental markets in rural China. *Journal of Comparative Economics* 30 (2): 395–414.

Landes, Rip, and Ashok Gulati. 2003. Policy reform and farm sector adjustment in India. Mimeo, International Food Policy Research Institute, Washington, D.C.

Lardy, Nicholas R. 1983. *Agriculture in China's modern economic development.* Cambridge, England: Cambridge University Press.

———. 1995. The role of foreign trade and investment in China's economic transition. *China Quarterly* 144 (December): 1065–1082.

Laxminarayan, H., and S. S. Tyagi. 1977. Inter-state variations in types of tenancy. *Economic and Political Weekly* 12 (22).

Li, Enping. 2003. Effects of economic status of the rural aging people on their utilization of medical services. Ph.D. dissertation, Chinese Academy of Social Sciences, Beijing.

Li, Guo, Scott Rozelle, and Loren Brandt. 1998. Tenure, land rights, and farmer investment incentives in China. *Agricultural Economics* 19 (1–2): 63–71.

Li, Hongbin, and Scott Rozelle. 2000. Saving or stripping rural industry: An analysis of privatization and efficiency in China. *Agricultural Economics* 23 (3): 4601–4612.

Li, Jing, and Yang Yao. 2002. Egalitarian land distribution and labor migration in rural China. In *Land settlement and land reform.* Rome: United Nations Food and Agriculture Organization (FAO).

Li, Jing, Justin Y. Lin, and Yang Yao. 2003. Credit constraints, land, and children's education in China's poor rural regions. *Chinese Journal of Population Science* 2 (April–May). Available at <www.cass.net.cn/chinese/s06_rks/erkkx.htm> (accessed November 2004).

Li, S., F. Zhai, and Z. Wang. 1999. The global and domestic impact of China joining the World Trade Organization. Project Report, State Council, Development Research Center, Beijing.

Li Shijun, Lihong Gao, Suping Zhou, Gaoqiong Liu, and Wei Liu. 1998. Diversification of vegetable growing in the middle and lower reaches of the Yangtze River. Proceedings of the 3rd International Symposium of Vegetables Crops. *Acta Horticultura* 467: 253–255.

Liang, Huixin. 1998. *A study of the property law*. Beijing: Legal Press.

Lieten, G. K. 1982. *The first Communist ministry in Kerala, 1957–59*. Calcutta: K. P. Bagchi.

———. 2003. Land reforms at centre stage: The evidence from West Bengal. In *Power, politics and rural development: Essays on India*, ed. G. K. Lieten. New Delhi: Manohar.

Lin, J. Y., and D. T. Yang. 2000. Food availability, entitlement, and the Chinese famine of 1959–61. *Economic Journal* 110 (460): 136–158.

Lin, Justin Yifu. 1988. The Household Responsibility System in China's agricultural reform: A theoretical and empirical study. *Economic Development and Cultural Change* 36 (3).

———. 1989. Rural reforms and agricultural productivity growth in China. UCLA Working Paper 576, December. Los Angeles: University of California.

———. 1990. Collectivization and China's agricultural crisis in 1959–1961. *Journal of Political Economy* 98 (6): 1228–1252.

———. 1991. Prohibitions of factor market exchanges and technological choice in Chinese agriculture. *Journal of Development Studies* 27 (4): 1–15.

———. 1992. Rural reforms and agricultural growth in China. *American Economic Review* 82 (1): 34–51.

———. 2003. WTO accession and rural development in China. Opening speech delivered at the Chinese Academy of Agricultural Sciences (CAAS)–International Food Policy Research Institute (IFPRI) International Conference of the Dragon and the Elephant, Beijing, November 10–11.

Lindal, B. 1973. Industrial and other applications of geothermal energy. In *Geothermal energy*, ed. H. C. H. Armstead. Paris: United Nations Educational, Scientific and Cultural Organization (UNESCO).

Liu, Minquan. 1993. Exit-right, retaliatory shirking, and the agricultural crisis in China. *Journal of Comparative Economics* 17 (2): 540–559.

Liu, Shouying, Michael Carter, and Yang Yao. 1998. Dimensions and diversity of property rights in rural China: Dilemmas on the road to further reform. *World Development* 26 (10): 1789–1806.

Liu, Yigao, Xiaoyi Wang, and Yang Yao. 2002. *The Chinese village inside and out*. Shijiazhuang, China: Hebei Renmin.

Liu, Yuanli, Keqin Rao, and Shanlian Hu. 2001. The necessity to establish the rural health protection system in China and relevant policies (in Chinese). Research Report presented at the international symposium Rural Basic Safety Nets in China, Beijing, July 9–10.

Lohmar, Bryan, and Jinxia Wang. 2002. Will water scarcity affect agricultural production in China? China's food and agriculture: Issues for the 21st century. Agriculture Information Bulletin 775. Washington, D.C.: Economic Research Service, United States Department of Agriculture (ERS/USDA).

Lu, Rong. 2001. The development trend of Chinese small private TVEs—A case study in Zhili township, Zhejiang province. Master's thesis, Center for Chinese Agricultural Policy, Chinese Academy of Sciences (CAS), Beijing.

Luo, Hanping. 2005. *A history of the land reform movement*. Fuzhou, China: Fujian Renmin.

Maddison, Angus. 2002. *The world economy: A millennial perspective*. Paris: Organisation for Economic Co-operation and Development (OECD).

Malviya, H. D. 1954. *Land reforms in India*. New Delhi: Economic and Political Research Department, All-India Congress Committee.

Martin, W. 2001. Implication of reform and WTO accession for China's agricultural policies. *Economies in Transition* 9 (3).

Maskus, K. E., and S. M. Dougherty. 1998. Intellectual property rights and economic development in China. Paper presented at the Sino–U.S. conference Intellectual Property Rights and Economic Development, Chongqing, China, September 16–18.

Mazumdar, Dipak. 1965. Size of farm and productivity: A problem of Indian peasant agriculture. *Economica* 32 (126).

McFadden, Daniel. 1974. Conditional logit analysis of qualitative choice behavior. In *Frontiers of econometrics*. New York: Academic Press.

McMillan, J., J. Whalley, and L. Zhu. 1989. The impact of China's economic reforms on agricultural productivity growth. *Journal of Political Economy* 97 (4): 781–807.

Mearns, Robin. 1999. Access to land in rural India: Policy issues and options. Working Paper 2123. Washington, D.C.: World Bank.

Meinzen-Dick, Ruth, K. V. Raju, and Ashok Gulati. 2000. What affects organization and collective action for managing resources? Evidence from canal irrigation systems in India. EPTD Discussion Paper 61. Washington, D.C.: International Food Policy Research Institute (IFPRI).

Mellor, John W. 1976. *The new economics of growth: A strategy for India and the developing world*. Ithaca, N.Y.: Cornell University Press.

Meng, Qingpu, and Lixin Yuan. 2006. Shenzhen: Health insurance for migrated Workers. *Jiang Kang Bao* (Health news) (Beijing), April 4, 7.

Meng, Xin. 2000. Institutions and culture: Women's economic position in mainland China and Taiwan. Manuscript, Department of Economics, Research School of Pacific and Asian Studies, Australian National University, Canberra.

Misra, V. N. 2004. Terms of trade. State of the Indian farmer: A millennium study, Vol. 15. New Delhi: Academic Foundation, under arrangement with Department of Agriculture and Cooperation, Ministry of Agriculture, Government of India.

Mitra, Arup. 1993. Rural non-farm employment, poverty and women. *Indian Journal of Labour Economics* 36 (3).

Mohan, R., D. Jha, and R. E. Evenson. 1973. The Indian agricultural research system. *Economic and Political Weekly* 8 (13): A21–A26.

NAAS (National Academy of Agricultural Sciences). 2002. Agricultural policy: Redesigning R&D to achieve its objectives. Policy Paper 18. New Delhi: National Academy of Agricultural Sciences.

Narayana, N. S. S., K. S. Parikh, and T. N. Srinivasan. 1991. Agriculture, growth and redistribution of income: Policy analysis with a general equilibrium model of India. In *Contributions to economic analysis series*, Indian edition. New Delhi: Allied.

Narayana Murthy, A. 1993. Competition for borewell water and its impact on tank: Some observations. Proceedings of the 15th Congress on Irrigation and Drainage, The Hague, The Netherlands. New Delhi: International Commission on Irrigation and Drainage.

———. 1994. Who sells more and who sells less on deep borewell water business in Pudukkottai District, Tamil Nadu: Some empirical analysis. *Journal of Indian Water Resources Society* 14 (1–4): 51–56.

National Dairy Development Board. 2002. *Annual report 2001–02*. Anand, India.

Naughton, B. 1995. *Growing out of the plan: Chinese economic reform, 1978–93*. New York: Cambridge University Press.

Nayyar, Rohini. 1996. New initiatives for poverty alleviation in rural India. In *Economic reforms and poverty alleviation in India*, ed. C. H. H. Rao and Hans Linnemann. New Delhi: Sage.

NBS (National Bureau of Statistics of China). 1999. *Household income and expenditure survey*. Beijing: Statistics Publishing House.

———. 2001 and 2002. *Poverty monitoring report of rural China*. Beijing: Statistics Publishing House.

———. Various years. *China education yearbook*. Beijing: Statistics Publishing House.

———. Various years. *China electronical power yearbook*. Beijing: Statistics Publishing House.

———. Various years. *China fixed asset investment yearbook*. Beijing: Statistics Publishing House.

———. Various years. *China science and technology yearbook*. Beijing: Statistics Publishing House.

———. Various years. *China statistical yearbook*. Beijing: Statistics Publishing House. Beijing: Statistics Publishing House.

———. Various years. *China transportation yearbook*. Beijing: Statistics Publishing House.

———. Various years. *China water conservancy yearbook*. Beijing: Statistics Publishing House.

Nian, L. 2001. *Participatory irrigation management: Innovation and development of irrigation system*. Beijing: China Water Resources and Hydropower Publishing House.

NIHWR (Nanjing Institute of Hydrology and Water Resources). 1998. *Water demand and supply in China in the 21st century*. Beijing: China Water Resources and Hydropower Press.

North, D. 1990. *Institutions, institutional change and economic performance*. New York: Cambridge University Press.

North, Douglas, and Robert Thomas. 1973. *The rise of the western world*. New York: Springer.

NSSO (National Sample Survey Organisation). 1954. Report on land holdings, rural sector, states. Report 66. 8th Round (1954–55). New Delhi: Department of Statistics.

———. 1961. Tables with notes on agricultural holdings. Number 113. 16th Round (1960–61). New Delhi: Department of Statistics.

———. 1962. Tables with notes on some aspects on land holdings in rural India. 17th Round (1961–62). New Delhi: Department of Statistics.

———. 1972. Tables on rural landholdings, all-India and states. Number 215. 26th Round (1971–72). New Delhi: Department of Statistics.

———. 1987. Report on land holdings (1987), 1: Some aspects of household ownership holding (state and all-India estimates). 37th Round. New Delhi: Department of Statistics.

———. 1992a. Morbidity and utilisation of medical service. In *Sarvekshana* 15 (51st). 42nd Round (1986–87). New Delhi: Department of Statistics.

———. 1992b. Operational land holdings in India, 1991–92, salient features. Report 407. 48th Round (January–December 1992). New Delhi: Department of Statistics.

————. 1992c. Some aspects of season-wise operation of holdings. Report 414. 48th Round (January–December 1992). New Delhi: Department of Statistics.

————. 1995. Some aspects of household ownership holdings. *Sarvekshana,* October–December. 48th Round (January–December 1992). New Delhi: Department of Statistics.

————. 1999. Common property resources in India. 54th Round (January–December 1998). Report 452, December. New Delhi: Department of Statistics.

————. 2000. Literacy and levels of education in India. Report 473. 55th Round (1999–2000). New Delhi: Department of Statistics.

Nyberg, A., and S. Rozelle. 1999. *Accelerating China's rural transformation.* Washington, D.C.: World Bank.

Paddock, William, and Paul Paddock. 1967. *Famine 1975, America's decision: Who will survive?* Boston: Little, Brown.

Paglin, Morton. 1965. Surplus agricultural labor and development—Facts and theories. *American Economic Review* 55 (4).

Pal, S., and D. Byerlee. 2003. The funding and organization of agricultural research in India: Evolution and emerging policy issues. Policy Paper 16. New Delhi: National Center for Agricultural Economics and Policy Research.

Pal, S., and Alka Singh. 1997. Agricultural research and extension in India: Institutional structure and investments. NCAP Policy Paper 7. New Delhi: National Center for Agricultural Economics and Policy Research (NCAP) of ICAR (Indian Council of Agricultural Research).

Pal, S., and R. Tripp. 2002. India's seed industry reforms: Prospects and issues. *Indian Journal of Agricultural Economics* 57 (3): 443–458.

Pal, S., P. K. Joshi Mruthyunjaya, and Raka Saxena. 2003. *Institutional change in Indian agriculture.* New Delhi: National Center for Agricultural Economics and Policy Research.

Pal, Suresh. 2004. Agricultural R&D reforms in China and India: Lessons learned and future challenges. Revised version of a paper presented at the Chinese Academy of Agricultural Sciences (CAAS)–International Food Policy Research Institute (IFPRI) International Conference of the Dragon and the Elephant, Beijing, November 11–12, 2003.

Palanisami, K. 1990. Tank irrigation—What next? *Water Resources Journal* ST/ESCAP/ SER.C/167, December, 50–54.

Palanisami K., and K. W. Easter. 2000. *Tank irrigation in the 21st century: What next?* New Delhi: Discovery.

Parikh, K. S. 1994. Who gets how much from PDS: How effectively does it reach the poor? *Sarvekshana* 39 (1). New Delhi: National Sample Survey Organization (NSSO).

Parikh Kirit, Mahendra, S. Dev, and Abusaleh Shariff. 2003. Anti-poverty programs in India: Are they pro-poor? Paper presented at the international JNU (Jawaharlal Nehru University)–IFPRI conference, New Delhi, March 25–26.

Parish, William, Xiaoye Zhe, and Fang Li. 1995. Non-farm work and marketization of the Chinese countryside. *China Quarterly* 143: 697–730.

Park, A., H. Jin, S. Rozelle, and J. Huang. 2002. Market emergence and transition: Transition costs, arbitrage, and autarky in China's grain market. *American Journal of Agricultural Economics* 84 (1): 67–82.

Park, Albert, Sangui Wang, and Guobao Wu. 1998. Regional poverty targeting in China. Working paper, Department of Economics, University of Michigan, Ann Arbor.

Parthasarthy, G. 1987. Changes in the incidence of rural poverty and recent trends in some aspects of agrarian economy. *Indian Journal of Agricultural Economics* 42 (1): 1–21.

Parthasarthy, R. P., P. S. Birthal, P. K. Joshi, and D. Kar. 2002. Agricultural diversification in India and role of urbanization. Paper presented at the workshop Agricultural Diversification in South Asia, Paro, Bhutan, November 21–23.

Pender, J., and P. Hazell. 2002. Promoting sustainable development in less-favored areas. 2020 Focus 4, Brief 1 of 9, November 2000. Washington, D.C.: International Food Policy Research Institute.

People's Daily. 2001. White paper on rural poverty alleviation. October 15. Available at <http://english.peopledaily.com.cn/>.

Perkins, D. 1988. Reforming China's economic system. *Journal of Economic Literature* 26: 601–645.

Pingali, P. L., and M. W. Rosegrant. 1995. Agricultural commercialization and diversification: Processes and policies. *Food Policy* 20 (3): 171–185.

Platteau, Jean-Philippe. 1991. Traditional systems of social security and hunger insurance. In *Social security in developing countries,* ed. Ahmad Ehtisham et al. Oxford: Clarendon Press for Wider.

Postel, S. L. 1999. *Pillar of sand—Can the irrigation miracle last?* New York: W. W. Norton.

Prabhu, S., M. Kathel, and S. Mahendra Dev. 2004. Reexamining human development outcomes: China and India. Paper presented at the Chinese Academy of Agricultural Sciences (CAAS)–International Food Policy Research Institute (IFPRI) International Conference of the Dragon and the Elephant, Beijing, November 11–12.

Pray, C., and R. Basant. 2001. India. In *Private investment in agricultural research and international technology transfer in Asia,* ed. C. Pray and K. Fuglie. AER-805. Washington, D.C.: United States Department of Agriculture (USDA).

Pray, C. E., B. Ramaswami, and T. Kelley. 2001. The impact of economic reforms on R&D by the Indian seed industry. *Food Policy* 26 (6): 587–598.

Putterman, Louis. 1990. Effort productivity and incentives in a 1970s Chinese people's commune. *Journal of Comparative Economics* 14 (1): 88–104.

————. 1993. *Continuity and change in China's rural development.* New York: Oxford University Press.

Qian, K. 1999. To share IPR of plant germ plasm together with public and private sector and farmers: Analysis of social welfare and incentives to innovation. Report to the Drafting Groups of the National People's Congress for China Seed Law, Beijing. Mimeo.

Qian, Z., ed. 1991. *China's water resources.* Beijing: China Water Resources and Hydropower Press.

Qu, Tianjun. 2002. Analysis of NGOs' contribution on Chinese antipoverty achievement and development suggestion for it. *Issues in Agricultural Economy* 9.

Radhakrishna, R. 2002. Agricultural growth, employment and poverty—A policy perspective. *Economic and Political Weekly,* January 19.

Radhakrishna, R. K., and S. Indrakant Subbarao. 1987. Effects of rice market intervention policies in Andhra Pradesh. Working Paper 15. Hyderabad, India: Center for Economic and Social Studies (CESS).

Radhakrishna, R. K., S. Indrakant Subbarao, and C. Ravi. 1997. India's public distribution system: A national and international perspective. World Bank Discussion Paper 380. Washington, D.C.: World Bank.

Rajaraman, Indira. 2001. Expenditure reform. *Economic Times,* May 10.

———. 2004. Growth-accelerating fiscal devolution to the third tier. In *Fiscal policies and sustainable growth in India,* ed. Edgardo M. Favaro and Ashok K. Lahiri. New Delhi: Oxford University Press.

Raju, K. V., Ashok Gulati, and Ruth Meinzen-Dick. 2003. *Innovations in irrigation financing: Tapping domestic financial markets in India.* MSSD Discussion Paper 58. Washington, D.C.: International Food Policy Research Institute (IFPRI).

Ramanna, A. 2002. Policy implications of India's patent reforms: Patent applications in the post-1995 era. *Economic and Political Weekly* 37 (21): 2065–2075.

Ramaswamy, Bharat. 2002. Efficiency and equity of food market interventions. *Economic and Political Weekly* 37 (12).

Ramchandran, V. K. 1997. On Kerala's development experiences. In *Indian development: Selected regional perspectives,* ed. Jean Dreze and Amartya Sen. New Delhi: Oxford University Press.

Randhawa, M. S. 1979. *A history of the Indian Council of Agricultural Research.* New Delhi: Indian Council of Agricultural Research (ICAR).

Rani, Usha. 1971. Size of farm and productivity. *Economic and Political Weekly,* Review of Agriculture, June.

Ranjitha, P. 1996. An analysis of investment in agricultural research and extension in India. Ph.D. thesis, Indian Agricultural Research Institute (IARI), New Delhi.

Rao, A. P. 1967. Size of holding and productivity. *Economic and Political Weekly,* November 11.

Rao, C. H. H. 1967. Alternative explanations of the inverse relationship between farm size and output per acre in India. *Indian Economic Review* 1.

———. 1992. Integrating poverty alleviation programs with development strategies: The Indian experience. *Economic and Political Weekly* 27 (48).

———. 2000. Watershed development in India: Recent experiences and emerging issues. *Economic and Political Weekly,* November 4.

———. 2002. Sustainable use of water for irrigation in Indian agriculture. *Economic and Political Weekly,* May 4.

———. 2003. Keynote speech given at the Chinese Academy of Agricultural Sciences (CAAS)–International Food Policy Research Institute (IFPRI) International Conference of the Dragon and the Elephant, Beijing, November 11–12.

Rao, D. R., and U. Muralidhar. 1994. *A study on agricultural universities on information system.* Hyderabad, India: National Academy of Agricultural Research Management.

Ravallion, Martin. 2003. Have we already met the Millennium Development Goal for poverty? Available at <http://team.univ-paris1.fr/teamperso/page/Ravallion_response_to_Bhalla.pdf> (accessed February 15, 2004).

Ravallion, Martin, and Gaurav Datt. 1995. Growth and poverty in rural India. World Bank Policy Research Working Paper 1405. Washington, D.C.: World Bank.

———. 1996. India's checkered history in fight against poverty: Are there lessons for the future? *Economic and Political Weekly,* Special Number, September.

Reidinger, R. 2002. Participatory irrigation management: Self-financing independent irrigation and rainage district in China. Paper presented at the Sixth International

Forum of Participatory Irrigation Management, held by the Ministry of Water Resources and the World Bank, Beijing, April 21–26.

Rosegrant, Mark, and X. Cai. 2002. Rice and water: An examination from China to the world. Paper presented at the First International Rice Congress, International Rice Research Institute, Beijing, September 16–20.

Rosegrant, Mark W., and Peter Hazell. 2000. *Transforming the rural Asian economy: The unfinished revolution.* Manila: Asian Development Bank.

Rosegrant, W. M., X. Cai, and S. Cline. 2002. *World water and food to 2025: Dealing with scarcity.* Washington, D.C.: International Food Policy Research Institute (IFPRI).

Rosen, S. 1974. Hedonic prices and implicit markets, production differentiation: In pure competition. *Journal of Political Economy* 82: 34–55.

Rozelle, Scott. 1996a. Gradual reform and institutional development: The keys to success of China's agricultural reforms. In *Reforming Asian socialism: The growth of market institutions,* ed. John McMillan and Barry J. Naughton. Ann Arbor: University of Michigan Press.

———. 1996b. Stagnation without equity: Changing patterns of income and inequality in China's post-reform rural economy. *China Journal* 35 (January): 63–96.

Rozelle, Scott, C. E. Pray, and Jikun Huang. 1999. Importing the means of production: Foreign capital and technology flows in China's agriculture. Paper presented at the 1999 International Agricultural Trade Research Consortium (IATRC) Conference, San Francisco, June.

Rozelle, Scott, Linxiu Zhang, and Jikun Huang. 1999. China's war on poverty. Report, Food and Agriculture Organization (FAO), Rome.

Rozelle, Scott, Guo Li, Minggao Shen, Amelia Hughart, and John Giles. 1999. Leaving China's farms: Survey results of new paths and remaining hurdles to rural migration. *China Quarterly* 158 (June): 367–393.

Rozelle, Scott, Albert Park, Jikun Huang, and Hehui Jin. 2000. Bureaucrat to entrepreneur: The changing role of the state in China's transitional commodity economy. *Economic Development and Cultural Change* 48 (2): 227–252.

Rozelle, Scott, Loren Brandt, Guo Li, and Jikun Huang. 2002. Land rights in China: Facts, fictions, and issues. *China Journal* 47: 67–97.

Ruben, R., M. Wesselink, and F. Saenz, 2001. Contract farming and sustainable land use: The case of small scale pepper farmers in northern Costa Rica. Paper presented at the Asociacion Espanole de Economica Agraria Seminar, Copenhagen, June.

Rudra, Ashok. 1968a. Farm size and yield per acre. *Economic and Political Weekly,* Special Number 3 (26–28).

———. 1968b. More on return to scale in Indian agriculture. *Economic and Political Weekly* 3 (43).

Ruttan, Vernon, and Yujiro Hayami. 1984. Toward a theory of induced institutional innovation. *Journal of Development Studies* 20 (4): 203–223.

Ryan, J. G., and D. C. Spencer. 2001. *Future challenges and opportunities for agricultural R&D in the semi-arid tropics.* Patancheru, India: International Crops Research Institute for the Semi-Arid Tropics.

SAI (Seed Association of India). 2001. *National seminar on seed sector reforms.* New Delhi.

Saini, G. R. 1969. Farm size, productivity and returns to scale. *Economic and Political Weekly,* Review of Agriculture 4 (26).

————. 1971. Holding size, productivity and some related aspects of Indian agriculture. *Economic and Political Weekly* 6 (26).

Saith A. 1992. *The rural non-farm economy: Processes and policies.* Geneva: International Labor Organization (ILO).

Saleth, R. Maria. 1996. *Water institutions in India: Economics, law and policy.* New Delhi: Commonwealth.

Sanyal, S. K. 1969. Size of holding and some factors related to production. *Economic and Political Weekly* 4 (33).

Schumacher, Katja, and Jayant Sathaye. 1999. India's fertilizer industry: Productivity and energy efficiency. Report for the U.S. Department of Energy, Ernest Orlando Lawrence Berkley National Laboratory, University of California Berkeley. Available at <http://eande.lbl.gov/EA/IES/iespubs/41846.pdf> (accessed November 2003).

Scott, G. J. 1995. *Price, product and people: Analysis of agricultural markets in developing countries.* Boulder, Colo.: Lynne Rienner.

Sen, Abhijit. 1996. Economic reforms, employment and poverty—Trends and options. *Economic and Political Weekly* 31 (35–37): 2457–2477.

Sen, Abhijit, and M. S. Bhatia. 2003. Cost of cultivation and farm incomes: A study of the comprehensive scheme for studying the cost of cultivation of principal crops in India and results from it. In *State of Indian farmers: A millennium study.* New Delhi: Ministry of Agriculture, Government of India.

Sen, Amartya. 1962. An aspect of Indian agriculture. *Economic Weekly* 14 (4–6): 243–246.

————. 1981. *Poverty and famines.* Oxford: Clarendon.

————. 1998. *Development as freedom.* New York: Random House. Reprinted by Oxford University Press, 2003.

Sen, A., and Himanshu. 2004. Poverty and inequality in India, II: Widening disparities during the 1990s. *Economic and Political Weekly* 39 (38): 4361–4375.

Sengupta, Nirmal. 1985. Irrigation: Traditional vs. modern. *Economic and Political Weekly* 20 (45–47): 1919–1938.

Shah, Tushaar. 1993. Groundwater markets and irrigation development. Bombay: Oxford University Press.

Shah, Tushaar, and K. Vengama Raju. 1987. Working of groundwater markets in Andhra Pradesh and Gujarat: Results of two village studies. *Economic and Political Weekly,* March 26, A23–A28.

Shah, Tushaar, Christopher Scott, and Stephanie Buechler. 2004. Water sector reforms in Mexico: Lessons for India's new water policy. *Economic and Political Weekly,* January 24.

Sharma, Ashok B. 2003. Is Indo-China trade pact a beginning for better? News article in Financialexpress.com, New Delhi. Available at <www.financialexpress.com/fe_full_story.php?content_id=37220> (accessed July 2003).

Sharma, H. R. 1994. Distribution of land holdings in rural India, 1953–54 to 1981–82: Implications for land reforms. *Economic and Political Weekly* 29 (13).

————. 1995. *Agrarian relations in India: Patterns and implications.* New Delhi: Har-Anand.

Sharma, Naresh, and Jean Dreze. 2000. Tenancy. In *Economic development in Palanpur over five decades,* ed. Peter Lanjouw and Nicholas Stern. New Delhi: Oxford University Press.

Shergill, H. S. 1989. Agrarian structure as a factor in rural poverty. *Economic and Political Weekly*, March 25.

Shiklomanov, I. A. 1998. World water resources: A new appraisal and assessment for the 21st century. International Hydrological Programme (IHP) report. Paris: United Nations Educational, Scientific and Cultural Organization (UNESCO).

————. 1999. Electronic data provided to the Scenario Development Panel, World Commission on Water for the 21st Century. Mimeo. Paris.

Shyam, Sundar, S. 1993. India in FAO forestry policies of selected countries in Asia and the Pacific. Rome: United Nations Food and Agriculture Organization (FAO).

Sicular, Terry. 1988a. Agricultural planning and pricing in the post-Mao period. *China Quarterly* 116: 671–703.

————. 1988b. Plan and market in China's agricultural commerce. *Journal of Political Economy* 96 (2): 283–307.

————. 1995. Redefining state, plan, and market: China's reforms in agricultural commerce. *China Quarterly* 144: 1020–1046.

Singh, Chhatrapati, ed. 1991. *Water law in India*. New Delhi: Indian Law Institute (ILI) Publications.

Smith, L. E. D., and I. Urey. 2002. Agricultural growth and poverty reduction: A review of lessons from the post-independence and Green Revolution experience in India. Report, Department of Agricultural Sciences, Imperial College at Wye, London.

Solinger, Dorothy. 1999. *Contesting citizenship in urban China: Peasant migrants, the state and the logic of the market*. Berkeley: University of California Press.

Srinivasan, T. N. 2003a. China and India: Growth and poverty, 1980–2000. Washington, D.C.: World Bank. A shorter version of a related paper. Available at <http://poverty.worldbank.org/files/12404_TNSrinivasan-Paper2+Tables.pdf> (accessed September 2004).

————. 2003b. Comments on Gulati and Mullen (2003). Mimeo, International Food Policy Research Institute, Washington, D.C.

Srinivasan, T. N., and Suresh D. Tendulkar. 2003. *Reintegrating India with the world economy*. Washington, D.C.: Institute of International Economics. Available at <www.iie.com> (accessed July 2003).

Srivastava, Ravi. 1989. Tenancy contracts during transition: A study based on fieldwork in Uttar Pradesh. *Journal of Peasant Studies* 16 (3): 339–395.

————. 1994. Planning and regional disparities in India: The uneven record of change and growth. In *The State and development planning in India*, ed. T. J. Byres. New Delhi: Oxford University Press.

————. 1997. Change and resilience in producer strategies in Indian agriculture. In *The village in Asia revisited*, ed. Jan Breman, Peter Kloos, and Ashwani Saith. Oxford: Oxford University Press.

————. 2000. Changes in contractual relations in land and labor. *Indian Journal of Agricultural Economics*, Keynote Paper, Conference Issue, October–December.

Srivastava, Ravi, and Yang Yao. 2004. Land institutions in India and China: Lessons for future reform for sustained agricultural growth and poverty reduction. Revised version of a paper presented at the Chinese Academy of Agricultural Sciences (CAAS)–International Food Policy Research Institute (IFPRI) International Conference of the Dragon and the Elephant, Beijing, November 11–12.

Sternquist, B., and Z. Chen. 2002. Food retail buyer behaviour in People's Republic of China: A model from grounded theory. Mimeo, Michigan State University.

State Science and Technology Commission. Various years. *China statistical yearbook on science and technology*. Beijing: China Statistical Press.

Sternquist, Brenda, and Zhengyi Chen. 2006. Food retail buyer behaviour in People's Republic of China: A grounded theory model. *Qualitative Market Research: An International Journal* 9 (3).

Stokes, E. 1983. Agrarian relations: Northern and central India. In *The economic history of India*, ed. D. Kumar and M. Desai, Vol. 2, *1757–1970*. Cambridge, England: Cambridge University Press.

Stone, I. 1984. *Canal irrigation in British India*. Cambridge, England: Cambridge University Press.

Sundaram, K. 2001a. Employment and poverty in the 1990s: Further results from the 55th NSS round survey on employment and unemployment, 1999–2000. *Economic and Political Weekly*, August 11.

———. 2001b. Employment-unemployment situation in the nineties: Some results from the 55th NSS round survey. *Economic and Political Weekly*, March 17.

Sundaram, K., and S. D. Tendulkar. 2002. Recent debates on database for measurement of poverty in India: Some fresh evidence. Paper presented at the workshop organized by the Indian Planning Commission and the World Bank, New Delhi, January 11–12.

———. 2003. Poverty among social and economic groups in India in the nineteen nineties. *Economic and Political Weekly* 38 (50).

Svendsen, Mark, A. Gulati, and K. V. Raju. 2003. *Financial and institutional reforms in Indian canal irrigation*. New Delhi: Books for Change.

Swain, Mamata. 1999. Agricultural tenancy and interlinked transactions I: Neoclassical and Marxist approaches. *Economic and Political Weekly* 34 (37).

Swallow, Brent M., and Daniel W. Bromley. 1994. Co-management or no management: The prospects for internal governance of Common Property Regimes through dynamic contracts. *Oxford Agrarian Studies* 22 (1): 3–16.

Taylor, J. Edward. 1998. Trade liberalization and the impact on small holders in rural Mexico. Working Paper, Department of Agricultural and Resource Economics, University of California, Davis.

Tendulkar, S. D., and L. R. Jain. 1993. Poverty in India: 1970–71 to 1988–89. ARTEP Working Paper, International Labor Organization (ILO), New Delhi.

Thorat, Sukhadeo. 1990. Farm size and access to institutional finance in India. Working Paper, Center for Rural and Agricultural Development, Department of Economics, Iowa State University, Ames.

———. 1993. *Technological change and regional differentiation*. New Delhi: Khanna.

———. 1994. Farm size and capital structure—Evidence from drought prone agriculture. *Productivity* 35 (2).

Thorner, Daniel. 1976. *Agrarian prospect in India*. New Delhi: Allied.

Tian, Chuanghao, and Hong Chen. 2003. The impacts of land fragmentation on agricultural productivity in Jiangsu and Shangdong provinces. Working paper, School of Economics, Zhejiang University, China.

Tong, P. 2002. *Seed industry in China: Who will dominate?* (in Chinese). Guizhou, Guilin: Guizhou Science and Technology Publication Company.

Tripathi, Kamlesh C. 1987. Local institutions involved in forest management: Panchayat case studies. In *Peoples' institutions for forest and fuelwood development: A report on participatory fuelwood evaluations in India and Thailand,* ed. Richard Morse et al. Honolulu: East West Center.

Tripp, R., and Suresh Pal. 2000. Information and agricultural input markets: Pearl seed in Rajasthan. *Journal of International Development* 12 (1): 133–144.

Turner, Mathew, Loren Brandt, and Scott Rozelle. 2000. Local government behavior and property right formation in rural China. Working paper, Department of Economics, University of Toronto, Toronto.

United Nations Development Program (UNDP). 1993. *Human development report.* Oxford: Oxford University Press.

UNDP (United Nations Development Program) and EU (European Union). 1999. Poverty and Environment Initiative Publications 1–6. New York.

UNDP (United Nations Development Program), LGPA (Leading Group for Poverty Reduction), and World Bank. 2000. China: Overcoming rural poverty. Joint report of the Leading Group for Poverty Reduction. Washington, D.C.: UNDP and the World Bank.

USDA (United States Department of Agriculture), Economic Research Service (ERS). 2001. *Rice yearbook 2001.* Available at <http://usda.mannlib.cornell.edu/reports/erssor/field/rcs-bby/rcs2001.pdf> (accessed October 2004).

Vaidyanathan, A. 1986. Labor use in rural India: A study of spatial and temporal variations. *Economic and Political Weekly* 21 (52): A130–A146.

———. 1991. Integrated watershed development: Some major issues. Foundation Day Lecture, Society for the Promotion of Wastelands Development, New Delhi, May.

———. 1999. *Water resources management: Institutions and irrigation development.* New Delhi: Oxford University Press.

van de Walle, Dominique. 1985. Population growth and poverty: Another look at the Indian time series data. *Journal of Development Studies* 21: 429–439.

Visaria P., and B. S. Minhas. 1991. Evolving an employment policy for the 1990s: What do the data tell us? *Economic and Political Weekly* 15 (April): 977.

von Braun, Joachim. 2003. Opening speech at the Chinese Academy of Agricultural Sciences (CAAS)–International Food Policy Research Institute (IFPRI) Conference of the Dragon and the Elephant, Beijing, November 11–12.

Vosti, S., and T. Reardon, eds. 1997. *Sustainability, growth and poverty alleviation: A policy and agro-ecological perspective.* Baltimore: The Johns Hopkins University Press.

Vyas, V. S. 1970. Tenancy in a dynamic setting. *Economic and Political Weekly,* June 27.

———. 1996. Diversification in agriculture: Concept, rationale and approaches. *Indian Journal of Agricultural Economics* 51 (4): 636–643.

———. 2001. Agriculture: Second round of economic reforms. First Professor Dantwala Memorial Lecture. *Economic and Political Weekly,* March 10.

———. 2002. Changing contours of Indian agriculture. In *Facets of the Indian economy,* ed. Rakesh Mohan. New Delhi: Oxford University Press.

Vyas, V. S., and Bingsheng Ke. 2004. Market reforms in China and India—Approach, impact and lessons learned. Revised version of a paper presented at the Chinese Academy of Agricultural Sciences (CAAS)–International Food Policy Research

Institute (IFPRI) International Conference of the Dragon and the Elephant, Beijing, November 11–12, 2003.

Waldman, Amy. 2003. Sizzling economy revitalizes India. *New York Times,* October 20, A1.

Walford, Veronica, Mark Pearson, Ravi Rannan Eliya, and Tharange Fernando. 2006. Future policy choices for the health sector in Asia. Background paper prepared for the conference Asia 2015: Promoting Growth, Ending Poverty, London, March 6–7. Available at <www.asia2015conference.org>.

Walinsky, L., ed. 1979. *Agrarian reform as unfinished business: Selected papers of Wolf Laadejinsky.* Oxford, England: Oxford University Press.

Wang, Jinxia, Jikun Huang, and Scott Rozelle. 2003. Evolution of tubewell ownership and production in the North China Plain. Brown bag seminar presentation at the International Food Policy Research Institute, Washington, D.C., May.

Wang, Jinxia, Zhigang Xu, Jikun Huang, and Scott Rozelle. 2003. Incentives in water management reform: Assessing the effect on water use, production and poverty in the Yellow River Basin. Brown bag seminar presentation at the International Food Policy Research Institute, Washington, D.C., May.

WDI (World Development Indicators). Various years. *World Bank statistics.* CD-ROM. Washington, D.C.: World Bank.

Weersink, Alfons, and Scott Rozelle. 1997. Market reforms, market development, and agricultural production in China. *Agricultural Economics* 17 (2–3): 95–114.

Wei Zhong. 2003. Analyses on rural health insurance system in Jiangyin city. Discussion paper, Institute of Economics, Chinese Academy of Social Sciences (CASS), Beijing.

Whitcombe, Elizabeth. 1971. *Agrarian conditions in Northern India: The United Provinces under British Rule, 1860–1900.* Vol. 1. Berkeley: University of California Press.

White, G., ed. 1991. *The Chinese state in the era of economic reform.* Armonk, N.Y.: M. E. Sharpe.

Williamson, O. E. 1986. *Economic organization: Firms, markets and policy control.* Brighton, England: Wheatsheaf.

Willig, R. D., and E. E. Bailey. 1981. Income distribution concerns in regulatory policy making. In *Studies in public regulation,* ed. G. Fromm. Chicago: University of Chicago Press.

Wilson, Dominic, and Roopa Purushothaman. 2003. Dreaming with BRICs: The path to 2050. Goldman Sachs Global Economics Paper 99, October 1. Available at <www.gs.com/insight/research/reports/99.pdf> (accessed April 16, 2004).

Wilson, Gordon. 1992. Diseases of poverty. In *Poverty and development in the 1990s,* ed. T. Allen and A. Thomas. Oxfod: Oxford University Press in association with Open University Press.

Working Group on Women's Rights. 1996. Reversing the option: Civil codes and personal laws. *Economic and Political Weekly* 31 (21): 1180–1183.

World Bank. 1990. *Agricultural research in India: Prologue, performance and prospects.* Washington, D.C.: World Bank.

———. 1993. Water resources management. A World Bank policy paper. Washington, D.C.: World Bank.

————. 1997a. At China's table: Food security options. Mimeo, World Bank, Washington, D.C.

————. 1997b. *Financing health care*. China 2020 Series. Washington, D.C.: World Bank.

————. 1997c. India achievements and challenges in reducing poverty, fifty years after independence. A World Bank country study. Washington, D.C.: World Bank.

————. 1999. *Inter-sectoral water allocation, planning, and management*. New Delhi: Allied.

————. 2000a. An assessment of China's poverty policy. Working Paper, World Bank, Washington, D.C.

————. 2000b. *China: Overcoming rural poverty*. Washington, D.C.: World Bank.

————. 2001. *China: Overcoming rural poverty*. Washington, D.C.: World Bank.

————. 2003a. Global economic prospects (GEP) and the developing countries 2003. Report, World Bank, Washington, D.C. Available at <://www.worldbank.org/prospects/gep2003/toc.htm> (accessed April 16, 2004).

————. 2003b. India: Sustaining reform, reducing poverty. A World Bank development policy review. Poverty Reduction and Economic Management Sector Unit, South Asia Region, World Bank, Washington, D.C.

————. 2006. *China Quarterly* update. February. Beijing: World Bank.

World Economic Forum. 2006. Global governance initiative: Annual report. Available at <www.weforum.org/pdf/Initiatives/GGI_Report06.pdf.>.

WRI (World Resources Institute). 1998. People and ecosystems: The fraying web of life. *World Resources 1998 1999*. Washington, D.C.: World Resources Institute.

WTO (World Trade Organization). Various years. Protocols of accession for new members since 1995, including commitments in goods and services. Available at <www.wto.org/english/thewto_e/acc_e/completeacc_e.htm>.

Xu, Z. 2001. Study on increasing water use efficiency. *Journal of China Water Resources* 455: 25–26.

Yang, Dennis. 1997. China's land arrangements and rural labor mobility. *China Economic Review* 8 (2): 101–115.

Yao, Yang. 1998. Tenure security and the application of green manures in Zhejiang and Jiangxi provinces. *China Rural Survey* 1998 (2): 1–10.

————. 2000a. Chinese land tenure and rural social security. *Chinese Social Sciences Quarterly* (Hong Kong), Fall, 19–26.

————. 2000b. The development of the land lease market in rural China. *Land Economics* 76 (2): 252–266.

————. 2002a. Efficiency or political impetus—A comment on the new Land Contract Law. *Nanfeng Chuang* (The south window), September.

————. 2002b. The rational versus the political model in collective decision: The case of land tenure choice in Chinese villages. CCER Working Paper E2002003, May 30. Beijing: China Center for Economic Research, Beijing University. Available at <http://old.ccer.edu.cn/workingpaper/paper/E2002003.doc> (accessed January 29, 2004).

Zai, H. 2002. Speech given at the national workshop on water-saving irrigation held by the Ministry of Water Resources, Beijing, October 16–19.

Zhang, Juwei. 2003. Nutrition, health and productivity—Evidence from poor areas of rural China. *Economic Research Journal* 1 (January).

Zhang, Linxiu. 2004. Social viability, gender and food security in China. Paper prepared for the Regional Workshop on Policy Issues and Investment Options to Avert Hunger and Food Insecurity in Asia, Cha-am, Thailand, March 25–26.

Zhang, Linxiu, Scott Rozelle, and Jikun Huang. 2000. *Poverty alleviation and economic growth.* Annual report on economic and technological development in agriculture—2000. Beijing: China Agricultural Press.

Zhong, Funing, and Zhu Jing. 2000. The role of structural adjustment in Chinese agricultural growth (in Chinese). *Chinese Rural Economy* 7.

Zhong, Funing, and P. K. Joshi. 2004. Rural diversification in developing countries: Lessons from India and China. Revised version of a paper presented at the Chinese Academy of Agricultural Sciences (CAAS)–International Food Policy Research Institute (IFPRI) International Conference of the Dragon and the Elephant, Beijing, November 11–12.

Zhong, Funing, Zhigang Xu, and Longbo Fu. 2001. Regional comparative advantage in China's grain production: Implications for policy reform. In *China's agriculture in the international trading system.* Paris: Organisation for Economic Co-operation and Development (OECD).

Zhou, Qiren, and Shouying Liu. 1998. Meitan: A case of traditional agricultural county with incomplete land tenure. In *Practices of rural reforms.* Guiyang, China: Guizhou Government.

Zhou, Z., X. Liu, and N. Perera. 2001. Nutritional poverty and role of PDS in India: An analysis. In *Indian agricultural policy at the cross road,* ed. S. S. Acharya and D. P. Chaudhari. Jaipur, India: Rawat.

Zhu, Ling. 2002a. Farmer preferences in choosing health programs with insurance components. *China and World Economy* 1.

———. 2002b. To invest in medical services and education for impoverished rural people as a countermeasure to ease the pressure of employment after China's accession into WTO. *Chinese Rural Economy* 1.

———. 2002c. The usage and management of village health service (in Chinese). *Zhongguo Renkou Kexue* (Chinese Journal of Population Science) 5.

Zhu, Ling, and Jiang Zhongyi. 1996. *Public works and poverty alleviation in rural China.* Commack, N.Y.: Nova Science.

Contributors

Alan de Brauw is a research fellow at the International Food Policy Research Institute, Washington, D.C., USA.

Ximing Cai is an assistant professor of civil and environmental engineering at the University of Illinois, Urbana-Champaign, USA.

G. K. Chadha is a former vice chancellor of Jawaharlal Nehru University, New Delhi, India.

Sara Dalafi is a consultant to the Academy of Sciences for the Developing World, Trieste, Italy.

S. Mahendra Dev is director of the Center for Economic and Social Studies, Hyderabad, India.

Shenggen Fan is director of the Development Strategy and Governance Division of the International Food Policy Research Institute, Washington, D.C., USA. He also serves as a class one economist at the Institute of Agricultural Economics and Development of the Chinese Academy of Agricultural Sciences (CAAS) and as director of the International Center for Agricultural and Rural Development, which was jointly set up by IFPRI and CAAS.

Ashok Gulati is director in Asia for the International Food Policy Research Institute, New Delhi, India.

Anwarul Hoda is a member of the Planning Commission of the Government of India.

Jikun Huang is director of the Center for Chinese Agricultural Policy, Chinese Academy of Sciences, Beijing, China.

Ramaswamy R. Iyer is an honorary research professor at the Centre for Policy Research, New Delhi, India.

Dayanatha Jha (deceased) was ICAR National Professor at the National Centre for Agricultural Economics and Policy Research, New Delhi, India.

P. K. Joshi is a former research fellow at the International Food Policy Research Institute, New Delhi Office, India.

Bingsheng Ke is director general of the Research Center for Rural Economy, Ministry of Agriculture, Beijing, China.

Bonwoo Koo is a former research fellow at the International Food Policy Research Institute, Washington, D.C., USA.

Erno Kuiper is an associate professor at Wageningen University, The Netherlands.

Hualiang Lu is a Ph.D. candidate at Wageningen University, The Netherlands.

Suresh Pal is a principal scientist at the National Centre for Agricultural Economics and Policy Research, New Delhi, India.

Philip G. Pardey is a professor of science and technology policy at the University of Minnesota, St. Paul, USA.

Kirit Parikh is a member of the Planning Commission for the Government of India.

Keming Qian is a former director of the Institute of Agricultural Economics, Chinese Academy of Agricultural Sciences, Beijing, China.

K. V. Raju is a professor in the Ecological Economics Unit of the Institute for Social and Economic Change, Bangalore, India.

Mark W. Rosegrant is director of the Environment and Production Technology Department, International Food Policy Research Institute, Washington, D.C., USA.

Scott Rozelle is a professor in the Department of Agriculture and Resource Economics, University of California—Davis, USA.

Ruerd Ruben is chair of development studies and director of the Centre for International Development Issues Nijmegen (CIDIN) at Radboud University—Nijmegen, The Netherlands.

N. C. Saxena is a former member of the Planning Commission for the Government of India.

C. S. C. Sekhar is a research fellow with the Indian Council for Research on International Economic Relations, New Delhi, India.

Abusaleh Shariff is principal economist for the National Council of Applied Economic Research, New Delhi, India.

Ravi Srivastava is a professor at the Center for the Study of Regional Development School of Social Sciences, Jawaharlal Nehru University, New Delhi, India.

Sukhadeo K. Thorat is a professor at Jawaharlal Nehru University and director of the Indian Institute of Dalit Studies, New Delhi, India.

V. S. Vyas is a professor emeritus at the Institute of Development Studies, Jaipur, India.

Jinxia Wang is an associate professor at the Centre for Chinese Agricultural Policy, Chinese Academy of Sciences, Beijing, China.

Yang Yao is a professor at the China Centre for Economic Research, Beijing University, China.

Linxiu Zhang is a professor at and deputy director of the Centre for Chinese Agricultural Policy, Chinese Academy of Sciences, Beijing, China.

Funing Zhong is a professor and dean of the College of Economics and Trade, Nanjing Agricultural University, China.

Jing Zhu is a professor at the College of Economics and Trade, Nanjing Agricultural University, China.

Ling Zhu is deputy director of the Institute of Economics, Chinese Academy of Social Sciences, Beijing, China.

Index

Page numbers for entries occurring in figures are suffixed by an f; those for entries in notes by an n; and those for entries in tables by a t.